The Design of the Psalter

The Design of the Psalter
A Macrostructural Analysis

PETER C. W. HO
Foreword by Gordon McConville

◆PICKWICK *Publications* • Eugene, Oregon

THE DESIGN OF THE PSALTER
A Macrostructural Analysis

Copyright © 2019 Peter C. W. Ho. All rights reserved. Except for brief quotations in critical publications or reviews, no part of this book may be reproduced in any manner without prior written permission from the publisher. Write: Permissions, Wipf and Stock Publishers, 199 W. 8th Ave., Suite 3, Eugene, OR 97401.

Pickwick Publications
An Imprint of Wipf and Stock Publishers
199 W. 8th Ave., Suite 3
Eugene, OR 97401

www.wipfandstock.com

PAPERBACK ISBN: 978-1-5326-5442-8
HARDCOVER ISBN: 978-1-5326-5443-5
EBOOK ISBN: 978-1-5326-5444-2

Cataloguing-in-Publication data:

Names: Ho, Peter C. W., author. | McConville, Gordon, foreword.

Title: The Design of the Psalter : a Macrostructural Analysis / Peter C. W. Ho ; foreword by Gordon McConville.

Description: Eugene, OR: Pickwick Publications, 2019. | Includes bibliographical references and index.

Identifiers: ISBN 978-1-5326-5442-8 (paperback). | ISBN 978-1-5326-5443-5 (hardcover). | ISBN 978-1-5326-5444-2 (ebook).

Subjects: LCSH: Bible. O.T. Psalms. | Hebrew poetry, Biblical.

Classification: BS1430.2 H62 2019 (print). | BS1430.2 (ebook).

Manufactured in the U.S.A.   AUGUST 14, 2019

Scripture quotations taken from the New American Standard Bible® (NASB), copyright © 1960, 1962, 1963, 1968, 1971, 1972, 1973, 1975, 1977, 1995 by The Lockman Foundation. Used by permission. www.Lockman.org

Scripture quotations are from The ESV® Bible (The Holy Bible, English Standard Version®), copyright © 2001 by Crossway, a publishing ministry of Good News Publishers. Used by permission. All rights reserved.

The arrangement of the Psalms seems to hold the secret to a great mystery to me, though, has not yet been revealed to me.

—Augustine

It is a literary question to what extent the editors of a biblical book, in putting together various sources of pieces of material, have created a meaning in the juxtaposition, as distinct from the meaning of the parts. 'The case for meaning must be decided on literary criteria: one must show that a unit is not just an anthology but is an intended structure with meaning'.

—James Barr

Contents

Figures / ix
Foreword by Gordon McConville / xiii
Preface / xv
Abbreviations / xvii

1. Introduction / 1
2. The Macrostructure / 82
3. Concentric and Linear Reading / 134
4. The Five Davidic Collections / 193
5. Numerical Devices, Alphabetic Acrostics or Compositions, and Superscriptions / 265
6. Conclusion / 331

Appendix / 343
Bibliography / 355
Scripture Index / 379

Figures

Figure 1: Wilson's Final Frame of the MT Psalter / 15

Figure 2: Auwers and Zenger's Parallel Structures of the Korahite and Asaphite Psalms / 22

Figure 3: Mitchell's Eschatological Program for the MT Psalter / 30

Figure 4: Formal Organizational Techniques of the MT Psalter / 36

Figure 5: Tacit Organizational Techniques of the MT Psalter / 37

Figure 6: Survey of Macrostructural Divisions of the Five Books / 39

Figure 7: Barton's Message-Author-Text-Reader Map / 42

Figure 8: Colon Division, Structure and the Numerical Centers of Psalms 1–2 / 66

Figure 9: Structural Divisions, Parallels and Contrasts of Psalms 1 and 2 / 69

Figure 10: Structural Parallels between 2 Sam 4–9 and 2 Sam 19–24 / 76

Figure 11: Comparison of Common Songs between 2 Samuel, Chronicles, and the Psalms / 78

Figure 12: Gianni Barbiero's Structure of Book I (with my modifications in Pss 35–41) / 85

Figure 13: Barbiero's Thematic and Genre Structures for Book I / 88

Figure 14: Parallel Genre Structures between the Two Korahite Subgroups / 91

Figure 15: Parallel Genre Structures between the Two Asaphite Subgroups / 92

Figure 16: Different Structural Divisions within Pss 51–72 / 93

Figure 17: A Proposal for the Macrostructure of Books II–III / 95

Figure 18: Superscription Tabulation in Books II–III / 100

Figure 19: Survey of Macrostructural Divisions of Book IV / 103

Figure 20: Structural Divisions, Methods and Arguments for Book V / 106

Figure 21: Wilson's Structure for Book V / 108

Figure 22: Zenger's Structure of Book V / 109

Figure 23: Hossfeld and Zenger's Structure of Pss 107–19 / 110

Figure 24: Survey of Structural Divisions of the Songs of Ascents / 111

Figure 25: Symmetric Structures of the Songs of Ascents / 112

Figure 26: Hossfeld and Zenger's Structure for Pss 135–50 / 114

Figure 27: A Proposal for the Macrostructure of Books IV–V (Pss 90–19) / 116

Figure 28: A Proposal for the Macrostructure of Books IV–V (Pss 120–50) / 116

Figure 29: Number of Occurrences, Locations, and Functions of Imperative Masculine Plural forms of הלל and ברך, ידה / 119

Figure 30: Interlocking Function of Doxological Vocabulary in Psalms 103–7 / 120

Figure 31: Chapter Length and the Unity of Psalms 104–7 / 121

Figure 32: Parallel Trajectories from Creation to Exile in Pss 104–7 and 135–37 / 125

Figure 33: Parallels between Pss 104–19 and 135–50 in Books IV–V / 126

Figure 34: Structure of Four Major Groups of Books IV–V / 127

Figure 35: Superscription Tabulation in Books IV–V / 128

Figure 36: Named and Unnamed Superscription-Type Count / 128

Figure 37: Vincent van Gogh's Cafe Terrace at Night / 131

Figure 38: Subjects who Praise Yhwh / 140

Figure 39: Central Motifs in the Asaphite Psalms / 143

Figure 40: Parallel Trajectories in Pss 104–7 and 111–19 / 148

Figure 41: Use of סתר in Psalms 88–119 / 150

Figure 42: Trajectories in Groups 9–10 of Books IV–V / 151

Figure 43: Central Motifs of the Songs of Ascents / 151

Figure 44: Prinsloo's Spatial Storyline of the Songs of Ascents / 156

Figure 45: Movement toward Zion in Books IV–V / 158

Figure 46: Central Motifs of all 12 Groups in the 3 Sections of the MT Psalter / 161

Figure 47: Concentric and Linear Structures of the Group Central Motifs / 162

Figure 48: Pan-Psalter Occurrence Scheme of שער / 169

Figure 49: Pan-Psalter Occurrence Scheme of יעקב / 174

Figure 50: Penultimate Locations of שיר חדש in Book I / 179

Figure 51: Concentric Structure of the Six Instances of שיר חדש / 180

Figure 52: Penultimate Locations of שיר חדש in Book V / 181

Figure 53: Pan-HB Occurrence Scheme of קומה יהוה ("Arise, O Lord!") / 188

Figure 54: Pan-HB Occurrence Scheme of שובה יהוה ("Return, O Lord!") / 188

Figure 55: ראש across the Psalter / 212

Figure 56: Parallel Thematic Development of Davidic Superscriptions with Historical Reference / 218

Figure 57: Pan-Psalter Occurrence Scheme of זבח / 223

Figure 58: Pan-Psalter Occurrence Scheme of עלה / 225

Figure 59: Highlights of Davidic Collections I and II / 230

Figure 60: Pan-Psalter Occurrence Scheme of ברית / 239

Figure 61: Summary of the Davidic Characterization from DC-I through IV / 248

Figure 62: Common Final Group Central Motif of Davidic Supplication in Every Section / 250

Figure 63: Common Motifs of the Distressed David in Supplication as Last Historical Superscriptions in Two Parallel Trajectories in DC-I and DC-II–V / 251

Figure 64: Summary of the Five Davidic Collections / 257

Figure 65: The Five Davidic Collections in the Horizon of the Psalter / 261

Figure 66: Labuschagne's Structure of the Psalter based on Numbers "7" and "11" / 272

Figure 67: Nexusword, Content/Genre Motifs, and Macrostructure Juxtaposition in Book I / 287

Figure 68: Nexusword Structure of Pss 15–24 / 290

Figure 69: Nexusword-Motif Structure of Pss 25–34 / 291

Figure 70: Nexusword Structure of Pss 35–41 / 292

Figure 71: Nexusword, Content/Genre Motifs and Macrostructure Juxtaposition in Books II–III / 294

Figure 72: Genre-nexusword Parallels in the Korahite Groups / 296

Figure 73: Genre-nexusword Parallels in Asaphite Groups / 299

Figure 74: Nexusword, Content/Genre Motifs and Macrostructure Juxtaposition in Books IV–V / 302

Figure 75: Distribution of Alphabetic Acrostics and Alphabetic Compositions Across the Three Main Sections of the Psalter / 318

Figure 76: Count of Alphabetic Acrostics, and (Probable) Alphabetic Compositions / 324

Figure 77: Numerical Techniques in the Superscriptions of the MT Psalter / 328

Figure 78: Central Motifs of all 12 Groups in the 3 Sections of the MT Psalter / 335

Figure 79: Concentric and Linear Structures of Group Central Motifs / 335

Figure 80: Summary of the Five Davidic Collections / 336

Foreword

THE BOOK OF PSALMS has a unique place in the life and thought of both church and synagogue. Since the earliest Christian centuries, the rich streams of these songs have fed both Christology and the practice of worship. While rooted in the history and experience of ancient Israel, they nevertheless defy reduction to religious-historical significance, but rather have shown an amazing capacity to convey and express deepest meaning to countless people in every time and place. The speakers in the Psalms enact human responses to what has befallen them on their particular life-journeys, yet in such a way that readers and hearers absorb them effortlessly into their own.

Part of the genius of the Psalms is a poetry that combines profundity and simplicity. While scholarly study of the book has benefited from various critical methods, notably form-criticism, it is the quality of their expression itself that gives them their undying power. This quality is evident at the levels of line and phrase, of structure and metaphor, the masterly interplay of form and sense. In recent years, scholars have recognized that the texture of the Psalms is a factor in their meaning, not only within the individual Psalm, but at the level of the whole canonical collection, conceived as a "Book," not just in name but with a book's capacity for coherence, thematic development, and intertextual allusion.

In the present volume, Peter Ho has made an enormous contribution to this aspect of the Book of Psalms. His "macrostructural analysis" understands that meaning-relations occur across the whole Psalter, and that there is an organic integrity between such relations at the local level of individual compositions and the wider environment of the canonical book. Description of such relations is a task that may occupy scholars for generations to come. But Peter Ho provides a timely and welcome stimulus to its furtherance, for the benefit of both church and academy. I am glad to have the opportunity to commend it.

GORDON MCCONVILLE
Professor of Old Testament Theology
University of Gloucestershire
October 2018

Preface

THIS IS A SLIGHTLY revised version of my doctoral dissertation that was defended in January 2017. The culmination of this volume is possible because of the help, patience, and wise guidance of many people to which I am indebted. Between my *viva* and this publication, I have had opportunities to interact with a number of Psalms scholars. Some of them have read an early version of this manuscript and responded with helpful comments and encouragement. Lynell Zogbo and Ernst Wendland, both of whom are passionate about the Psalter, have welcomed my research and extended an invitation to share my work at the Jerusalem Center for Bible Translators in 2018. Lynell, especially, has offered many suggestions to make this book more readable. I am also humbled that Walter Bruegguemann was willing to read my manuscript and even write an endorsement for me. Other Psalms scholars such as David Howard, David Mitchell, Gianni Barbiero, Pieter van der Lugt, Casper Labuschagne, Greg Goswell, and Marco Pavan are positive of my work and have given me useful feedback. Others such as Martin Leuenberger, Marco Pavan, Christine Jones, Shirley Ho, and K. C. Hanson, have exuded kind generosity by sharing their dissertations with me when I reached out to them. As I write this, I have met none of them except Greg Gosswell and David Mitchell in person.

My days spent at the University of Gloucestershire are probably the most special amongst my academic pursuits. I can still remember the serendipitous unarranged first meeting my family and I had with my *Doktorvater*, Gordon McConville, at a church on the first Sunday we arrived in Cheltenham. It turned out that the day I first met my supervisor was also the day we worshiped together. It has been a great privilege and blessing to be supervised by Prof. McConville. He has more than thirty doctoral students supervised unto completion, and his deep and broad scholarship did not get in way of his sincere and kind disposition toward his students. I can still remember the conversations with Gordon on biblical texts and life at the University's refectory over a cuppa. (He takes Americano topped with a little milk!) I have yet to meet a student of his who is not happy under his supervision!

I would also like to thank Prof. Philip F. Esler, my second supervisor, for offering a perspective on my work that I would otherwise miss. His sensitivity to the socio-communal aspects of the ancient world has expanded my perspectives. The encouragement of Prof. Andrew Lincoln and Dr. John Hockey is like a warm beverage on a cold winter night, uplifting and refreshing. A special thanks to my examiners, Dr. David Firth, and Dr. Pekka Pitkänen, who have strengthened and sharpened my methodology by their thoughtful questions and comments. The few who fought alongside me in the trenches of the research student office: Andy Dvoracek, Kyung Ho, Mark Arnold, and Choi Yong Joon will be sorely missed. Friends at the regular post-graduate Hebrew reading class are my constant inspiration. The post-class *Chiquito* sessions have taught me that Hebrew (personal devotions) and light brews (fellowship) need not be separated.

Although we knew very few people when we first arrived at Cheltenham, we quickly found friendship at Cambray Baptist Church. Under the shepherding of pastors Tim Welch and Tim Martin, and the selfless service of the children church leaders, my family was able to settle down quickly. Conversations and prayers shared with Henning Schmidt, Dr. Fredrick Hugh and his wife, Vivian, are too precious to forget.

The crucial intercessory support we received from Lap, Sam, and Waichan, reflects the posture of longsuffering prayers I have learned from the Psalter. It is also the encouragement of Dr. Jerry Hwang and Dr. Samuel Goh from the Singapore Bible College that sparked my journey into Old Testament studies and the Hebrew Bible. Hopefully, this book is a testimony to their tutorship and inspiration.

The love, gifts, care and prayers of our parents and siblings, Sum Yuen and Geok Wah, Chong Ho and Mooi Choo, Levi and Hui Hui, Terence and Joreen, and our home church in Singapore kept us going. Without the generous financial help from the Brash Scholarship and love gifts from Magdalene, Mabel, Raymond, Audrey, Richard, Enoch, William, Connie, Ruby and others, this journey would not have been possible.

Wendy, my wife, is a valiant companion on this journey (and still is!). No one else reads more of my writings than her. Together with my three children, Priscilla, Ezra, and Jereann, they taught me love, servanthood, patience, and trust. This book is dedicated to them, whose God is Yahweh (Ps 144:15)! Lastly, a special record of thanks to Waitrose supermarkets for providing their customers, especially poor research students, with a daily, complimentary, and *necessary*, caffeine fix. It is little wonder why you have been voted one of the best supermarkets in the U.K.!

PETER C. W. HO
October 2018, Singapore

Abbreviations

AB	Anchor Bible
ABD	*Anchor Bible Dictionary*. 6 vols. Edited by David Noel Freedman. New York: Doubleday, 1992
ABib	Academia Biblica Series
AIL	Ancient Israel and Its Literature
AnBib	Analecta biblica
ANE	Ancient Near East
AOAT	Alter Orient und Altes Testament
AOTC	Abingdon Old Testament Commentaries
ASOR	American School of Oriental Research
ATANT	Abhandlungen zur Theologie des Alten und Neuen Testaments
AThR	*Anglican Theological Review*
ASB	*Austin Seminary Bulletin*
AUSS	*Andrews University Seminary Studies*
BASOR	*Bulletin of the American Schools of Oriental Research*
BBB	Bonner biblische Beiträge
BBR	*Bulletin of Biblical research*
BCOTWP	John Goldingay, *Baker Commentary on the Old Testament Wisdom and Psalms*. 3 vols. Grand Rapids: Baker Academic, 2006–2008
BDB	Francis Brown, S. R. Driver, and Charles A. Briggs. *A Hebrew and English Lexicon of the Old Testament*. Oxford, 1907
BETL	Bibliotheca Ephemeridum Theologicarum Lovaniensium
BHQ	*Biblia Hebraica Quinta*
BHS	*Biblia Hebraica Stuttgartensia*
Bib	*Biblica*
BibInt	*Biblical Interpretation*
BLS	*Bible and Literature Series*
BN	*Biblische Notizen*
BRev	*Bible Review*
BSac	*Bibliotheca sacra*

Abbreviations

BT	*Baptistic Theologies*
BTB	*Biblical Theology Bulletin*
BthSt	Biblisch-theologische Studien
BZ	*Biblische Zeitschrift*
BZAW	Beihefte zur Zeitschrift für die alttestamentliche Wissenschaft
CahRB	Cahiers de la Revue biblique
CAS (I–III)	Pieter van der Lugt, *Cantos and Strophes in Biblical Hebrew Poetry*. 3 vols. Leiden: Brill, 2006–2013
CBQ	*Catholic Biblical Quarterly*
CBQMS	Catholic Biblical Quarterly Monograph Series
CBW	*Conversations with the Biblical World*
CEJL	Commentaries on Early Jewish Literature
CQ	*Covenant Quarterly*
CTJ	*Calvin Theological Journal*
CTM	Calwer theologische Monographien
CurTM	*Currents in Theology and Mission*
CV	*Communio viatorum*
DCH	David J. A. Clines, ed., *Dictionary of Classical Hebrew*. 9 vols. Sheffield, 1993–2012
DCLS	Deuterocanonical and Cognate Literature Studies
DOTP	*Dictionary of the Old Testament: Pentateuch*. Edited by T. Desmond Alexander and David W. Baker. Black Dictionaries on the Bible. Downers Grove, IL: IVP Academic, 2003
DOTWPW	*Dictionary of the Old Testament: Wisdom, Poetry & Writings*. Edited by Tremper Longman III and Peter Enns. Black Dictionaries on the Bible. Downers Grove, IL: IVP Academic, 2008
EDB	*Eerdmans Dictionary of the Bible*. Edited by David Noel Freedman. Grand Rapids: Eerdmans, 2000
EHP	Gerald H. Wilson, *The Editing of the Hebrew Psalter*. SBLDS 76. Chico, CA: Scholars, 1985
Enc	*Encounter*
ESV	English Standard Version
ETS	Evangelical Theological Society
ExAud	*Ex auditu*
ExpT	*Expository Times*
FAT	Forschungen zum Alten Testament
FB	Forschung zur Bibel
FOCI	Foundations of Contemporary Interpretation
FOTL	Forms of Old Testament Literature
HALOT	Ludwig Koehler, Walter Baumgartner, and J. J. Stamm, *The Hebrew and Aramaic Lexicon of the Old Testament*. Translated and edited

	under the supervision of M. E. J. Richardson. 4 vols. Leiden: Brill, 1994–1999
HAR	*Hebrew Annual Review*
HAT	Handbuch zum Alten Testament
HB	Hebrew Bible
HBM	Hebrew Bible Monographs
HBOT	Hebrew Bible/Old Testament Studies
HBS	Herders biblische Studien
HBT	*Horizons in Biblical Theology*
HKAT	Handkommentar zum Alten Testament
HOL	*A Concise Hebrew and Aramaic Lexicon of the Old Testament* based on the Lexical Work of Ludwig Koehler and Walter Baumgartner. BibleWorks10 Electronic Version. Leiden: Brill, 2000
HS	*Hebrew Studies*
HThKAT	Herders theologischer Kommentar zum Alten Testament
HTR	*Harvard Theological Review*
HTS	Harvard Theological Studies
IBC	Interpretation: A Bible Commentary for Teaching and Preaching
ICC	International Critical Commentary
Int	*Interpretation*
IOTS	Introduction to the Old Testament as Scripture
JAAC	*Journal of Aesthetics and Art Criticism*
JAJSup	Journal of ancient Judaism, Supplements
JAOS	*Journal of the American Oriental Society*
JBL	*Journal of Biblical Literature*
JBQ	*Jewish Bible Quarterly*
JESOT	*Journal for the Evangelical Study of the Old Testament*
JETS	*Journal of the Evangelical Theological Society*
JSNT	*Journal for the Study of the New Testament*
JSOT	*Journal for the Study of the Old Testament*
JSOTSup	Journal for the Study of the Old Testament Supplementary Series
KSTS	Kohlhammer Studienbücher Theologie Series
L	Codex Leningradensis
LB	*Linguistica Biblica*
LD	Lectio divina
LEC	Library of Early Christianity
LHBOTS	Library of Hebrew Bible/Old Testament Studies
LM	*Liturgical Ministry*
LQ	*Lutheran Quarterly*
LTP	*Laval théologique et philosophique*

Abbreviations

LTQ	*Lexington Theological Quarterly*
LXX	Septuagint
Maarav	*Maarav*
MasS	Masoretic Studies
MNTS	McMaster New Testament Studies Series
MPHB	J. P. Fokkelman, *Major Poems of the Hebrew Bible*, 4 vols. SSN 37, 41, 43 and 47. Assen: Van Gorcum, 1998–2004
Ms(s)	Medieval Hebrew manuscript(s)
MT	Masoretic Text
NAC	New American Commentary
NAU	New American Standard Bible (1995)
NEA	*Near Eastern Archaeology*
NIB	New Interpreter's Bible
NICOT	New International Commentary on the Old Testament
NIDOTTE	*New International Dictionary of Old Testament Theology and Exegesis*. Edited by W. A. VanGemeren. 5 vols. Grand Rapids, 1997
NIV	New International Version
NRSV	New Revised Standard Version
NTSI	New Testament and the Scriptures of Israel
Numen	*Numen: International Review for the History of Religions*
ÖBS	Österreichische biblische Studien
OTE	*Old Testament Essays*
OTG	Old Testament Guides
OTL	Old Testament Library
OtSt	*Oudtestamentische Studiën*
PBM	Paternoster Biblical Monographs
PRSt	*Perspectives in Religious Studies*
RB	*Revue biblique*
RCT	*Revista catalana de teología*
ResQ	*Restoration Quarterly*
RevExp	*Review and Expositor*
RevQ	*Revue de Qumran*
RelS	*Religious Studies*
RelSRev	*Religious Studies Review*
RevScRel	*Revue des sciences religieuses*
RSR	*Recherches de science religieuse*
RTR	*Reformed Theological Review*
SBB	Stuttgarter biblische Beiträge
SBL	Society of Biblical Literature
SBLDS	Society of Biblical Literature Dissertation Series

SBLMS	Society of Biblical Literature Monograph Series
SBS	Stuttgarter Bibelstudien
SHS	Scripture and Hermeneutics Series
SJT	*Scottish Journal of Theology*
SR	*Sewanee Review*
SSN	Studia Semitica Neerlandica
ST	*Studia theologica*
StBibLit	Studies in Biblical Literature
STDJ	Studies on the Texts of the Desert of Judah
STR	*Southeastern Theological Review*
SubBi	Subsidia Biblica
SVT	Supplements to Vetus Testamentum
TDOT	*Theological Dictionary of the Old Testament*. 16 vols. Edited by G. Johannes Botterweck, Helmer Ringgren, and Heinz-Josef Fabray. Translated by Geoffrey W. Bromiley et al. Grand Rapids, 1974–2018
Them	*Themelios*
Theol	*Theology*
TJ	*Trinity Journal*
TLOT	*Theological Lexicon of the Old Testament*. 3 vols. Edited by Ernst Jenni and Claus Westermann. Translated by Mark Biddle. Peabody, MA: Hendrickson, 1997
TOTC	Tyndale Old Testament Commentaries
TR	Textus Receptus
TTE	*The Theological Educator*
TynBul	*Tyndale Bulletin*
VT	*Vetus Testamentum*
VTSup	Supplements to Vetus Testamentum
WBC	Word Biblical Commentary
WTJ	*Westminster Theological Journal*
WUNT	Wissenschaftliche Untersuchungen zum Neuen Testament
WW	*Word and World*
ZAW	Zeitschrift für die Alttestamentliche Wissenschaft
ZTK	Zeitschrift für Theologie und Kirche

Mishnaic, Talmudic Tractates and Other Rabbinic Texts

b.	*Babylonian Talmud*
Pesaḥ.	*Pesaḥim*
Qid.	*Qiddushin*
Ber.	*Berakhoth*

Abbreviations

Bik.	*Bikkurim*
Pes. de-Rav Kah.	*Pesikta de Rav Kahana*
Mid.	*Middot*
Midr. Pss.	*Midrash on Psalms (Midrash Tehillim)*
Sifre	*Sifre*
Sop.	*Sopherim*
Sukk.	*Sukkah*

Latin/Greek Texts

Enarrat. Ps.	*Enarrationes in Psalmos*
Hom. Ps.	*Homiliae in Psalmos*

Other abbreviations used in this book

AA	Alphabetic Aacrostic
AC	Alphabetic Composition
CM	Central Motif
DC	Davidic Collection
GCM	Group Central Motif
PAC	Probable Alphabetic Compositions
POS	Pan-Psalter Occurrence Scheme
SOA	Song of Ascents

1

Introduction

The question about the Psalter as a book is ... rather a question whether each psalm, with its inherent and specific language, may have yet another dimension of meaning by its given position in the book of Psalms. It is whether the book as a whole has a program, which cannot be precisely detected with a mere glance at the individual texts.[1]

—Erich Zenger

Poetry is a series of discrete units upon the field and at the same time, it is also the total. There are factors operating in every poetic text that lend varying degrees of connectedness to the discrete units of the work. The predominant formal feature of the poem is its articulation of these distinct units into a series of organized parts that are both distinct from and related to each other that together form a unified whole.[2]

—Daniel Grossberg

"Blessed," as the first word in the Psalter, provides a significant clue to the message of the Psalms when the entire book is read with an overarching logic.[3] An overarching compositional design, or logic, of the Masoretic (MT) Psalter, if any, is in the sequence

---

1. Zenger, "Der Psalter als Buch," 12.
2. Grossberg, *Centripetal and Centrifugal*, 5.
3. The Hebrew אשרי is typically translated as "blessed." Hanson has argued that it does not belong to the wordfield of blessing and curse. Rather, this word had a Mediterranean social setting and is to be understood as a social endorsement for "honor" (as antipodal to "shame"). Hanson's translation of אשרי is "honorable," though others have translated as "commendable," or "admirable." See Hanson, "How Honorable! How Shameful!," 87–93; Seow, "An Exquisitely Poetic Introduction to the Psalter," 278–79.

of its one hundred and fifty psalms. Formal, tacit and, thematic literary devices incorporated within the text either conjoin or delimit a unit of adjacent psalms, according it distinctive structural form and theme. However, the inquiry into the design (or logic) of the Psalter lies in whether these successive units of psalms come together under the broader text horizon to unveil a coherent macrostructure and metanarrative at the level of the book. The aim of this book is to understand the logic and *design* of the MT Psalter and whether any overarching architectural schema can be assigned to it.

If Psalms scholarship over the last hundred and twenty years were to be defined by its dominant approach, we would find ourselves at an interesting overlap between two major *revolutions*.[4] The *Formgeschichte* (or *Gattungforschung*) defines the first revolution and remains methodologically entrenched even among the most recent major commentaries on the Psalms.[5] At the same time, the second revolution, the canonical approach (or understanding the Psalter as a complete text), set ablaze by B. S. Childs, G. H. Wilson, and E. Zenger in the 1980s, is still growing strong even after about four decades. Despite a clear shift in mainstream Psalms research toward the latter, this approach *has not* achieved the same kind of influence *Formgeschichte* has had. There seems to be a growing impatience to reap what was promisingly sown forty years ago, and this is for several reasons. Perhaps the first and clearest reason is a lack of consensus in finding a coherent structure and dominant message in the entire Psalter based on the organization of the Psalms. Is the motif of the temple in the Psalter primarily theological or historical?[6] Does the book of Psalms have an overarching shape defined by Torah (didactic) or kingship (eschatological)?[7] Can various motifs be unified under some overarching theme?

Second, methodological choices adopted by scholars have affected the search for the Psalter's structure and logic. For instance, following David Howard's method of exhaustive lexical analysis of a structural unit of psalms in *The Structure of Psalms 93–100*, a host of similar studies have been undertaken and almost every psalm unit in the Psalter has been analyzed. While the positive impact of these studies is a clearer appreciation of how certain psalm units are connected through recurring lexemes or motifs, the downside is that these studies offer an equal number of competing conclusions on different parts of the Psalter, making an overall coherent analysis difficult.

Third, macrostructural analyses of the *entire* Psalter as a coherent unit are also rare, and the few available are primarily based on more subjective thematic arguments loosely supported by formal and structural evidence.[8] The function of formal poetical

---

4. Wenham, "Towards a Canonical Reading," 335.

5. deClaissé-Walford, *Book of Psalms*, 13–21; Longman, *Psalms*, 38–42.

6. Zenger has made an interesting argument for the Psalter functioning as the sanctuary in "Der Psalter als Buch," 35–43. For a more historical, socio-political view, see deClaissé-Walford, "Meta-Narrative of the Psalter," 363–75; Gillingham, "Zion Tradition," 308–41.

7. This polarization is surmised by Gillingham, "Zion Tradition," 307–8.

8. One of the latest macrostructural treatments of the Psalms as a coherent work is Robertson, *Flow of the Psalms*. See also Parrish, *Story of the Psalms*.

devices (e.g., superscriptions) and higher level poetic structural analyses (beyond a single psalm) are usually not central to the overall argument of these treatments. Thematic and poetical analyses of the Psalms remain disconnected, partly because poetical structural studies are, in general, limited to the level of a single psalm,[9] while thematic analyses traverse across individual psalms easily. Although there are works that argue for a coherent organization of entire biblical books based on poetical techniques,[10] such arguments for the Psalter are scant.[11]

Fourth, the search for the coherence of the Psalter is also complicated by the intertextual link between the Psalms and other books in the OT (even without considering diachronic issues of dependency), which affects how the Psalter is viewed.[12] When the Psalter is seen as being influenced by Prophetic books, the former can be seen as having a messianic thrust.[13] If the Pentateuchal/Historical books are seen to be predominately influential, the Psalms can be seen as oriented towards fostering Torah-piety.[14] Hence, how should the reader think about intertextual elements in the Psalms? Is the Psalter simply borrowing certain motifs in an ad hoc manner or are these motifs used definitively under certain overarching logic in the Psalter?

Finally, various textual evidence of differing arrangements of the psalms may be reframing the canonical question altogether. The contention, based on evidence of Qumran and medieval Hebrew Psalms manuscripts, that "no standard MT configuration of the premodern Hebrew psalter ever existed," presents a dilemma to the study of the arrangement of the MT Psalter.[15] As such, it is not surprising that a number of

---

9. See esp. the works of Van der Lugt, *CAS I–III*; Fokkelman, *MPHB I–III*; *Reading Biblical Poetry*; *Psalms in Form*.

10. William Shea's and Wolfe's macrostructural chiastic views on large segment of texts are helpful. See Shea, "Chiastic Structure of the Song of Songs," 378–96; "Chiasmus and the Structure of David's Lament," 13–25; "Further Literary Structures in Daniel 2–7"; "Chiasm in Samuel," 21–31. See also Wolfe, "Chiastic Structure of Luke–Acts," 60–71; Bertman, "Symmetrical Design in the Book of Ruth," 165–68.

11. Consider the two works by Labuschagne, "Significant Compositional Techniques," 583–605; and Koorevaar, "Psalter as a Structured Theological Story," 579–92.

12. Tanner, *Book of Psalms*.

13. Mitchell argues that the Psalter follows a messianic program as identified in Zechariah 9–14 while Creach sees the dependence of Ps 1:3 on Jer 17:8. Cf. Mitchell, *Message of the Psalter*; Creach, "Like a Tree," 34–46.

14. Grant, *King as Exemplar*; Weber, "Die Doppelte," 14–27.

15. Perhaps the most recent discussion is found in an important article by Yarchin, in which his bold summary is telling: "This survey has produced evidence showing that, while the semantic content of *sēpher təhillîm* did indeed become the fixed text known as the MT, the ways in which the content was configured into discrete psalmic compositions varied widely among the medieval manuscripts. Drawing from medieval halakists, the article offers a partial explanation for the variety in psalter configurations centered on different liturgical customs. *By applying the evidence from hundreds of Hebrew medieval Psalms manuscripts, the article concludes that, since no standard MT configuration of the premodern Hebrew psalter ever existed*, framing the question about scrolls from Qumran as either true psalters or as secondary collections finds no basis in the manuscript evidence." (Yarchin, "Were the Psalms," 775–89, emphasis added). See also Seybold (and Howard's response) on this issue. These

important Psalms scholars (e.g., John Goldingay, Tremper Longman III, Erhard S. Gerstenberger)[16] remain cautiously reserved in adopting the canonical approach, or in positing any overarching structure and metanarrative in the Psalms.

The factors above have contributed to a serious impasse, with regards to the seminal question of the logic of the Psalms. This book seeks to address the question of design and logic by adopting a macrostructural and literary approach to the entire book of Psalms based on the received Hebrew MT Psalter (TR-150).[17] Diachronic or canonization issues, while important, are beyond the scope of this book. By macrostructural and literary, I pay attention to how and where leitmotifs, especially in the Prologue (Pss 1–2) of the Psalter, recur and develop, and whether metanarratival developments are present. I seek to understand delimitation and structuring of major psalm groups, and provide a synchronic analysis and comparison of all the Davidic Collections in the Psalter.

As poetry, the form of the Psalter is as important as its thematic content. If an overarching design of the entire Psalter does exist, it is highly plausible that poetic techniques at work in individual poems are also expressed beyond a single psalm. I will study how superscriptions, numerical symbolism and acrostic/alphabetic compositions function macrostructurally, explicating the roles they play in the design of the Psalter.

---

two authors have noted that despite more scholars viewing the Qumran tradition as having its own canonical nature, "the Jerusalem tradition" (that is, a Jerusalem *vorlage* that MT probably depended on) is a "forerunner" of the LXX and the Qumran tradition and hence, the normative MT tradition remains an important aspect for study. See Seybold, "Psalter as a Book," 178–80; Howard, "Proto-MT Psalter," 184. See also Flint, "Dead Sea Psalms Scrolls," 11–34; *Dead Sea Psalms*; "Book of Psalms," 453–72; Swanson, "Qumran and the Psalms," 247–61.

16. Goldingay, in his magisterial three-volume commentary, registers that "Psalms study that focuses attention on the arrangement of the Psalter still seems to me to involve too much imagination in connecting too few dots. I remain of the view that the main focus of Psalms study needs to be the individual psalm" (Goldingay, BCOTWP, 3:11–12). Longman also notes, "The fact that this arrangement was not noticed before 1985 should make us pause and suggest that it was imposed rather than described from what is there" (Longman III, "Messiah: Explorations," 24). See also Gerstenberger, "Der Psalter Als Buch," 3–13.

17. Textus Receptus-150, coined by Yarchin, is the text on which modern edition (e.g., *BHS*) rely. This specificity is important because the configurations of psalms in the MT-150 (P. Flint's term) remains fluid up to the printing of the rabbinic bibles. In this study, I have used these two terms interchangeably for two reasons: First, Yarchin's study does not affect the *text* (or its order), only delimitations and the total count of the psalms. This does not, in general, affect our main argument in the book. Second, the definition of "TR-150" has not received widespread acknowledgment in Psalms scholarship and Yarchin's method of delimitation requires further clarity (William Yarchin, "Is There an Authoritative Shape," 359–61). Specifically, I have used the *BHS* (which is based on the Leningradensis Codex B19A) and all word searches in this book are undertaken electronically through BibleWorks v.10 WTT/WTM Hebrew texts (which is also based on Leningradensis Codex B19A and tagged with the Groves-Wheeler Westminster Morphology and Lemma Database. Neither the Psalms texts from the *BHQ* nor the *Hebrew Bible: A Critical Edition* (formerly known as the *Oxford Hebrew Bible*, an eclectic text) were available at the time of writing.

Three key research questions that guide this study are as follow: (1) What are the main organizing techniques of the Psalter? (2) How is the Psalter organized macrostructurally? (3) Is there a consistent, coherent, and overarching logic to the design and arrangement of the Psalter?

In the remainder of this chapter, I will further contextualize the study and consolidate recent proposed key organizing techniques and structures. I will also present four hermeneutical perspectives on reading the Psalter. First, I will briefly discuss the connections between the text, implied reader, and author of the Psalter, and how text unity is perceived. I am interested in the extent to which we can postulate the authorial intent of the Psalter based on various rhetorical features that readers can discern from the text. Second, I will discuss the views of several scholars who do not consider the Psalter as a unified book and then explain why I think the contrary is more reasonable. Third, I argue that the Prologue is programmatic and functions as the exordium for the entire Psalter. Finally, I propose that the Psalter be viewed through the theme of the Davidic covenant, contemporaneously with the books of Samuel and Chronicles.

In the second chapter, I will delve into the macrostructure of the five Books of the Psalter, proposing three main Sections (Books I, II–III, IV–V), each containing four Groups (see nomenclature in 2.1) that parallel each other. In the third chapter, I will highlight how leitmotifs are located centrally in the twelve Groups of the Psalter and explain how the Psalter can be read *concentrically,* *linearly,* and *contemporaneously.* I posit an interesting lexical-poetical technique, termed the Pan-Psalter Occurrence Scheme (POS), which shows the careful design and unity of the Psalter. In the fourth chapter, I offer a macrostructural analysis of the five Davidic Collections (Pss 3–41; 51–70 [and 86]; 101–103; 108–110; 138–145), which trace a cogent metanarrative. This cogency is also found in the design of the thirteen historical superscriptions in the Davidic psalms. I conclude that we need not preclude a Messianic shaping of the Psalter at the time of final composition. In chapter five, I will analyze three formal poetical devices: numerical compositions, acrostic, and alphabetic compositions, and superscriptions. I posit an alternative method of counting words in the Psalms and compare my findings with the works of Labuschagne and van der Lugt. I have found that these formal devices were carefully designed to mark structural units and leitmotifs of the MT Psalter. The final chapter summarizes this monograph and posits the implications and future work that could arise from this study.

My conclusion is that the design of the Psalter is an intertwining structure of at least three narratives expressed via the garbs of Hebrew poetry. The first is a larger metanarrative of God's purposes expressed through the prophetic (mantological exegesis[18]) understanding and unfurling of the Davidic covenant. Within this metanarrative, two

---

18. Perhaps we can apply Fishbane's understanding here. By mantological, it refers to a "pattern of inner-biblical exegesis, with its own configurations and dialectics, ... the reinterpretation of prophetic oracles." He adds, "With respect to oracles, however, the issue is more extreme: reinterpretation is necessary precisely because the original oracle-revelation was not yet—or not conclusively—actualized" (Fishbane, "Revelation and Tradition," 354). See also Fishbane, "Inner-Biblical Exegesis," 33–48.

smaller narratives representing the life-journeys of the Davidic king and the *chasidim* of God to the paradisical garden-city of bliss, are skillfully interwoven (legal and aggadic exegesis[19]). The reader's own journey becomes the unspoken fourth narrative that is fused with the above three as the Psalter is read.

Historical Survey of The Psalms as an Ordered and Unified Book

According to Goulder, "The oldest commentary on the meaning of the Psalter is the manner of their arrangement in the Psalter."[20] Jesus's words in Luke 24:44 could have been one of the earliest statements with regards to the design of the Psalter—what is written about Jesus in the Psalms "is necessary to be fulfilled" (ὅτι δεῖ πληρωθῆναι).[21] In other words, the Psalter is a prophetic text with a *telos*. The early church understood this design by emphasizing Jesus as the descendant of David (Acts 13:22–23) through whom the sure blessings of David promised by God are fulfilled through the resurrection. Thus, Jesus is the Son of Yhwh and the king of Psalm 2 (Acts 13:33–35).[22]

Very early on, in the first few centuries after Christ, the logic of arrangement of individual psalms was already of interest. According to G. Braulik, "*Hippolytus's Homily* 'On the psalms' (*HomPs*) is the oldest known systematic reflection on the Psalter."[23] Rabbi Abbahu, Eusebius, Basil, and Jerome discussed the ordering of the Psalms and how Ps 1 could function as an introduction to the entire Psalter.[24] Also noted in the Babylonian Talmud, psalms were grouped according to the approximation of the ideas they contain.[25] The *Midrash Tehillim*, with references dating to the first few centuries,

---

19. Fishbane writes, "Legal provisions regarded as having been revealed by God and viewed as authoritative divine utterances came to constitute Sinaitic revelation as given by God to man. In the course of time this revealed law was viewed as definitive. Yet its very authoritativeness underscores the dilemma caused by the inevitable inability of the first revelation to deal with all new situations and unforeseen contingencies. This problem was variously resolved in different biblical genres and narratives." Hence, Legal exegesis is the expression of "ongoing legal *traditio*" (transmission) of the received authoritative *traditum* (tradition). In similar ways, Aggadic exegesis is the "later homiletical transformations of authoritative texts" (Fishbane, "Revelation and Tradition," 343, 351; "Inner-Biblical Exegesis," 38–43).

20. Goulder, *Psalms of the Sons of Korah*, 1.

21. Dale Brueggemann notes that Luke 24:44 tells us that Jesus "was not looking at select messianic predictions but referring to a message written 'in all the scriptures' (v. 27). This encourages us to see the New Testament finding a messianic maximum in the Old Testament rather than a minimum" (Brueggemann, "Evangelists and the Psalms," 243).

22. Acts 13:33–35 cites Isa 55:3; Pss 2:7; 16:10 (cf. Heb 1:5). It must be noted, however, that the name "Jesus" does not appear in the Psalms.

23. Braulik notes that the text was written "in Rome at the beginning of the third century," and that Hippolytus "presumably considered the arrangement of the Psalms to be of hermeneutical relevant, because he reflects upon their position in the Psalter: 'Two psalms were read to us and it is necessary to state why they are the first.' (*Hom. Ps. 18*)" (Braulik, "Psalter and Messiah," 31).

24. Auwers, *La Composition*, 12–14. Wenham, "Towards a Canonical Reading," 335.

25. Vesco, *Le psautier de David*, 1:32.

provides one of the earliest explicit understanding of the five-book arrangement of the Psalter.[26] Although the significance of the order in the Psalms had been recognized in the writings of early rabbinic literature,[27] further clarity on the Psalter's overall shape and message, remained elusive.[28]

According to Labuschagne, "the German scholar, Friedrich Köster [1837] was the first in modern times to explicitly address the problem of the arrangement of the psalms."[29] Köster notes that "from its beginning, it is to be expected that this [the arrangement of the Psalms] will not be a work of chance, but of a certain ordering."[30]

Dorsey traces interests in the structural order of the Psalms back to Thomas Boys (1824),[31] an English scholar, who "seems to have been the first modern structural analyses of entire biblical books, studying the internal organization of 1 Thessalonians, 2 Thessalonians, Philemon, 2 Peter, and some of the Psalms."[32]

Ernst Hengstenberg (1845), J. Stähelin (1859), F. Hitzig (1863, 1865), B. Jacob and F. Delitzsch are a few nineteenth-century scholars who addressed structural features, links and the order of the Psalms.[33] John Forbes's *Studies on the Book of Psalms* (1888), applying the techniques of Robert Lowth's principles of parallelism to the entire Psalter (1825), is another early work in English.[34] However, as Wenham notes, they remained "lone voices crying in the wilderness."[35]

At the dawn of the twentieth century, Gunkel's (1926) revolutionary genre/form-critical approach (*Gattungsforschung, Formgeschichte*) took the center stage of Psalms scholarship.[36] Following and expanding on Gunkel's approach, Mowinckel, Kraus, Weiser, and Gerstenberger continue to influence generations of Psalms scholars with

---

26. "As Moses gave five books of laws to Israel, so David gave five Books of Psalms to Israel, the Book of Psalms entitled Blessed is the man (Ps 1:1), the Book entitled For the Leader: Maschil (Ps 42:1), the Book, A Psalm of Asaph (Ps 73:1), the Book, A Prayer of Moses (Ps 90:1), and the Book, Let the redeemed of the LORD say (Ps 107:2)" (Braude, *Midrash on Psalms*, 1:5). See Wilson, *EHP*, 200.

27. Vesco also writes, "according to the *Midrash Tehillim*, regarding Ps 3, when Rabbi Joshua ben Levi tried to put the psalms in order, a heavenly voice replied: 'Do not wake that which is asleep.' And when Rabbi Ishmael, in the presence of his master, wanted to arrange the Psalms according to their own order, his teacher said, 'it is written: All His commandments are sure. They remain forever, they are done in truth and uprightness' (Ps 111: 7–8)" (Vesco, *Le psautier de David*, 1:32).

28. Zakovitch, "Interpretative Significance," 215; Barton argues that the rabbis were seldom concerned with holistic interpretation and that "the rabbis treat biblical books as wholes in the sense that they do not divide them up into sources" (Barton, *Old Testament Canon*, 48).

29. Labuschagne, "Compositional Structure of the Psalter," 1–29.

30. Köster, *Die Psalmen*, x.

31. Boys, *Key to the Book of Psalms*.

32. Dorsey, *Literary Structure of the Old Testament*, 19.

33. Labuschagne, "Compositional Structure of the Psalter," 1.

34. Forbes, *Studies on the Book of Psalms*; Lowth, *Lectures on the Sacred Poetry*.

35. Wenham, "Canonical Reading," 335.

36. Gunkel and Begrich, *Einleitung in die Psalmen*; *Introduction to Psalms*; *Die Psalmen*. The ideas present in the *Einleitung* were already found in an earlier article in the second edition of *Die Religion in Geschichte und Gegenwart* (1927–31). See also Gunkel, *Psalms*.

Formgeschichte.³⁷ It can be said that from its inception to the mid-twentieth century, Psalms scholarship was defined by concerns of the text's compositional history.³⁸ However, in the decades that followed, there was a gradual shift to more text-centered studies.³⁹ Reviewing several volumes produced by the Forms of the Old Testament Literature project, David Petersen notes that two important articles were reformulating the prevailing methodologies of Psalm studies.⁴⁰ James Muilenburg (1969) sought to give more attention to rhetorical and literary features of the biblical text.⁴¹ Rolf Knierim raised questions on the fluidity of the genre and relationships between the genre and "its content, mood, function, intention, or concern on the other."⁴² Since then, there has been a growing concern of the *individuality* of the text as a unit in biblical scholarship.

John Barton reasons that a concentration on genre and form criticism is also due to a rise in interest in reading the Bible "as literature" from the late 1940s.⁴³ The adoption of structuralism in linguistic studies, in the wake of Ferdinand de Saussure, and in literary studies in the early 1960s, coupled with various new theories in literary studies further rattle the base of classical form-criticism.⁴⁴

From the 1960s, the early vestiges of a burgeoning of critical methods that moved from diachronic to synchronic⁴⁵ concerns could be seen in Psalms scholarship. It is likely that the works of G. von Rad (1962), W. Zimmerli (1972), J. Brennan (1976), C.

---

37. Various interpretations in the 1960s expanded on the postulations of enthronement cult-settings by Mowinckel. For example, Kraus (royal Zion festival); Weiser (covenant renewal ceremony); Gerstenberger (liturgical sermons). See Mowinckel, *Psalmenstudien* (1924); *Psalms in Israel's Worship* (1962); Kraus, *Worship in Israel* (1966); *Psalms* (1988); Weiser, *Psalms* (2000); Gerstenberger, *Psalms, Part 1* (1991).

38. Petersen notes that even in the late 1960s, the "Hebrew Bible scholarship could, in many circles, be described as involving a discrete set of readily identifiable methods: lower [textual] and higher [historical] criticisms" (Petersen, "Hebrew Bible Form Criticism," 29). See also Gillingham, "Studies of the Psalms," 209–16.

39. Sweeney and Ben Zvi, introduction to *Changing Face of Form Criticism*, 3; Stensvaag, "Recent Approaches to the Psalms," 195–212.

40. The Forms of the Old Testament Literature (FOTL) project seeks to produce a series of volumes that cover the entire Old Testament using a common format and methodology of form analysis. Each volume examines the genre, setting, structure, and intention associated with the biblical literature. See "Forms of Old Testament Literature (FOTL)"; Petersen, "Hebrew Bible Form Criticism," 30.

41. Muilenburg, "Form Criticism," 1–20.

42. Knierim, "Old Testament Form Criticism Reconsidered," 442, 449.

43. While Barton provides a good overview and analysis of how this transition had occurred, Knierim, who wrote in 1973, has already suggested such assimilation. See Barton, "Classifying Biblical Criticism," 25; Knierim, "Old Testament Form Criticism," 440–41.

44. Barton, "Classifying Biblical Criticism," 29.

45. The term, "synchronic," can be defined as "the approach which aims at the definition and description of the structure of a text in the final form in which it is handed down to us." On the other hand, "diachronic" is understood as "the approach which aims at the definition and description of the compositional/redactional history of this text" (Hoftijzer, "Holistic or Compositional Approach?" 98). See Hong, "Synchrony and Diachrony," 521–39.

Westermann (1981), and J. Reindl (1981) on the Psalter foreshadowed the "second" revolution of Psalms study in the twentieth century.[46] Von Rad considers the Psalms to be Israel's personal theological responses to God, having experienced Yhwh's mighty saving acts and his choice of the house of David for perpetuity and blessings.[47] Westermann downplayed the prevailing occupation with *Sitz im Leben* and emphasized the Psalter as an entire unit.[48] Zimmerli uncovers the pairing of psalms (twin-Psalms) connected by keywords and motifs.[49] He has shown that the juxtaposition of two psalms can bring about a richer understanding when both psalms are considered together.[50] Brennan made three important observations: First, there is an attempt "to impose some sort of logical order upon the various collections" which extends to the entire Psalter. Second, there is an effort "to adapt and apply much earlier material to later conditions." Third, "Such a reading of the Psalter opens the way to an eschatological and messianic interpretation of many texts which had originally only a limited national and historic setting."[51] These scholars set the stage for what would come.

By the 1980s, the "second" revolution of Psalms research was clearly underway. According to Barton, this "real shift of perspective" (from the "author" to the "text,")[52] was pioneered by B. S. Childs (1978)[53] and brought to mainstream Psalms scholarship by his student, G. H. Wilson.

---

46. Von Rad, "Israel Before Jahweh"; Westermann, *Praise and Lament*, 250–58; Zimmerli, "Zwillingspsalmen," 105–16; Reindl, "Weisheitliche Bearbeitung," 333–56; Brennan, "Some Hidden Harmonies," 126–58; "Psalms 1–8," 25–29.

47. Bosma, "Discerning the Voices in the Psalms,"185.

48. For example, he concluded that praise psalms "find fulfillment in Christ." The praise of God is fulfilled when Christ praised God the Father at the completion of his work on the cross by his death (he noted that this is a twist because, in the Psalms, the "dead" do not praise God). In similar ways, the Laments find a culmination in Christ when he took on the words of lament in Ps 22 on the cross. See Westermann, *Praise and Lament*, 161. Separately on methodology, Westermann writes, "an individual psalm can be adequately understood only in the context of the group to which it belongs, i.e., by comparing it with psalms of the same genre" (Westermann, *Psalms*, 28).

49. For example, he briefly points out the "twinning" of Pss 1–2; 32–33; 38–39; 39–40; 43–44; 69–70; 74–75; 77–78; 79–80; 80–81; 105–106; 127–128. See his detailed analysis on Pss 111–112 in Zimmerli, "Zwillingspsalmen,"106–7.

50. E.g., Pss 111–112 are joined by the term "the fear of the LORD." At the end of both psalms, there is a shift in the subject of discussion (from Yhwh to לכל-עשיהם in 111:10; from the "righteous" to the רשע in 112:10). These psalms, when seen individually, describe the works and fate of its subjects mentioned in the final verse. However, when both psalms are seen in juxtaposition, the enriched perspective is a contrast between the outcome of the righteous and the wicked. See Zimmerli, "Zwillingspsalmen," 109.

51. Brennan, "Psalms 1–8," 28–29.

52. By "author," Barton means one of the four coordinates of his critical theory schema, which is modified from the schema presented by Abrams, *Mirror and the Lamp*. Related to the *text* is, on one side, the *content* (the subject matter); on the other side, the *author* (his experiences, emotions, and settings); and on the third side, the *audience* (the rhetoric in persuasion). See Barton, "Classifying Biblical Criticism," 22–24.

53. A year before the publication of his well-known *Introduction to the Old Testament as Scripture* (1979), Childs published the concept of the canonical approach in Childs, "Canonical Shape of the

The Design of the Psalter

Since Wilson's seminal work (*EHP*, 1985), the questions of the shape and message of the Psalter have captured the imagination of Psalms scholarship on both sides of the Atlantic. The works of Childs and Wilson were quickly picked up by scholars such as P. D. Miller (1980),[54] J. L. Mays (1987),[55] D. Howard (1989),[56] J. C. McCann (1993),[57] J. Creach (1996),[58] F.-L. Hossfeld and E. Zenger (2000),[59] and others,[60] who focused on the Psalms in its final composition as a "literary unity,"[61] and offered nuanced propositions on the editorial shape and shaping of the Psalter. Martin Klingbeil's survey of major commentaries on the Psalms from 1935–2003 reveals that from the 1970s, commentators had indeed moved towards more literary approaches.[62] By 2014, deClaissé-Walford found that a new generation of Psalms commentators had taken canonical and editorial arrangements of the psalms into account.[63]

An important methodology that has recently taken root is the lexical/thematic links analysis. Howard's method of exhaustive examination of lexical links within a group of neighboring psalms, coupled with the growing sophistication of biblical software, has spawned an increasing number of doctoral theses adopting a similar

---

Prophetic Literature"; See also Childs "Analysis of a Canonical Formula," 357–64.

54. Miller, "Beginning of the Psalter," 83–92; "End of the Psalter," 103–10; "Synonymous-Sequential Parallelism in the Psalms," 256–60.

55. Mays, "Place of the Torah-Psalms," 3–12; "Question of Context," 14–20.

56. Howard, *Structure of Psalms 93–100*; "Editorial Activity in the Psalter," 274–85; "Contextual Reading of Psalms 90–94," 108–23; "Psalm 94," 667–85.

57. McCann, "Books I-III and the Editorial Purpose," 93–107; "Wisdom's Dilemma," 18–30; "Shape of Book I," 340–48; "Reading from the Beginning (again)," 129–42; "Single Most Important Text," 63–75; "Shape and Shaping," 350–62.

58. Creach, *Yahweh as Refuge*; "Shape of Book Four," 63–76; "Like a Tree," 34–46; "Destiny of the Righteous," 49–61.

59. Hossfeld and Zenger, *Psalmen*; *Psalms 2*; *Psalms 3*; "Neue Und Alte Wege," 332–43.

60. Mitchell, *Message of the Psalter*; "Lord, Remember David" (2006); Grant, *King as Exemplar* (1997); Davis, "Contextual Analysis of Psalms 107–118," (1996).

61. An example of a commentary that viewed the Psalms as a literary unit and work of art is Ridderbos, *Die Psalmen* (1972). See also Kugel, *Idea of Biblical Poetry* (1981); Berlin, *Poetics and Interpretation* (1983); Alter, *Art of Biblical Poetry* (1985); *Dynamics of Biblical Parallelism* (1985); Schökel, *Manual of Hebrew Poetics* (1988).

62. Klingbeil, "Off the Beaten Track," 29–33. He adds that from the 1980s, fewer Psalms commentators adopted comparative methodologies. He calls this trend, a "going off the beaten track" (of form-critical analysis), revealing an "increasing dissatisfaction" with the method among commentators. This dissatisfaction was not merely rhetorical. He cites Hans-Joachim Kraus, who changed his approach from the fourth to the fifth revised edition of his Psalms commentary, moving from form-critical to "descriptive categories, based on the content and context of the various psalms."

63. She cites McCann's work in Doran et al., *New Interpreter's Bible*; Hossfeld and Zenger, *Psalms*; deClaissé-Walford et al., *Book of Psalms*; deClaissé-Walford, "Canonical Approach to Scripture," 8–9, and I add to her list with Vesco, *Le psautier de David traduit*.

methodology.[64] Almost every literary unit in the Psalter has been studied exhaustively by this approach.[65]

However, this methodology seems to be increasingly counterproductive. For instance, the plethora of lexical links generated made it increasingly harder to find the dominant idea across the unit of concern, let alone the entire Psalter. To address the problem of numerous lexical links and the inability of distinguishing a truly significant connection, scholars typically sharpen the criteria for claiming intentional links. Such solutions, in general, provide distinctions between strong or weak connections.[66] Perhaps one of the most recent solutions proposed is M. Snearly's (and C. Richards) statistical criterion based on a lexeme's frequency of occurrence and its associated location.[67] Nonetheless, it is difficult for such studies to expand beyond the single literary unit. Moreover, the research of formal poetic devices has not yet been thoroughly integrated into such lexical/semantic studies.[68] Often, it is not clear how conclusions reached via lexical/thematic studies correspond with poetical devices or the macrostructure of the Psalms. Different conclusions reached for separate collections highlight different emphases and there is currently little effort to integrate these studies.[69]

Thus, consolidating these studies is a much-needed endeavor,[70] which is possible thanks to various studies on the Psalms carried out in the last two decades. In the following section, we will survey several important works and consolidate their proposed

---

64. Davis, "Contextual Analysis of Psalms 107–118"; Kimmitt, "Shape of Psalms 42–49"; Cha, "Psalms 146–150"; Smith, "Redactional Criteria and Objectives"; Jones, "Psalms of Asaph"; Todd, "Poetic and Contextual Analysis"; de Hoog, "Canonical Reading of Psalm 119"; Snearly, "Return of the King." The theses above generally have a similar methodology. Notably, Todd and Snearly have included poetics as part of their analyses in the theses.

65. Usually, conjunctions, prepositions, particles, negative adverbs, interrogative, demonstrative, personal and relative pronouns are excluded in such analyses.

66. This has been variously defined. For instance, Howard classifies links into three main groups: "Key-word links," "thematic" and "structure/genre" similarities. Kimmitt divides them into "Key-lexeme links" and "Thematic-lexeme links." It is somewhat a subjective endeavor of grouping common lexemes as strong or weak (incidental) links. Hoog applied Leonard's criteria for grading lexical connections ("quality"). His work focuses on Ps 119 within Book V. See Howard, *Structure of Psalms 93–100*, 99; Hoog, "Canonical Reading of Psalm 119," 60–62; Leonard, "Identifying Inner-Biblical Allusions," 245–57.

67. He notes, "key-word links, which is defined as a word or phrase for which at least half of all occurrences in Book V are in one group and/or at least 20 percent of all occurrences in the Psalter are in one group." Snearly, "Return of the King," 210; *Return of the King*, 1, 120, 187; Richards's dissertation is plausibly one of the latest. See Richards's SBL presentation, "Toward the Kingdom."

68. Works that try to integrate formal and tacit analyses of the Psalms include Maloney, "Word Fitly Spoken"; "Intertextual Links," 11–21; Todd, "Poetic and Contextual Analysis."

69. Wilson notes that the relationships between groups of psalms within the Books of the Psalter are an area of research that requires focus. See Wilson, "Understanding the Purposeful Arrangement," 43.

70. Gillingham's article is a helpful piece of work in this area. See Gillingham, "Zion Tradition."

approaches, structures and programs in an attempt to bring together a macro study of the whole Psalter.

Survey of Key Studies on The Psalms as an Ordered and Unified Book

Brevard S. Childs

Childs's works have been well studied.[71] He defined his canonical approach as "interpreting the biblical text in relation to a community of faith and practice for whom it served a particular theological role as possessing divine authority."[72] The final form of text or book has an important hermeneutical function.[73] It establishes a "peculiar profile of a passage,"[74] emphasizing certain elements and reducing the importance of others, so as to bring to the forefront the theological message that needs to be heard.[75] This is well illustrated in a short article of Childs where he cites Ps 102:19, remarking that the final redactors had intended "the divine word of promise, which was first given to a generation in exile, to be written down for the sake of the coming generation."[76]

Childs highlights six methodological concerns on reading the Psalms: First, the introduction of the Psalms provides a hermeneutical refocus. Psalm 1 functions as a call to Israel to meditate upon the Torah[77] in the written form. Second, composite

---

71. Recent studies include Sumpter, "Substance of Psalm 24," (2011); Driver, "Brevard Childs," (2009); Olson, "Zigzagging through Deep Waters," (2009); Xun, *Theological Exegesis* (2010); Seitz, *Bible as Christian Scripture* (2013). Perhaps the sharpest criticism of Childs work is by Barr, especially in his *Holy Scripture* and *Concept of Biblical Theology*. Others—such as Barton, McEvenue, and Brueggemann—have also registered their reservations on the canonical approach. See McEvenue, "Old Testament, Scripture or Theology," 229–42; Brueggemann, "Brevard Childs's Canon Criticism," 311–26; Barton, *Reading the Old Testament*, 77–103, 208–11; *Old Testament Canon*, 43–51.

72. Childs, *IOTS*, 74.

73. Childs, *IOTS*, 73. Childs was not so much concerned with "aesthetic unity" or coherency of a work. Barton understands this holistic "theological shape" as having "an edifying meaning, a 'confessional' meaning, a worthy meaning, a consistent meaning . . . Different criteria of meaning, truth and consistency apply in reading Scripture from those we regularly employ in reading other books." Barton, *Old Testament Canon*, 48–49.

74. Childs, *IOTS*, 77; "Canonical Shape," 47–48.

75. Childs, *Biblical Theology*, 71.

76. Childs, "Analysis of a Canonical Formula," 361.

77. In Childs's view, the entire Psalter, as introduced by Ps 1, is to be read as the Torah. Scholars have understood the term, "Torah" in Ps 1:2 in different ways. LeFebvre summarizes the meaning of "Torah" in Ps 1:2 as such: "(1) a certain, individual precept (*a* torah); (2) the whole Deuteronomic law collection (*the* Torah); or (3) the complete Pentateuch (also *the* Torah)." A fourth suggestion is a more general term, "instruction" rather than "law." LeFebvre's own definition is interesting. He notes that when Moses composed two documents, a song, and a book of the law before he died (Deut 31:22–24). The reciting of the song involves the observation of the book of the law as well. In other words, "Deut 31–32 identifies law-contemplation with song-singing. It is the song which will be forever known by the people (Deut 31–32), while the book is not accessible to them." Lefebvre then applies this concept to the Psalmody. He argues that the "Psalmody served as a means of torah-meditation . . . Based on

psalms (e.g., Ps 108) illustrate that "psalms have been loosened from a given cultic context" and reappropriated for a different context.[78] Third, original settings identified for Royal psalms are given messianic significance. Childs considers it likely that the final redactors had provided a "new meaning" (messianic) for reading the Royal psalms.[79] Fourth, Childs argues that at times, eschatological elements are abruptly placed in complaint psalms, which signals an eschatological impetus, not "different in kind from the prophetic message."[80] Fifth, many psalms (e.g., Pss 14; 25; 51) that began as an individual prayer shift toward a communal orientation at the end. Childs argues that this is evidence of collective reception by later generations.[81] Finally, Childs notes that superscriptions alter the way the psalms were understood. He argued that late[82] psalm superscriptions are often used in association with David.[83] This Davidization allows the Psalms to "testify to all the common troubles and joys of ordinary human life in which all persons participate."[84] The Davidic psalms become a representative psalm of the common person.

While Childs raised important concerns about reading the Psalms, he did not postulate any macrostructure or theological program for it. This work, however, was taken up by Childs's protégé, Gerald H. Wilson.

---

the paradigm in Deut 31–32 it can be seen that Israel used surrogate texts for torah-contemplation, particularly songs" (LeFebvre, "Torah-Meditation and the Psalms," 220–25). Elsewhere, Kratz also argues that the person who reads Ps 1 and five-books of the Psalter is learning and living a life under the Torah. See Kratz, "Die Tora Davids," 32.

78. He also cited how 1 Chr 16 used parts of Pss 105, 96, and 106 in a new setting. Childs, *IOTS*, 515.

79. For instance, the superscription attributed to Solomon and the concluding subscript, "the prayers of David are ended," suggest that the redactor wanted Ps 72 to be "understood in the context of the biblical story found in Kings and Chronicles" rather than "an example of ancient Near Eastern royal ideology" (Childs, *IOTS*, 517).

80. E.g., complaint elements in Ps 102:2–12, 24–25a are separated by an eschatological segment with little literary connection. Childs also notes that various scholars explained that the phenomenon arose because the psalms were likely "reworked" in the postexilic period. See Childs, *IOTS*, 518.

81. Childs, *IOTS*, 520.

82. Mays points out that because "the Greek text has added to Psalm 95 (MT 96) 'of David when the house was built after the captivity,' it is apparent that these editors were not thinking historically. Such practices make it very clear that what is at work in the later history of the '*le dàwid*' attributions is some kind of canonical ordering and defining that proceeds oblivious of any sort of historical or autobiographical concerns" (Mays, "David of the Psalms," 153). For a discussion on superscriptions as a "late" phenomenon, see Sheppard, "Theology and the Book of Psalms," 147.

83. For instance, the superscriptions of Pss 51 and 56 draw the reader to the historical setting in Samuel rather than the cultic setting in the psalms themselves. By reading the psalm within the context of the historical events, the reader is given access "into his [David's] emotional life," connecting the reader's context with the historical context of the superscriptions (Childs, *IOTS*, 521). See also Childs, "Psalm Titles and Midrashic Exegesis," 137–50.

84. Childs, *IOTS*, 521.

Gerald H. Wilson

Wilson's approach is both historical-comparative and literary. He believes that there is "an editorial movement to bind the whole [Psalter] together."[85] The first two-thirds of his landmark work, *The Editing of the Hebrew Psalter*,[86] consists of comparative studies of explicit editorial markers found in Mesopotamian hymnic literature and Qumran psalms manuscripts. However, after 140 pages of such study, Wilson concedes that "any organizational concern or purpose of the editor(s) must be inferred from the *tacit* arrangement of the pss."[87] Several techniques of tacit editorial organization are given in Wilson's works. One of the clearest is the use of thematic parallels within the Psalms.[88] Abrupt authorship changes in the superscriptions are also used to mark "strong disjunctions" in the Psalter, especially in Books I–III.[89] Certain words in the superscriptions identifying genre "designations"[90] can mark a disjuncture.[91] There is a tendency to use verbal parallels,[92] employed as "identical first lines," to unite psalms in Books IV–V (105:1; 106:1; 107:1).[93] Doxological phrases at the end of major divisions (e.g., 104–106; 111–117; 135) and the use of הודו phrases to "introduce the next segment of psalms" are important evidence of editorial arrangements.[94] Even "the absence of a superscript function as an editorial method of . . . [combining an] 'untitled' psalm with its immediate predecessor."[95]

---

85. Wilson, "Shape of the Book of Psalms," 129.

86. Parts of this book are also expanded and published as separate articles. Wilson, "Evidence of Editorial Divisions," 337–52; "Qumran Psalms Scroll [11QPsª] Reconsidered," 624–42; "Use of Royal Psalms," 85–94; "Use of 'Untitled' Psalms," 404–13.

87. Wilson, *EHP*, 142, emphasis added. Wilson argues that it does not mean that Psalms superscripts do not contribute in any way to the organizational purposes of the Psalms. He notes that "while there is no evidence that the final editor produced the s/ss to serve editorial ends in the organization of the psalter, there are indications that they actively utilized these fixed s/ss in their purposeful arrangement of the pss" (Wilson, *EHP*, 144).

88. Wilson cites the parallels between Pss 90 and 106, evident in the emphasis on the character of Moses, and the narration of the punishment of Israel because of their sins. See Wilson, *EHP*, 187.

89. Authorship changes, as an organizational technique, occur mainly in Books I–III and are less obvious in Books IV–V of the Psalter. See Wilson, "Evidence of Editorial Divisions," 339, 349; For a list of differences in the organization techniques between Books I–III and IV–V, see Wilson, "Use of Royal Psalms," 87.

90. They are distinct from genre categories defined by form criticism.

91. He cites, "1. *šgywn* (Ps vii); 2. *mktm* (6 psalms); 3. *tplh* (5 psalms); 4. *mśkyl* (13 psalms); 5. *thlh* (Ps cxlv); 6. *hllwyh* (16 psalms)" and that "the major distinguishing characteristic of these terms is that they never occur together in the same superscript" (Wilson, "Evidence of Editorial Divisions," 340).

92. For example, both Pss 136 and 145 are concerned with Yhwh's "wondrous works," his "steadfast love," and praise Yhwh for his provision to his creatures. See Wilson, *EHP*, 189.

93. Wilson, *EHP*, 195.

94. Wilson, *EHP*, 190.

95. Wilson, "Use of 'Untitled' Psalms," 404.

Wilson also posits an interesting "interlocking" technique that binds the entire Psalter together.[96] The whole Psalter is bound by a final Wisdom frame (1; 73; 90; 107; 145) which interlocks with a Royal Covenant frame (2; 72; 89; 144). This is shown graphically below:

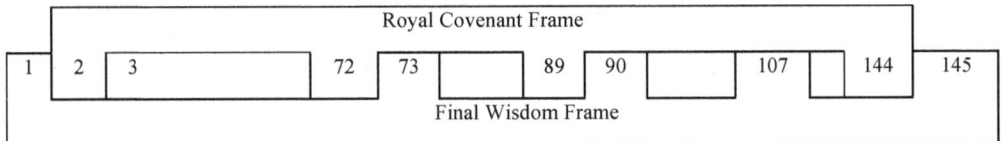

Figure 1: Wilson's Final Frame of the MT Psalter[97]

Three elements, namely, the introduction (Ps 1), the five-book divisions and the final Hallel serve as the basic trajectory of the editorial agenda.[98] Books I–III trace the establishment of Yhwh's covenant with the Davidic king (2), celebration of Yhwh's faithfulness to his covenant (72), and apparent failure of the covenant because of Israel's sin (89:38–39, 44). Book IV opens with a hopeful response to the pessimism at the end of Book III. It focuses on the kingship of Yhwh who had been the refuge of Israel. In Book V, the two Davidic segments at the beginning and end show that David is the model exemplar who places this trust in Yhwh. The massive Torah Ps 119 serves to "emphasize the primacy of the law in man's relationship to Yhwh," and that access to God (120–134) and his blessings is "through the appropriation of and obedience to Torah."[99] The final Hallel is a response to Ps 145:21 by all the recipients of Yhwh's promises.[100] The final result is "a Psalter that recalls the foundational pre-monarchical faith of Israel (90; 105–106) and directs the faithful to trust in Yahweh as king rather than in fragile and failing human princes."[101]

---

96. Wilson, "Shaping the Psalter," 72–82.

97. Redrawn from Wilson, "Shaping the Psalter," 81.

98. Wilson's redactional theory is further elaborated and crystallized in an article published a year after his book. Wilson, "Use of Royal Psalms," 85–94.

99. Note that in 11QPs^a, Ps 119 comes after the Songs of Ascents. Wilson notes that "the placement of this psalm after the [Songs of Ascents] psalms, rather than before them as in the canonical Psalter, has a significant effect. Rather than Torah precipitating pilgrimage to Jerusalem and the temple pilgrimage, in effect, leads to the Torah." Wilson, "Qumran Psalms Scroll (11QPs^a)," 460; Wilson, *EHP*, 223.

100. According to Wilson, the final text of the Psalter is most likely a composition developed under the "social matrix" of the "last century BC and the first century AD" (Wilson, "Use of Royal Psalms," 93). Elsewhere, Wilson writes, "I would like to suggest that events surrounding the first Jewish war with Rome in 66–70 CE, as well as the activities of Johanan ben Zakkai and the great Academy of Yavneh following the war, may well have influenced the distinctive characteristics of the final form of the Psalms" (Wilson, "First Century CE," 106).

101. Wilson, "King, Messiah," 392–93; "Structure of the Psalter," 240.

The Design of the Psalter

Two issues stand out in Wilson's work.[102] First, Wilson has foregrounded the study of colophonic and explicit editorial markers as organization techniques. Wilson may not have successfully explained the use of such explicit data in the Psalter,[103] but his proposals on the use of superscriptions, doxologies, formulaic phrases as explicit and tacit evidence of organization have piqued immense interests in Psalms scholarship. Second, the study of the Psalter as a coherent editorial organized work has taken form. Wilson's postulations of the macrostructural agenda of the five Books have found widespread acceptance though they continue to be interpreted and nuanced in various ways.[104]

Erich Zenger

Writing from Germany, Zenger blazed the trail of reading the Psalter as a "book" in continental Europe. His voluminous works on the Psalter and his three-volume commentary (co-written with F.-L. Hossfeld)[105] quickly became important references.[106]

As early as 1987, Zenger had expressed the view that the Psalter is increasingly being considered as a book of prayer and contemplation (*Gebets- und Betrachtungsbuch*) as opposed to a Second Temple songbook.[107] In "Was Wird Anders bei Kanonischer Psalmenauslegung," Zenger lists four observations of the canonical interpretation.[108]

---

102. Over the last three decades, Wilson's work has been well documented and sometimes, sharply criticized. See esp. Mitchell, "Lord, Remember David"; Howard, *Structure of Psalms 93–100*.

103. Wilson was not too confident of how superscriptions worked, especially in Books IV and V of the Psalter. He confessed, "the absence of superscripts reflects an awareness on the part of the Psalter editor(s) of alternate traditions for the combination/division of these pss and represents a purposeful technique employed to preserve them [in Books I–III]. This inference can be extended to other examples of such pss in Books 4 and 5, with *varying degrees of confidence*" (Wilson, *EHP*, 181, emphasis added).

104. Wilson's reasoning of Book V as a pious portrayal of David rather than his kingship has not received rigorous affirmation because Books IV–V continue to portray a positive view of the Davidic kingship (101; 103; 108; 110; 144–145) and Zion (120–134).

105. Hossfeld and Zenger, *Die Psalmen*. Volumes two and three have been translated as part of the Hermeneia series, which include a number of excurses that analyze various collections of psalms.

106. A brief list of Zenger's thoughts on the canonical concepts of the Psalms and various methods he employed to formulate his thoughts in several of his works from 1991 to 2010: Zenger, "Was Wird Anders," 397–413; "Das Buch der Psalmen," 348–70; "Der Psalter als Buch," 1–58; "Psalmenforschung," 399–435; "Psalmenexegesis und Psalterexegese," 17–65. Beyond these references, other related articles are also consulted. See Zenger, "Der Jüdischer Psalter," 95–105; "Der Zion als Ort der Gottesnähe," 84–114; "Torafrömmigkeit," 380–96; Hossfeld and Zenger, "Neue Und Alte Wege," 332–43. See also Wenham's appraisal of Zenger's article, "Towards a Canonical Reading," 334–46.

107. Zenger, "Was Wird Anders," 397.

108. Zenger avoids a lengthy discussion on the term "canonical" in most of his works. It is not clear to what extent he has adopted the term entirely as conceived by Childs. However, Zenger is clearly interested in the intent and message through the arrangement of individual psalms in the Psalter and the location of the Psalter in the larger context of the Hebrew Bible.

First, canonical psalm interpretation observes the relationship between neighboring psalms, in particular, the end of one psalm and the beginning of the next.[109] Concatenations of psalms provide additional meaning to an individual psalm that is not explicit when it is considered on its own.[110]

Second, canonical psalm interpretation observes the position of the psalm (as intended by the editor) within its compositional unit.[111] Interpretation of a psalm is enriched when it is considered within the context of a group of psalms around it.[112]

Third, psalm superscriptions are to be read along an interpretive horizon.[113] Reading the Davidic collections in connection with the figure David and the biblical narrative through the superscriptions allow the reader to personalize the psalm and respond with hope in times of suffering and affliction in their own lives.[114] These superscriptions become an interpretive horizon from which one learns to see the collective and individual concerns of the psalms.[115]

---

109. Zenger, "Was Wird Anders," 399. He cites existing examples of "twin-psalms" such as Pss 1–2; 111–112; 90–92; 135–136. Other examples include the "binding" (*Zusammenbindung*) of Pss 50; 51 through Ps 51:18–21 and Pss 84; 85 through Ps 84:9–10. See also Zenger, "Der Psalter als Buch," 13–18. The technique concatenation (or "pearling") has been described by D. H. Müller as early as 1896. See Müller, *Die Propheten*.

110. We have seen this in Zimmerli's works. Zenger cites the example of Ps 8. This hymn-like wisdom psalm that sings of God's power and provision in creation receives a fuller meaning when it is viewed with the laments in Ps 7 and in the context of the oppressed and afflicted in Pss 9–10. Psalm 8, thus, becomes the central pillar of hope. Keyword and thematic connections in Pss 12:2, 6 and 13:3b, likewise, link Pss 12 and 13 together, highlighting God's imminent action to deliver the poor and the oppressed. Bar-Efrat also argues that structure "serves to express or accentuate meaning" (Bar-Efrat, "Some Observations," 172).

111. Zenger, "Was Wird Anders," 403.

112. For instance, the group of Pss 25–34 is framed by two forms of the acrostics Pss 25 and 34. Zenger cited the correspondences of four verses in each psalm (Pss 25:13 // 34:12; 25:15 // 34:16; 25:16 // 34:17; 25:22 // 34:23). With Ps 29 at the center (highlighting Yhwh as the king of the universe), the three psalms before (Pss 26–28) and after it (Pss 30–32) form a concentric pattern. Psalm 33, seemingly out of place (without superscription), is clearly connected with Ps 32. A second example is the group, Pss 3–14. This group is framed by Pss 3:9b and 14:7 where Israel, God's people, will receive blessings from Yhwh and rejoice. Psalms 3–7 are supplications of a worshiper seeking judgments against personal threats whereas Pss 9–14, as a whole, highlights the socially-poor oppressed in the midst of a hostile world. At the center, Ps 8 shows that Yhwh is the majestic creator God whom Israel places her hopes. Zenger, "Psalmenforschung," 422–24; "Der Psalter als Buch," 19. Another example cited is Ps 149, which by itself, can be misconstrued as a military battle song. However, when this Psalm is set in context within Pss 146–150, it reflects Yhwh's invitation to his godly ones who were afflicted, in solidarity with his universal reign, to execute on the hostile powers the written judgments of Yhwh. See Zenger, "Was Wird Anders," 403.

113. Zenger, "Was Wird Anders," 407. We have also seen this principle in the works of Childs and Wilson.

114. As a further example, Zenger notes that the Asaphite psalms (Pss 50, 73–83) have a common "historical-theological" interest. On one hand, they contain descriptions of the history of Israel (her exodus, exile, and destruction of the Temple); on the other hand, all these events are gathered into Yhwh's "eschatological court" by the psalmist, seeking Yhwh, the creator and judge of the new world order, to set it right. See Zenger, "Das Buch der Psalmen," 353.

115. At the macro-level, editors use the arrangements of superscriptions and framing devices (e.g.,

Fourth, canonical interpretation pays careful attention to the intra-biblical connections and repetitions of the psalms.[116] Zenger sees that a single text must always be heard within the concerted voice of the canonical context. When the Psalter is read in these four ways, a fuller theological message is revealed, binding the psalms together as a "book."

Hossfeld and Steiner[117] recast Zenger's methodological formulation into seven increasing text pericopes: (1) literal continuation from the end of a psalm to the beginning of the next; (2) "literal resumption" with a development of meaning in the following psalm; (3) "twin-psalms" with meaning understood from the entirety of both psalms (Pss 111–112); (4) "cluster compositions" of perceivable "editorial concatenation" (Pss 3–7); (5) "group compositions" perceived by the group's compositional structure (Pss 15–24, with 19 at the center); (6) "psalm collections" through editorial superscriptions or formulas (e.g., Davidic psalms); (7) "collections by theme" (e.g., Yhwh *Malak* psalms).

In "Das Buch der Psalmen," Zenger points out that the Psalms should be read through the characteristic "parallelism" of Hebrew poetry.[118] Unlike prose, poetry works with lines (cola) "strung together on a consistent basis."[119] Each line approaches the intended meaning via a slightly different perspective and together, they produce a "fuzzy and plastic" sense of meaning that can only be grasped as a whole.[120] Hebrew poetry requires both aesthetical and holistic appreciation of the patterns and structures of the texts in order to plumb the theological intents of editorial shaping.

In this same work, he laid out the architecture of the Psalter.[121] With Pss 1–2 as the "programmatic overture,"[122] Book I is structured into four main units (3–14, 15–24, 25–34, 35–41). Book II is divided into three main units (42–49; 50; 51–72). Book III consists of two units (73–83; 84–89).[123] Book IV is divided into three sections (Mosiac 90–92; Yhwh's kingship 93–100; and Davidic 101–106). Book V is arranged in a chiastic A-B-C-B'-A' structure (107; 108–110; 111–137; 138–145; 145).[124]

Pss 1–2; 146–150). Zenger sees that new Books of the Psalter are marked by a significant change in the headings of the initial psalms (e.g., Pss 3, 42, 73, 90, 107). Furthermore, the first three Books close with a Royal psalm that has messianic concerns (Pss 41, 72, 89) and the last two Books end with the program of Yhwh's kingship (Pss 106, 145). Seen with Ps 144 (another messianic Royal psalm), Book V ends in the same way as Books I–III, which corresponds to Ps 2.

116. Zenger, "Was Wird Anders," 409.

117. For specific examples, see Hossfeld and Steiner, "Problems and Prospects," 241.

118. Zenger, "Das Buch der Psalmen," 348–70.

119. Zenger, "Das Buch der Psalmen," 360.

120. Zenger, "Das Buch der Psalmen," 360.

121. Psalms 107 and 145 (A and A') are "Lobpsalm" celebrating the "königtum YHWHs." Psalms 108–110 and 138–145 (B and B') are Davidic psalms. At the center, Pss 111–137 are divided into five small groups (Pss 111–112; 113–118; 119; 120–134; 135–137). Zenger, "Das Buch der Psalmen," 356.

122. Zenger, "Das Buch der Psalmen," 36–39.

123. Apart from Ps 86, a Davidic psalm.

124. For further details on the structure of Book V, see Hossfeld and Zenger, *Psalms 3*, 1–7; Zenger,

For Zenger, the editorial program of the Psalter is the theme of Torah wisdom and the praise of God, seen in the horizon of the whole creation, Israel and the universal rule of Yhwh.[125] Reading the Psalter within this framework gives its reader the ability to resist wicked powers in the world and rely on the saving strength of Yhwh. The entire function of the Psalter is a theological proposition: "the editorial formative sapiential theology of the Psalter is the sanctuary itself; in God, it is to be searched and lived and through which one can expect God's blessing and salvation."[126] In other words, Zenger argues that the Psalter is not used as a Second Temple liturgical composition, but rather functioned theologically as the *sanctuary*, through which one approaches God by reading, meditating and singing its words.

Zenger's work on the Psalter is extensive. On one hand, he is concerned with the diachronic formation of the Psalter as a book and on the other, how the book functioned for the postexilic reader. Zenger is perhaps the first to systematize the techniques of editorial shaping with a complete study of structural units of the entire Psalter.[127] He raised the profile of reading the Psalter as a "book." Second, Zenger highlights important arguments for the Prologue (Pss 1–2) as the "programmatic overture" of the Psalter. His argument that the Psalter itself functions as the sanctuary, not just as the songbook of the Second Temple period, seems significant. Finally, he emphasizes the importance of reading the Psalter through the hermeneutical lenses of poetry and aesthetics, which remains to be further integrated with canonical-literary approaches at this time.[128]

Jean-Luc Vesco

Vesco's two-volume commentary on the Psalter is an important French contribution to the study of the structural and thematic unity of the Psalms. Like Zenger, Vesco agrees that the Psalter must be interpreted as a book. He notes, "It is in this [book] form that reached us finally. Only a holistic reading allows us to connect the parts that bind together the various psalms, and to better identify the theology of their mutual relationship and ultimate meaning."[129] Vesco identifies several organizational

---

"Komposition Und Theologie," 97–116, which also has an English counterpart in 1998 (Zenger, "Composition and Theology," 77–102). This will be further discussed in chapter 2.

125. Zenger, "Der Psalter als Buch," 31.

126. Zenger, "Der Psalter als Buch," 47.

127. The Hossfeld-Zenger Psalms commentary is likely the first of its kind that gave serious attention to the Psalms as a book. For instance, the structuring of Book I into four units has been largely adopted. See Barbiero, *Das erste Psalmenbuch als Einheit*.

128. It is interesting that the aesthetic approach to the Psalter has almost developed into a subject of its own within Psalms scholarship. Consider the works of Alonso-Schökel, *Manual of Hebrew Poetics*; Watson, *Classical Hebrew Poetry*; Berlin, *Dynamics of Biblical Parallelism*; van Grol, "Emotions in the Psalms," 69.

129. Vesco, *Le psautier de David*, 1:34.

principles similar to those we have seen in Wilson and Zenger's works. First, he sees that collections of psalms are arranged by attributed authorship. Second, psalms are grouped according to their intended use (e.g., the Songs of Ascents). Third, psalms that begin with the formulaic *hallelujah* are often grouped together (e.g., 104–106; 111–113; 115–117; 146–150). Fourth, there are indications that psalm "genres [by the designations in the superscriptions] were used as transitions between collections."[130] Fifth, Vesco also sees that certain psalms are placed together because of their dominant motifs (e.g., 65–68 are centered on praise).[131]

Like Zenger, Vesco emphasizes Pss 1–2 as the introduction of the Psalter. He argues for the notion that the "spirituality of the Torah as divine teaching that guides man in his life [in Ps 1] structures the Psalter as a whole."[132] Significantly, sapiential psalms are strategically located at the centers of collections (e.g., 8 in 3–14; 19 in 15–24), at the beginning of a book (1; 73; 90; 107) or at the end (89; 106).[133] As a result, the Psalter takes on the appearance of a book of wisdom reflecting the influence of the wisdom circles in its final form. Equally significant is the emphasis of the messianic king, to whom God promises a universal dominion (Ps 2). Messianic or Royal psalms are also strategically distributed across the Psalter, suggesting certain deliberate organization.[134] In sum, the function of the prologue emphasizes the judgment of Israel (Ps 1) and of the nations (Ps 2), evoking the concept of eschatological judgment following Mal 3:18. They set the tone for their readers, with the promise of being blessed on one hand and Yhwh's judgment on the other, consistently resounding throughout the Psalms. Vesco considers Pss 148–150 as the conclusion of the Psalter because Ps 148:11 harks back to 2:10–12 where the kings of the nations would take heed and render praise to Yhwh.[135]

Vesco's attention to structure in the Psalter is also revealed in the organization of his commentary. Vesco divides Book I into four groups of Davidic Psalms (3–14; 15–24; 25–34; 35–41), concentrically structured around Pss 8; 19; 29; and 38.[136] Book II is divided into Pss 42–49; 50; 51–71; 72.[137] Book III is divided into the Asaphite (73–83) and Korahite (84–89) collections. Book IV consists of three main collections: Pss 90–92; 93–100; 101–106. Book V is divided into Pss 107; 108–110; 111–117; 118–119;

---

130. Vesco, *Le psautier de David*, 1:47. He cites the use of *mizmor* in the superscriptions of Pss 47–51 and the use of *Miktham* in the series of Pss 56–60 as examples. This is similar to one of Wilson's arguments.

131. Vesco, *Le psautier de David*, 1:48.

132. Vesco, *Le psautier de David*, 1:59.

133. At the end of Pss 89 and 106 (end of Books III and IV), the sapiential motif (divine teachings) is connected with descriptions of the fall of the Davidic monarchy.

134. Vesco, *Le psautier de David*, 1:68.

135. Vesco, *Le psautier de David*, 1:72–74.

136. Vesco, *Le psautier de David*, 1:95.

137. Vesco further divides the second Davidic collection (Pss 51–71) into Pss 51; 52–55; 56–60; 61–64; 65–68; 69–71.

120–134; 135; 136–150.¹³⁸ Vesco links Ps 118 to 119 rather than Ps 117, and groups the entire Pss 136–150 as a unit under the title, "The wonders of God."¹³⁹ The editorial agenda of the entire Psalter "reveals the route of salvation."¹⁴⁰ It is a divine teaching in the form of human prayers which, ultimately, are praises to God.

While Vesco's methodology echoes much of Wilson's and Zenger's, Vesco writes with a clear disposition toward an integrated reading of the Psalter. He takes a key motif found in a particular psalm and analyzes it across the entire Psalter.¹⁴¹ He tends to devote a short section in his commentary to a group of psalms before discussing the individual psalms that make up the group. Another important aspect of Vesco's work is his distinctions between man and the king; Israel and the messiah; blessedness and judgment in two journeys based on the Prologue. These twin motifs, expressed in the forms of Sapiential and Messianic/Royal psalms are strategically distributed across the Psalter. I think Vesco's dual-themed emphasis is an important proposition, though an entire coherent structure based on this approach has not been exhibited.

Jean-Marie Auwers

By the dawn of the twenty-first century, Auwers had already consolidated much research relating to the composition of the Psalter. In his monograph, *La Composition Littéraire Du Psautier: Un état de La Question*, and two separate book sections in the BETL series,¹⁴² Auwers captures important arguments on the historical¹⁴³ and literary dimensions in the composition of the Psalter. He argues that one should not interpret the Psalter only from a redactional point of view, but also from the intent and context of the final form. Interpreters must not only understand the individual parts, but the whole, in which the individual parts are interconnected.¹⁴⁴ In general, Auwers follows the methodology posited by Zenger and highlights techniques of juxtaposition¹⁴⁵ (a pair of psalms) and concatenation (linking one psalm to the next).¹⁴⁶ He argues that

---

138. Pss 136–150 is subdivided into Pss 136–37; 138–145; 146–150.

139. He further divides the final Davidic collection into Pss 138–139; 140–143; 144–145. Vesco, *Le psautier de David*, 2:1417–19.

140. Vesco, *Le psautier de David*, 1:75.

141. For instance, he provides a lengthy study of the figure of David across the entire Psalter (even in LXX and Qumran texts) in his comment on Ps 2. He argues that David is both the prototype of the future messianic king and his prayers become that of the people. The people prayed as their king. Whoever reads the Psalms becomes the new David. Likewise, he studies the motif of Zion across the entire Psalter in his analysis of Ps 3. Vesco, *Le psautier de David*, 1: 77–93, 102–11.

142. Auwers, "Les Voices," 5–26; "Le Psautier." See also Auwers, "L'organisation," 37–54; "Les Psaumes 70–72"; "Le David Des Psaumes," 187–224.

143. His book section summarizes an updated version of the historical development of the Psalter. See Auwers, "Le Psautier," 67–90.

144. Auwers, *La Composition*, 177.

145. He cites Pss 3–4; 20–21; 32–33; 103–104; 105; 111–112. See Auwers, *La Composition*, 42.

146. He traces various lexemes that occur in Pss 2–9 and notes that some recurrences can hardly

such techniques of binding "successive parts of the Psalter are meaningful only if the final editors wanted to encourage reading the book *per ordinem ex integro* [from the beginning to the end in one reading]."[147] While there is no single consistent principle of organization, groups of psalms are arranged by techniques such as juxtaposition, concatenation, genres, and chiastic structural patterns.

Auwers structures Book I in the same way as Zenger and Vesco.[148] Book II is divided into the Korahite (42–49), Asaphite (50) psalms, and three Davidic subgroups (51–64, 65–67, 69–72).[149] Book III is divided into two main groups, the Asaphite (73–83) and Korahite psalms (84–89). Auwers also identifies a parallel between the two Korahite and Asaphite groups in Books II and III shown below.

Korahite Psalms	**Pss 42–49**	**Pss 84–85, 87–88**
Lamentation	42/43 ("I")–44 ("We")	84 ("I")–85 ("We")
Divine Response	45–48	87
Lamentation	49 ("I")	88 ("We")
Asaphite Psalms	**Pss 73–77**	**Pss 78–83**
Didactic	73	78
Lamentation	74 ("We")	79–80 ("We")
Divine Response	75–76	81–82
Lamentation	77 ("I")	83 ("I")

Figure 2: Auwers and Zenger's Parallel Structures of the Korahite and Asaphite Psalms[150]

Auwers structures Book IV into three parts (90–92; 93–100; and 101–106) and Book V into four parts (107–117; 118–135; and 136–150) based on the doxological elements at the end of a group and the *hodu* phrase at the beginning of a group.[151]

While the Psalms was once a songbook of the Second Temple period (1 Chr 16), Auwers argues that its function today is found through reading the Psalter as a book and as such, "the *Sitz im Kult* has been replaced by a *Sitz in der Literatur*."[152] Auwers

---

be accidental. See Auwers, *La Composition*, 89–91.

147. Auwers, *La Composition*, 92–93; "Les Voices," 7.

148. Auwers, *La Composition*, 43–47.

149. These three Davidic subgroups are understood as "individual petitions, hymns or collective thanksgiving and complaints." Auwers, *La Composition*, 47.

150. Auwers, *La Composition*, 49; Zenger, "Das Buch der Psalmen," 354.

151. Note that this follows Wilson's structuring of Book V. Auwers, *La Composition*, 64.

152. Auwers doubts if the Levites really sang hymns such as Pss 51:18; 40:7; 50:9–13. He questions if Pss 1 and 119 were part of the Levites' song list. Furthermore, what purpose could the Royal psalms serve after the demise of the Davidic monarchy? The Psalter does not begin with a call for the liturgical

reads the program of the Psalter from its Prologue (1–2) and sees a democratization of the Davidic psalms. He suggests that "the Jewish community is like the voice of David and continues to apply to itself the extension of the benefits previously granted to David and to his successors. What was once given to David and his offspring is now granted to all the people."[153] He places the messianic reading of Ps 2 under the sapiential framework of Ps 1[154] and the latter alludes to Josh 1:7–8. Being the first chapter and book of the Former Prophets, Josh 1:7–8 invites readers to read the book with a view of keeping the Torah. In the same way, Ps 1 invites readers to view the Psalter with a view of the Torah's way of life. "The psalms that follow [Ps 1] are not only read as prayers to God but above all, a word addressed by Yhwh to his people which they are to meditate diligently."[155] The final composition of the Psalter is thus set up as a book of the Bible,[156] configured to foster a change of behavior (*conversio morum*) in its readers.

Auwers's work on the Psalter is well-researched. His characterization of the historical development and summary of various references bring about a greater depth to our understanding of the Psalms. Although he has not advanced a new methodology for reading the Psalter, his proposal to read the Psalter via the hermeneutical perspectives provided by its Prologue, and consequently as a biblical book, deserves further attention.

J. Clinton McCann

McCann has edited an important volume, *The Shape and Shaping of the Psalter*, authored a commentary on the Psalms, and several important books and articles relating to the shape of the Psalter.[157] He considers the use of literary links, genres, individual/communal psalms, repetitions, structure, and the Prologue as key techniques for reading the Psalms.[158] He subordinates questions of "form and settings" to that of "content

---

participation at the Temple day and night, rather, it begins with a call for meditation on the Torah. Although liturgical usage needs not be excluded, he concludes that the canonical Psalter is not the hymnal of the Temple and that the overall emphasis is not participation in worship. See Auwers, "Le Psautier," 86–87.

153. Auwers, "Le Psautier," 85.

154. He notes that "even if Ps 2 were the collection that prefaced a national *Kampf-Liederbuch* [battle songbook], Ps 1 makes all *Gebetbuch das der Gerechten* [Prayerbook of the righteous]" (Auwers, *La Composition*, 127). See Auwers, "Les Voices," 14.

155. Auwers, *La Composition*, 128.

156. Auwers, "Les Voices," 21.

157. McCann, "Shape and Shaping," 350–62; "Single Most Important Text," 63–75; "Reading from the Beginning (again)," 129–42; "Shape of Book I," 340–48; "Wisdom's Dilemma," 18–30; "Books I–III," 93–107; *Theological Introduction*; "Psalms as Instruction," 117–28.

158. McCann, "Books I–III," 96, 104; *Theological Introduction*, 19.

and theology."[159] The Book of Psalms is to be understood by how it can "address *us* in our time and place."[160]

In one of his most recent works on the shape of the Psalter, McCann follows Wilson's thesis: "Books I–III took shape first and have a messianic orientation, and Books IV–V respond to the crisis articulated in Psalm 89."[161] McCann considers the Prologue as the key to reading the Psalms, but adds that it contains motifs of happiness, justice, Torah, kingship, Zion, and refuge, which are not only repeated throughout the Psalter, but are often situated at strategic locations.[162] As a whole, Book I of the Psalter is to be heard and interpreted in relation to David, a suffering "messiah" who is God's son depending on Yhwh's protection.[163] Book II, ending with a Solomonic psalm, suggests that "the promise of God to David is good for Solomon and all other Davidic descendants as well."[164] Despite that, Book III ends with a failed covenant. McCann views Books II and III together, highlighting the phenomenon of the Elohistic Psalter (42–83).[165] Seen together with Ps 89, Books I–III end with the fall of both the Davidic monarchy and the temple at Jerusalem.[166] Book IV reveals a turning point in the state of affairs. By comparing the ends of Books III and IV, McCann notes that while both speak of the exile, in Ps 89:48, 51, David pleads for Yhwh to "remember" whereas "Ps 106 has affirmed that 'God "remembered his covenant.""'[167] Hence, Book IV is a response to the tragedy at the end of Book III.

According to McCann, Book V presents a vision of restoration. The dominant literary feature in this Book is the Torah Ps 119. Chiastically centered in Book V, McCann suggests that the use of the motifs of the Egyptian Hallel (113–118), as well as the Davidic psalms (108–110) leading to the Torah psalm (Ps 119) and references to

---

159. McCann, *Theological Introduction*, 19.

160. McCann, *Theological Introduction*, 10.

161. McCann, "Shape and Shaping," 351; "Psalms as Instruction," 122–23.

162. For instance, he cites the use of "refuge" in Pss 16–18, which is connected to "happiness" in Pss 2:12; 40:5; 41:2 (beginning and end of Book I). Psalm 40 is related to a Royal psalm and Pss 40–41 echo Pss 1–2. The word, "happy" (*ashre*) is also found at the concluding sections of Books II–IV and Ps 146. McCann, "Shape and Shaping," 352–53.

163. See also McCann, "Books I–III," 94.

164. McCann, "Books I–III," 94.

165. Following Burnett's suggestion, the use of the number "42" was probably meant "to lament the destruction of the temple in 587 BCE and to express hope for renewal beyond the crisis." He notes that the first psalm of the collections that frame the Elohistic Psalter (Pss 42; 73) are laments concerning the "absence of the temple" and "divine favor" (McCann, "Shape and Shaping," 355).

166. Elsewhere, McCann argues that "Books I–III themselves *already* begin to answer the problem posed by the exile, dispersion, and oppression of Israel by the nations in the post exilic era." This is seen in the final form of these books with the juxtaposition of lament and hope psalms at the beginning of Books I–III, having a collective orientation that functions to address the concerns of the exilic/postexilic community, and reorientating them against the apparent failure of the Davidic/Zion theology. See McCann, "Books I–III," 95, 103, 106.

167. McCann, "Shape and Shaping," 358.

Zion (120–134), capture the idea that "one may enter into Zion through the Torah."[168] The Davidic psalms in Book V present a *different* Davidic king that is priestly. The collection, as a whole, is also *predicated* on the people. Instead of a Davidic ruler, "the whole people of God have become the new agency for the enactment of God's will in the world."[169]

The last two points above deserve more attention. If the first three Books of the Psalter have a communal function of reorientating exilic/post exilic Israel in light of the failure of the Davidic/Zion theology, it heightens the question of how Books IV–V respond to this failure. The response identified in the last two Books is the onset of a *different* Davidic king and the democratization of God's purposes for a community which recalls the Davidic Covenant (2 Sam 7:8–16).

Jerome Creach

In *Yahweh as Refuge and the Editing of the Hebrew Psalter*, Creach's thesis is that the concepts expressed by חסה/מחסה ("refuge," 2:12; 91:9) and their related word field represent an "intentional schema, not a subjective structure imposed on the collection."[170] He concludes that "central to the *ḥāsâ* field is the idea that Yahweh is the only reliable source of protection and that an attitude of dependence upon Yahweh is the most basic element of piety."[171]

Important for our study is how Creach argues for the shaping of the Psalter via the concept of refuge.[172] It must be noted that Creach's approach is primarily semantic. Creach analyzes frequencies of the word field use,[173] verbal connections and parallels

---

168. McCann, "Shape and Shaping," 360.

169. McCann, "Shape and Shaping," 361.

170. He makes the caveat, "To say that the Psalter is organized around the idea of 'refuge' does not mean that every psalm contains *ḥāsâ/maḥseh* or a related word; nor does it mean that the psalms of the Psalter have been completely ordered (or reordered) with this concept in mind" (Creach, *Yahweh as Refuge*, 17–18).

171. Creach, *Yahweh as Refuge*, 37.

172. See Creach, *Yahweh as Refuge*, 74–105.

173. For instance, Creach captures the high usage of חסה/מחסה and associated word field in Book I (Creach, *Yahweh as Refuge*, 75). Gillmayr-Bucher takes the word field analysis a step further. She notes that words in the Psalms can be tagged to a certain semantic domain (e.g., "cries" or "tears" in the right context can be tagged under a larger domain called, "misery"). The result of this tagging is that the entire Psalter can be searched and analyzed not merely by individual lexemes, but by semantic domains. Gillmayr-Bucher, "Relecture of Biblical Psalms," 259–82.

The Design of the Psalter

within the Book(s) of the Psalter in light of its distinctive contexts,[174] and emphasizes the use of the refuge concept at the beginning and end of a unit of psalms.[175]

Structurally, Book I has an overarching editorial shape that characterizes the piety of seeking refuge in Yhwh. The emphasis of the Torah in the Prologue (1–2) and Ps 19 reflect the importance of "displaying one's dependence on Yahweh."[176] Books II–III characterize "a confession of confidence in Yahweh's refuge with a protest that Yahweh has rejected or 'cast off' Israel."[177] For Book IV, Creach argues that it answers the trauma of the exile by recognizing "the limitation of the human condition and especially human rulers, and [to] seek refuge in Yahweh."[178] Although he highlights the associated concepts of dependence and Torah piety in Book V, he posits no clear program for the use of the חסה/מחסה word field in Book V.[179]

Creach's approach and method are uncommon in the study of the Psalms. While he reads the shape of the Psalms via the study of a semantic concept, other structural or formal poetical devices are not key to his arguments regarding the editing of the Psalms. Several issues come to light. First, there is a difference between arguing for editorial shaping *around* a concept versus the presence of a concept in service of the final editorial shape. In the former, the Psalter's shape is defined by the concept but

---

174. Creach argues that "every occurrence of *ḥāsâ* and associated terms in David 1 [Pss 3–41] is either a confession of faith in Yahweh, a record of how Yahweh protects those faithful to him, or a description of how one is pious... In contrast, David 2 [Pss 51–72] contains several discussions of misguided trust with an emphasis on the resulting rejection of Yahweh" (Creach, *Yahweh as Refuge*, 83).

175. He notes, "It is interesting that book three of the Psalter begins like book two with two psalms (Pss 73; 74) that contain a confession of trust in Yahweh's refuge (Ps 73:28) and a complaint of being rejected by God (Ps 74:1). This may be an indication that this section of the Psalter took shape in a community that was concerned with its being 'cast off' by Yahweh, that is, a community that interpreted exile as God's rejection for their lack of faith." In analyzing Pss 90–91; 92; 94, Creach notes that "these works share many thematic and verbal parallels. The relationship between the psalms is so close that it is hard to avoid the conclusion that they are placed together purposefully. Their position at the beginning of book four, perhaps the 'editorial center of the Psalter,' in Wilson's words, indicates the importance of these works for the present shape of the book" (Creach, *Yahweh as Refuge*, 90, 96).

176. Creach notes that Book I contains the highest concentration of חסה/מחסה field members. His "preliminary assertion [is] that Pss 2–41 are organized in part around the portraits of the righteous with 'seeking refuge in Yahweh' as a key organizing feature." He concludes "that David 1 [3–41] was drawn together with Psalms 1–2 as a series of reflections on the nature of the righteous over against the godly... Given the nature of Psalms 1–2 and these emphases in David 1, it seems plausible that book one of the Psalter should be read as an extended picture of true piety, seen in total reliance on Yahweh and exemplified by David" (Creach, *Yahweh as Refuge*, 75, 77, 80, 103).

177. Creach notes that in Books II–III, there is a "shift in editorial interest, from a dominant focus upon the faithful believer in David 1 to the presentation of examples of misappropriated trust and struggle over God's rejection of those who claim him as refuge" (Creach, *Yahweh as Refuge*, 92, 104).

178. Creach, *Yahweh as Refuge*, 100.

179. He admits, "it is more difficult to show any ongoing purposeful arrangement in these psalms [Pss 90–150], especially book five. However, it has been shown that this vocabulary is every present and seems to express some of the most prevalent ideas in the book" (Creach, *Yahweh as Refuge*, 100, 104).

in the latter, the shape is defined by another overarching logic to which the concept serves. While Creach notes that the contexts for the refuge concept have shifted from Books I (e.g., piety) to II–III (confidence in Yʜᴡʜ) and to IV–V, he does not seem able to thread them coherently through to Book V. Creach may have successfully argued for the prominence of the refuge concept but in order to claim an editorial shaping of the Psalter around this word field, the relationship between the "shaping" (use of the refuge word field) and the "shape"[180] (macrostructure, metanarrative) needs to be integrated.

Second, it is not impossible that the Psalter is shaped around other concepts. For instance, Gillingham has identified a number of "Zion markers" across the entire Psalter and at strategic locations.[181] Ramon Ribera-Mariné has also argued that the Psalter is structured (retrospectively) around the theme of "praise" found in the most heightened state at the end.[182] Both of these concepts, *Zion* and *praise*, are likewise good candidates for studying the editorial shaping of the Psalter.

Third, Creach's concept of refuge has become so expansive that it is hard not to find links anywhere in the Psalter. For instance, refuge is associated with the concepts of trust, protection, kingship,[183] Zion and Torah piety,[184] thus weakening his argument. This limitation, nonetheless, has been admitted in his work.[185] Creach's unique approach may have uncovered an important technique in the editing of the Psalter, but his methodology has not been adopted by many.

---

180. For Creach, "'shape' refers to both the particular cast provided by distinct language, and to literary structure, that is, the purposeful arrangement of that language" (Creach, "Shape of Book Four," 64).

181. Gillingham, "Zion Tradition," 308–41.

182. Ribera-Mariné, "'El Llibre de les Lloances,'" 1–19. See also James Hutchinson's ten propositions for the motif of praise in the Psalms in Hutchinson, "Psalms and Praise," 85–100.

183. This is especially clear in how Creach argues for Pss 90–92; 94 as editorial activity to show that Yahweh, the king, is a refuge and protection. Creach argues that "for ancient Near Eastern people, acknowledgment of someone as king is inextricably bound to the choice of that person as a means of protection" (Creach, *Yahweh as Refuge*, 96–97).

184. He notes, "The presence of psalms that emphasize the protective role of *tôrâ* suggests that mediation on *tôrâ* had become an important way of expressing devotion to Yahweh and a means of proving oneself worthy of the sheltering care of God. The fact that the Psalter begins with this idea (Ps 1) and contains similar concepts in some of the latest psalms (19, 119) as well as in parts of the Psalter recognized for editorial activity (Ps 94) indicates further that the idea of 'refuge in *tôrâ*' is important for reading and understanding the completed book" (Creach, *Yahweh as Refuge*, 102).

185. "Admittedly, the parameters of the 'ḥāsâ field,' as presented here, are not (and perhaps cannot be) neatly and definitively drawn. Nevertheless, it seems clear that the Psalter contains a 'refuge piety,' in which dependence upon Yahweh is the supreme virtue and this virtue is communicated with a multitude of terms" (Creach, *Yahweh as Refuge*, 48).

The Design of the Psalter

Nancy deClaissé-Walford

DeClaissé-Walford has written extensively on the shape and shaping of the Psalter.[186] Adopting Wilson's methodology, she analyzes various psalms at the seams of the collections and books of the Psalter and prescribes a coherent storyline across the five Books of the Psalter that traces Israel's canonical history from the Davidic monarchy to the postexilic period. This storyline is recapitulated in two of her most recent works:

> It begins in Book I with the story of the reign of King David. Solomon's reign is recounted in Book II. Book III tells the story of the divided kingdoms and their eventual destructions by the Assyrians and the Babylonians. Book IV relates the struggle of the exiles in Babylon to find identity and meaning in a world of changed circumstances. Book V celebrates the return to Jerusalem and the establishment of a new Israel with God as sovereign.[187]

DeClaissé-Walford argues that "the story of the shaping of the Psalter is the story of the shaping of survival."[188] This struggling community had to find an "identity and structure for existence that extended beyond traditional notions of nationhood. King and court could no longer be the focal point of national life. Temple and worship took center stage, and Yhwh, rather than a Davidic king, reigned as sovereign over the new 'religious nation' of Israel."[189]

DeClaissé-Walford's works trend toward a socio-historical interpretation. She assigns the entire shape of the Psalter to Israel's canonical history and explains it with the existential needs of the postexilic community who tried to make sense of their life experiences. Though plausible, some issues remain. The five-book storyline does not correspond well with the literary evidence. She claims that Books I and II contain the stories of David and Solomon but Book II has only one psalm (at the end) that relates to Solomon. Moreover, while she claims that these two figures characterize a "flourishing" period in Israel's nationhood, Books I–II have the highest percentage of Lament psalms.[190] This percentage declines in Books III–IV, despite the fact that Books II–III encapsulate the fall of Jerusalem and the exile. We might also ask, how likely does the final Hallel, the crescendo of praise in the Psalms, represent the historical

---

186. deClaissé-Walford, "Canonical Approach to Scripture," 1–11; "Meta-Narrative of the Psalter," 363–75; deClaissé-Walford et al., *Book of Psalms*; "Psalm 145," 55–66; "Reading Backwards from the Beginning," 119–30; "Intertextual Reading of Psalms," 147; "Canonical Shape of the Psalms," 93–110; *Reading from the Beginning*.

187. deClaissé-Walford, "Meta-Narrative of the Psalter," 368; "Reading Backwards from the Beginning," 120; deClaissé-Walford et al., *Book of Psalms*, 29–38.

188. deClaissé-Walford, "Meta-Narrative of the Psalter," 374.

189. deClaissé-Walford, "Meta-Narrative of the Psalter," 368; deClaissé-Walford et al., *Book of Psalms*, 28–29.

190. See the percentages listed in deClaissé-Walford, "Meta-Narrative of the Psalter," 366–67.

circumstances in postexilic Israel? Her views of the Davidic kingship in Book V remain historical and she interprets the transcendental king in Ps 110 as Yhwh.[191]

David C. Mitchell

Mitchell sees the entire Psalter as a purposeful well-crafted five-book design with Books I–III skillfully joined to Books IV and V of the Psalter.[192] For him, the Psalter was not shaped with a historical-oriented agenda (contra Wilson, Gillingham, and deClaissé-Walford), but with an eschatological agenda under a context "dominated by eschatological concerns."[193] Crucial to Mitchell's thesis is the identification of an "eschatological programme" in Zech 9–14 which he believes the Psalter is based on. In this "programme," there will first be an ingathering (אסף or קבץ) of scattered Israel by an eschatological king (Zech 9:11–10:12). This is followed by a gathering of nations warring against Israel (Zech 12:3/14:1). Then the king dies and an eschatological exile ensues (Zech 12:10–14; 13:7–9). Israel is gathered again and delivered by divine help (Zech 14:2–15). Eventually, Israel and the survivors of all the nations will gather and ascend (עלה) in festal Sukkoth worship of Yhwh in Jerusalem (Zech 14:16–21).[194]

Mitchell illustrates the entire eschatological program of the Psalter, seen in light of Zech 9–14, as follows:

---

191. deClaissé-Walford is hesitant to view the Davidic king in Book V as messianic. Besides ascribing the king in Ps 110 as Yhwh, her discussion of kingship in Ps 132 is also framed historically. See deClaissé-Walford et al., *Book of Psalms*, 838, 936. See also Ho, "Review of deClaissé-Walford et al.," 496–97.

192. Mitchell, "Lord, Remember David"; *Message*, 69–82.

193. He points out four concerns: (1) The Psalter is finalized between the end of the exile and the translation of the lxx. In this Second Temple period, biblical literature looks for a "sudden dramatic divine intervention in history that will restore the nation's fallen fortunes." Books of Ezekiel and Zechariah, likewise, anticipate "a golden age prosperity." (2) Figures that the Psalms are attributed to (e.g., David, Asaph, Jeduthun, Heman, and Moses) are often regarded as "future-predictive prophets." (3) Certain psalms (e.g., Pss 2, 21, 45, 72, 110) describing a person or event use language that "far exceeds the reality of any historical king or battle." (4) The Royal psalms included in the Psalter at a time where Israel had no king are to be understood as referring to a future anointed king. See Mitchell, *Message*, 82–87.

194. Mitchell, *Message*, 215.

Ps	Asaph				89	Book IV	110	Hallel	Ascents
	45	50	72	73–83		90–106		111–118	120–134
Zech 9–14	Bridegroom king comes to Daughter Zion	Gathering of scattered Israel to Jerusalem	Temporary messianic *malkut*	Hostile nation gather against Jerusalem	The king cut off	Israel exiled in desert. Gathered and return to Zion	Rescue by king messiah	Paeans of messianic victory; the hero's welcome	Ascent of Israel and all nations to Sukkoth on Zion in messianic *malkut*

Figure 3: Mitchell's Eschatological Program for the MT Psalter[195]

Mitchell's unique contribution is linking the redaction of the Psalter with the eschatological program found in Zech 9–14. However, to accept his thesis, several difficulties must be resolved. We need to first assume an "established" program in Zech 9–14 and presume the Psalms had depended on Zech 9–14. We also need to understand the differences between the two programs. Mitchell admits that many strategic or even eschatological psalms are not included in his final eschatological proposal. For instance, the final Hallel (146–150) is eschatological but not integrated into his plan. Mitchell has also excluded a large number of psalms (esp. wisdom/Torah-themed psalms), weakening his overall thesis.[196]

Walter Brueggemann and John Kartje

Presenting an analysis on the other side of the spectrum, Brueggemann and Kartje argue for a certain "wisdom shaping" of the Psalter based on sapiential elements prominently located in the Psalms.[197] Interestingly, these two scholars arrive at the same conclusion from different approaches. Brueggemann focuses on the theological intention of psalm locations, whereas Kartje analyzes the social-epistemological development of four strategic psalms.[198]

For Brueggemann, the Psalter is bound and shaped by a trajectory defined by its two ends (1, 150)—from obedience to praise. Within this boundary, there is a move from "willing duty" to a "self-abandoning" delight in the praise of God. However, this move is characterized through suffering, doubt and trust before arriving at praise.

---

195. Mitchell, *Message*, 298.

196. Mitchell, *Message*, 267.

197. Brueggemann and Kartje's arguments for a wisdom shaping of the Psalter are also adopted by deClaissé-Walford. Cf. deClaissé-Walford, "Reading Backwards from the Beginning," 125; Brueggemann, "Bound by Obedience and Praise," 63–92; *Message of the Psalms*; "Psalms and the Life of Faith," 3–32; Brueggemann and Miller, "Psalm 73 as a Canonical Marker," 45–56; Kartje, *Wisdom Epistemology in the Psalter*.

198. See also Ho, "Review of Kartje," 100–1.

Bruggemann cites Ps 25 as describing a realistic life situation which does not correspond to the confidence of Torah-piety depicted in Ps 1. However, Ps 103 voices confidence and hope despite the realities of life, made possible because of Yhwh's חסד. Within this drama of life, the pivotal role is played by Ps 73 which captures the "theological move from *ḥesed* doubted (as in Psalm 25) to *ḥesed* trusted (as in Psalm 103)."[199]

By comparing Pss 1; 73; 90; and 107, Kartje traces a trajectory of "epistemological progression" in how the Psalter depicts human suffering.[200] Psalm 1 posits the worldview of two different journeys of the righteous and the wicked as a binary state of affairs. Psalm 73 complicates the wisdom-based proposition of Psalm 1 by showing that the wicked *can* prosper and the righteous *can* suffer. In Ps 90, the seeming impossibility of moving across the fixed categories of blessedness and cursedness (in Ps 1) becomes surprisingly possible. By Psalm 107, "suffering is not necessarily tied to moral culpability and even the wicked have access to divine salvation."[201]

Brueggemann and Kartje's analyses are similar in several ways. Their works focus on the issues of human flourishing vis-à-vis covenantal faithfulness to Yhwh as they appear in the Psalter. Both of these scholars identify strategically-located psalms that capture these issues and trace a certain trajectory across these psalms. Their propositions are, however, impressionistic as only a few psalms are selected. The trajectories posited might well vary if different psalms were selected.[202] In contrast to Mitchell, important kingship or Zion psalms are not featured.

Casper Labuschagne, Duane L. Christensen, and Hendrik J. Koorevaar

Several scholars have taken a numerical approach to understanding the macrostructure of the Psalter. The use of symbolic numbers in the HB has been recognized by various scholars,[203] and, according to some, brings a serious challenge to source criticism.[204] Counting words are first associated with the Masoretic divisions of text (e.g.,

---

199. Brueggemann, "Bound by Obedience and Praise," 81.

200. Kartje, *Wisdom Epistemology in the Psalter*.

201. Kartje, *Wisdom Epistemology in the Psalter*, 157.

202. For instance, in Kartje's case, if Psalm 112 with a similar proposition to Psalm 1, were analyzed, the epistemological "progression" that he proposes would be undermined since Psalm 112 is canonically located after Psalm 90.

203. Joffe, "Answer to the Meaning of Life," 223–35; Haakma, "Die Zahlenmässige Strukturanalyse," 273–83; Bazak, "Numerical Devices in Biblical Poetry," 333–37; Schedl, "Die Alphabetisch-Arithmetische Struktur," 489–94; *Baupläne des Wortes Einführung*; Labuschagne, "Neue Wege Und Perspektiven," 146–62.

204. "With Schedl, says Labuschagne, the key to exegesis does not lie on the historical sources of the text but on the final form. One may move from the subjective criteria for dividing the text to a new, objective criteria. The logotechnique can provide such an objective criteria." Haakma, "Die Zahlenmässige Strukturanalyse," 274.

setuma, petuchah, athnak).[205] But one of the most ambitious applications of numerical methods on the Psalter, and beyond the level of a single poem, is Labuschagne's Logotechnique[206] analysis. By counting words and seeing how the word count of a certain literary unit is a factor of recurring numbers such as "7" and "11," he argues that these numbers function as a macrostructuring device for the entire Psalter[207] (more discussion in chapter 5).

Christensen posits a redactional process of the Psalter using the number "17."[208] He highlights the fact that Books III and IV contain 17 psalms and that, at an early stage of the Psalter, Books I, III, IV, V plausibly contained 119 (17x7) psalms.[209] The two Books at the center are framed by an original Davidic Psalter (Books I and V) which consists of 51 (17x3) Davidic psalms and 34 (17x2) non-Davidic psalms. The five Books of the Psalter form a chiasm with Book III at the center focusing on "Israel and the nations."[210] Each Book of the Psalter is also arranged in a chiastic manner, with a single center psalm (19, 50, 81, 98, 119), though the numerical technique is not a clear feature of these chiasmi. For Christensen, the Psalter's final design is closely related to the Pentateuch with the possibility of the Psalter following a triennial lectionary cycle of ancient Palestinian Judaism reading of the Pentateuch.

By counting the number of psalms, Koorevaar argues that the numbers "17" and "43" are used in the structuring of the books of the Bible.[211] When Pss 9–10, 42–43 and 114–15 are seen as single compositions, Books I and II consist of 70 (40+30) psalms, and Books III–V consist of 77 (17+17+43), making a total of 147 psalms.[212] Books I–II is Davidic in orientation as the numbers "40" and "30" signify the number of years David reigned and the age when David began to rule (2 Sam 5:4). Books III–V is Yahwistic in orientation based on the symbolic use of the numbers "7" and "11." Furthermore, the 13 historical psalms of David are distributed as 4, 8 and 1 respective

---

205. Haakma, "Die Zahlenmässige Strukturanalyse," 275.

206. Labuschagne notes, "Claus Schedl coined the term 'logotechnique' to describe the art of numerical composition, which he derived from the Greek term logotechnia meaning 'literature,' more particularly a skillfully designed literary work of art conforming to certain laws governing its form. So 'logotechnique' denotes, in fact, 'word-art,' 'language-art,' 'compositional art'" (Labuschagne, *Numerical Secrets of the Bible*, 94).

207. Labuschagne, "Significant Sub-Groups," 623–34.

208. Christensen, *Unity of the Bible*, 132–33; "Book of Psalms," 421–32 [423].

209. He notes, "When book 2 is removed, all of the 'doublets' noted by scholars disappear (i.e., Ps 14 = Ps 53; Ps 70 = Ps 40:13–17; Ps 108 = Ps 57:7–11 and Ps 60:5–12). A reasonable working hypothesis posits the insertion of book 2 as the final addition to the Psalter when the seventeen books of the deuteronomic canon were expanded to make the twenty-two books of the pentateuchal canon in the time of Ezra" (Christensen, *Unity of the Bible*, 132).

210. Christensen argues that Ps 81, located at the structural center of the entire Psalter, is a liturgy that reviews Israel's canonical history from Jacob to the Exodus under Moses. See Christensen, *Unity of the Bible*, 133.

211. Koorevaar, "Psalter as a Structured Theological Story," 579–92.

212. Koorevaar cites 147 as the total number of psalms in the Jerusalem Talmud tractate Sabbath 16. Koorevaar, "Psalter as a Structured Theological Story," 582–83.

psalm(s) in Books I, II and V. Symbolically, the numbers 4-8-1 is the reverse of אחד ("one"), representing the oneness of Yhwh. (Deut 6:4).²¹³

Koorevaar prescribes a theme to each book and assigns center psalm(s) for each book as follows:

> Introduction: Pss 1–2
>
> Book I: David flees from Absalom; center: Ps 19
>
> Book II: Cause of the crisis, sin, Solomon becomes king; center: Ps 50
>
> Book III: National crisis, exile, temple and messianic king lost; center: Ps 86
>
> Book IV: Above the crisis in exile, Yhwh is king; center: Ps 97
>
> Book V: Victory over crisis, return to Yhwh and land; center: Pss 119, 127
>
> Conclusion: Pss 149–150²¹⁴

For Koorevaar, the message at the center (86:8–10) is the central message for Israel as they go into exile. Although Koorevaar's treatment in his book section is too brief for further analysis, like Labuschagne, he has shown how numerical analyses can function in the structuring of the Psalter.

O. Palmer Robertson

Robertson's *The Flow of the Psalms*²¹⁵ is one of the latest macrostructural treatments of the Psalter. As the title suggests, Robertson sees an "organized development of thought progression" flowing across the book of the Psalms.²¹⁶ In his methodology, similar to what we have seen above, Robertson considers how lexemes are used, their frequency of occurrence and connections. He summarizes twelve elements that define the basic structure of the Psalter, indicating purposeful arrangement.²¹⁷ The entire Psalter is to be seen under a "redemptive-historical" framework of king David, after which no

---

213. Moreover, the total number of words in these historical superscriptions add up to 100 (10x10), a number symbolic of "completeness, perfection and full measure" (Koorevaar, "Psalter as a Structured Theological Story," 587).

214. The center psalms are usually numerically weighted. For instance, Ps 86 contains 17 verses and 147 words, corresponding to the number of psalms in Book III and the entire Psalter respectively (according to Koorevaar's count). See Koorevaar, "Psalter as a Structured Theological Story," 589–90.

215. Robertson, *Flow of the Psalms*; "Strategic Placement of the 'Hallelu-Yah' Psalms," 265.

216. Robertson, *Flow of the Psalms*, loc. 1293.

217. These twelve elements are: (1) Five book structure; (2) Grouping by reference in titles to individuals; (3) Two thematic "Pillars" in Pss 1 and 2–Torah and messiah; (4) Coupling of three Torah psalms with three messianic psalms (Pss 1,–2; 18–19; 118–19); (5) Eight acrostic psalms; (6) Groupings that celebrate the kingship of Yhwh and his messiah (e.g., Pss 20–24; 45–48; 93; 96; 97; 99); (7) Psalms of Ascents; (8) Psalms of historical recollection (e.g., Pss 105–106); (9) Focal messianic psalms (e.g., Pss 22; 45; 69; 72; 80; 110; 118); (10) Psalms confessing sin (e.g., Pss 38–41; 51); (11) "Poetical pyramid" (symmetrically) structure collection of psalms; (12) *Hallelujah* psalms (e.g., Pss 111–117). See Robertson, *Flow of the Psalms*, loc. 477–729.

The Design of the Psalter

further OT covenants were realized,[218] with the essential core of the covenant resting on two areas: the perpetual Davidic dynasty and Yhwh's permanent dwelling place at Zion.[219]

The editorial flow of the Psalms begins with the *confrontation* of David with his enemies (Book I). This is followed by the *communication* of the supremacy of Yhwh to the nations and the reign of David's son, Solomon (Book II). Book III encapsulates the *devastation* of Yhwh's people and the messianic crown. The sapiential psalms and the Yhwh *Malak* psalms in Book IV underscore Israel's *maturation* in their understanding of Yhwh's kingdom. Finally, Book V describes the *consummation* of Yhwh's purposes, culminating in praise.[220] The entire Psalter is designed to "provide a framework for God's people to approach the Lord properly in worship."[221]

Robertson's structural understanding is perhaps the most unusual in our survey.[222] Positively, he views the Psalter as thematically coherent and provides several important structural insights. For instance, his arguments for Pss 18–19 functioning as structural markers in Book I is significant. The connection between the dramatic declaration of Yhwh's kingship over all gods (Pss 93–100) and the bringing of the ark to Zion (1 Chr 16) is also pertinent.[223] A weakness, however, seems to be an overdependence on thematic arguments in structuring the Psalter. This is also reflected by the relegating of Robertson's significant chiastic macrostructures within the Psalter (which are termed, "poetical pyramids") as an "excursus" in his work, rather than keeping them in the main body.

---

218. Robertson notes that "After God's covenant with David, no further covenants were realized. The promise of a "new covenant" came through the Lord's prophets (Jer. 31:31–34; Ezek. 37:21–28). But it never was the intent of the Lord to institute any covenants for his Old Testament people as a national entity beyond the covenant with David. In David, the king had come and the kingdom had come" (Robertson, *Flow of the Psalms*, loc. 742–46).

219. Robertson, *Flow of the Psalms*, loc. 1241.

220. Robertson, *Flow of the Psalms*, loc. 454–70.

221. Robertson, *Flow of the Psalms*, loc. 854.

222. This follows from several insights. (1) Each of the Five Books begins with one or two psalms as the introduction [Pss 1-2; 42-44; 73-74, 90-91; 107]; (2) Three pairs of Torah-messianic psalms are structurally significant; (3) Acrostic psalms function to divide the largest books of the Psalter into smaller sections. (4) Certain thematic motifs are more important as a structuring principle than superscriptions (e.g., Pss 49–52). (5) The "Poetic pyramid" structuring principle in a collection of psalms, arranges psalms symmetrically about a center psalm. The function of these pyramids, like the acrostics, serves to aid memorization. Robertson identifies several of these "pyramids" across the Psalter: Pss 120–134; 111–117; 92–100; 77–83; 20–24. Robertson, *Flow of the Psalms*, loc. 1856, 5038–121.

223. Cf. Ps 96:1–13 // 1 Chr 16:23–33; Ps 105:1–15 // 1 Chr 16:8–22; Ps 106:1, 47–48 // 1 Chr 16:34–36. Robertson also points out that the phrase, עַל-כָּל-אֱלֹהִים, is found only in three locations in the entire HB (1 Chr 16:25; Pss 95:3; 96:4; 97:9). See Robertson, *Flow of the Psalms*, loc. 3335–68.

Introduction

Summary and the Status Quaestionis

The preceding survey provides a short glimpse into current research on the field of macroanalyses of the entire Psalter, which touch on our three research questions: *organizing technique, structure*, and *overarching design*. Two following figures consolidate 32 organizational principles (13 formal and 19 tacit) and macrostructural divisions of the Psalter. They are representative, though not exhaustive.[224]

The boundary between *formal*[225] and *tacit*[226] organization principles is not always clear as they can overlap at different levels of composition. For completeness, I have included my own findings and elaborations on certain organizational techniques in the lists below (marked with an asterisk). Most, if not all, of these techniques will be discussed further in this book.

	Formal Techniques	**Observations**
1	Book Divisions	Major divisions of the Psalter (Pss 1–41, 42–72, 73–89, 90–106, 107–150).
2	*Prologue (Pss 1–2)	Identifies the leitmotifs in the Psalms and three major divisions. Provides the programmatic outlook for the entire Psalter.
3	Epilogue	Provides closure to the metanarrative of the Psalter (Pss 146–150).
4	*Symmetrical/concentric structures (chiasmus/"pyramid"/ "centering") at different levels of composition	At the highest level, the Psalter is concentrically arranged in three Sections (Books I, II–III and IV–V). At the lowest level, they can occur within a poetic phrase (see esp. chapter 3).
5	*Five Davidic Collections	Pss 3–41, 51–70, 101–103, 108–110, 138–145. Reveals the Metanarrative of the Psalter and how the Davidic covenant develops (see chapter 4).
6	Elohistic/YHWH Psalter	The predominant use of *elohim* over YHWH in Pss 42–83.
7	*Acrostics & Alphabetical Psalms	Their locations mark leitmotifs of the Prologue, the beginning and end of the Psalter, and the seams of literary units (see chapter 5).

---

224. Cf. Grossberg's list of techniques in Grossberg, *Centripetal and Centrifugal*, 9–12.

225. With the use of the designation, "formal," I refer to the use of literary devices in a particular and distinct format. I do not mean it as the literary *type* (as in form criticism). Formal techniques could represent existing poetic structuring conventions existing at the time of the composition. Tate, *Biblical Interpretation*, 186.

226. As a literary form, I treat "tacit" devices as less distinctive. Rather, they are associated with motifs and themes. Wilson uses the terms, "explicit" and "tacit," which differ from mine. For him, "explicit" techniques are those that make plain "statements of organizational intent" or purpose. "Tacit" techniques are those that require the understanding of the broader horizon of the Psalter to be able to perceive the implied editorial purpose. See Wilson, *EHP*, 139–40, 182.

The Design of the Psalter

	Formal Techniques	Observations
8	*Superscriptions (with authorship attribution)	Key to the structuring of the Psalter. Such as the psalms of David, Solomon, Moses, Asaph, Korah and the YHWH *Malak* psalms (see chapter 2).
9	*Historical superscriptions	These are found in 13 Davidic psalms collaborating with the Metanarrative of the Davidic Collections (see chapter 4).
10	*Superscriptions without authorship attribution	Key to the structuring of the Psalter. Formulaic phrases that begin a psalm (e.g., *hallelujah, hodu* in the imperative plural) as a form of special superscription, marking a unit of psalms (see chapter 2).
11	*Postscript (72:20)	Marks a structural point in the Metanarrative. Psalm 72:20 identifies a closure of David's kingship when seen in parallel with the Samuel narratives
12	Doxological postscripts/motifs	Pss 41:14; 72:18–19; 89:53; 106:48 mark the conclusion of a Book.
13	*Numerical Devices and Symbolism	Associated with the number of words or the number of superscription type. Locate certain *nexusword* and help to locate the structure of the larger collective unit in collaboration with the Metanarrative of the Psalter (see chapter 5).

Figure 4: Formal Organizational Techniques of the MT Psalter

	Tacit Techniques	Observations
1	*Leitmotifs in the Prologue	Three main motifs in the Prologue that recur throughout the Psalter: YHWH and the Davidic/Messianic kingship; Zion-temple; YHWH's Torah and Torah-fidelity.
2	*Central Motifs of a Group	The trio-motifs of Kingship, Zion and Torah usually mark the structural center of a Group for emphasis (see esp. chapter 3).
3	Genre Motifs	A generalization assigned to the literary form/content of a psalm. A series of psalms arranged as a chiasmus by their genre.
4	*Verkettung* ("chain-linking"), concatenation	Lexical or certain phonological, semantic, thematic, syntactical, grammatical parallels that connect *adjacent psalms* (e.g., *ashre* in Pss 1–2; "righteous" in Pss 111–112).
5	**Vernetzung* ("networking")	Lexical or certain phonological, semantic, thematic, syntactical, grammatical parallels that connect and bind *a group of psalms* (e.g., YHWH *Malak* psalms; the motif of Zion in Pss 120–134, see chapter 3).

	Tacit Techniques	**Observations**
6	*Fernverbindung* ("distant-binding")	Lexical or certain phonological, semantic, thematic, syntactical, grammatical parallels that connect *distant psalms* (e.g. "to reject" in Books II–III).
7	*Composite Psalms	Psalms that are composed by reusing existing psalms texts. They indicate a development or re-reading of earlier psalms in a latter context in the Psalter (e.g., Pss 57, 60 in 108. See chapter 5).
8	*Intertextual reading (extratextual references)	Reading the Psalms against texts outside the Psalter (e.g., reading the motifs associated with the completion of the temple with the narratives in 1–2 Chronicles).
9	*Theological development or Metanarrative *progression* (*Steigerung*)	A development or progression of a motif or concept (e.g., the concept of Zion eventually as an social-reality of peace and bliss. See chapter 3).
10	*Messianic and eschatological perspective	The Davidic Collections Pss 101–103 and 108–110 present a *different* Davidic king who is blameless, afflicted and victorious (see chapter 4).
11	*Shift from individual to communal psalms	More individual psalms in the earlier Books compared to later ones.
12	Interlocking framework	One frame "interlocks" with another via the presence of one or more psalms occurring in the other collection (esp. G. Wilson).
13	Psalms 18–19 in Book I and Pss 18–144.	These two psalms mark a decisive change in the use of certain terminologies and motifs The motifs of deliverance and security are heightened and bounded by these two locations (Pss 18, 144) based on similar terminologies.
14	*Narrative and prophesy-fulfilment	The place of Ps 51 and its role in the Second Davidic Collections unite a unit of text (Pss 51–66, 69).
15	*Pan-Psalter occurrence scheme (POS)	The careful use and placement of certain word/phrases at strategic locations across the entire Psalter to make or reinforce a rhetorical point in collaboration with the Metanarrative of the Psalter (see chapter 3).
16	Figurative/Metaphorical devices	The use of the "rock" metaphor occurs only between Pss 18 and 144, binding the kingship psalms.
17	*Maqqep*	Counting words linked by *maqqep* as a single word. Affects total word count in a psalm.
18	*Nexusword	Nexusword identifies the word(s) at the center of a psalm by word count. Traced across the psalms, they collaborate with the macrostructural shape of the Psalter (see chapter 5).
19	Alternation	Alternating motifs and consecutive psalms binding a group of psalms. For instance, the use of "day" and "night" psalms in Pss 3–14 could be a response to Ps 1:2.

Figure 5: Tacit Organizational Techniques of the MT Psalter

The Design of the Psalter

From the above techniques, the structure can be understood. Figure 6 below provides a summary and comparison of several structural divisions of each Book of the Psalter. This summary provides a snapshot of representative divisions. From them, we can identify areas of consensus or disagreement in various parts of the structure of the entire Psalter.

Book I

Zenger	1–2	3–14		15–24		25–34		35–41
Vesco	1–2	3–14		15–24		25–34		35–41
Auwers	1–2	3–14		15–24		25–34		35–41
Koorevaar	1–2	3–14		15–24		25–34		35–41
Christensen	1	2–6	7–11	12–18	19	20–26	27–31	32–36	37–41
Labuschagne	1	2–8		9–18		19–29	30–31	32–41	
Robertson	1–2	3–17		18	19	20–24	25	26–32	33	34–41

Book II

Zenger	42–49		50	51	52–55	56–60	61–64	65–68	69–71	72
Vesco	42–49		50	51	52–55	56–60	61–64	65–68	69–71	72
Auwers	42–49		50	51–64				65–67	69–71	
Koorevaar	42–49		50	51–72						
Christensen	42–44	45–49	50	51–70					71–72	
Labuschagne	42–49		50	51–57		58–64		65–71		72
Robertson	42–44	45–48	49–52	53	54–60		61–68		69–71	72

Book III

Zenger	73–83			84–89			
Vesco	73–83			84–89			
Auwers	73–77	78–83		84–85	86	87–89	
Koorevaar	73–83			84–85	86	87–88	89
Christensen	73–79	80	81	82	83–89		
Labuschagne	73–83			84–89			
Robertson	73–74	75–76	77–83	84–87		88–89	

Book IV

Zenger	90–92	93–100		101–103	104–106
Vesco	90–92	93–100		101–106	
Auwers	90–92	93–100		101–106	
Koorevaar	90–92	93–100		101–106	
Christensen	90–96	97	98	99	100–106
Labuschagne	90–100			101–106	
Robertson	90–91	92–100		101–103	104–106

				Book V					
Zenger	107	108–110	111–112	113–118	119	120–134	135–136	137	138–145	146–150
Vesco	107	108–110	111–117		118–119	120–134	135	136–137	138–145	146–150
Auwers		107–117			118–119	120–134	135	136–137	138–145	146–150
Koorevaar	107	108–110	111–117		118	119	120–134	135	136	137	138–145	146–150
Christensen	107	108–112		113–118	119	120–134	135–145			146–150
Labuschagne		107–117			118–119	120–134	135–145			146–150
Robertson	107	108–110	111–117		118	119	120–134	135–137		138–145	146–150

Figure 6: Survey of Macrostructural Divisions of the Five Books

For Book I, there is a general consensus that Pss 1–2 is the Prologue. Most scholars also identify four major groupings (3–14, 15–24, 25–34, 35–41). Christensen, Labuschagne and Robertson's groupings are significantly different because they are driven by a particular technique (numerical or thematic). In Book II, apart from Robertson's structure, there is a common consensus of grouping according to the Korahite, Asaphite and Davidic Collections (42–49, 50, 51–72). The main structuring disagreement lies within the Davidic psalms, since Christensen and Robertson have identified Pss 42–44 as a group based on thematic observations.

Likewise, in Book III, the major consensus is to organize according to the overtly noted Asaphite and Korahite Collections (73–83, 84–89). However, main structuring differences occur within the Collections. Christensen's structure stands out again because he considers Pss 80, 81, 82 to be framed by seven psalms on each side.

In Book IV, a similar phenomenon recurs. Scholars generally agree, however, on the three main sections: Pss 90–92, 93–100 and 101–106. Christensen applies a similar technique of a 7+3+7 structure in Book IV. Labuschagne's structure is based on his Logotechnique argument for eleven psalms (90–100). Robertson groups Ps 92 with 93 based on thematic reasons and considers a collection of nine psalms (92–100) with Ps 96 functioning as the apex. In Book V, the problematic areas occur around Pss 117–18 and between 135–137. There is unanimous agreement on a structural break after Pss 119; 134; and 145.

Macrostructural divisions underlie the overarching editorial design proposed by various scholars. Wilson highlights the role of the Davidic covenant. Arguing from the Prologue, Zenger sees that the book of Psalms functions theologically as a sanctuary. Robertson's view is similar. He argues that the book of Psalms provides a framework for God's people to approach him in proper worship. Also arguing from the Prologue, Vesco concludes that the Psalter reveals the route to Salvation. Those who read the Psalms become the new David.

With these, our research questions for this book can be summarized as follow:

(1) *Organizing principles*—It is clear that a variety of techniques were used in the shaping of the Psalter. We observe that certain methodologies produce very different structural divisions. (e.g., numerical vs. thematic). They cannot all be right at the same time. A presumption we make is that the final editor(s) would have some ability and freedom to shape the Psalter based on these literary organizing techniques. If such freedom were available, and if the final form (or "original text")[227] of the Psalter were organized with some intentional design, we would expect correspondence in the expressions of techniques, content, and structure. Hence, an important consideration in this book is to observe whether *organizing techniques, form*, and *content* cohere.

(2) *Macrostructure*—While there is some consensus in the major grouping of psalms (e.g., in Book I), structural difficulties remain in certain subcollections (esp. within Pss 51–72; 117–119; and 135–137). Since structural arguments affect the design and focus of the book, we need to identify the most coherent structural design based on literary evidence.

(3) *Overarching design and logic*—As we address the coherence of organizing principles and macrostructure, we regularly question why the entire Psalter fits together as it stands. Can we detect a consistent overall design of the Psalter? Can we confirm a programmatic role for the Prologue (Pss 1–2)? Is there a metanarrative across the Psalter? How do structuring techniques, macrostructure, and the vantage point of the Prologue (etc.), come together to reveal the design and message of the Psalter?

Approach and Methodology

My general interpretive approach in this book can be situated under the titles of "Rhetorical Criticism," "New Criticism," and "Close Reading" as defined by David Clines:

> Rhetorical criticism, often operating under the banner of "the final form of the text," concerns itself with the way the language of texts is deployed to convey meaning. Its interests are in the devices of writing, in metaphor and parallelism, in narrative and poetic structures, in stylistic figures ... New Criticism was especially an Anglo-American movement in general literary criticism, regarding texts as unitary works of art, paying close attention to the internal

---

227. In textual criticism, the terms, *original text*, *original version*, and *final text* are differentiated. A composition, when it is first completed, is the *original version*. However, this original version can be published later with some changes or re-published with changes as a new edition. At some point, these versions culminate with a final version that may be quite different from the very first version when the composition was first written. This final version is the *original text*. The *final text* is not associated with individual biblical books but with the "completed canon that was accepted by the church(es) as authoritative and definitive for the Christian faith about 100 CE" (cf. Childs's definition). My use of the phrase "final form" denotes the *original text* rather than the *final text* since this book is concerned primarily with the individual biblical book of the Psalms. For a good discussion of these nuances, see Fischer and Würthwein, *Text of the Old Testament*, 158–62.

characteristics of the text itself and abjuring the use of data extrinsic to a text in its interpretation . . . "Close reading" is a term for the method of New Criticism; it refers to a paying of special attention to theme, imagery, metaphor, paradox, irony, ambiguity, keywords, motifs and the like.[228]

However, my approach is not strictly limited to observations in the text. I make inferences about the text in relation to its final editors and readers. As such, it is also a canonical-literary or editorial criticism approach.[229] My interests are primarily in the literary shape[230] of the hundred-and-fifty Hebrew poems and how they are designed as a single composition, if at all, in shaping a coherent theological program for its readers who may belong to a later generation (102:19). It is not far-fetched to postulate, from observing the rhetorical features of the text, possible authorial intent conveyed by such features and how they would affect its readers.[231]

My approach will also be macrostructural, that is, instead of focusing on detailed exegesis of a limited number of adjacent psalms, this volume will investigate how certain lexemes or motifs, superscriptions, Davidic collections, and other poetical features function within the entire Psalter. Structural centers and distant thematic parallels are of interest. Such a macrostructural study of the entire Psalter avoids the difficulties associated with analyses of a limited number of psalms, yet at the same time, takes advantage of their gains by consolidating them under a macroanalysis. As Körting notes, "the macro study of the book of Psalms [is] fundamental for further research."[232]

In the rest of this chapter, four higher level hermeneutical issues associated with my approach are discussed. First, after clarifying my approach, I will briefly discuss how this book is situated within the hermeneutical framework of author–text–reader. Second, I will state how the Psalter can be read as a unified whole. Third, the Prologue (Pss 1–2) will be studied. I argue that the poetical structure (form), key motifs (content) and structuring techniques observed in the Prologue cohere with one other so that the Prologue provides the hermeneutical key to reading the Psalter. Finally, we explore how fundamental motifs found in the books of Samuel and Chronicles, specifically the Davidic covenant in 2 Sam 7, relates intertextually to the reading of the Psalter. I propose that the Psalter is the unfurling of Yhwh's covenant with David.

---

228. Clines, "Contemporary Methods," 151–52.

229. Editorial criticism emphasizes evidence of editorial shaping of a biblical text and the significance or meaning of the shape of that text. For a definition of "editorial criticism," see Grant, "Editorial Criticism," 149–56.

230. The "shape" of the Psalter refers to identifiable "editorial activities" of various extents in unifying the book. "Shaping" emphasizes the "editorial purpose that governs the organization process" (deClaissé-Walford, "Canonical Approach to Scripture," 7).

231. My methodology is similar to that of Dorsey, *Literary Structure of the Old Testament*.

232. Körting, "Psalms," 553.

Author–Text–Reader Framework

From my demonstration of various observations and readings of the structural design of the MT-150 text, important questions relating to *warrant* (justification for claims) would inevitably be raised. For instance, we may ask if an *implied*[233] author of the Psalter had indeed intended a particular structure? Could the reader (even the informed reader) be reading something that the author never intended, unwittingly imposing an "artificial order on an unwilling text"?[234] If structures demonstrated above were intended by the author, how and why would the reader(s) recognize them? While these questions are impossible to answer with absolute certainty, it is necessary to provide some preliminary discussions before beginning with more detailed analyses of the Psalter's form and structure.

One way to clarify the interrelationships between the theological message, author, text, and reader, is via a diagram from John Barton.[235]

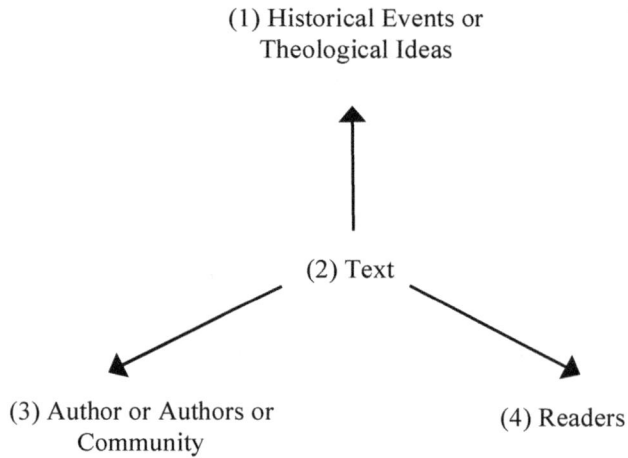

Figure 7: Barton's Message-Author-Text-Reader Map

---

233. The "implied author" is a construct, namely one who "would possess the necessary competence in the conventions assumed by the text in order to 'decode' the text." The implied author is an imaginary author constructed from the text alone. In Wolfgang Iser's terminology, the "implied reader" is one who "embodies all those predispositions necessary for a literary work to exercise its effect. These predispositions are laid down, not by an empirical outside reality, but by the text itself. Consequently, the implied reader as a concept has its roots firmly planted in the structure of the text." However, it is also possible that the implied reader is not completely defined by the text. "The implied author may assume on the part of the implied reader a set of values, literary competence, and background." (Tate, *Biblical Interpretation*, 192, 195). See Tate, *Interpreting the Bible*, 176; cf. Iser, *Act of Reading*, 38.

234. Wilson, *EHP*, 3.

235. This model has been redrawn from Barton's "Classifying Biblical Criticism," 23; *Reading the Old Testament*, 201. Barton developed this model from Abrams, *Mirror and the Lamp*. Cf. Longman, *Literary Approaches*, 18.

The figure above shows four different loci where meaning can be centered. Critical methods that place the locus of meaning on the author (locus 3)[236] state that interpretation is enhanced when all can be uncovered about the minds of the author(s), redactor(s) or community, and the (socio-political and ideological) world in they are situated in. The basic assumption is that the text (locus 2) will reflect the authorial intent, which, in turn, is shaped by the complex matrix of events and theological ideas (locus 1) as understood by the author. Thus, the meaning of the text is primarily associated with the author. An understanding of the world that shaped the worldview of the author is crucial to ascertain the meaning of the text. Complicating this approach, however, is the question of whether the world of the author(s) and his intent can be reasonably reconstructed.[237]

Text-centered methods (locus 2) view the text as an artifact.[238] Meaning is found only within the forms and content of the text while the world behind the text (e.g., author) is irrelevant. "Any interpretation of the text must treat it as a coherent and complex whole."[239] Literary conventions govern how texts are to be understood. Meaning is derived not so much from the text but by the linguistic rules through which the text is constructed. The genre of poetry is not the same as that of prose and hence, meaning is derived differently. In other words, "meaning of the work is found [primarily] in the convention rather than the intention of the author."[240] Rhetorical criticism (or stylistic analysis), as a text-centered method, isolates a discrete literary unit for analysis, and focuses on the structure and balance of the text, giving attention to certain keywords or theme.[241] The text is the artistic artifact to be examined without necessarily presupposing or dismissing its history. Nonetheless, many scholars have pointed out that texts do not have absolute autonomy. It begs the question of the extent to which the forms and structures (or conventions) of the text can be universally accepted.[242]

Reader/audience-centered methods are concerned with the effects the text produces in relation to the reader or community.[243] There is little concern with the

236. E.g., Source, Form, and Redactional criticisms.

237. Authorship anonymity is common in the Bible. Pseudonymity is also practiced when the real author speaks through a constructed persona. See Lim, *Strategy for Reading Biblical Texts*, 32–33; Nonetheless, Hirsch argues that the author's intent remains important as it provides a "kind of anchor in the sea of interpretive relativity." The authorial intent is to be inferred through "a careful study of the text in relationship to other closely related text" (Longman, *Literary Approaches*, 20–21). See also Hirsch, *Validity in Interpretation*.

238. E.g., Structuralism, New Criticism, and Rhetorical Criticism.

239. Tate, *Biblical Interpretation*, 205.

240. Longman, *Literary Approaches*, 32.

241. Berry, *Psalms and Their Readers*, 81.

242. Berry, *Psalms and Their Readers*, 139.

243. E.g., feminist or liberation theology. For Stanley Fish, meaning is the "direct result of the strategies [structures] applied to the text by the reader [or the interpretive community]" (Tate, *Interpreting the Bible*, 193). Fish argues that "in this formulation, the reader's response is not *to* the meaning; it *is* the meaning, or at least the medium in which what I wanted to call the meaning comes into being"

intention of the authors. Meaning is primarily the construct of the implied/informed/ideal reader. The implied reader is the "imaginary person who should completely understand a TEXT as an AUTHOR intended him or her to do and who thereby respond as the author expects."[244] Reader response critics highlight the "gaps" in the texts (ambiguities) which the reader must respond to in order to make sense. The text provides the "directives" (ideologies, forms or content) through which the implied reader is constructed.

There is a continuum between those who hold on to text-centered methods and those who locate meaning in the readers. Somewhere in the midpoint is Wolfgang Iser's approach.[245] In his view, the implied reader is limited by the text. Although the reader interacts with the text to form meaning, the reader is still under the control of the text. In extreme forms of reader response methods, it is not the text that controls the reader but the *interpretive community* in which the reader is situated.[246]

In this mediating position, meaning arises from a dialogical communication process, between the textual signals (forms, structure or content) and the reader's interpretation of these textual signs. Meaning is "a product of interaction between the enabling structures of a text and a reader's acts of comprehension, [and] meaning must be something other than what is found on the printed pages of the text."[247] In other words, meaning is only *apparently* present in the text. The reader cannot freely determine meaning because of various text directives, and yet the text only establishes meaning through the reader's interaction. Although there are indeterminacies, not every meaning is legitimate. The more gaps or differing directives in the text, the harder it is for the reader to come to a consistent perspective of meaning.

Poetry is *lacunous* in character. In a compilation of 150 poems, this characteristic is multiplied. Any consistent perspective to meaning in the Psalter, if any, would be the result of interactions between the text directives and the reader. The question is whether the Psalter contains these text directives and whether they provide the reader with a *consistent* perspective.

With the brief sketch of author–text–reader framework above, my response is as follows: (1) I will first explore what is known of the world of the authors and readers based on extant historical information. From this information, inferences about the author(s)' compositional skills and readers' literary competence can be made. (2) Since my methodology does not differ in large measure from the works of Wilson, Howard, Grant, Labuschagne, Freedman, van der Lugt, and others, I will explore the

---

(Fish, *Is There a Text in This Class*, 3).

244. In contrast, a real reader, conditioned socially and historically, can only understand what his or her worldview affords. Hence, no real reader can fully exhaust the meaning of the text. See Tate, *Interpreting the Bible*, 173, 176.

245. Iser, *Implied Reader*; Berry, *Psalms and Their Readers*, 11–13.

246. Tate, *Interpreting the Bible*, 304.

247. Tate, *Interpreting the Bible*, 305.

Introduction

controls these scholars have adopted in their works and their arguments on authorial intent and readers' responses.

We begin by asking what we know about the world of implied authors and readers of Hebrew poetry. Extrabiblical evidence provides a good source of supporting information. Archaeologists have found, from excavating various sites in Palestine such as Lachish, Arad, and Kuntillat Ajrud, "a number of practice alphabet texts, as well as isolated letters, or letters apparently grouped by similarity of shape, and other materials indicative of elementary instructions,"[248] most of which, can be dated to the eighth century BCE or earlier.[249] Besides such abecedary materials, inscriptions of names, formulaic headers of letters, lists of months of the year, symbols, and sequences of signs, and various drawings have been found.[250] The study of scribal education and curriculum in Kuntillat Ajrud has been recently updated, leading Schniedewind to conclude the following, "Already by the end of the ninth century BCE, even remote desert fortresses would have scribes who were trained in basic skills relating to trade and state bureaucracy. The Kuntillet ʿAjrud inscriptions illustrate a main role of scribes in the ancient world, namely, they work in the service of the state and its bureaucracy."[251]

This epigraphic evidence not only suggests common literacy and training in the preexilic period across Palestine but indicates that specific literary elements of abecedaries, formulas, genre collections, symbols and sequences were prevalent in ancient Hebraic literature. This correlates well with the use of such literary features found in the Psalter. (e.g., alphabetical acrostics and formulaic expressions; cf. Pss 9; 10; 119; 106:1). Moreover, by the seventh and sixth century BCE, ancient Israel's scribal training "required extensive knowledge beyond Hebrew and Aramaic" which would include knowledge of Egyptian or Akkadian.[252]

Biblical acrostics are clearly not the innovation of Hebrew poets. A number of extrabiblical Mesopotamian and Egyptian acrostic poems are extant. Believed to have been composed around the time of 1000 BCE, the Akkadian acrostic, "the Babylonian theodicy," is the result of a poetic technique in which the initial syllables of horizontal lines spell out a message when they are read vertically.[253] The message, *a-na-ku sa-ag-gi-il ki-[i-na-am ub]-bi-ib maáš—ma-šu ka-ri-bu ša i-li ú šar-ri* ("I Saggil-kinam-ubbib,

---

248. Kugel and Greer, *Early Biblical*, 52; Crenshaw, *Education in Ancient Israel*, 100–8.

249. Shea points out that Proto-Sinaitic alphabetic scripts found in the early twentieth century CE have been dated to the fifteenth century BCE. Shea, "Earliest Alphabetic Inscription," 48. See also Albright, *Proto-Sinaitic Inscriptions*.

250. Crenshaw, "Education in Ancient Israel," 605.

251. Schniedewind, "Understanding Scribal Education," 293.

252. Crenshaw, *Education in Ancient Israel*, 88.

253. Brug notes that the poem "apparently consisted of 27 eleven-line stanzas. Each of the 11 lines of a given stanza begins with the same sign. The stanzas are separated by horizontal lines, but there is no other indication of the acrostic" (Brug, "Near Eastern Acrostics," 5).

the exorcist, am a worshipper of god and king"),²⁵⁴ when decrypted, shows the poet's character (a worshipper) is at odds with the poem's content.

Another Akkadian acrostic, probably composed around the same time, is the Prayer of *Nabu-ushebshi*. Recognized as an acrostic only in 1969, this acrostic consists of acrostic signs, half of which occur at the beginning and the other half at the end.²⁵⁵ This is the poetic technique of "telostics" or "mezostics" in which the poem uses signs or words acting as frames around the text.²⁵⁶ In another acrostic connected with King Nebuchadnezzar and dated between 605–562 BCE, each line of four sets of ten/eleven stanzas begins with a sign that forms a cryptic identification of Nabu, the god invoked in the poem.²⁵⁷ Akkadian poets have also used number patterns or line counts as symbolic features in poems. Brug notes that a hymn to the goddess Ishtar consists of 15 stanzas, and the number 15 is "the symbolic number of Ishtar."²⁵⁸

Chiasmus is another technique used as early as the third-millennium BCE. Smith notes,

> Most of the essential features of chiastic form and function were available to Mesopotamian authors from the late third millennium through the mid-first millennium BC, and that chiastic usage in Ugaritic and Hebrew should not be considered unique–except insofar as local eccentricities are exhibited.²⁵⁹

Consider also Dorsey's observation on the Akkadian "Descent of Ishtar to the Nether World":²⁶⁰

a   Ishtar reaches the *first* gate and takes off her *great crown*
  b   Ishtar reaches the *second* gate and takes off her *earrings*
    c   Ishtar reaches the *third* gate and takes off her *necklaces*
      d   Ishtar reaches the *fourth* gate and takes off her *breast ornaments*
        e   Ishtar reaches the *fifth* gate and takes off her *birthstone girdle*

---

254. Brug, "Near Eastern Acrostics," 5.

255. Brug notes, "The clue to the acrostic is provided by the colophons that read, "The beginning and the ending of the writing are to be read twice," that is, horizontally as part of the prayer and vertically as an acrostic. The text consists of two prayers, one to Marduk for offspring and one to Nabu for life" (Brug, "Near Eastern Acrostics," 5).

256. Brug has shown that Mezostics is already an established technique in the Egyptian literature of the nineteenth through twenty-second Dynasties." He points out that "the tomb inscription of Neb-wenenef from the time of Ramses II is written in horizontal columns. However, it is divided by two vertical lines. When the signs between these lines are read vertically, they form an acrostic, or I suppose we should say a mesostic, since the message is in the middle of lines" (Brug, "Near Eastern Acrostics," 6–7).

257. Brug, "Near Eastern Acrostics," 5.

258. Brug, "Near Eastern Acrostics," 6.

259. Smith, "Chiasm in Sumero-Akkadian," 35. For an extensive definition of chiasmus, see Breck, "Biblical Chiasmus," 70–74; *Shape of Biblical Language*.

260. This abridged form of the poem is found in Dorsey, *Literary Structure*, 30. Cf. Pritchard, *Ancient Near East*, 77–81.

    f   Ishtar reaches the *sixth* gate and takes off her *bracelets*

        g   Ishtar reaches the *seventh* gate and takes off her *breechcloth*

            h   Ishtar enters Hades and dies

            h′   Ishtar comes alive and exits Hades

        g′   Ishtar comes to the *seventh* gate and puts on her *breechcloth*

    f′   Ishtar comes to the *sixth* gate and puts on her *bracelets*

  e′   Ishtar comes to the *fifth* gate and puts on her *birthstone girdle*

 d′   Ishtar comes to the *fourth* gate and puts on her *breast ornaments*

c′   Ishtar comes to the *third* gate and puts on her *necklaces*

b′   Ishtar comes to the *second* gate and puts on her *earrings*

a′   Ishtar comes to the *first* gate and puts on her *great crown*

This example also shows that the extended chiastic structure, incorporating the use of numbers such as "seven," is already an established technique in the ancient Near East. The poem centers on the turning point of Ishtar's dying and coming back to life.

Brug points out that quasi-acrostics are also found in Ugaritic poems. It has been observed that Ugaritic poets placed the same word (anaphora/alliteration) or letter at the beginning of several consecutive lines. These poetic effects are similar to those found in the acrostic Ps 119.[261] Certain Egyptian acrostics, by their use of numbers and wordplay, also provide an early attestation of such poetic methods. The hymn to Amon, from the Leiden Papyrus I 350 (dated to thirteenth century BCE),[262] shows that the poem is structured by numbered units. Signs at the beginning and the end of these literary units are actually puns or words that mimic the phonetic value of a number. This Egyptian acrostic is also structured by a number sequence (the first ten chapters are numbered 1 to 10, and subsequent chapters numbered by 10s and 100s). Brug notes that "this format seems to have the same stylistic motive suggested for the biblical acrostic, namely, depicting completeness."[263]

From the brief survey above, we note how Akkadian, Ugaritic, and Egyptian poets were able to encrypt messages, invoke the names of deity, apply various techniques for structuring, and embed numerical sequences within acrostics.

Many of these poems are either contemporaneous to or predate biblical psalms. Without downplaying their differences or specifying the direction of dependence, it is reasonable to assume that poetical techniques seen in the ANE were also practiced and established in ancient Israel because they share a common historical and cultural milieu. Hence, we can assume that the Hebrew poets were conversant with most, if not

---

261. Brug, "Near Eastern Acrostics," 4.
262. Brug, "Near Eastern Acrostics," 6; Zandee, "Le Roi-Dieu," 230.
263. Brug, "Near Eastern Acrostics," 6.

all, the techniques described above and at least some of the readers of the Psalter would also have the necessary literary competency to understand these poetic features.

There is internal evidence that supports the high level of compositional skills of poets, as well as high levels of reading competency of readers of the Psalter. Crenshaw has provided a list of OT references and argues that this "evidence clearly points to the existence of literate persons at an early period in Israel" (e.g., Isa 28:9–13; 50:4–9; Prov 22:17–21).[264]

It is likely that many poetic techniques observed in the Psalter were established early in the Hebraic community. David Freedman's analysis of several early poems of Israel confirms the use of certain poetic techniques by the time of earliest biblical psalms (tenth century BCE?). Dated to the twelfth century BCE,[265] the Song of the Sea (Exod 15) and the Song of Deborah (Judg 5), were of central importance to Israel's social fabric and "could not be lost or forgotten."[266] Even if we grant later editorial hands at work in the Song of the Sea, scholars consider the *terminus ad quem* of its final textual form to be in the pre-monarchic period.[267] From Freedman's study of the Song of the Sea, we note at least six different poetical techniques employed: (a) the use

---

264. Crenshaw cites at least ten further examples: "(1) the existence of a city named Qiriath-Sepher (City of the Book, or City of the Scribe); (2) the story in Judg 8:13–17 about Gideon enlisting the aid of a local youth to write down the names of the city officials; (3) Isaiah's determination to bind up the testimony and seal the teaching among his disciples (8:16); (4) Job's desire to have the charges against him written on a document so that he could display them and demonstrate his innocence (31:35–37); (5) Habakkuk's reference to a vision that could be read while one ran through the streets (2:2); (6) allusions to buying knowledge, which *is* understood as tuition (Prov 4:5; 17:16); (7) presumed scribes and courtiers in the royal court, particularly in the time of David, Solomon, and Hezekiah; (8) references to parental instruction in Proverbs (especially 4:1–9; 8:32–36); (9) scattered references to writing (e.g., Isa 10:19; 29:11–12; Prov 3:3; 7:3 [the tablet of the heart]; Jer 8:8 [the false pen of scribes]; Deut 24:1, 3 [a bill of divorce]; Jer 32:12 [deed of purchase]; Josh 18:9; 2 Sam 18:17); (10) vocabulary for teaching and knowledge in Proverbs (cf. also the Oak of Moreh in Gen 12:6; Deut 11:30)" (Crenshaw, "Education in Ancient Israel," 603–4).

265. Freedman, *Pottery, Poetry, and Prophecy*, 118, 160, 226.

266. Freedman identified a number of songs dated from the twelve to tenth century BCE. He notes three different phases of compositions. These compositions, he argues, were central and basic to Israel's life. He notes, "I distinguish three phases of composition, which may be assigned to the twelfth, eleventh, and tenth centuries respectively: (i) the period of militant Mosaic Yahwism: the Song of the Sea (Exodus 15), during the first half of the twelfth century, and the Song of Deborah (Judges 5), during the second half of the same century; (ii) the archaic period, with the revival of patriarchal names and titles for God: the Testament of Jacob (Genesis 49), during the first half of the eleventh century, and the Testament of Moses (Deuteronomy 33), during the later part of the same century; the Oracles of Balaam (Numbers 23–24), perhaps in the middle of the century; (iii) the period of the monarchy: the Song of Moses (Deuteronomy 32), difficult to date, but there are tell-tale signs of later composition in the selection of divine names, which indicate that it belongs to phase iii, not earlier than the tenth to ninth centuries, perhaps around 900 BC" (Freedman, "Pottery, Poetry, and Prophecy," 18).

267. The absence of monarchical references and various associations to Canaanite mythic *topoi* are elements that suggest that the Song of the Sea was composed at least as early as the pre-monarchic period. For a recent discussion of the historicity of Exod 15, see Leuchter, "Eisodus as Exodus," 321–46.

of divine name and titles as rhetorical devices;[268] (b) strophic structures;[269] (c) the use of inclusions;[270] (d) pyramid (chiastic) structures with a central focus on Yhwh's kingship and his victories over his enemies;[271] (e) the use of "Exordium" [or introduction];[272] (f) metric and symmetry in the structure of a poem.[273]

Specifically for (d), the heart of the Song (Exod 15:9–11) highlights the final expressions of Yhwh's victory over Pharaoh before the poet moves on to a different motif: that of Yhwh leading his people to the Promised land. Freedman argues, "These data indicate the pyramidal structure of the main part of the poem with the apex in the center of the poem. So far as the content is concerned, it coincides with the final destruction of Pharaoh's host in the turbulent waters."[274]

Moreover, the Song of the Sea depicts not just Yhwh's deliverance of Israel but their passing over into the land of Canaan and eventual dwelling in the mountain where Yhwh's sanctuary is established by his own hands (Exod 15:17–18). There is a movement in the Song, a trajectory that captures Israel's relationship with God, their struggle and eventual arrival to a place of promise and security. The language of praise in the first person (Exod 15:1 cf. Pss 13:6; 104:33);[275] the arboreal language

---

268. For Freedman, the name "yhwh" is used "exclusively or predominantly" in the "militant Mosaic Yahwism" period (twelfth century). In the Song of the Sea, Exod 15:1 and 21 are seen as the refrain, enveloping the main section of the poem. Freedman notes that in these two framing verses, "the only divine name which occurs is Yahweh." For him, "the selection and distribution of divine names do not appear to be haphazard but follow a traceable evolutionary pattern" (Freedman, *Pottery, Poetry, and Prophecy*, 79, 107).

269. "Starting from an extremely important and completely convincing observation of Professor Muilenburg, we can proceed at once to an examination of the strophic pattern of the poem. He points out that a special poetic device (of great antiquity since it is a common feature of pre-Mosaic Canaanite poetry) is used to separate the poetic units of stanzas of the composition. These dividers [Exod 15:6, 11, 16b], or refrains (since they employ repetitive pattern), are very much alike in structure or pattern." Freedman concluded, "The existence of a strophic structure in this poem may be regarded as highly probable if not virtually certain" (Freedman, *Pottery, Poetry, and Prophecy*, 179, 188).

270. "The rhetorical device known as *inclusion* is shown by the repetition of the name 'Yahweh' in vss. 3 and 19—a continuity maintained in the refrains [vv.1, 21]." Elsewhere, Freedman added, "the second refrain stands at the center of the poem, and is an elaborate apostrophe on the incomparability of Yahweh. It serves to link not only the two major parts of the poem, but also the thematic statements at the beginning and end: vs 3, Yahweh the warrior, and vs 18, Yahweh the king who will reign over his people" (Freedman, *Pottery, Poetry, and Prophecy*, 182, 216).

271. Freedman, *Pottery, Poetry, and Prophecy*, 180.

272. "The conclusion of the investigation into the strophic structure of the Son of the Sea is that it is a well-ordered poem, with a single inclusive design. The Song consists of an Exordium [introduction], followed by an opening stanza which is complemented by a parallel closing stanza, each one corresponding in length and pattern to the stanza-units of the body of the poem" (Freedman, *Pottery, Poetry, and Prophecy*, 183, 217).

273. "I further suggest that the poem—a gem of metrical symmetry and artistic simplicity—belongs to the same period, Phase I, as the Song of the Sea, Psalm 29, and the Song of Deborah" (Freedman, *Pottery, Poetry, and Prophecy*, 235).

274. Freedman, *Pottery, Poetry, and Prophecy*, 180.

275. The exact phrase, אשירה ליהוה, is found only in these three places.

of Yhwh's "planting" (נטע) of his people at "the mountain of [Yhwh's] inheritance" (cf. Pss 1:3; 52:10; 92:13–15); the recurring rhetorical question of "who is like you, O Lord" (Exod 15:11; cf. Pss 35:10; 71:19; 89:9; Deut 33:29); and the final conclusion of Yhwh's eternal kingship (יהוה ימלך לעלם ועד; Exod 15:18; cf. Pss 10:16; 29:10; 93:1; 96:10; 97:1; 99:1),[276] are significant literary motifs that later poets seemed to have adopted and used in the Psalter.

The parallel features between the Song of the Sea and the Psalms are significant. Granting the antiquity and centrality of the Song of the Sea (and other early poems) in Israel's history, it is reasonable to assume that the readers of the Psalter were not only familiar with such poetic techniques and competent to understand them, but were also familiar with the theological metanarrative and motifs inherent in biblical poems such as the Song of the Sea.

We move on to explore how Psalms scholars understand issues of authorial intent and readers' response related to the Psalter. We begin with Wilson's *Editing of the Hebrew Psalter*. In his work, Wilson argues for *intentional editorial design* based on various literary features observed in the MT-150.[277] This is clearly evident by the use of "editing" in the title of his book. Under the hermeneutical framework of author-text-reader, Wilson's interest was primarily in the first two loci, the author and the text. Now, the issue of whether an implied or informed reader would be able to pick

---

276. The juxtaposition of the two lexeme, מלך יהוה, is found only in these texts: Exod 15:18; 1 Chr 16:31; Pss 10:16; 29:10; 93:1; 96:10; 97:1; 99:1; Isa 33:22; 44:6; Jer 17:20; 19:3; 22:2. Note also that the phrase with the defective spelling, לעלם, is found only in Exod 15:18 and Ps 45:18 (cf. Pss 9:6; 119:44; 145:1–2, 21; Dan 12:3; Mic 4:5).

277. Jamie Grant calls this "editorial criticism." For his definition of "editorial criticism," see Grant, "Editorial Criticism," 149–56. Consider the following statements that Wilson frequently adopts in *EHP*: "I am convinced by the data that there are clear indications of editorial activity throughout MT 150. These are not isolated examples of limited editorial concern, but are part of a broader editorial movement to unify the 150 pss into a coherent whole" (Wilson, *EHP*, 11); "evidence ... of editorial use" (Wilson, *EHP*, 167); "how the editor(s) of the Psalter used the pss-headings" (Wilson, *EHP*, 167); "method and purpose of the Psalter editor(s)" (Wilson, *EHP*, 170); "explicit statements in the pss-headings were employed by the editor(s) to organize and structure the Psalter" (Wilson, *EHP*, 182); "my study of the distribution of the technical terms ... is a real and purposeful division which is indicated internally by the editorial use of author designations ... not fortuitous, but represent editorially induced methods of giving 'shape' to the pss corpus" (Wilson, *EHP*, 186); "the results [Wilson's analysis] indicate that the positioning of the opening and closing pss of these segments reflects *purposeful* choice and arrangement of pss rather than chance juxtaposition" (Wilson, *EHP*, 190); "I have been able to show (1) that the "book" divisions of the Psalter are real, editorial induced divisions and not accidentally introduced; ... All these findings demonstrate the presence of editorial activity at work in the arrangement of the pss" (Wilson, *EHP*, 199); "it is possible to show that the *final* form of the MT 150 is the result of a purposeful, editorial activity which sought to impart a meaningful arrangement which encompassed the whole" (Wilson, *EHP*, 199); "the curious conjunction of such large number of "untitled" pss in Book Four, as well as its other distinctive features, lead me to suggest that this book is especially the product of purposeful editorial arrangement" (Wilson, *EHP*, 215); "close correspondence between the concluding summary in Ps 106:40–46 and the continuing refrain of 107:6–8 ... leaves little doubt of the purposeful juxtaposition of these two pss" (Wilson, *EHP*, 220); "two groups of Davidic pss preserved in this final book ... Their placement at beginning and end implies purposeful editorial arrangement" (Wilson, *EHP*, 221).

up Wilson's observations of the text is not discussed. To be sure, Wilson had set up his study with an objective control to avoid imposing "non-existent structure on the text."[278] This is achieved by a preliminary study of several comparative ANE texts which, in turn, allowed him to "set parameters for the kind of editorial techniques and concerns one might expect to find active in the organization of a group of hymnic texts such as the Psalter."[279] For Wilson, this is an adequate methodological control. Although Wilson's work has been widely discussed, this important methodological stance is not often highlighted and neither is it vehemently contended. Hence, the editorial techniques found in Mesopotamian hymnic literature[280] warrant the assumption that the editors of the MT-150 possessed similar poetic skills.

In his study of Sumerian Temple Hymns, Wilson notes "the collection indicates that at a very early date (2334–2279 BCE, if not earlier), it was possible to enter into a complex arrangement of individual literary compositions (each maintaining its own integrity) on the basis of a larger schema (in this case the campaign of Sargon of Akkad)."[281] Specifically, it is suggested that techniques such as genre categories, author designations, colophons, song type, characteristic language, size of a partial collection, deity addressed in the hymn and chiastic structures[282] were well-established techniques.

Instead of focusing on the editor/author, Jamie Grant emphasizes certain assumptions about the readers' sensitivity to the text and connects these assumptions with the editor. His dissertation, "The King as Exemplar," argues for intentional juxtaposition of Torah and kingship psalms in the shaping of the Psalter and postulates possible meanings for the ancient readers. He identifies three types of features in the text—canonical, lexical and theological—which he contends readers would have discerned and understood.[283] Canonically, he notes that "whoever placed Pss 1 and 2 as the dual introduction [Torah and kingship] to the Psalms wanted the readers of the book to view its varied content from the perspective of a Deuteronomic worldview,"[284] that is, a perspective guided by the Deuteronomic Law of the King in Deut 17:14–20.[285] Readers were assumed to be aware of the "typical role of kingship in the ancient Near East."[286] In this way, the juxtaposition of Torah and kingship psalms would elicit a

278. Wilson, *EHP*, 5.

279. Wilson, *EHP*, 5–6.

280. Two Mesopotamian hymnic materials (third-millennium BCE) used for comparison are the Sumerian Temple Hymn Collection and the Catalogs of Hymnic Incipits. See Wilson, *EHP*, 7.

281. Wilson, *EHP*, 23.

282. Wilson, *EHP*, 38, 47, 53–57, 126, 196–97.

283. Grant, "King as Exemplar," 146. Note that his dissertation is also published with the same title under the Academia Biblica Series of SBL.

284. Grant, "King as Exemplar," 43.

285. Readers were expected to perceive lexical repetitions and thematic overlaps of Torah and kingship motifs between adjacent Pss 18–21. See Grant, "King as Exemplar," 86.

286. Grant, "King as Exemplar," 157.

"substantial degree of cognitive dissonance for the reader of the psalms" at the time when the Davidic kingship is no longer present.[287] Grant argues, "The reasons for this paradigm being placed at the head of the Psalter reflect two of the primary theological concerns of the period of the Psalter's closure: 1. The Torah, as the proper rule for the life of Israel, and 2. Eschatological hope for the 'renewal' of the Davidic king."[288]

By positing these socio-theological concepts behind the text shared by the composers and readers alike, Grant links authorial intent (by the arrangement of psalms and their contents) and readers' reception of the text.[289] The readers' ability to derive meaning from paratextual features, such as the peculiar juxtapositions of Torah and kingship psalms, is an interaction between the text's *directives* and readers' socio-theological worldview, a proposition we have seen in Iser's theory.

David Howard, in his important work, *The Structure of Psalms 93–100*, has performed a systematic and exhaustive analysis on all lexical connections between these eight psalms. He makes several claims on how the implied reader could detect such connections. Noted only briefly in the methodological chapter, Howard says that "the rabbis traditionally were more attuned to ... connections between neighboring psalms, ... Their [the early Jewish rabbis] works especially reflected attention to key-word links between consecutive psalms."[290] Like Wilson, Howard appeals to early Jewish literature in trying to understand the readers and composers of the Psalms. Howard classifies the lexical connections found within the Yhwh *Malak* psalms into three categories with decreasing significance ("*Key-Word Links*"; "*Thematic Connections*"; and "*Structure/Genre Similarities*").[291] Only in the first category, *Key-word Links*, did Howard suggest that "they were undoubtedly present in the editors' thinking as they made decisions about bringing the Psalter together."[292] In the second category, he sees connections arising from a "general vocabulary" existing at the time of composition. Apart from the *Key-word links* category, which Howard insists that the choice of lexemes was "undoubtedly present" in the minds of the implied authors at the time of the final composition, Howard provides little clarity on how such lexical connections can be perceived by the readers.

Howard's method of studying lexical connections has been followed by others who continue to sharpen the distinction between what might constitute intentional lexical links and what might be accidental. For instance, Michael Snearly proposes a statistical criteria in his study of Book V of the Psalter and identifies a significant

287. Grant, "King as Exemplar," 27.

288. Grant, "King as Exemplar," 56.

289. Grant also notes, "The placement of Pss 1 and 2 at the beginning of the Psalter was designed to draw the *attention of the reader* to themes which were *important to those who had put the book of Psalms together*; the intention being that *awareness of these motifs should remain prominent in the mind of the reader* throughout their reading or hearing of the Psalter" (Grant, "King as Exemplar," 96).

290. Howard, *Structure of Psalms*, 2.

291. Howard, *Structure of Psalms*, 100–1.

292. Howard, *Structure of Psalms*, 100.

key-word (or phrase) as one having "at least half of all occurrences in Book V" located in one group "and/or at least 20 percent of all occurrences in the Psalter are in one group."²⁹³ How Snearly arrives at 20 percent and how he draws the boundary of the "group" remain sticking points.

If Snearly's quantitative method is unhelpful, Jeffrey Leonard's eight qualitative guidelines for judging the strengths of literary links between texts may provide an alternative.

> (1) Shared language is the single most important factor in establishing a textual connection. (2) Shared language is more important than nonshared language. (3) Shared language that is rare or distinctive suggests a stronger connection than does language that is widely used. (4) Shared phrases suggest a stronger connection than do individual shared terms. (5) The accumulation of shared language suggests a stronger connection than does a single shared term or phrase. (6) Shared language in similar contexts suggests a stronger connection than does shared language alone. (7) Shared language need not be accompanied by shared ideology to establish a connection. (8) Shared language need not be accompanied by shared form to establish a connection.²⁹⁴

David Willgren further refined this list and arrived at six methodological points with some overlap with Leonard's list.²⁹⁵

> (1) Verbatim similarities featuring rare words establish stronger connection than those including common or very common words. (2) Verbatim similarities occurring in similar contexts establish a stronger connection than similarities based on shared words only. (3) Declared citations establish a stronger connection than undeclared citations. (4) Shared phrases establish a stronger connection than shared words. (5) Shared phrases featuring formulaic or idiomatic language establish a weaker connection than shared phrases that do not. (6) Multiple shared phrases establish a stronger connection than single shared phrases.

Dorsey has also identified several methodological errors associated with the technique of chiastic structures.²⁹⁶ He provided ten guidelines to alleviate subjectivity as follows:²⁹⁷

---

293. Snearly, "Return of the King," 210; *Return of the King*, 1, 120, 187. One of the latest works using a statistical method of identifying significant links is Richards, *King and the Kingdom*.

294. Leonard, "Identifying Inner-Biblical Allusions," 246.

295. Willgren, *Formation of the "Book" of Psalms*, 291. Cf. Lange and Weigold, *Biblical Quotations and Allusions*.

296. (1) Creative titling: units made to match by imaginative wordings. (2) Illegitimate word-linking: use of common words in connecting units. (3) Illegitimate theme-linking: use of common motifs in connecting units. Dorsey, *Literary Structure*, 33–34.

297. I have retained Dorsey's titles for the ten points (in italics) but shortened the descriptions. For examples of these guidelines, see Dorsey, *Literary Structure*, 34–35.

(1) *Objective links*. Connections should be based on verbatim or near verbatim words. (2) *Prominent links*. Connections should be based on prominent echoes rather than obscure ones. (3) *Multiple links*. Multiple connections should be given more weight. (4) *Unique links*. Rare and unique connections not found in surrounding texts should be given more weight. (5) *Easily perceived links*. An easily perceived link is more likely for the readers to perceive. (6) *Author's agenda*. Connections that correspond to the composer's agenda are more convincing. (7) *Danger of forcing loose ends*. Exceptions should not be forced to fit as they may be suggestive of other authorial design. (8) *Danger of rearranging the text*. This should not be undertaken just to fit a proposed structural scheme. (9) *Danger of reductionism*. The tendency to identify the same structural scheme in every text should be avoided. (10) *Analyses of other scholars*. Consulting the structural analyses of others will help reduce subjectivity.

These qualitative criteria provide additional controls to claims of textual connections in the texts and will underlie the basis of my study of the Psalter. Nonetheless, I accept that some subjectivity will always be present. This is why scholars such as Labuschagne and van der Lugt, despite their extensive work on the Psalter, only connect loosely their observations in the text with the implied authors (or readers). After about 1700 pages in van der Lugt's three-volume magisterial work on canto and strophic structures of the Psalter, he concluded with a brief paragraph, connecting his observations of the text to the Hebrew poets themselves. He notes,

> I conclude that the Hebrew poets used a limited number of basic canto patterns to shape their compositions. In the book of Psalms, these patterns can be clearly discerned. At the same time—by their poetic craftsmanship—the Hebrew writers handled these canto patterns in a creative way. Despite the fact that they imposed particular restrictions on themselves, they freely varied them, with the result that already on the level of the overall framework hardly any two poems of some length have exactly the same canto structure in terms of verselines.[298]

Labuschagne's work on the Psalter focuses on numerical features functioning as structuring devices. His proposition is that poets had organized the content of texts by a selected number of words such that important features are often located at the mathematical center of the text unit.[299] This phenomenon occurs not just in the Psalter but throughout the OT.

Labuschagne also argues that the numerical technique he observes would not have been written for the general reader, but for those within the guild—craftsmen of poetry themselves. With the passage of time, these techniques were substantially

---

298. Van der Lugt, *CAS III*, 3:606.

299. He reasons that poets and transmitters of the texts had incorporated these poetic devices so that the text can be checked and preserved. Labuschagne, *Numerical Secrets of the Bible*, 11.

lost or forgotten.³⁰⁰ Labuschagne's point should be noted. It is possible too that certain poetic techniques have gone into disuse. In other words, the repertoire of poetic techniques at the disposal of ancient poets could have been substantially more than what scholars today have uncovered.

In general, my methodological stance does not differ substantially from the scholars listed above. Where I have remarked certain observations of the text as evidence of authorial intent in this book, I see them as secondary inferences. I am aware of what Wimsatt and Beardsley call "intentional fallacy" (a confusion between what the text *is* and the intent of the author) or the "affective fallacy" (a confusion between what the text *is* and what the text *does* to its readers).³⁰¹ I like to think that we can "avoid the two extreme views of authorial intention being irrelevant or that authorial intention is decisive."³⁰²

In conclusion, we summarize our discussion above with six points: From comparative ANE poetic literature and inscriptions found in Palestine, it is highly plausible that composers and readers alike would have been familiar with (1) certain poetic compositional techniques such as the use of colophons, superscriptions, numerical and symbolic devices, abecedarian acrostics, names or epithets of God, chiastic structures, inclusions, exordiums, and strophic structures. Since similar poetic techniques are found in the Psalter, our assumptions on the poetic skills of the final editors and literary competency of readers can be sustained. (2) If the Song of the Sea provides an early example of Hebrew poetry, we can assume ancient readers of the Psalms would be familiar with the use of metanarratival progression in a poem. Israel will eventually be "planted" by God in the mountain of God, where God's sanctuary, built by his own hands, is established. The emphasis of Yhwh's kingship, and the phrase, מלך יהוה in the Song of the Sea, could have been one of the earliest poetic expression the Psalms composers had drawn on. (3) Poetry, as a literary genre, is aesthetic and lacunous. Meaning is often expressed and understood via gaps in the text. Meaning is not merely found in the text, but also in the paratext—everything else alongside the text (the shapes, gaps, stylistic arrangements, structure, etc.). Since the explicit text does not exhaust the meaning of the text, we need not assume that the composers had made everything consistently detectable nor assume that the readers could uncover every intended meaning. For instance, it has been shown that chiastic structures have been

---

300. Labuschagne, *Numerical Secrets of the Bible*, 11–12.

301. Wimsatt and Beardsley argue "that the design or intention of the author is neither available nor desirable as a standard for judging the success of a work of literary art, and it seems to us that this is a principle which goes deep into some differences in the history of critical attitudes." For them, "intention is design or plan in the author's mind. Intention has obvious affinities for the author's attitude toward his work, the way he felt, what made him write." This intention needs to be separated from the work itself. See Wimsatt and Beardsley, "Intentional Fallacy," 468–69. Cf. Dickie and Wilson, "Intentional Fallacy," 234; Lim, *Strategy for Reading*, 38.

302. Lim, *Strategy for Reading*, 73.

used by Hebrew poets in the Psalms (e.g., Ps 67).[303] The rhetorical feature of concentricity may even harbour mathematical precision. Van der Lugt cites Ps 79:7, noting how this verse is not only the mathematical center colon, but that the texts themselves are arranged in a chiastic manner ("predicate + object // object + predicate").[304] However, his observations cannot be sustained in every psalm (or even in the majority of most psalms). This does not mean that a mathematically precise technique, as an established form, is thus implausible because chiastic forms are not always expressed in a rigid, consistent way.[305] In other words, text directives may not always present exacting (consistent) perspectives for the reader and the burden is on the exegete who requires them to be. Hence, our observations are descriptive rather than prescriptive. Moreover, it is conceivable to assume, as Labuschagne has, that poets sometimes use techniques that were privy to poets themselves and that the general readers were not expected to access.[306]

(4) It is reasonable to say that not all connections carry the same weight. We can assume some form of distinctions between intentional or incidental lexical connections are possible. The choice and use of certain words or motif should not always be judged as incidental. Particularly in poetry, we can assume that the choice of words by the poets is often thoughtful. (5) We also see that ancient readers of the text would have possessed some level of literary competence in reading. They were already familiar with literary elements that are common to the biblical Psalms. By the time of the Rabbis, concerns with the sequence and arrangements of psalms were extant. Even before the advent of modern computers, the scribal techniques employed by the Masoretes, especially from their marginal notes and word counting, reflected a high level of familiarity with the Hebrew Scripture. They were able to reference the locations and frequencies of certain word forms across the entire Hebrew (MT) canon and locate midpoints of entire books such as the Psalter.[307] Such skills suggest that the Masoretes were highly sensitive to text structure, word forms, and their occurrence. (6) The socio-political environment of the readers at the time of the final composition of the Psalter fits well with the postexilic existential needs and theological hopes of Israel. Moreover, as Grant noted, readers would have been familiar with the Deuteronomic worldview and the concepts of kingship in the ANE. Hence, kingship and Torah

---

303. deClaissé-Walford et al., *Book of Psalms*, 538.

304. Van der Lugt, "Mathematical Centre," 649.

305. Similarly, there is a consensus in reading Pss 42–83 as the Elohistic Psalter since the name, "Yhwh," has been replaced by "Elohim" in numerous places. The reading of these psalms as "Elohistic Psalter" is maintained by Psalms scholarship even though not every occurrence of "Yhwh" in these psalms were replaced by "Elohim."

306. In a good piece of painting, it is reasonable to assume that a skilled audience (i.e., professionally trained artists) would find observations that an untrained audience would not. While the latter may identify the painter of a painting, the skilled audience may pick up unique brush or framing techniques.

307. See the Masorah parva note of Ps 78:36 in L (הספר חצי).

motifs prominently located in the Psalter provide the necessary fodder for theological reflection and readers' responses. It is safe to assume that the dissonance between the missing Davidic king in postexilic Israel and the Davidic covenantal promises would have had a major theological contemplation for the reader. It is also logical to assume that eschatological and messianic emphases in the early Jewish and Christian works at the turn of the era would have had their roots planted in the theological fabric of the postexilic period.

Where I have made certain original observations or claims in this book, it will be shown that they are consistent with the above assumptions on the composers or readers. Finally, this long quote from Freedman is helpful:

> It is difficult if not impossible to draw the line between the conscious intention of the poet and what the attentive reader finds in a poem. On the whole, I think we have given insufficient credit to the poet for the subtleties and intricacies in his artistic creation, and it is better to err on that side for a while. If we find some clever device or elaborate internal structure, why not assume that the poet's ingenuity, rather than our own, is responsible? It is a different matter if it is our ingenuity in restoring or reconstructing the text. In many cases, however, I believe that the process by which the poet achieves an effect is different from the process by which the scholar recognizes and describes it. What is the result of conscious effort on our part may be spontaneous in the poet, or second nature. For one who is steeped in the tradition and draws on long experience in creating poems, it is not necessary to start from scratch, and the associations and intricate arrangements, which we discover only painstaking investigation, may be byproducts of which he is not fully aware, while he centers attention on other aspects of composition. Since there is no way to finally resolve such questions about the intention of the poet, it is safer and better procedure to restrict or extend ourselves to the visible data and describe what we see there, rather than to probe to recesses of the poet's mind.[308]

Unity of the Psalter?

Careful readers of the Bible have often noted the "inconsistency in historical information, moral teaching and theological understanding" of the Bible.[309] Where the Psalter is concerned, scholars such as Whybray, Gerstenberger, and others argue against reading the Psalter as a *book*.[310] Whybray argues that "there is no tangible evidence of a

---

308. Freedman, *Pottery, Poetry, and Prophecy*, 8. Cf. Berry, *Psalms and Their Readers*, 85.

309. Barton, *Old Testament Canon*, 54.

310. Day notes, "any attempt to find one grandiose scheme to account for the ordering of the Psalter is bound to end in failure" (Day, *Psalms*, 111). Anderson concludes, "the book itself shows little evidence of deliberate internal ordered placement" (Anderson, "Division and Order," 219–41). Similarly, Nogalski echoes these thoughts by noting that "no single organizational principle can adequately explain every aspect of Psalms . . . The lack of a single organizing principle further suggests a complex

The Design of the Psalter

consistent and systematic attempt to link the whole collection of psalms together by editorial means."[311] There is a loose sense of progression in the trajectory of the Psalter rather than intentional effort to arrange every psalm. For Whybray, it is difficult to dismiss "the impression of randomness" in the Psalms.[312]

Similarly, Gerstenberger registers his resistance by saying that "the Psalter is not a 'book' in our sense of the word, and certainly not a theological textbook of progressively unfolding of God's statement."[313] He also casts doubt on keyword connections, pointing out that the questions remain whether such links represent "conscious connection of the texts or [are] merely a random result of the array of related texts in a writ."[314] Gerstenberger's view on the Psalter is driven by socio-historical concerns that underlie the composition of individual psalms.[315] For him, the distinctive message of individual psalms must be preserved and examined under its *Sitz im Leben*.[316] As a whole, Gerstenberger rejects a single unified theological message behind the Psalter but posits the Psalter as a compendium of experiences collected over time and used as a hymnal for the Jewish diaspora.

In seeking to answer *how* and *why* the "Book" of Psalms was formed, an important monograph, *The Formation of the "Book" of Psalms*, by David Willgren needs to be addressed.[317] He argues that the Psalter is an *anthology* (compilation) and the "book" of Psalms is *not* a coherent whole. Moreover, the final form of the Psalter does not provide any interpretive context to understanding an individual psalm.[318]

Like Wilson, Willgren first contextualizes his study in an ancient Near Eastern scribal and material culture, comparing the Psalms with the Sumerian Temple Hymns, the Hodayot, and the "psalms" scrolls from the Judean desert. He observes that various paratextual elements (e.g., superscriptions and colophons) often serve preservation and canonization purposes.[319]

---

development of the psalter" (Nogalski, "From Psalm to Psalms," 52–53). See also Whybray, *Reading the Psalms*, 84; Gerstenberger, "Der Psalter Als Buch," 3–13.

311. Whybray, *Reading*, 84, emphasis added.

312. Whybray, *Reading*, 85–86, emphasis added.

313. Gerstenberger points out several pitfalls of this approach. He sees that all texts have a concrete communicative environment ("ein konkretes kommunikatives Umfeld"). Taking a text out from this historical and social environment makes interpretation harder. He views the diachronic socio-historical anchor as necessary in understanding the Psalter. He notes, "The canonical final form of the Hebrew scripture is entirely connected to the specific, historically unique setting of sufferings, joys and visions of the postexilic Jewish communities in Palestine and in the Diaspora" (Gerstenberger, "Der Psalter Als Buch," 3–4, 9). My translation.

314. Gerstenberger, "Der Psalter Als Buch," 5.

315. Gerstenberger, "Die 'Kleine Biblia,'" 391.

316. For him, this concrete environment relates to the Jewish synagogal diaspora of the postexilic period.

317. Willgren, *Formation*.

318. Willgren, *Formation*, 19–20.

319. Willgren, *Formation*, 79.

Introduction

Willgren provides five major points[320] against a unified reading of the Psalter: (1) Psalm 1 (or Pss 1–2) did not provide any interpretative framework for the rest of the Psalter; (2) Superscriptions were added later and were not indicative of earlier existing collections, nor served any organizing function; (3) The colophon in Ps 72:20 preserved "the end of the first [of two] scroll of a collection of psalms"; (4) The ברך doxologies in Pss 41:14; 72:18–19; 89:53; and 106:48 were incorporated to "create a conceptual similarity with the Pentateuch," resulting in some authoritative status; (5) The הלל doxologies (Pss 146–150) superseded the ברך doxologies framework and belonged to a late formation period.

At the end of his work, Willgren lays out *how* the "Book"[321] of Psalms was formed. There was no "Ursammlung" (primitive collection) of psalms with fixed sequence or content at the early stages of reconstructing the book of Psalms. He argues that individual psalms could be "easily rearranged, or new psalms inserted (and probably removed from) anywhere in the sequence" and that the collection then grew to two full scrolls with a sizable amount of psalms.[322] By the early postexilic period, the first scroll would contain Pss 1–119 (not necessarily the same MT Pss 1–119 we are familiar with), and Ps 72:20 was incorporated at the end of the scroll following Ps 119. Then Korahite and Asaphite psalms were then included at this stage. By the Persian period, longer sequences of psalms linked to David via superscriptions appeared. When 1–2 Chronicles were composed, the Song of Ascents, the doxologies of Pss 135–136, and Pss 2:12; 41:14; 89:53 were added to the collection of psalms. Eventually, Ps 72:20 was left as a frozen colophon at the end of the first scroll, following Ps 72. Thereafter, the entire "Book" of Psalms was divided into five parts. The final stage of formation is the incorporating of the Hallelujah framework and is dated to the "late third or early second century BCE."[323] Willgren concludes that the formation process was driven by practical issues such as scroll sizes and preservation needs, and there were no single purpose or theological motivation that could be identified and ascribed to the final text.[324]

While Willgren should be commended for his detailed work, several issues dampen his argument. First, Willgren's propositions are highly speculative.[325] His con-

320. Willgren, *Formation*, 147, 170, 186, 192, 199, 225, 250.

321. For Willgren, the "book" is always enclosed with parenthesis because he argues for reading the Psalter as an anthology rather than a "book."

322. Willgren, *Formation*, 376.

323. Willgren, *Formation*, 383.

324. Willgren, *Formation*, 388.

325. An example of the lack of hard evidence and the conjectural aspects of Willgren's argument on how the musical notations in superscriptions are deemed later addition (or added over a long period of time) can be seen here: "As the distribution and variation of these terms show, they are not to be considered as important to the organization of psalms, but their presence could nevertheless give some indications about its formation. If understanding the irretrievability of the meaning of many of these terms as caused by some change in use and historical circumstances, rather than being an indication of, say, a redactional purpose, there is an important observation to be made. Throughout

59

clusions are not based on any textual evidence (at most, ancient parallels) and there is no concrete way to prove or deny his arguments. Moreover, Willgren's reconstruction of the formation process is a linear process chain in which one speculation is built on another. If any developmental stage in the formation process is unsustainable, subsequent stages in the process would require another theory.

Second, it remains unclear in his reconstruction if there were a larger set of extant *authoritative* psalms from which a subset was selected to be incorporated into the final form of the Psalter, or *only* those selected psalms were considered authoritative. If the former were true, then the selection was independent of the authoritative status of selected psalms. However, this goes against Willgren's view that the selection of psalms for inclusion is motivated by the status of a psalm's relative importance and material limitations. Now, if the latter is to be sustained, it would be difficult to freely include or exclude selections because of their authoritative status. Based on Willgren's reconstructions, MT Pss 119–134 were absent in the second scroll before the Persian period. That meant that many psalms originally in the *second scroll* (by his proposal) would have to be excluded subsequently to make way for MT Pss 119–134 later. Either way, such massive content changes or arbitrary selections logically contradict Willgren's own views on the formation process that is motivated by the status of psalms authority and material limitations.

Third, the methodology adopted by Willgren and how he addressed the canonical issues are problematic. On the one hand, Willgren adopts a comparative approach leveraging on selective and extant textual evidence (e.g., DSS) to build arguments against canonical/editorial approaches to the Psalter, which generally proceed from the final text. On the other, Willgren reconstructs the formation of the Psalter based on literary approaches to the final text! In other words, there is a methodological disconnect, and to some extent, fluidity. I have found that it is unnecessary for him to dismiss editorial/literary methods to justify his proposals since he also uses them to reconstruct the formation process. He wants to shift the discussion of the MT Psalter to the DSS Psalms and deemphasizing the canonical nature of the former, but he has

---

Pss 4–88, these terms are fairly widely distributed, although clustered especially around Pss 53–62, but as for Pss 89–150, they are nowhere to be found. Since the pattern is so clear, it would reasonable reflect some change in how these psalms were perceived and used, rather than being the result of mere chance ... *it would be reasonable to assume that the function of these paratexts has changed from specifying some musical performance to instead provide a general notion of antiquity and status to the psalms to which they were attached.* It also indicates that the overall tendency is that superscriptions are added over time, and that previous elements are seldom removed, even if unintelligible ... *The psalms could just as well have been juxtaposed without superscriptions for a long period of time.* If this approach is reasonable, the occurrence of a Davidic psalm in the middle of a cluster of Korahite psalms (Ps 86) need not be interpreted as an 'interlocking' device, but as ... similar addition of a Davidic superscription to Ps 43 in the LXX. *It would have been added at a time when that particular sequence of psalms was fairly fixed ... The sequences now found in the MT 'Book' of Psalms seem to have become increasingly fixed, so that new areas of use for various psalms did not necessarily lead to rearrangement, but simply to the adding of superscriptions to the psalms in question*" (Willgren, *Formation*, 183, 191–92, emphasis added).

not shown, methodologically speaking, how an anthology is formed historically. In other words, the methods through which Willgren formulates the formation of the MT Psalter is primarily literary, and are not different from those of canonical approaches. While Willgren rejects the editorial approaches to the Psalter that support a unified logic for its formation, his proposals for the formation process include so much intentional content changes that it seems to support *editorial shaping* for coherency rather than a mere *selection* and inclusion of psalms in the formation of the Psalter.

In sum, Whybray's argument is one of degree and not of substantial disagreement. Gerstenberger's argument is more of a methodological disagreement rather than a negation by literary analysis. Willgren's methodology is fluid and his conclusions remain highly conjectural.[326]

Notwithstanding the diachronic process of the Psalter's composition into its final unified form as a book,[327] our interests are focused on the editorial handiwork that brought about the final form of the Psalter as received. We do not begin with the premise that the Psalter is unified and work back to it, but we argue how a unified document should look like and whether the Psalter fits such a description. What differentiates intentional design as opposed to mere anthological juxtapositions of texts? As Barr notes, "It is a literary question to what extent the editors of a biblical book, in putting together various sources of pieces of material, have created a meaning in the juxtaposition, as distinct from the meaning of the parts. 'The case for meaning must be decided on literary criteria: one must show that a unit is not just an anthology but is an intended structure with meaning.'"[328]

Barr's quote echoes that of Zenger's at the beginning of this chapter. Since the Psalter is made up of 150 self-delimited individual poems, the case for meaning as a whole would have to emerge from meaning that is developed from its macrostructure. The argument for literary unity in the Psalms would require a display of certain thematic inter-development (meaning) across the entire macrostructure.

By "inter-development," concepts seen in one discrete unit undergo contrast, expansion, or explanation in another. This argument is of methodological importance to Richard Schultz who identifies it as the "control" for arguments of the unity of texts. He writes:

326. As Bellinger observes, most Psalms scholars, nonetheless, agree that the Psalter is intentionally shaped as a book. See Bellinger, "Psalter as Theodicy," 151.

327. For a discussion on how the Psalter gradually grew as a "book" from the perspective of redactional process, see Seybold, "Psalter as a Book," 168–81.

328. Barr, *Holy Scripture*, 160, emphasis added. In this quote, Barr brought together several elements. First, he situated the context as the "editing of a biblical book." Second, he identified the limitations and the criteria of inquiry with a literary methodology. Third, he brought together the concepts of "meaning," "unity" and "structure." Fourth, he posited a distinction between the meaning of the whole and its parts. The first, third and fourth occurrence of "meaning" in the quote is different from the second. The second represents meaning of individual texts. The first, third and fourth represent meaning at the level beyond that of the parts; meaning that arises from a unified structure as a whole and extends beyond meaning of the parts.

> In seeking significant verbal parallels, one should look for verbal and syntactical correspondence that goes beyond one key or uncommon term or even a series of commonly occurring terms, also evaluating whether the expression is simply formulaic or idiomatic. Thus one should look for indications of contextual awareness, including interpretive re-use, which indicates verbal dependence which is conscious and purposeful, even though one may not be able to determine the direction of borrowing with any certainty. If such dependence can be posited, one's knowledge of the quoted text will facilitate the proper interpretation of the quoting text.[329]

Schultz's essential point is that one has to ascertain a "contextual awareness" and "interpretive re-use" between the texts to show a macro-development, which properly unify two different texts. In an important article on the unity of narratives, Bar-Efrat notes, "Structural arguments can be and in fact have been used to prove the unity of a given narrative or to determine the boundaries of a literary unit. Moreover, structure has rhetorical and expressive value: it is one of the factors governing the effect of the work on the reader and in addition it serves to express or accentuate meaning."[330]

In view of Barr's, Schultz's and Bar-Efrat's points above, we can make an interim case for the Psalter as a unity at this point of the investigation.

Prologue:
Structure, Motifs, Alphabetical Thinking & Numerical Technique

If the Psalter is designed with an overarching program, the content and elements of its shape should cohere in the final outlook. This unity of design is displayed in the Prologue (Pss 1–2) functioning as the programmatic prelude to the Psalter. To understand this, we will first discuss how alphabetical and numerical techniques function in the Psalms.

In general, there are two kinds of alphabetic poems, which are broadly termed as the *alphabetical acrostic* (hereafter AA) and the *alphabetic composition* (hereafter AC).[331] The AA usually has a clear abecedarian (or *alefbetic*) structure in which each poetic line (or colon, strophe) begins with a successive letter of the Hebrew alphabet. Barring missing or reversed letters in the sequence, there are, as commonly accepted, eight standard AAs in the Psalter (9–10;[332] 25; 34; 37; 111; 112; 119; 145). The second

---

329. Schultz, "Ties That Bind," 32.

330. Bar-Efrat, "Some Observations," 172.

331. Parts of the following section will be published as Ho, "Macrostructural Logic." This article consolidates the materials here and in chapter 5. It argues that alphabetical poems, by their locations in the Psalter, carry structuring functions.

332. Psalms 9 and 10 are separate psalms in the MT-150 Psalter on which this study is based. These two separate psalms are, however, considered two halves of a single alphabetic acrostic. In other words, one alphabetic acrostic poem can transverse across two separate psalms. We will count them as two separate psalms but a single AA.

kind of alphabetic poem is non-standard and has been given various names ("semi-acrostics" or "quasi-acrostics"). For consistency, it is here defined as the *alphabetic composition* (AC). These poems do not have a full set of alphabetic sequence and hence they are not called "acrostics." Nonetheless, they display elements of alphabetical thinking, or mezostics, which are clearly connected to the AA.

Since the AA is the most complete form alphabetic poem, characteristics of AAs form the basis for our understanding and exploration of ACs. Unfortunately, there is currently no consensus in the definition of ACs nor is there an agreed set of criteria available for its definition. In the following, certain quintessential characteristics of the AAs are analyzed and from these analyses and available literature on AAs and ACs, a set of criteria is proposed for the ACs. This set of criteria is then used to identify psalms that are clearly ACs and a number of other psalms that are *probable* ACs (which we will call, "PAC").

We begin by noting that alphabetic acrostics tend to use three Hebrew alphabets (א, ל, and פ) to mark the beginning, middle and end of a psalm. In the AAs Pss 25 and 34, Ceresko points out the additional 23rd letter פ at the end. The adding of the פ line forms a 23-line poem such that the ל becomes the "middle letter of the series."[333] Thus, the first, middle and last lines of the acrostic in Ps 25 begin with א, ל, and פ, forming the consonants of *aleph* which are also the root of the verb, אלף ("to teach/learn" or "to increase").[334]

It has also been shown that prominent structural locations in AAs (and ACs) can be identified by syllable counts, though certain criteria of counting are debated.[335] By counting syllables in Ps 34, Ceresko finds that the middle of Ps 34:12, where ל occurs, is almost the "exact middle of the poem."[336] Interestingly, if letters that function as *matres lectionis* are removed in Ps 34:2, the entire verse consists of "23 consonants, the first consonant being א, the twelfth or middle consonant being ל, and the final one פ."[337] Hurowitz uncovered a similar phenomenon on four "sides" of Ps 34.[338] The

---

333. Ceresko, "ABCs of Wisdom," 102. See also Skehan, "Structure of the Song of Moses," 100.

334. As a verb, it occurs exclusively in the Wisdom Books (Job 15:5; 33:33; 35:11; Ps 144:13; Prov 22:25). On the "lateness" of this word, see Hurowitz, "Additional Elements of Alphabetical Thinking," 326n3, 331–33. For the concept of "teaching" in Ps 25, see Abernethy, "God as Teacher," 339–51.

335. There are different criteria for identifying a single syllable. For example, Bee notes that "full" syllables take "no account of simple or augmented shewa, the definite article and the conjunctive prefix, and counting a segholate as a monosyllable" (Bee, "Use of Syllable Counts," 68–70). See Freedman, "Acrostics and Metrics," 369; Fokkelman, *MPHB*, 1:16.

336. Ceresko, "ABCs of Wisdom," 100.

337. Ceresko, "ABCs of Wisdom," 101.

338. According to Hurowitz, the consonants א, ל, and פ were also found in reverse sequence in the last word of the א, ל, and ת poetic lines (cf. בפי v. 2; אלמדכם v. 12 and יאשמו v. 22) in Ps 34. The last line in the psalm is also framed with the letters א, ל, and פ in the reverse. Furthermore, Hurowitz sees that the first consonant of the word (root) in the second respective cola of Ps 34:2–4 begin with the last three letters of the alphabet ת, ש, and ר respectively (תמיד in the second colon of v. 2, ישמעו in the second colon v. 3 and ונרוממה in the second colon of v. 4). This is a form of reverse acrostic. See Hurowitz, "Additional Elements," 328–29.

use of consonants forming vertical and horizontal patterns in a poem is a technique known as *mezostics* or *telestics*.[339] Working together with numerical features, the array of א, ל, and פ consonants functions as an editorial signature to indicate alphabetical thinking of a psalm.

In addition to using Hebrew alphabets, certain words in AAs also display structural significance. Barré finds "terminative" words such as כלה ("to come to an end"), תמם ("to be finished"), and אבד ("to perish") being used "to mark off sections of the acrostics or whole poems that have reached their end" (cf. Pss 25; 37; 112; 119; Nah 1:2–9; Lam 1, 2, and 4).[340]

Consider Ps 150. After the formulaic inclusio, הללו יה, the poem begins with הללו-אל. This is the *only* instance of הלל having the suffix אל in the entire Hebrew Bible. At the end of the psalm, the הלל is prefixed with a ת, which is significantly the "only jussive of הלל in the Psalms."[341] The choice of these two unique phrases at the beginning and end of the poem is likely intentional. Concomitant with the theme of totality in Ps 150, it is reasonable to assume that the editor wanted to express the same concept with the use of the consonants of א and ת with הלל. If the inclusio הללו-יה is temporarily ignored in Ps 150,[342] the first and last words of Ps 150 are now suffixed and prefixed with the letters א and ת respectively. Psalm 150 contains 34 words,[343] of which the two middle words (17th and 18th) are בנבל וכנור (150:3) and a ל is close to the center of these two words.[344] Based on these alphabetical thinking, Ceresko considers Ps 150 an AC.

Taking a leaf from the alphabetic thinking of marking the front and end of a textual unit, we now turn our attention to Pss 1 and 150.[345] Prima facie, both psalms consist of six verses each. Both begin with a word that starts with א and ends with a word that starts with ת.[346] Consequently, the entire Psalter starts with א and ends with ת. Given these emerging parallels, is it plausible that Ps 1, like 150, is an AC?

---

339. These techniques were also featured in Akkadian texts in biblical times. Hurowitz, "Additional Elements," 327. Cf. Watson, *Classical*, 191–92; Brug, "Biblical Acrostics," 283–30; Soll, "Babylonian and Biblical Acrostics," 305–23.

340. Barré, "'Terminative' Terms in Hebrew Acrostics," 207–15; Ceresko, "Endings and Beginnings," 34.

341. Ceresko, "Endings and Beginnings," 44. However, it is possible that one other jussive 3fs reference of הלל is found in Ps 119:175.

342. Some scholars consider them as an "extrametrical syllables," which refers to words that do not belong to the poem proper but are "added by the singing community or by tradition" (Fokkelman, *MPHB*, 1:16).

343. I have counted words linked by *maqqef* as one word. However, even if words joined by *maqqef* are counted separately, there is a total of 37 words and the center word is וכנור, which just follows the ל.

344. If we consider the two words, בנבל וכנור, consisting of a total of eight consonants (ignoring *matres lectionis*), we have two letters, ל and ו at the center.

345. For a discussion on the introduction to the Psalter (Pss 1–2) and the conclusion (Pss 146–150 or 149–150), see Gillingham, "Entering and Leaving the Psalter," 383–93.

346. We see the poet working on several poetical techniques. On one level, he was illustrating the

Psalms 1–2 as a Unit

Instead of Ps 1, I propose seeing Pss 1–2 as a single AC. Much has been discussed on whether Pss 1 and 2 are to be seen as a single composition or distinct from each other.[347] Arguments on both sides appeal to content, historical evidence, theological and ideological elements in the two psalms. While it has been widely acknowledged that the אשרי that begins the first colon of Ps 1 forms an inclusio with the last colon of Ps 2, not many have recognized additional poetical features that bind them together.

The plausibility of seeing Pss 1–2 as one AC is based on the characteristic features of the AAs Pss 9–10. Among the eight AAs in the Psalter, Pss 9–10 is the only AA that is combined by two individual psalms (in the MT).[348] Note that only two psalms (Pss 2 and 10) in the entire Psalter begin with the interrogative phrase, למה.[349] These unique features help us see further parallels that occur between Pss 2 and 10. On closer scrutiny, there is a host of lexical and thematic parallels at the transitions between Pss 1 and 2, and between Pss 9 and 10. For instance, the contrasts of two groups of people ("wicked" versus the "poor" and "righteous") are seen.[350] Common lexemes, such as "why" (למה), "perish" (אבד), "wicked" (רשע), "nation" (גוי), "judgment" (משפט), "to stand" (קום) and "YHWH," are found in the few verses packed tightly around both transitions. Common motifs of the wicked plotting against God's people are also clear in Pss 2:1–2 (as a collective group) and 10:1–2 (as an individual). Such hostilities are both expressed through speech (cf. 2:3; 10:4).

There are further literary features that support seeing Pss 1–2 as a single AC. Consider Figure 8 showing Fokkelman's poetical structure of Pss 1–2.[351]

---

alphabetical technique and on another, he was keeping the inclusio הללו יה, binding the section of Pss 146–150 together.

347. With regards to the first two psalms, those who maintain Ps 1 as distinct from Ps 2 include John Willis, Benjamin Sommer, and recently, David Willgren. It is interesting to note that even Gerald Wilson, who sees the Psalter as an edited and integrated whole, sets apart Psalm 1 and 2. Wilson maintained the distinction between these two psalms because he argues for a separate wisdom (Pss 1; 73; 145) and royal (Pss 2; 72; 144) framework that binds and interlocks the entire Psalter. Those who see Psalms 1–2 as integrative include Jesper Høgenhaven, Erich Zenger, and Robert Cole. Both sides have appealed to literary features, comparison of ancient texts and theological/ideological arguments for the distinctiveness or unity of Pss 1 and 2. See Sommer, "Psalm 1," 211, 214. Cf. Willis, "Psalm 1," 381–401; Wilson, "Shape of the Book," 132–33; Willgren, *Formation*, 136–71; Zenger, "Der Psalter als Buch," 31–32; Høgenhaven, "Opening of the Psalter," 169–80; Cole, *Psalms 1–2*.

348. While Pss 9–10 in the LXX and Vulgate are considered as one psalm, they are separate in the MT-150 and likely in 5/6Ḥev.

349. Psalm 74:1 also begins with למה, though preceded by the two words, משכיל לאסף. Moreover, the two non-superscript psalms in Book I (apart from the prologue) are juxtaposed to, or are part of an acrostic (cf. Pss 9/10; 33/34).

350. Cf. Pss 1:5–6; 9:18–19.

351. The Roman numerals on the right indicate strophe units. The Arabic numerals indicate verse units. Spaces in the texts separate cola/versets. The text and the colon divisions are Fokkelman's, but all the box-markers are mine. See also Fokkelman, *Psalms in Form*, 16.

The Design of the Psalter

		Psalm 1		
I	1	אַשְׁרֵי־הָאִישׁ אֲשֶׁר ׀	לֹא הָלַךְ בַּעֲצַת רְשָׁעִים	
	2	וּבְדֶרֶךְ חַטָּאִים לֹא עָמָד	וּבְמוֹשַׁב לֵצִים לֹא יָשָׁב:	
		כִּי אִם בְּתוֹרַת יְהוָה חֶפְצוֹ	וּבְתוֹרָתוֹ יֶהְגֶּה יוֹמָם וָלָיְלָה:	
II	3	וְהָיָה כְּעֵץ שָׁתוּל עַל־פַּלְגֵי מָיִם	אֲשֶׁר פִּרְיוֹ ׀ יִתֵּן בְּעִתּוֹ	
		וְעָלֵהוּ לֹא־יִבּוֹל	וְכֹל אֲשֶׁר־יַעֲשֶׂה יַצְלִיחַ:	
III	4	לֹא־כֵן הָרְשָׁעִים	כִּי אִם־כַּמֹּץ אֲשֶׁר־תִּדְּפֶנּוּ רוּחַ:	
	5	עַל־כֵּן ׀ לֹא־יָקֻמוּ רְשָׁעִים בַּמִּשְׁפָּט	וְחַטָּאִים בַּעֲדַת צַדִּיקִים:	
	6	כִּי־יוֹדֵעַ יְהוָה דֶּרֶךְ צַדִּיקִים	וְדֶרֶךְ רְשָׁעִים תֹּאבֵד:	

		Psalm 2		
I	1	לָמָּה רָגְשׁוּ גוֹיִם	וּלְאֻמִּים יֶהְגּוּ־רִיק:	
	2	יִתְיַצְּבוּ ׀ מַלְכֵי־אֶרֶץ	וְרוֹזְנִים נוֹסְדוּ־יָחַד	עַל־יְהוָה וְעַל־מְשִׁיחוֹ:
	3	נְנַתְּקָה אֶת־מוֹסְרוֹתֵימוֹ	וְנַשְׁלִיכָה מִמֶּנּוּ עֲבֹתֵימוֹ:	
II	4	יוֹשֵׁב בַּשָּׁמַיִם יִשְׂחָק	אֲדֹנָי יִלְעַג־לָמוֹ:	
	5	אָז יְדַבֵּר אֵלֵימוֹ בְאַפּוֹ	וּבַחֲרוֹנוֹ יְבַהֲלֵמוֹ:	
	6	וַאֲנִי נָסַכְתִּי מַלְכִּי	עַל־צִיּוֹן הַר־קָדְשִׁי:	
III	7	אֲסַפְּרָה אֶל חֹק יְהוָה	אָמַר אֵלַי בְּנִי אַתָּה	אֲנִי הַיּוֹם יְלִדְתִּיךָ:
	8	שְׁאַל מִמֶּנִּי	וְאֶתְּנָה גוֹיִם נַחֲלָתֶךָ	וַאֲחֻזָּתְךָ אַפְסֵי־אָרֶץ:
	9	תְּרֹעֵם בְּשֵׁבֶט בַּרְזֶל	כִּכְלִי יוֹצֵר תְּנַפְּצֵם:	
IV	10	וְעַתָּה מְלָכִים הַשְׂכִּילוּ	הִוָּסְרוּ שֹׁפְטֵי אָרֶץ:	
	11	עִבְדוּ אֶת־יְהוָה בְּיִרְאָה	וְגִילוּ בִּרְעָדָה: 12 נַשְּׁקוּ־בַר	
		פֶּן־יֶאֱנַף ׀ וְתֹאבְדוּ דֶרֶךְ	כִּי־יִבְעַר כִּמְעַט אַפּוֹ	אַשְׁרֵי כָּל־חוֹסֵי בוֹ:

Figure 8: Colon Division, Structure and the Numerical Centers of Psalms 1–2

Fokkelman divides Ps 1 into three strophes and Ps 2 into 4 strophes (Roman numerals), with each strophe consisting of two or three verselines.[352] Each verseline, in turn, consists of 2 or 3 cola. The אשרי that begins the first colon of Ps 1 also begins the last colon of Psalm 2, forming an inclusio.[353] The use of ל at the beginning of 2:1 indicates

---

352. By "verse," Fokkelman means a "full poetic line" which may or may not coincide with divisions of verses in L.

353. See the last box-marker in Figure 8. There are four strophes and 28 cola in Ps 2. The last colon is the 28th, אשרי כל־חוסי בו (Ps 2:12). See also Fokkelman *Reading Biblical Poetry*, 21, 37–41 for defining and delimiting a colon.

Introduction

it is at the middle point or the second-half of a single composition.³⁵⁴ Also the phrase, פֶּן־יֶאֱנַף (2:12), possibly begins the last verseline.³⁵⁵ When viewed together, we have א in the first verseline (1:1), ל at the half-way mark (2:1) and פ in the final verseline (2:12). These three consonants are the alphabetical signature we have seen in Ps 34 earlier. In other words, Pss 1–2, taken together, display features of a single AC.

Certain numerical features connect these two psalms as well. There are 57 words in Ps 1 when we count words connected by *maqqef* as a single word.³⁵⁶ The use of *maqqef* is usually associated with scansion but issues of meter remain.³⁵⁷ It is possible that the use of *maqqef* is more fluid than assumed and is not limited to accentuation or prosodic concerns.³⁵⁸ The 29th word of Ps 1, אשר (1:3), is not only at the numerical center, but also begins the 8th colon of the 16-cola psalm.³⁵⁹ The choice of the אשר recalls the אשרי־האיש אשר at the beginning of Ps 1:1.³⁶⁰

Psalm 2 has 77 words. The word at the center (39th) is בני (2:7), referring to Yhwh's son, the anointed king. When Pss 1 and 2 are viewed as a single composition (57+77=134 words), the pair of words at the center is the 67th and 68th word, על־יהוה ועל־משיחו ("against the Lord and against his anointed one"; 2:2). This phrase identifies the dual figures of "Yhwh" and "his anointed" (son), which are also the dual figures identified by the center word of Ps 2 (when counted on its own) as indicated

---

354. This has been pointed out by scholars such as Seow, "Exquisitely Poetic," 292–93.

355. Variant readings are given in *BHS* with the suggestion of deleting the phrase, נשקו־בר, as dittography. For a full discussion on the division of cola on 2:11–12, see Fokkelman, *Psalms in Form*, 156; *MPHB*, 3:56.

356. Lambdin points out that the use of *maqqef* "indicates that these words are proclitic, ie, have no stress of their own, but are pronounced as the first syllable of the whole group taken as a single word!" However, he recognized that the use of *maqqef* is not consistent without offering clear reasons. This will be discussed further in chapter 5. See Lambdin, *Introduction*, 5–6, 207–8; Watson, *Classical Hebrew Poetry*, 101–4.

357. Scansion is "the rhythmic reading and/or division of a poetic line." The use of *maqqef* thus affects the number of rhythmic counts (meter) and word count (word division) rather than syllable count. In recent studies, Fokkelman makes an important critique of "metrics" and Lowth's "*parallelismus membrorum*" in classical Hebrew poetry. He argues that the stalemate on metrics makes it difficult to reach any conclusive consensus between scholars. See Fokkelman, *Reading Biblical Poetry*, 22–23, 227.

358. For instance, the presence of *maqqef* linking the אם to the following word with the use of the conjunction כי אם is frequently found in the HB (cf. Ps 1:4, כי אם־כמץ). Almost all uses of כי אם in the OT Prophets have a *maqqef* following the אם to the next word. The absence of it is very rare (cf. Gen 15:4; Num 35:33; Esth 2:15). However, we find the occurrence of כי אם without the *maqqef* linking the אם to the following word in Ps 1:2 and one *with* the *maqqef* which does, just two verses away in Ps 1:4.

359. The central position of the cola opened by this word is also underscored by van der Lugt and Labuschagne from a numerical perspective. Van der Lugt notes, "from this point of view, the seven words of v. 3b–c ('which brings forth its fruit in due season and whose foliage does not fade') constitute the centre of the poem (>30+7+30 words)" (Van der Lugt, *CAS III*, 580).

360. Note that the consonant אשר opens the Psalter and cola 1, and the relative particle closes cola 1. Standing at the head of a clause, Lambdin notes that אשר can carry the force of the phrase, "'the fact that…' and further may require the translation value of 'since, because'" (Lambdin, *Introduction*, 65).

by the word, בני.³⁶¹ In other words, the words at the mathematical center of the two introductory psalms, seen combined or separate, respectively identify the "blessed man," "Yʜᴡʜ" and "Yʜᴡʜ's anointed son."³⁶²

Moreover, the poetical and thematic structures of Pss 1–2 are both concentric in shape and parallel each other thematically. Fokkelman points out that the middle strophe of Ps 1 is a short strophe,³⁶³ with the "long strophes flanking the center . . . The first strophe 'defines' the righteous by contrasting him with the wicked and the opposite happens in the third strophe."³⁶⁴ The second strophe characterizes the attributes of the "blessed man." The final strophe identifies the outcomes of the wicked and the righteous.

Psalm 2, likewise, can be seen as concentric with a corresponding thematic and poetic structure. The first strophe (2:1–3) highlights the conspiracy and actions of the nations, and the kings of the earth (i.e., the wicked) going against Yʜᴡʜ and his anointed. The last strophe (2:10–12) shows the outcome of the kings and judges of the earth and their destruction before Yʜᴡʜ's son. The final colon also characterizes the destiny of the blessed. Strophes II and III (2:4–9) form the center frame. The two center strophes capture the attributes of Yʜᴡʜ's king who has been installed on Zion and will rule victoriously. The disjunctive markers, לא־כן (1:4) and ועתה (2:10) mark an emphatic transition into the final frame in both psalms. The following figure illustrates the corresponding poetical and thematic structures of both psalms, listing the various parallel/contrasts in each of the frames.

---

361. *BHS* suggests that the entire phrase על־יהוה ועל־משיחו is "probably a gloss" which could suggest some form of editorial processing.

362. They also refer indirectly to the wicked nations conspiring against Yʜᴡʜ. Cole argues that "the righteous one compared to a tree in Psalm 1 is further defined in Psalm 2 as the divinely chosen king, installed on the holy mountain of Zion." If Cole's understanding is right, then all the words at the center, seen separately or combined, identify Yʜᴡʜ and his anointed. See Cole, "Integrated Reading," 76.

363. Highlighted with dotted line.

364. Fokkelman, *Reading Biblical Poetry*, 28; Van der Lugt likewise sees a three-part concentric structure in Psalm 1. He notes, "Psalm 1 is a highly sophisticated composition, opening the book of Psalms. Its concentric design is one of the most conspicuous features in terms of structure. Vv. 3–4 represent a pivotal 3-line strophe and stand out on the grounds of their allegorical character. This 3-line strophe is enveloped by 2-line strophes at both sides, vv. 1–2 and 5–6" (Van der Lugt, *CAS III*, 583).

Psalm 1:1–2, Strophe I	Psalm 2:1–3, Strophe I
• The "ways" of the "*blessed man*" • The essence of his "way" = *Torah piety*	• The "ways" of the *kings and nations* • The essence of their "way" = *against YHWH and his anointed*
Psalm 1:3, Strophe II (Center)	**Psalm 2:4–9, Strophes II–III (Center)**
• Attributes of the "*blessed man*" • Located at the *heavenly* "Zion" • Center word = "*that blessed man*"	• Attributes of the "*anointed king.*" • Located at Zion • Center word = "*my* [YHWH's] *son*"
Psalm 1:4–6, Strophe III	**Psalm 2:10–12, Strophe IV**
• Outcome of both the wicked and the righteous • Judgment before the righteous • Ends with the wicked perishing	• Outcome of both the kings and judges of the earth • Destruction before the Son • Ends with the blessed under YHWH's refuge

Figure 9: Structural Divisions, Parallels and Contrasts of Psalms 1 and 2

In Fokkelman's taxonomy of poetic hierarchy, the "whole poem" is situated at the highest level for consideration.[365] But in our study, we observe poetic structuring, word-count phenomenon and alphabetical thinking can occur beyond the level of a single psalm.

Our brief study of the Prologue has uncovered three points pertinent to our interim argument. First, Pss 1–2 can be seen together as a single AC. The use of alphabetical techniques binds them as a single composition. Together with Ps 150, the entire Psalter is poetically framed by ACs. Second, a variety of techniques (thematic and numerical) are at work in coherence. By counting words, certain words at the numerical center of the psalm correspond to the central focus and macrostructure of each and both psalms combined. When the appropriation of different techniques corresponds, the plausibility of intentional shaping increases.

We must also note that the poetic and thematic structures of Pss 1–2 reveal a certain trajectory that may be programmatic for the Psalter.[366] Shaped concentrically, the forms of these two psalms highlight a central motif. Yet when they are seen as a whole, their structures reveal a linear reading as well. The first and last panes of each psalm characterize the *way* and *outcome* of the righteous and the wicked respectively. At the center of both psalms, the attributes of the righteous and the messianic king are highlighted respectively. In Ps 1, the motif of the blessed one being planted and flourishing at the center pane *bridges* the way and outcome of the righteous. Similarly, in Ps 2, the motif of the messianic king ruling supremely in the center *bridges* the way and outcome of the wicked (as well as for the righteous).

---

365. At the lowest level is "sounds," followed by "syllables"; "words"; "versets" (or colon); "verses"; "strophes"; "stanzas"; "sections" and "the poem as a whole." See Fokkelman, *Reading Biblical Poetry*, 30.

366. Cole argues that Pss 1–2 and 3 provide the "gateway" to the entire Psalter. His work deals primarily with the connections found in the first three psalms. While his analysis is detailed and impressive, Cole's study remains at this "gateway" since he posits little on how this gateway affects the shape and reading for the rest of the Psalter. See Cole, *Psalms 1–2*.

The Design of the Psalter

In short, the use of various techniques, poetical structures and thematical developments in Pss 1–2 not only connect them together but provide an impetus to read the Prologue as the programmatic overture to the Psalter—a hypothesis we will return back to soon.

Intertextual Reading and the Design of the Psalter

Almost half of the Psalter is Davidic psalms. The predominant Davidic profiling and structural arrangements of Davidic psalms are crucial to the understanding of the Psalms. The presence of many Royal psalms also adds to the Davidization of the Psalms.[367] Primarily, our understanding of the Davidic characterization of the Psalter is achieved through the historical narratives in the books of Samuel, Kings and Chronicles. Besides references to the figures of David, Solomon and various Levites in Psalm superscripts, the 13 historical titles presume knowledge of the narrative of David's life based on the Historical books.[368]

As such, intertextuality[369] between the Psalter and other texts in the HB are well noted. For our purposes here, we will not address the diachronic development, dependency, or formulation of certain criteria for such reading.[370] Instead, we will explore how the rereading the Psalter in view of the Davidic Covenant in 2 Sam 7 and the Davidic Song narratives in 2 Sam 6 and 1 Chr 16 deepens our understanding of the thematic shape of the Psalter.

2 Samuel 7 (Davidic Covenant) and the Design of the Psalter

If the Prologue is the programmatic prelude to the Psalter, then it should, in some way relate to the Davidic psalms that make up almost half of the psalmody. The primary way through which the Prologue provides a Davidic profiling of the Psalter is the motif of the messianic king, located centrally in Ps 2. In turn, this motif of the anointed

---

367. For a recent discussion on the issues of the classification of Royal psalms, see Grant, "Psalms and the King," 101–18.

368. See esp. chapter 4. The 13 historical superscriptions are Pss 3; 7; 18; 34; 51; 52; 54; 56; 57; 59; 60; 63; 142.

369. The term "intertextuality" was originally coined by J. Kristeva in Kristeva, *Desire in Language*. I have used this term "intertextuality" as understood in the study by Tanner, *Book of Psalms through the Lens of Intertextuality*. In it, she studies how Ps 90 and the Yʜᴡʜ *Malak* psalms are viewed intertextually. She also draws correspondences between Ps 112 and Prov 31; Ps 88 and Judg 19, respectively.

370. Russel Meek has written a helpful article explaining the terminologies of intertextuality, inner-biblical exegesis, and inner-biblical allusion. In his prescription, intertextuality is less concerned with the direction of influence and diachronic concerns. Rather, it focuses on the reader's ability to sense connections between texts. Intertextuality is differentiated from inner-biblical exegesis (which seeks to show that a receptor text had deliberately used and interpreted an earlier text) and from inner-biblical allusion (which seeks to show that an earlier text has been alluded to, but not necessary re-interpreted). See Meek, "Intertextuality," 280–91.

kingship, described in excessive language of universal rule and power (2:6–12), is most clearly depicted by the Davidic covenant found in the historical narratives.

There is a close relationship between the Davidic covenant[371] of 2 Sam 7 and the Psalter. In fact, the leitmotifs of the Psalter parallels the major motifs of the Davidic covenant. The Davidic covenant, set within the larger context of the Deuteronomic history,[372] provides the hermeneutical key to understanding the program of the Psalter.[373] Seven motifs found in both the Davidic covenant and the Psalter are highlighted below.

(1) *A secure dwelling and rest with* Yhwh *at Zion*. After David's reign over all Israel had been established, he brought the ark of God to dwell with him in the city of Zion (2 Sam 5–6). The concept of God bringing about rest and security to his people, and dwelling with them at a place of his choice (2 Sam 7:10),[374] is an important motif in the Psalms. The paradisical garden described in Ps 1:3–4 and mount Zion in 2:6 encapsulate this concept of flourishing in the presence of God, reveling in his security. Just as Yhwh will plant (נטע) his people in a place of security (2 Sam 7:10), the blessed ones will be planted (שתול) and rest peacefully by streams of water (Ps 1). This search for a place to dwell is a key concern in Book V of the Psalms (cf. Pss 107; 132; 144).

(2) Yhwh *cutting off all the enemies of David*. Second Samuel 7:1 (cf. 2 Sam 7:9, 11) begins with the description that Yhwh had given David rest from all his enemies, specifically, Saul (2 Sam 7:15). While the enemy motif is prevalent in the Psalter, the specific description of Yhwh cutting off the king's enemy can be seen in the Royal Ps 18 (cf. 110:1–2; 143:12), a structurally important psalm as noted by Robertson.

(3) *The building of the House of God*. Second Samuel 7 starts with the premise of building a physical house for God's dwelling in Jerusalem. Yet it was not David, but his descendant who eventually built Yhwh's house (2 Sam 7:13). The Psalms, likewise, highlights the building of Yhwh's house with the same dilemma of who would build it. Even under the postexilic historical context of the Second Temple (cf. 126.1), there remains a better house and city that Yhwh himself will build (127:1). Psalm 30 contains the only reference to Yhwh's house in all the superscriptions of the Psalter. Like 2 Sam 7, this unique allusion to the house of God is set within the immediate context

---

371. Note that the term, "covenant," is not used in 2 Sam 7. However, it is referred to as a "covenant" elsewhere (ברית; 2 Sam 23:5, Ps 89:4, 29, 35, 40) or an "oath" (שבע; Ps 89:4, 36, 50). On the connection between 2 Sam 7 and Ps 89, see Mullen, "Divine Witness," 209.

372. For how 2 Sam 7 contributes to the Deuteronomic history, see McCarthy, "2 Samuel 7," 131–38.

373. Gillingham notes, "Given that the prophets drew a good deal from other traditions, from earlier prophets, from the Deuteronomistic literature and the Priestly material, it would be surprising if the now known psalms were not also part of this postexilic practice of 'inner-biblical exegesis' used to reassure the people of the ultimate vindication of the earlier prophetic promises" (Gillingham, "From Liturgy to Prophecy," 473–74).

374. McCarthy notes that the hiphil הניח "is practically a technical term in the Deuteronomic writings for Yahweh's ultimate blessing on Israel: rest from the enemies in the promised land" (McCarthy, "2 Samuel 7," 132).

The Design of the Psalter

of Yhwh's kingship, his establishment and destruction of the human king and his enemies respectively (cf. 29:10–30:1). Structurally, both Pss 29–30 and 127 are also significantly located (see chapter 2).

(4) *The language bestowed on the king*. In 2 Sam 7, Yhwh establishes the anointed king as the ruler, servant, and shepherd over the people (2 Sam 7:7, 26, 29). Yhwh and the anointed king are intimated as father and son (2 Sam 7:14). The king's rule and kingdom will be forever (2 Sam 7:13, 16, 24–26). This covenantal language has a futuristic[375] orientation, similar to messianic and eschatological descriptions found in the Prophets (ותדבר גם אל-בית-עבדך למרחוק ["and you spoke also of the house of your servant concerning the distant future"], 2 Sam 7:19; cf. Isa 40:11; Ezek 37:23–24; Mic 5:4).[376] In similar ways, such language is bestowed on the king in Pss 2;[377] 45; 89; and 110. The Messianic king, Yhwh's son, will reign victoriously, universally and forevermore.[378]

(5) Yhwh's חסד *with the king*. The perpetuity of the Davidic dynasty is ascertained through Yhwh's enduring lovingkindness despite human failings (2 Sam 7:14–15; Ps 89:20–38). The Davidic covenant, like a "royal grant,"[379] is secure because of Yhwh's unconditional promises to David and his offspring.[380] In the Psalms, the concept of Yhwh's חסד is most clear in Pss 89 and 136. In fact, these two psalms contain the highest frequency of the word חסד in the Psalter.[381] Bookwise, the Psalter and 2 Sam have the highest occurrences of the lexeme חסד in the HB.[382] In Ps 89, חסד is used in

---

375. Besides the waw consecutive perfect tense (imperfect sense) associated with 2 Sam 7:10, Murray argues that the "place" (מקום) in 2 Sam 7:10 is the eschatological temple (Murray, "*Mqwm* and the Future of Israel," 299).

376. Piotrowski, "'I Will Save My People,'" 239.

377. Forbes argues that the king in Psalm 2 is unlikely to be David or Solomon. "The language of the Psalm, by whomsoever composed, could not have been meant for David, since the words, 'Thou art my son, this day have I begotten thee' (ver. 7), are evidently borrowed from the great promise made to David (in 2 Sam. vii. 12–16) with reference, not to himself, but to a 'seed' to be set upon his throne when he should 'sleep with his fathers,' and of whom the Lord says, 'I will be his Father, and he shall be my son' (ver. 1–4), Neither could the Psalm be meant for Solomon (the Peaceful), since the king designed is evidently to be a man of war, against whom 'the nations and peoples rage, and their kings and rulers take counsel together'—whom he shall 'break with a rod of iron, and dash them in pieces like a potter's vessel'" (Forbes, *Studies*, 4).

378. Clements, "Psalm 72," 336.

379. It is has been proposed that the Davidic covenant is a royal grant "which depicts the unconditional promise of the king to the vassal as a reward for faithful service to the suzerain" (Mullen, "Divine Witness," 207). See also Levenson, "Davidic Covenant," 205–19; Weinfeld, "Covenant of Grant," 184–203.

380. Gundersen notes, "The promise of permanence deeply embedded in Psalm 89 requires the view that the covenant with David eventually will be fulfilled. The question is not *whether* but *when, how,* and *who*" (Gundersen, "Davidic Hope," 89). For a comparison of the Davidic covenant in 2 Sam 7 and its later manifestations in the OT, see Angel, "Eternal Davidic Covenant," 83–90.

381. Psalm 136 has 26 instances; Psalms 89 and 119 follow with 7 occurrences each. This is followed by Pss 107 and 118.

382. In 247 instances, the word חסד occurs 126 times in the Psalms (51 percent) followed by 13

the context of the Davidic covenant. In Ps 136, חסד is used in the formulaic refrain כי לעולם חסדו. This phrase is associated especially with the re-establishment of the temple.³⁸³

(6) *David's prayer, praise, and blessings.* In the opening line of 2 Sam 7:5, the king's attitude and action before Yhwh is called to question.³⁸⁴ The second half of 2 Sam 7 describes David's responses to Yhwh after receiving God's word through Nathan. David expressed gratitude for Yhwh's promises concerning his house, prayed and praised Yhwh (2 Sam 7:18–29) for his great deeds of salvation for his people in the past. In a similar way, the Psalter expressed the king's gratitude, prayers, and praise to God. Westermann argues that psalms of lament eventually give way to psalms of praise toward the end of the Psalter.³⁸⁵ This praise is often done in the context of recounting Yhwh's salvific deeds in Israel's history (cf. Pss 78; 104–106; 146–150). Second Samuel 7 concludes with a doxology. The striking parallel is that all five Books of the Psalms also conclude with doxologies (41:14; 72:18–19; 89:53; 106:48; 145:21).

(7) *David and the people of God.* One of the promises of Yhwh given to David was the establishment (כון; 2 Sam 7:12, 13, 16) of his kingship and the planting of the people of Israel in a secure place (2 Sam 7:10). This could arise from the concerns of the community in postexilic times.³⁸⁶ The motif of establishing (כון) David's house and the people *as God's people* is repeated in David's response to God (2 Sam 7:23–26).³⁸⁷ In the Psalms, Yhwh's establishment (כון) of the king and his people is most clearly seen in 89:5, 22; 102:29. By 144:12–15, the phrase, "blessed are the people, whose God is Yhwh" (העם שיהוה אלהיו), solidifies this promise of establishing the people.

These seven motifs, which can be expanded from the motif of the Messianic kingship in the Prologue, add to our hermeneutical understanding of the Psalter's design. If we can reduce the Psalter into one single theme, the most accurate one would be the Davidic covenant. The covenant theme is wide enough to encapsulate all these seven interlocking motifs as God's word *to* both David and his people to be meditated upon (דבר-יהוה; cf. 2 Sam 7:4, 17; Ps 149:19). At the same time, it is not too generic

---

times (5 percent) in 2 Samuel.

383. Cf. 1 Chr 16; 2 Chr 5–7; Ezra 3:11; Pss 106:1; 107:1; 136:1–26; Jer 33:11. See chapter 3.

384. George, "Fluid Stability in Second Samuel 7," 22.

385. Westermann, *Praise and Lament*, 257; *Psalms*, 10.

386. George argues that "precisely because it was edited during the exile in light of the exilic community's experiences, 2 Samuel 7 addressed the anxieties, needs, and concerns of that community, with particular reference to both its identity and its theology as a community" (George, "Fluid Stability in Second Samuel 7," 19).

387. With regards to the "house" (בית) in 2 Sam 7:13, it is possible that the word means more than David's house *per se*. George notes, "By recognizing and using the fluidity and indeterminability of בית, the exilic editor would have seen in this oracle a promise to the people. What was promised to David was not just something for him and his family alone, but a radically new and different promise for the people. They were *still* Yhwh's chosen people, for they were his descendants and kin. The בית being promised in 2 Sam 7:13 was the people *themselves,* independent of any particular place or family (i.e., the Davidides)" (George, "Fluid Stability in Second Samuel 7," 29, 34).

such that it can be appropriated for any text. In this respect, the single motif of refuge (Creach), praise (Ribera-Mariné) or Zion (Gillingham) is insufficient, but to say that the Psalter is a book about the "route of salvation" (Vesco) may be too general. The Davidic covenant not only includes these motifs but gives flesh to the cause, plot, and *telos* of Yʜᴡʜ's purposes for his people.

David's Songs in 2 Samuel 22; 1 Chronicles 16; 2 Chronicles 6 and the Design of the Psalter

Literary connections between David's songs in 2 Sam 22:1–51; 1 Chr 16:8–36; 2 Chr 6:41–42; and the Psalter have been noted.[388] Psalm 18 and 2 Sam 22:1–51 are clearly parallel poems and scholars generally accept that the former depended on the latter.[389] Scholars also argue that 1 Chr 16:8–36 depended on Pss 105:1–15; 96:1–13; 106:1, 47–48.[390] The formulaic expressions, "Give thanks to the LORD" (1 Chr 16:8) and "For he is good; for his steadfast love endures forever!" (1 Chr 16:34), clearly parallel 105:1, 106:1.[391] The desire for Yʜᴡʜ's ark to "rise to its resting place" in Solomon's prayer in 2 Chr 6:41–42 alludes to Ps 132:8–10.[392] Moreover, intertextuality between Pss 18 (2 Sam 22) and 144 have been ascertained.[393] As noted, our concern is how intertextual connections between these David songs and the Psalms help elucidate the design of the Psalter.[394]

---

388. Butler, "Forgotten Passage," 142–50; Doan and Giles, "Song of Asaph," 29–43; Van Grol, "1 Chronicles 16," 97–121; Klein, "Psalms in Chronicles," 264–75; Rezetko, *Source and Revision*; Weber, "Das Königlich-Davidische Danklied," 87–204; "'Gelobt Sei Der HERR, Mein Fels …!'" 195–220; "Die Doppelte Verknotung Des Psalters," 14–27; Shipp, "'Remember His Covenant Forever,'" 29–39.

389. The direction of dependence is argued based on Psalms superscriptions, which require knowledge of the Samuel narratives (tradition) and not the other way round. Weber argues, "Der Psalter verweist auf die Samuelbücher, besonders auf dessen David-Texte 'zurück' und setzt die Kenntnis der narrativen, in Sam aufbehaltenen Überlieferung voraus—nicht umgekehrt" (Weber "'Gelobt Sei Der HERR, Mein Fels …!,'" 199). See also Weber, "Die Doppelte Verknotung," 18.

390. They are all taken from Book IV of the Psalter. See Klein, "Psalms in Chronicles," 264.

391. Cf. Isa 12:4; Pss 118:1, 29; 136:1.

392. Klein, "Psalms in Chronicles," 271; Weber, "Die Doppelte Verknotung," 20; Shipp, "'Remember His Covenant Forever,'" 33. For an interesting discussion on the ark in the Psalms, see also Broyles, "Psalms and Cult Symbolism," 139–56.

393. Weber, "'Gelobt Sei Der HERR, Mein Fels …!,'" 213–14; On dependency issues, Shipp argues, "Chr [the Chronicler] is apparently invoking the traditions reflected in 2 Samuel 7 and Psalm 132, where God's covenant with David is expressed in terms of an eternal dynasty, forever associated with the temple and its service. This point may help explain the commonly accepted view that Chr's theology rests on the 'two pillars' of temple and king, with the caveat that to Chr these two pillars are like *Jachin* and *Boaz* (the two pillars of Solomon's temple) and ought not to be separated, as earlier commentators have done. It is obvious, then, that for Chr kingship had not disappeared, never to return. Chr, in the appropriation of Psalmic sources, is calling upon the people to remember God's faithfulness to the covenant and is calling upon God to remember the covenant with David, the choice of king and temple" (Shipp, "'Remember His Covenant Forever,'" 39).

394. See Weber, "'Gelobt Sei Der HERR, Mein Fels …!'" 199.

Second Samuel 22 begins with a characteristic heading, "in the day the LORD delivered him from the hand of all his enemies and from the hand of Saul" (2 Sam 22:1), and ends with reiteration of Yhwh's covenantal promise "to his anointed, to David" (2 Sam 22:51). This characteristic inclusio, highlighting David's victory, recalls Yhwh's promises to deliver David from his enemies and Saul in 2 Sam 7:9, 15.

As a psalm of deliverance, 2 Sam 22 begins with thanksgiving (2 Sam 22:2–7) and ends with praise (2 Sam 22:47–51) through descriptions of Yhwh's power, Torah commitment, confidence, and victory (2 Sam 22:8–46).[395] The song and its inclusio fit well within the literary horizon of 2 Sam 21–23. In 2 Sam 21, David buried the bones of Saul and his sons and defeated the Philistines, dovetailing nicely with 2 Sam 22:1. Immediately following the song, 2 Sam 23:1 records "David's last words" (דברי דוד האחרנים) and the military legacy he was leaving behind. The final chapter in 2 Sam 24 records David's census, punishment and how an altar was built on the threshing floor of Araunah for the aversion of the plague. The record of David's sin in the last chapter of 2 Sam (24:17) seems to suggest that the song's victorious and salvific expressions are not final.

It is important to connect the headings of 2 Sam 22:1 and 7:1 (cf. 7:9, 11), where the latter notes, "Yhwh gave him [David] rest from all his surrounding enemies." Furthermore, these two headings and their immediate literary horizons can be seen together. The following figure captures the thematic sequential parallels between 2 Sam 4–9 and 19–24.

---

395. Anderson divides it into a "Psalm of Deliverance" (vv. 2–20), "Connecting Material" (vv. 21–28), "Royal Psalm of Victory" (29–51b) (Anderson, *2 Samuel*, 262).

The Design of the Psalter

2 Sam 4	Ish-bosheth murdered (Saul's son)	2 Sam 19	Absalom killed (David's son); David began to return to Jerusalem
2 Sam 5	(1) David's anointed reign over all Israel and Judah; (2) Verbal challenge against David by Jebusite who were overcome behind a fortified city; (3) David built his house and God established his kingdom; (4) David took more concubines; (5) David struck down the Philistines	2 Sam 20	(1) David returned to Jerusalem as king; (2) Verbal challenge against David by Sheba who was overcome behind a fortified city; (3) David came to his house in Jerusalem; (4) David's concubines shut up (5) David destroyed rebellion within Israel.
2 Sam 6	David tried to bring the ark to Jerusalem but error at "threshing floor of Nacon" (6:6) caused Yhwh's wrath to break forth; David brought the Ark to Jerusalem with sacrifice, shouting and celebration.	2 Sam 21	David's kindness to Mephibosheth; Buried Saul's bones; Victory over Philistines
2 Sam 7	Davidic Covenant. *When Yhwh gave him rest from all surrounding enemies*, David wanted to build a house for the ark, but God would build a house for him instead. His offspring would build the house.	2 Sam 22	David's song of deliverance. *When Yhwh delivered him from all his enemies and Saul.*
2 Sam 8	David's victories and a list of his officials	2 Sam 23	David's victories and a list of mighty men
2 Sam 9	David's kindness to Mephibosheth	2 Sam 24	David's error with the census, Yhwh's wrath broke out. Plague ceased at the "threshing floor of Araunah," the Jebusite (24:16); David offered sacrifice and built an altar.

Figure 10: **Structural Parallels between 2 Sam 4–9 and 2 Sam 19–24**

Both 2 Sam 4 and 19 mark the death of a prince. At least five thematic parallels occur between 2 Sam 5 and 20. In both cases, David was requested by the tribes of Israel to return to Jerusalem to be their king (cf. 5:1–3; 19:12—20:3). In both cases, the tribes referred to themselves as the "bone and flesh" of David (cf. 5:1; 19:12-13). On these two returns to Jerusalem, David faced verbal challenges, one by the Jebusites (5:6) and the other by Sheba (20:1), against whom David eventually overcame despite them hiding behind fortified walls. The allusions to building David's house (cf. 5:11; 20:3) and his concubines (cf. 5:13; 20:3) in successive sequences in these two places of 2 Sam are uncanny.

The four successive chapters from 2 Sam 6–9 and 2 Sam 21–24 also parallel each other with an interesting inversion between the first and last chapters of both groups (i.e., 2 Sam 6 // 24 and 2 Sam 9 // 21). The distinct parallels between 2 Sam 6 and 24 are explicated by the word, גרן ("threshing floor"),[396] which occurs only in these two places in 2 Sam. In both cases, Yhwh's wrath was unleashed due to errors committed

---

396. 2 Sam 6:6; 24:16, 18, 21–22, 24.

by David; however, the punishment fell on others (Uzzah in 6:6–7 and seventy thousand Israelites in 24:15). In both cases, sacrifices were made to the LORD (6:13, 17–18; 24:25) with immediate contexts associated to the ark and house of God (6:2; 24:25; cf. 2 Chr 3:1). It is important to note that these two texts mark the establishment[397] and wane of David's kingship (2 Sam 6; 24), thus framing his kingship.

As observed above, parallels between 2 Sam 7 and 22 can be identified by their similar headings (7:1; 22:1) and their common motif of David's deliverance from his enemies. The use of the noun זרע ("offspring"), which appears only in three instances in 2 Sam, highlights not just the affirmation of Yhwh's covenantal promises to the kingship of a Davidic progeny (2 Sam 7:12; 22:51), but compares it with the progeny of Saul who would not be established (4:8). The parallels between 2 Sam 8 and 23 are clear in the lists of David's officials and mighty men. Finally, a parallel between 2 Sam 9 and 21 can be found in David's kindness to Mephibosheth, Jonathan's son.

Further observations can be made for the parallels between 2 Sam 4–9 and 2 Sam 19–24[398] but the point that is pertinent to our argument relates to the structural and thematic parallels of 2 Sam 7 and 22. They connect the Davidic covenant (victory over enemies, establishment of kingship, dynasty) and the moving of the ark (building of Yhwh's house) at two definitive points in the Samuel narrative—the establishment and wane of the Davidic kingship.

An interesting case can be made with the contextual order of David's victory songs in the books of Samuel, Chronicles, and the Psalter and how they suggest intertexual rereading at work. The song of thanksgiving in 1 Chr 16:8–36 is recorded in the narrative after *David* moved the ark to Jerusalem and placed it in a tent. The Levites were assigned to minister before the ark to give thanks to God. The first part of the song follows Ps 105:1–15,[399] which ascribes to Yhwh's wonderous deeds, judgments, his covenant with his chosen servants and his promises to bring them into Canaan. Subsequently, the song in 1 Chr 16 follows Ps 96:1–13, characterizing Yhwh's universal kingship. Then it concludes with the invocation to give thanks based on the doxological formula in Ps 106:1, 47–48.[400] The primary motifs of 1 Chr 16:8–36 are Yhwh's power, kingship and his covenantal expressions to his chosen people.

A second song in 2 Chr 6:41–42 (which follows Ps 132)[401] is also recorded in the narrative after the ark was brought to the temple that *Solomon* had built. This is

---

397. The lemma, כון ("to establish"), occurs only in 2 Sam 5:12; 7:12–13, 16, 24, 26 in the book of 2 Samuel and are all associated with the establishment of kingship and nation.

398. E.g., David's sins, the outbreaking or aversion of Yhwh's wrath on a "threshing floor."

399. For detailed textual comparisons between the song in 1 Chr 16:8–36. See Klein, *1 Chronicles*, 359–70.

400. Klein argues that all these psalm references are taken from Book IV of the Psalter and the use of the doxology indicates that Book IV "was completed by the time of the Chronicler." See Klein, "Psalms in Chronicles," 269.

401. For a comparison of the differences between the two texts, see Japhet, *I & II Chronicles*, 600–1.

The Design of the Psalter

followed immediately by 2 Chr 7 in which YHWH appeared to Solomon and renewed the covenant first given to David (2 Chr 7:12–22).

When we consolidate these similar motifs in the songs of 2 Sam 22, 1 Chr 16 and 2 Chr 6 and their immediate contexts, and then revisit their parallels in the Psalter, we see an interesting intertext, illustrated in the figure below.

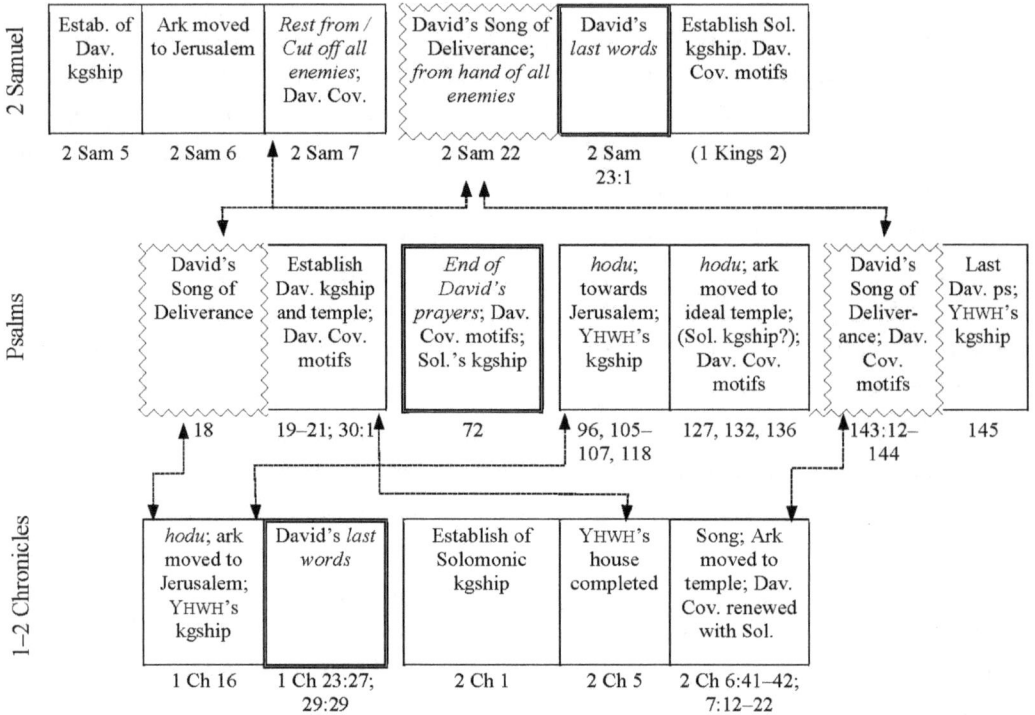

Figure 11: Comparison of Common Songs between 2 Samuel, Chronicles, and the Psalms

In the figure above, the wriggly boxes connect 2 Sam 22 with the Psalms. The boxes that contain songs of *hodu* (הודו) connect the Psalms with 1 Chr 16 and 2 Chr 6 while the double lined boxes locate references to David's last words or prayers (wane of his kingship). Intertextual rereadings of the above provide two hermeneutical insights: (1) *Structural frames of books*. The statements of rest/deliverance from the hands of David's enemies (2 Sam 7:1, 9, 11; 22:1) and the song in 2 Sam 22 frame two important points of David's life—the establishment (2 Sam 7) and wane of his kingship (2 Sam 22). It is plausible that the final editors of the Psalms understood the design of 2 Sam and adopted the motifs of David's deliverance at these two definitive periods of David's life, and then arranging them as Pss 18 and 144 to form a similar inclusio in the literary horizon of the Psalms.

The two songs in 1–2 Chronicles are situated with the two movements of the ark, along with the narratives of David and Solomon's kingships. First Chronicles 16 parallels 2 Sam 6, which indirectly identifies itself with Ps 18 whereas 2 Chr 6 draws on Ps 132 which locates itself at the end of the Songs of Ascents (SOA) in the Psalter. The thematic contents of 1 Chr 16 and 2 Chr 6, and the specific use of the formula, "for he is good, for his *hesed* endures forever," are found between Pss 96 and 136 (cf. 105–107; 118; 127; 132).

If Chronicles had drawn on the Psalms, then the Chronicler would have understood the designs of the Psalter and Samuel, choosing to adopt from the Psalms for its own purposes, the motifs of Yhwh's kingship (choosing the Yhwh *Malak* and Zion-centered, rather than the Davidic kingship psalms) and the building of Yhwh's house.

The references of David's last words (double-lined boxes) also help us locate the wane of David's kingship along each of the three trajectories. The connections seen in the structural parallels, the inclusions, thematic content, and their distinctiveness provide clues to understanding the design of the Psalter.

(2) It follows then that intertextual reading deepens the understanding of how parallel themes develop structurally in the Psalms. The seven key motifs identified in 2 Sam 7 are affirmed in the above intertextual review of the songs common to the books of Samuel, Chronicles, and the Psalms. This leads us to focus on how these prominent motifs, associated with Yhwh's covenantal promises given to David, unravel across the Psalter.

For instance, the integral concept of secure dwelling (for the king and people) and deliverance from enemies is clearly characterized in Pss 18 and 144. The proliferation of the eight nouns and two verbs with first person suffix highlighting secure dwelling and deliverance in Ps 18:1 is not sustained anywhere else in the Psalter.[402] The lexemes associated with the Davidic king's "deliverance" (נצל) from the "hands" (יד) of "all" (כל) his "enemies" (איב) are specifically found between Pss 18 and 143:12–144,[403] reinforcing this frame. The actual social reality of such security and deliverance is also well envisioned in 144:9–15.

Following the references to David's last words, the moving of the ark is associated with Solomon in 2 Sam and Chronicles. However, in the Psalms, the association of the ark with Solomon is less clear. Psalm 132:8 is the only reference in the Psalms to the ark but in this context, an offspring of David rather than Solomon is mentioned. We may ask why is this so? By comparison, the Psalter seems to also have an *extended association* with the Davidic kingship beyond the establishment of the temple and

---

402. The eight nouns are סלעי ("my rock"), מצודתי ("my stronghold"), צורי ("my rock"), אלי ("my God"), מגני ("my shield"), קרן-ישעי ("horn of my salvation") and משגבי ("my fortress"), while the two verbs are מפלטי ("one who delivers me") and אחסה-בו ("I seek refuge in him"). Note how the two verbs bring together the concept of seeking refuge in the one who delivers. The word, "stronghold" (מצודה) is found only 7x in the Psalter and occurs between Pss 18 and 144 (18:3; 31:3–4; 66:11; 71:3; 91:2; 144:2).

403. Pss 18:1; 22:21; 31:16; 82:4; 97:10; 143:12; 144:7, 11. While this specific motif may be seen in Ps 7:1, the idea of Davidic kingship is not prominent.

The Design of the Psalter

the moving of the ark (after Pss 120–134).[404] While 2 Chronicles, a post-exilic work (2 Chr 36), continues the narration of Judahite kings and concludes with an interest in the rebuilding of the house (2 Chr 36:23), the Psalter does not sustain a similar interest in temple building beyond Ps 136. Rather, it brings back Davidic psalms, concluding again with the emphases of kingship, deliverance and secure dwelling.[405] The final Davidic Ps 145 is a focus on Yhwh's kingship. This distinctive focus of the Psalter draws our attention to its structural and theological thrust, especially in relation to the Davidic characterization in Books IV–V of the Psalms.

Summary

- In this chapter, we have located our study in the context of Psalms scholarship and addressed key hermeneutical issues. We have also identified helpful avenues into our three research questions.

- The three research questions guiding this book pertain to the literary methods (or techniques), macrostructure, and message (logic) of the Psalter.

- The design of the MT Psalter is to be understood via a macrostructural perspective. Such macrostructural study of the Psalms remains lacking in Psalms research. The main issues currently faced by Psalms scholarship are due to difficulties associated with a plurality of techniques, differing structural divisions, and themes.

- A number of organizing techniques (at least 32 formal or tacit) are observed. If the final editor(s) of the Psalms had the freedom to edit the texts toward a certain design, then it is logical to assume that organizing *techniques*, structural *form*, and *content* should cohere and correspond.

- Psalms 1–2 are concentrically structured. Their poetical and thematic structures correspond. They are a single alphabetical composition. Their poetical and

---

404. Mitchell argues that the ark represents the "the footstool of the Holy One . . . For the footstool, like the sceptre and crown, is a perennial symbol of royal estate. The king puts his royal feet up, while others attend him, standing in the dust. No self-respecting monarch goes without one. Tut-ankh-amun had a footstool. The king of Megiddo . . . has one. The kings of Israel had footstools . . . The idea of the ark as a footstool is confirmed by other ancient texts which show that a covenant or treaty was placed in a chest beneath the feet of the god who served as witness to it" (cf. Pss 99:5; 132:7; 1 Chr 28:2; Isa 60:13; Lam 2:1) (Mitchell, *Songs of Ascents*, 49–50).

405. Klein argues that the Chronicler no longer felt the need to reinstitute feelings for the monarchy. This deviates from the Psalter's thrust. He notes, "By the time of the Chronicler the post-exilic community had existed for a century and a half with a fully functioning temple but without a king. If the Chronicler had felt any need for the reinstitution of the monarchy, he would have had to make a strong case for it. Instead, his additional paragraph in 2 Chronicles 7 puts the onus of responsibility exclusively on the people. Yahweh promises to forgive and to heal provided that Israel humbles itself, prays, seeks Yahweh's face, and repents. The promise in this programmatic verse is that there will always be forgiveness and healing for those who wholeheartedly participate in Israel's religious life and in the temple's worship" (Klein, "Psalms in Chronicles," 274).

numerical centers highlight the righteous man planted in the paradisical garden and the Messianic king reigning in Zion respectively.

- Psalms 1–2 form the Prologue of the Psalter and could function programmatically via its formal structure and thematic development. The Prologue's concentric shape (central motif) and linear trajectory (metanarrative) could express the overarching design of the Psalter.

- The Davidic characterization of the Psalms should be read alongside the historical narratives of David in the HB (i.e., 2 Sam 7; 1 Chr 16; 2 Chr 6). The Psalter shows that it has reread and adapted 2 Sam for its own structural design. The Chronicler's selective use of the Psalter indirectly reveals the design of the Psalter.

- The Psalter can be read as a unified book when discrete units of texts show a meaningful macro-interdevelopment of motifs (program).

2

The Macrostructure

The arrangement of the Psalms seems to hold the secret to a great mystery to me, though, has not yet been revealed to me.[1]

—Augustine

The psalms are then seen as the parts of a single book, each playing its role by providing a contribution in harmony with the whole, to which it is welded. The order of the psalms within them is not indifferent, it is wanted, consciously organized by the final editors, it is not the product of chance, but on what principles it had been established remains unknown.[2]

—Jean-Luc Vesco

THE MAIN CONCERN OF this chapter is to understand the structural and thematic shape of the five Books of the Psalter based on insights gained in the last chapter regarding the programmatic nature of the Prologue, various organizing techniques and intertextual reading. For the Prologue to be programmatic of the Psalter, we would expect features of the Prologue to be developed in the rest of the Psalms. A crucial insight gained in chapter 1 is the three-part concentric structure of Pss 1–2. The first and last sections of Pss 1–2 identify the *ways* and *outcomes* of the righteous and the wicked. The dominant image of the center sections is the *characterization* of the righteous man and the anointed king. We have also shown that the composers of the psalms would have adopted various rhetorical skills such as inclusions, anaphora, word plays,

---

1. "Quamvis Ordo Psalmorum, qui mihi magni sacramenti videtur continere secretum" (Augustine, *Sancti Aurelii Augustini Opera*, 81). My translation.
2. Vesco, *Le psautier de David*, 1:32. My translation.

alliteration, meter, and the use of introductions (exordium). Such rhetorical features would have been identified by readers of the Psalter who were equipped with the relevant literary competency. These informed assumptions will provide helpful controls for our analysis of the text. At the end of this chapter, we conclude that the entire Psalter is also organized in a three-part concentric structure with similar thematic development (Books I, II–III, IV–V). At the onset, I will define a nomenclature of psalms-delimitation (beyond a single psalm) to be used consistently throughout this book.

Nomenclature of Psalms-Delimitation

We define eight compositional levels from a single psalm to the entire Psalter as illustrated below. When they are capitalized in this book, they refer to the delimitation defined here.

1. Individual psalm
2. Pair or Twin-psalm (Prologue = Pss 1–2)
3. Subcollection[3]
4. Collection/Subgroup[4]
5. Group[5]
6. Book (Masoretic book divisions)
7. Section (Books I, II–III and IV–V)
8. Psalter

Barbiero's Macrostructural Analysis of Book I

A number of detailed studies focus on partial groupings within Book I, as well as giving a general view of Book I.[6] An important structural proposal for Book I, adopted by a number of Psalms scholars (e.g., Zenger, Vesco), views Pss 1–2 as the Prologue, followed by a four-part division (3–14; 15–24; 25–34; 35–41). One of the most important monographs on Book I, in my opinion, is Gianni Barbiero's *Das erste Psalmenbuch als*

---

3. This may be several adjacent psalms linked by content genre or superscription-genre (e.g., *mikhtam*).

4. A literary unit made up of Subcollections linked by a common superscription, genre, or formula.

5. There are usually three Collections within a Group of psalms. The center Collection typically forms the central motif for the Group. The Group defines a major unit within a Section. Each Section is made up of four Groups.

6. Smith, "Redactional Criteria"; McCann, "Shape of Book I"; "Books I–III"; Bellinger, "Reading from the Beginning (again)," 114–26.

The Design of the Psalter

Einheit: Eine synchrone Analyse von Psalm 1–41.[7] His understanding of how superscriptions in Book I play a role in structuring is crucial. Certain structural concepts he proposes for Book I will be adapted and they provide the basis for our analyses of Books II–V. In the following, we will look closely at his arguments and highlight pertinent insights.

We begin with Barbiero's view on the Prologue.[8] In the MT, Psalms 1–2 logically continue from the book of Malachi, sharing its major concepts.[9] Thus Barbiero argues that the Prologue of the Psalter is to be read as a "wisdom-prophecy," which is "on the one hand, as written wisdom [Ps 1], and on the other, as a prophetic book that speaks of the hope of Israel [Ps 2]. The history of Messiah and his people becomes the paradigm for humanity."[10] Barbiero also notes that the "man" in Ps 1 remains distinct from the messianic figure in Ps 2.[11] The Davidic psalms are "firstly the prayer of the Messiah of Ps 2 and secondly, the prayer of the 'man' in Psalm 1."[12] Psalms 1–2 and 40–41 are seen to form an inclusio for Book I of the Psalter.

---

7. Barbiero, *Das erste Psalmenbuch*. A shortened version of his original thesis, in article form, is published in French: Barbiero, "Le Premier Livret Du Psautier," 439–80. Barbiero is not the first person to have identified the four-part structure in Book I. However, I have found Barbiero's treatment detailed and his discussion on the superscriptions of the psalms is insightful. His shortened version is used in our discussion below.

8. Barbiero considers Pss 1–2 as a strong redactional unit functioning as the Prologue of the Psalter. "Les Ps 1 et 2 constituent donc une unité rédactionnelle forte au début du Psautier; ils servent d'introduction ou de prologue à celui-ci" (Barbiero, "Le Premier Livret Du Psautier," 447).

9. E.g., the nations' rage (Mal 3:12); Yhwh's eschatological reign (Mal 4:1); the separation of the righteous and wicked (Mal 3:18–4:2); Torah-piety (Mal 4:4).

10. Barbiero, "Le Premier Livret Du Psautier," 448.

11. For a detailed treatment of understanding the "man" in Ps 1 as the anointed king in Ps 2, see Cole, *Psalms 1–2*, 93. I think Barbiero's treatment is more balanced.

12. Barbiero, "Le Premier Livret Du Psautier," 450.

The Macrostructure

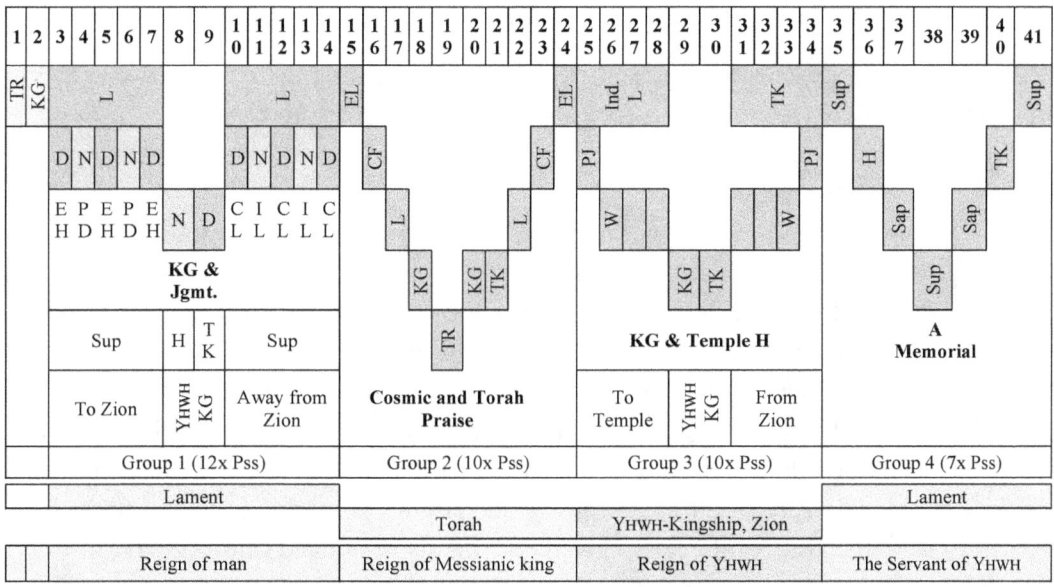

Figure 12: Gianni Barbiero's Structure of Book I (with my modifications in Pss 35–41)

In Figure 12 above,[13] I have drawn up the macrostructure of Book I by following Barbiero's understanding in general, and adding my modifications for the Group Pss 35–41. In the first Group of 12 psalms (Pss 3–14), Barbiero sees two Subgroups of five Supplication psalms (Pss 3–7, 10–14), binding Pss 8 and 9 at the center which are, in turn, Praise and Thanksgiving psalms.[14] Within Group 1, there is a thematic movement from an absence of salvation to the presence of salvation (Ps 8), followed by thanksgiving (Ps 9). Then the thematic genre returns to Supplications (10–14). Barbiero understands this thematic development to mean that "salvation is not something definitive ('already but not there yet')."[15]

Barbiero argues that the superscriptions of Pss 3 and 7 bind the first Subgroup (3–7). Note how the titles of Pss 3–7 form a chiastic structure.[16]

A: מזמור לדוד; historical superscript regarding Absalom (3)

B: למנצח; with stringed instrument (נגינה) (4)

C: למנצח; with the flutes (נחילות) (5)

B′: למנצח; with stringed instrument (נגינה); eight-stringed lyre (6)

---

13. Legend: D: Day Psalm; N: Night Psalm; EH: External Hostilities; PD: Personal Distress; CF: Confidence Psalms; CL: Communal Laments; IL: Individual Laments; Sup: Supplication; TK: Thanksgiving Hymn; TR: Torah Psalm; Z: Zion Psalm; KG: Kingship Psalm; EL: Entrance Liturgy; PJ: Motifs of the poor and justice; W: Motif of the wicked; Sap: Sapiential Psalms; H: Hymn of Praise; L: Lament.

14. Barbiero sees the acrostics Pss 9–10 as two separate psalms according to the MT tradition.

15. Barbiero, "Le Premier Livret Du Psautier," 467.

16. Smith, "Redactional Criteria and Objectives," 240; Smith and Domeris, "Arrangement of Psalms 3–8," 371.

The Design of the Psalter

A′: שגיון לדוד; historical superscript regarding Cush (7)

The superscriptions of Pss 8–9 are very similar, highlighting them as the two center psalms of Group 1. Psalms 11–14 are also chiastically structured (ABB′A′) based on their superscriptions.[17] Hence, Group 1 (3–14) is concentric with Pss 3–7 with 10–14 framing 8–9 at the center.

Moreover, the two Subgroups of five psalms (3–7, 10–14) are composed as alternating sequence of "day-night-day-night-day" psalms.[18] At the center, Psalms 8–9 are "night-day" psalms,[19] where "Day" psalms correspond to the motif of "external hostility" (EH), and the "night" psalms correspond to the motif of "personal distress" (PD).[20] Psalms 10–14 are also structured as an *alternation* between Communal (10, 12, 14) and Individual Laments (11, 13). Barbiero argues that this alternation technique is a "composition principle."[21] At the center, Pss 8–9 are both a response to the Laments (in Pss 3–7) and an expression of thanksgiving for Yhwh's deliverance. Finally, Barbiero describes a thematic "centripetal movement" that is orientated *towards* Zion in Pss 3–7 and a "centrifugal movement" that is orientated *away* from Zion in Pss 10–14.[22]

Group 2 (15–24) consists of 10 psalms. Like Group 1, it has a symmetrical structure around the center Ps 19 which is a Hymn of the Torah. Genre categories provide the structural basis for Group 2. It is bound by two Entrance Liturgies (15, 24) followed by a second outermost ring of two Confidence psalms (16, 23), a third ring of two Supplication psalms (17, 22), and a fourth ring (immediately surrounding the center) of psalms with kingship motifs (18, 20–21). When Ps 19 is seen together with Pss 18–21, the central motifs of Group 2 recapitulate the motifs of Torah and kingship in the Prologue.

The superscriptions of Pss 15–24 are arranged symmetrically.[23] Longer titles are found at the center of Group 2 (cf. 18–22). They are flanked by Subgroups of psalms with shorter titles on both sides (15–17, 23–24).[24] The titles of Pss 14 and 25 are of a different construction, framing Group 2.[25]

---

17. Note two shorter and identical superscriptions in Pss 11 and 14, bounding two longer superscriptions in Pss 12 and 13. Barbiero, "Le Premier Livret Du Psautier," 468.

18. Cf. Pss 3:6, 8; 4:5, 9; 5:4, 6:7; 7:7; 10:12; 11:2; 12:6; 13:4; 14:2, 5.

19. Cf. Pss 8:4; 9:20.

20. Personal distress of the psalmist in Ps 4 relates to his poverty, and in Ps 6, his disease.

21. Barbiero, "Le Premier Livret Du Psautier," 468.

22. There is a thematic trajectory developing across Group 1. In Pss 3–7, the psalmist looks towards the temple and enters Yhwh's house (3:5; 5:8). At the center of the entire Subgroup, Yhwh is enthroned in Zion (9:12–15). In Pss 10–14, the psalmist calls upon the eternal kingship of Yhwh (10:16) and declares Yhwh's rule at the temple and in heaven (11:4). By Ps 14:2, 7, Yhwh's gaze and salvation *come* out from Zion. Barbiero, "Le Premier Livret Du Psautier," 469.

23. McCann, "The Shape and Shaping of the Psalter: Psalms in Their Literary Context," 354.

24. Furthermore, Barbiero sees a chiasmus in the superscriptions of Pss 23 and 24. Note that this is not visible in the English translations. Psalm 23 begins with מזמור לדוד and Ps 24 with לדוד מזמור.

25. Barbiero, "Le Premier Livret Du Psautier," 465–66.

Group 3 in Book I is another 10 psalms arranged concentrically and bound by two AAs (25, 34). Two pairs of four psalms (25–28; 31–34) frame a Thanksgiving and Praise hymn at the center (29, 30). Barbiero observes that Pss 25–28 express a movement *towards* the temple.[26] This movement culminates at Ps 29, a hymn, praising Yhwh's enthronement in the temple (29:9–11). Psalm 30:1 then begins with a significant superscription: "a song at the dedication of the house." Psalms 31–34 highlight the protection and watchful eye of Yhwh *from* Zion (31:21–22; 33:13–15; 34:16). These centripetal (25–28) and centrifugal movements (31–34) in relation to Zion on both sides of Pss 29–30, emphasize Yhwh's enthronement at the Zion-temple (Pss 29–30), also seen in Group 1.

Barbiero argues that the second half of Groups 1 and 3 (10–14; 31–34) are characterized by a similar vocabulary associated with poverty. The difference is that in Pss 31–34, this poverty is understood in a spiritual sense and associated with personal sin.[27]

In Group 3, the superscriptions follow a three-part symmetric structure. The similarity in the construction of the titles in Pss 25–28 binds them as a Subgroup. This also applies to Pss 29–31.[28] The superscriptions of Pss 32–34, beginning with לדוד, likewise form a unit.[29] It is important to note that the structural shape of the Groups, accorded by the superscriptions, corresponds to the shape accorded by its theme. In other words, the poetical form corresponds with its thematic content.

Group 4 (35–41) consists of seven psalms arranged symmetrically. It is framed by two Supplication psalms (35, 41), followed by a second ring of Thanksgiving hymns (36, 40) and a third ring of Sapiential psalms (37, 39). For Barbiero, the center psalm, Ps 38, another Supplication psalm, is associated with the Supplication Pss 35, 41. He considers Pss 37 and 39 functioning as two centers in the Group.[30] In general, the first half (35–37) focuses on motifs of "external evil and oppression of enemies" while the second (39–41) highlights motifs of "inner misfortune, sickness and sin."[31] This phenomenon is similar to the alternation sequence of external hostilities and personal distress seen in Pss 3–7.

The לדוד in the superscriptions of Pss 35 and 37 form an inclusio around the Subgroup (35–37) just prior to the center Ps 38. The other Subgroup (39–41) is united by למנצח in the superscriptions.

As a whole, Barbiero sees the structure of Pss 35–41 following an A-B-C-A'-C'-B'-A'' configuration with two centers (Pss 37, 39). However, it is likewise possible to

---

26. Barbiero, "Le Premier Livret Du Psautier," 471.

27. Barbiero, "Le Premier Livret Du Psautier," 472.

28. Note that the מזמור in the superscriptions of Pss 29–31 is absent in the rest of Group 3.

29. Barbiero points out that although Ps 33 has no superscription, Pss 32 and 33 are a unit. Barbiero, "Le Premier Livret Du Psautier," 471.

30. Barbiero, "Le Premier Livret Du Psautier," 473–75.

31. Barbiero, "Le Premier Livret Du Psautier," 472.

see Ps 38 functioning as the center of Group 4. Barbiero's analysis of the superscriptions above suggests a distinctive Ps 38. Hence, I have modified Barbiero's structure, viewing Ps 38 as the central psalm in this Group.

Looking at Book I as a whole, Barbiero argues that the four Groups form a chiastic structure according to genre categories. Groups 1 and 4 are Laments. Groups 2 and 3 at the center are Praise and Thanksgiving hymns. He notes that this structure is already evident within Pss 3–14.[32]

The following figure summarizes the key motifs across the Prologue and the four Groups in Book I:

Psalms	1–2 Prologue		3–14 Group 1	15–24 Group 2	25–34 Group 3	35–41 Group 4
Poetic and Thematic Structure	Torah, "man"	Reign of Messiah	Reign of man	Reign of the Messianic king	Reign of Yhwh	The Servant of Yhwh

Figure 13: Barbiero's Thematic and Genre Structures for Book I

In Barbiero's opinion, the Prologue centers on the motifs of the Torah and the kingdom of God.[33] Group 1 represents the "reign of man" (8:3–6).[34] Group 2 is seen as the "reign of the Messiah." Just as the story of Abraham is the answer to the spread of sin in the world, Pss 15–24 and 25–34 are the answers to the evil depicted in Pss 10–14. The answer to this sin is found in the "institutions of salvation for the chosen people," that is, the institutions of kingship, law and the temple which are emphasized in the centrally located Pss 18–21.[35]

Group 3 represents the "reign of Yhwh." This is clearly seen from the emphasis on Yhwh's reign in Ps 29:9–11 located at the center of this Group. Although the reign of Yhwh is the primary focus at the core, the reign of a human king is not completely absent (cf. 24:10; 33:12, 16). What is seen is a subordination of the human king to the reign of Yhwh.

The final group, Group 4 (35–41), can be seen through the motif of the "Servant of Yhwh," a name which David assumes in 36:1 and 35:27. Interestingly, Barbiero notes that the term, מלך, does not occur either as a verb or noun in this Group.[36] The

32. Barbiero, "Le Premier Livret Du Psautier," 476.

33. Barbiero, "Le Premier Livret Du Psautier," 477.

34. Barbiero argues that there is a connection between Pss 1, 3–14 and Genesis 1–11. Both identify human beings in general rather than the chosen people of God. Barbiero, "Le Premier Livret Du Psautier," 478.

35. Barbiero, "Le Premier Livret Du Psautier," 478.

36. For instance, Ps 40:7–9 speaks of an inner attitude of obedience to the law that is within the heart. Not only is kingship "absent," the sacrificial system, as a whole, is in crisis (40:7–9). Sacrifices and offering are now substituted with the expression of obedience to Yhwh, a motif already implicit in Ps 1.

concern of forgiveness of sin, while absent in Group 1, is remarkably dominant in Group 4 (38:4, 19; 39:2; 41:5). These emphases point to the theological motif of the New Covenant in Jeremiah and Ezekiel.[37] Barbiero concludes by saying that Book I of the Psalter provides the theological trajectory of the whole Psalter.[38]

Evaluation of Barbiero's Thesis

In my view, Barbiero's structural and thematic views of Book I provides a good framework to understand the Psalter. I highlight six insights helpful for our study:

(1) *Concentric structures working at different levels of composition.* Barbiero's arguments for a concentric structure in each of the four Groups show that the Psalter is carefully organized even at the level of the Subgroups. His thematic proposition for the entire Book I is symmetric, with Pss 3–14 and 35–41 framing Pss 15–24 and 25–34. Barbiero's understanding of Book I reinforces my proposal of a three-part concentric structure of the Prologue which is also programmatic.

(2) *Central focus.* Concentricity directs the reader to a central focus. The common focuses at the *centers* of Groups 1–3 are the recurring motifs of Torah, Kingship and the Zion-temple. These motifs are also found at the central segment of the Prologue (cf. 1:3, 2:4–9).

(3) *A trajectory in relation to Zion.* Barbiero detects a thematic movement in relation to Zion. The psalms before and after the centrally-located psalms (in Groups 1 and 3) are orientated *towards* and *away* from Zion respectively. At the center, Yhwh or the Davidic kingship at Zion, is emphasized.

(4) *A Symbolic number of psalms in each group.* Including the number of psalms in the Prologue, the number of psalms for the four Groups is sequenced as (2x7)-10-10-7. These numbers can be considered symbolic, as relating to completeness and totality (see chapter 5), in support of a concentric shape of Book I with two Groups of 10 psalms at the center.

(5) *Psalm superscriptions* show that their design corresponds to the genre and thematic shapes in Book I. This is an important argument. Form and content are not in opposition to each other. This raises the profile of the function of *superscriptions as macrostructuring devices*. Psalms are not only united at the level of large Groups (e.g., Asaphite/Korahite Collections) but also at the compositional level of the Subgroups.

(6) *Reading the Psalter after Malachi.* Barbiero's observation of the canonical arrangement of the Psalter following Malachi in the *BHS* and characterizing a thematic flow between them is significant.[39] Based on the L tradition, the Book of Psalms follows 1–2 Chronicles.

---

37. Barbiero, "Le Premier Livret Du Psautier," 480.

38. Barbiero, "Le Premier Livret Du Psautier," 480.

39. It shows the interaction of the Psalms with other biblical texts and the technique of binding two texts separated by literary divisions with a common vocabulary. However, the Psalter's location

The Design of the Psalter

The motifs of eschatological kingship, Torah-piety, and separation between the righteous and the wicked are traced through the last two chapters of Malachi and the first two chapters of the Psalms. This arrangement accords the eschatological perspective to the Prologue of the Psalms. As such, the Torah-kingship motifs in the Psalms need not only be connected with a Deuteronomic understanding of Torah-kingship (Deut 17),[40] but also with eschatological interests of the postexilic period.

As we conclude our review of Book I based on Barbiero's study, these six summary points collaborate and confirm our propositions in the first chapter. The Prologue's programmatic nature, specifically its poetical and thematic macrostructures and its central focuses (of the righteous man and the messianic king), are affirmed in Book I. This structural and thematic correspondence between the Prologue and Book I provide the impetus for studying the rest of the Psalter in a similar fashion. Now since the Prologue is programmatic for Book I, it follows that it is also plausibly programmatic for the rest of the Psalms, which we will next explore.

Macrostructural Analysis of Books II–III

Books II and III of the Psalms can be seen together via the formal poetical device of the Korahite and Asaphite superscriptions that link them. They form a general chiastic Korahite-Asaphite-Davidic-Asaphite-Korathite (A-B-C-B'-A') arrangement (42–49, 50, 51–72, 73–83, 84–89).[41] Furthermore, the Elohistic Psalter that begins Book II (42) extends all the way to Ps 83 in Book III, binding them together.[42]

---

is attested to in at least eight different ways, occurring also within different categories of Writings, Prophets or Hagiographa. In L and the Aleppo Codex, the Psalms comes after Chronicles. In the works of Eusebius and Origen, the Psalms comes after Ezra-Nehemiah. Elsewhere, the Psalms are listed following Job, Ruth, 1–4 Maccabees or Judith. See Auwers, *La Composition*, 172–73.

40. Grant, *King as Exemplar*, 6–7.

41. Mitchell, *Message of the Psalter*, 71; Erich Zenger, "Das Buch der Psalmen," 354.

42. Mitchell notes that there is "an old Hebrew tradition which uses *elohim* with God's judgment and YHVH with his mercy." He cites "*Sifre* §27; *Pes. De-Rav Kah.* 149a; *Midr. Pss.* 74.2; *Zohar, Shemot* 173b–174a" and quotes A. P. Hayman: "The doctrine of the two divine attributes, Justice and Mercy, runs like a thread through all the rabbinic writings. It is the basis of a fundamental exegetical rule, namely that the divine name *Yahweh* denotes the attribute of Mercy, the name *Elohim*, the attribute of Justice" (Hayman quoted in Mitchell, *Songs of Ascents*, 6).

Research on these two books, whether in part or whole, includes the works of Burnett,[43] Kimmitt,[44] Goulder,[45] Cole,[46] Jones,[47] Gillingham[48] and others.[49] Gillingham's article provides a good starting point for understanding the macrostructure of Books II–III.

One of the ways Books II and III are seen as a single unit is the parallel genre structures between the two Korahite Subgroups.[50] In both Korahite Groups, there is a common sequence of Individual Lament (42–43, 84),[51] Communal Lament (44, 85), Kingship Psalm (45, 86); Divine Response (46–48, 87), and Individual Lament (49; 88). This parallel is illustrated below.

Korahite Subgroup I	Genre	Korahite Subgroup II
42–43	Individual Lament	84
44	Communal Lament	85
45	Kingship	86
46–48	Divine Response (YHWH's kingship)	87
49 (Wisdom)	Individual Lament	88, 89 (Kingship)

Figure 14: Parallel Genre Structures between the Two Korahite Subgroups

This parallel goes beyond the genre categories. Gillingham argues that there is a thematic motif of longing for Zion (42–43; 84) and a prevalence of "Zion markers" (42; 43; 46; 48; 84; and 87) uniting the Korathite Subgroups. There are also many common words/phrases between these two Korahite Subgroups.[52]

---

43. Burnett, "Forty-Two Songs for Elohim," 81–101; "Plea for David and Zion," 95–113.

44. In addition to his PhD diss., see also Kimmitt, "Psalms 44, 45, 46," 1–33.

45. Goulder, "Social Setting of Book II," 349–67; *Prayers of David*; *Psalms of Asaph*.

46. Cole, *Shape and Message*.

47. I am thankful to Christine Jones who supplied a copy of her dissertation for this research. See Jones, "Psalms of Asaph"; "Message of the Asaphite Collection," 71–85.

48. Gillingham, "Zion Tradition," 322–26.

49. Attard, *Implications of Davidic Repentance*; McCann, "Books I–III"; Nasuti, *Tradition History*; Buss, "Psalms of Asaph and Korah," 382–92; Houston, "David, Asaph," 93–111.

50. Gillingham, "Zion Tradition," 323; Zenger and Auwers have also noted this parallel. Auwers, *La Composition*, 49; Zenger, "Das Buch der Psalmen," 354.

51. Strictly, Ps 43 does not have the Korahite superscript.

52. For example, the phrase, אל חי ("living God"), occurs only in Pss 42:3 and 84:3 in the Psalms; משכן as a second person noun only in Pss 43:3; 84:2; connections between בית אלהים (42:5) and ביתך (84:5); עיר־אלהים (46:5; 48:2, 9) and עיר האלהים (87:3); עליון (46:5; 47:3; 87:5); הר־קדשו (48:2) and בהררי־קדש (Ps 87:1); יכוננה (48:9) and יכוננה (87:5); אלהי יעקב (46:8) and משכנות יעקב (87:2). Gillingham, "Zion Tradition," 323.

The Design of the Psalter

Kimmitt's detailed study of Pss 44–46 within the first Korahite Subgroup reinforces the above observations about their genre.[53] He concludes that Ps 44 is a Communal Lament of God's "abandonment," Ps 45 pictures an anointed king and Ps 46 is the Divine Response: Yhwh is savior and king! There is also a thematic "interlocking" phenomenon between Pss 45, 47 and Pss 46, 48. These psalms are interlocked by the motifs of kingship and Zion.[54]

Remarkably, this parallel phenomenon is also seen in the two Subgroups of the Asaphite Psalms (50, 73–77 and 78–83).[55] They contain a parallel sequence of Didactic, Communal Lament, Divine Response and Individual Lament psalms as illustrated in Figure 15.

Asaphite Subgroup I	Genre	Asaphite Subgroup II
50, 73	Didactic/Sapiential	78
74	Communal Lament	79–80
75–76	Divine Response	81–82
77	Lament	83

Figure 15: Parallel Genre Structures between the Two Asaphite Subgroups

The separation of Ps 50 from the main Asaphite Group is regarded as structurally deliberate, allowing the entire Books II–III to be a chiasmus. Thematically, Ps 50 bridges the Korahite Group to the Davidic Collection.[56] Zenger argued that the entire Asaphite Group develops the theme of "God's judgment."[57] The Asaphite Group could be associated with the northern kingdom (77:16; 80:2, 3; 81:6).[58]

---

53. Kimmitt identifies 46 common lexemes within Pss 44–46, of which 28 are "incidental" while 18 are significant. See Kimmitt, "Psalms 44, 45, 46," 1.

54. Creach, *Yahweh as Refuge*, 87.

55. This has been concluded by Hossfeld and Zenger as well (Zenger, "Das Buch der Psalmen," 354; Hossfeld and Zenger, *Psalms 2*, 2).

56. Jones suggests that Ps 50 functions as a shift of tone to God's role as the judge for the wicked and the righteous (Jones, "Psalms of Asaph," 136–39, 141, 177). Consensus has not been reached on the placement of Ps 50. Gillingham finds it hard to understand why Ps 50 is set away from the rest of the Asaph collection. She suggests that this psalm provides a "commentary to the end of Ps 51" and notes various connections between Ps 50 and Pss 73–83. See Gillingham, "Zion Tradition," 325; Mitchell, *Message of the Psalter*, 72.

57. Zenger, "Das Buch der Psalmen," 353.

58. Gillingham notes that the presence of an Exodus tradition (Pss 77:11–22; 78:11–53; 80:9–12; 81:5–8) and the use of אל "especially (although not exclusively) in the northern circles" are indications of northern associations. See Gillingham, "Zion Tradition," 325; Goulder, "Asaph's History of Israel," 72–76.

Moreover, between the Korahite and Asaphite Groups, an interesting contrast can be seen. The 12 Korahite psalms[59] emphasize Yhwh's presence in Zion whereas the 12 Asaphite psalms lament his absence. Asaphite psalms are associated more with Yhwh's judgment against Israel, the nations, and have a warlike context. The Korahite psalms, in contrast, are associated with worship and Zion.[60] It is certainly not fortuitous that both the Asaphite and Korahite Groups consist of exactly 12 psalms each.

While scholars generally agree on how the Korahite and Asaphite psalms are structured, there is less agreement with regards to the Davidic psalms in Book II. Figure 16 summarizes divisions within Pss 51–72 by various scholars.

Psalms	51	52	53	54	55	56	57	58	59	60	61	62	63	64	65	66	67	68	69	70	71	72
Zenger	51	52–55				56–60					61–64				65–68				69–71			72
Vesco	51	52–55				56–60					61–64				65–68				69–71			72
Auwers	51–64														65–67			68	69–72			
Christensen	51–70																				71–72	
Labuschage		51–57						58–64							65–71							72
Robertson	49–52		53	54–60							61–68								69–71			72
Goulder	51	52–55				56–59				60–64					65–68				69–71			72

Figure 16: Different Structural Divisions within Pss 51–72

For Zenger and Vesco, the Davidic Group is bound on both ends by two Petition psalms (51, 72). Psalms 52–55 is a unit of Laments with the common superscription, משכיל לדוד. A symmetric group of Laments occurs in Pss 69–71. These two Subcollections of Lament frame a further sequence of Petition (56–60), Confidence (61–64) and Thanksgiving (65–68) psalms. These three Subcollections at the center are characterized by לדוד מכתם (56–60), לדוד (61–64), and שיר (65–68) in their superscriptions respectively.[61] Again, we see a correspondence between the genre (thematic) and formal structures of this Group.

Auwers divides the Davidic Group into three segments (51–64, 65–67, 68–72) corresponding to the genres of Individual Petitions, Thanksgiving, and Complaints. However, he provides little reasons for doing so.[62] As noted in the last chapter, Labus-

---

59. Psalm 43 is seen as a separate psalm of Korah, though it does not have a "Korahite" superscription. However, the almost identical verses of Pss 42:6, 12 and 43:5 suggest they are likely to belong together (though a separate psalm). Note the recurrence of the symbolic number 12, as seen in Book I. For a discussion of Pss 42–43 as a single composition, see van der Lugt, *CAS II*, 16–18.

60. Gillingham, "Zion Tradition," 325.

61. Hossfeld and Zenger, *Psalms 2*, 2; Vesco, *Le psautier*, 1:480, 505, 541, 565, 602.

62. It is unclear how he structures this, apart from genre designations based on the referenced work. Psalm 68 stands alone. Auwers, *La Composition*, 47.

The Design of the Psalter

chagne's division is based on numerical considerations. Christensen[63] and Robertson's divisions are primarily thematic-based, but Christensen viewed the Davidic Group as part of a chiasmus with Ps 50 at the center, and 51–70, 71–72 forming the second half.

Goulder argues that the narrative flow of David's life, spanning from Uriah's death (2 Sam 11) to the ascension of king Solomon (1 Kg 1), forms the basis for Pss 51–72.[64] He prescribes a thematic structure, beginning with Ps 51 which describes David's sin and atonement, followed by 52–55, highlighting David's retreat from Zion to Olivet. Then in Pss 56–59, David retreats to Mahanaim and 60–64 reflect a period of civil war and siege at Mahanaim. In Ps 65, the fortunes of David begins to change (cf. 65:9–13). The positive turn of events culminates in Psalm 68 with David's victory over Absalom, though this upturn is not sustained. Psalms 69–71 describe David's continuing woes in his later years and the final Ps 72 is associated with the ascension of a new king. Goulder views the motivation of this composition as liturgical.[65]

Goulder's structure is similar to Vesco and Zenger's, but with certain nuances. For Goulder, Ps 60 begins a new subgroup (60–64) and Pss 69–72 are taken as one Subcollection rather than two in Zenger's proposal (69–71, 72). This is because Goulder was interested in the narrative events of David's life, hence adopting a structure based on common motifs that best correspond to the narratival structure. I highlight four observations from the above survey.

(1) *There is some consensus to consider Pss 56, 61, 65, 69 as psalms that begin a new unit based on thematic, genre and poetic concerns.* Furthermore, Pss 51 and 72 are somewhat distinct from the entire Davidic Group. As a whole, the Davidic Group is best seen through the life of David in the Samuel-Kings narratives. This reinforces our proposals in chapter 1.

(2) *There is a concentric genre structure in the Davidic Group of Book II* comprised of (A) Petition, (B) Lament, (C) Petition-Confidence-Praise, (B′) Lament, and (A′) Petition. The use of Laments to frame a unit of centrally located psalms is a recurring structuring technique found in Book I, and more particularly, the Asaphite and Korahite Groups (cf. 3–14, 17–22). Again, this reinforces our analyses of the Prologue and Book I.

(3) *The most convincing basis of division, in my opinion, is the convergence of various superscriptions, poetic and thematic devices, and genre arguments in support of the proposed shape.* It is likely that the final editors of the Psalms had used specific terms in the superscriptions to differentiate groupings: לדוד (51, 61–64, 69–70), משכיל (52–55), מכתם (56–60), and שיר (Pss 65–68).

(4) *There is a period of weakness just before the end of the trajectory.* Goulder's argument that such a period described in Pss 69–71 before the end of the entire

---

63. Christensen, *Unity of the Bible*, 135.

64. Goulder, *Prayers of David*, 27.

65. He notes, "The Prayers were chanted liturgically in a procession one day in the autumn festival at Jerusalem" (Goulder, *Prayers of David*, 28).

narrative corresponds to Barbiero's "already-and-not-yet" proposal in Book I. This is an interesting and important phenomenon that will be explored subsequently.

A Proposal for the Macrostructure of Books II and III of The MT Psalter

Based on the major structuring techniques seen in Book I (the use of superscription, genre theme, three-part concentric structure, central motifs of kingship and Torah, thematic trajectory related to Zion, symbolic numbers [e.g., Pss 7, 10, 14], and interconnecting lexemes), along with the survey of Books II–III, a proposal for the macrostructure of Books II–III is given in Figure 17.[66]

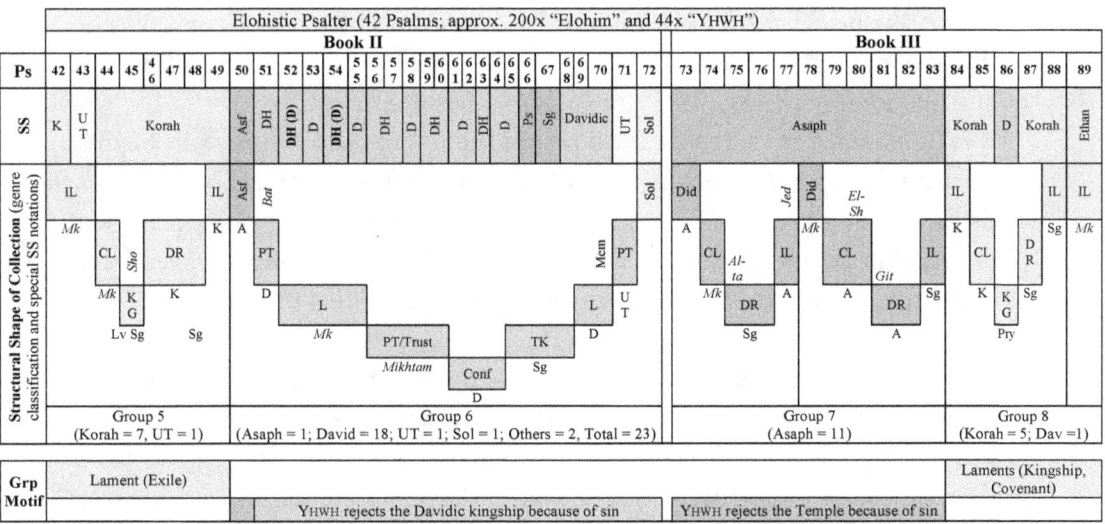

Figure 17: A Proposal for the Macrostructure of Books II–III

The following arguments are in order:

(1) *Carefully structured Superscriptions.* In the "Superscript" row of Figure 17, I have designated psalms according to their superscriptions. For instance, Pss 43 and 71 are often considered as part of the Korahite and Davidic Psalter respectively, but they are also psalms without superscription (hence, they are labeled "UT" or "Untitled"). It is also common to find Pss 71–72 grouped together, but by keeping them specific to their description (Ps 71= "UT," Ps 72 = "Sol"), the poetical structure of Book II is

---

66. Legend: SS: Superscription; Ps: A Psalm; UT: Untitled Psalm; IL: Individual Lament; CL: Communal Lament; DR: Divine Response; SAP: Sapiential Psalm; KG: Kingship Psalm; K: Psalm of Korah; DH: Psalm of David with historical superscription; D: Davidic Psalm; (D): Name "David" occurs in the historical superscription; PT: Petition Psalm; Conf: Confidence Psalm; A: Asaph Psalm; Sol: Solomonic Psalm; Mem: "a memorial" in the superscription; Pry: Prayer; Did: Didactic Psalm; TK: Thanksgiving psalm; Lv Sg: Love song; Sg: A Song; "*Sho*," "*Bat*," "*Jed*," "*El-Sh*," "*Al-ta*," "*Git*," "*Mk*": Musical/instrumental/genre notations in the superscription.

The Design of the Psalter

sharpened. The Davidic psalms in Book II (51–70, excluding 66–67) are framed by non-Davidic psalms (Pss 50, 71–72). Furthermore, the two UT psalms are skillfully arranged in the second, and second to last psalm of Book II (43, 71). From the design of the superscriptions, Book II contains three pairs of non-Davidic/Korahite psalms—two UT psalms (43, 70); two psalms with superscriptions attributed to someone other than David (50, 72); and two psalm superscriptions without name attribution within the Davidic Group (66, 67).

It is also interesting that the Davidic psalms in Book I (3–41) also contain exactly two untitled psalms (10, 33). The Davidic psalms in Books I and II are framed by two UT psalms (2, 71), or a pair of psalms where one is UT and the other, a Kingship psalm (1–2, 71–72). The "DH" in this row marks eight superscriptions with historical references to David's life (discussed further in chapter 4).[67]

The row below the Superscription illustrates the shape of various Collections (or Subgroups) within Books II–III. The subdivisions are coded and identified by its dominant motif/genre (e.g., "KG" for Ps 45 = Kingship psalm).[68]

(2) *Concentric arrangements and central motifs*. The last two rows in Figure 17 summarize the central motifs for each of the Groups. Like Book I, Books II–III can be divided into four major Groups (5–8). The last row captures the shape of the entire Section and its central idea. Because of their central motifs, Groups 5–8 can be seen as a chiasmus. Groups 6–7 underscore the fall of the Davidic king temple in Zion. In turn, they are framed by Groups 5 and 8.[69]

Although the Asaphite Group as a whole has a parallel rather than concentric structure (73–77 // 78–83), a concentric structure can be seen within the Subgroups of Pss 73–77; 78–83. At the center of these subgroups (75–76; 81–82), two pairs of psalms associated with Yhwh's kingship and deliverance are found. In other words, the structuring principles and shape of the Korahite and Asaphite psalms in Book II–III are remarkably similar. They are generally concentric and have a central focus on either the Davidic kingship or Yhwh's kingship. This phenomenon is consistent with our macrostructural study.

(3) *The fall of the Davidic kingship in Book II*. Goulder's postulation that the Davidic psalms in Book II trace David's life from the death of Uriah to the ascension of Solomon deserves further attention. Specifically, within the frames of Pss 51 and

---

67. The "DH(D)" in Pss 52 and 54 denotes a double occurrence of David's name in the superscription. The double occurrences in Pss 52, 54 supply two more references to "David" in the superscriptions, perhaps in replacement of Pss 66–67, making a total of 20 references to David in the superscriptions in Book II. Together with the Davidic reference in Ps 86, there is a total of 21 (7x3) references to David.

68. Certain words in the superscription that characterize a Subgroup is labeled above or below it (e.g., For Ps 45, the "*Sho*" above identifies the phrase, על־ששנים, and the "love song" below identifies the phrase, שיר ידידת, which are distinctive for this psalm. In the box, the label "KG" identifies this psalm with the genre of kingship).

69. Furthermore, Kingship and Divine Response psalms are centrally located in both the Korahite psalms (45, 46–48; 86, 87).

72, we see David's downfall and the wane of his kingship (cf. 2 Sam 12–1 Kgs 1). This imagery of ruin and decline associated with David's kingship is at the structural center of the Davidic Group in Book II. The superscription of Ps 59 describes David fleeing for his life. Even with the apparent victorious superscription of 60:1–2, the psalm proceeds with אלהים זנחתנו פרצתנו אנפת ("O God, you have rejected us, broken us and you were angry") in 60:3. The next verse brings this brokenness further to the cosmic level. The psalmist repeatedly highlights Yhwh's rejection with the rhetorical question, הלא־אתה אלהים זנחתנו ("have you not, O Lord, rejected us?") in 60:12 (cf. 43:2; 74:1; 77:8). Psalms 61–64 that follow continue the bleak depiction of David's life.[70]

A sense of rejection and brokenness pervade these psalms. David's life is hanging by the thread (54:5; 55:5–6; 56:3; 57:5; 59:4; 61:7). David is pictured as a suffering and broken king in need of God's help. The place of the postscript in 72:20, "the prayers of David, the son of Jesse, are ended," functions to underscore the message that the reign of the human king in the Davidic Psalter of Book II has come to an end and that hope no longer lies in David's kingship but in his posterity's. I argue that the presence of Davidic psalms beyond this postscript is not due to a gradual process of psalms amalgamation but by careful design (more discussions in chapter 4).

Crucially, this motif of the brokenness of Davidic kingship is remarkably expressed by the lexeme, "to reject" (זנח). I define this editorial technique as the Pan-Psalter Occurrence Scheme (POS), that is, the careful use and placement of certain word/phrases at strategic locations across the entire Psalter to make or reinforce a rhetorical point. In the case of זנח, this word is carefully chosen and located such that they speak of Yhwh's apparent rejection of the human king and earthly temple, specifically in Books II–III of the Psalter.[71]

All ten instances of זנח in the Psalter are found, fittingly and interestingly, only in Books II–III.[72] Their locations also mark the beginning and end of Books II and III respectively (43:2; 89:39).[73] About half of the instances of זנח are found in the Laments of the two Korahite Groups that frame Books II–III (43:2; 44:10, 24; 88:15; 89:39). They also mark the Laments in the Davidic Group of Book II and the Asaphite Group in Book III respectively (60:3, 12; 74:1; 77:8). They are precisely located where acute brokenness is portrayed. זנח occurs twice in Ps 60:3, 12 and twice in Pss 74:1 and 77:8, where Zion lies downfallen. All occurrences are found in literary contexts that highlight the pain of the exile (43, 44), David's kingship (60, 88) and Zion (74, 77). The presence of זנח in Ps 89 at the close of Book III consolidates this multiple "brokenness"

---

70. Cf. Pss 61:1–3; 62:1–4; 63:1–2; 64:1–3.

71. Hence, deClaissé-Walford's postulation that Book II depicts king Solomon's reign is not accurate. It is more accurately the fall of the Davidic kingship.

72. Cf. Pss 43:2; 44:10, 24; 60:3, 12; 74:1; 77:8; 88:15; 89:39; 108:12.* Note that Ps 108:12 is a reuse of Ps 60. Hence, we can say that all of זנח are found properly in Books II and III.

73. Creach, *Yahweh as Refuge*, 91.

under the perspective of the Davidic covenant (89:39–52).⁷⁴ In other words, the use of זנח in Books II–III is characteristics of the painful experiences of the exile, fallen kingship and temple, and understood as a whole, YHWH's apparent rejection of the Davidic covenant. We can trace the trajectory of this brokenness with the captivity, collapse of David's kingship and the Zion temple, culminating with the uncertainty surrounding the Davidic covenant by the end of Book III.

From this perspective, the postscript at 72:20, marking the end of David's prayer, and the sapiential Ps 73 that begins Book III would not be the "acclaimed" turning point of the entire Psalter as Brueggemann and others have argued.⁷⁵ Admittedly the psalmist's hope is reawakened at the temple (73:17). By virtue of its location (beginning Book III and somewhat in the middle of the Psalter), it suggests some sort of renewal.⁷⁶ Yet two contextual issues go against this interpretation. From the literary horizon of Book III, this hope that arises in the beginning, however, ends in ruin. The purported turning point of Ps 73 does not come to a sustained fruition by the end of the Book. Moreover, within the more immediate context, the hope awakened at the temple (73:17–28) is quickly quashed by descriptions of the destruction of the temple a few verses later (74:3–4). The destruction of the temple (79) and YHWH's people (80) effectively negate any sustained prospects of Ps 73.

How do we explain this element of turning in Ps 73? Perhaps it is a structural one. There is a motif of a similar turning at the beginning of the Davidic and Asaphite Groups (cf. 51, 73). Psalm 51 highlights the penitent inner posture of David after his sin with Bathsheba. While Nathan's rebuke rightly marks the beginning of David's downfall from a macro-perspective, David's responses to Nathan in 2 Sam 12 and the Davidized response in Ps 51 express an inward awakening and change of perspective. Through YHWH's cleansing, the Davidic king finds acceptance with God (51:9–15). This motif of inner awakening in Ps 51 finds its parallel in 73:17 where the psalmist's worldview is reversed, as he worships in the sanctuary.⁷⁷

Nonetheless, these mere glimpses of awakenings at the beginning of the second Davidic Collection and the Asaphite psalms, in the form of hope of a human king and Jerusalem sanctuary, will not materialize in Books II–III.⁷⁸ Bound by the two Kora-

---

74. See also Creach's treatment of the idea of being "cast off" in Creach, *Yahweh as Refuge*, 85–86.

75. Brueggemann and Miller, "Psalm 73 as a Canonical Marker"; "Psalms and the Life of Faith," 1–25.

76. Clayton, "Examination of Holy Space," 120.

77. Kartje argues that Pss 1; 73; 90; 107 develop an understanding of human suffering and flourishing vis-à-vis how one lives before God. See Kartje, *Wisdom Epistemology in the Psalter* (cf. Ho, "Review of John Kartje," 100–101).

78. Jones, likewise, notes, "The locus of change for the psalmist in Psalm 73 is the sanctuary of God, but what the exilic reader knows is confirmed in Psalm 74—the sanctuary has been destroyed. Psalm 74 elaborates on the confusion presented at the beginning of Psalm 73 by communicating the distress of the people in the face of the destruction of the sanctuary. The place where one went to be in the presence of God, the temple, has been destroyed, thus the psalmist must turn to another source to find comfort" (Jones, "Psalms of Asaph," 178).

hite Groups as inclusio, the twin motifs of the brokenness of the human king David (the Davidic Psalter) and the brokenness of the Zion-temple (the Asaphite psalms) form the core message and center of Books II–III. The lone Asaphite Ps 50, placed away from the main Asaphite Group,[79] serves to bind Pss 50–83, highlighting the twin focuses on brokenness.

In short, the occurrence of the lexeme זנח confirms and reinforces the proposed structural shape, highlighting the fall of the Davidic kingship and the temple at the centers of Books II and III. The POS of זנח corresponds and integrates well with the overall shape and Metanarrative. Since Yhwh's apparent rejection of the human monarch and the Zion-temple is apparently due to sin, the placement of Ps 51 at the beginning of the Davidic Psalter serves to highlight sin and disobedience as the precursor to brokenness and Yhwh's rejection.

This proposal is in line with Wilson's view that Book III ends with the apparent fall of the Davidic covenant and Books IV–V answer this problem. Nevertheless, Books I–III, as McCann also adds, have already begun to answer the problem with glimmers of hope.[80]

(4) *Hope at the center.* There is always an element of hope in the midst of apparent brokenness. This hope is often associated with the triumph of Yhwh and the messianic kingship. As noted, the superscription of Ps 60 is at odds with its content. The superscription alludes to David's victories in 2 Sam 8:1–14/1 Chr 18:1–13 but the psalm is more of a Lament and Petition.[81] Zenger offers a solution for this incongruity by noting that the presence of the term, ללמד (60:1), suggesting that the psalm could have been used as an instruction at a time of war.[82]

Similarly, even in the bleak outlook of the Korahite and Asaphite Groups, there are psalms that depict Divine Responses at the center (45, 75–76, 81–82). The presence of the lone Davidic Ps 86 is not haphazard. It is the only Davidic psalm in Book III and is carefully placed at the center of the second Korahite Group to highlight the central motif of the Davidic kingship.[83]

---

79. For links between Pss 49 and 50, see Attard, "Establishing Connections," 413–42.

80. Wilson, *EHP*, 209–15; McCann, "Books I–III," 95; "Shape and Shaping," 350–62.

81. Zenger notes that "on the whole, the situation described in the psalm's superscription does not appear to fit the corpus." See Hossfeld and Zenger, *Psalms 2*, 98.

82. He argues that the psalm could have recorded an earlier defeat (60:3–7), but 60:8–11 is a divine oracle emphasizing Yhwh's victory.

83. Koorevaar argues that Ps 86 is at the center of the entire Psalter that has 147 psalms (by combining Pss 9, 10; 114, 115; and 42, 43 based on textual variants). Furthermore, Ps 86 consists of "147" words. Koorevaar notes, "Psalm 86, as the center of the Psalter, contains 17 verses and 147 words. The number of 17 verses corresponds to 17 as the number of psalms in Book III, the central book in which it stands. The number of 147 words corresponds to 147 as the number of psalms in the entire Psalter. Coincidence seems improbable. It is more likely that the final editor arranged this deliberately. On the basis of Ps 86, he builds first a dome over Book III and then a superdome over the whole Psalter" (Koorevaar, "Psalter," 591).

The Design of the Psalter

This centering of the kingship motif is a repeated feature in the Psalter (cf. 1–2, 8–9, 18–21, 29–30). The triumphant superscript of 60:1–2 in the middle of the Davidic Group is likely an intended design, a case of adopting the same pattern in an otherwise bleak depiction of the Davidic king. Thus, despite the portrayal of David's fall in Book II, Yhwh's presence and promise of victory are not absent.[84]

(5) *Numerical symbolism.* Another important piece of evidence that unifies Books II and III structurally is the use of numerical devices in Psalms superscriptions. Psalms superscriptions are carefully chosen so that they add up to figures with symbolic value.

Books II–III have a total of 48 psalms (31+17, or 12x4 psalms respectively). On its own, Book II contains strictly 7 Korahite and 18 Davidic psalms; two UT psalms; one Asaphite; one Solomon psalm and two other psalms without authorship in the superscriptions. I have also classified Ps 89 as a Korahite superscription in connection with 88:1.[85] Book III contains 11 Asaphite psalms, one Davidic psalm and five Korahite psalms.

Within each Book, these numbers are not exactly significant or symbolic. However, when Books II and III are combined, we have a total of 19 Davidic psalms, 12 Korahite psalms and 12 Asaphite psalms, 2 untitled psalms, 2 titled non-authorship psalms and 1 psalm of Solomon. The following figure summarizes these numbers:

Superscription	Psalm	Subtotal	A	B	C
Asaphite	50, 73–83	12	24	24	44 (11x4)
Korahite	42, 44–49, 84–85, 87–89	12			
David	51–65, 68–70, 86	19	20	24	
Solomon	72	1			
Untitled (no clear superscript)	43, 71	2	4		4
Psalms without attributive named figures	66, 67	2		4	
	Total	48			

Figure 18: Superscription Tabulation in Books II–III

In Figure 18, column "A" shows the numbers for three different groups of superscription (Levites, kings, unnamed attribution). If we consider the Levites representing

---

84. The reuse of part of this psalm in Ps 108 functions to bring out a different emphasis (more discussion in chapter 4). Gundersen argues that even in Ps 89, the Davidic covenantal hope persists. This is seen in the repeated contrast between God's persistence in keeping the covenant and man's failure (cf. 89:29, 31, 32, 35, 36). Gundersen, "Davidic Hope," 83–84.

85. There is a possible association with "Ethan" of the Korahite in 1 Chr 6:17–32, 42. Hossfeld and Zenger, *Psalms 2*, 402, 407; deClaissé-Walford et al., *Book of Psalms*, 675.

Zion symbolically and the rest of the psalms representing the Davidic kingship/people of Israel, then column "B" shows that there is an equal number of psalms (24 =12x2) representing (the fall of) Zion and Davidic kingship in Books II–III. If we divide the superscriptions into psalms with and without attributed authorship (in column "C"), we have 44 (11x4) psalms with names in the superscriptions and 4 psalms without.

Scholars have identified the Elohistic Psalter (42–83) due to its prevalent use of "elohim" over "Yhwh."[86] The number of 42 psalms in the Elohistic Psalter is possibly associated with the "name(s) of god(s) and curses in ancient tradition.[87] Joffe argues that the motivation of such a redactional phenomenon brings together a "triangular relationship" between the number 42, the name(s) of god(s), and curses.[88]

The number 42 (and 72) is also associated with Yhwh in the Jewish and Talmudic traditions (*b. Qid.* 71a) and its use in Jewish amulets "for protective function, especially in childbirth," is attested.[89] Joffe argues that the symbolic number 42 in the Elohistic Psalter "was commissioned in order to ward off the curse of 42 [note that Ps 42 also begins the Elohistic Psalter], to turn it into a blessing."[90] If Joffe is right, then her analysis reinforces our point regarding the emphasis of the ominous demise of the human king and the Zion-temple in Books II–III.

Summary

Our analysis of Books II–III of the Psalter recalls the structuring techniques of Book I. The characteristics of the three-part structure, symmetry of collections, central motifs, symbolic number of superscriptions, lexeme occurrences scheme, and placement of seemingly odd psalms (e.g., untitled or lone psalms) are important in elucidating the macrostructural shapes of Books I–III of the Psalter. Furthermore, they follow the programmatic nature of the Prologue.

The crucial key that unravels much of the structural riddles is the surprising importance and value of superscriptions. While superscriptions are often considered secondary additions, with "no use as critical guides"[91] or omitted totally in translation,[92]

---

86. Goulder notes that "Book I shows an overwhelming preference for Yahweh over Elohim for God (272 times to 15), whereas the second Davidic collection prefers Elohim (122 times to 23)" (Goulder, *Prayers of David*, 11).

87. Joffe, "Answer to the Meaning of Life," 221.

88. Joffe notes, "42 is a number of disaster and ill-omen. 42,000 Ephraimites were slain for not being able to say 'shibboleth' in Judg 12.6. In 2 Kgs 10:14, 42 relatives of Ahaziah were killed by Jehu. . . . Rev. 11.2 gives the period of rampage to be 42 months (or put differently, 1260 days in Rev. 11.3; 12.6)" (Joffe, "Answer to the Meaning of Life," 228–29). Burnett offers additional evidence of the use of the number 42 in Ancient Egyptian texts and how "42" is used in Mesopotamian Tradition as a way of organizing texts. See Burnett, "Forty-Two Songs," 95–99.

89. Joffe, "Answer to the Meaning of Life," 229, 231.

90. Joffe, "Answer to the Meaning of Life," 231; Burnett, "Forty-Two Songs," 87.

91. Toy, "On the Asaph-Psalms," 73.

92. In the *New English Bible* (1970), superscriptions in the psalms are altogether omitted. This was

our analysis shows the reverse! They possess the macrostructural key to unveiling the Psalter's shape. Our analysis suggests that superscriptions are *unlikely* to function *merely* for historical or cultic purposes.[93] The symbolic value of numbers associated with a particular group of superscriptions should not be dismissed. Superscriptions (or the lack thereof) provide structural and interpretive value to the shape of the Psalms.[94]

At this point, we have determined that the Prologue is programmatic for Books I and II–III. We will now examine Books IV and V to see if they follow a similar program.

Macrostructural Analysis of Books IV–V

A number of recent studies have focused on the canonical order and function of various Collection or Subgroups in Books IV[95] and V.[96]

Macrostructural Analysis of Book IV

Figure 19 summarizes several major studies on Book IV (17 psalms in total).

---

because, "as G. R. Driver, Professor of Semitic Philology at the University of Oxford, and Joint Director of the project, explained in the preface, they contain musical instructions which are no longer intelligible, as well as 'historical notices' which are sometimes incorrect, and because they 'are almost certainly not original'" (Sawyer, "Psalms in Judaism and Christianity," 134).

93. Weiser, *Psalms*, 96–97.

94. Hence, I disagree with Charles and Emile Briggs who propose that superscriptions serve to organize groups of psalms but as a whole, do not have value in the interpretation of the texts of the Psalms. See Fraser's thesis for a good discussion on the antiquity, authenticity, issues with LXX and Syriac Peshitta on Psalms titles. Fraser, "Authenticity of the Psalms Titles"; Briggs and Briggs, *Critical and Exegetical Commentary*, 1:lviii.

95. Gundersen, "Davidic Hope"; Creach, "Shape of Book Four," 63–76; Howard, *Structure of Psalms*; "Contextual Reading," 108–23; Kim, "Strategic Arrangement of Royal Psalms," 143–57; Kim, "Structure and Coherence"; Ndoga, "Revisiting the Theocratic Agenda," 147–60; McKelvey, *Moses, David*.

96. Virtually all major Groups of Book V have been treated at length. For Pss 107–118, see Crutchfield, *Psalms in Their Context*; Moon, "Sapiential Reading of Psalms 107–118"; Davis, "Contextual Analysis"; For Ps 119: de Hoog, "Canonical Reading"; Soll, *Psalm 119*; Reynolds, *Torah as Teacher*; Zakovitch, "Interpretative Significance," 215–27; For Pss 120–134: Seybold, *Die Wallfahrtpsalmen*; Crow, *Songs of Ascent*; Keet, *Study of the Psalms*; Mitchell, *Songs of Ascents*; Grossberg, *Centripetal and Centrifugal Structures*; For Pss 135–137: Todd, "Poetic and Contextual Analysis"; Zakovitch, "On the Ordering of Psalms," 214–28; For Pss 138–145: Buysch, *Der letzte Davidpsalter*; For Pss 146–150: Cha, "Psalms 146–150"; Entire Book studies: Goulder, *Psalms of the Return*; Brennan, "Some Hidden Harmonies," 126–58; Snearly, "Return of the King"; Tucker, "Empires and Enemies," 723–32; *Constructing and Deconstructing Power*; Zenger, "Composition and Theology," 77–102; Studies involving Book IV and V as a unit: Ballhorn, *Zum Telos Des Psalters*; Leuenberger, *Konzeptionen des Königtums Gottes*. I am thankful to Martin Leuenberger for graciously providing me with a copy of his thesis.

Book IV	90	91	92	93	94	95	96	97	98	99	100	101	102	103	104	105	106
Zenger	90–92			93–100								101–103			104–106		
Vesco	90–92			93–100								101–106					
Auwers	90–92			93–100								101–106					
Koorevaar	90–92			93–100								101–106					
Christensen	90–96							97	98	99	100–106						
Labuschagne	90–100											101–106					
Robertson	90–91		92–100									101–103			104–106		
Gundersen	90–92			93–100								101–104*			104*–106		
Kim	90–100											101	102–106				
McKelvey	90–92			93–100								101–104				105–106	
Howard	90–94*					95–100						101–106					

Figure 19: Survey of Macrostructural Divisions of Book IV

There is a general consensus concerning Pss 90–92, 93–100, 101–106 as the main divisions of Book IV. Within these divisions, several differences can be observed. For instance, scholars identify Pss 101, 104 as Janus-psalms. They are related to the psalms that come before and after them. Christensen, Labuschagne and Robertson differ radically from the others because of their specific methodologies.

The unity of Pss 90–92 has been noted by Zenger, Vesco, Auwers, Gundersen, McKelvey and others.[97] There is a general acceptance that Pss 90–92 is grouped together by numerous lexical/thematic links with a thematic trajectory. Zenger argues that these three psalms develop a lament on "human subjection to death and the suffering of divine wrath" in Ps 90, followed by a "double assent and promise" in Ps 91, and culminate in thanksgiving in Ps 92.[98] Gundersen highlights verbal interconnections between Pss 90–92 and the Moses Song (Deut 32, 33),[99] adding a further layer of support to the binding of Pss 90–92.

Howard considers that Book IV to be structured around three major groups of psalms (90–94; 95–100; and 101–106).[100] He argues that Ps 94 is linked to 90–92 with its common wisdom vocabulary in several places, which is unique to only this group

---

97. See footnote 5 in Howard, "Psalm 94," 669; Zenger, "Das Weltenkönigtum," 151–78; Hossfeld and Zenger, *Psalms 2*, 420; Gillingham, "Zion Tradition," 326–28; Reindl, "Weisheitliche Bearbeitung," 350–54; Gundersen, "Davidic Hope," 91–145.

98. Hossfeld and Zenger, *Psalms 2*, 424, 442.

99. Gundersen, "Davidic Hope," 91–145. At the time of writing, Andrew Dvoracek, a fellow research student at the University of Gloucestershire currently studying the "rock" metaphor in the Song of Moses (Deut 32), has also pointed out this connection to me in a conversation.

100. See footnote 5 in Howard, "Psalm 94," 669.

of psalms.[101] Psalm 94 functions as a bridge connecting the earlier part of Book IV and the Yʜᴡʜ *Malak* psalms.[102] However, Howard admits that Ps 94 belongs to a group of 8 community psalms (93–100) that is framed by Pss 92 and 101.[103] His monograph, *The Structure of Psalms 93–100*, confirms the unity of these eight psalms.[104]

As with Howard, Kim regards Pss 95–100 as a unit.[105] He argues that Ps 101 stands alone between Pss 90–100 and 102–106 as it is loosely connected with either Pss 100 or 102.[106] For him, Ps 101, placed after the Yʜᴡʜ *Malak* psalms, has an important message: "The anticipation of Yahweh's coming as king can be correlated with the advent of a human king."[107]

Hossfeld and Zenger note that in the final redaction of the Psalter, the "Hallelujah acclamations" were added to Pss 104–106, such that the entire group (101–106) is divided into two triads of Pss 101–103 and 104–106.[108] Hossfeld also points out that the first triad (101–103) begins with a "royal prayer" (101) followed by descriptions of the king in distress (102) and ends with "praise and thanksgiving"[109] (103).

---

101. Howard, "Psalm 94," 671.

102. Howard, "Psalm 94," 668.

103. Howard, "Psalm 94," 674–75.

104. Auwers follows the grouping of Pss 93–100. However, he points out different opinions on the grouping of Yʜᴡʜ kingship psalms. He notes, "for L. Jacquet, it would include Pss 93, 96–100; for Cl. Westermann, it's 93, 95–99, 100; H.-J. Kraus includes Ps 93–99; É. Beaucamp extends it to Ps 92–100, and P. Auffret, to Pss 93–101. Howard considers Pss 93–100 form a structural unit. C. A. and E. G. Briggs had previously hypothesized that Pss 93, 96–100 have originally formed a single psaume" (Auwers, *La Composition*, 29, 31, 51).

105. Kim, "Structure and Coherence," 410–11.

106. He further argues that "the small units in the first section (90–91; 92–93 [94]; 95–100) are respectively paralleled to the psalms in the second section (102–3; 104 and 105–6), and Psalms 94 and 101 are seen as exceptional cases." For an illustration of his entire schematic of Book IV, see Kim, "Structure and Coherence," 413.

107. Kim, "Structure and Coherence," 414.

108. Hossfeld and Zenger, *Psalms 3*, 2.

109. Both Hossfeld and Gundersen view Ps 104 as a Janus psalm, connecting Pss 103 and 105. See Hossfeld and Zenger, *Psalms 3*, 28, 58, 75, 95; Gundersen, "Davidic Hope," 151.

Macrostructural Analysis of Book V

Author	Structure of Book V	Dominant Method	Key Thesis and Unique Contribution
Egbert Balhorn	105–107 | 108–10 | 111–118 | 119 | 120–134 | 135–136 |137 | 138–45 | 146–150	Canonical-literary, Teleological	When one moves from Book IV to the end of the Psalter, there are several major shifts such as (1) Temple to Zion; (2) David to YHWH's rule; (3) individual to collective Israel as the fulfillment of the covenant. The Psalter ends with an eschatological focus. The *telos* of the Psalter is the kingdom of God.
Nancy deClaissé-Walford	107 | 108–110 | 111–112 | 113–118 | 119 | 120–134 | 135–136 | 137 | 138–145 | 146–150	Canonical-literary, Historical	Book V forms part of the larger understanding of the metanarrative of the Psalter which traces the story of the reign of David (Book I), Solomon (Book II), the divided kingdom and their fall (Book III), the exile in Babylon (Book IV) and return to Jerusalem (Book V). The Psalter, as a whole, is a rationale for existence so that Israel can continue to survive under the rule of foreign nations.
Michael Goulder	107–119 | 120–134 | 135–150	Intertextual / Cultic-liturgical	Three major units of Book V represent the three "ascents" or return from Babylon as described in the Books of Ezra-Nehemiah. Psalms 107–118 celebrate the first return and restoration of the temple under Sheshbazzar, Zerubbabel and Jeshua; Psalms 120–134 celebrate the second return and represent 15 episodes of the Nehemiah Testimonies. Psalms 135–150 celebrate the third return under Ezra.
Jamie Grant	107 | 108-110 | 111–117 | 118–119 | 120-134 | 135–137 | 138–145 | 146–150	Canonical-literary / Intertextual	There are three groups of psalms where the motif of Torah and Kingship are juxtaposed (Pss 1–2; 18–21; 118–119). Influenced by the "Kingship Law" stipulated in Deuteronomy, the Psalter orients the reader to the "eschatological king" and fosters the reader's devotion to YHWH.
Jinkyu Kim	90–110 | 111–118 | 119 | 120–134 | 135–145 | 146–50	Canonical-literary	Books IV and V are structured as three parallel groups of psalms, each consisting of a sequence of Royal psalm(s) followed by doxological psalm(s). Books IV and V also have a chiastic structure with Ps 119 at the center. Together, Books IV–V serve to highlight the concept of kingship in the post-exilic period.
Martin Leuenberger	107 | 108–110 | 111–117 | 118 | 119, 120–134 | 135 | 136 | 137, 138–145 | 146–150	Literary / Redactional, Theological	The final form of the Psalter is shaped with the concept of the kingdom of God. Through an investigation of the redactional process, there is an expanding "theocratic" concept in Books IV–V in response to human kingship in Books I–III. The YHWH *Malak* Psalms bring the praise of God's reign to the forefront, reaching a high point in Ps 145 and climax in Ps 150.
Matthias Millard	107–118 | 120–137 | 138–150	Redactional, Form-critical	The entire Psalter is divided into 14 compositional arches. In Book V, there are three compositional arches (107–118; 120–137; 138–150). The Psalter as a book of instruction and prayers has a text-pragmatic function. It helps the individual to seek God, recall YHWH's past deliverances, hope in God, pray and praise him.

The Design of the Psalter

Author	Structure of Book V	Dominant Method	Key Thesis and Unique Contribution
David Mitchell	110 | 111–118 | 120–134	Intertextual/ Redactional/ Eschatological	The Psalter is shaped eschatologically rather than historically and follows an eschatological program found in Zech 9–14. The Psalms of Asaph highlight preexilic concerns of distress and war and emphasize pending judgment. The Songs of Ascents anticipate postexilic restoration with a joyful pilgrimage to Jerusalem and the hope of a messianic king.
Klaus Seybold	107 | 108–110 | 111–118 | 119 | 120–134 | 135–136 | 137 | 138–145 | 146–150	Redactional-historical/ Non-unifying	The formation of the Psalter drives its shape. The agenda of the Psalter is constantly being redefined at various stages of the formation. There is no single editorial agenda but several key themes (messianic, wisdom, hymnic).
Michael Snealy	107–118 | 119 | 120–137 | 138–145 | 146–150	Literary, Statistical (Computer-aided)	Book V signals a "renewed hope in the Royal/Davidic promises." Five keywords connect "dominant themes" in Book V with Pss 1–2 and 89. A variegated mix of text-linguistics, poetics literary theories; computer-assisted analysis and statistical criterion for keyword searches techniques are used. The criteria for keyword study limits roots that have "at least 50 percent of [its] usage within Book V and/or 20 percent of [its] usage within the Psalter."
Dennis Tucker	107 | 108–110 | 111–118 | 119 | 120–134 | 135–136 | 137 | 138–145 | 146–150	Socio-historical, Literary	The Psalter is set in the context of Persian imperial ideologies. Book V seeks to deconstruct these imperial ideologies with a negative critique of them. At the same time, Book V constructs the power ideologies of YHWH primarily through three major concepts: Zion, YHWH's creation and YHWH's kingship.
Gerald Wilson	107–17 | 118–35 | 136–45	Literary	The first three Books trace the establishment (Ps 2), celebration of YHWH's faithfulness to His covenant (Ps 72), and its eventual failure because of Israel's sin (Ps 89:38–39, 44). Book IV answers the pessimism at the end of Book III and focuses on the kingship of YHWH. Book V shows that David is the model exemplar who reflects trust in YHWH. Book V is based on the *hodu*-opening and *hallelujah*-ending structure. At the center is Psalm 119 which emphasizes the Torah and shows that access to God (Pss 120–34) is through Torah-piety.
Erich Zenger	107, 108–110 | 111–112, 113–118 | 119 | 120–136, 137 | 138–144, 145 | 146–150	Literary / theological-liturgical	Book V is unified in three ways: First, it consists of a liturgical shaping of the three feasts which are to be read as post-cultic, literary pilgrimages. Second, Book V is also a "meditative actualization of the canonical history" of Israel's origins, nationhood and exodus (113–118); Sinai and the giving of the law (119) and entry into the Promised land (120–136). Third, Book V is to be read eschatologically with messianic and cosmic themes (110, 144, 146–150).

Figure 20: Structural Divisions, Methods and Arguments for Book V[110]

110. There is considerable literature pertaining to Book V and almost every Group or Collection within Book V has been treated at length. In the figure below, I summarize thirteen structures,

Book V is perhaps the most difficult to analyze not only because it is the longest Book with the most variegated superscription types, but also due to the different methods adopted by scholars.[111] Scholars also posit a number of different theological themes in Book V.[112]

---

methods and main arguments on Book V. **Ballhorn's** work includes both Book IV and V of the Psalter. My summary pertains primarily to his discussion on Book V of the Psalter. See *Zum Telos Des Psalters: Der Textzusammenhang Des Vierten Und Fünften Psalmenbuches* (Ps 90-150); "Das Historische Und Das Kanonische Paradigma in Der Exegese," in *Der Bibelkanon in Der Bibelauslegung: Methodenreflexionen Und Beispielexegesen* (eds. Egbert Ballhorn and Georg Steins; Stuttgart: Kohlhammer, 2007), 9–30; In addition to the references of **deClaissé-Walford** works that are cited in chapter 1, see "The Structure of Psalms 93-100," RevExp 95, no. 2 (1998): 290–91; "Anzu Revisited : The Scribal Shaping of the Hebrew Psalter," WW 15, no. 3 (1995): 358–66; **Goulder**, *The Psalms of the Return (Book V, Psalms 107-150)*; "The Songs of Ascents and Nehemiah," 43–58; **Grant**, *The King as Exemplar: The Function of Deuteronomy's Kingship Law in the Shaping of the Book of Psalms*; **Kim**, "The Strategic Arrangement of Royal Psalms in Books IV–V," 143–57; **Leuenberger**, *Konzeptionen des Königtums Gottes im Psalter: Untersuchungen zu Komposition und Redaktion der theokratischen Bücher IV–V im Psalter*; **Millard**, *Die Komposition Des Psalters: Ein Formgeschichtlicher Ansatz*; **Mitchell**, *The Message of the Psalter an Eschatological Programme in the Books of Psalms*; *The Songs of Ascents: Psalms 120 to 134 in the Worship of Jerusalem's Temples*; **Seybold**, *Die Psalmen*; *Introducing the Psalms*; "Zur Geschichte Des Vierten Davidpsalters (Pss 138-145)," 368–90; **Snearly**, "The Return of the King: An Editorial-Critical Analysis of Psalms 107-150," now published as *The Return of the King: Messianic Expectation in Book V of the Psalter*. His thesis is also summarized in a book chapter: "The Return of the King: Book V as a Witness to Messianic Hope in the Psalter," 209–17; **Tucker**, "A Polysemiotic Approach to the Poor in the Psalms," 425–39; "Empires and Enemies in Book V of the Psalter," 723–32; *Constructing and Deconstructing Power in Psalms 107-150*; "The Role of the Foe in Book 5: Reflections on the Final Composition of the Psalter," 147–60; **Wilson**, "Shaping the Psalter: A Consideration of Editorial Linkage in the Book of Psalms," 72–82; "Understanding the Purposeful Arrangement of Psalms in the Psalter: Pitfalls and Promise," 42–51; *EHP*; "The Use of Royal Psalms at the 'Seams' of the Hebrew Psalter," 85–94; "The Shape of the Book of Psalms," 129–42; **Zenger**, "The Composition of the Book of Psalms: Neue Wege Der Psalmenforschung: Der Psalter Als Buch: Colloquium Biblicum Lovaniense LVII (2008)," 625–35; "Psalmenexegesis Und Psalterexegese: Eine Forschungsskizze," 17–65; "Der Psalter Als Wegweiser Und Wegbegleiter: Ps 1-2 Als Proömium Des Psalmenbuchs," **Hossfeld et al.**, *Psalms 3: a commentary on Psalms 101-150*, Hermeneia; *Psalms 2: A Commentary on Psalms 51-100*; **Hossfeld and Zenger**, *Psalmen*; "Der Psalter als Buch," 1–58; 29–47; "Der Zion als Ort der Gottesnähe. Beobachtungen zum Weltbild des Wallfahrtspsalters Ps 120-134," "Das Buch der Psalmen"; "Was Wird Anders Bei Kanonischer Psalmenauslegung," 397–413.

111. For instance, Tucker uses both socio-historical and literary methods in his analysis while Ballhorn adopts a synchronic approach. Seybold and Leuenberger understand the Psalter primarily through a redactional process.

112. (1) Wisdom and Torah-piety; (2) Vindication of the poor and needy from their wicked oppressors; (3) Davidic (messianic)-Yʜᴡʜ kingship and judgment; (4) Collective Israel in praise of Yʜᴡʜ; (5) Festal pilgrimage; (6) Restoration of temple and Zion. Crutchfield surveyed eight important works written on the arrangement and editorial agenda of the Psalter (J. Brennan, B. S. Childs, G. H. Wilson, J. Walton, W. Brueggemann, G. T. Sheppard, J. Creach, and D. Mitchell), and concludes that "the search for a single agenda is a misguided search because there is not one dominant, driving agenda, but rather, a collection of themes." He posits three major dominant themes running through the entire Psalter: wisdom, eschatology, and a trajectory from Lament to Praise (Crutchfield, "Redactional Agenda," 43–44, 47). Gillingham further reduced the themes to two such that the Psalter is shaped primarily through an "eschatological" or "didactic" significance. Scholars who emphasized the former point out that despite a "failed national covenant with king David, . . . a new world order would be established where God himself would be acknowledged as king," Scholars who emphasized

The Design of the Psalter

Structural divisions in Book V are argued primarily through a combination of superscriptions, formulaic phrases (e.g., *hodu/hallelujah*) and thematic motifs. Basic structural recognition is first given to the Davidic psalms (108–110; 138–145), the Song of Ascents (120–134) and the final Hallel (146–150). They are generally accepted as units of composition. However, main structural disagreements are associated with Pss 107; 118; 119; and 135–137.

Barring this diversity, the structures of Book V can be summarized by two major divisional structures presented by Zenger and Wilson. The key lies in how Pss 118 and 136 are viewed (as the start of a new unit or the end), which also affects how immediate psalms (119; 135; 137) are grouped.

In Wilson's case, the use of doxological phrases concludes major divisions (104–106; 111–117; 135) and the use of הודו phrases starts a new unit of psalms.[113]

107–117			118–35				136–45		
107	108–110	111–117	118	119	120–34	135	136–137	138–145	146–150
הדו	Dav	הללו יה	הודו	Trh	SOA	הללו יה	הודו	Dav	הללו יה
107:42–43			Wisdom Frame				145:19–20		

Figure 21: Wilson's Structure for Book V[114]

Enclosed by two "wisdom frames" (107:42–43, 145:19–20), Book V consists of three major units, each opened by a הודו and closed by a הללו-יה. The first and third units are centered by a Davidic frame. The second unit consists of the massive Ps 119 which emphasizes access to God at Zion (SOA) "through the appropriation of and obedience to Torah."[115] The two Davidic segments at the beginning and end of Book V show that David is the model exemplar who reflected this trust in Yhwh.

However, the הודו and the הללו-יה phrases are not consistently applied as openings or closings as Wilson would like.[116] Wilson's focus on the הודו-הללו-יה method

---

the latter highlight the "personal needs of individuals within the community," and that the Psalter was composed primarily as a reflective book with wisdom and Torah concerns (Gillingham, "Zion Tradition," 308–9).

113. Wilson, *EHP*, 190.

114. This has been reconstructed by Zenger, "Composition," 83.

115. Note that in 11QPs^a, Psalm 119 comes after the Songs of Ascents. Wilson notes that "the placement of this psalm after the [Songs of Ascents] psalms, rather than before them as in the canonical psalter, has a significant effect. Rather than Torah precipitating pilgrimage to Jerusalem and the temple, pilgrimage, in effect, leads to the Torah." Wilson, "Qumran Psalms Scroll," 460; Wilson, *EHP*, 223.

116. Psalms 105, 106, 107 all begin with הודו phrases. Based on his arguments, Psalm 105 begins a new unit with the use of הודו and Ps 106 ends it (with a הללו-יה) and therefore, Ps 107 can be said to begin a new unit. Moving backward from Ps 105, we observe a concluding הללו-יה in Ps 104 but we

of delimitation also led him to undervalue other lexical or thematic evidence.[117] His structural thesis, nonetheless, remains appealing to some (e.g., Leuenberger).[118]

Zenger's structural view on Book V is reproduced in Figure 22.[119]

R A		A		R A
107, 108–110, 111 and 112	113–118	119	120–136, 137	138–144, 145
David (eschatological/ messianic)	Exodus (Pesach)	Torah (Shabuoth)	Zion (Sukkoth)	David (eschatological /messianic)

Figure 22: Zenger's Structure of Book V[120]

Contra Wilson, Zenger separates Pss 111–112 from 113[121] and links Ps 118 with 117. Psalm 113 is also grouped within 113–118 based on the "Pesach-Hallel" tradition (or Egyptian Hallel). This unit develops a "theology of the Exodus with Ps 118, focusing on the sanctuary on Zion as goal of the Exodus."[122] For Zenger, Ps 118 ends a literary unit.

---

cannot find an opening הודו. Wilson collaborated his arguments of הודו-opening and הללו-יה-closing with a similar phenomenon in 11QPsª, but the difficulty of fitting the הודו-הללו-יה is also present. Wilson posited five groups of psalms separated by the hwdw/hllwyh phrases. As an example, one of the segments is structured as such: Group 1: Psalms 101, 102, 103; Group 2: Psalms 109, 118 (hd/hd), 104 (/hl); Group 3: Psalms 147 (hl/hl), 105 (hd/hl), 146 (hl/hl); Conclusion of the segment: Psalm 148 (hl/hl). From this structure, Group 1 has no opening or closing hwdw/hllwyh phrases. Psalms 105 and 118 (which have the hwdw opening) are in the middle of the groups and not at the front. While there is a hllwyh that closes the entire segment (Ps 148), it is not opened by a hwdw psalm (Ps 101). Hence, prescribing a consistent hwdw-hllwyh structure (both in the MT and Qumran Psalter) is difficult. Wilson, "Qumran Psalms Scroll," 458–59.

117. For example, the three-part repetitions, "Israel," "house of Aaron" and "one who fears the LORD," in Pss 115:9–11; 118:2–4 and 135:19–20 are to be seen in connection with one another. Wilson linked Ps 118 with 135 because these phrases and the *hwdw* fit well as frames of the entire section from Pss 118–35. However, he ignored the connections to these phrases in Ps 115. If the connections with Ps 115 had been adduced, Pss 115 and 118 can also be seen to unite the Egyptian Hallel (most scholars break between Pss 118 and 119 instead, but this would mean that the *hwdw* psalm 118 closes a group, which would break down Wilson's structure).

118. Leuenberger, *Konzeptionen des Königtums Gottes*, 276, 299.

119. In analyzing the composition of Book Five, Zenger first reviewed the theses of Gerald Wilson, Klaus Koch and Reinhard Kratz. He disagreed with Wilson and Kratz's separation of Psalms 117 and 118, and assessed that the sub-collections of psalms have not been sufficiently examined. Zenger also saw that these scholars were not able to explain Psalm 119's position in their structuring of Book Five. Zenger, "Composition," 87–88.

120. "R" = Royal psalm; "A" = Acrostic psalm; Zenger, "Composition," 98.

121. This is despite being linked by the *hallelujah* superscriptions. Hossfeld and Zenger, *Psalms 3*, 178.

122. Within Pss 113–118 (or the Egyptian Hallel), Hossfeld and Zenger further divided it into two smaller groupings of Pss 113–115 and 116–118, which is accented "theologically or monotheistically" and "universalistically [sic] (anthropologically)" respectively. Zenger, "Composition," 92; Hossfeld and Zenger, *Psalms 3*, 178, 210, 220, 224.

The Design of the Psalter

Standing between "two liturgically inspired collections [Pss] 113–118 and 120–136,"[123] Ps 119 represents the Jewish festival of Shabuoth (Feast of Weeks) which commemorates the giving of the Torah at Sinai. Together, these three festive-collections trace the canonical history with the Exodus (Pesach), the giving of the Torah at Sinai (Shabuoth) and entry into Zion (Sukkot). The acrostic Psalm 119 reflects the Torah-pious attitudes that enabled one to enter the gates of righteousness into Zion.[124]

Zenger's structure of Book V is symmetric. Groups and Collections within Book V are arranged as triads based on genre or thematic motifs. The Davidic Pss 108–110 are a triptych distinguished by their superscriptions and genre sequence of Plea-Lament-Divine Response.[125] Likewise, Pss 111–119 are also seen as a triptych. The acrostic Torah wisdom Pss 111–112 and 119 frame the Egyptian Hallel (113–118) in a three-part structure.[126] The Egyptian Hallel at the center can be further divided into two parts with a theocentric and universal focus respectively (113–115, 116–118). The following summarises Hossfeld and Zenger's structure of Pss 107–119.

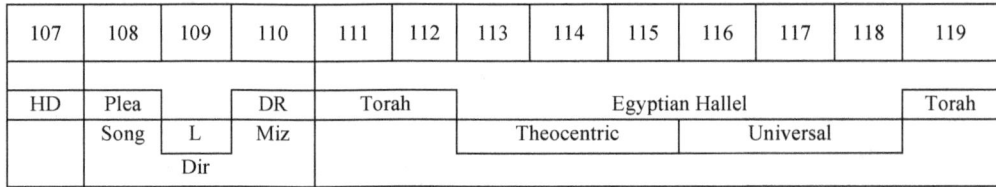

Figure 23: Hossfeld and Zenger's Structure of Pss 107–119[127]

The SOA[128] have been well-studied and are generally accepted as a unified group with a symmetrical structure. Certain linguistic peculiarities, such as the use of words with

---

123. Zenger, "Composition," 97.

124. They provide a "meditative actualization of the canonical history of the origin of Israel." Zenger, "Composition," 101; See also Hossfeld et al., *Psalms 3*, 4, 284.

125. While they all have לדוד in their superscriptions, each is distinguished by certain words or arrangement. Psalm 108 is characterized differently by the שיר ("song") in the superscription and 109, by למנצח ("for the choir director"). As such, these three psalms can be seen as a triptych based on their superscriptions.

126. Hossfeld et al., *Psalms 3*, 284.

127. HD = הודו Psalm; L = Lament; DR = Divine Response; Dir = למנצח; Miz = מזמור.

128. Grossberg lists at least seven ways through which the superscription שיר המעלות has been variously interpreted: (1) It is associated with the term, המעלה, in Ezra 7:9, describing the return from the exile. The plural use of the term in Pss 120–134 is supported by multiple returns from Babylon to Jerusalem. (2) This term is also interpreted as a pilgrimage to Jerusalem, but not associated with the exile. The pilgrimages to Jerusalem are made during the three festivals of the year (Exod 23:17; 34:18–23; Deut 16:16). (3) In the Mishnah, the 15 psalms were associated with a Levitical procession on the 15 steps leading from the Court of the Women to the Court of the Israelites on the first day of *Sukkot* (Exod 20:26; 1 Kgs 10:19–20; m. *Mid*. 2:5; *Sukk*. 5:4). (4) As a literary poetical structure in which a word or phrase from a clause is repeated and elaborated in the following (Pss 121; 122:2–4; 123:2–4; 124:1–5; 125:2, 3; 126:2, 3; 129:1, 2). (5) An ascending of voices of praise based on 2 Chr 20:19 where the Levites praised Yhwh with "greatly raised voices." (6) A plurality of ascending up

high frequency relative to the rest of the Psalter, bind the entire SOA.[129] In Figure 24, a survey of structural divisions in the SOA is represented.

Zenger	120–124		125–129		130–134	
Vesco	120–124		125–129		130–134	
Gillingham	120–122	123–125	126–128	129–131	132–134	
Van der Lugt	120–122	123–125	126–128	129–131	132–133/4	
Prinsloo	120–122	123–125	126–128	129–131	132–134	
Satterthwaite	120–122	123–125	126–128	129–131	132–134	
Beaucamp	120–122	123–128			129–134	
Auwers	120–122	123–126	127–129	130–131	132	133–134
Viviers	120–122	123–126	127–129	130–131	132–134	
Hengstenberg	120–126		127		128–134	
Labuschagne	120–126		127		128–134	

Figure 24: Survey of Structural Divisions of the Songs of Ascents[130]

Most scholars identify a three/five-part (3-3-3-3-3/5-5-5/7-1-7) symmetric structure in the SOA. Located at the center of the symmetry is Ps 127 which focuses on the Zion city. This symmetry is extended to Subgroups within the SOA too. Zenger argued for a three-part symmetric structure in all three Subgroups of five psalms (120–24, 125–29, 130–34). The concern at the center in all three Subgroups is Zion ("Z"; 122, 127, 132). The first and last psalm in the first Subgroup are Lament and Praise ("L," "P"; 120, 124). This phenomenon is repeated in the third subgroup ("L," "P"; 130, 134). The first and last psalm in the second Subgroup have a common focus on the wicked ("W"; 125, 129). The entire SOA is a remarkable triptych-within-a-triptych, with a movement from Lament to Praise. For Zenger, it is a "search for a place of safety and protection in the midst of a hostile world ... [and finding] its fulfilment in the cultic house and life community on Zion."[131]

---

and out of distresses repeatedly by Yhwh's salvific deliverances rather than the return from exile. (7) Rising into "higher walks of faith" or growing in spirituality. (8) The 15 Songs of Ascents is linked to the 15-word Aaronic Blessing in Num 6:24–26. The use of four keywords, "may he bless you" (יברכך), "may he protect you" (וישמרך), "may he be gracious to you" (ויחנך), "peace" (שלום), in the Aaron Benediction is repeatedly seen in the Songs of Ascents. Grossberg sees that the most commonly accepted interpretation is that of pilgrimage to Jerusalem during the three yearly festivals. For the study of the Songs of Ascents as a collection, see Grossberg, *Centripetal and Centrifugal Structures*, 15–54.

129. For instance, Grossberg cites הנה (Pss 121:4; 123:2; 127:3; 128:4; 132:6; 133:1; 134:1) and the preference of the abbreviated relative particle, ש (Pss 122:3–4; 123:2; 124:1–2, 6; 129:6–7; 133:2–3), over אשר (Pss 127:5; 132:2). See Grossberg, *Centripetal and Centrifugal Structures*, 49.

130. Hossfeld et al., *Psalms 3*, 296; Vesco, *Le psautier de David*, 2:1251–52; Van der Lugt, *CAS III*, 422–40; Viviers, "Coherence of the Ma'alôt Psalms," 284–87; Labuschagne, "Significant Sub-Groups," 633; Satterthwaite, "Zion in the Songs," 105–28; Beaucamp, "L'unité du recueil des montées," 13–15; Prinsloo, "Role of Space," 457–77; Auwers, *La Composition*, 58; Gillingham, "Zion Tradition," 318; One of the latest studies on the SOA is Mitchell, *Songs of Ascents*.

131. Zenger, "Composition," 99; See also Millard, *Die Komposition*, 30–32, 35–41, 227–28; Hossfeld and Zenger, *Psalms 3*, 296.

The Design of the Psalter

		120	121	122	123	124	125	126	127	128	129	130	131	132	133	134
	Organizing Principles			D		D			Sol				D	D		
Zenger	Thematic Genre	L		Z		P	W		Z		W		L	Z		P
Hengstenberg	Thematic Numerical	12x "YHWH" 1x "YH"			12x "YHWH"				3x "YHWH"	12x "YHWH" 1x "YH"			12x "YHWH"			
Prinsloo	Thematic Spatial	To earthly Zion			Heaven, Hell, YHWH				Zion built by YHWH	Heaven, Hell, YHWH			Eschatological Zion			
Satterthwaite	Thematic Lexical	Journey to Zion			Hostility to Zion				Restoration of Zion	Waiting for YHWH			The Found Vision and the Future			

Figure 25: Symmetric Structures of the Songs of Ascents[132]

The symmetry of the SOA can also be seen in the four attributions to David ("D"; 122, 124, 131, 133) with two on each side of Ps 127. Labuschagne, Hengstenberg and Mitchell also arrive at a three-part structure (7-1-7) based on numerical methods. Hengstenberg's structure deserves further attention.[133] He observed that the centrally-placed Ps 127 is bound by two groups of seven psalms, each of which can be further separated into two groups of psalms (Figure 25). In each of these groups, there are 12x "YHWH," each making 24x "YHWH" on each side of Ps 127. There is a total of 48x "YHWH" and 2x "YH" around Ps 127, which itself, consists of three references to "YHWH." Mitchell's finds that there are 26x "YHWH" (10+5+6+5) between the two "YH" (10+5) in Pss 122:4 and 130:3. There are also 26x "YHWH" before the word, ידידו ("his beloved," 127:2), which is the central word in Ps 127.[134] These findings show that the entire SOA is a remarkable triptych shaped by numerical design.

The symmetric shape of the SOA is not limited to genre and poetical characterization. Scholars such as Prinsloo and Satterthwaite have argued for thematic spatial movement *toward* and *away* from Zion based on five triads of psalms (recall this feature in Barbiero's work earlier).[135] The imagery of Zion, as YHWH's dwelling place, is

---

132. L = Lament psalm; P = Praise psalm; Z = Zion psalm; D = "David" in superscription; Sol = "Solomon" in superscription.

133. Joffe, "Answer to the Meaning of Life," 227; Hengstenberg, *Commentary on the Psalms*, 3:410. Mitchell argues that the "YH," located in Pss 122 and 130, is "the third psalm of each heptade" (hence seeing the structure as 7-1-7). See Mitchell, *Songs of Ascents*, 17.

134. Omitting the superscription, Mitchell counts a total 57 words in the Ps 127 with 28 words before and after ידידו (the 29th word). Mitchell's method of count is similar to Labuschagne and van der Lugt's (see chapter 5). Mitchell, *Songs of Ascents*, 22.

135. Pss 120–22, 123–25, 126–28, 129–31, 132–34. Prinsloo, "Role of Space," 457–77. Satterthwaite, "Zion," 105–28.

seen as the place of intersection between God and man, heaven and earth.[136] For Prinsloo, the beginning of the SOA shows a pilgrimage to the earthly temple in Jerusalem. The movement is further seen as a "spiritual pilgrimage" from hell to heaven, and ascending into the embrace of Yhwh.[137] Satterthwaite suggests there is a future eschatological vision associated with Zion at the end of the Songs of Ascents.

Figure 25 shows how the SOA, as a unit, is concentric with various structuring techniques of genre characterization, thematic development, and poetic, spatial devices (numerical) corresponding to its symmetric structure.

Between the SOA and the final Davidic Collection lie three psalms that often resist clear groupings. While Wilson begins a new segment with Ps 136, Zenger notes that Pss 135–36 are thematically concatenated to Ps 134.[138] This is followed by Ps 137, described as a "theological commentary" of 120–136.[139]

The Davidic psalms (138–145) are framed on both ends. The frames (138, 145) are Praise psalms containing the theme of "glory" and "greatness." Hossfeld argues that this group of eight Davidic psalms is concentric based on genre categories. At the center are four Individual Laments (140–143). Although the two remaining Pss 139 and 144 are harder to define by genre designation, they fit well thematically between the frames and with the Laments at the center.[140] Hossfeld argues that the "concept of the fifth Davidic Psalter can be perceived from the concluding function of Psalm 145," that Yhwh is king.[141] The concluding doxology (v. 21) of this psalm also functions as the closing psalm of the five-part "Torah of David."[142]

The last five psalms in the MT Psalter (146–150) are known as the "Little" or "Final Hallel," united by the imperative plural form of הלל. As headings and codas, they occur 10x in total, representing the "totality and the perfection of the praise of God."[143] There is also a progressive expansion of subjects in this Collection, beginning

---

136. He notes, "In a very special sense temple in Jerusalem becomes the meeting point between the human (concrete) world and the divine (mythological) world. Jerusalem becomes the centre of the universe. There the cosmic planes intersect to create a three-story universe: a vertical plane intersects earth and extends down into the chaotic waters below, and the same plane extends upwards into heaven" (Prinsloo, "Role of Space," 461).

137. Prinsloo, "Role of Space," 473.

138. Hence, it is possible that the twin Pss 135–36 (instead of just Ps 136) is referred to as the "Great Hallel" in Jewish tradition (b. Pesaḥ. 118a). See Hossfeld and Zenger, Psalms 3, 491.

139. Zenger, "Composition," 96; Psalm 137 also functions as a "transitional psalm," bridging 135–36 and 135–45, and serving as the "Sitz im Leben" for the compositions of 120–134; 135–136. See Hossfeld and Zenger, Psalms 3, 520–21.

140. Hossfeld and Zenger, Psalms 3, 524.

141. Hossfeld and Zenger, Psalms 3, 524.

142. Doxology also concludes the first four Books in Pss 41:14; 72:18–19; 89:53; 106:48.

143. Note also that in the final Psalm 150, "Hallelujah" is used 10x within the psalm itself. Zenger views Pss 146–150 as a separate editorial work. See esp. the "excursus" section on "The Function of 'Hallelujahs' in the redaction of the Psalter," and "The Composition of the So-called Little Hallel or Concluding Hallel, Psalms 146–150." Hossfeld and Zenger, Psalms 3, 7, 39–41, 605–7.

with an individual "I" (146) and ending with "all who has breath" (150) praising God.[144] Zenger argues that these five psalms "not only constitute a linear-progressive context, but at the same time, they are structured concentrically with Psalm 148 at the center."[145] Psalm 148 highlights a "cosmic order" and evokes the "special position" of Israel within that order. Psalms 147 and 149 address issues of justice and the violence of the wicked. As frames, Pss 146 and 150 celebrate Yʜᴡʜ's universal kingship. Zenger concludes that the Final Hallel projects an "eschatological vision whose realization is already in progress and whose completion is proleptically celebrated in a cosmic liturgy."[146] Figure 26 captures our discussion of Pss 135–150 above:

135	136	137	138	139	140	141	142	143	144	145	146	147	148	149	150
Great Hallel		Trans				Final Davidic Collection							Final Hallel		
Great Hallel		Trans	K							K	I	W		W	Uni
				Med		I-Laments			P			Isr		Chas	
			PoD	Dir	Dir	PoD	Msk	PoD	PoD	P			Cos + Chas		

Figure 26: Hossfeld and Zenger's Structure for Pss 135–150[147]

As noted, Hossfeld and Zenger have argued for an organizational structure of Book V that deviates from Wilson's *hodu-hallelujah* structure. Both structures have their merits. Hossfeld and Zenger's arguments are more convincing with considerations given to thematic, genre connections and development. There is a coherent macrostructural theme to the shaping of Pss 107–136 (as a celebration of Israel's restoration) and Pss 138–145 (as the last Davidic-Psalter). On the other hand, Wilson's emphasis on the combined הודו and הללו-יה phenomena cannot be dismissed. Despite these differences, Book V is *still* seen as concentric by both. At the center of Wilson's concentric structure is both the Torah Ps 119 and the SOA. At the center of Hossfeld-Zenger's structure is the Torah Ps 119.

---

144. In Ps 147, this is expanded to a group of subjects in Jerusalem and to Israel as a whole. In Ps 148, the entire cosmos is called to praise God, and the psalm ends with a group of *chasidim*, sons of Israel, in the praise of God. In Ps 149, Israel is called to praise God but through her praise, the entire cosmos will be transformed in praise of God.

145. Hossfeld and Zenger, *Psalms 3*, 605.

146. Hossfeld and Zenger, *Psalms 3*, 605.

147. Trans = Transitional psalm; K = Kingship psalm; Med = Meditative psalm; Isr = the people of Israel or Jerusalem; P = Praise psalm; Chas = the special role of faithful Israel within the cosmic subjects; Cos+Isr = Cosmic subjects and *chasidim*; I = Individual psalm; W = psalm with an emphasis on the wicked and justice. Uni = Universal subjects, all that has breath; PoD = לדוד; Dir = למנצח; Msk = משכיל.

One of the key reasons for these differences is the overarching delimitation principle that Wilson and Zenger/Hossfeld had chosen for Pss 118–37. Another reason is the place of the הודו and הללו-יה formula and how they function as a poetical device to mark a collection. In the following section, I offer my proposal for Books IV and V of the MT Psalter.

A Proposal for the Macrostructure of Books IV–V of the MT Psalter

Ballhorn and Leuenberger have shown that Book IV is closely related to Book V and that these should not be viewed in isolation from each other.[148] My proposal is that the structural mystery of Book V is revealed when it is viewed together with Book IV (like Books II and III). I further posit that Pss 104–106 at the end of Book IV serves not just as the final Collection in that Book, but also functions as a Janus ("two-faced") unit. Its thematic trajectory straddles across the end of Book IV into the beginning of Book V. Together with Pss 107–119, the entirety of Pss 104–119 functions structurally as the second Group in Books IV–V with three Groups formed by 104–119; 120–134; and 135–150 respectively. Books IV and V, in total, consist of four Groups (9–12) and can be seen as symmetric.

Figure 27 and Figure 28 set out my proposal for the structure of Books IV and V:

---

148. Ballhorn notes that "if you follow the sequence of psalms and their collections, a transformation within the Psalter is visible. The corpus of the first three books is recognized primarily as a school of prayer. From the first psalm, it is a Torah-meditation book, and the royal psalms that recur in the book (Ps 72; 89) allow us to read the book from the perspective of the Davidic kingship. The fourth and fifth book shift the focus to the dominant theme of the kingdom of God, which begins and ends Book IV and V book respectively" (Ballhorn, *Zum Telos Des Psalters*, 382). Leuenberger also sees that Books IV–V are shaped according to the theme of the kingdom of God. See Leuenberger, *Konzeptionen des Königtums Gottes*, 4.

The Design of the Psalter

Psalm	Book IV																	Book V											
	90	91	92	93	94	95	96	97	98	99	100	101	102	103	104	105	106	107	108	109	110	111	112	113	114	115	116	117	118	119
Superscript	Mo	UT	Ps	*mlk*	UT		*mlk*	Ps	*mlk*		Thk	Dav	Aff	Dav	*brk*	HD	HLL	HD	Dav		HLL			UT		HLL	HD			Ash
Occurrences of certain words or formulaic phrases				BRK			HD		Mo		BRK HD			Mo BRK BRK BRK	Mo BRK BRK	HLL Mo	HLL Mo Mo Mo HLL					HLL HLL HLL	HLL	HLL	HLL	HLL	HD			
Shape of Collections	Sup	Tr-ust Sg	Thk				YHWH *Malak*					P PoD	Sup PoD	Thk POD	*brk*	HD HLL	HL L	HD Sg	Plea L Dir, PoD		DR PoD		Torah			HLL Theocentric			Universal	Tor-ah

	Group 9																	Group 10											
	90	91	92	93	94	95	96	97	98	99	100	101	102	103	104	105	106	107	108	109	110	111	112	113	114	115	116	117	118	119
Shape of Groups	Mosaic. Moses sings (Deut 32). The ideal "righteous one." Brink of entry											Davidic. David sings. The ideal afflicted Davidic king in Zion			Canonical Hist: Creation to Exile. Brink of entry			Praise of YHWH. Creation to Exile. Enter gates of Zion at Ps 118, End with Torah Praise. Acrostic											
	Take refuge in YHWH's house			YHWH's kingship in Zion								Live righteously in YHWH's house										YHWH establishes afflicted, Davidic King in Zion								

Shape of Section (Books IV–V); Central motif	YHWH's cosmic kingship; judgment from Zion	A Victorious Messianic king; Torah glorified
	The "righteous" walking right in the Torah (90–92) > YHWH's Kingship (93–100) > A Davidic king that walks right (100–103) > Time of Blessings begins (101)	Alphabetical Psalm (103) > Canonical history (104–107) > Victorious David (108–110) > Acrostic (111–112) > Hallelujah (113–117) > "Righteous" enter earthly Zion (118) > Acrostic; Perfect Praise of Torah (119). Righteous David at the Zion-Temple

Figure 27: A Proposal for the Macrostructure of Books IV–V (Pss 90–119)

Psalm	Book V																															
	120	121	122	123	124	125	126	127	128	129	130	131	132	133	134	135	136	137	138	139	140	141	142	143	144	145	146	147	148	149	150
Superscript																HLL	HD	UT	Dav						h	Dav	HLL	HLL	HLL	HLL	HLL
				Songs of Ascents																											
Occurrences of certain words or formulaic phrases			D		D			Sol					D		D BRK	BRK HLL HLL HLL BRK BRK BRK BRK HLL	HD HD		HLL						HLL	HLL	HLL HLL HLL HLL HLL HLL	HLL HLL HLL HLL HLL HLL HLL HLL	HLL HLL HLL HLL HLL HLL HLL HLL HLL	HLL HLL HLL HLL HLL HLL HLL HLL HLL HLL	HLL HLL HLL HLL HLL HLL HLL HLL HLL HLL
Shape of Collections	L	Z	P W		Z W		L		Z		P					Great Hallel PoD	Jns Dir	KG Dir	Med PoD	Ind. Lament Msk		P PoD		KG P		I Isr	W Cos + Chas		W Chas	Uni

	Group 11															Group 12															
	120	121	122	123	124	125	126	127	128	129	130	131	132	133	134	135	136	137	138	139	140	141	142	143	144	145	146	147	148	149	150
Shape of Groups	Lament-Zion-Praise. Center: Arriving at Zion					Lament-Zion-Praise. Center: The eschatological Zion										Canonical Hist: Creation to Exile			Supplication of afflicted David								Praise YHWH, Creation to Restored Zion. People in Zion in Ps 149. End with the Praise of YHWH. Alphabetic				
			YHWH establishes Zion. Center: Not a house/city built by man													Praise in house of God			Supplication								Praise in house of God				

Shape of Section (Books IV–V). Central motif	A Zion-City-Temple built by YHWH	Supplication of afflicted David
	Earthly Zion (120–124) > An ideal Zion built only by YHWH (125–129) > Ideal Zion built (130–134)	Praise in God's house and back into exile (135–137) > Alphabetic (138) > Davidic (138–145) > Acrostic (145) > Praise; creation to Zion; Righteous Israel in Zion (148–150) > Perfect Praise of YHWH; Alphabetic (150)

Figure 28: A Proposal for the Macrostructure of Books IV–V (Pss 120–150)

Figure 27 and Figure 28[149] illustrate the macrostructure of Books IV–V at three/four compositional levels: (a) The "superscript" row identifies each psalm according to its

149. M: Moses; UT: Untitled psalm; Ps: a psalm; *mlk*: YHWH *Malak*; Thk: Thanksgiving psalm; B:

superscription. The row below it characterizes certain words or formulaic phrases that occur in the psalm. For instance, Ps 103 is a Davidic psalm ("Dav") and within this psalm, there is one reference to "Moses" and three references of "B" (ברך in the *piel* imperative masculine plural). I have also underlined instances when a reference occurs as a coda. Hence, in Ps 103, "B" (with an underline) denotes that the psalm ends with ברך of the same conjugation. These references show graphically the extent to which such formulaic phrases are used. They give us a visual sense where praise is heightened macrostructurally. This effect is clearest in Ps 150 where there are eleven occurrences of הללו in addition to one in the superscription making a total of 12. I have also labeled the superscription of a psalm according to its characterization in the text. Phrases such as יהוה מלך (93:1), הודו (105:1) and הללו (106:1) that begin psalms are considered a form of editorial superscription, and not as "untitled psalms" as some scholars regard them.[150] Common superscriptions are marked with the same colors.

(b) The row denoted by "Shape of Collections" illustrates subdivisions at the Collection level. They are marked by their dominant thematic motif/genre. For instance, I have grouped Pss 125–29 as a unit. The first and last psalm (125, 129) in the unit are psalms with the dominant motif of the wicked ("W"). The center psalm (127) is focused on Zion ("Z").

(c) In the row denoted by "Shape of Groups," I have further generalized Groups 9–12 by their central motifs. Hence, the central motif of Group 12 is the final Davidic Collection (138–145), which can be characterized as "Supplication" since the four psalms at the center are Supplication psalms. Each Group can be divided concentrically into three Collections. Psalms 104–107 (which cuts across Books IV–V) is the first Collection in Group 12, a viewpoint that will be subsequently discussed.

(d) Finally, the row denoted by "Shape of Section" further generalize the entire shape of Groups 9–12, which has an A-B-A'-B' symmetric structure.

Psalms 104–106 as a Janus Collection

A crucial undertaking in analyzing the shape of Books IV–V is understanding the function of Pss 104–106.[151] Psalms 101–103 is clearly a unit (Davidic triad) and sepa-

---

piel imperative mp ברך; HD: *hiphil* impv mp ידה; H: *piel* imperative mp הלל; Aff: A psalm of affliction; Dav/PoD: Davidic psalm; Sol/D: Solomonic/Davidic superscriptions following the שיר המעלות; brk: "bless the LORD" as superscription (*piel* imperative, fs); Ash: אשרי as superscription; P: Praise psalm; Sup: Supplication psalm; Z: Zion-focused psalm; W: Wicked motif in psalm; Med: Meditative psalm; Uni: Universal in scope; KG: Kingship psalm; Jns: Janus psalm; Cos: Cosmic; Chas: *Chasidim*; Sg: a song.

150. Wilson considered Pss 90–99, 114–19 as groups of "untitled psalms." He notes that there is a "tendency toward combination of these untitled pss into larger compositions ... This wholesale combination most frequently takes place in two groups of pss (90–99 and 114–19). Such large-scale unification of several consecutive pss results in extremely awkward constructions and probably reflects a secondary development rather than original unity" (Wilson, *EHP*, 177).

151. Linsay Wilson has argued that Ps 103 is also connected to Pss 104–106, and together, they

rate from Pss 104–106 (Hallelujah triad).[152] Disjunctures are often marked by a shift in the superscription type.[153] Doxology is also a feature in the conclusion of a unit of psalms. Hence, doxological references at the end of Ps 103 bind the group 101–103 and conclude this segment with a spectacular fourfold ברך in the last three verses of Ps 103.[154] The term, ברך (*piel* imperative mp), is found in Pss 96, 100, 103–104,[155] 134–135, likely functioning to mark the end of a compositional unit. It is possible to see their occurrences in Pss 96 and 100 marking the end of a unit of UT and Yhwh *Malak* psalms.

There is a remarkable parallel between the pairs of Pss 103–104 and 134–135.[156] Psalms 103 and 134 are located at the end of the Davidic Psalms (101–103) and the SOA (120–134) respectively. Psalms 104 and 135 each begin a new Collection of three psalms with three different superscriptions (104–106; 135–137). Hence, Pss 104–106 and 135–137 have a common feature—they function as Collections of Janus psalms linking Groups 9 and 10, Groups 11 and 12 respectively in Books IV–V.

As previously noted, Wilson's view on הללו-יה and הודו psalms concluding and introducing a segment of psalms does not work because Ps 104 (with a *hallelujah* conclusion) does not seem to conclude a segment and Ps 105 (as a הודו psalm) does not introduce any new segment.

I propose that three verbal forms of doxologies (not just two in Wilson's view) have been used as structuring techniques to shape Books IV–V. The first form is the *piel* imperative mp of ברך. The second is the *hiphil* imperative mp of ידה and the third is the *piel* imperative mp of הלל. They might have cultic or liturgical origins, but when specifically used in imperative and plural forms, these three terms are carefully appropriated as a literary formula for structuring purpose in the final text of the Psalter. These doxological phrases serve to unite groups of psalms, and mark beginnings or endings in individual psalms as well as a group of psalms in the Psalter. They also mark Yhwh *Malak* or enthronement psalms. Figure 29 identifies these terms, their locations, and functions.

---

serve as a "focus on God's kingship" closing the entire Book IV. See Wilson, "On Psalms 103–106," 765.

152. Hossfeld and Zenger, *Psalms 3*, 96.

153. While this is affirmed in Books I–III, Wilson argues that "for obvious reasons, author-change can no longer serve as an effective indicator of disjuncture. In this segment [Pss 90–150], therefore, we find hllwyh and hwdw pss performing the same function" (Wilson, *EHP*, 157–58).

154. Wilson showed that "in the Mesopotamian hymns and catalogues, 'praise' and 'blessing' (Hallel and Doxology) frequently concluded documents or sections within documents. It is not surprising then to discover a similar technique in the Hebrew hymnic literature . . . There we find four groups of hllwyh pss, all of which mark the conclusion of Psalter" (Wilson, *EHP*, 181).

155. The opening line in Ps 104:1 is a deviation from the imperative plural. This is likely intentional, not just from the inclusio point of view (cf. 104:35). My argument is that it is shaped by a numerical design. This will be clear by the end of this chapter.

156. The ברך in Psalm 104 is in *piel* imperative feminine singular.

Possible Functions	YHWH Malak/ enthronement	End a unit of psalms	Begin a unit of psalms	Unite a group of psalms	Occurrences in Psalter
ברך piel imperative masculine plural	96:2	100:4; 103:20–22; 134:1–2	135:19–20	66:8; 68:27	13
ידה piel imperative masculine plural	30:5; 97:12;	33:2; 100:4; 106:1; 118:1, 29	136:1–3, 26; 107:1	105:1; 106:1; 107:1	13
הלל piel imperative masculine plural	22:24	150:1–6; 106: 48; 113:9; 117:2	111:1; 135:1, 3, 21; 146:1	104:35; 105:45; 106:1, 48; 111:1; 112:1; 113:1; 115:18; 116:19; 117:1; 146:1, 10; 147:1, 20; 148:1–4, 7, 14; 149:1, 9	48

Figure 29: Number of Occurrences, Locations, and Functions of Imperative Masculine Plural forms of ברך, ידה and הלל

The numbers in the far right column are based on an exhaustive electronic search on the imperative masculine plural of the three doxological phrases in the Psalms. Neither Wilson and Zenger have accounted for all the occurrences of these forms, nor do they differentiate their occurrences in the imperative forms. While there are other occurrences of these three verbs in construct and non-imperative forms, the distinction of the imperative plural forms is based on morphological parallels to the formulaic imperative plural הללו-יה and הודו forms which mark certain psalms in Books IV–V.

Although the phrase, ברכו, is never used in the superscription of the Psalms, their specific occurrences in the Psalter are important. This is shown by how they function to link two psalms across the seam of Collections (e.g., Pss 103–4, 134–35). In Pss 103–4, it does so with the use of ברכי. The phrase, ברכי נפשי (fem imperative), occurs only in two psalms (103:1–2, 22; 104:1, 35) in the entire HB.[157] The parallel between Pss 103–4 and 134–35 is distinctive in that the first psalm of the pair (103, 134) contain only the imperative plural ברכו but the second psalm in the pair (104, 135) contain the imperative ברכו as well as a concluding הללו-יה.

When we consider the imperative doxologies in the superscriptions functioning as intentional structural markers, the macrostructure of Books IV–V is revealed. These doxological superscripts function to connect and distinguish psalm groups. While Ps 104 is connected to Ps 103, the triad (104–106), marked by these doxological superscriptions, is also distinguished from the Davidic Pss 101–103. Yet, the same

---

157. Interestingly, the pairing of ברך and נפש (though not in the same form) is only found elsewhere in Gen 27:4, 19, 25, 31, where they describe Isaac blessing his sons before he died.

The Design of the Psalter

triad (104–106), at the end of Book IV, is also connected to Ps 107 in Book V by הודו with the common superscription.

The four psalms (Pss 104–107) that begin with the phrases הללויה, ברכי, הודו and הודו respectively highlight these three doxological formulaic superscription. Psalms 104–106 all end with הללויה. Yet Pss 105–7 contain the הודו phrase (*hiphil* imperative, 105:1; 106:1; 107:1) in their first verse. With the use of the הודו and הללויה at the beginning and end of psalms Pss 104–107, these four consecutive psalms are interlocked in spite of the Book division between Pss 106 and 107. Moreover, the use of ברכי,[158] also binds Pss 103–104 to the entire Pss 103–107. When Psalms 104–107 is observed against the horizon of Pss 101–10, these four psalms function as a Janus-Collection not just between Books IV and V, but also between the two Davidic Collections (101–103; 108–110).

The following figure illustrates this graphically.

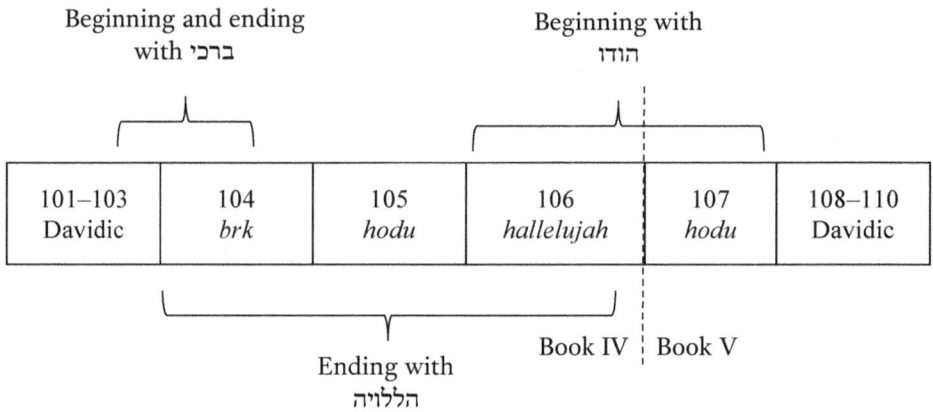

Figure 30: Interlocking Function of Doxological Vocabulary in Psalms 103–107

Role of Psalms 104–107

A number of reasons help us see how Psalms 104–107 are plausibly designed as a unit:

(1) *Superscriptions and doxological vocabulary.* In light of how superscription is used to organize various units of psalms Books I-III, we argue that Pss 104–107 are organized as a unit of psalms using doxological vocabulary that function as superscripts. This is not new since it has been generally agreed that the doxological

---

158. For Psalm 104, the superscription is given in the LXX, 11QPs[a] and Aquila's translation of the Psalms. Wilson suggested that the absence of superscription "functions as an editorial method of preserving a *tradition* for the combination of the 'untitled' psalm with its immediate predecessor." However, he admitted that this does not imply that "*all* occurrences of such 'untitled' psalms throughout the Psalter are to be so combined" (Wilson, "Use of 'Untitled' Psalms," 404).

vocabulary הלל link Pss 146–150 as a unit. Unfortunately, ברכי and הודו were not understood as superscripts and since Gerald Wilson, psalms such as Pss 104–107 are generally considered "untitled" (or lacking superscription). As such, their organizing function had been largely ignored. However, in view of our discussion, such psalms that begin or end with the doxological-imperative formula can be viewed as editorial features that aid macrostructural organization.

(2) *Length of Pss 104–107*. They are considerably longer in words than the psalms in adjacent groups. Psalms 104–107 are four psalms with a total of 171 verses (approx. 43 verses per psalm). The two adjacent Davidic triads have a total of 59 (101–103) and 52 (108–110) verses, with an average of 19.7 and 17.3 verses per psalm respectively. Clearly, the two Davidic triads are very similar in length. Psalm 107, however, is similar to Pss 104–106 in length and verse density. These numbers clearly bind Ps 107 to Pss 104–106 as an editorial unit.[159] Figure 31 summarizes these numbers.

	Psalm	Verses	Total	Average
Davidic	101	8	59	19.7
	102	29		
	103	22		
Doxological Superscription	104	35	171	42.8
	105	45		
	106	48		
	107	43		
Davidic	108	14	52	17.3
	109	31		
	110	7		

Figure 31: Chapter Length and the Unity of Psalms 104–107

(3) *Genre of the Psalms*. Psalms 104–107 are similar in genre and carry a different tone as compared to the Davidic Pss 101–103, 108–110. Dominant in Pss 104–107 is *descriptions* or *recounts* of Yhwh's works as opposed to petitions or prayers in the Davidic psalms. Psalms 104–107 emphasize the mighty deeds of God in Israel's history and statements of the psalmist's lament *against* his enemies in Pss 104–107 are few.[160] In contrast, the Davidic triads are filled with personal pleas for vindication and deliverance (cf. 101; 109).

(4) *Metanarrative and thematic progression through Pss 104–107*. Psalm 104 focuses on God's creation.[161] This Psalm is also used in various traditions associated

---

159. Labuschagne notes, "It is important to note that Book IV has an apparent open end. There is no clear break between 106 at the end of Book IV and 107 at the beginning of Book V because 107 is very closely related to 105–6, all three being 'episodic poems,' as I have shown in my analyses. This means that the seam between Book IV and Book V is rather artificial, in contrast to the strong caesura between Psalm 89 and 90, and between Psalm 119 and the Songs of Ascents" (Labuschagne, "Compositional Structure of the Psalter," 19).

160. Perhaps only in Pss 104:34–35; 106:10; 107:2, 42.

161. God *stretched out* (נטה, v. 2) the heavens like a curtain; *made* (עשה, v. 19) the stars; set the

The Design of the Psalter

with new life.¹⁶² Psalm 105 describes God's covenant with the patriarchs (Abraham, Isaac, Jacob and Joseph, vv. 9–23), how God turned Israel into a nation in Egypt and brought them out through Moses and Aaron (vv. 26–43).¹⁶³ Psalm 106 describes Israel's rejection *of* God (vv. 6–39) and her rejection *by* God (vv. 41–44).¹⁶⁴ By the end of the Ps 106, Israel was in captivity (v. 46), scattered, and looked forward in time to be gathered from the nations (v. 47). Psalm 107 begins by with descriptions of Israel's redemption and gathering from four corners of the lands (107:2). God broke their bondage (107:14), shattered "gates of bronze and cut bars of iron asunder" (v. 16)¹⁶⁵ and has led them to an "inhibited city" (107:4, 7, 36) where the people would flourish, multiply and be secure (107:38, 41). This trajectory of Israel's canonical history across Pss 104–107 binds them together as an editorial unit.

(5) *Thematic and lexical interconnections.* Psalm 104 is connected to Psalm 105 with the lexemes שיר and זמר (אשירה ליהוה אזמרה לאלהי [104:33]; שירו־לו זמרו־לו [105:2]). The word שמח is used consecutively in Pss 104:31, 34; 105:3, 38; 106:5; 107:30, 42¹⁶⁶ as a concatenation technique binding Pss 104–107 (*Verkettung*).

Psalm 105 is concatenated to Psalm 106 with the formulaic *hallelujah* (105:45; 106:1).¹⁶⁷ Clifford points out that the words "desert/wilderness," which occur thrice in Pss 106 and 107, serve to link both of them.¹⁶⁸ Kim shows exhaustively that Pss 105–6 have 55 words in common and these two adjacent psalms have the highest lexical interconnections in the whole of Book IV.¹⁶⁹ Certain words/phrases are found only in these two adjacent psalms.¹⁷⁰

Psalm 106 is further connected to 107 via the word קבץ. This word occurs only four times in the Psalter (41:7; 102:23; 106:47; 107:3). Of these four occurrences, only

---

earth on its foundation (יסד־ארץ על־מכוניה, v. 5); and *established* the boundary for the mountains, valleys (גבול־שמת בל־יעברון, v. 9). Cf. Gen 1:7; 2:8; Job 38:4. Goldingay, citing P. Miller, sees this psalm as perhaps the "most extended explication of God's work of creation outside of Genesis" (Goldingay, *Psalms*, 3:196).

162. In the Jewish tradition, this psalm is sung on the morning of Yom Kippur and in the evening of the new moon. It is also recited from the feast of Sukkoth to Pesach, looking forward to new life as spring draws near. In the Orthodox tradition, this psalm is recited at "vespers at the setting of the sun, with the lighting of lamps, signifying the beginning of the new day." In the *Book of Common Prayer* of the Church of England, this psalm is associated with the Pentecost, to link the giving of God's spirit "when people are born and when they are born anew." Goldingay, *Psalms*, 3:199.

163. Goldingay, *Psalms*, 3:203.

164. Note that זנח is not used here.

165. Johnston notes that "bars and gates" (e.g., Ps 107:16, 18) are "quasi-physical features" that are associated with *sheol*, or "a land of no return." See Johnston, "Psalms and Distress," 71.

166. Prior to Pss 104–107, the word is only found in Ps 97 and in Ps 109 after.

167. LXX omits the *Hallelujah* in Ps 105:45. Goldingay thinks it might be a "dittography from Ps 106." Goldingay, *Psalms*, 3:217.

168. Cf. Pss 106:9, 14, 26; 107:4, 33, 35. Clifford, *Psalms 73–150*, 162.

169. See Kim, "Structure and Coherence," 305–10.

170. Cf. "Land of Ham" (105:23, 27; 106:22); "Canaan" is found only in these two adjacent psalms and once elsewhere in the Psalter (105:11; 106:38; 135:11).

106:47 and 107:3 are associated explicitly with the motif of ingathering of scattered Israel "from among the nations" and "from the land, east and west, north and south." Furthermore, in both psalms, there are explicit references to Israel's enemies. Israel is given "into the hand of the nations" (ביד-גוים, 106:41); to "all their captors" (כל-שוביהם, 106:46); and to the "hand of adversary" (מיד-צר, 107:2). Their connection is further explicated by the use of three common vocabularies in the last three lines of Ps 106 and the first three of Ps 107.

⁴⁶ויתן אותם לרחמים לפני כל-שוביהם
⁴⁷הושיענו יהוה אלהינו וקבצנו מן-הגוים להדות לשם קדשך להשתבח בתהלתך
⁴⁸ברוך-יהוה אלהי ישראל מן-העולם ועד העולם ואמר כל-העם אמן הללו-יה

¹ הדו ליהוה כי-טוב כי לעולם חסדו
² יאמרו גאולי יהוה אשר גאלם מיד-צר
³ ומארצות קבצם ממזרח וממערב מצפון ומים

Psalms 106 and 107 are clearly juxtaposed with each other despite being divided across Books IV–V. At the seam between these two psalms lie the message of praise and thanks to God for he *is to gather* (*piel* imperative; 106:47) and *has gathered* (*piel* perfect; 107:3) his scattered people from the nations and the lands. In other words, the significance of this division between Pss 106–7 within the horizon of Pss 104–107 suggests that Book V is to be read, at least in its opening, with the perspectives of the return and ingathering of scattered Israel.[171] From a larger horizon, Book III depicts Israel's ejection from Zion, and Book IV describes Yhwh's kingship (93–100) and descriptions of the righteous Moses and David (90–92, 101–103). Book V begins to depict Israel's return and restoration.

(6) *Use of ἀλληλούια in the* LXX. It is possible that the LXX links these groups of psalms by an interconnecting phrase, ἀλληλούια ἐξομολογεῖσθε, between two psalms. The ἀλληλούια phrase is absent at the end of the LXX Ps 103:35 [MT 104:35] but this verse is concatenated to LXX 104:1 [MT 105:1], where the first two words are ἀλληλούια ἐξομολογεῖσθε ("Hallelujah, give praise"). This phenomenon recurs between the pairs of LXX Pss 104:45—105:1, 105:48—106:1, 116:2—117:1 and 134:21—135:1. This concatenation also occur between LXX Pss 145:10 and 146:1 [MT 146:10 and 147:1] with a different second word, ἀλληλούια Αγγαιου.

- a. LXX 103:35 ... εὐλόγει ἡ ψυχή μου τὸν κύριον—[LXX 104:1] <u>ἀλληλούια ἐξομολογεῖσθε</u> τῷ κυρίῳ ...

- b. LXX 104:45 ... καὶ τὸν νόμον αὐτοῦ ἐκζητήσωσιν—[LXX 105:1] <u>ἀλληλούια ἐξομολογεῖσθε</u> τῷ κυρίῳ ὅτι ...

---

171. Other literary evidence of postexilic orientation can be seen in Pss 126, 137. This does not mean that all the psalms in Book V are composed in the postexilic period.

The Design of the Psalter

c. LXX 105:48 ... καὶ ἐρεῖ πᾶς ὁ λαός γένοιτο γένοιτο—[LXX 106:1] <u>ἀλληλούια ἐξομολογεῖσθε</u> τῷ κυρίῳ ὅτι ...

d. LXX 116:26 ... καὶ ἡ ἀλήθεια τοῦ κυρίου μένει εἰς τὸν αἰῶνα—[LXX 117:1] <u>ἀλληλούια ἐξομολογεῖσθε</u> τῷ κυρίῳ ...

e. LXX 134:21 ... ὁ κατοικῶν Ιερουσαλημ —[LXX 135:1] <u>ἀλληλούια ἐξομολογεῖσθε</u> τῷ κυρίῳ ὅτι ...

f. LXX 145:10 ... εἰς γενεὰν καὶ γενεάν—[LXX 146:1] <u>ἀλληλούια Αγγαιου</u> καὶ Ζαχαριου αἰνεῖτε τὸν κύριον ...

The five identified concatenations of two psalms with the phrase, ἀλληλούια ἐξομολογεῖσθε, do not occur elsewhere in LXX Psalter (cf. LXX 113:26—114:1; 115:10; 116:1). They are found only towards both ends of Books IV-V (104; 146).[172] While our concern is primarily in the MT, these concatenations in the LXX suggest that the LXX translators considered the MT Pss 104-107; 117-118; 146-147 linked by ἀλληλούια ἐξομολογεῖσθε.

(7) *Numerical and thematic connections between Pss 105-107*. Labuschagne makes an interesting observation of the use of 34 words in three separate texts of Pss 105:40-44; 106:23-27; 107:23-26, 40 (last five verses in Ps 107 marked by the inverted *nun*). The number "34" is significant as it is a factor of "17" (divine name number). These 34 words are also divided into a 19+15 sequence, separated by *'athnach* or verse division.[173]

The preceding reasons sustain the structural unity of Pss 104-107. This unity helps us see a striking macrostructural thematic parallel between Pss 104-119 and 135-150 (discussed next), which provides the key to understanding how Books IV and V are designed as a unity.

Reading Books IV and V together

Like Books II and III, there is form-structural (and thematic) support to show that Books IV and V are designed as a compositional Section. This does not suggest that the division between Books IV and V is in any way diminished in significance, yet, in spite of the division, readers can detect the rhetorical and literary features when they read the last two Books of the Psalter together. The following four structural arguments help us understand how these two books can be read together and thereby enriching our understanding of the message of the Psalter.

(1) *Parallel trajectories between Pss 104-107 and 135-137*. As previously detailed, a trajectory is traced from Pss 104 to 107, revealing the canonical history of creation, to Israel's exile, and to her impending return. Interestingly, Pss 135-137 contain a

---

172. Cf. LXX Pss 113:26—114:1

173. On the specific numerical technique of 34 (19+15) words, see Labuschagne "Psalm 95," 1.

parallel trajectory. Like Pss 104–107, there is no authorship attribution in the superscriptions of Pss 135–137.[174] Motifs of creation and providence are found in Ps 135:6-7 (cf. 104:2–32). The motif of a chosen people is also found in 135:4 (cf. 105:6–24).[175] We observe the motif of Yhwh's deliverance of his people from Egypt and leading them into Canaan in Ps 135:8–12 (cf. 105:25–43). Israel's rebellion and idolatry are characterized next in Ps 135:14–18 (cf. 106:6–7). The entire trajectory of creation, deliverance and entry into the land of Canaan is reimagined in the form of praise in Ps 136. By Ps 137, Israel's exile to Babylon is clear and there is a longing for hope at the end (137:1, 5–6, 9; cf. 107:1–43). These remarkable parallels are summarised below.

Pss 104–107	Common Motifs in the Trajectory	Pss 135–137
104:2–32	Yhwh's creation and providence	135:6–7; 136:4–9
105:6–24	Yhwh's choosing and forming a people	135:4
105:25–43	Yhwh's deliverance of Israel from Egypt	135:8–9
105:44	Yhwh's giving of the land to Israel	135:9–12
106:6–7, 19–22, 35–39	Israel's persistent idolatry	135:14–18
106:41–47	Yhwh's giving up of Israel to the Babylonian exile	137:1–4
107:1–43	Israel's hopes for restoration in Zion	137:1, 5–6, 9

Figure 32: Parallel Trajectories from Creation to Exile in Pss 104–107 and 135–137

(2) *Parallels between Pss 104–119 and 135–150.* The parallel in the trajectories between Pss 104–107 and 135–137 above leads us to see a wider parallel between two broader compositional units (Pss 104–119 and 135–150) as depicted in Figure 33.

---

174. Todd, likewise, sees Pss 135–137 as a unit. See Todd, *Remember, O Yahweh*, 122–23.

175. For connections between Pss 135–136 on the motif of creation, see Todd, *Remember, O Yahweh*, 87–90.

The Design of the Psalter

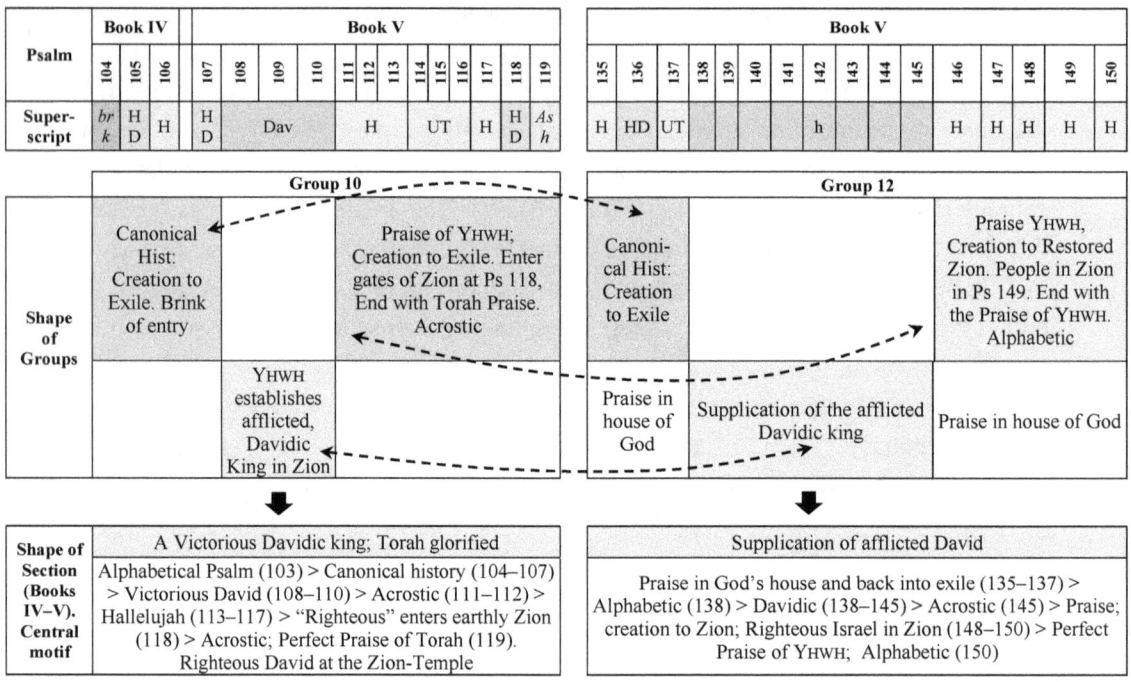

Figure 33: Parallels between Pss 104–119 and 135–150 in Books IV–V

Both Pss 104–119 and 135–150 consist of a three-part symmetric structure. In both Groups, we observe first a collection without authorship attribution (104–107 // 135–137). This is followed by the Davidic Collection (108–110 // 138–145), and another Collection of psalms without authorship attribution but characterized by *hallelujah* (111–119 // 146–150). In other words, the entirety of 104–119 and 135–150 follow a common sequence of canonical history, Davidic and *hallelujah* psalms. This structural shape suggests that Books IV–V intentionally trace a (repeated) storyline that begins with the creation, followed by the formation of Israel as the people of God, through a Davidic Collection (cf. chapter 4), before arriving at the consummative hallelujah psalms. Thus, it is through the Davidic psalms that Israel's history moves into consummative praise.

Groups 10 and 12 (104–119; 135–150) begin with a concentrated occurrence of plural imperative doxological vocabulary (cf. 104–107; 135–136), then go through a series of *hallelujah*-superscription psalms (111–117; 146–149), and interestingly, conclude with an AA and AC composition respectively (119; 150). Furthermore, Pss 119 and 150 at the end of the Groups culminate with the motifs of Torah (119) and kingship (150), recalling the Prologue (Pss 1–2). It is also striking that the two seams between the Davidic and *hallelujah* Collections are marked by two AAs (111–112; 145).[176] The convergence of these multiple parallel features is unlikely to be incidental.

---

176. The function of AA and AC will be further discussed in chapter 5.

The final third Collections of both Groups (111–119; 146–150) are bound by AA/AC which is a poetical device symbolizing "perfection" or "completeness." This totality concept is also implicit within the content of Pss 119 and 150 (119:96; 150:1). Psalm 150 also consists of a total of 12 instances of the imperative plural הלל, further reinforcing the motif of completeness.

(3) *Symmetric shape of Books IV–V.* The entire Books IV and V can be grouped into four major Groups (9–12). All four Groups have a three-part concentric structure. The dominant motifs at the center of each Group are (a) Yhwh *Malak* psalms (93–100), (b) the ideal triumphant Davidic king (108–110), (c) the ideal Zion-temple built by Yhwh (122; 127; 132) and (d), a final Davidic group with the motif of supplication (138–145).

When we consider the dominant motifs at the center of each Group under the horizon of Books IV–V, they are also symmetrical with a focus on the idealized Davidic kingship and Zion at the center (Groups 10–11), framed by Yhwh's kingship (Group 9) and Supplication (Group 12). The following figure illustrates this:

	Books IV-V											
	Group 9			Group 10					Group 11			Group 12		
	90–92	93–100	101–103	104–106	107	108–110	111–119	120–124	125–129	130–134	135–137	138–145	146–150
Shape of Groups	Moses' Song; Righteous dwell in Yhwh's house	David's Song; Righteous and afflicted Davidide in Zion	History Creation to Exile; Brink of entry				*Hallelujah*; Creation to Exile; King and the righteous enters gates	Lament to Zion to Praise Center: Jerusalem		Lament to Zion to Praise Center: ideal Zion	History Creation to Exile		*Hallelujah*; Creation to heavenly Zion; Chasidim in Zion
	Take refuge in Yhwh's house	Yhwh's kingship in Zion	Live in Yhwh's house				Yhwh estab. King in Zion		Yhwh estab. Zion		Praise in Yhwh's house (135, 136)	Supplication	Praise in Yhwh's house (150)
Central Motif	Yhwh's kingship											Supplication
				Ideal Davidic Figure					Ideal Zion-city				

Figure 34: Structure of Four Major Groups of Books IV–V

(4) *Symbolic numbers are seen when superscriptions are totaled.* In our discussions of Books I–III, we noted that the number of psalms based on their specific superscriptions adds up precisely to symbolic numbers (see Figure 18). The symbolism is present *only* when the numbers in Books II–III are added, reinforcing our contention that these books are designed as a unit. The question, then, is whether the same phenomenon is observed in Books IV and V. However, ascertaining symbolic numbers

The Design of the Psalter

in Books IV–V is a more complex endeavor because of the variegated superscription types, many of which have no attributed authorship.

The mystery is revealed when the superscriptions are grouped into five main categories: (a) YHWH *Malak* psalms that begin with the formula, יהוה מלך; (b) Psalms with named figures in superscriptions (e.g., Moses, David); (c) Psalms containing superscriptions but without attributed names or psalms without clear superscriptions; (d) Psalms that begin with either *hodu* or *hallelujah* in the imperative plural; (e) The שיר המעלות superscription.[177]

The tabulated figures for these five categories of superscription add up to interesting figures (3+14+14+15+15 = 61). When we further classify these superscriptions into two main groups—those with names and those without names, we arrive at the numbers 17 and 44 (11x4) respectively. These two numbers are symbolic of YHWH's presence and totality (see chapter 5).

Superscription Categories			Sub-total	
(a) YHWH *Malak* (divine name; 93, 97, 99)			3	17
(b) Psalms with names present in superscription	Davidic (101, 103, 108–110, 138–145)	13	14	
	Moses (90)	1		
(c) Psalms with superscription but without names present or psalms without obvious superscription	Without clear superscriptions (91, 94–96, 114–116, 137)	8	14	44 (11x4)
	Ashre (119)	1		
	A Psalm / Thanks / Afflicted / *brk* (92, 98, 100, 102, 104)	5		
(d) *Hodu* and *Hallelujah*	*Hodu* Hiph Impv mp (105, 107, 118, 136)	4	15	
	Hallelujah piel impv mp (106, 111–113, 117, 135, 146–150)	11		
(d) Songs of Ascents (120–134)			15	
Total Psalms in Books IV and V			61	

Figure 35: Superscription Tabulation in Books IV–V

Superscription Type	Book I	Books II–III	Books IV–V	Total
Names *present* in Superscription	37 (26+11)	44 (11x4)	17	98 (7x7x2)
Names *absent* in Superscription	4	4	44 (11x4)	52 (26x2)
Total	41	48	61	150 (10x15)

Figure 36: Named and Unnamed Superscription-Type Count

177. To avoid double-counting, the "David" and "Solomon" references in Pss 122, 124, 127, 131, 133 are not included in the category of "names." I have considered all these psalms as belonging to the Collection of the Songs of Ascents.

As shown in Figure 36, both Books I and II–III have four psalms that do not have names in their superscriptions. Books II–III and IV–V have a common number "44" (11x4). The category of superscription without names in the three Sections of the Psalter (Books I, II–III, IV–V) are linked to the number "4" (or a factor of "4"). The numbers "17" and "26" are divine name numbers[178] while numbers "7," "11" and "10" are associated with completeness. The numerical correspondences show that formal and thematic devices correspond.

Before we conclude this chapter, we return to the question of validity of interpretation. The most important techniques seen at work in this chapter can be reduced to parallelisms (recurrences of common words, ideas, structures or trajectories, close or distant), concentricity (leitmotifs in the Prologue), intertextuality (Davidic covenant) and perhaps, numerical symbolism. We have discussed at length in chapter 1 how the editor(s) would have the required literary ability to compose such poems and how readers could, to some extent, appreciate the key motifs of Yhwh's kingship, messianic deliverance and establishment of a flourishing Zion. In light of our observations in this chapter, we will further reflect on the plausibility of these techniques (from the perspective of the composer) and the readers' ability to decipher their meaning.

We started our analysis based on Barbiero's structural analysis of Book I and observed how concentric structures work at different levels of composition via the use of superscriptions and content to display a central motif. These central focuses, or motifs, often highlight the leitmotifs in the Prologue, which we have analyzed independently. We have moved beyond Book I and extended our observations through the Psalter.

In our analyses of Books II–V, we have observed surprising consistency in the use of literary techniques and development of content. Moreover, these observations fit remarkably well with our proposal that the Prologue is programmatic structurally and thematically. We have seen the three-part concentric structures across Books II–III, IV–V and observed a thematic movement from a distressful situation to a secure and blessed city through victorious kingship at the center of that concentric structure (or turning point). These features are all found in the Prologue and unfurled across the macrostructure as discussed in this chapter. As such, the Prologue is shown to be programmatic for the Psalter.

This internal literary consistency is important because it suggests an authorial coherent design. Such design, in terms of literary technique or content development, is highly plausible because it was already seen in Israel's oldest poetry, the Song of the Sea (Exod 15). The original readership of the Psalter would have experienced a prevailing circumstance of distress, hoped for Yhwh's promises of blessing and anticipated a messianic deliverance. The Psalter's specific contribution, as opposed to

---

178. "17" and "26" are also the gematria of the Tetragrammaton. Books III and IV each contain 17 psalms.

The Design of the Psalter

the Song of the Sea, is the recasting the storyline with Davidic kingship (rather than Yhwh) and Zion (rather than Canaan).

The use of the numerical technique is a bit of an enigma because it requires a lot more from the audience. The use of chiasmus, recurring motifs, and macrostructural storyline can be appreciated aurally but numerical devices require not just a *reading* audience, but one who had the entire text in hand and could work through the material. For readers to recognize the symbolic numbers associated with different kinds of superscriptions, they would have to keep track of all their different counts through the entire book of Psalms. This would naturally require a meticulous and focused reading of the Psalter in its entirety (or large sections of it). It is unclear if the Psalter was used in such a way, but in the postexilic period, it is likely that copies of the Psalter as a "book of praises," rather than separate loose collections, were circulated. The numerical devices were probably not intended for the general audience. They could, nonetheless, be established techniques of the scribal profession and understood by those in the guild. Perhaps with some instruction, more advanced readers were able to recognize them.

The use of numerical devices as symbols is theologically significant and should not be ignored. They may not be *essential* to the overarching design or content but they function in a complementary way, adding depth to meaning. Numbers symbolizing completeness, such as "7," "10," and "14," recur often in the HB. The numbers "17" and "26" are associated with God's name and thus symbolize Yhwh's covenantal relationship with his people through all generations (Exod 3:15).

A good piece of artistic work often consists of different levels of meaning that may not be plain to every person. Perhaps we can illustrate this with a modern analogy using Vincent Van Gogh's famous painting, *Cafe Terrace at Night*.

Figure 37: Vincent van Gogh's Cafe Terrace at Night[179]

At first sight, the painting is a simple café scene with a few diners, as its title suggests. But Van Gogh was the son of a minister, and it is highly likely that he might include Christian symbols in his paintings. Critics of this painting have observed that the café scene is actually a rendition of Leonardo da Vinci's Last Supper. In other words, a visual "intertextuality" is at work. The twelve persons seated at the café represent the twelve disciples and the waiter (with long hair and white robe) standing at the center represents Jesus. Other critics have argued that there are a number of crosses hidden in the painting (other than the cross painted just above the shoulder of the waiter).

Once these elements are observed, the painting takes on a different meaning. The visual framing and color composition further confirm such an interpretation. In the painting, the edges of the terrace awning; the edges of the cafe flooring and the

---

179. The painting is currently housed at the Kröller-Müller Museum in the Netherlands. See Van Gogh, *Terrace of the café*.

tracks of the cobblestones (at the lower forefront) all extend towards a focal point (or "vanishing point")—the waiter in white and the cross behind him (that is, Jesus!). This man and the area immediately surrounding him is painted with a bright glow (under a lamp), providing a contrast against the outer darker hues. The bright spot, a standing man in white amongst twelve seated diners, the convergence of perspectival lines, their centralized location in the painting, and the idea of a meal at night, all confirm clear connections to the Last Supper interpretation.

In other words, the coherency of composition techniques, form, content, symbolism, and circumstances concerning the life of Van Gogh provide a good basis to argue for the painter's intent. It is not difficult to see how his original audience in nineteenth-century Europe would be familiar with Da Vinci's famous painting, *The Last Supper*. One may argue that such reading may be coincidental or perhaps a kind of "reader-response" understanding. However, we cannot deny that this interpretation is derived from the features afforded by the painting itself (recall our discussion of Iser's reader response method in chapter 1).

The above discussions on Van Gogh's painting parallel our argument thus far. In similar ways, the literary composition (concentric structures), content, intertextuality, numerical symbolism, and historical circumstances provide coherency and unity to the Psalter, pointing to skillful editorial design.

Summary

- In this chapter, we have analyzed the entire macrostructure of the Psalter and shown how the Prologue's program is expressed through Books I, II–III and IV–V.

- Book I can be structured into four main Groups (Pss 3–14; 15–24; 25–34; 35–41). Each Group can be further divided into three concentric Collections with a central focus.

- Several important structuring techniques in Book I include: (1) concentric structures working at different levels of composition; (2) central focuses of Torah-fidelity, kingship and Zion-temple; (3) trajectories in relation to Zion; (4) number of psalms in each group that add up to symbolic numbers; (5) psalm superscriptions designed to delimit Subgroups; (6) alternation techniques (day–night); (7) an "already-but-not-yet" phenomenon.

- The most convincing principle of division occurs when the poetic form (e.g., superscription), thematic features and genre (content) structures cohere.

- Books II–III can be seen as a compositional unit with four main Groups (Pss 42–49; 50–72; 73–83; 84–89).

- The *Pan-Psalter Occurrence Scheme* is an editorial technique based on careful use and placement of certain word/phrases at strategic locations across the entire Psalter to make or reinforce a rhetorical point. The use of זנח in the Psalter is carefully appropriated and located to underscore the message of Yhwh's apparent rejection of the human king and earthly temple specifically in Books II–III.

- Books IV–V can be seen as a compositional unit with four main Groups (Pss 90–103; 104–119; 120–134; 135–150). Group 10 (Pss 104–119) parallels Group 12 (Pss 135–150).

- The compositional unity of Pss 104–107 is important for understanding Books IV–V as a unit. Psalms 104–106 function as a Janus collection.

- Poetical, thematic and genre techniques of structuring in Books I are repeated in Books II–III and IV–V.

- Superscriptions (or the lack thereof) assign important structural, interpretive and symbolic value to the shape of the Psalms. The imperative plural of *Hallelujah*, *Hodu*, and the יהוה מלך opening invocations are a form of superscription.

- In its entirety, the Psalter is divided into three Sections (Books I, II–III, IV–V) and each Section consists of four Groups (1–4, 5–8, 9–12). Each Section, Group, or Collection has a concentric/symmetric shape, emphasizing a central motif.

- This deliberate shape confirms that the Prologue is programmatic, both in structure and theme, for the 150 psalms. Our macrostructural analyses of all five Books have shown how formal and tacit techniques work coherently in shaping the Psalter with striking consistency.

3

Concentric and Linear Reading

It is not enough to receive the text only in 'linear' fashion, line by line (the first dimension). Simultaneously, its passages must be read 'palindromically,' from the outer edges to the center (the second dimension), and citations and allusions to other places in Scripture allowed to contribute to the text's meaning (the third dimension).[1]

—Martin Mark

It is a literary question to what extent the editors of a biblical book, in putting together various sources of pieces of material, have created a meaning in the juxtaposition, as distinct from the meaning of the parts. 'The case for meaning must be decided on literary criteria: one must show that a unit is not just an anthology but is an intended structure with meaning.'[2]

—James Barr

WE HAVE SEEN HOW the entire Psalter can be divided into three major Sections (Books I, II–III, IV–V). Each of these Sections, in turn, consists of four major Groups. In this chapter, the three Sections will be studied together, revealing a remarkable macrostructural design that is both *concentric* and *linear*. These two macrostructural dimensions of reading not only cohere and correspond to each other, but they confirmed that the design of the Psalter is an "intended structure with meaning"!

---

1. Mark quoted in Weber, "Toward a Theory," 157.
2. Barr, *Holy Scripture*, 160.

A concentric reading is characterized by structural symmetry,[3] and is often called a chiasmus.[4] Concentricity usually highlights a significant motif at the center of a structural unit. As such, the key motif located at the center of a *Group* will be termed as the *Group Central Motif* (GCM). Based on three Sections of four Groups in the Psalter, there is a total of 12 GCMs. Motifs occurring at other compositional levels of concentric units will simply be known as the central motif (CM).

A linear reading is defined by a coherent thematic trajectory or the development of a certain motif across the Psalter. Linearity provides the forward thrust along the trajectory. The general Metanarrative (capital "M") across the three main Sections can be summarized as the establishment (Book I), fall (Books II–III) and re-establishment (Books IV–V) of the Davidic kingship and Zion. This is the *linear reading* across the three Sections of the Psalter. In this chapter, we will also observe how the *Pan-Psalter Occurrence Scheme* (POS), an editorial technique that traces the exhaustive occurrences of certain lexemes/phrases across the Psalter sequentially, supports this linear dimension of reading. The linearity of the Psalter is further understood by analyzing the five Davidic Collections across the Psalter, which is the focus of chapter 4.

Concentric and linear dimensions of reading are intertwined in the design of the Psalter. The concentricity of the structure and the CM and GCM provide the macro-structural shape and locate prominent motifs pertinent to the message of the Psalter. At the same time, when these central motifs are traced across the structure (linearly), the Metanarrative and message of the Psalter are revealed. In turn, this Metanarrative, once understood, establishes the hermeneutical horizon (*Sitz im Psalter*) for understanding individual psalms across the Psalter.

Concentric Reading

The "palindromical" reading highlighted by Martin Mark at the beginning of this chapter characterizes the concentric phenomenon. Weber calls such an interpretation "centering."

> The pattern, . . . characterized by the fact that the stressed, strongly underlined pronouncement of the poem is not located (only) at the end, but in the center, in the 'heart.' . . . Interpreting a poem that is structured in this way requires one to identify the central pronouncement as such and to unlock its

---

3. Alonso Schökel notes, "a *concentric* structure is one where words are repeated in inverse order on both sides of a central point. This is also called a symmetrical structure. Others see it as a kind of augmented chiasm. Such structures may be indicated thus: ABC X CBA, or ABCD DBCA" (*A Manual of Hebrew Poetics*, 192).

4. A "concentric" structure/reading is also called "alternation," "inversion," "pyramid" or "introverted parallelism." For perhaps the most extensive bibliography on chiasms, see Murphy, "Welch Chiasmus Papers Collection." For a review of chiastic reading and its application to specific psalms, see Alden, "Chiastic Psalms," 11–28; "Chiastic Psalms (II)," 191–200; "Chiastic Psalms (III)," 199; Zogbo and Wendland, *Hebrew Poetry in the Bible*, 44–46.

significance in a dual movement from the periphery to the center and from the center to the periphery.[5]

The argument that the weight of the poem is not only at the end, but "in the "center, in the 'heart'" is important. For poetry, the "'what' of communication is bound up with the 'how.'" The "form in poetic texts such as the psalms is therefore extraordinarily important" in interpretation.[6] Weber is correct and our analyses of the Psalter in the preceding chapters have confirmed this.[7]

The concentric structure can be formed by formal and thematic features in the text.[8] Christensen's chiastic reading of the Psalter is primarily thematic (chapter 1) but his work on the Psalter is too brief, and the structural shape that he has proposed is based on loose thematic arguments. Labuschagne and van der Lugt have taken "centering" to the level of mathematical precision. They argue that "one of the techniques commonly used was to organize the contents of a text in such a way that the *most important element* was situated [by word count] in the *mathematical center* position."[9] For Alonso Schökel, this "*semantic center*, . . . is frequently an image or symbol"[10] of significance.

Most Psalms scholars[11] whose work assume the canonical approach (overtly or not) adopt a linear reading. One clear proponent is Egbert Ballhorn who argues that the Psalter has come to us in the form of a book and therefore, the "book form of the Psalter is the subject of interpretation, including the layout and structures contained therein."[12] Reading the Psalter as a book helps to see that the overall presentation is made up of not just the relationship between texts, but also the *order* of psalms. It is through these *successions* that a statement of the book is made.[13]

However, based on the structural shape of the Psalter uncovered, I am inclined to conclude that Ballhorn's methodology of linear reading across the entire Psalter as a book, while correct and necessary, is insufficient. The Psalter has to be read not just linearly, but concentrically as well, such that its structural form also informs its meaning. The third dimension, intertextual reading (see Mark's quote above), is also necessary. We have seen glimpses of this in the preceding chapters, but this will become

---

5. Weber, "Toward a Theory," 183, emphasis added.
6. Weber, "Toward a Theory," 164.
7. Weber, however, did not present a thesis for the entire Psalter in his article.
8. See our discussion of Barbiero's work in chapter 2.
9. Labuschagne, *Numerical Secrets of the Bible*, 11, emphasis added. The technique of numerical analyses will be discussed in chapter 5.
10. He cited Pss 37; 102; 4; 23; 8; and 65 in the Psalms. Alonso Schökel, *A Manual of Hebrew Poetics*, 197–98.
11. E.g., G. H. Wilson, N. deClaissé-Walford, C. McCann, W. Brueggemann, D. Howard, etc.
12. Ballhorn, *Zum Telos des Psalters*, 11.
13. Ballhorn, *Zum Telos des Psalters*, 11.

clearer in chapter 4 when we discuss how the Psalter is read alongside the Davidic narratives and covenantal promises.

Macrostructural chiasmi at the level of entire biblical books have been studied and shown to be plausible.[14] Nonetheless, identification of chiasmus, especially at the macrostructural level, must be done with caution, especially when it is constructed by generalized motifs or selected lexemes rephrased by the interpreters.[15] Being aware of this pitfall, our structural arguments are based on explicit/formal marking techniques such as superscriptions, formulaic phraseology and genre categories that are consistently observed.

Concentric reading highlights a central motif (CM).[16] This is the weight or the heart of a compositional unit of psalms. It is important for us to understand the phenomenon of the CM at the composition units of the Collection, Group, and Section.[17] This is because these compositional units function as the major structural components in the literary horizon of the entire Psalter revealing its shape.[18] The overall design of the Psalter remains obscure when the exegetical focus is too limited (smaller than a Collection) or partial (not the entire Psalter).

In chapter 1, we have shown from Freedman's analyses that chiastic arrangement with a central focus of Yhwh's triumphant kingship is a poetic technique found in the earliest of Hebrew poetry such as the Song of the Sea (Exod 15). There is a trajectory of Israel's journey from Egypt to the Promised land, where the people of God can dwell with Yhwh, is also observed (cf. Exod 15:1–11, 12–18). At the center (Exod 15:11–13), the poet highlights Yhwh's superior nature over all other gods.

The centralizing technique is also seen in the Akkadian poem, the "Descent of Ishtar to the Nether World," which spelled out the progression of seven gates to and fro from Hades. At the center of this chiasmus, the focus is on Ishtar entering and rising from hades—a thematic crucial event capturing also the turning point of the poem. The concentric structure is an important rhetorical device that draws the reader's attention to the heart of the psalm, emphasizing the victory that comes through Yhwh.

---

14. Symmetric structures for entire books, such as Song of Songs, have been proposed (Shea, "Chiastic Structure"). See also Ceresko, "Function of Chiasmus," 1–10; Watson points out that chiasmus occurring in long passages has "structural" and "expressive" functions. See Watson, *Classical Hebrew Poetry*, 205–7.

15. For a good discussion on over-zealousness in identifying chiasmus as a macrostructural technique and its pitfalls, see DeSilva, "X Marks the Spot?," 362.

16. Ronald Man notes two ways through which "chiasm help interpreters understand the meaning of biblical passages: (1) the presence of either a single central or two complementary central elements in the structure, which generally highlight the major thrust of the passage encompassed by the chiasm; and (2) the presence of complementary pairs of elements, in which each member of a pair can elucidate the other member and together form a composite meaning" (Man, "Value of Chiasm," 147–48).

17. Entire individual psalm (e.g., Ps 67) has already been shown to be concentric and linear. See deClaissé-Walford et al., *Book of Psalms*, 538–40.

18. Perhaps we can compare them to strophes and cantos poetic units within a single psalm.

The Design of the Psalter

In the Psalter, this CM is often associated with Yhwh's kingship, his rule from Zion, and the destruction of his enemies. From our analysis in the last chapter, we have observed that this technique has been applied beyond a single psalm. Thus, concentric and linear reading of poetry were rhetorical devices familiar to ancient readers.

Group Central Motifs (1–4) of Book I

In chapter 1 (Figure 12), we see significant motifs located at the concentric center of the four Groups of Book I (cf. 8–9, 19, 29–30, 38). Group 1 (3–14) is characterized by the genre of Lament.[19] For Barbiero, the central motif of Pss 3–14 is "the reign of man" based on Ps 8 (*Le règne de l'homme*).[20] Barbiero picks up the important elements of the בן־אדם ("son of man") whom God has set on earth to rule over creation (8:7–9). However, this motif does not capture the full thrust of both Pss 8–9 as the central psalms of Group 1. This can be seen in two ways. First, the universality of Yhwh's kingship frames Ps 8 (8:2, 4, 10).[21] Structurally, descriptions of human reign are subsumed under Yhwh's overarching purposes and power. The psalmist characterizes Yhwh's power over the enemies and his establishment of the heavenly orders (8:2–3) before describing the reign of man. Yhwh is also the one who *causes* man's rulership (תמשילהו; note the use of *hiphil* impf). In other words, the reign of man in Ps 8 is set under the auspices of Yhwh's overarching reign.

Second, the overall imagery in Ps 9 is, on one hand, Yhwh's siting on his throne in Zion judging triumphantly over the nations and the wicked (9:4–9, 16–18, 20–21), and on the other hand, establishing divine salvation for his people (9:10–15). The idea of Yhwh's judgment is repeated at least eight times in this psalm (9:5, 8, 9, 17, 20). No other psalm in the entire Psalter uses the term אבד ("to perish"; 9:4, 6-7, 19) to characterize the wicked more than Ps 9.[22] Clearly, the rhetorical weight of Ps 9 lies in the divine judgment over the wicked and providence for the righteous from Zion. Hence, in my view, Pss 8–9 underscore Yhwh's splendor,[23] his universal kingship in his establishment of the human king, his judgment over the wicked, and his providence for those who trust and seek him (9:11). In short, we modify Barbiero's view for the GCM of Group 1. It is more accurate to see it as "Yhwh's cosmic kingship and his judgment from Zion" rather than the "reign of man."

---

19. Barbiero, "Le Premier Livret Du Psautier," 475.

20. Barbiero, "Le Premier Livret Du Psautier," 477.

21. The phrase, "Yhwh, our God, how great is your name in all the earth!" (8:2, 10), stands at both ends of the psalm.

22. The lemma אבד occurs 26x in the Psalter. Psalm 9 contains 9 instances. This is followed by Ps 119 with 3 instances. These are the only two psalms with multiple instances.

23. Labuschagne argues that the central message is Yhwh's presence based on numerical analysis of Psalm 8. See Labuschagne, *Numerical Secrets of the Bible*, 146.

Concentric and Linear Reading

The second GCM can be summarized as: "Victorious Messianic king and Torah glorified" according to the main motifs of Pss 18–21 which are at the concentric center of Group 2. Psalms 18–21, instead of Ps 19, are the structural center of Group 2 for two reasons.

(1) *Psalms 18 and 22 are connected by common motifs of the Davidic kingship.* This has been well-argued by Grant who has shown that motifs such as Yhwh's chosenness, the king's dependence on Yhwh, and kingship law bind them together.[24] Apart from Ps 24 within Pss 15–24, the word "king" (מלך) is found only in Pss 18:51; 20:10; 21:2, 8. The unique form of משיח with the third-person suffix is found only in four places in the entire Psalter and in Group 2, it is found only in 18:51; 20:7. The similar words, ישע and ישועה ("salvation") recur often in Pss 18–22 linking them together.[25] The use of these common lexemes in Pss 18–22 bind these psalms together.

(2) *The Technique of inclusio in these psalms.* The use of anaphoras and inclusions is an established poetic technique. Psalms 18–19, 20, 21 are framed by certain recurring words. Psalms 18–19 is framed by the phrase, "O Yhwh, my rock" (צורי; cf. 18:3, 19:15). This phrase is found immediately after the superscription in Ps 18 and in the concluding line in Ps 19:15. A similar phenomenon of framing occurs in Pss 20 and 21. In Ps 20, the verb ענה ("to answer") is found at the beginning and end (cf. 20:2, 7, 10). In Ps 21, the word עז ("strength") is, likewise, found only at the two ends of the psalm. This structural phenomenon is seen *only* in these four psalms in Group 2 (15–24).

Within Pss 25–34 (Group 3), the GCM represented by Pss 29 and 30, is that of the historical Zion-temple and Yhwh's kingship. Barbiero has shown how Pss 29–30 are set apart at the center of the concentric structural unit.[26] Centered between Laments on the left (25–28) and Thanksgiving on the right (31–34), Pss 29–30 highlight Yhwh's enthronement at Zion. While Yhwh's kingship is clear in Ps 29, the distinguishing element in Ps 30 comes from its superscription. Apart from the superscription, Ps 30 is a typical Davidic Lament. Yet this superscription, שיר-חנכת הבית, is unique. It is the only superscription in the Psalter that specifically mentions Yhwh's house.[27] Furthermore, the editorial move to link the dedication of the House in Ps 30 with David rather than Solomon is clearly forced. This editorial move requires reading Pss 29–30 together.

There is also an interesting development regarding the subjects giving praise to Yhwh in the first three GCM. In Ps 8, it is the "heavens" and "all the earth" that declare the majesty of Yhwh (8:1, 9). In Ps 9, those who dwell in Zion are the ones who give praise to Yhwh (9:12, 15). In the second GCM, it is the anointed king (18: 3, 50) and

---

24. Grant, *King as Exemplar*, 175–78.
25. Pss 18:3–4, 28, 36, 47, 51; 20:6–7, 10; 21:2; 22:2, 22.
26. See chapter 2.
27. The phrase, "the house" (הבית), occurs in Pss 30:1; 59:1; 113:9, but only in Ps 30:1, it refers to the temple. The noun, "dedication" (חנכת), occurs only once (30:1) in the Psalter.

creation that give praise to both Yhwh and the Torah (19:1–11). In the third GCM, the "heavenly beings," (בני אלים; 29:1) are to "ascribe" (יהב) to Yhwh. This phrase, בני אלים, occurs only once in the HB. At the end of Ps 29:9, all in Yhwh's temple are to give "glory." The common factor in the subjects of praise in these three GCMs is the cosmic nature in all creation (cf. 8:1, 9; 19:1–2; 29:3–9).[28] It is also interesting that these subjects called to praise in the first three GCMs correspond with those found in Pss 145–150. The following figure illustrates this comparison.

First three GCMs	Subjects of Praise	Pss 145–150 (Final Hallel)
18: 3, 50	"I" or the Davidic king	145:1, 146:1–2
9:12, 15	People in Zion and Temple	147:12; 149:2; 150:1
29:1	heavenly beings	148:2
8:1, 9; 19:1–11	Cosmic expanse	148:3–10

Figure 38: Subjects who Praise Yhwh

The GCM of Group 4 (Ps 38) is a departure from the trend. It highlights the motif of David's supplication and contains an interesting phrase (להזכיר; "for a memorial") in the superscription that occurs once more in Ps 70:1. Barbiero has shown how Ps 38, a Supplication psalm, is set within two Sapiential psalms. The three psalms at the center (37–39) of Group 4 highlight the motif of patience, waiting in hope and prayer, desiring to be delivered from sin (38:4, 19).[29] The lexeme קוה ("to wait") occurs repeatedly in close succession over three psalms (37:9, 34; 39:8; 40:2).[30] Likewise, the motifs of Yhwh's שמר ("keeping") and the psalmist's שמר ("perseverance") occur repeatedly (37:28, 34, 37; 39:2; 41:3). These words, repeated with such frequency in these few psalms, reinforce the motif of supplication.

The GCM of supplication is further emphasized by the vocabulary of hastening Yhwh's deliverance under the wicked's derision.[31] The Qal imperative חוש ("to make haste") in Ps 38:23 occurs only seven times in the Psalms and only in Davidic psalms.

---

28. The word, רקיע ("expanse"), is found only in Pss 19:2; 150:1. In both instances, they are used in the context of praising Yhwh.

29. Note repetitions of similar motifs such as עון ("iniquity") in Pss 38:5, 19; 39:12; 40:13 and פשע ("transgression") in Pss 36:2; 37:38; 39:9.

30. The word דמם ("to be silent") and the phrase, והתחולל לו ("wait patiently for him"), in Ps 37:7 add to this motif.

31. The expression האח ("ah ha!") occurs only in Group 4 of Book I (35:21,25; 40:16; 70:4). Psalm 70:4 is a reuse of Ps 40:14–18.

In Book I, it occurs only in the second (22:20) and fourth (38:23; 40:14) Groups.[32] All seven instances are used in the contexts of the Davidic king seeking expedient deliverance of Yhwh. This motif of hastening Yhwh's deliverance connects three psalms (38, 40, 70) in an interesting way. As noted, the phrase, "for a memorial" (להזכיר), connects Pss 38:1 and 70:1 (both in superscriptions).[33] Furthermore, these two psalms are ACs.[34] The entire Ps 70, on the other hand, is an exact reuse of Ps 40:14–18, apart from changing the use of יהוה, אדני, and אלהי (40:14, 18) to אלהים in Ps 70.[35] Psalm 70 is also a Supplication psalm at the end of the Davidic Psalter in Book II. With the connections of these three psalms, the net effect is a heightening of the motif of supplication at the end of Book I (Group 4).

The GCMs of Groups 1–4 are not only understood via genre or thematic considerations, but certain unique poetic editorial moves (e.g., peculiar superscription) help to distinguish them. In summary, we propose that the four GCMs in Book I are: (a) Yhwh's cosmic kingship; judgment from Zion; (b) Victorious Messianic king and Torah glorified; (c) Dedication of the historical Zion-Temple and Yhwh's kingship; (d) Supplication of the afflicted David.

Group Central Motifs (5–8) of Books II–III

Groups 5–8 in Books II–III are Pss 42–49; 50–72; 73–83; and 84–89.[36] Group 5 is bound by Laments and its GCM is a kingship song (45) celebrating the military reign of the messianic king.[37] Psalm 45 is a unique psalm. Schroeder notes, "Whereas hymns of praise in the psalter are normally addressed to Yhwh, this psalm is a song of praise and promise to the *human* king who is seen in godlike features."[38] The central position of this psalm is again made evident by its unusual superscription. As a *maskil*, it is set apart from preceding psalms with an additional על-ששנים ("according to the lilies")

---

32. In Book II, it occurs once as part of the superscription in the Davidic Psalter (70:2, 6; 71:12). This imperative recurs once more as a superscription at the center of the final Davidic Collection in Ps 141:1.

33. Outside the Psalter, it is found only in 1 Kgs 17:18 and Amos 6:10. For a good study on the word זכר in the Psalms and how it unifies Book III, see Pavan, "He Remembered," 234–37. Special thanks to Marco Pavan for sharing a softcopy of his revised dissertation for this research.

34. See chapter 4.

35. This deliberate change in the use of the name of God in Ps 70 adds credibility to the proposition of an Elohistic Psalter. The peculiar use of להזכיר in the superscription in Ps 38 distinguishes it from the surrounding psalms. Its connection with Ps 70 highlights the motif of petition and the hastening of Yhwh's deliverance in Ps 38.

36. For the structural divisions of Books II–III, see chapter 2.

37. The Aramaic Targums and the early Christian community have interpreted Ps 45 messianically (cf. Heb 1:8–9). deClaissé-Walford et al., *Book of Psalms*, 416–17.

38. Schroeder argues that the messianic king imagery in Psalm 45 is depicted in two parallel strophes. While the first strophe shows the king's dominion through victory over his enemies (45:3–7), the second describes the king's dominion through marriage (45:8–16). Schroeder, "'Love Song,'" 417.

The Design of the Psalter

and שיר ידידת ("a song of love") in the superscription. No other psalm has these descriptions. In fact, the form, ידידת ("love"), is an *hapax legomenon*. Psalms that follow in this Group (46–49) are *not* marked as *maskil*.[39] Hence, from the perspective of the superscription, Ps 45 stands out as the Group's structural center as well as its motif of the victorious messianic king who takes a bride. The GCM of Group 5 in Books II–III can be summarized as the "Messianic king and his bride."

The GCM (61–64) of Group 6 (50–72) describes the threat to David's life and fall of his kingship. We have shown how Pss 61–64 is centrally located under a larger pericope (56–68) consisting of three Subgroups with superscriptions marked by "*mikhtam*" (56–60), "for the choir director, a psalm of David" (61–64), and "a song" (65–68), respectively. These three Subgroups are symmetrically bound by Laments and Supplication psalms (51–55, 69–71) on both sides. The overall thrust in Pss 56–64 is the bitter description of threats to David's life and the fall of his kingship. The mood, however, turns positive in Pss 65–68 with the foregrounding of Yhwh's power over nature, enemies and his deliverance of Israel. Psalm 68 ends with a celebration of Yhwh's victory over the kingdoms of the world at Zion.

As David's kingship and glory fade in Pss 56–64, Yhwh's kingship and power comes to the foreground in Pss 65–68. This weakening of the image of the Davidic king can be seen by the use of the adjective משיח, or the verb, משח. It is important to note that the adjectival form, משיח, ("anointed") does not occur in Pss 51–70, despite its ten instances in the Psalter.[40] Ironically, it is found in every Book of the Psalter except Book II where the historical depictions of David are most heightened.[41] The verbal form, משח, likewise, occurs only twice in the entire Psalter (45:8; 89:21), and is surprisingly also absent in the Davidic Pss 51–70. Perhaps this omission is deliberate in conjunction with the fall of the Davidic kingship in Book II. It suggests a conscious effort to disassociate the fallible human "David" depicted in the second Davidic Psalter from the transcendental, victorious "anointed" Davidic king.[42] These literary features and the organization of the three Subgroups, Pss 56–60, 61–64, 65–68 (particularly Pss 61–64), highlight the central motif of the fall of the Davidic king in Group 6.

The GCM of Group 7 (73–83) underscores the fall of Jerusalem and the Zion-temple (Figure 17). The motif of the fall of Jerusalem is introduced in Pss 42–44, setting the tone for the rest of Books II–III. This fall motif is also revealed by the strategic use of the term זנח as discussed in the last chapter.[43] The fall of Zion is most graphically pictured in Pss 74; 79–80. The word, משאות ("ruin"), referring to Zion in 74:3,

---

39. It is also possible to see Pss 45–48 as a Subgroup with a common motif of celebrating the messiah and Yhwh's kingship at Zion. Note that שיר also occur in the superscription of Ps 48. The two locations of שיר frame this Subgroup.

40. Cf. Oswalt, "משח."

41. Pss 2:2; 18:51; 20:7; 28:8; 84:10; 89:39, 52; 105:15; 132:10, 17.

42. We will revisit this issue in our discussion of the five Davidic Collections in chapter 4.

43. This fall of Zion motif is seen especially in the Laments Pss 74; 77; 79–80.

is an *hapax legomenon*. Everything in the sanctuary has been broken by the enemy (74:3). Extremely vivid descriptions are given in 74:3–9. The "engravings" (פתוחיה) of the sanctuary are smashed with "axe" (כשיל) and "hammer" (כילף). These words occur within a single verse and they are all *hapax legomena*. All meeting places of God in the land are burnt (74:8), the temple carvings smashed and its symbols removed. Foreign nations have taken over the house and set up their banners over it.

In a similar way, Ps 79 captures a lucid description of the destruction of Zion. It begins with the nations taking over the inheritance of Israel, defiling the temple and reducing Jerusalem to rubbles. The noun, עי ("rubbles/ruins") in 79:1, is the only instance found in the book of Psalms. In Ps 79:2, the bodies of Yhwh's servant are given to the birds for food and the flesh of the *chasidim* are "given to the wild animals of the earth." The lexeme, חסיד, occurs 25x in the Psalms and is 25x more than any other books of the HB.[44] The reference in Ps 79:2 is the most graphic and negative in all of the Psalter. This is in vivid contrast with Ps 16:10 where Yhwh would not let his *chasid* see decay.[45] These graphic depictions in Pss 74 and 79 emphasize the fall of Zion in the Psalms. Consider Figure 39 below.

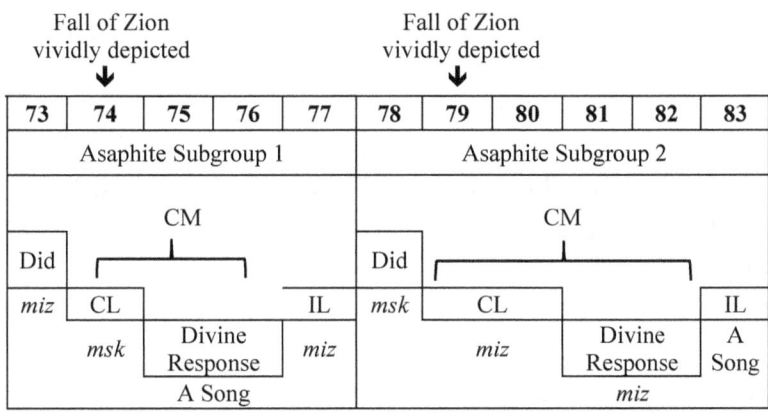

Figure 39: Central Motifs in the Asaphite Psalms[46]

Structurally, there are two parallel Subgroups within this Asaphite Group (73–77; 78–83). At the center of these Subgroups, we find two sets of psalms (74–76; 79–82) bound by a Didactic (73; 78) and Individual Lament (77; 83). These two sets of psalms at the center (74–76; 79–82) are parallel to each other. They depict the fall of the

---

44. Apart from the Psalms, this word occurs 7 more times. Deut 33:8; 1 Sam 2:9; 2 Sam 22:26; 2 Chr 6:41; Pss 4:4; 12:2; 16:10; 18:26; 30:5; 31:24; 32:6; 37:28; 43:1; 50:5; 52:11; 79:2; 85:9; 86:2; 89:20; 97:10; 116:15; 132:9, 16; 145:10, 17; 148:14; 149:1, 5, 9; Prov 2:8; Jer 3:12; Mic 7:2.

45. Cf. Pss 97:10; 116:15.

46. Legend: Did: Didactic psalm; *miz*: *mizmor* as superscription; msk: *maskil* as superscription; IL: Individual Lament; CL: Communal Lament.

The Design of the Psalter

Zion-temple (74; 79–80), and is followed by psalms of Divine Response (Yhwh's judgment in 75–76; 82).[47]

These central psalms are also marked differently by their superscriptions. Psalms 74–76 are distinguished with "*maskil*" and "a song" in their superscriptions. Psalms 73 and 77, framing 73–76, are marked with "a *mizmor* of Asaph." In a striking reversal, Pss 79–82 are linked by "a *mizmor* of Asaph,"[48] with Pss 78 and 83 distinguished by a "*maskil*" and "song" respectively. The organization of the superscription and genre of these psalms is unlikely to be fortuitous. And by their arrangement, the central position of Pss 74–76; 79–82 can be discerned.

Group 8 in Books II–III is the second Korahite psalms (84–89).[49] Interestingly, the central psalm is the solitary Davidic psalm (86) surrounded by Korahite psalms. Psalm 86 is the only psalm with a Davidic superscription in Book III and is titled as תפלה לדוד. The idea of a Davidic prayer, occurring after the postscript at 72:20 ("the prayers of David, son of Jesse, are completed"), is somewhat unexpected.[50] But there is a significant structural parallel—like the last GCM of Book I (Ps 38 in 35–41), the last GCM in Books II–III (Ps 86 in 84–89) highlights the supplication of an afflicted Davidic figure. The motif of supplication is clear in Ps 86:1–7, 11–13, 16–17.[51] The use of the absolute noun תפלה ("A prayer") in the superscription of 86:1[52] and תחנון ("plea") in 86:6[53] clearly chacterize the psalm as a Supplication.

The central position of Ps 86 is similarly revealed by its distinguishing superscription תפלה לדוד. On its left, the common phrases that characterized the superscriptions are "for the choir director, . . . a psalm of the sons of Korah" (cf. 84:1; 85:1). On its right, the superscriptions are characterized by the phrase "a song" (שיר; cf. 87:1; 88:1). Hence, Ps 86 is differentiated not only by its attribution to David but also by the characteristic difference of the two pairs of Korahite superscriptions around it.[54]

---

47. Note that the verb שפט ("to judge"), occurs six times in the entirety of Book III and only in the two sets of central psalms (Pss 75 and 82). The motif of "judgment" is associated with Yhwh's response to the fall of Zion (Cf. Pss 75:3, 8; 82:1–3, 8).

48. Psalm 81 does not have the *mizmor*. However, Pss 81–82 have the למנצח in their superscriptions which bind them (the למנצח is not found in the superscriptions of 78–83 apart from these two psalms).

49. Strictly speaking, Ps 86 is not a Korahite psalm. As such, I have avoided using Korahite "Collection" but have adopted the phraseology of "Group" which has structural, rather than genre connotations. See chapter 2 for a nomenclature of different compositional units in the Psalms.

50. DeClaissé-Walford et al., *Book of Psalms*, 659.

51. March shows how Ps 86 exudes various features of a "Complaint" psalm. March, "Psalm 86," 17–25.

52. In the absolute state, it occurs only in Pss 17:1; 42:9; 65:3; 86:1; 90:1; 102:1; 109:4; 142:1 within the Psalter.

53. As a common noun, it occurs only in Pss 28:2, 6; 31:23; 86:6; 116:1; 130:2; 140:7; 143:1.

54. Labuschagne highlights אדני, which occurs 7x in Ps 86 as the psalm with the highest frequency of the word in the Psalter. Since the Prophetic books adopt this term more frequently than other genres, Labuschagne suggests that there is a "prophetic provenance" in Ps 86. See Labuschagne "Psalm 86," 1–5.

In sum, the GCMs of Groups 5–8 in Books II–III are: (a) Messianic king and his bride; (b) fall of Davidic kingship (and Yhwh's response); (c) fall of Zion-temple (and Yhwh's judgment); (d) supplication of the Davidic figure.

Group Central Motifs (9–12) of Books IV–V

Referring to our macrostructural proposals for Books IV–V earlier (Figure 27 and Figure 28), the Yhwh *Malak* psalms (93–100), which highlight the motif of Yhwh's kingship,[55] is at the center of Group 9 (90–103). This centering of Yhwh's kingship is an established poetic technique and its central emphasis has been noticed by Howard and others.[56] Structurally, Pss 90–92 (to the left of the Yhwh *Malak* psalms), are sapiential in tone, emphasizing the motifs of living righteously before God and dwelling in him. Mournet points out that the use of מעון ("dwelling") in 90:1 (cf. לצור מעון ;71:3) implies that at the beginning of Book IV, the Israelites are seeking for a secure dwelling in God.[57] This motif of dwelling in Yhwh is sustained at the beginning of Ps 91 (ישב בסתר עליון; "one who dwells in the secret place of Elyon").[58] The word, מעון, recurs in 91:9 but the following verse reveals that the psalmist is dwelling in a "tent" (אהל). The imagery presented in 92:13–16 further heightens the imagery of dwelling securely in Yhwh's refuge. Here, the "righteous" (צדיק) will flourish like a palm tree and grow like a cedar in the house of God in Zion.

Crucially, Zion is depicted as the ultimate destination for Israel's longing to dwell securely in Yhwh. Together, Pss 90–92 recall the Moses' song and prayer in Deut 32–33.[59] Gundersen argues that these three psalms "activate the purpose and content of Deuteronomy 32–33."[60] Deuteronomy 32–33, as we know in their larger canonical context, envisage the impending entry into the Promised land by a new generation of Israelites.

To the right of the Yhwh *Malak* psalms are three psalms termed as the third Davidic Collection (DC-III; 101–103). Psalms 101–103 describe a Davidic figure who gives heed "in the blameless way" בדרך תמים; 101:2 and walks in his house with integrity. Psalm 102 is a prayer of affliction that looks forward to the *appointed time* for Yhwh's grace to be upon Zion when her people will be established (102:13–28). Psalm

---

55. Tanner argues that the enthronement Pss 93–99 form the "heart of Book Four" of the Psalter. See deClaissé-Walford et al., *Book of Psalms*, 706.

56. Howard, *Structure of Psalms 93–100*; Mitchell, *Message of the Psalter*, 284–91.

57. She argues that the LXX term is used elsewhere in the Psalter "to describe a place of refuge" and that the "message overwhelmingly at the beginning of Book IV is one of refuge in God, the ultimate source of the Israelites' security" (Mournet, "Moses and the Psalms," 70).

58. See the repetitions of synonymous nouns such as סתר ("covering," 91:1); מחסי ומצודתי ("my refuge and fortress," 91:2, 4, 9); צנה וסחרה ("shield and buckler," 91:4); מעון ("dwelling place," 91:9).

59. For parallels between Deut 32–33 and Pss 90–92, see Gundersen, "Davidic Hope," 116–36.

60. He adds, "Psalms 90–92 invoke an ancient lyrical witness against Israel, a witness that explains their exile while anticipating their exodus" (Gundersen, "Davidic Hope," 135).

103 underscores Yhwh's *hesed* to those who fear him and keep his ways (103:17–19). The word, ברך (*hiphil* imperative verb), occurs 5x in Ps 103, framing the psalm and accounts for the highest number of instances in any chapter of the Psalter. Led by the Davidic songleader, Ps 103 looks forward to a time when all creation is called to "bless the LORD" for the establishment of his throne and reign over all (103:19).[61] Hence, the Yhwh *Malak* psalms are framed by the voices of two "song leaders"—Moses on the left and David on the right.

Furthermore, several key terms connect the Subgroups Pss 90–92 and 101–103 with the effect of further distinguishing the Yhwh *Malak* psalms at the center. The verb, צוץ ("to flourish/spring up"), occurs only 5x in the Psalms.[62] Four out of five of its occurrences in the Psalms are used in arboreal analogies. The first four instances (72:16; 90:6; 92:8; 103:15) link Pss 90, 92 and 103 with the motif of mankind's temporal well-being in contrast to the lasting weal in Yhwh's city (72:16). The fifth use of צוץ in Ps 132:18 is associated with the messianic king planting humans in the paradisical garden (72:16).[63]

The strongest evidence for Pss 90–103 as a Group (rather than 90–106) is the spectacular use of the theme of man's frailty before Yhwh's eternal nature at the beginning of Ps 90 and end of Ps 103. Psalm 90 begins with the superscription of "Moses." This is followed by a description of Yhwh's "everlasting" nature. Psalm 90:3–6 describe mankind's returning to "dust" (90:3) and passing away over the night. They are quickly "swept away like a flood," and like "grass" (חציר; 90:5), they sprout anew in the morning and wither in the evening. These verses describe the temporary nature of human life in contrast with the everlasting nature of Yhwh (90:1–2). The main reason for the fleeting nature of human life is human iniquity (עון; 90:8) before Yhwh's anger (90:7).

Psalm 90 thus begins with four related motifs in this order: (a) the use of Moses's name; (b) characterization of Yhwh's everlasting nature; (c) the fleeting nature of mankind; (d) man's sins and the wrath of God. Remarkably, there is a striking reversal of these motifs at the end of Ps 103. In Ps 103:7, the name "Moses" reappears. This is followed by several verses describing Yhwh as being "slow to anger" (103:8) and not

---

61. Willis argues that the overall purpose is praising God for his love and mercy (103:1–2), in spite of difficulties (103:3–5) and in view of Yhwh's trustworthiness and character (103:6–19). Willis, "'So Great Is His Steadfast Love,'" 534, 537.

62. Pss 72:16; 90:6; 92:8; 103:15; 132:18.

63. Interestingly, Pss 72 and 92 use a different word, פרח (72:7; 92:8), to describe the concept of flourishing. Like פרח, צוץ is a rare word in the Psalter, found only in four places (72:7; 92:8, 13–14). In Ps 72:7, פרח is used in relation to the "righteous" under the rule of a transcendental and universal king (72:8–17). Its use in Ps 92:13–14 speaks of the righteous flourishing like palm trees. In the Psalms, the word, שתל ("planted"), occurs only in Pss 1:3; 92:14. They are "planted" (שתל) in the house of God and "flourish" (פרח) in the courts of God. The rare but repeated uses of צוץ and פרח at these common locations (Pss 72; 90; 92; 103; 132) seek to contrast mankind's fleeting nature with Yhwh's (and the Messiah's) reign and those who will flourish in Yhwh's house. This recalls the Prologue where the righteous will flourish in the paradisical temple (Ps 1) through the Messianic king (Ps 2).

"angry" forever (103:9). Moreover, Yhwh does not deal with his people according to their iniquities (עָוֹן; 103:10) and he will remove their transgressions (103:12). These descriptions of Yhwh's dealings with humans is followed by the same description of mankind's temporal nature in 103:15–16. Human beings are but "dust" (עָפָר; 103:14) and his days are as fleeting as "grass" (חָצִיר; 103:15). Finally, the temporal human nature is contrasted with Yhwh's everlasting and universal nature in Ps 103:17–19. This stunning parallel at the beginning of Ps 90 and end of Ps 103 is illustrated as follows:

A "Moses"
   B Yhwh's everlasting and universal nature
      C Fleeting nature of mankind
         D Yhwh consumes mankind in his anger because of their sins and iniquities

A' "Moses"
         D' Yhwh removes mankind's transgressions and will not be angry
      C' Fleeting nature of mankind
   B' Yhwh's everlasting and universal nature

The structural evidence above reinforces our proposition that Pss 90–103 is designed as a Group made up of three Subgroups (90–92; 93–100; 101–103). The GCM of the entire Group is Yhwh's kingship (93–100) at the center. This GCM is nicely flanked by the representations of two figures (Moses and David) on its left and right. Yhwh's kingship is also neatly balanced by two triads of psalms that describe, in general, (a) right living before Yhwh (90, 101); (b) affliction and refuge in Yhwh (91, 102), and (c) praise of Yhwh's *hesed* (92, 103) through which the righteous will flourish.

Group 10 (104–119) includes the fourth Davidic Collection (DC-IV) consisting of three psalms (108–110). These three psalms highlight Yhwh's deliverance and victory (108) through the affliction (109) and vindication of the Messianic king (110).[64] The centrality of Pss 108–110 is revealed by the parallelism of the thematic trajectories in Subgroups 104–107 and 111–119 that frame it (see Figure 40). Both Pss 104–107 and 111–119 trace a trajectory of the canonical history of Israel. Psalms 104–107 recapitulate the canonical history from creation to the Exile, culminating in a psalm of hope of Yhwh's restoration of Zion (107).

---

64. Crutchfield has made a strong case in identifying the victimized speaker in Psalm 109 and the "God-fearer" in Psalm 112 as the "Davidic messiah" of Psalm 110. As such, he views the entirety of Psalms 109–12 as messianic. Furthermore, Crutchfield argues that the "celebrant" in Psalm 118 is "likened to Moses" and when seen together with Pss 109–112, "[the] only person who could be referred to with such language in this context is the expected messiah" (Crutchfield, *Psalms in Their Context*, 28–35, 54). See also Ho, "Review of Crutchfield," 219–21.

104	105	106	107	108	109	110	111	112	113	114	115	116	117	118	119
brk	HD	H	HD	Dav			H				UT			H	HD	*Ash*
Canonical History: Creation to Exile. Brink of entry into Zion							Canonical History: Creation to Exile. Enter gates of Zion at Ps 118.								
				YHWH establishes afflicted, Davidic King in Zion											

Figure 40: Parallel Trajectories in Pss 104–107 and 111–119

In the same way, Pss 111–119 recall a trajectory from Egypt to Zion as well. This is seen via the Egyptian Hallel (113–117) which highlights the Exodus tradition.[65] Psalm 118 encapsulates various motifs in Pss 113–117,[66] culminating with the righteous' entry into Zion (118:27). Prinsloo has also argued for a *spatial* movement toward Zion in the Egyptian Hallel. He notes,

> Read as a single literary composition, the Egyptian Hallel tells a spatial story suggestive of a climactic movement from captivity to Jerusalem to the house of the LORD to the sanctuary to the altar. It is exactly this emphasis on Jerusalem and the sanctuary that raises the reader's suspicion that more than the exodus from Egypt is at stake.[67]

As such, DC-IV (108–110) is framed by two similar presentations. The presentation to its left (104–107) has a trajectory that ends with Israel at the brink of entering an inhabited city. The presentation on its right (111–119) recalls the Exodus tradition and has a trajectory that ends with the messianic figure and the righteous entering the Zion city (118:19–20).

The former (104–107) highlights the canonical story of the nation Israel *as a community* journeying toward a secure dwelling place (105:43–45; 106:47–48; 107:4–7). The latter (111–119) not only identifies Israel as a nation, but envisions *a righteous*

---

65. Crutchfield writes, "clearly Psalm 114, with its focus on the proper reaction to the Exodus event, introduces Psalm 115, which also focuses the spotlight not on Israel as a nation but on the God of the nation. In other words, these psalms foreground the importance on God in Israel's history" (Crutchfield, *Psalms in Their Context*, 92).

66. Crutchfield cites Mays and agrees with his thesis that "every one of the first five psalms in the cycle [of the Egyptian Hallel] anticipates themes and motifs of Psalm 118" (Mays, *Psalms*, 378). See also Crutchfield, *Psalms in Their Context*, 54.

67. He further argues that "Psalms 113–118 is a reflection upon deliverance from bondage, not only from the bondage of Egypt, but also the bondage of captivity and exile. It is a reinterpretation and a re-application of the exodus narrative for the postexilic community" (Prinsloo, "Šeʾôl→Yerûšālayim←Šāmayim," 755–56).

people (who fears the LORD) entering Zion and led by a divine warrior.⁶⁸ The warrior-like figure is not accentuated in Pss 104–107. This difference is important because, despite the common trajectories toward Zion, the latter presentation has taken on the characteristic of the warrior-king in the Davidic Collection in Pss 108–110 just before it. As such, it highlights Yhwh's deliverance through the vindication and victory of the messianic king. Another noteworthy feature is that in both Subgroups (104–107; 111–119), there is no definitive description of a final and utopic bliss state at the Zion city. This ideal Zion is sustained only toward the end of the SOA.

This movement to Zion also allows us to perceive the design of the larger textual pericope of Groups 9–10 (90–103, 104–119). Consider three structural parallels below.

(1) The entirety of Groups 9–10 are framed on one end by a Mosiac psalm and on the other, a Torah psalm (90, 119, cf. Figure 27).⁶⁹ Hence, on both ends of Pss 90–119 are two psalms that highlight wise-living and the fear of Yhwh (90:11–12; 119:63, 98). This framing suggests that the call for a wise and reverent living is associated with a movement to the Zion city.⁷⁰ When Groups 9–10 are seen together, the movement to Zion is traced by at least three Subgroup presentations (90–92; 104–107; 111–119). At the cores of Groups 9–10 lie Yhwh's universal kingship (93–100) and the Davidic kingship (108–110).

(2) The preceding point is reinforced by the use of the words, חכמה (90:12; 104:24; 107:27; 111:10) and חכם (esp. 105:22; 107:43; 119:98). They are found exactly in the three Subgroups associated with Israel's movement toward Zion (90–92; 104–107; 111–119). These two wisdom terms are not found elsewhere in Books IV–V.⁷¹

(3) There is another editorial move that binds Pss 91 and 119. In Ps 119, the psalmist praises Yhwh in his "house" (119:54) and finds Yhwh as "my hiding place and shield", סתרי ומגני, 119:114. The *nominal* form of סתר (indicating a "place of hiding") occurs interestingly at Pss 91:1 and 119:114.⁷² Their strategic presences in Pss 90–119 fit well with the developing motifs of seeking refuge in Yhwh and the desire for an inhabitation of rest.

---

68. Cf. Ps 106:3, 31 vs. Pss 111:3, 5; 112:1, 3, 4, 6, 9; 115:11, 13; 116:5; 118:4, 15, 20; 119:40, 63, 74, 79, 120, 137, 142.

69. Though not in the superscript, Ps 106 contains three references to "Moses," which is the highest in the Psalter. Mournet also points out that the root, נחם in Ps 106:45, connects with Ps 90:13. In Book IV, this word occurs only in Pss 90 and 106. These two references highlight Yhwh's relent toward Israel and faithfulness to his covenant. These repetitions also function to bookend Book IV. See Mournet, "Moses and the Psalms," 73.

70. This call to wise living is also present at the beginning of Book V in Ps 107:43, highlighting a parallel between the first psalms of Books IV and V.

71. Both words are rare in the Psalter. They occur six times each. חכם is found elsewhere in Pss 19:8; 49:11; 58:6 and חכמה is found elsewhere in Pss 37:30; 51:8.

72. Between Pss 91:1 and 119:114, the root סתר occurs as adverbs or verbs in Pss 101:5; 102:3; 104;29; 119:19.

Viewed through the ironic wordplay of the *verbal* form of סתר ("to hide") in Pss 88:15; 89:47; 102:2; 104:29; 119:19, there is a development of the motif of סתר from Lament to Confidence through Petition and sapiential reflections. At the end of Book III, the psalmist complains that Yhwh has *hidden* his face from him (89:47) and questions why he has done so (88:15). Four instances that follow, arranged in alternation, express the inner struggle between reflection (91:1; 104:29) and petition (102:2; 119:19). Finally, the last instance of סתר expresses the psalmist's confidence in Yhwh as his *hiding place* (119:114). These references of סתר are a display of the POS technique. Figure 41 presents this phenomenon graphically.

Location	Ref	Development of the Motif of סתר	Genre
End of Book III	88:15	Why do you hide your face?	Lament
	89:47	How long, will you hide yourself?	Lament
Book IV	91:1	He who dwells in the hidden place of Most High.	Reflection
	102:3	Do not hide your face!	Petition
	104:29	When you hide your face, they are dismayed.	Reflection
Ps 119 in Book V	119:19	Do not hide your commandments!	Petition
	119:114	You are my hiding place!	Confidence

Figure 41: Use of סתר in Psalms 88–119

We have noted that Book III, as a whole, highlights the fall of the Zion-temple and city. This is reflected in the lament that Yhwh has hidden his face. Groups 9–10 respond to the fall of Jerusalem by reframing a trajectory towards a "different" Zion-temple. This Zion-temple will be a *hiding place* and *refuge* for the psalmist, and is effective only for the "righteous." The call to live a life of wisdom, to embark on a Yhwh-fearing pilgrimage and to arrive at Yhwh's house, frame Groups 9–10. Between these bookends, Yhwh's universal rule (93–100) and the triumphant Davidic kingship (108–110) characterize the GCMs of Groups 9–10. Figure 42 summarizes our discussions.

Concentric and Linear Reading

90–92	93–100	101–103	104–106	107	108–110	111–119
Mosaic; Moses the song leader; At the brink of entry into Canaan.		Davidic; David the song leader; The Davidic king rules in Zion	Canonical History: Creation to Exile. Brink of entry			Creation to Exile. The king and the righteous enter gates of Zion (Ps 118)
↑ Living righteously is to dwell in the hiding place of YHWH (house of God)	GCM (GROUP 9) YHWH's kingship in Zion	↑ King rules righteously in house of YHWH			GCM (Group 10) Davidic Kingship in Zion	↑ Living the Torah-pious life means hiding in YHWH

Figure 42: Trajectories in Groups 9–10 of Books IV–V

The motif of dwelling securely at Zion with YHWH, as seen in Groups 9–10, develops in Group 11 (120–134). The CM of Group 11 is the establishment of an ideal Zion city. This is found at the structural and mathematical center (122; 127; 132) of the three Subgroups (120–124; 125–129; 130–134) as illustrated in Figure 43.[73]

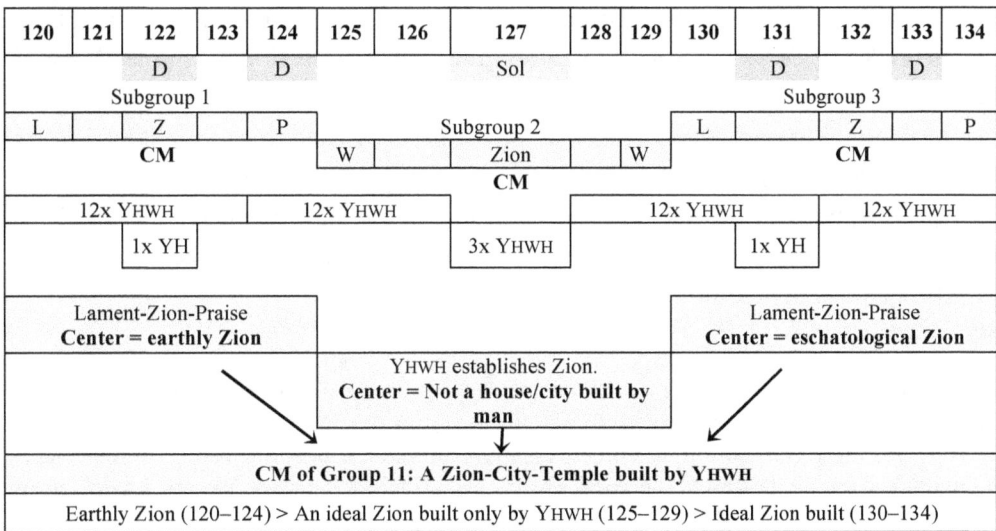

Figure 43: Central Motifs of the Songs of Ascents

In 122:2–3 and 126:1, postexilic Zion had been restored and the community of Israel is now settled in Jerusalem.[74] Israel might have resumed festive processions (or

---

73. For a discussion on the structural breakdown of the Songs of Ascents, chapter 2.

74. Booij identifies various evidence of a settled communal life with expressions of daily living in the Songs of Ascents. "First, there is a notable preference for scenes from daily life: slaves watching their master's gesture (Ps 123); people sowing and reaping (Ps 126); men discussing at the city gate (Ps 127); children sitting around the table (Ps 128); an infant at rest with its mother (Ps 131). Secondly, some terms, relevant to the community and its well-being, are found in remarkable frequency: 'Israel' nine times (and that in eight psalms), 'Zion' seven times (seven psalms), 'Jerusalem' five times (three

pilgrimage at the annual festivals) to the temple.⁷⁵ Booij suggests that the SOA, as a whole, *describes a procession to the sanctuary* for he sees that "[the] linkage of daily forms and images to words of consecration and friendly authority suits a ritual that, essentially, is a passage from common reality to the dwelling place of God."⁷⁶

Booij's argument that there is a movement towards the dwelling place of God in the SOA is a technique we have already seen in Barbiero's work on Book I. This progression is not limited spatially, but it can progress conceptually. We observe that depictions of the Zion-city at the end of the trajectories in Pss 104–107 and 111–119 do not reflect an ideal Zion. But in the three-part structure of the SOA, we see a development of a city that moves from an earthly Jerusalem (122) to an eschatological Zion (132) built by Yhwh alone (127).⁷⁷

The name, "Solomon," in the superscription of Ps 127 at the center of the SOA is a *dislegomenon* in the Psalter (72:1; 127:1).⁷⁸ Psalm 127 begins the motif of building a "house" and "city" in connection with Solomon (cf. 1 Kg 5). This connection between Solomon and the building of the sanctuary is heightened by the use of a *paronomasia*.⁷⁹ The words בית, בנה, and בנים are used in close proximity. The consonance of these words links the concepts of "building," "house," and "children."⁸⁰

While there is a *prima facie* connection between Solomon and the building of the temple in Ps 127, certain literary difficulties hinder this connection. First, the ideal and blissful depictions of Zion in Ps 127 remain elusive even within the psalm. Implicit in Ps 122 is an imperfect Zion city. Peace and prosperity need to be sought by prayers (122:6–9) and Ps 127 highlights the futility of human endeavor in building this ideal Zion-city. Although the psalm envisions a house of strength that is fruitful and "not be ashamed" before the enemies (127:5), the verity of this ideal is only certain through Yhwh's hands, not Solomon's.

---

psalms), 'bless' / 'blessing' ברך pi., pu. / ברכה nine times (five psalms), 'peace' (שלום) seven times (four psalms)" (Booij, "Psalms 120–136," 241–55).

75. Cf. Ps 126:1. Goulder postulates these psalms as liturgical sequences in parallel to Nehemiah's testimony and used at the feast of Tabernacles in 445 BCE. Goulder, "Songs of Ascents," 57; deClaissé-Walford et al., *Book of Psalms*, 917.

76. Booij, "Psalms 120–136," 246.

77. I am not alone in this proposition. Rohde points out that the expression "let Israel say" in Pss 124.1 and 129:1 supports a "tripartite division of Psalms 120–134 (three groups of five) at the end of each one the summons is repeated." He offers a good study of these three subgroups of psalms and argues that the Songs of Ascents argue for a metaphysical Temple. Zenger, likewise, argues for the same tripartite structure. See Rohde, "Observations," 25; Hossfeld and Zenger, *Psalms 3*, 394.

78. Zenger notes that the final redactors "placed Ps 127 at the center of the composition of the Pilgrim Psalter, as a 'royal' lesson for life by Solomon." See Hossfeld and Zenger, *Psalms 3*, 394.

79. A *paronomasia* is a kind of wordplay using two (or more) different words that sound alike. See Watson, *Classical Hebrew Poetry*, 242.

80. Miller discusses the meaning of "building a house" in Ps 127:1. He points out that the activity of building a "house" can refer to a "dynasty" (1 Sam 2:35; 2 Sam 7:27) or a "family line" (Deut 25:9; Ruth 4:11). Miller, "Psalm 127," 123–24.

Second, the absence of a righteous and powerful king building the Zion-city in the postexilic context is disconcerting. Psalm 72 is a prayer for the progeny of the messianic king of Israel.[81] It pictures righteous and powerful rule by a Davidic scion.[82] However, neither Pss 72 nor 127 can be easily applied to the historical Solomon or any king in the Davidic dynasty. In fact, Ps 127 seems to negate even the deeds of Solomon. The transcendental overtones applied on the messianic king in 2 Sam 7:12–16, 1 Chr 17:11–14[83] and in the Psalms add to the difficulties of identifying a specific king in the Davidic line.[84] Psalms 72, 122, 127 and 132 all envision a blissful state of life in Zion that is brought about by a victorious king whose identity, unfortunately, remains mysterious in the text.[85]

Thus, Ps 127 subverts a clear and direct connection to the historical Solomon as the king who will build Yhwh house and Zion-city. Why, then, is there a strategically important psalm at the center of the SOA possibly redacted for postexilic Israel at a time when hopes of rebuilding the nation is high, and yet downplays the role of a human king?

The answer I offer is to view Pss 122, 127 and 132 to understand the rationale of the SOA. Psalms 122 and 132[86] are two psalms in the entire Psalter with the highest number of "Zion/temple markers."[87] The presence of "Zion markers" would "indicate the Zion tradition in the minds of the editors."[88] These three psalms are centrally located in the three Subgroups of the SOA (Figure 43). The centering technique and their common focus on Zion are not incidental.

Contextually, Ps 120 is set at a distance from Jerusalem.[89] However, Ps 121 pictures an approach to the hills of Jerusalem with singing and praise. Then in Ps 122, the psalmist arrives at the gates of Jerusalem with jubilant joy (v. 2). Prinsloo notes that

81. Longman, *Psalms*, 270.

82. For a discussion on "Solomon" and the redaction of Ps 72, see Barbiero, "Risks of a Fragmented Reading," 67–91.

83. Barbiero, "Risks of a Fragmented Reading," 89.

84. Barbiero concludes that it is unlikely that the psalm refers to "a concrete reigning figure of the postexilic period" (Barbiero, "Psalm 132," 258). Cf. Ps 126:1.

85. Barbiero argues that "'Solomon' thus comes to personify the messianic hope of the community of the עֲנָוִים, according to the prophecy of [Zech] 9:9–10. Clearly, behind 'David' and 'Solomon' are two diverse models for understanding the Messiah. The first represents the Messiah as warrior perhaps alluding to the option chosen by the Maccabees. The author of Psalm 72 consciously keeps his distance from this typology. The Messiah will not be 'David,' but 'Solomon.'" See Barbiero, "Risks of a Fragmented Reading," 89–90.

86. Psalm 132 is also the longest psalm in the SOA.

87. Gillingham identifies at least 21 words and phrases that she (or rather, John Day) termed as "Zion Markers." These are identified by words/phrases that parallel "Zion" in the psalms. From these 21 words and phrases, she identifies 75 psalms that "bear clear marks" of the Zion tradition. In a later article, she uses the term, "temple marker," instead. See Gillingham, "Zion Tradition," 313–14; "Levitical Singers," 92.

88. Gillingham, "Zion Tradition," 315.

89. deClaissé-Walford et al., *Book of Psalms*, 899.

Pss 120–22 "describe a journey (Psalm 121) from negative space (Psalm 120) towards positive space (Psalm 122), an ascending movement, from the depths of despair and exile to the joyous arrival in Jerusalem."[90] This journey is marked with geographical and physical landmarks (120:5; 121:1, 122:1–3, 6–7, 9).[91] Although the terms, "Zion" and "Jerusalem," can take on different connotations, Goldingay suggests that the use of "Jerusalem" in Ps 122 identifies "more to an earthly city, the capital of Israel, a city of stone and brick, inhabited by people."[92] Zion, on the other hand, has a more "religious" connotation in association to the temple of Y<small>HWH</small>.

Psalm 122 is framed by the phrase, "the house of the L<small>ORD</small>" (122:1, 9). The verse at the center of the psalm (122:5) highlights the Davidic thrones of justice in Jerusalem.[93] This recalls the motifs of kingship and justice of 2 Sam 8:15—"David reigned over all Israel; and David administered justice and righteousness for all his people." However, the city has not yet become the just and righteous society longed for in Ps 122. This can also be seen by the need to pray for peace (122:6–8).

The just and blissful society envisioned in Ps 127 requires us to look beyond the Davidic monarchs in Israel's pre-exilic history.[94] It is in Ps 132 where the imagery of this blissful Zion is depicted in greater clarity. Psalm 132 identifies a time of no kingship (132:17) in postexilic Zion. This ideal Zion only takes shape with the advent of the "horn of David."[95]

Barbiero argues that Ps 132 is an expression of the messianic hope envisioned on a messianic-Solomon figure based on three points: (1) Ps 132:8–9 identify a kingdom of Y<small>HWH</small> with messianic perspectives. The "vision of 'peace' (v. 8) and of 'justice' (v. 9) echo that of Psalm 72, which is clearly "messianic."[96] (2) The use of Solomon's prayer from 2 Chr 6:41–42 in Ps 132:8–10 makes the prayer Solomonic. (3) Despite not using

---

90. Prinsloo, "Role of Space," 465, 472–73.

91. From "Meshech" and "Kedar" in Ps 120 to the "hills" in Ps 121, and to "House of Y<small>HWH</small> in Jerusalem" in Ps 122. Grossberg argues that "this pair, Meshech and Kedar, is to be taken as a merism expressing the totality of the menacing diaspora, even its most far-flung regions" (cf. Gen 10:2; 25:13; Ezek 27:13; 32:26; Isa 41:11). Grossberg, *Centripetal and Centrifugal Structures*, 24.

92. Goldingay, *Psalms*, 3:462.

93. The plurality of "thrones" suggests the Davidic dynasty (king and his sons). Goldingay, *Psalms*, 3:466.

94. German argues that the Solomonic superscription in Ps 127 provides the context of the Davidic dynasty for the entire psalm, emphasizing the Davidic lineage. He identifies the "blessed man" in 127:5 as David himself. While I agree that this superscription functions to highlight the Davidic lineage, I think German has not addressed the dilemma of the futility of building a house and watching a city in relation to that lineage. See German, "Contexts for Hearing," 196.

95. Zenger argues that the concept of "horn" represents "a revival of the powerful kingship of David in Jerusalem ('horn' as a metaphor for royal power: cf. especially Pss 18:3; 33:15; Zech 3:8; 6:12; Isa 11:1) and thus joins with corresponding postexilic hopes." See Hossfeld and Zenger, *Psalms 3*, 466.

96. Barbiero, "Psalm 132," 249.

the name "Solomon," the transition from משכנותיו ("his dwelling place"; 132:7) to מנוחתך ("his resting place in 132:8) alludes to Solomon's work of building the temple.[97]

As noted, the association to the historical Solomon in Ps 127 is problematic but seen messianically, Pss 127 and 132 make sense. It will be through this messianic-Solomonic figure which the ark (132:8) would find ultimate rest, and that the kingdom of peace and justice, envisioned in Ps 122, would be established. The kingdom of Yhwh and the kingdom of this messiah is "one and the same kingdom."[98]

In short, Pss 122; 127; and 132 become a triptych for Zion. A journey to the earthly gates of Jerusalem is first seen (122). The Jerusalem city and administration for justice pictured in Ps 122 is not ideal. The earthly Jerusalem can only become the ideal and utopic Zion-city-temple through Yhwh's deliverance (126), building (127) and blessing (128). Although the temple had been built by Solomon and rebuilt by the postexilic community, human hands cannot build the ideal Zion. Rather, the entire SOA, seen through these central motifs (122; 127; and 132), show that the ideal Zion will be ruled by a righteous, divine Solomonic-Messianic figure (127:1; 132:11–12) who will usher *shalom*, unity and blessing into Zion.

Prinsloo's spatial analysis of Pss 120–134 reinforces our proposals above. He argues that Pss 120–122 is a movement towards the earthly Jerusalem on the horizontal plane moving from strife to peace. Psalm 123, set "symbolically" in heaven (123:1), shows that the danger is still present. The spatial imagery in Ps 124 is symbolic of Sheol (124:3–4). Psalm 125 brings the spatial imagery back to earthly Zion. The following Pss 126–28 is a triad that forms the core of the SOA with Ps 127 at the center. Spatially located at Zion and around Ps 127, Pss 125–129 emphasize Yhwh's deliverance and protection surround Israel so that she can flourish in peace. Psalms 129–31 mirror 123–25 symmetrically.[99] Psalms 132–134 form a final triad in parallel to 120–122. Psalm 132, like 122, focuses on Zion. Psalm 133, like 121, brings out the imagery of the "mountains of Zion" (133:3) while Ps 134 contrasts with Ps 120, depicting a positive house of the LORD. Prinsloo's entire spatial map of the SOA is illustrated in Figure 44.

---

97. Barbiero's argument is convincing. He notes, "In context, this term [מנוחה] suggests the temple built by Solomon. David's משכנותיו [Ps 132:7] was a provisional dwelling, not a permanent one. The מנוחתך [Ps 132:8] is meant to express the stability offered by a solid building, a construction in stone. But this term is a pregnant one that goes beyond the concrete reference. It occurs again with respect to the temple, in Deut 12:9; 1 Kgs 8:56; Ps 95:11 and Isa 66:1 (מקום מנוחתי)" (Barbiero, "Psalm 132," 246).

98. Barbiero, "Psalm 132," 258.

99. Psalm 129, like 125, highlights Yhwh's protection on earth. Psalm 130, like 124, is spatially located in the "depths" (130:1). Psalm 131, like 123, highlights Yhwh's redemption of Israel's sin and Israel finding "calmness in Yhwh's arms (131:2). The use of "lifted up" (גבה) and "high" (רום) in Ps 131:1 may suggest a "heavenly" spatial frame though the content identifies Yhwh's bosom. Although Prinsloo identifies Ps 131 spatially in "heavens" in his final graphical summary, his arguments stop short of situating the "complete contentedness in the presence of Yhwh" in the heavenly realm. See Prinsloo, "Role of Space," 470, 473–74.

The Design of the Psalter

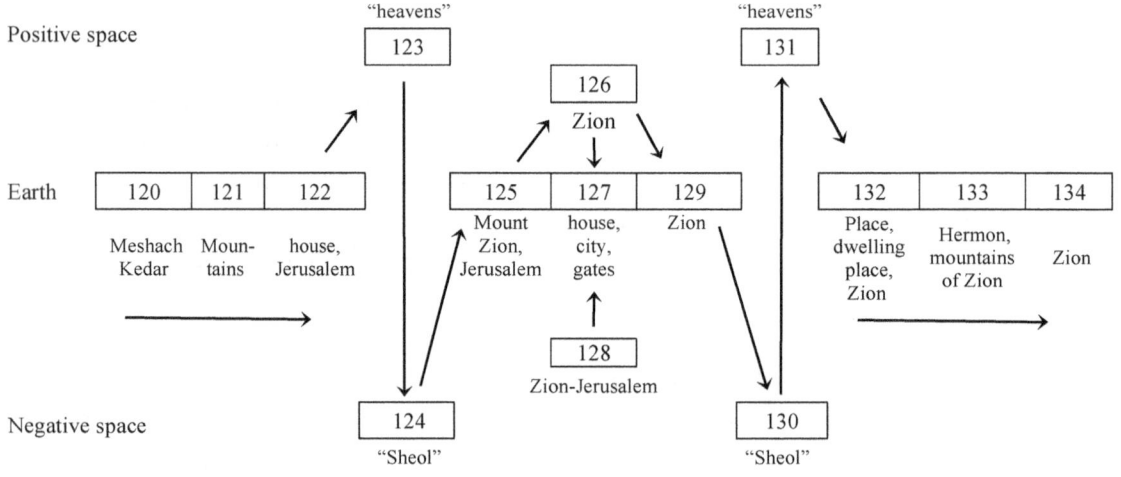

Figure 44: Prinsloo's Spatial Storyline of the Songs of Ascents[100]

Although Prinsloo's structural map is grouped into five triads as opposed to our triad of five psalms each, the final effect is similar—the SOA is still structured concentrically with Pss 125–29 as the core. It is also possible to see Pss 120–22 and 132–34 as parallels. While Pss 120–22 capture a troubled situation leading to rejoicing at earthly Jerusalem, 132–34 identify a blissful eschatological state in Zion.

In short, the GCM of the SOA (Group 11) depicts the development of the Zion-temple. A three-step development of Zion is captured by the triptych Pss 122, 127 and 132, which are located at the respective centers of the three Subgroups Pss 120–24, 125–29, 130–34.

Moving on to Group 12 (135–150), the GCM is the recurring concept of supplication found within the fifth Davidic Collection (138–145).[101] This last Davidic Collection sits between the Great Hallel (135–136) and the final Hallel (146–150). Bound by two Kingship psalms (138, 145) four Supplication psalms (140–143), united by the words, תחנון ("plea"; 140:7; 143:1) and תפלה ("prayer"; 141:2, 5; 142:1; 143:1)[102] and their literary contexts of affliction, form the CM of DC-V and the entire Group 12.

---

100. This is redrawn from Prinsloo, "Role of Space," 474.

101. There is some disagreement between scholars in naming Pss 138–145 as the "fifth/last" Davidic Psalter (Zenger, Tucker, Buysch), "fourth" David Psalter (Seybold, Singer) or "third Davidic Collection" (Wenham, cf. Auwers). In this volume, I am in agreement with Buysch's argument, considering Pss 101–103 and 108–110 as two Davidic Collections (third and fourth). See Buysch, *Der Letzte Davidpsalter*, 15; Cf. Hossfeld and Zenger, *Psalms 3*, 524; Tucker, "Role of the Foe," 186; Seybold, "Zur Geschichte," 368–90; Singer, "Literary Context," 373; Wenham, *Psalms as Torah*, 48; Auwers, *La Composition*, 27.

102. The word תפלה occurs 11x in Books IV–V (Pss 90:1; 102:1–2, 18; 109:4, 7; 141:2, 5; 142:1; 143:1), of which three times are in superscriptions (90:1; 102:1; 142:1). All the occurrences of תפלה in Books IV–V are always followed closely by Divine Response psalms which emphasize Yhwh's

With this focus of supplication in the last GCM of Group 12, we observe a striking parallel in all fourth GCMs of the three Sections of the Psalter (cf. Figures 12, 17, 27 and 28)—a common motif of supplication. Moreover, these GCMs are all Davidic (cf. 38; 86; 140–143). In other words, there is a recurring motif of Davidic supplication skillfully located in the fourth GCMs of the three Sections (1–41; 42–89; 90–150). The significance of this final CM of supplication will be discussed in chapter 4.[103]

Parallel between Groups 10 and 12 in Books IV–V of the Psalter

The amazing structural design and significance of the GCMs' location and function can be further understood by remarkable distant parallels between Groups 10 and 12 (104–119; 135–150). The following observations are in order. (1) Both Groups begin with *hallelujah* psalms (104–106 // 135) and end with psalms that characterize an all-encompassing praise of Yhwh and his Torah (119 // 150). The "totality" of praise in these two ending psalms are also partly exuded by their acrostic (or alphabetical) poetical structure. At the center of both Groups is a Davidic Collection (108–110; 138–145).

(2) Groups 10 and 12 (104–119; 135–150) also share a thematic trajectory from creation to exile (cf. Subgroups 104–107 // 135–137). From the parallel of the trajectories between 104–107 and 135–137, we can now understand the location of Ps 137, with its exilic focus, immediately after Ps 136. Psalm 137 completes this thematic movement from creation to exile.

Psalms 104–107 trace the canonical history of Israel and the trajectory that ends at Ps 107 envisages the establishment of a secure dwelling at Zion (107:4, 7, 36). Similarly, Pss 135–136 recapitulate the canonical history (135–136) and ends with the exile in Babylon (137). Hence, at the end of both Subgroups Pss 104–107 and 135–137, the settings in Pss 107 and 137 are exilic. The exilic imageries in Pss 107:3, 7, 14, 16, 28–30, 36; 137:1 reflect a desire for a better Zion, and not merely an inhabited city. This yearning for a movement toward Zion is expressed as conceptually as opposed to an actual movement, suggesting that an ideal, rather than earthly Zion, is in view.[104]

---

kingship, deliverance and blessings (93–100; 103:19–22; 110; 144–145; cf. 74–76; 79–82).

103. This is supported by Gillmayr-Bucher's word field analysis of the concept of "misery" in the Psalms. See Figure 1 in her article, where there is a perceivable high frequency of occurrences of the concept of "misery" in psalms located near the end of Section 1, 3 and 5 by our structural definition. Gillmayr-Bucher, "Relecture of Biblical Psalms," 314.

104. An alternative way of viewing the two trajectories of Pss 104–107 and 135–137 is to consider that the latter is a development from the former. That is, Pss 104–107 could refer to the historical return from exile while Pss 135–137 pertain to an *ongoing* return because postexilic Israel remains under foreign rule. An additional point on the parallel pertains to the inverted *nun* which occurs only in nine places in the HB (Num 10:34, 36; Pss 107:20–25, 39). While I am not positing any definitive solutions, the occurrences in Numbers 10 and Ps 107 are connected by a movement toward the Promised Land. There is a common motif of Yhwh leading the people from a place of misery towards a place of blessing (cf. Num 10:29; Ps 107:14, 28, 39). The setting of wilderness connects the two passages as well

The Design of the Psalter

Groups 10 and 12 also end with a destination at Zion (111–119 // 146–150). A similar trajectory to Zion is also traced in the Egyptian Hallel (113–118). In the Final Hallel (146–150), it is possible to detect a movement that begins from Yhwh's creation (146:6), followed by deliverance of his people (146:7–9) from exile (נדחי ישראל; "the exiles of Israel"; 147:2), and Yhwh's building of Zion (146:10; 147:2, 12–14), before ending with praise of Yhwh in the ideal Zion (149:1–2; 150:1).

Therefore, we can trace at least six such movements toward Zion in Pss 90–150. This trajectory to Zion (whether earthly or ideal) is found in every Group of Books IV–V. These recapitulations reinforce the centrality of the motif of Zion from Ps 90 to the end of the Psalter. The following figure illustrates these movements towards Zion in Groups 9–12 graphically. The symbol "→Z" indicates the presence of such movement.

Group 9			Group 10			Group 11			Group 12		
90–92	93–100	101–103	104–107	108–110	111–119	120–124	125–129	130–134	135–137	138–145	146–150
Mosaic	Yhwh *Malak*	DC-III	Canonical histoty	DC-IV	Hallelu-jah psalms	Songs of Ascents			Canonical history	DC-V Suppli-cation	Final Hallel
→Z ideal		At earthly Zion?	→Z earthly		→Z earthly?	→Z earthly	Ideal Zion estab.	At ideal Zion?	→Z ideal?		→Z Ideal

Figure 45: Movement toward Zion in Books IV–V

(3) There are four lexical parallels between Subgroups Pss 111–119 and the Final Hallel. (a) The phrase, "maker of heaven and earth" (עשה שמים וארץ), occurs only in six places in the Psalter.[105] All six instances of this phrase are associated with God's creation and are located in Book V of the Psalter. Apart from the SOA, this phrase occurs only in the Egyptian Hallel (115:15) and Final Hallel (146:6).[106] The use of this formulaic phrase and the creation motif bind the Egyptian and Final Hallels.

(b) The Egyptian and Final Hallels are the only two literary units with the most sustained recurrences of the *piel* imperative הלל.[107] With the exception of Ps 114, Pss

(Num 10:12, 32; Ps 107:4, 33, 35). This view of Pss 135–137 will fit well with either Jewish or Christian reading. For a comparison of Christians and Jewish readings on Ps 137, see Gillingham, "Reception of Psalm 137," 64–82.

105. Pss 115:15; 121:2; 124:8; 134:3; 135:6; 146:6. Inclusive of prefixed prepositions or conjunctions on any of the lexemes.

106. When we expand the search to include these three lexemes occurring separately within a single verse in the HB, the result significantly recalls Yhwh's creation. Cf. Gen 1:26; 2:4; Exod 20:11; 31:17; 2 Kgs 19:15; 2 Chr 2:11; Neh 9:6; Ps 102:25; Isa 37:16; 44:24; 45:12; 45:18; Jer 32:17; 51:15–16. Another associated motif based on these lexemes is Yhwh's universal power, though occurring less frequently than the creation motif. Cf. Deut 3:24; 28:12.

107. Cf. the occurrences in Pss 104–106 and 135.

111–117 are framed with הלל either at the beginning of the psalm (111–113), at the end (115–116), or at both ends (117). Furthermore, both Hallels contain a symbolic number of the *piel* imperative הלל (10x in Pss 111–117 and 28x in the Final Hallel).[108]

(c) Both Hallels are bound by AAs and/or ACs. Psalms 111–112 and 119 are clearly acrostics psalms. Psalms 145 and 150, framing the Final Hallel, are AA and AC respectively.

(d) Psalms 111–119 and 146–150 are the only two Subgroups in Book V that sustain the motif of the Torah extensively. The words, פקודים ("precepts"),[109] מצוה ("commandment"), אמרה[110] ("utterance"),[111] and משפט ("judgment")[112] are found almost exclusively in these two Subgroups in Book V.

(4) Psalms 135–136 parallel Pss 104–106 as Janus psalms. While Pss 135–136 can be read as the first two psalms of Group 12 (135–150), it is also possible to read them as the celebration of the completion of Yhwh's house in Ps 132. The Pentateuch records that soon after the completion of the Tabernacle, Aaron is consecrated and the Levites are set apart to serve in the sanctuary (Exod 40; Num 3–4). This sequence of events is mimicked in Pss 132–136. First, the completion of the house of God is seen in Ps 132 with the ark arriving at its resting place (cf. 132:7, 14). Then the anointing of Aaron in Ps 133:2 corresponds to the Exodus account in which Aaron is anointed after the completion of the Tabernacle (Exod 40:1–15). Psalm 134 highlights the temple servants who minister in Yhwh's house day and night. This has clear parallels to the giving of laws and instructions of the ministry of the Levites at the Tabernacle "day and night" in the entire Book of Leviticus after the Tabernacle is completed (Num 3–4; Exod 30:7; Lev 8:35; cf. 1 Chr 23:28–30). Moreover, at the completion of the temple (a parallel of the Tabernacle), Aaron and his sons are to burn incense before the Lord and minister to Him. They are called "to bless in His name forever" (1 Chr 23:13). It is striking that a similar benediction is seen in Ps 135:19–20, where "Israel," "Aaron" and "Levi"[113] are called to "bless the Lord"!

---

108. We have seen the recurring numbers "10," "7" and "4" in our study of superscriptions earlier. More discussion on numerical devices are in chapter 5.

109. Pss 111:7; 119:4, 15, 27, 40, 45, 56, 63, 69, 78, 87, 93–94, 100, 104, 110, 128, 134, 141, 159, 168, 173.

110. Pss 112:1; 119:6, 10, 19, 21, 32, 35, 47–48, 60, 66, 73, 86, 96, 98, 115, 127, 131, 143, 151, 166, 172, 176.

111. Pss 119:11, 38, 41, 50, 58, 67, 76, 82, 103, 116, 123, 133, 140, 148, 154, 158, 162, 170, 172; 138:2; 147:15.

112. Pss 111:7; 112:5; 119:7, 13, 20, 30, 39, 43, 52, 62, 75, 84, 91, 102, 106, 108, 120–121, 132, 137, 149, 156, 160, 164, 175; 122:5; 140:13; 143:2; 146:7; 147:19–20; 149:9.

113. "Levi" in Ps 135:20 is the only instance found in the Psalms.

The Design of the Psalter

From the Chronicles, we see how the formula כי טוב כי לעולם חסדו was used.[114] It was sung when David celebrated the bringing of the ark to Jerusalem (1 Chr 16:34).[115] This formula is recited again when the ark is moved into the temple that Solomon had built (2 Chr 6:41—7:3). The sons of Israel, upon seeing the glory of the Lord filling the temple, "gave praise [ידה] to the Lord," and invoked the exact formula, כי טוב כי לעולם חסדו (2 Chr 7:3, 6).

Thus, this formula is associated with the climactic celebration of the completion of Yhwh's house.

The 26 instances of this formulaic expression in Ps 136 fulfill a similar role in the Psalms.[116] Psalm 136 contains 26 verselines and 52 (26x2) cola.[117] These two figures are "symbolic representation of the Tetragrammaton (10+5+6+5)."[118] Significantly, the connection between the name of Yhwh (the number 26) and the completion of the temple recalls the Davidic covenant in 2 Sam 7:13 (הוא יבנה-בית לשמי).[119] What a fitting finale to the completion of the Zion-temple!

Psalm 136 is structured in two halves. The first half of every line recapitulates the canonical trajectory from God's creation to the deliverance of his people. This trajectory connects Ps 136 to 137. However, the second half of every verse in Ps 136 contains the formula, כי טוב כי לעולם חסדו, and connects with the preceding Pss 132–135. Seen under this horizon, Ps 136 functions as the climactic praise at the completion of the sanctuary. Hence, Pss 135–136, like 104–107, function as a unit of Janus-psalms.

These four literary character show how Group 10 parallels Group 12 in Books IV–V and supports our structural argument that the fourth and fifth Davidic Collections are at the center of both Groups. In sum, the GCMs for Books IV–V are: (a) Yhwh's universal kingship and judgment from Zion (93–100); (b) victorious Davidic king and Torah glorified (108–110); (c) the establishment of the eschatological ideal Zion-Temple (122; 127; 132) by a messianic king; and (d) the supplication of the afflicted David (140–143).

---

114. On the origins of this phrase, Shipp suggests that "(1) the historical background and setting for the refrain was corporate temple worship; (2) it figured prominently in the temple dedications or cultic installations; (3) it was intoned in response to present crises, persecution, or recent deliverance; and (4) it called upon the community and the Lord to remember the everlasting nature of the Covenant commitment of the Lord to Israel, to remind God of his promise to deliver Israel in light of the present distress, and to remind them that they could rely on God for covenant faithfulness because he is good" (Shipp, "Remember His Covenant Forever,'" 31).

115. Cf. 2 Chr 5:13; 7:3; Ezra 3:11.

116. We have discussed how Pss 135–36 function as Janus psalms, linking Pss 120–134 and 135–150 together. Seen in this way, Pss 135–36 opens the final Group, highlighting the completion of Yhwh's house and framing the entire final Group with Ps 150.

117. Van der Lugt, *CAS III*, 455.

118. Van der Lugt, *CAS III*, 455.

119. Cf. 1 Kgs 5:5; 8:18–19; 1 Chr 22:10; 28:3; 2 Chr 6:8; Mal 1:11.

Summary of Group Central Motifs in the MT Psalter

The GCMs of the three Sections of the MT Psalter are summarized in Figure 46.

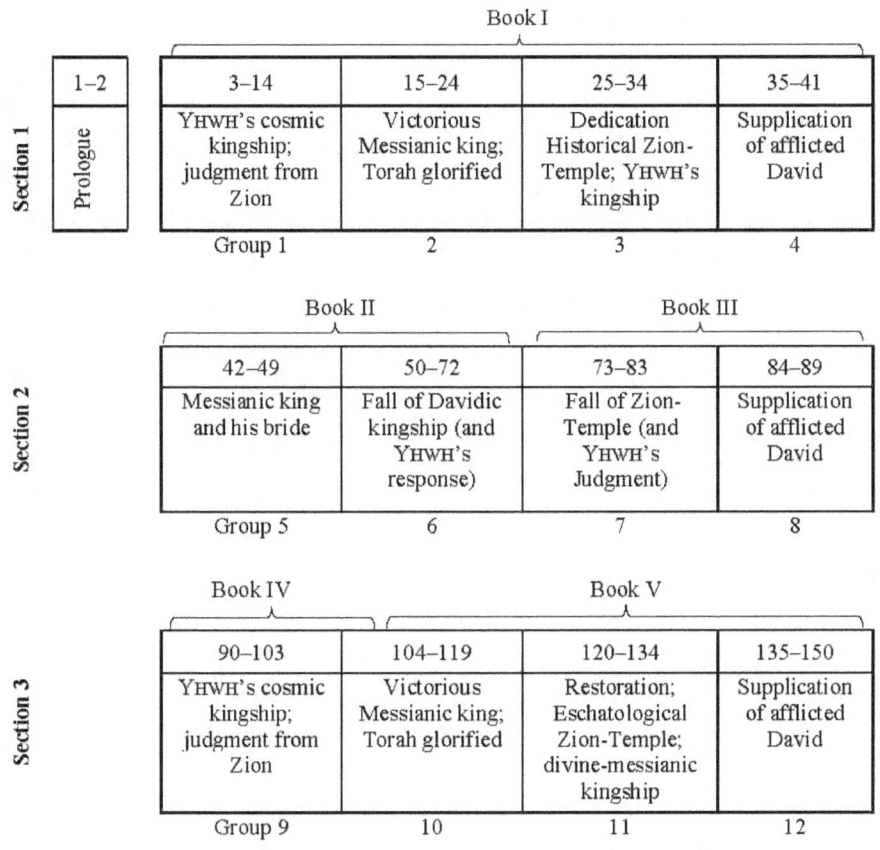

Figure 46: Central Motifs of all 12 Groups in the 3 Sections of the MT Psalter

Based on the GCMs, the MT-150 reveals a structure of three Sections, each consisting of four Groups that parallel one another. The three Sections are also concentric. In the first chapter, we argue that the Prologue identifies two central motifs: (1) the blessed man flourishes in the paradisical garden because of his Torah-pious life, and (2) YHWH's universal victorious reign from the eschatological Zion through his son, the vicegerent Messianic king. These two leitmotifs are recapitulated in various GCMs throughout the Psalter (e.g., 15–34; 104–34).

From Figure 46, the first GCM of each Section is the glorification of YHWH and/or the Messianic king. This can be seen vertically down Groups 1, 5 and 9 with minor nuances. In the first Section, YHWH's kingship is seen in his creative powers and universal rule (Group 1). In the second Section, the highlight is the marriage celebration of the God-like Messianic king (Group 5). In the third Section, the focus is on YHWH's kingship and his universal judgment over nations and powers (Group 9).

The Design of the Psalter

On the other end, the fourth GCM in each Section (Groups 4, 8 and 12) highlights the supplication of an afflicted David. This motif of supplication consistently recur down Groups 4, 8 and 12. Hence, the GCM in the first and fourth Groups in all Sections are recurring focuses on Yhwh/Messianic kingship and Davidic supplication. They form the bookends across each Section.

Horizontally across each Section, the second and third Groups lie at the center. Following the development of the two center Groups down the three Sections, the crucial Metanarrative of the entire Psalter us revealed. The second GCMs down the three Sections in Groups 2, 6 and 10 emphasize the Davidic king. Specifically, they trace the establishment, fall, and the (re)establishment of an ideal Davidic king. A distinction between the Messianic king and historical Davidic monarch has previously been noted. The term, משיח ("anointed"), which was avoided deliberately throughout Book II, is likely one aspects of the distinction. The third GCMs down the three Sections in Groups 3, 7 and 11 emphasize the Zion-temple. Likewise, they trace the establishment, fall and (re)establishment of Zion.

In short, concentricity occurs horizontally across the four Groups in each of the three Sections. A three-part concentricity also occur vertically down the three Sections. Linearity occurs down the Sections along the two center Groups 2, 6, 10 and Groups 3, 7, 11.

The Metanarrative of the MT Psalter is formed by a concentric-linear parallel macrostructure that celebrates Yhwh-Messianic kingship by tracing the establishment, fall of the Davidic kingship and Zion-temple at the center, and their subsequent reestablishment. We can further summarize our discussion with Figure 47 below.

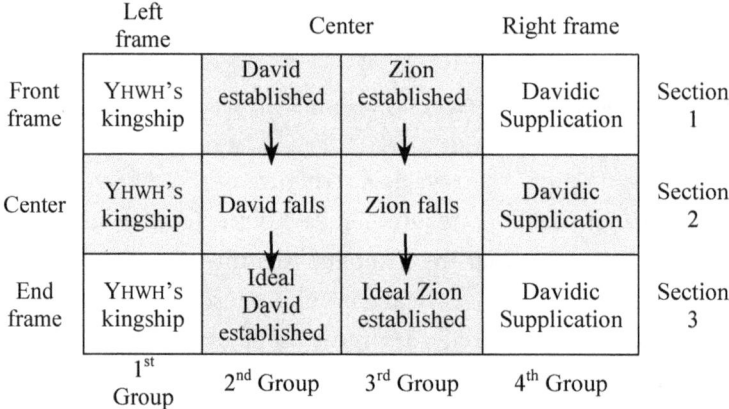

Figure 47: Concentric and Linear Structures of the Group Central Motifs

We highlight two peculiarities in the macrostructure. First, there are unchanging motifs of Yhwh's universal kingship and supplication down the Left and Right frames (first and fourth Groups). These two "static" motifs bind two developing motifs of the Davidic kingship and Zion in the second and third columns. The Davidic supplication along the right frame suggests a persistent presence of afflictions and distresses, but they are counter-balanced by the persistent restatement of Yhwh's kingship along the left frame. This persistence of Davidic supplication in affliction recalls 1 Kings 11:39 where God raised up Jeroboam because of Solomon's rebellion, saying "I will afflict the offspring of David because of this [turning from Yhwh], but not forever." In the last phrase of 1 Kings 11:39, this supplication will not be "forever." That is why the laments give way to praise in the Psalter. Praise, not affliction or supplication, is the consummative end to the Psalms. This is expressed by the Final Hallel (146–150) *after* the Davidic Collection (138–145).

Second, our analyses show that the macrostructural shape of the MT Psalter is an ingenious design integrating poetical (e.g., superscription, inclusion, numerical) and thematic (e.g., genre) techniques. In this chapter, we also see the use (or absence) of certain lexemes plays a role in the macrostructure. Correspondence, collaboration and coherence of technique, form and content consistently across the entire macrostructure of the Psalter make a strong case for our proposal.

Barr's quotation at the beginning of this chapter deserves a repetition: "The case for meaning must be decided on literary criteria: one must show that a unit is not just an anthology but is an intended structure with meaning."[120] It is helpful to reflect on the extent to which our structural analysis "is an intended structure with meaning."

Our study shows that the concentric structuring technique is a major literary tool employed by the final editors to explicate meaning. The chiasmus, expressing parallelism and symmetry in various forms, is more prevalent in the Hebrew Bible than we had perceived.[121] This technique, as noted, has been widely practised in ancient Mesopotamia.[122]

Large sections of texts can also be arranged linearly as well as concentrically. For instance, Dorsey points out that the Book of Judges is one that consists of both a linear and a "secondary symmetric scheme, in which the introduction (1:1–3:6) is matched by the conclusion (17:1–21:25); and the body itself presents the seven major judges in an order that has a conspicuous touch of symmetry."[123] There are rhetorical advantages

---

120. Barr, *Holy Scripture*, 160.
121. See especially the work of Dorsey, *Literary Structure*; Welch, *Chiasmus in Antiquity*, 9–16.
122. For instance, in the Akkadian hymn, the "Descent of Ishtar to the Nether World."
123. The following structure has been identified by Dorsey, *Literary Structure*, 31:

for such structures[124]: They provide (a) aesthetical beauty and compositional balance to the text; (b) coherence based on a structured text; (c) a sense of completeness; (d) a central focus which indicates a climax or turning point; (e) memory aid to the successive points in the text; (f) opportunities to develop parallels and repetitions.

These six advantages of concentric structures are audience-centered, and they help foster understanding and remembering. Since the second half of the symmetric structure is never completely synonymous to the first but develops it,[125] the concentric structure is actually linear! The pivot of the concentric structure, besides being a focal point, explains how the second half of the concentric structure develops.

The Metanarrative afforded by our analysis is a story about how the Davidic kingship and Zion are established (Book I), broken (Books II–III), and would be re-established (Books IV–V; see Figure 47). The Central Motifs of different compositional units connect the dots of the Metanarrative across the entire Psalter. If this were the Metanarrative intended for the original postexilic readers (and even so for readers today), then the story is yet to be finished since the final idyllic social reality has not taken place. If this is indeed the story expressed by the Psalter, how should the reader respond? What is the theological message for the audience? The answer to these questions is found in the macrostructural shape. The theological message to the reader, in view of this Metanarrative, is both a *hope* and *exhortation*. The hope, expressed between the fall at the end of Book III and final re-establishment at the end of Book V, is the powerful display of Yhwh's kingship and the triumph of a ideal Messianic king—an unfurling of the Davidic covenant. The exhortation, as seen from the frames of the structure in Figure 47, is to persist in recognizing Yhwh's kingship and in patience supplication. The Davidic covenant calls for patience and redirects the people's vision onto God's triumphant kingship and his anointed king in post-exilic Israel.

Returning to Barr's quote, we have briefly shown how the Macrostructure can function as an "intended structure with meaning." Our interim argument (in chapter 1) that the Prologue is programmatic of the entire Psalter can now be ascertained with more confidence. However, discussions thus far have focused on a concentric reading of the Psalter (which I argue, is also linear). In the following, our discussion will focus on a linear reading of the Psalter to reveal how it further collaborates with the design of the Psalter.

    a   Othniel and his good *wife* (3:7–11; cf. 1:11–15)
        b   Ehud and the victory *at the Jordan fords* (3:12–31)
            c   Deborah: *enemy's skull crushed by woman* (4:1—5:31)
                d   Gideon: turning point (6:1—8:32)
            c′   Abimelech: *judge's skull crushed by woman* (8:33—10:5)
        b′   Jephthah and civil war *at the Jordan fords* (10:6—12:15)
    a′   Samson and his bad *wives* (13:1—16:31)

124. These six points are those of Dorsey, *Literary Structure*, 31.

125. For discussion on the idea that no parallelism is truly synonymous, see Jebb, *Sacred Literature*; Kugel, *Idea of Biblical Poetry*.

Linear Reading

While concentric reading identifies structural core focuses of compositional units in the Psalter, a linear reading tracks a trajectory. In the Psalms, they complement each other to reveal a skillful design of the Psalter.

We are not unfamiliar with arguments associated with the linear dimension of reading. The trends toward Communal and Praise psalms as one moves from the beginning to the end of the Psalter are well documented.[126] There is also an culminating of praise at the end. Citing Reindl, Ballhorn notes that in Ps 146, the individual figure of "David" is called to praise, But in Ps 147, this call is expanded to all "Israel" and Jerusalem.[127] By Ps 148, "God's angels" and all created hosts of heaven are called to praise. In Ps 149, the subjects of praise return to "Israel" and the "congregation" of the *chasidim*. In the final Ps 150, it is "everything that breathes!" This expanding body of praise, from the local to the universal, traces the accentuation of praise of Yhwh as the Psalter concludes.

The increasing prosody of praise as we move to the end of the Psalter is also shown via the formulaic use of ברך, הלל (*piel* imperative mp), and ידה (*hiph* imperative mp). Their occurrences are weighted heavily in Books IV–V of the Psalter. In Books I–III, these three terms occur only 5x (none in Book III), but in Books IV–V, they occur a total of 69x. The frequency of occurrence also increases from Book IV to V.[128]

Brueggemann captures another trajectory (theological) in the Psalter. He argues that the Psalter characterizes the people of God moving from "obedience" to "praise" through a sequence of "orientation," "disorientation" and "reorientation."[129] Brueggemann's proposition has found general acceptance in Psalms scholarship.[130]

Linear/sequential readings of the Psalter that identify developing storylines have been treated by several scholars.[131] "A sequence may be seen as a series of connected elements whose order is significant for meaning."[132] Just as there are various central motifs working at different compositional levels, linear trajectories working at various compositional levels can be found in the Psalter.

Trajectories may be detected by "shifts" in storylines and a movement toward resolution. By "shifts," we mean the detectable *change* of an existing concept. These

---

126. Westermann, *Praise and Lament*, 257; Nasuti, "Interpretive Significance," 311–39; *Defining the Sacred Songs*, 174.

127. Ballhorn, *Zum Telos des Psalters*, 299.

128. There are 4x הלל, 5x ברך (*piel* imperative mp), and 4x ידה (*hiph* imperative mp) in Book IV. These numbers increase to 45, 6 and 7 respectively in Book V.

129. Brueggemann, "Psalms and the Life of Faith," 3–32; "Bound by Obedience and Praise," 63–92.

130. See a nuanced understanding of this trajectory in Parrish, *Story of the Psalms*.

131. Apart from Ballhorn's *Zum Telos des Psalters*, see Nasuti, "Interpretive Significance"; *Defining the Sacred Songs*, 173–74, for a good discussion on "linear" reading of the Psalter.

132. Nasuti, "Interpretive Significance," 313.

"shifts" can be understood historically, theologically or conceptually. For instance, the *fall* and *re-establishment* of Zion are such identifiable "shifts." The idealized Zion is the final resolution of the plot. Storylines like these are often observed and appropriated by its implied readers because they, likewise, look forward to these resolutions in postexilic Israel.[133]

Nonetheless, the linearity of the Psalter is not presented in a continuous unbroken sequence. The nature of poetry is lacunous. There is both "contraction" of form and "compaction" of content.[134] Between two texts, readers' imagination is required to fill in the gaps in plot development. Hence, the question is not whether the Psalter is loosely connected (since by its nature, poetry is lacunous), but whether a coherent Metanarrative develops across the entire macrostructure.

We have discussed briefly how a Metanarrative is developed across the three major Sections of the Psalter, tracing the establishment, fall and (re)establishment of the Davidic kingship and Zion. In the following, I will demonstrate a number of linear trajectories that support this Metanarrative.

Canonical History of Israel

With Wilson's pioneering work on the editing of the Hebrew Psalter, there is general acceptance that the Psalter traces a progression of the Davidic covenant.[135] Wilson argues that the establishment of the Davidic covenant in Book I (esp. Ps 2) is now "passed on to his descendants" by the end of Book II (Ps 72).[136] This covenant "is viewed as broken, [and] failed" in Book III.[137] However, Book IV begins to address the problem of the failed covenant. Book V answers the problem by presenting "an attitude of dependence and trust in Yhwh alone."[138] The intent was for its readers to respond with the same attitudes. Wilson's proposal identified a trajectory that describes the canonical story of Israel through the Davidic kingship, dynasty, exile and restoration. His proposal has been nuanced in various ways[139] and recast as Israel's postexilic search for identity.[140]

---

133. Nasuti argues that "readers are inclined to interpret the Psalter sequentially because of the sequential nature of their own lives . . . and a sequential understanding of the Psalms means that one must be aware of and open to psalms beyond those that express one's current point of standing" (Nasuti, "Interpretive Significance," 334–35).

134. Wendland, *Analyzing the Psalms*, 160–64.

135. Wilson, *EHP*, 209.

136. Wilson, *EHP*, 211.

137. Wilson, *EHP*, 213.

138. Wilson, *EHP*, 227.

139. McCann, "Books I–III," 93–107; deClaissé-Walford, *Reading from the Beginning*.

140. For example, deClaissé-Walford summarizes, "The Psalter begins with the story of the reign of King David in Book One, moves to the reign of Solomon in Book Two, and onto the divided kingdom and destruction of the northern kingdom by the Assyrians and the southern kingdom by the

Independently, we have also observed how trajectories tracing the canonical history of Israel are repeatedly found in various Groups in the Psalter. This canonical history begins from (a) Yhwh's creation to the formation of a chosen people, (b) their historic deliverance from Egypt, (c) their settlement in Jerusalem, (d) the establishment of the Davidic kingship, (e) Israel's exile and return, and (f) her desire for to enter the ideal Zion city-temple. This linear movement is not merely historical or geographical, but conceptual as well. It is a departure from slavery and exile (negative state) towards an ideal, secure, blissful and flourishing Zion-city (positive state).[141]

Development of the Zion City-Temple

Besides movement toward (or away from) the Zion-city, we have also noted a linearity in the development of Zion itself. Several scholars have dealt with the motif of Zion in the Psalter. For instance, Ballhorn finds an emphasis on *theocracy* in relation to the temple motif (90–100) at the beginning of Book IV. This theocracy is said to emanate from the temple (95, 100). The physical nature of the temple is then transcended when it is being referred to as "Judah" (114:2). By Pss 120–134, the temple concept is subsumed under the greater Zion concept. This Zion-temple is understood in several ways. It can refer to topology (125:1), the temple mount (128:5), the people of Israel (126:1), a metaphor for Yhwh's dwelling (132:13) or a *social-reality* (122:8; 149:2; "*soziale Wirklichkeit*").[142] In the Final Hallel (146–150), Zion is given an idealized form. By idealized, I do not mean spiritualized. It is clearly depicted within a social-reality in Ps 149:2 where the community at Zion gathers to judge all human governments and in praise of God.[143] With the establishment of the idealized or eschatological sanctuary, the final editor(s) of the Psalms paints an inviolable sanctuary, one that no human hands can destroy.[144]

In chapter 2, we have shown how the Zion-temple motif develops across the CM of the third Groups in each of the three Sections. This development of Zion is

Babylonians in Book Three; Book Four recounts the struggles of the exiles in Babylon to find identity and meaning, and Book Five celebrates the return to Jerusalem and the re-establishment of a new Israel with God as sovereign" (deClaissé-Walford et al., *Book of Psalms*, 29). Cf. McCann, "Shape and Shaping," 350–62; "Meta-Narrative of the Psalter," 363–75.

141. See esp. our earlier discussions on Pss 113–118.

142. "Jerusalem stellt immer auch eine soziale Wirklichkeit dar, wie in Ps 122,8 ausdrücklich gesagt wird" (Ballhorn, *Zum Telos des Psalters*, 248).

143. Ballhorn, *Zum Telos des Psalters*, 378.

144. For Ballhorn, this is "a deliberate final" conception and "a metaphor for God's future dealings with Israel and to humanity" (Ballhorn, *Zum Telos des Psalters*, 379). My translation. However, Gillingham's study on "Zion" is quite different. Although she finds that a "Zion tradition" well integrated into the entire Psalter (in at least 75 psalms dispersed through Books I–V), she does not posit a coherent trajectory of "Zion" in the Psalter. Instead of arguing for an "eschatological sanctuary" at the end of the Psalter, she argues that "the compilers' focus is on the Zion tradition as an actual place, with a this-worldly dimension" (Gillingham, "Zion Tradition," 334).

observed at the highest compositional level of the Psalter. The two center-psalms in the third Group of Book I (25–34) highlight Yhwh's glorious enthronement at his temple (29:9) and "the dedication of the House [of God]" (30:1). What is interesting is that the content of Ps 30 relates little to the temple itself. It is a Praise psalm intermixed with supplication and thanksgiving.[145] This mismatched superscription in Ps 30:1 could have "originally read *a Davidic psalm*."[146] Regardless of the historical processes that shaped the superscription, the term "dedication" (חנכה; 30:1) presumes the presence of a physical temple.

As we move to the third Group of Section 2, we observe a vivid depiction of the fall of the earthly Zion-temple (esp. 74, 79). The earthly Zion-temple has turned from a glorious "dedication" to a humiliating destruction. However, by the third Group of Section 3, Ps 126:1 depicts a "restored" Zion (120–22; cf. 126:1).[147] This Zion-temple is further depicted as one that is not "built by human hands" (127:1). The descriptions of the postexilic Zion-temple take on an eschatological ring by Ps 132:15–18. The ark of God ultimately finds its dwelling place at this Zion.

We have also discussed how Zion is transformed from an earthly Jerusalem to an ideal or eschatological one in the SOA. The three Pss 122, 127, 132 form a triptych, showing this development of the motif of Zion in the MT Psalter.

An interesting development of the Zion-temple can be seen in the word "tent" (אהל). David's desire to find a permanent dwelling place for Yhwh (2 Sam 2:2, 6), whose presence was originally associated with a "tent" (אהל), is eventually accomplished by Solomon building the temple. In the Psalms, the lexeme, אהל, first occurs in Ps 15:1 with the question of who may enter into the presence of God. The last instance of the 18 occurrences of אהל is in Ps 132:3.[148] In this psalm, Yhwh's dwelling place was finally established and he arose to this "resting" place. Interestingly, from Ps 132 onwards, אהל no longer appears in the Psalter. The אהל has become the Zion-city-temple that Yhwh has built![149]

It is plausible that a development of the Zion motif occurs across the MT Psalter. It is established initially as an earthly Davidic city (29, 30; Book I). However, it fell into ruins and was destroyed by Israel's enemies (74, 79; Books II–III). Yet Yhwh's steadfast love remains on Zion. Despite the apparent restoration of the postexilic Jerusalem

---

145. deClaissé-Walford et al., *Book of Psalms*, 289.

146. From ancient sources, two possibilities were proposed for the insertion of the phrase. Historically, it could have functioned as the dedication of the temple "after the exile ca 515 BCE, as described in Ezra 6," or a "rededication of the temple in 165 BCE under Judas Maccabeus following its profanation ca. 167." Cf. Talmud (*b. Sop.* 18:3; *Bik.* 3.4). deClaissé-Walford et al., *Book of Psalms*, 230, 289–90.

147. Scholars generally agree on the unity of the Songs of Ascents as a collection. In Ps 126:1, the destruction of Jerusalem and the exile is clearly an event in the past. Even if we do not agree that the "Jerusalem" in Ps 122 is postexilic, by Ps 126, the references to the Zion-Temple is clearly so.

148. Pss 15:1; 19:5; 27:5–6; 52:7; 61:5; 69:26; 78:51, 55, 60, 67; 83:7; 84:11; 91:10; 106:25; 118:15; 120:5; 132:3.

149. Cf. 1 Chr 15:1.

and its temple, there remains a greater, flourishing eschatological Zion-city ruled by a messianic king, which only the righteous will enter. It will be a Zion that no human hands can build, save YHWH (127, 132–136). The final imagery of Zion depicts an idealized social reality with its righteous inhabitants praising YHWH and executing judgment on the nations (144–150).

"Gate"

In chapter 2, we introduced the Pan-Psalter Occurrence Scheme (POS) with the lexeme זנח. The POS is the careful use and sequential placement of certain word/phrases strategically and exhaustively across the entire Psalter to make or reinforce a rhetorical point that collaborates with the Metanarrative of the Psalter. We have also seen interesting ways certain lexemes are used throughout the Psalter. In the following, we will see how linear reading and the Metanarrative across the Psalter can be traced by the lexeme שער ("gate"), occurring 13x in the Psalter. Consider the following figure which summarizes the occurrences.

Trajectory	Text	Reference
Introductory	Gates of death and gates of the daughter of Zion	9:14–15
Begin: Davidic monarchy	Celebrating victory at the "gates" of the city	24:7, 9
Ashamed	Psalmist ashamed at the city "gates"	69:13
Turning point	YHWH's love for the "gates of Zion"	87:2
Call to enter	The call to enter "YHWH's gates"	100:4
Gates restored	Recalling the "gates of death" during the exile	107:18
Righteous enter	The righteous will enter the "gates of righteousness"	118:19–20
Within the gates	The psalmist is standing at the "gates of Jerusalem"	122:2
Unashamed	The psalmist is unashamed at the city "gates"	127:5
End: Toward ideal Zion	YHWH strengthens the "bars of [Zion's] gates"	147:13

Figure 48: Pan-Psalter Occurrence Scheme of שער

In Ps 9:14,[150] the psalmist calls out to YHWH to "lift him up from the gates of death [מות]." This "gate" refers to YHWH's deliverance from a "near-death experience."[151] The reference, "gates of the daughter of Zion" in the following verse is the antithetical-parallel to the "gates of death." According to Jacobson, the expression, "daughter of Zion" (בת-ציון),"[152] is a "metaphor that portrays the city [of Jerusalem] as a woman

---

150. *BHS* notes that the Targum and Ms are missing the yod suffix (construct form). This textual note does not affect the POS of שער.

151. deClaissé-Walford et al., *Book of Psalms*, 137.

152. Stinespring provides a detailed argument on why this phrase should be translated as an

who embodies what it is for the people of Israel to be God's people."[153] To praise Yhwh at the gates of the daughter of Zion exemplifies life as God's people, standing in stark contrast to the "gates of death." These two instances introduce and encapsulate the message of the rest of the occurrences of שער.

The next two instances of שער (24:7, 9) are set within the literary contexts of warfare. Craigie notes that the historical context "may have been the arrival of the Ark in Jerusalem in David's time (in 2 Sam 6:12–19), which marked on the one hand, the establishment of the sanctuary in Jerusalem, and on the other hand, the crowning achievement of Israel's war."[154] If this interpretation is correct, the word שער identifies with the early Davidic monarchy in Israel's canonical history. We can then trace the beginning of the trajectory defined by שער from the beginning of the Davidic monarchy.

The next instance of שער is found in Ps 69:13. Here, the psalmist sits at the city gates in vivid public humiliation. Zenger argued that the reason for the humiliation is the psalmist's "zeal for the house of God."[155] This psalm, according to Zenger, is likely situated in the postexilic period "after the reestablishment of the temple, or rather of the sacrificial cult."[156] Even if we do not accept Zenger's view, there is good reason to see that the psalm clearly alludes to Zion in jeopardy (69:10, 36). This motif of Zion in jeopardy corresponds to the metanarrative depicted in Books II–III of the Psalter which underscores both the fall of the Davidic monarchy and the Zion temple.

In Ps 87:2, the שער takes on a ruminative character. With the humiliation at the city gates, the psalmist now proclaims Yhwh's chief love for the "gates of Zion." For Longman, Psalm 87 celebrates Zion where "God makes his glorious presence known in the world."[157] Zion may still be in jeopardy but Ps 87 highlights Yhwh's timeless love for her (87:2) and that Yhwh "will establish" her (יכוננה; 87:5). This instance of שער indicates a turning point along the trajectory.

Coming at the end of the Yhwh *Malak* psalms (93–100), the שער in 100:4 is a call for the people of God to enter Yhwh's gates with thanksgiving and celebratory praise. The appointed time for Yhwh's restoration of the Zion city is at hand (102:14). The restoration of Zion's gates is described in a concrete way as Israel looked to a

---

appositive genitive "daughter Zion" as opposed to "daughter of Zion." The appositive-genitive interpretation is well countered by Dobbs-Allsopp and Floyd. See Stinespring, "No Daughter of Zion," 133–41; Dobbs-Allsopp, "Syntagma of Bat," 451–70; Floyd, "Welcome Back, Daughter of Zion!," 484–504. This phrase is most extensively used in the Book of Lamentations but occurs only once in the Psalms. Cf. 2 Kgs 19:21; Ps 9:15; Isa 1:8; 10:32; 16:1; 37:22; 52:2; 62:11; Jer 4:31; 6:2, 23; Lam 1:6; 2:1, 4, 8, 10, 13, 18; 4:22; Mic 1:13; 4:8, 10, 13; Zeph 3:14; Zech 2:14; 9:9.

153. deClaissé-Walford et al., *Book of Psalms*, 138;
154. Craigie, *Psalms 1–50*, 214. See also deClaissé-Walford et al., *Book of Psalms*, 252.
155. Hossfeld and Zenger, *Psalms 2*, 178.
156. Hossfeld and Zenger, *Psalms 2*, 179.
157. Longman, *Psalms*, 319.

restored inhabited city (107:18). Those who are qualified to enter into the "gates of righteousness" and the "gates of the LORD" are called the "righteous" (118:18–19).[158]

By the SOA, the psalmist now stands "in your gates, O Jerusalem" (בשעריך ירושלם; 122:2).[159] In a starking reversal, the psalmist who was earlier humiliated before his foes at the gates in Ps 69:13 is now rendered as those who are "unashamed" (לא־יבשו) before his enemies at the gate (127:5). This spectacular reversal is emphasized by one last instance of שער in Ps 147:13. Here the word, "gate," recalls the "bars" (בריח) of Ps 107:16,[160] referring to Yнwн's breaking of Israel's captivity and leading them to an inhabited city. However, the "bars" and "gates" in Ps 147:13 refer to the restored and secure Zion city (cf. 147:12). Thus, this last instance of שער in the MT Psalter identifies a flourishing and life-giving Zion city (147:13). Therefore, we have moved from the "gates of death" to the "gates of the daughter of Zion" (cf. 9:14–15) by Ps 147:13. The 13 instances of שער identify a general historical trajectory of Israel's fate represented through the motif of Zion's gates. This trajectory begins with the establishment of the Davidic kingship, followed by her captivity and restoration. The trajectory traced by שער also corresponds to the Metanarrative across the five Books of the Psalter.

"Jacob"[161]

Different books of the Hebrew Bible characterize the name יעקב in distinctive ways.[162] The name, יעקב in the Genesis narratives refer to the individual patriarch, the son of Isaac, or the "Jacob people," a seminomadic tribe or community seeking for permanent settlement. According to Zobel, the earliest use of יעקב, as a designation of the people of Israel,[163] can be traced back to the early Davidic period in 2 Sam 23.1, 3.[164] Here, the name Jacob takes on "national and religious" connotations. In Deuteronomy, יעקב is often cast positively, standing alongside the patriarchs "Abraham" and "Isaac" as "servants of God" (Deut 9:27). However, it is in the story of Jacob that the

---

158. Zenger notes that the phrase, "gates of the righteousness," refers to the "gates to the inner court of the Temple." See Hossfeld and Zenger, *Psalms 3*, 241.

159. *BHS* notes that Greek has ἐν ταῖς αὐλαῖς σου ("in your courtyard"), but this is not attested by any Mss.

160. This Lemma occurs only twice in the entire Psalms.

161. The following study on יעקב is also published in my article, "Pan-Psalter Occurrence Scheme of 'Jacob' and 'Covenant.'" I like to thank *JSOT* for giving me permission to reprint them here.

162. The name "Jacob" occurs 349 times in the Hebrew Bible. The majority of these occurrences, 205 of them, refer to the individual patriarch. See Zobel, "יעקב," *TDOT*, 6:187–88.

163. The origins of the name of "Israel" is associated with Jacob's first encounter with God ("El"; Gen 32:23–33). This new name of Jacob thus has religious notions in connection with the worship of El and is not to be seen as an independent group of "Jacob people and later merging with them" (Zobel, *TDOT* 6:185–208, [195]).

164. Zobel, *TDOT*, 6:208.

The Design of the Psalter

history of the people of God identified with rather than Abraham or Isaac.[165] In the Prophets, the name יעקב predominantly takes on the meaning of the chosen people of God or "the community of Yahweh" (cf. Isa 2:5–6; Jer 31:7; Amos 9:8; Obad 1:17; Mic 2:12; Mal 1:2).[166] This characterization of Jacob in the prophetic books, for Zobel, is "substantially the same" as that in the poetry of Israel.[167]

Apart from Genesis and Isaiah, the Book of Psalms contains the highest occurrences of Jacob in the Hebrew Bible. There are 34 instances of יעקב in the Psalms.[168] It is striking that almost all of these 34 instances of Jacob (barring two instances[169]) are found either at the beginning,[170] end,[171] or center (Ps 44:5) of a strophic unit in a psalm.[172] It is also found at the beginning and end of an entire psalm.[173] In many instances, יעקב is immediately followed by a "*selah*."[174] In short, יעקב is often situated prominently within a psalm.

These poetic features suggest that the use of יעקב is not haphazard at least within a single psalm. Strategic placement of certain terms within a psalm, such as the use of an inclusio, is common literary technique that we are familiar with. However, apart from the need to trespass the boundaries of distinct poems, there is little to prevent us from considering the possibility of strategic placement of terms beyond the single composition if we accept the possibility of a final editor.

The following figure lists all the sequential occurrences of יעקב in the Psalter.

---

165. Foulkes, "Jacob," *NIDOTTE*, 4:738–743 [743].

166. This is not to say there are no references to Jacob the patriarch (Isa 58:14; Eze 28:25). See Zobel, *TDOT*, 6:202–204.

167. Zobel, *TDOT*, 6:207.

168. Pss 14:7; 20:2; 22:24; 24:6; 44:5; 46:8, 12; 47:5; 53:7; 59:14; 75:10; 76:7; 77:16; 78:5, 21, 71; 79:7; 81:2, 5; 84:9; 85:2; 87:2; 94:7; 99:4; 105:6, 10, 23; 114:1, 7; 132:2, 5; 135:4; 146:5; 147:19.

169. Pss 105:23; 135:4.

170. Pss 20:2; 22:24; 75:10; 78:5; 78:21; 79:7; 81:2, 5; 85:2; 94:7; 99:4; 105:10; 146:5.

171. Pss 24:6; 46:8, 12; 59:14; 76:7; 77:16; 78:71; 105:6; 132:5; 147:19.

172. Cf. Terrien, *Psalms*, 162, 217, 228, 244, 357, 371–373, 443, 546, 547, 552, 558, 559, 563, 570–571, 581, 603, 619, 661, 685, 719, 766, 845, 980, 913; Hossfeld and Zenger, *Psalms 2*, 257, 259, 275, 295, 302, 323, 348, 451; Hossfeld and Zenger, *Psalms 3*, 192, 461, 613.

173. Pss 14:7; 46:12; 53:7; 87:2; 114:1, 7.

174. Pss 24:6; 47:5; 59:14; 77:16; 84:9.

Concentric and Linear Reading

	Structure	Key Motifs	Ref.	Text (my translation)	No.
Introduction and Frame 1	A	Introduction; Frame 1 & 2 Begin. Motifs: Zion; Restoration of captives; LORD answers	14:7	Who will bring from Zion the salvation of Israel when the LORD <u>restores his captive people</u>, Jacob will rejoice, Israel will be glad.	1
			20:2	May the LORD <u>answer</u> you in the day of distress! May the name of the God of Jacob set you on high!	2
	B	YHWH in 3rd person singular. Jacob to YHWH.	22:24	You who fear the LORD, praise <u>him</u>; All descendants of Jacob, glorify <u>him</u>, And revere <u>him</u>, all you descendants of Israel.	3
			24:6	This is the generation of those who seek <u>him</u>, who seek Your face, O Jacob. Selah.	4
	C	Center: YHWH as victorious king	44:5	You are he, my <u>King</u>, O God; Command <u>salvation</u> for Jacob.	5
	B'	Jacob as 1st person plural. YHWH to Jacob.	46:8	Yahweh of hosts is with <u>us</u>; The God of Jacob is <u>our</u> stronghold. Selah.	6
			46:12	Yahweh of hosts is with <u>us</u>; The God of Jacob is <u>our</u> stronghold. Selah.	7
			47:5	He chooses <u>our</u> inheritance for <u>us</u>, The exaltation of Jacob whom he loves. Selah.	8
	A'	End of Frame 1 / Start of Frame 2	53:7	Who will bring from Zion the salvation of Israel when the LORD <u>restores his captive people</u>, Jacob will rejoice, Israel will be glad.	9

	Structure	Key Motifs	Ref.	Text (my translation)	No.
Frame 2	J	Frame 2a: YHWH punishes nations (victory)	59:14	Completely destroy <u>them</u> [nations] in wrath, completely destroy <u>them</u> that they may be no more; That they may know that God <u>rules</u> in Jacob to the <u>ends of the earth</u>. Selah.	10
	K	*Praise*	75:10	But I, I will declare it forever; I will sing praises to the God of Jacob.	11
	L	***Destruction of Egypt (victory)***	76:7	At your <u>rebuke</u>, O God of Jacob, rider and horse are fast asleep.	12
	M	*For Jacob*	77:16	You have by your power redeemed your people, the sons of Jacob and Joseph. Selah.	13
	N	*Law*	78:5	But he established a testimony in Jacob, and set a law in Israel, which He commanded our fathers to declare them to their children.	14
	J'	Frame 2b: YHWH punishes Jacob (victory)	78:21	Therefore, Yahweh heard and was <u>full of wrath</u>; and a fire was kindled against Jacob, and anger also went up <u>against Israel</u>.	15
	M'	*For Jacob*	78:71	From following nursing ewes, he brought him to shepherd Jacob his people, and Israel his inheritance.	16
	L'	***Destruction of Jacob (victory)***	79:7	For they have devoured Jacob, and laid waste his dwelling.	17
	K'	*Praise*	81:2	Sing for joy to God our strength, shout joyfully to the God of Jacob.	18
	N'	*Law*	81:5	For it is a statute for Israel, an ordinance of the God of Jacob.	19
	A''	End of Frame 2. Motif: Restoration of Captives; LORD hears; Zion (cf. A, A')	84:9	Yahweh, the God of hosts, <u>hear</u> my prayer; give <u>ear</u>, O God of Jacob! Selah.	20
			85:2	Yahweh, you showed favor to your land; You <u>restored the captivity</u> of Jacob.	21
			87:2	Yahweh loves the gates of <u>Zion</u> more than all the other dwelling places of Jacob.	22

The Design of the Psalter

Structure	Key Motifs	Ref.	Text (my translation)	No.
Turning Point	LORD has seen (cf. 20:1; 78:21; 84:8); King executes justice.	94:7	They have said, "Yah does not see, nor does the God of Jacob discern."	23
		99:4	The strength of the king loves justice; You have established uprightness; You have executed justice and righteousness in Jacob.	24

Frame 3	W	Start of Frame 3. Chosenness	105:6	O seed of Abraham, his servant, O sons of Jacob, His chosen ones!	25
	X	YHWH's faithfulness	105:10	Then he confirmed it to Jacob for a statute, to Israel as an everlasting covenant.	26
	Y	Israel sojourns	105:23	Israel also came into Egypt; Thus Jacob sojourned in the land of Ham.	27
			114:1	When Israel went forth from Egypt, the house of Jacob from a people of strange language.	28
	Z	YHWH's kingship (victory)	114:7	Tremble, O earth, before the Lord, before the God of Jacob.	29
	X'	David's faithfulness	132:2	How he (David) swore to Yahweh, and vowed to the Mighty One of Jacob.	30
	Y'	Ark sojourns	132:5	Until I find a place for Yahweh, a dwelling place for the Mighty One of Jacob.	31
	W'	End of Frame 3: Chosenness	135:4	For Yahweh has chosen Jacob for himself, Israel for his own possession.	32

Conclusion	Beatitude	146:5	How blessed is he whose help is the God of Jacob, whose hope is in Yahweh his God.	33
	YHWH's word	147:19	He declares his words to Jacob, his statutes and his ordinances to Israel.	34

Figure 49: Pan-Psalter Occurrence Scheme of יעקב

The entire sequence of these 34 occurrences fit into three frames and has an introduction, turning point and conclusion. Consider Frame 1. This frame is arranged concentrically (A-B-C-B'-A'). It is bounded by two instances of "Jacob" on one end in 14:7; 20:2 and on the other end in 53:6.[175] Apart from the change of יהוה to אלהים, note that the two verses in 14:7 and 53:7 are identical.[176] As such, they form the bookends around Frame 1. The second reference, 20:2, with its motif of YHWH and his answering of the people's call, forms part of the introduction and this will become clear when we come to the end of the second frame.

Within Frame 1, the parallel B-B' structural units describe Jacob in a right relationship with YHWH as worshipers, and YHWH's as their God who cares for them. Note that the B units repeatedly use the syntax of the *third person singular* when referring to God (22:24; 24:6). The descendants (or "generation") of Jacob is to "praise him," "seek him," "glorify him" and "stand in awe of him." In contrast, the B' unit repeatedly use

---

175. Terrien sees ambiguity in the translation of Ps 14:7 (and 53:7) and depending how one reads it, the "name Israel would would mean the 'northern kingdom' with its sanctuaries at Shechem or Bethel associated with Jacob" (Terrien, *Psalms*, 166).

176. This is a phenomenon of the Elohistic Psalter. Psalm 53:7 has ישעות instead of ישעת in 14:7.

of the syntax *first person plural* in reference to יעקב (46:8, 12; 47:5).[177] Interestingly, all these three references, are confessions of the people's allegiance and trust in the God of יעקב.[178] As such, the B-B' units highlight the attitudes of the worshipers before Yhwh.

At the structural center of Frame 1 stands 44:5, which is a victorious declaration of Yhwh's kingship.[179] This triumphalism of Yhwh over his enemies is a recurring motif at the center of compositional units (cf., Song of the Sea). The message of Frame 1 tells us that salvation and restoration of Jacob (shown by A-A') is bounded by a right inter-relationship between God and Jacob (shown by B-B') and underscored by the central place of Yhwh's triumphant kingship.

Frame 2 is bounded on the left by 53:7 and on the right by three psalms (84:9; 85:2; 87:2).[180] As a whole, Frame 2 can be divided into two halves highlighting God's wrath on the nations in the first half, and on Jacob in the second.

The two halves are two parallel sequences. The first sequence consists of five instances of "Jacob" (2a: JKLMN). As indicated by the first instance of "Jacob" in this sequence, 59:14 identifies the *wicked nations* as objects of God's wrath.[181] This is followed by four psalms that carry the motifs of *praise* (75:10; K), *destruction of Egypt* (76:7; L), *care for Jacob* (77:16; M) and *Yhwh's law* (78:5; N). At the center of these five psalms stands Ps 76:6, which again emphasizes Yhwh's triumphant destruction of Egypt.

There is a remarkable parallel in the second sequence as shown in Frame 2b ([JKLMN]'), which also consists of five instances of יעקב. It is first introduced by 78:21 (J'), which indicates *Jacob*, rather than the nations as the object of God's wrath. This is followed by four psalms carrying the same four motifs of *care for Jacob* (78:71; M'); *destruction of Jacob* (79:7; L'), *praise* (81:2; K') and *law* (81:5; N'). With skillful

---

177. In 46:8, 11; 47:5, Terrien sees "Jacob" as the "congregation of Israel" or the "holy people." See Terrien, *Psalms*, 374.

178. Divine appellatives compounded with "Jacob" has been deemed a "Jerusalemite theologoumenon operating the time of David." In 2 Sam 23:1, 3, the phrase, "God of Jacob" refers "to the people of the Davidic state, who worship Yahweh as the God of this state." While distinctions can be made between אלוה יעקב or אל יעקב, אלהי יעקב, לאביר יעקב, they convey the same meaning. Zenger argues that the title "God of Jacob" is a "specific feature" of both the Korahite and Asaphite Psalms (cf. Pss 46:8, 12; 75:10; 76:7; 81:2, 5; 84:4). Zobel points out "God of Jacob" could have been an extension of the "archaic phrase, 'the mighty one of Israel.'" Zobel, *TDOT*, 6:201, 206–207. Cf. 20:2; 46:8; 46:12; 75:10; 76:7; 81:2; 81:5; 84:9; 94:7; 114:7; 132:2; 132:5; 146:5; Isa 2:3; Mic 4:2.

179. The centrality of Ps 44:5 is also observed within its immediate literary context. Terrien sees Ps 44:5 standing as the concentric center verse in the first strophe (vv. 2–9) of the psalm. Terrien, *Psalms*, 357, 359.

180. The use of "'Jacob' instead of 'Israel' may be significant" in Ps 87:2, though Terrien did not elaborate. Terrien, *Psalms*, 621.

181. The "missing" object of the verbs in 53:14 refers to the psalmist "enemies" This is contrasted with "Jacob" in Ps 53:14 refers to the nation Israel. Tate, *Psalms 51–100*, 98.

precision, the center of these five psalms (79:7) now accounts *Jacob's destruction by the nations*.[182]

Frame 2 concludes with three instances of יעקב (A″; 84:9; 85:2; 87:2). Note that the motifs in these three verses describing the deliverance and restoration of the captive people of Jacob are the exact motifs found in the bookends of Frames 1 (cf. 14:7, 20:2, 53:7).[183] The reference in 84:9, with the psalmist's petition for God to hear his prayers parallels 20:2, where God "answers in the day of trouble." As such, the end of Frame 2 (A″) parallels the bookends of Frame 1 (cf. A, A′). By the use of repeated motifs, the poet has skillfully structured the first 22 instances of יעקב into two main frames.

As a whole, the message of Frame 2 suggests that salvation and restoration of יעקב would involve Yhwh's punishment of the nations and even Jacob. However, God has provided redemption for Jacob and his people through a shepherd in this process. Reading along this trajectory, God is to be praised and his statutes are to be kept. Note that Yhwh's triumphant power remains at the structural center of the Frames 2a and 2b.

The turning point of the entire trajectory of יעקב can be seen in 94:7 and 99:4 immediately after Frame 2. These two references are a play on motifs of the bookends of Frames 1 and 2 (cf. A, A′, A″). Note how 94:7 captures the taunting of the wicked, accusing Yhwh of being blind or unable to pay heed. This wilful accusation is in direct contrast to 20:2 and 84:9 where Yhwh answered in the day of trouble when his people cried out to him. Psalm 99:4 now declares that Yhwh has clearly heard the taunts of the wicked and the disobedient children of Jacob (78:21) and will act righteously. These two psalms, identified as the Turning point of the POS, highlight YHWH's response in the face of the wicked's derision and rejection.

The third frame consists of seven instances associated with Jacob. The bookends of this Frame, 105:6 and 135:4, are clearly linked by the nominal and verbal forms of בחיר ("chosen one") and בחר ("to choose") respectively. Using the technique repeating motifs to mark the structural bookends of a compositional unit, as observed in Frames 1 and 2, the poet repeats this technique in Frame 3. The common motif in the bookends of Frame 3 is is Yhwh's special choice of Jacob. Coming after the Turning point, the entire Frame 3 depicts a positive outlook and speaks of Jacob's blessed status in God. This Frame makes no direct mention of Jacob's afflictions or rebellion. Moreover, the concept of "chosenness" is found only in this Frame.

It is important that the idea of Jacob's "chosenness" is associated with Yhwh's covenants with the patriarchs and David (cf. 89:4; 105:6–10) in the HB, which is

---

182. Harold notes, "the Divine Warrior motif often depicted a close association between the warrior and the earthly king. The Divine Warrior was called upon in times of national distress and disaster to provide protection and defense for the nation of the king" Ballard, *Divine Warrior Motif*, 28.

183. The translation and interpretation of Ps 85:2b has been debated due to the *ketiv* שבות. It could be translated as "captivity" (cf. Num 21:29) or "return/allow to return." Zenger translates it as "You have restored the first beginnings of Jacob" (Hossfeld and Zenger, *Psalms 2*, 359, 362).

remarkably expressed here. Clearly, the poet is fully cognizant of Israel's covenant theology. The X-Y units in Frame 3 focus on Yhwh's *covenantal faithfulness* and Jacob's sojourn to the Promised Land. In contrast, the (X-Y)' units focus on the *Davidite's covenantal faithfulness* and the ark's sojourn to Zion. Like Frames 1 and 2, Frame 3 is carefully-structured, focusing on the concepts of covenant and chosenness. Using the same poetic technique, the motif of 114:7 at the structural center of Frame 3, is Yhwh's victorious power over the land.

As a whole, the message of Frame 3 is Yhwh's covenantal faithfulness to his chosen people, Jacob, and expressed by two distinct journeys. The first journey is associated with the people of God and their journey to the Promised Land. The second is associated with the resting place of the ark the journey to its dwelling place.

The remarkable sequence of all 34 instances of יעקב is concluded by two verses (146:5; 147:19). The first of these is a beatitude for those "whose help is the God of Jacob." Beatitudes are usually located at the end each book of the Psalter (cf. 2:12; 41:14; 72:17–19; 89:16, 53; 106:48; 144:15). The appropriation of beatitude at the end of structural units shows that those responsible for the יעקב schema-design were clearly aware of the concluding praises and blessings at the end of each book and had adopted a similar technique.

The final instance of יעקב in 147:19 reads, "He declares his words to Jacob, his statutes and his ordinances to Israel." This final instance recalls the prophetic formula ("thus said the Lord") usually located at the beginning or end of a prophetic speech (cf. Jer 33:14; Ezek 12:28; Zech 12:1). Hence, the message of the two verses in the Conclusion is both a blessing and a call for Yhwh's people to keep his word.

In sum, the 34 sequential occurrences of יעקב form a skillful poetic design of a three-part concentric-linear structure with a coherent message. Careful observation of these instances highlights the plausibility that the POS is an intended editorial compositional technique as opposed to fortuitous arrangement.[184] The entire metanarrative of the POS can be seen as such: Frame 1 encapsulates what it means to have a right relationship with Yhwh. Frame 2 highlights an apparent broken relationship with Yhwh punishing the wicked nations as well as his people, Jacob. Glimpses of hope are embedded within this Frame. This is followed by the Turning Point of the POS, which is a call for God to act in view of the wicked's mockery of God's apparent inaction. The final Frame 3 now sets the story of Jacob in the right perspective. The hope of Jacob ultimately lies in Yhwh's covenantal relationship with his chosen people. God will lead Jacob, his people, to the Promise Land. The POS concludes with both a blessing and call for Jacob to continue to obey God.

The metanarrative of the POS of Jacob is about Yhwh's dealings with his people and converges with our proposals for the entire Psalter. It is a message to the chosen people of God that salvation will come from Zion and that Yhwh will restore them

---

184. It is also striking that there is not a single textual note in the *BHS* on these 34 instances of יעקב.

The Design of the Psalter

by his covenantal faithfulness. The repeated and consistent use of parallel motifs as bookends to structure the POS and the placement of YHWH's triumphant rule at the center of a unit are established poetic techniques (e.g., inclusio and chiastic structures) that provide credence to the plausibility this literary phenomenon. It is unlikely that the elaborate and precise occurrences of יעקב in the Hebrew Psalter is random. The POS for יעקב is also significant if it can be sustained because it shows us an ancient literary technique that hitherto, has not been explored.

Important "Turning points" in Yhwh's Salvific Work

Linear developments throughout the Psalter are identified by *shifts*. A trajectory is discerned because some element has shifted or developed along a continuum. In view of our understanding of the linear development of Israel's canonical history, I have identified four words/phrases of shifts that also display the POS technique. The first is the phrase "new song" (שיר חדש). The second is a pair of associated word-phrases, "appointed" time (מועד), and "from now to forever more" (מעתה ועד-עולם). The third is associated with Yhwh's "change of mind/heart" (נחם) and the fourth is another pair of associated phrases, "Arise O LORD!" and "Return O LORD!" (קומה יהוה and שובה יהוה).

"New Song"

(a) The phrase, שיר חדש, occurs only six times in the Psalter and are all in connection to praising Yhwh.[185] It occurs twice in Davidic psalms (40:4; 144:9), twice in Yhwh *Malak* psalms (96:1; 98:1), once in an untitled psalm (33:4) and once in a psalm without attributed authorship in the title (149:1). The only instance of this phrase found outside the Psalter is Isa 42:10.

Kraus notes that the expression is an "eschatological song that breaks out of the category of space and time and embraces all things" (cf. Rev 5:9).[186] Craigie argues that this expression represents "ever-new freshness of the praise of God in his victorious kingship (96:1, 98:1; 149:1)."[187] Tate, likewise, points out that the expression "praises the coming new and unprecedented intervention of Yahweh in history."[188] Patterson examines four of the six instances in the Psalms and argues that Pss 33, 96, 98 and 149 are considered a "subgenre" of praise psalms because of their similarities in theme, structure and vocabulary used in relation to the expression.[189] Our primary concern is to explore if the phrase, "new song," (as opposed to simply "a song"; cf. 46:1; 48:1;

---

185. Patterson, "Singing the New Song," 416.
186. Kraus, *Psalms 60–150*, 252; Craigie, *Psalms 1–50*, 272.
187. Craigie, *Psalms 1–50*, 272.
188. Tate, *Psalms 51–100*, 507.
189. Patterson, "Singing the New Song," 431–32.

69:30) located in six places in the Psalter displays a certain development or trajectory. Consider the six arguments given below.

(1) The six instances are located as three separate pairs found in Books I, IV and V respectively. In Book I, the two instances occur as the penultimate psalms of Groups 3 and 4. The first "new song" occurs after Yhwh's enthronement and is found in the Thanksgiving hymn (33) just before the end of the Group. The following figure illustrates this trajectory.

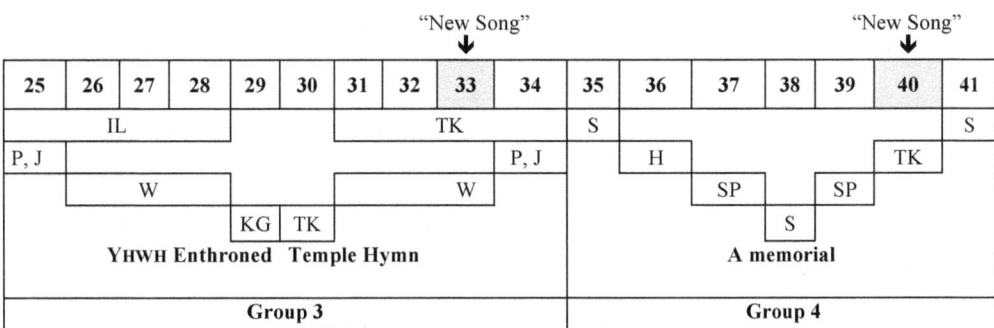

Figure 50: Penultimate Locations of שיר חדש in Book I[190]

Psalm 40, which contains the second instance of "new song," is situated on the right-half of the concentric structure in Pss 35–41. It is located after the center Ps 38, which is a supplication for salvation. Given the shape of these two Groups described in chapter 2, we observe that the first two instances of "new song" occur just before the final psalm in both Groups. Both instances are found in Thanksgiving hymns and appear after the presentations of Yhwh's kingship (29–30) and supplication for salvation. This sequence suggests that the singing of a "new song" is a development from Yhwh's response to the supplication for salvation.

(2) The six instances of שיר חדש in the Psalter form a three-part AB-CC-B′A′ configuration based on their superscription type. The first and last instances are found in psalms without attributed authorship. The second and fifth instances are found in the first and last Davidic collections in Books I and IV respectively. The two center instances are found in the Yhwh *Malak* psalms. The phrase, "new song," is absent in Books II–III of the Psalter. This is probably intentional since Books II–III defined the fall of the Davidic kingship and the Zion–temple.[191] The following figure shows this structure graphically.

---

190. Legend: IL: Individual laments; S: Supplication; TK: Thanksgiving hymn; TR: Torah psalm; P, J: Motifs of the poor and justice; W: Motif of the wicked; SP: Sapiential psalms; H: Hymn of praise.

191. Coincidentally, all thirteen instances of the *polel* verb רום ("to exalt") in the Psalms occur in all the Books except Books II and III as well. Cf. Pss 9:14; 18:49; 27:5; 30:2; 34:4; 37:34; 99:5, 9; 107:25, 32; 118:16, 28; 145:1. Note that the *polel* verb occurs 25x in the HB. Psalms contain the highest number of such occurrences, followed by Isaiah with 3 instances.

The Design of the Psalter

Superscription Type		Distinct Literary Context		Text (NAU)	Ref
No author-ship	A	Waiting and trusting	X	Sing to Him a new song; Play skilfully with a shout of joy.	33:3
Davidic	B			He put a new song in my mouth, a song of praise to our God; Many will see and fear, and will trust in the LORD.	40:4
YHWH *Malak*	C	YHWH's kingship and judgment	Y	Sing to the LORD a new song; Sing to the LORD, all the earth.	96:1
YHWH *Malak*	C			A Psalm. O sing to the LORD a new song, For He has done wonderful things, His right hand and His holy arm have gained the victory for Him.	98:1
Davidic	B'	Ideal city and final justice	Z	I will sing a new song to You, O God; Upon a harp of ten strings I will sing praises to You,	144:9
No author-ship	A'			Praise the LORD! Sing to the LORD a new song, And His praise in the congregation of the godly ones.	149:1

Figure 51: Concentric Structure of the Six Instances of שיר חדש

(3) The two instances in the superscripts of 96:1 and 98:1 are situated within the YHWH *Malak* psalms (93–100). The literary contexts surrounding the "new song" (Y) highlight the praise of YHWH's universal victorious kingship (96:1; 98:1–2);[192] his nature (96:6, 13; 98:1–3), deliverance (96:2; 98:2–3), works of creation (96:5),[193] and his impending judgment (96:13; 98:9). Patterson argues that both Pss 96 and 98 are thematically similar.[194]

When we compare the literary contexts (X) of the expressions in Pss 33:3 and 40:4, we see the common motifs of praising YHWH's universal kingship (33:8; 40:4); nature (33:4–5; 40:11–12); salvation (33:16–19; 40:3, 11, 18); and creation (33:6–7, 15; 40:6). But there are also differences. The motif of YHWH's impending judgment in Pss 96 and 98 is not present in Pss 33 and 40. Conversely, the high view of YHWH's word and truth in 33:4, 11 and 40:8–9, 12 is absent in Pss 96 and 98. In Pss 33 and 40, there is also the motif of waiting (33:20; 40:2) and trusting (33:21; 40:4–5), which are not apparent in Pss 96 and 98. Neither are they present in the contexts of Pss 144 and 149.

In the last two literary contexts (Z) of the expression "new song" (144:9 and 149:1), we notice, first, a strong emphasis on YHWH's theophanic deliverance (144:5–11), and second, a paradisiac description of a people living in a city of utopic bliss (144:12–15). Booij argues that this utopic description is *the* "new song" itself.[195] Psalm

---

192. *BHS* notes that the entire phrase, שירו ליהוה שיר חדש, is absent in the parallel text, 1 Chr 16:23.

193. Van Leeuwen, "Why Do the Trees," 28.

194. Patterson, "Singing the New Song," 423; For a detailed study of the singing a "new song" in Ps 98 and what it means in a local African context, see Wendland, *Studies in the Psalms*, 244–321.

195. Booij, "Psalm 144," 175.

149:5–9 describe a situation where the *chasidim*[196] hold a "two-edged" sword in their hands exacting vengeance and punishment on the nations. These imageries are *not* found in the literary contexts of the first four occurrences (X, Y).

In other words, when we compare the immediate contexts surrounding the 3 pairs of "new song," we observe the content developing linearly with an X-Y-Z structure. Through characteristic emphases in each context, there is a movement from waiting and trusting in Y{\scriptsize HWH}'s deliverance (Book I), to a climactic vision of Y{\scriptsize HWH}'s universal kingship and impending judgment (Book IV), and finally to the prospect of Y{\scriptsize HWH}'s theophanic deliverance of his people, bringing them into a paradisiac blissful city (Book V). The last instance of "new song" (149:1) leads the reader into a conclusive time when ultimate judgment and vengeance are executed on God's enemies (Figure 51).

(4) Like the first two instances in Book I, the last two instances in Book V are found in the penultimate psalms of the Subgroups they are situated in. Psalm 144 comes just before Ps 145 which is the final Davidic psalm exalting Y{\scriptsize HWH}'s kingship. Likewise, the last instance in Ps 149 comes just before the final Ps 150 where the Psalter ends in a consummation of universal and perfect praise (Figure 52).

							"New Song" ⬇				"New Song" ⬇	
137	138	139	140	141	142	143	144	145	146	147	148	149	150
UT	Davidic (D)								Final Hallel				
Jns	KG							KG	I	W		W	Uni
		Med	Individual Lament					P		Isr		Chas	
	D	Dir	Dir	D	*Msk*	D	D	P			Cos + Chas		

Figure 52: Penultimate Locations of שיר חדש in Book V[197]

Theologically, this characteristic penultimate location of the "new song" marks an important point in the trajectory from Lament to Praise. Their locations may be understood as follows: the "new song" of the psalmist (and the readers) is situated after witnessing Y{\scriptsize HWH}'s power in history. This calls for trusting and waiting in spite of the fall of the Davidic kingship and the Zion-temple. Y{\scriptsize HWH}'s victorious kingship is the

---

196. Cha notes, "In 1 Maccabees 2:42 the Hebrew term "Hasidim" appears. While derived from the Hebrew term, חסידים, the 'Hasidim' here refers to a Jewish military group in the 160s BCE. By this time the Hebrew term חסידים had become a proper noun specifically referring to those who fought along with Judas Maccabees in their war against the Seleucids. חסידים in the Psalter should not be identified with this later Jewish military group" (Cha, "Psalms 146–150," 92).

197. D: Davidic psalm; P: Praise psalm; UT: Untitled psalm; Sup: Supplication psalm; I: Individual psalm; Med: Meditative psalm; Uni: Universal in scope; W: psalm with a motif of the wicked; KG: Kingship psalm; Jns: Janus psalm; Isr: Israel is called to praise; Cos: Cosmic; *Chas*: *Chasidim*; Sg: a song.

climactic turning point. He will bring about the utopic life in the ideal city and execute just revenge on his enemies and the oppressors of his people. The place of the "new song" is situated just before that consummative end. It anticipates the realization of a new era in the eschaton. The "new song" is the psalmist's song for an impending new world order that is dawning.[198]

(5) The one other occurrence of "new song" outside the Psalter is in Isa 42:10. Scholars have pointed out that from Isaiah 40 onwards, the judgment of spiritual insensitivity (the motifs of "blindness and deafness," cf. Isa 6:9–13) is now past (cf. Isa 40:2).[199] Isaiah 42 begins by describing the servant of YHWH upon whom his spirit rests. This servant will establish justice throughout the nations and the earth. YHWH will appoint him to "open blind eyes" and "bring out prisoners from the dungeon and those who dwell in darkness" (Isa 42:7). Then in Isa 42:9, YHWH said, "Behold, the former things have come to pass and new things [חדש] I now declare . . . " This is followed by the call to sing a שיר חדש in Isa 42:10.

The motif, YHWH will "do something new" (עשה חדשה), continues in Isa 43:19, beckoning praise.[200] Robinson argues that Isa 43:8–13 "in some ways represents a transition between judicial blindness and total restoration of sight. The former is associated primarily with preexilic times; the latter in some future eschatological time."[201] Furthermore, eschatological imageries in Isaiah are also expressed by the lexeme חדש (cf. "something new," Isa 48:6; "a new name," 62:2; "new heaven and new earth," 65:17; 66:22).[202] In other words, the single occurrence of the phrase, "new song" outside the Psalter is used in a similar semantic context, collaborating with its meaning and use in the Psalms.

(6) Culley identifies the four instances of the phrase, שירו ליהוה שיר חדש in 96:1; 98:1; 149:1; Isa 42:10, as a formula.[203] Culley finds that Pss 96 and 98 have at least 65 percent and 50 percent of its text containing formulaic expressions[204] which according to him, come "from a period very close to the time when oral formulaic composition was being practiced."[205] As an "oral formulaic" expression, they are likely part of a set

---

198. Dietterich, "Sing to the LORD," 26.

199. Rendtorff and Kohl, *Canon and Theology Overtures*, 170–89; Robinson, "Motif of Deafness and Blindness," 167–86; Clements, "Beyond Tradition-History," 95–113.

200. Dietterich, "Sing to the LORD," 26.

201. Robinson, "Motif of Deafness and Blindness," 181.

202. The LXX translation of שיר חדש takes two forms: ᾆσμα καινόν (in LXX Ps 32:3; 39:4; 95:1; 97:1; 149:1) and ᾠδὴν καινὴν (in LXX 43:9; Rev 5:9; 14:3). The latter's use in Rev is clearly eschatological.

203. With the inclusion of the variation in Ps 33:3, it becomes a "formulaic phrase." A "formula" by his definition, is a phrase (a colon long or a verseline) and "recurs at least once." "Formulaic phrases" contain certain variations to the formula, such as addition or omission of particles or pronominal suffixes. Culley defined another category, "free substitutions," in which a formulaic phrase contains a different lexeme. These three categories are increasing in variation. Culley, *Oral Formulaic Language*, 22, 32–33, 58.

204. Culley, *Oral Formulaic Language*, 103, 105.

205. Culley, *Oral Formulaic Language*, 114.

of "stock phrases" an oral prophet would use and reuse. It is plausible that the phrase, שירו ליהוה שיר חדש, is employed as a formula and carefully appropriated in 96:1; 98:1; 149:1; Isa 42:10. This idea that the phrase, "new song," was an established oral formula strengthens our proposition that the phrase has a specific connotation and is used in specific circumstances.

In conclusion, these six points demonstrate that שיר חדש is a carefully chosen formula, plausibly appropriated to form a remarkable schema. The shape of the six occurrences is carefully designed in collaboration with the Metanarrative of the Psalter. Together, they tell of an impending decisive shift in Yhwh's deliverance, bliss and justice at the final consummation.

"Appointed Time/Place" & "From Now to Forever"

The second lexeme that marks a milestone and disjuncture in the development of Yhwh's purposes for his people is the motif of an "appointed time/place" (מועד). This motif is also highlighted by a similar phrase, מעתה ועד-עולם ("from now to forever more").

מועד has multiple meanings. It can mean "appointed place" or "appointed time."[206] In the Pentateuch, it is usually connected to the "appointed feasts" (e.g., Passover; Num 9:2–3) of Israel where the people gather and offer sacrifices to Yhwh.[207] This lexeme occurs only 5x in the Psalms and carries the meaning of "appointed time" in three psalms (75:3; 102:14; 104:19). The "appointed time" in Psalm 75 is found in a Divine Response psalm immediately after the Lament in Ps 74. Likewise, מועד in 102:19 comes after supplication prayers in 102:1–12.[208] The temporal contexts expressed in Pss 75:3 and 102:19 are oriented to the "future."[209] At the same time, the literary contexts in both instances of מועד are associated with the divine response to the fall of Zion.

The third instance of מועד in Ps 104:19 describes Yhwh's appointing of the moon to its circuitry order. In this context, it represents Yhwh's power to order, to provide and care for his creation at the right "time."[210] However, we observe that Ps 104 comes just after the end of the third Davidic Collection (101–103) and is located at the beginning of another series of psalms marked with doxological terms (104–107). This

---

206. "מועד" *HOL*, 186; "מועד" *BDB*, 417.

207. Exod 13:10; Lev 23:2; Num 9:2–3.

208. Historically, Israel blows the trumpet over their offerings and sacrifices as an act of reminder before Yhwh (Num 10:10) at "appointed times." The silver "trumpet" (חצצרה) in Numbers 10 is found only once in the Psalter (98:6) and is located just prior to Ps 102:19. It is interesting that מועד, with connotations of sacrifice and trumpet call, is found near each other in the Psalter.

209. Hossfeld determined this "appointed time" in Pss 75:3 and 102:14 as a time in the future. See Hossfeld and Zenger, *Psalms 2*, 255.

210. Perhaps as a polemic against Aton, in the Great Hymn to Aton. Hossfeld and Zenger, *Psalms 2*, 53–54.

series, Pss 104–107, traces a trajectory from creation (104), the formation and captivity of Israel (105–106), to her entry into an inhabited city (107). The use of מועד in Ps 104 thus sets forth a series of psalms leading into Book V with positive expectations of Israel's restoration to the city of Zion.[211]

The three instances of מועד ("appointed time") in the Psalms share a common feature. They underscore Yhwh's power and surety to act positively at an "appointed time" to reverse the afflictions and difficulties experienced by his people. They mark the dawning of change or a turning of tide in the misfortunes of the Davidic kingship and Zion.

Similarly, the formulaic phrase, מעתה ועד-עולם, reinforces this view.[212] This merism occurs 8x in the HB, five of which occur in the Psalms and interestingly, all of them in Book V of the Psalter (113:2; 115:18; 121:8; 125:2; 131:3).[213] The first two instances are found within the Egyptian Hallel, framing the center Ps 114.[214] They are located in the Hallelujah superscript of Ps 113 and the postscript of Ps 115, forming a frame around 113–15. This framing connects the motifs of Israel's deliverance from Egypt and Judah, and Yhwh's sanctuary in Ps 114 with the special mention of מעתה ועד-עולם.

The three other instances of מעתה ועד-עולם are found in the SOA. In these three instances, there is a common motif highlighting the psalmist's dependence on Yhwh's protection. This is depicted by the imagery of Jerusalem's "mountains" (121:1; 125:2) and a "weaned child resting against his mother" (131:3).[215] Together, these three texts reveal that a special period of Yhwh's providence that has occurred will continue. Yhwh will protect and surround his people in Zion from this time and forevermore so that they can rest in God like a weaned child resting in his or her mother.[216]

---

211. Psalm 104 follows a series of ברך at the end of Ps 103 and is the first of the three psalms that begins with ברכי, ("I bless," Ps 104:1), הודו ("Give thanks" Ps 105:1) and הללויה ("hallelujah," Ps 106:1). Psalm 104 are also the first psalms of the collection of Hallelujah psalms (Pss 104–106, 111–113; 115–117; 135; 146–150) with the "Hallelujah" coda. Hossfeld and Zenger, *Psalms 3*, 39–41.

212. Hossfeld notes that this expression is related to the formula, "forever and ever," which he termed as "eternity formula in doxologies" (Hossfeld and Zenger, *Psalms 3*, 182). Cf. Pss 45:7; 48:15.

213. This phrase is not captured in Culley's analysis.

214. The centrality of Ps 114 can also be seen in the placement of the hallelujah formula. It is located as superscripts in Pss 111, 112; as postscripts in 115, 116 and as frames in 113 and 117. Psalm 114 is set apart without any instance of hallelujah. This is not denying other coherent structural designs or formats that include Ps 118. Our earlier discussion of Prinsloo's spatial study on Pss 113–118 is a case in point.

215. Goldingay, *Psalms*, 3:485.

216. Goldingay points out that "the psalm commends a quietism that lasts forever. Israel needs to be prepared to settle down for the long haul with the circumstances such as those of the Persian period described in Ezra and Nehemiah and forgo any attempt to bring in the kingdom of God, which is the venture of a lofty heart and eyes that look high. It needs to be prepared to wait forever" (Goldingay, *Psalms*, 3:538).

Also noteworthy is that the three instances outside the Psalter (Isa 9:6; 59:21; Mic 4:7) are set within contexts that are considered messianic.[217] Isaiah 9:5–6 describes a messianic figure king who will rule on the Davidic throne, and who will be called "wonderful counselor, mighty God, eternal Father and prince of peace."[218] Isaiah 59:20–21 identifies a time when a "redeemer will come to Zion," and Yhwh's word will never depart from the mouth of "those [and their offspring] who turn from transgression." It has been argued that Isa 59:15b–21 carries a "divine warrior motif" linked directly with Isa 63:1–6, framing the eschatological renewal of Zion.[219] Likewise, Mic 4:1–2 begins with a futuristic[220] depiction of Zion as the chief of mountains where people converge to learn the word of Yhwh. In Mic 4:7–8, the lame and weak will become the remnant and strong nation.

These eschatological connotations surrounding the formula מעתה ועד-עולם, as well as its strategic presences in Book V of the Psalter should not be dismissed as mere coincidence. The motifs of deliverance (114), peace and the rule of a messianic king (120:6–7; 122:6–8; 125:5; 128:6; 132:10–12), and his protection all collaborate with the Metanarrative of the Psalter.

The three phrases, מועד, שיר חדש, and מעתה ועד-עולם, do not come at the end of the Psalter. Interestingly, all the occurrences of מועד and מעתה ועד-עולם lie between Pss 75:3, which is the divine response to the fall of the Zion temple, and 131:3 which comes just prior to the completion of the ideal Zion-temple.[221] Thus, their specific locations and associated literary suggest a turning of fortunes for Zion in the larger sweep of the storyline.

"Relent"

A third lexeme that illustrates a turning point in the Metanarrative is the *niphal* form of נחם. The use of the verb in *niphal* expresses (i) some kind of comfort in the midst of sorrow (77:2; Ezek 14:22) or (ii) "to be sorry, repent or change one's mind" (1 Sam 15:11).[222] In the Psalms, the *niphal* form occurs only 4x. The first two instances iden-

---

217. Goswell concedes that Isa 9:6–7 (and Mic 4:6–7) is "futuristic" and "messianic" despite his qualifications of the messianic figure. See Goswell, "Shape of Messianism," 106–7. Tate, likewise, views the figure as "essentially messianic, in the sense that it expects a new Davidic king whose reign will fulfill the ideals of the Davidic kingship; and since his reign is to extend 'from this time forth and forevermore,' he is to be the last (note 'the latter time' in vs. 1) king to sit on the throne of David and not merely as Ahaz's successor" (Tate, "King and Messiah," 417, 421).

218. For a discussion and debate on the compound five titles ("noun clauses or asyndetic phrases") functioning as theophoric names describing God (rather than the child), see Goswell, "Shape of Messianism," 107; Goldingay, "Compound Name in Isaiah 9:5(6)," 242; Schunck, "Der Fünfte Thronname Des Messias," 108–10; Wegner, "Re-Examination of Isaiah IX 1–6," 103.

219. Lynch, "Zion's Warrior and the Nations," 244–63.

220. Kapelrud, "Eschatology in the Book of Micah," 403; Marrs, "'Back to the Future,'" 93.

221. Cf. Pss 75:3; 102:14; 104:19; 113:2; 115:18; 121:8; 125:2; 131:3.

222. Butterworth, "נחם," *NIDOTTE*, 3:82.

The Design of the Psalter

tify the psalmist seeking "comfort" (77:3) and for God to "have compassion" (90:13). Thus, נחם connects *comfort* with Yhwh's *compassion*. The third instance describes Yhwh's "turning"[223] (106:45) from his anger against his own people. Despite their rebellion, Yhwh "relented" in response to their distress and supplications. The final instance describes Yhwh swearing an "unchanging" oath (לא ינחם) to the messianic king in Ps 110:4.[224]

The development of the motif across these four *niphal* instances and their associated contexts tell a story. The psalmist longs for a "turning/comfort" in his distress (77:2). He beseeches God to have "compassion" on him in his distress (90:13). Yhwh eventually "relents." This "relenting" involves Yhwh leading his people to dwell in an inhabited city (107) and ushers in the triumphant reign of the messianic king from Zion. This king receives Yhwh's "unchanging" oath as priest forever (110).

These four instances are also pegged carefully to the Metanarrative of the Psalter. The first instance (77) is set in Book III, which underscores the fall of Zion. The second and third instances are found in Book IV, highlighting Yhwh's reign and his steadfast love. The last instance in Ps 110 occurs in the fourth Davidic Collection which highlights the triumphant rule of the messianic king.

"Arise, O Lord!" & "Return, O Lord!"

The expressions, קומה יהוה and שובה יהוה, are special literary constructions that display the POS technique and the linear dimension of the Psalter. Both verbs in the expressions are imperatives and suffixed with the paragogic *heh*. The consonance and assonance between them are obvious. The two expressions also have exactly the same vowels. Seven out of eight consonants of these two phrases are identical. Furthermore, they are located only in three Books of the HB. The form, קומה יהוה, is found 8x in the HB and outside the Psalter, they are attested only in Num 10:35 and 2 Chr 6:41. The form, שובה יהוה, is found only 4x in the HB and the only instance outside the Psalter is Num 10:36.

These references outside the Psalter are all associated with the literary contexts following the completion of the Tabernacle at the time of Moses, or the Temple at the time of Solomon. Both are associated with the moving of the ark in search of a "resting place" (Num 10:33; 2 Chr 6:41).[225]

---

223. Hossfeld understands this as a "turning." See Hossfeld and Zenger, *Psalms 3*, 92.

224. Davis argues that Ps 110 is not simply a Royal or enthronement psalm because (a) no human king sits at the right side of Yhwh; (b) no human king is given the order of eternal priesthood; (c) no human king will be able to judge the nations. He argues from poetical, contextual and theological perspectives and concludes that Ps 110 is messianic and the identity of the אדני in Ps 110:1 is Jesus the Messiah. See Davis, "Is Psalm 110 a Messianic Psalm," 160–73.

225. Numbers 10:33 uses מנוחה whereas 2 Chr 6:41 uses the word נוח (rest). Both can be translated as "resting place."

The significance of its occurrence in Num 10 lies in Israel moving out for the first time (Num 10:12–13) in the wilderness of Sinai after the Tabernacle was completed and regulations pertaining to the transportation of the ark were given. The destination of the journey is specified as "the place of which the LORD said, 'I will give it to you'" (Num 10:29), recalling the Abrahamic covenant (Gen 12:7). The two verses, Num 10:35–36, are also known as "The Song of the Ark."[226] As the ark began to move, Moses would say, "קומה יהוה and let your enemies be scattered, and let those who hate you flee before you." As the ark came to rest, Moses would say, "שובה יהוה *to* the myriad thousands of Israel." Cole argues that this couplet in Num 10:35–36 reflects a "holy war motif" and "bespeaks the magnitude of the forces of Israel as they prepare to launch into the victory march leading to holy war against Canaan."[227]

The reference of קומה יהוה in 2 Chr 6:41 is the Chronicler's account of the Solomonic transfer of the ark to its final resting place at the Temple (cf. 1 Kgs 8), which is a literary parallel to David's transfer of the ark to Jerusalem in 1 Chr 16:7–36.[228] Japhet argues that the phrase "the ark of your might" in 2 Chr 6:41 is derived from the "original battle cry" in Num 10:35.[229] This association is clearly valid and connects Num 10:35–36 and 2 Chr 6:41. Hence, apart from the Psalms, the forms, קומה יהוה and שובה יהוה, are associated only with the movement of the ark either with reference to Moses or Solomon. However, these formulaic phrases *outside* the Psalms seem to *program* all their exact sequence of occurrences *within* the Psalms (3:8; 7:7; 9:20; 10:12; 17:13; 132:8; 6:5; 90:13; 126:4). The following figure illustrates this phenomenon.

---

226. Milgrom notes "that the poem [Num 10:35–36] does not belong to its context is indicated by the inverted nuns that frame it." Leiman discusses Num 10:35–36 as a text "borrowed from an apocryphal or pseudepigraphical book of Eldad and Medad." Levine argues that the scribal convention of the inverted nuns around the two verses "parallels the practice of the Alexandrian scribes in their copies of Greek texts, where similar markings are evident." See Milgrom, *Numbers*, 81; Leiman, "Inverted Nuns at Numbers," 354; Levine, *Numbers 1–20*, 319.

227. Cole, *Numbers*, 179.

228. Japhet, *I & II Chronicles*, 601.

229. Japhet, *I & II Chronicles*, 603.

The Design of the Psalter

Location	Motif	Text (NAU) on קומה יהוה	Ref
Num	Ark moves. Destruction of enemies.	Then it came about when the ark set out that Moses said, "Rise up, O LORD! And let Your enemies be scattered, And let those who hate You flee before You."	Num 10:35
2 Chr	Ark moves to dwelling place, favor for Israel	Now, therefore, arise O LORD God, to Your resting place, You and the ark of Your might; let Your priests, O LORD God, be clothed with salvation and let Your godly ones rejoice in what is good.	2 Chr 6:41
Psalms (Book I)	Petition for the destruction of enemies and deliverance for the afflicted	Arise, O LORD; save me, O my God! For You have smitten all my enemies on the cheek; You have shattered the teeth of the wicked.	3:8
		Arise, O LORD, in Your anger; Lift up Yourself against the rage of my adversaries, And arouse Yourself for me; You have appointed judgment.	7:7
		Arise, O LORD, do not let man prevail; Let the nations be judged before You.	9:20
		Arise, O LORD; O God, lift up Your hand. Do not forget the afflicted.	10:12
		Arise, O LORD, confront him, bring him low; Deliver my soul from the wicked with Your sword.	17:13
Psalms (Book V)	Ark moves to dwelling place	Arise, O LORD, to Your resting place, You and the ark of your strength	132:8

Figure 53: Pan-HB Occurrence Scheme of קומה יהוה ("Arise, O LORD!")

Location	Motif	Text (NAU) on שובה יהוה	Ref
Num	Ark rests. Petition for YHWH's favor to the people of Israel	When it came to rest, he said, "Return, O LORD, To the myriad thousands of Israel."	Num 10:36
Psalms (Books I, IV, V)	Petition for deliverance of the people.	Return, O LORD, rescue my soul; Save me because of Your lovingkindness.	6:5
		Do return, O LORD; how long will it be? And be sorry for Your servants.	90.13
		Restore our captivity, O LORD, As the streams in the South.	126:4

Figure 54: Pan-HB Occurrence Scheme of שובה יהוה ("Return, O LORD!")

Figure 53 lists all the occurrences of קומה יהוה in the HB. The first two occurrences (Num 10:35 and 2 Chr 6:41) carry two separate motifs in association with the movement of the ark. Numbers 10:35, connected to Moses, has a specific focus on YHWH's rising against his enemies. In contrast, 2 Chr 6:41 relates to YHWH's servants and his *chasidim*. Remarkably, these two references parallel two different sets of phrase occurrences in the Psalms as shown by the arrows. Numbers 10:35, with its combative focus, corresponds with the first five occurrences in the Psalms, all found in Book I. Interestingly, all five psalms (3:8; 7:7; 9:20; 10:12; 17:13) express YHWH's triumphant power and judgment over the nations and wicked adversaries. 2 Chronicles 6:41, with its phraseology on resting place and the priests clearly alludes to Ps 132:8–9 in Book V, carrying the tone of Yhwh's care and covenantal faithfulness to David (cf. 2 Chr 6:42; 132:10).

In Figure 54, the expression, שובה יהוה in Num 10:36 also corresponds to the three instances in Psalms (6:5; 90:13; 126:4). In Num 10:36, the particle, "to," in the phrase, "return O Lord, *to* the myriad thousands of Israel," is supplied by most English versions (e.g., NIV, ESV, NAU) but is not found in the Hebrew text. The New Revised Standard Version (NRSV, 1989) uses the genitive "of" instead. When it is translated without the particle "to," it is an epithet for Yhwh—"Return O lord, You who are Israel's myriads of thousands!"[230] Thus, for NRSV and Milgrom, the phrase "Israel's myriads of thousands" functions as an apposition to Yhwh. However, the appropriation of the particle "to" is not unwarranted. This translation, "to the myriad thousands of Israel," describes the people of God rather than Yhwh. This understanding works well in the couplet Num 10:35–36 since there is a contrasting parallel following both phrases, קומה יהוה and שובה יהוה, identifying the enemies and servants of God respectively.

From the above, we can see how Num 10:35–36 and 2 Chr 6:41 relate to the occurrence scheme for קומה יהוה and שובה יהוה in the Psalms. The correspondences of the use of קומה יהוה between Book I and Num 10:35, and between Book V and 2 Chr 6:41, bookend all the occurrences of the phrases, קומה יהוה and שובה יהוה, in the Psalter.[231] The final instance in Ps 132:8 collaborates well with our earlier proposition that the ideal Zion-temple is now completed along the horizon of Pss 132–136.

Features of the POS Technique

Based on the examples that exemplify the POS phenomenon above, we will systematize several common features of the POS as follows:

1. Specific words/phrases are selected.
2. These words may be of a certain grammatical construction or forms (e.g., *niphal* forms; paragogic *heh*); formulaic phrases; rare occurrences or theologically-loaded words/phrases (e.g., "Arise O lord!"). There are no significant textual issues associated with POS words identified so far.
3. The POS technique is usually an *exhaustive* display of all occurrences of the word in the Psalms. A careful analysis of all its occurrences is necessary to see the schema.

---

230. Milgrom, *Numbers*, 81. Milgrom's translation.
231. There are no critical notes for all the references of קומה יהוה and שובה יהוה in *BHS*.

The Design of the Psalter

4. The POS technique is always consistent and displays a spectrum of depth. Certain words, such as זכר ("remember"), סתר ("hiding place"), מעתה ועד-עולם ("from this time to forevermore") and נחם ("to relent"), do not form water-tight shapes. However, words like ברית and קביע Jacob are well-developed and consistent.

5. The number of occurrences is carefully chosen and located. They can be intentionally located (or omitted) at strategic places of the macrostructure (e.g., "new song"). The number of occurrences is usually symbolic (e.g, 34 [17x2] instances of "Jacob").

6. The words/phrases within the Psalms that exemplify the POS technique collaborate with the same words/phrases found outside the Psalms (e.g., "new song").

7. The POS of a certain expression is itself a skillfully-designed structure (e.g., "Jacob") and are usually concentric in shape, with inclusions and containing a central motif highlighting Yhwh's victorious kingship.

8. The POS technique converges with the organization principles, Metanarrative and macrostructural shape of the Psalter. The use of poetic features, concentric-linear structures, introductions, turning points, bookends and central motifs correspond exactly to the organizing principles of the MT Psalter.

9. It is not clear why certain words/expressions are chosen. However, those that we have detected relate to the major storyline of the canonical history of Israel and correspond generally to the Metanarrative. This suggests that those who were responsible for the POS were likely the same group/individual who composed the final text of the Psalter.

10. The POS technique suggests that the entire Psalter is edited as a unity and that a complete corpus of the Psalter was present for the editorial work. From the perspective of the reader, the POS demands a focused reading of the entire Psalter with a view on one single word. Therefore, it is less likely that an audience who depended on partial recitation of the Psalms could appreciate the POS. However, this does not necessitate that the POS is implausible. The use of theological significant words (e.g., "Jacob," 34x) and their symbolic recurrences work for the POS in this regard. This may be the first hint for the readers or hearers to identify an important POS lexeme.

11. As a whole, the POS captures both concentric and linear dimensions of reading. The linear aspect looks proleptically to an eschatological final consummation where the wicked nations are judged and the universal praise of God becomes a reality. It emphasizes the *telos* of the Psalter.

Summary

- In this chapter, we have shown how the Psalter is explicated via at least three dimensions of reading: Linear, Concentric and Intertextual. These three dimensions are intertwined and are in sync with each other. There is a remarkable harmony between the Psalter's form and content.

- A concentric reading identifies Central Motifs (CM) at different compositional levels (e.g., Collection, Group, and Section). The macrostructure of the Psalter displays a total of twelve Group Central Motifs (GCM) with four in each of the three Section of the Psalter (Books I, II–III, IV–V). The concentric structure, with the second half pivoting and developing from the first, is also a form of linear reading.

- The four GCMs in Book I (Section 1) are: (a) Yhwh's cosmic kingship; judgment from Zion; (b) Victorious Messianic king and Torah glorified; (c) Dedication Historical Zion-Temple and Yhwh's kingship; and (d) Supplication of the afflicted David.

- The four GCMs in Books II–III (Section 2) are: (a) Messianic king and his bride; (b) Fall of Davidic kingship (and Yhwh's response); (c) Fall of Zion-temple (and Yhwh's judgment); and (d) Supplication of the Davidic figure.

- The four GCMs in Books IV–V (Section 3) are: (a) Yhwh's universal kingship and judgment from Zion; (b) Victorious Davidic king and Torah glorified; (c) Establishment of the eschatological ideal Zion-Temple ruled by a messianic king; and (d) Supplication of the afflicted David.

- GCMs are characterized by formal (e.g., superscription) and thematic features (corresponding to leitmotifs), which correspond well with each other. In our observations, form and content correspond well with each other.

- A linear reading identifies the trajectory of the Psalter. Linear trajectories may be detected by "shifts" in storylines and a movement toward resolution. For instance, the *fall* and *re-establishment* of Zion are such identifiable "shifts."

- The overarching trajectory (or the Metanarrative) is seen when we move across the three Sections of the Psalter. These three Sections trace the establishment, fall and re-establishment of the Davidic kingship and Zion. This movement encapsulates the fate of the people of God. As such, the Metanarrative can be understood as the unfurling and development of Yhwh's promises to David in 2 Sam 7—a *compositional reception* of the Davidic covenant found in the Historical narratives.

- The Pan-Psalter Occurrence Scheme (POS) is an editorial poetic technique. It is the selection, location and arrangement of certain distinct words/phrases via all their sequential occurrences in the Psalter to emphasize a rhetorical message that corresponds to the overarching Metanarrative of the Psalms. The POS itself is a skillfully-designed structure (e.g., "Jacob"). They are usually concentric in shape, with inclusions and containing a central motif highlighting Yhwh's victorious kingship.

4

The Five Davidic Collections

[T]he more closely we examine the final shape of the Hebrew Bible (Tanak), the clearer it becomes that its shape and structure are not accidental. There are clear signs of intelligent life behind its formation. If that is so, we should be asking what is the theological message behind this shape. My answer to that question is that it is strongly messianic. I do not mean by that that the earlier forms of the Bible are not also messianic. What I mean is that in the later stages of the formation of the Hebrew Bible its authors were primarily concerned with making more explicit the messianic hope that was already explicit in the earliest texts.[1]

—JOHN SAILHAMER

What can have been the purpose of retaining such a relatively large number of royal psalms for a religious community that had no king and was compelled to live under the jurisdiction of foreign rulers? Surely we have here, as B. S. Childs has argued, a strong indication that these ancient compositions, which had themselves originated in a period when Israel had a reigning king, were being reinterpreted in expectation of a time when a new Davidic ruler would appear.[2]

—RONALD CLEMENTS

ACCORDING TO GORDON MCCONVILLE, "the validity of a Christian understanding of the Old Testament must depend in the last analysis on the cogency of the argument that the Old Testament is messianic."[3] It is likely that this messianic character

---

1. Sailhamer, "Messiah and the Hebrew Bible," 22.
2. Clements, "Messianic Hope," 14, emphasis added.
3. McConville, "Messianic Interpretation," 2.

The Design of the Psalter

of the Psalter is not merely an anachronistic reading of late Jewish or Christian understanding but a compositional reception (or re-reading) of the Davidic covenant in the Historical books (e.g., 2 Sam 7) in the postexilic period, taking the form of poetic garb.

In this chapter, we will analyze psalms that only carry the name "David" in the superscriptions. Surprisingly, there are very few works that look at all the Davidic psalms alone. If the Psalter has a logic of arrangement and that superscriptions play an important role as we have seen, then there should be an explanation why the Davidic psalms are distributed across the MT Psalter as we have received it.

As noted in chapter 1, the postexilic reader of the Psalter would have experienced substantial cognitive dissonance as they engaged with the rhetorics, structure, and content of the Psalms vis-à-vis their *Sitz im Leben*. The realities of life (absent Davidic king) apparently run counter to God's promises. Yet, postexilic prophetic texts, early Jewish literature, and the LXX have shown that biblical and non-biblical writers, translators and readers had held to messianic hopes. Grant's proposition that the juxtapositions of Torah and kingship psalms (Pss 1–2; 18–19, 118–19), which evoke Deuteronomic perspective of kingship (Deut 17:15–20), help to explain how postexilic Israel responded to the failures of Israel and Judah's kings with their persistent yearning for a victorious and Torah-pious king (Pss 89:50–51; 101:1–8; 110:1–7). In other words, the final form of the Psalter, as a postexilic composition, is not a nostalgic reminiscence of David who once ruled Israel. More importantly, king David functioned as a central figure in the life, thought, and aspiration of the postexilic reader.

The five Davidic Collections (DC I–V) in the Psalter have been described in various ways. While the first, second and last DCs (or Davidic Psalters) are generally understood by scholars to be Pss 3–41, 51–70[4] and 138–145, there is no clear consensus regarding Davidic Pss 101–103 and 108–110. For my analysis, I adopt Buysch's view that these two sets of psalms are DC-III and IV respectively, making a total of five DCs in the Psalms.

From the preceding two chapters, it is evident that the arrangement and placement of the DCs are not haphazard. An important issue that has often been raised is the "return" of Davidic psalms after Ps 72:20 where it clearly states that "the prayers of David, the son of Jesse are ended." Surely, the phrase, תפלה לדוד, occurring in the Davidic Ps 86:1 negates this claim. It is often assumed that the present arrangement of the Psalter is the result of a process of gradual historical amalgamation of texts.[5]

---

4. Auwers considers Pss 71–72 to be part of the second Davidic collection. This is due to the coda in Ps 72:20 which suggests that the prayers of David had ended at the end of Ps 72. However, I have taken strictly those psalms with a Davidic superscript in this delineation. So I have included Ps 86 in the discussion on Davidic Collections as we will show that all Davidic-superscriptioned psalms are carefully ordered. Auwers, *La Composition*, 30–31.

5. See especially Seybold's work on the historical process of the formation of the Psalter. He notes, "editors found old texts in the archives and were surprised and impressed, they thought they had found the songs of David, the great poet of the past and on . . . so they selected many of these texts

However, this does not explain the interesting location of the lone Davidic Ps 86. Why did the final collector(s) of the Psalms not simply place Ps 86 after Ps 70 or along with Pss 101–103 since the Psalter is, within the horizon of Books I–IV, already arranged in collections? The eight Davidic psalms (138–145) near the end of the Psalter could have been grouped with Pss 108–110 but they were not. It is more probable that the final editors of the Psalms did not simply splice newer collections with existing ones but ordered them intentionally. Armed with a macrostructural understanding of the Psalms in the last three chapters, we are in a good position to explore the DCs, starting with the concept of "Messiah in the Psalms."

Messiah in the Psalms?

Gillingham's article, "The Messiah in the Psalms,"[6] provides an excellent starting point. Her primary premise is that the eight psalms containing the term משיח ("the anointed one"),[7] the five Royal psalms,[8] and the fourteen psalms associated with a "royal ideology,"[9] whether at the time of their composition or at the later stages of assembling and arrangement, cannot be found to contain any futuristic, eschatological and "Messianic" interpretations.[10]

Gillingham uses the term, "Messianic" (capital "M"), to indicate a "once-for-all figure coming either at the end of time or heralding it."[11] If any text appears to be future oriented, Gillingham asserts that they are at most "short-term, contemporary and immediate."[12] Instead, *all* these psalms identify a particular person in ancient Israel's cult, assuming a particular historical role (as king, priest or prophet). Repeatedly, Gillingham emphatically states that,

> It is difficult to propose that any Messianic interpretation was intended, both in the earliest stages of the composition of individual psalms and in the later stages of the assembling of the Psalter as a whole.[13]

with the stamp of *le David*, . . . and arranged them in a meaningful order, bound them together and copied them" (Seybold, "Psalter as a Book," 170).

6. Gillingham, "Messiah in the Psalms," 209–37.

7. Pss 2, 18, 20, 28, 84, 89, 132, 45.

8. Pss 21, 72, 101, 110, 144.

9. Pss 9, 10, 22, 40, 41, 49, 56, 59, 68, 69, 86, 88, 91, 116.

10. Gillingham is clearly not alone in this position. In fact, this is a major position in recent OT scholarship relating to the "messiah." Longman notes, "it is impossible to establish that any passage in its original literary and historical context must or even should be understood as portending a future messianic figure." For him, transcendental descriptions of the anointed king, such as in Ps 2, "may simply be the type of hyperbole generated by the beginning of a new reign" (Longman, "Messiah," 13, 18).

11. Gillingham, "Messiah in the Psalms," 211.

12. Gillingham, "Messiah in the Psalms," 210.

13. Gillingham, "Messiah in the Psalms," 209.

> [Where] *māšîaḥ* is used in the 6 royal psalms, it concerns the living, reigning monarch and his successors. Its meaning is entirely political and immediate.
>
> They look back to ancient days using the memory of the monarchy as a means of evoking new faith in God's protection in the present. In none of these psalms, the term *māšîaḥ* is used with any eschatological orientation.... whether these five psalms are royal psalms or later imitation of royal psalms, the figure they consistently refer to is the Davidic king, whether as a contemporary ruler, or as King David himself as the focal point of God's covenant made in earlier days.[14]

For Gillingham, any expressions of futuristic eschatological elements in the Enthronement psalms found in Books IV–V of the Psalter are interpreted as expressions of Yʜᴡʜ's kingship rule. Furthermore, "*none of them* suggests the idealized eschatology depicting a new era, with a Coming Deliverer who will bring about a new and different future at a time known only to God . . . [Consequently] other fragmentary Davidic collections included *in Books Four and Five* do not serve any Messianic purpose."[15]

In other words, Gillingham believes that the canonical composition and arrangement of the Davidic psalms and its theology are primarily historically oriented. Any Messianic references in these psalms are late[16] "receptions" of the psalmody tradition and anachronistic re-readings of the HB texts which include: (a) the ʟxx translation between the second to first century BCE; (b) Qumran texts (e.g., *Hôdāyôt* or 1QH); and (c) Jewish apocalyptic writings in the Second Temple period (e.g., Psalms of Solomon).[17] She concludes that it is possible to "talk about the Messiah in the Psalms—not as a theological agenda arising out of the psalms themselves, but as one which has been imposed upon them."[18] However, it is possible that Gillingham's argumentation has some weaknesses. Consider the following issues:

(1) In unequivocal terms, Gillingham has argued that the title, משיח, in all the Davidic psalms refers to a historical figure rather than an eschatological Messiah. However, this viewpoint does not seem based on solid evidence. Gillingham cites the works of scholars such as Roberts, Kraus, and Craigie in support of her arguments,[19] but neither Roberts,[20] Kraus nor Craigie has amassed any unequivocal evidence for

---

14. Gillingham, "Messiah in the Psalms," 220–24, emphasis added.

15. Gillingham, "Messiah in the Psalms," 228, emphasis added.

16. Many scholars have followed Mowinckel's work in this regard. He argues that the title, "Messiah" (not "messiah"), which originated in later Judaism and the NT, is eschatological, and to apply it to mythical kingship concepts that exalt Israel's kings and ANE kings is to "misuse" the term. Mowinckel goes further to say that the term, used in reference to the king of the final age, does not occur even once in the OT. Mowinckel, *He That Cometh*, 3–4, 7.

17. Gillingham notes that the Psalms of Solomon 17 "offer the first really clear example of a Messianic interpretation of the Davidic psalms" (Gillingham, "Messiah in the Psalms," 231–33, 235).

18. Gillingham, "Messiah in the Psalms," 237.

19. Gillingham, "Messiah in the Psalms," 210.

20. Roberts makes the claim that all 39 occurrences of the term "anointed" (with the exception of

this notion. Interpretation by Kraus was based on parallel analogy to ANE royal ideologies.[21] Craigie's proposition of Ps 2 as a liturgical piece is, likewise, by his own admission, an uncertainty.[22]

While Gillingham uses unequivocal and indicative language to negate any presence of eschatological and Messianic concepts in the Psalms, alternative arguments she has proposed are written in the *subjunctive* mood. She repeatedly uses words such as "probably,"[23] "seem,"[24] and "likely"[25] in her alternate proposals that weaken the Messianic argument.

(2) Gillingham's arguments for postexilic redactions of messianic psalms (e.g., Pss 84, 144) as past-oriented reflections of pious kings aimed at legitimizing the temple traditions do not undermine the possibility of a postexilic editing of the Psalms that was understood eschatologically or messianically. She reasons that the psalmody

---

Isa 45:1) refer to the "contemporary Israelite king." However, he cites little evidence to support this claim in the article. See Roberts, "Old Testament's Contribution," 39.

21. Kraus posited that the "singer and speaker" in Ps 2 is the "king only." Where Ps 2 is concerned, the universal reign of the Davidic king is explained as an "imitation of foreign poems of pomp and circumstance or the excessive claims of glory in ancient Near Eastern 'court style.'" This argument is based on ANE parallel of "conventional" figurative speech, bringing together a royal enthronement ideology and the universal feature of "mythological cosmology." But Kraus was interpreting Ps 2 as a parallel analogy, and not citing solid evidence. See Kraus, *Psalms 1–59*, 126–28.

22. Craigie was careful to note that "the scant nature of the evidence, however, makes any such analysis [different voices identified in Ps 2 are part of a coronation liturgy] uncertain; it is equally uncertain whether the psalm may reflect the coronation liturgy of the temple or a later ceremony in the palace." Craigie notes that in Ps 2, the "world-wide authority always remained an ideal rather than a reality," and that the concept of the eschatological "Messiah" only came after the exile when "rethinking" of such ideal was needed with respect to the "earthly kings." Craigie dated the beginning of the concept of eschatology as early as after the exile. Craigie, *Psalms 1–50*, 65, 68.

23. Emphasis added throughout: "Most *probably* composed for use by any Davidic king"; "*probably* at the time of the coronation of the king"; "*probably* by a cultic prophet, and vv. 8–10 (ET 7–9) are the praise from the congregation. The psalm *may* well belong to an annual festival commemorating the various victories of the king, or it *could* have a more specific use at a service before a critical time of battle" (Gillingham, "Messiah in the Psalms," 212–14); "Like Psalm 84, it is a means whereby the psalmist (*probably*, on account of the borrowings, after the exile) picks up older forms" (Gillingham, "Messiah in the Psalms," 221).

24. Emphasis added throughout: "[The] term *māšiaḥ seems* to have meant, quite simply, an 'anointed one,' referring to one who held an office, whether that of a prophet, a priest or a king" (Gillingham, "Messiah in the Psalms," 210); "as in Psalm 28, the term here does *seem* more *likely* to recall the memory of the king: the parallelism of *māginnēnû* ('our shield') with *mᵉšîhᵉkā* ('thine anointed') *seems to suggest* a royal designation" (Gillingham, "Messiah in the Psalms," 219–20); "It *seems* safer to assume, with Mowinckel, . . . the so-called royal psalms might also include a much larger group on the basis that the suppliant *seems* to have some authority over the people as well as that degree of intimacy with God which would be expected of a king" (Gillingham, "Messiah in the Psalms," 224); "Between the period of the editing and collecting of the psalms, when the royal Messianic interpretation *seems* to have been peripheral" (Gillingham, "Messiah in the Psalms," 229).

25. Emphasis added throughout: "Therefore it could still be quite *likely* that, on account of the intercessory language, the psalm has been composed for a Davidic monarch" (Gillingham, "Messiah in the Psalms," 223); "it is more *likely* that their purpose was to portray David as the ideal figure of piety" (Gillingham, "Messiah in the Psalms," 226).

The Design of the Psalter

at that time was "orientated backwards" to the Davidic dynasty, and not forward to some future Messianic era.[26] She also claims that the historical information in the thirteen Davidic superscriptions serves as pious reflection, and "as a 'type' for others to follow."[27] Concerning the fifty-seven *ledāwid* psalms, their "main purpose . . . is to uphold the legitimacy of the temple, and with that, the worship of God there."[28] This argument, while plausible, cannot explain why there were not more Davidic psalms if the intention was to highlight the legitimacy of the temple or to bolster pious reflections on David, since, the addition of Davidic superscriptions had also been practiced in the LXX. However, in the LXX, the adding of τῷ Δαυιδ titles to non-Davidic titled psalms in the MT has a Messianic rather than a temple focus.[29] How do we then reconcile the Messianic emphasis in the LXX[30] with the piety of David or the legitimization of the temple in the MT?

The majority of the thirteen Davidic historical superscriptions (8 out of 13)[31] occur in Book II, related primarily to the dire situations David finds himself in. These historical superscriptions correspond to the *content* of these psalms which, in essence, identify the distressing experiences of the psalmist (or of David) and how he petitioned God for deliverance. They do not appear to be written for the legitimization of the Second Temple.[32]

As we have also ascertained, the historical superscriptions and literary contexts of these psalms in Book II identify the low points of David's life. Their frequent occurrences in Book II highlight a faltering Davidic monarch rather than a pious one. They depict the sin of David (51:1); plots against his downfall (52); the exposure of David to his enemies (54); his captivity (56); an escape (57); a persisting threat (59); and his wilderness wanderings (63). Since these historical titled psalms identify the low points of David's life, they are not likely used to celebrate or reminiscence about the glories of historical kingships. Pious reflections of David in these literary contexts make sense when readers make a link between David's dire circumstances and their own and find strength in David's future hope for YHWH's deliverance.

---

26. Gillingham, "Messiah in the Psalms," 225–26.

27. Gillingham, "Messiah in the Psalms," 226.

28. Gillingham, "Messiah in the Psalms," 228; see also "Levitical Singers," 122.

29. LXX psalms with Davidic titles not found in the MT include: LXX Pss 9:1; 32:1; 42:1; 70:1; 90:1; 92:1; 93:1; 94:1; 95:1; 96:1; 97:1; 98:1; 103:1; 136:1.

30. For example, Schaper notes that Ps 45:7 (LXX 44:7) is addressed to the king by the vocative address of ὁ θεός; He also points out that the LXX suggests the pre-existence of the king in Ps 110:3 (LXX 109:3). Schaper, *Eschatology in the Greek Psalter*, 80, 140.

31. Pss 3; 7; 18; 34; 51; 52; 54; 56; 57; 59; 60; 63; 142.

32. E.g., Pss 51; 52; 54; 56; 57; 59; 60; 63. Separately, Mays notes, "They all concern situations of need and the deliverance of the LORD as its resolution. They are either prayers for salvation or praise for salvation from trouble or songs of trust on the part of one who must and can live in the face of trouble in reliance on God" (Mays, "David of the Psalms," 151).

On this point, the historical information in Ps 60:1–2 is helpful. This superscription highlights David's victory (through Joab) and interestingly, provides a clue to its purpose. It is a מכתם לדוד ללמד ("a *miktham* of David, to teach").³³ Contrary to Gillingham's suggestion that such a superscription functions as a backward reflection, this superscription identifies the function as "to teach." As a teaching, the psalm has a present and forward thrust. In this psalm, what is observed is not the supremacy of David's victorious pursuits. The psalm clearly downplays human deliverance (60:13). Despite the historical information of victory in the superscription, verses 3–7 identify an earlier defeat.³⁴ What is taught, rather, that the believer should petition Yhwh despite his apparent "rejection" (זנח, 60:3, 12) and "breaking" (פרץ, 60:3) of his people. In other words, reflections on David's piety contrast Davidic weakness (and sin) vis-à-vis Yhwh's deliverance and restoration. They function as teachings and appropriations of faith for its readers under foreign masters in the postexilic period. As Mays argued,

> The psalm titles do not grow out of or function on behalf of a historical interest of any kind. They are rather hermeneutical ways of relating the psalms to the lives of those who lived in the face of threats from enemies within and without and from their own sin, and who sought to conduct their lives according to the way of David.³⁵

It is also difficult to make clear distinctions between what Gillingham means by the "immediate future" or a more "distant future" from the standpoint of the composition. Under the prolonged and severe conditions of Israel's vassalage, first through Babylon's seventy years of exile and then under Persian rule, notwithstanding the harsh threats and danger of rebuilding the postexilic community, we can only imagine that any deliverance sought must have been made with immediate and fervent zeal. An urgent, transcendental and mighty deliverance brought about by Yhwh resonates well with the expressions of strong emotions and aspirations found in the Psalmody.

Reflections on the piety of exemplar kings cannot be an end in itself. It is more plausible that in times of great distress, the community of postexilic Israel looks back at past promises of God to anchor their hope for a future deliverance (that is both immediate and ultimate) rather than a mere celebration of the piety of past kings. Only an ultimate establishment of Yhwh's kingdom and reign can satisfy.

(3) Gillingham's argument for the legitimization of the temple requires further discussion. She notes,

> An appeal to David was an appeal to the founding of Zion, and from this, a justification for the reinstating of Zion theology by the building of the Second Temple. To reflect upon the promises once made through the Davidic

---

33. On the teaching function of the Psalms, see Firth, "Teaching of the Psalms," 159–74; Firth, "More than Just Torah," 63–82.
34. Hossfeld and Zenger, *Psalms 2*, 98–99.
35. Mays, "David of the Psalms," 152.

covenant made some sense of the present conflict between faith and experience: hence to look back to David was in part a means of evoking a typical figure of piety, but more importantly, in socio-political terms, it was also a means of gaining legitimization for the Second Temple cult.[36]

The appeal to the Davidic covenant, however, is as much a choice of a Davidic king reigning on the throne of David (2 Sam 7:14–17)[37] as with the establishment of Zion.[38] In other words, any reflection on the Davidic covenant cannot be limited to "Zion theology" alone, unless the "Zion theology" is understood as one without the Davidic king. Even in the SOA in Book V which is focused on the restoration of Zion,[39] the Davidic kingship is an important and indispensable aspect. In the SOA, Davidic "thrones" are set and a Davidic "lamp" and "horn"[40] will spring forth (esp. 122:5; 132:10–12, 17). As Ollenberger points out, "David and Zion are the central symbols of two different traditions and cannot simply be identified, or the one reduced to the other."[41] Gillingham's argument that the Davidic psalms in the postexilic period function primarily to legitimize the Second Temple raises the question of the absent Davidic king since Israel had no king during that period.

While the concern for Zion and the temple is present in the Psalter, it seems that early Jewish compositions in the Second Temple period were already thinking beyond the physical restoration of the temple. For instance, Tobit 13:9–18, which is believed to be composed in third century BCE,[42] is concerned with the building of the eschatological temple.

(4) A gap remains in Gillingham's argument concerning how Messianic interpretations of these psalms arose between the early postexilic period (late fifth century BCE) and the first and second century BCE.[43] Gillingham argues that at the time of the final editing and collecting of the Psalms, "royal Messianic interpretation seems to have been peripheral."[44] While messianic prophecies were important in early Judaism and in the Qumran community,[45] Gillingham admits (following Schaper) that by the time of the LXX, eschatology and messianic thoughts were already present.[46] Schaper

---

36. Gillingham, "Messiah in the Psalms," 227.

37. Balentine, "Royal Psalms," 57.

38. Sergi, "Composition of Nathan's Oracle," 261.

39. By Gillingham's own acknowledgment. See Gillingham, "Zion Tradition," 320.

40. Note that Pss 130, 131 and 132 contain Davidic references in the superscription. Waschke was quoted, "The images of 'horn' and the 'lamp' are expressions for the power, strength and mighty posterity of the Davidic line; they represent a shortened form of the dynastic promise in the form of metaphors" (Hossfeld and Zenger, *Psalms 3*, 466). Cf. Waschke, *Der Gesalbte*, 70.

41. Ollenburger, *Zion*, 59.

42. Fitzmyer, *Tobit*; Brooke, "Psalms in Early Jewish Literature," 17–18.

43. Gillingham, "Messiah in the Psalms," 230.

44. Gillingham, "Messiah in the Psalms," 229.

45. Gillingham, "Messiah in the Psalms," 229; "Messianic Prophecy," 119.

46. Gillingham, "Messiah in the Psalms," 230–32; Schaper, *Eschatology in the Greek Psalter*, 26–30,

posits that the LXX originated by the "second half of the second century BC."⁴⁷ He points out that "messianic hope first and foremost meant hoping for the restoration of Israel's glories" and that it was "by nature, politically motivated."⁴⁸ While Schaper states that Messianic hopes took center stage in Jewish thinking at the time of the Hasmonean revolt, he makes no claims about when and how these concepts were originally conceived or understood, which would have begun earlier than the aforementioned period.

Schaper has shown that in no less than twenty instances,⁴⁹ the LXX translates the Hebrew texts with eschatological and messianic tendencies. He understands that these were not simply translational difficulties or textual issues but they reflect an established hermeneutic of the Hebrew Psalms and are at times, given "deliberate renderings" that depict an eschatological Messiah who is preexistent and God-like (cf. 72:17; 110:3; LXX 71:17; 109:3).⁵⁰

The *terminus a quo* of any messianic or eschatological thought, even if we deny its origins in the preexilic period (following Craigie), can be taken to be exilic or the early postexilic period (fifth century BCE). It is generally accepted that the final composition and compilation of the MT Psalter is completed in the postexilic period.⁵¹

Gillingham and Schaper have merely identified the period in which Messianic thoughts flourished. Its conception is likely earlier. It is unlikely to have risen suddenly at the composition of the LXX or during the Hasmonean revolt. It is also insufficient to link Jewish messianic and eschatological thought found in the LXX or Qumran literature with ancient Mesopotamian mythology by ignoring altogether its exilic and postexilic development in the HB.

144–64; Williams, "Towards a Date," 248–76.

47. He based his dating on three main evidence: "the use of the term βαρις, the occurrence of proto-rabbinic exegetical methods and the significance of 'Moab' in Jewish eschatology." For further details, see Schaper, *Eschatology in the Greek Psalter*, 34–45.

48. These messianic interpretations took on nationalistic expression at the "first stages of the Hasmonean revolt." Schaper, *Eschatology in the Greek Psalter*, 27, 29.

49. Cf. the following with its LXX counterparts. Pss 1:5*; 2:10–12*; 8:5; 16:9–10; 22:30–32; 45:5, 7*, 12; 46:9; 48:15; 49:12; 56:9; 59:14; 68:7, 13; 72:17*; 73:4; 80:15–18; 87:5; 110:3* See Schaper, *Eschatology in the Greek Psalter*, 46–107. See especially texts marked with asterisks that show such eschatological and messianic interpretations.

50. The eschatological and messianic interpretations in the LXX are made under careful translation work. Schaper states that the LXX and MT have an "astonishing degree of similarity . . . by and large [the LXX] constitute a faithful rendering of a Hebrew text that must have been quite close to the one produced and secured by the Masoretes" (Schaper, *Eschatology in the Greek Psalter*, 13, 15). Pietersma concurs. He states three non-negotiable points: "a. That the Greek translation of Psalms typically makes sense. b. That at times the Greek translator exegetes the source text. c. That messianic interpretation can be found in the Greek Psalter" (Pietersma, "Messianism and the Greek Psalter," 50).

51. Or as late as the first century BCE, argued from the fluidity of canonical arrangements found in the Qumran Psalms. Longman, *Psalms*, 33. An even later date of first century CE has also been proposed. See also Wilson, "Qumran Psalms Scroll," 624–42.

The Design of the Psalter

It is more plausible that Messianic and eschatological hermeneutics and interpretations had already been developed by the early second century BCE, or earlier, before the final editing of the Psalter. Furthermore, the concept of the ideal king who is anointed in Dan 9:25 shows that messianic expectations had already gained ground at around the same time.[52]

We also know that messianic expectations were reinterpreted[53] in the early postexilic times as evident in the prophecies of Zechariah (cf. 3:8, 6:9–15) and Haggai (2:20–23).[54] In view of Jer 23:5, Rose argues that the imagery provided by the term, צמח ("sprout"), "is used to evoke the idea of an intervention by Yhwh as the only means for guaranteeing the restoration of the monarchy"[55] and that its use *before* and *after* the exile shows that "the situation and prospects with regard to the Davidic dynasty at the time of the prophet Zechariah were not much different from that at the time of the prophet Jeremiah."[56]

This reinterpretation of Davidic kingship may have even been conceptualized in the Book of the Twelve. Petterson argues that although the Book of the Twelve presents a negative view of kingship, it contains hope for restoration through the Davidic house and in particular, a future Davidic king. This concept,

> occurs at key points in the Twelve: at the beginning, middle, and towards the end with a sustained treatment in Zechariah. This strongly suggests that those who compiled the Twelve sought to preserve a robust hope for a future king from the house of David, rather than overturning or muting these earlier hopes.[57]

In other words, it is possible that Messianic interpretations and compositions have already begun in the early postexilic period (fifth to fourth century BCE).[58] If such Messianic and eschatological interpretations had begun earlier than the second century BCE and with Yhwh's personal intervention and deliverance envisioned in the

---

52. That is, if we accept Balentine's second-century BCE dating of Dan 9:25. Balentine, "Royal Psalms," 61.

53. Concerning "reinterpretation," it is commonly held that later biblical writers understood the non-messianic biblical texts written by earlier writers as Messianic. Sailhamer understands "reinterpretation" as the "OT reads and interprets itself, as is happening in Daniel 7, it does so by drawing on the real, historical intent of the other OT authors. There is no need to speak of a re-interpretation of texts" (Sailhamer, "Messiah and the Hebrew Bible," 14, emphasis added). In other words, the Messianic reading was already present, and later writers *expanded* on such understanding. Sailhamer argues that the entire HB can be interpreted messianically.

54. Rose, "Messianic Expectations," 373; *Zemah and Zerubbabel*. See also Balentine, "Royal Psalms," 61.

55. Rose, "Messianic Expectations," 373.

56. Rose, "Messianic Expectations," 374.

57. Petterson, "Shape of the Davidic Hope," 246. See also Petterson, *Behold Your King*.

58. We have already seen how the Book of Tobit 13:9–18 reflect an eschatological view of the temple. On the use of the Psalter in *Apocalypse of Abraham*, *Testament of Levi*, the Wisdom of Solomon and the writings of Philo, see Brooke, "Psalms in Early Jewish Literature," 15–23.

Prophetic books composed in the early postexilic period, it is not unlikely that a Messianic understanding would have been incorporated in the Davidic or Royal psalms at the final editing and arrangement of the Hebrew Psalter. Granting the possibility that individual psalms may be originally composed for a particular officeholder historically or in court-style rhetoric based on ANE parallels (such as Zion theology based on Ugaritic Zaphon myth),[59] it is not necessary to preclude any eschatological or Messianic conceptual understanding *at the time of the final compilation* of the Hebrew Psalter. As Clements said,

> [it] is in any case singularly worthy of note that none of the other nations which cherished such a high doctrine of kingship, in many cases far more pretentious and ideologically exalted than that of Israel, carried this forward into the formation of a messianic expectation. This, so far as we know, was a unique achievement of the Old Testament.[60]

Messianic and eschatological traditions found in later Judaism[61] and the New Testament, as Clements rightly points out, "does not stand isolated and distinct from what has preceded it. Instead, it marks the end of a long process of what we have come to describe as 'inner-biblical' exegesis."[62]

In other words, Messianic and eschatological arguments in the Psalms are the result of re-readings, expositions, and interpretations of Historical/Prophetic texts under the exilic/postexilic circumstances. It can be seen as a poetic reception of the Davidic promises. Auwers argues, "it is possible that the editors of the Psalter have intentionally dismembered preexisting collections to redistribute the psalms according to other criteria, and that the distribution of 'Psalms of David' throughout the collection has to another purpose than to extend the patronage of musician-king to the entire Psalter."[63]

To be sure, the question of the origins of messianism raised by Clements has been answered by Mowinckel in his work, *He That Cometh*,[64] which is deemed "one of the great books of twentieth-century scholarship" by Collins.[65] Mowinckel makes two important distinctions in this work. First, he differentiates between a Messiah that is understood as a future, eschatological coming ideal king (capital "M" as in Gillingham's version), and that of an "idealized and empirical king in Israel."[66] This "ideal-

---

59. See especially Levenson, *Sinai and Zion*, 102–37; Clifford, "Temple in the Ugaritic Myth," 137–45; "Tent of El," 221–27; Clements, "Messianic Hope," 11.

60. Clements, "Messianic Hope," 13.

61. Mitchell argues that the messianic tradition is not only Davidic, but Josephite. For a discussion of how the Rabbis view the Psalter as messianic, see Mitchell, *Messiah ben Joseph*, 53–56.

62. Clements, "Messianic Hope," 15–16. See also Fishbane, *Biblical Interpretation*, 33–48.

63. Auwers, *La Composition*, 28.

64. See Mowinckel, *He That Cometh*.

65. Collins, "Mowinckel's He That Cometh Revisited," 3.

66. Mowinckel, *He That Cometh*, 123.

ized kingship" was a national concept and historically oriented. This concept probably arose at the time of Assyrian and Chaldean threats.[67] It emphasized a historical king that could deliver the Israelite nation and bring about political and social well-being. It was not formally associated with a future, final Messianic king.

Second, Mowinckel also differentiated what he calls, "eschatology" and "future hope."[68] Future hope is a concept that came before eschatology. It was a hope associated with the idealized historical king which remained elusive with each successive king. Eschatology, on the other hand, is associated with the "last things" and "dualistic conceptions" that originated only after the exile in the Persian period and later Judaism.[69]

The origins of messianism began with Israel desiring her own king, much like the kings of neighboring nations. Mowinckel assumes that Israel assimilated not just the concept of a king, but the myth, cult, formulaic phrases and practices associated with royal ideology in the ANE religion.[70] What Israel had as the earliest form of messianism, like her ANE counterparts, was an idealized kingship ideology which was historical and future-oriented, but not eschatological. Mowinckel postulates an annual enthronement festival of Yhwh, which at times coincided with the enthronement of a new king in Israel. During these festivals, Israel revisited and renewed their hopes for the idealized Davidic king who would bring about political and national deliverance. However, with the Babylonian exile, historical reality continued to fall short of such expectation, causing the people to turn towards Yhwh and his promises. They looked back at Yhwh's mighty deliverance in the Exodus event and consequently looked to the future with faith. The state of affairs had come to a point where "there appeared to be no future hope for the representatives of David's line."[71] It was under such circumstances that Messianic faith began to take shape. Mowinckel maintains that any eschatological and Messianic concept only took shape during the Persian (539–330 BCE) and early Hellenistic period. Mowinckel's understanding differs from Gillingham's argument in at least two ways. First, he allows a *future-oriented* idealized king (not merely historical). Second, the Messianic hope arose earlier than what Gillingham suggests.

---

67. Mowinckel, *He That Cometh*, 141.

68. Mowinckel, *He That Cometh*, 125.

69. Mowinckel defines "eschatology" as "a doctrine or complex of ideas about 'the last things' which is more or less organically coherent and developed. Every eschatology includes in some form or other, a dualistic conception of the course of history, and implies that the present state of things and the present world order will suddenly come to an end and be superseded by another of an essentially different kind" (Mowinckel, *He That Cometh*, 125, 264).

70. Mowinckel compared and highlighted similarities between Israel's kingship and those found in Sumerian, Babylonian, Egyptian, Hittite, Ugaritic and other Canaanite religions. See Mowinckel, *He That Cometh*, 23–55, 124.

71. Mowinckel, *He That Cometh*, 158.

However, there are several issues associated with Mowinckel's overall thesis. First, Mowinckel's reconstruction rests on the two foundations of traditional and literary criticism.[72] Using "traditional" criticism, Mowinckel depends on historical data, reconstructions, and comparisons between Israel and ANE religions for the interpretation of biblical texts. With "literary" criticism, Mowinckel adopts the conclusions of Documentary Hypothesis and Noth's Deuteromistic History in his dating and understanding of various messianic texts (esp. in Isaiah). These two foundations are not unshakable.[73] How ANE parallels are interpreted is often disputed[74] and could possibly fail based on new archaeological evidence.[75] Furthermore, some of Mowinckel's arguments cannot be falsified or verified. His datings based on source-critical arguments are often taken as actual historical evidence.[76]

Second, it must be noted that Mowinckel's distinction of the future-idealized and eschatological Messianic king cannot be ascertained from the texts of the Psalms. This distinction is a theoretical construct rather than a literary discernment. Moreover, Mowinckel's final interpretation of how Messianism (capital "M") came about is not dissimilar to our proposition that Messianism would have been the central occupation in the minds of the people of Israel in the postexilic period. Mowinckel's dating of Messianism to the Persian and early Hellenistic period also coincides well with our

---

72. Mowinckel admitted, "The work of tradition criticism and of literary criticism in distinguishing between earlier and later elements in the material handed down to us, and in attempting to arrange the tradition according to the changing periods in revelation history, and to discover the line of development in that history, is an absolute necessity if the historical study of theology is to be carried on" (Mowinckel, *He That Cometh*, 129).

73. Of various points deemed as "facts," Mowinckel admitted that "we have little direct knowledge of the royal ideology, and of the part played by the king as god's representative in the cult and in the mind of the community" (Mowinckel, *He That Cometh*, 21–26, 52, 56).

74. Mowinkel's understanding of the late, postexilic eschatology in the Messianic concepts is by his own admittance, contended by Gressmann, Sellin, Gunkel and others. Writing half a century after Mowinckel, Collins points out new historical evidence that links Egyptian mythological traditions to Israel's kingship ideology more closely than Mowinckel had thought. Becker, in his study of Messianic expectations in the OT, contends that "the concept of kingship, an important category for sacral history, was not integrated until late in Israel's history." This is in opposition to Mowinckel's thesis which sees kingship ideology as early. See Mowinckel, *He That Cometh*, 13–15, 123, 128; Collins, "Mowinckel's *He That Cometh* Revisited," 5–7; Becker and Green, *Messianic Expectation*, 17.

75. The *Ketef Hinnom* inscriptions (Num 6:24–26) found in 1979 is dated to the eighth/seventh century BCE undermining the dating of supposedly P text often assumed in source criticism and by Mowinckel as well. Writing against the Documentary Hypothesis, Cassuto argues that there is no factual evidence of the text sources. Source criticism is primarily a literary argument rather than empirical. See Barkay et al., "Challenges of Ketef Hinnom," 162–71; "Amulets from Ketef Hinnom," 41–71; Waaler, "Revised Date for Pentateuchal Texts?," 29–55; Cassuto and Berman, *Documentary Hypothesis*.

76. For instance, Mowinckel argues that different parts of Isaiah were written by Isaiah and that his circle of disciples has combined earlier and later prophetic sayings into one. At one point, Mowinckel notes that "there is clear evidence of this from the circle of Isaiah's disciples . . . in the circle of Isaiah's disciples the poem Isa. xxxii, 1–8 was interpreted as a prophecy about the ideal future king, and in the course of transmission it was put together with earlier and later prophetic utterances by Isaiah and his successors" (Mowinckel, *He That Cometh*, 174).

proposal that Messianic hope is present at the time of the final editing and composition of the Psalter.[77]

Hence, assumptions that post-OT readings have imposed Messianic concepts on the Psalms must be reviewed. The plausibility that a prevailing Messianic understanding was present at the time of the final composition of the Psalter cannot be simply be dismissed.[78]

Certainly, a number of scholars have also argued for a Messianic interpretation of the Psalms. Starling argues that the Royal psalms are not simply a "hyperbolic court-rhetoric associated with sacral kingship in its various forms, both in Egypt and Mesopotamia."[79] The descriptions of the reign of the messianic king in the Psalms far surpass historical realities even in the "best of times under the monarchy."[80] For instance, the descriptions of Ps 2 are presented "ahistorically," and attempts to locate this psalm within the history of Israel's monarchy remain unfruitful.[81]

David Mitchell argues that the final form of the Psalter was likely completed between the end of the exile and the translation of the LXX at "a time of growing eschatological hope" in anticipation of the restoration of Israel.[82] He makes an interesting point regarding the "future-predictive" nature of the figures attributed in the superscriptions of the Psalms. He argues that David, Asaph, Jeduthun, Heman and Moses are "future-predictive" prophets.[83] Various descriptions of kings or events are

---

77. For a good defense against Mowinckel's argument on the absence of an early Messianism and eschatology in the Psalms, see Starling, "Messianic Hope in the Psalms," 121–34.

78. Mowinckel believed that the conception of "a coming 'Anointed of Yahweh' existed in Israel quite early [though Mowinckel was uncertain] in the monarchic period . . . It comes from a time when the common oriental ideal of kingship had been naturalized in Israel, and when the tension between ideal and reality was making itself felt, so as to prompt the wish that in spite of the unpleasant facts the ideal of kingship would be realized." Mowinckel, however, deemed this stage as the "preliminary stage of the true Messianic faith." In a similar way, the postexilic period, where promises of the prophet Zechariah was made concerning Zerubbabel, "cannot be taken as expression of the Messianic hope, for they neither presuppose nor proclaim it; but they lay the foundation for it and create it." Mowinckel argues that "the message of Haggai and Zechariah has nothing to do with eschatology." But this has been contended by Rose. See Mowinckel, *He That Cometh*, 97–99, 119, 121; Rose, *Zemah and Zerubbabel*.

79. Starling, "Messianic Hope," 123.

80. Starling, "Messianic Hope," 125.

81. This is conceded by Tremper Longman who notes, "[on Ps 2] we are somewhat at a loss to understand exactly what kind of historical background generated such a thought . . . This may be the type of hyperbole generated by the beginning of a new reign" (Longman, "Messiah," 468). See Brownlee, "Psalms 1–2 as a Coronation Liturgy."

82. Mitchell, *Message of the Psalter*, 82.

83. Cf. 2 Sam 23:2–4; 7:11–16; 2 Chr 29:30; 35:15; 1 Chr 25:5; Deut 18:15; 31:19–22. Mitchell, *Message of the Psalter*, 83. Scholars such as Gunkel and Begrich have also made connections of eschatological features between the Prophetic Books and the Psalms. Gunkel and Begrich listed seven motifs of eschatological joy envisioned in the Psalms in connection with the Prophetic books: (1) Restoration of the city of Jerusalem (Ps 147:2); (2) Yhwh breaking the rule of the nations and his universal judgment (Pss 9:16; 76:9; 96:13); (3) The overthrowing of great natural calamities at the end time (Pss 46:3; 75:4; 93:1; cf. Isa 24:19; Hag 2:6); (4) The overthrowing of roaring waves which are the

also made in a language that "far exceeds the reality of any historical king or battle."[84] More recently, he argues for a messianic tradition in the Psalter that is Josephite, citing support from the Rabbinic literature.[85]

David Howard sees that despite various evidence presented for the "failure" of the Davidic covenant, the Royal psalms are arranged to reflect a "continuing hope that is focused on both Zion and the Davidic kingdom."[86] Marvin Vincent concludes that at the time of the final redaction when Israel was without king, the place of Ps 2 is significant because its treatment of Zion and the messianic king, cast against descriptions of the failure of the Davidic kingdom in subsequent pages of the Psalter, "makes it almost certain that this Psalm is to be given an eschatological interpretation."[87]

This long discussion, in response to Gillingham's and Mowinckel's work, together with the observations of Schaper, Clements, and others, brings us to this point: We need not accept the proposition that Messianic and eschatological concepts are entirely absent at the time of the final collection and editing of the Hebrew Psalter. It is not implausible that postexilic Israel, in the midst of various political, social and existential struggles, had reflected deep and hard theologically, and had received and written the biblical texts with a certain coherent, Messianic and eschatological thrust, on which subsequent Jewish and Christian communities built (despite their different interpretations of who that Messiah might be).

My argument is that the five DCs unfurl the crystallized form of Messianic hopes envisioned in the Prologue (Pss 1–2) and seen together, they tell the story of the establishment (DC-I), fall (DC-II) and re-establishment (DC-III–IV) of an ideal Davidic king who will usher in a new era at the end times (Pss 144–145 in DC-V). The central characterization of DC-V, however, depicts a period of prayer and waiting for the people of God, represented by the democratized Davidic figure, before Yhwh's consummative kingship takes over in Ps 145.[88]

First Davidic Collection (Pss 3–41)

Since DC-I consists of Book I minus the Prologue, our discussion for DC-I presupposes the results of our analyses of Book I. Our conclusions from chapters 2–3 are that Books I, II–III and IV–V are three Sections, forming a three-part concentric

---

attacking nations (Ps 46); (5) The fall of the great world empires with Yhwh ruling over the nations (Ps 10:18); (6) The transfiguration of Zion and the temple as the place of asylum (Ps 46:5, 6, 8; cf Isa 7:14; 31:5; Zech 12:8); (7) Greater things happening in heaven. Yhwh subdues humanity as well as all the gods (Ps 97:7). See Gunkel and Begrich, *Introduction to Psalms*, 252.

84. Mitchell, *Message of the Psalter*, 85.

85. Mitchell cites *Pirqei de Rabbi Eliezer* 22.a.ii; *Pesikta Rabbati* 36–37; Midrash *Tehillim* 60.3; The *Zohar*, Mishpatim 479. Mitchell, *Messiah ben Joseph*, 53–56.

86. Howard, *Structure of Psalms 93–100*, 202.

87. Vincent, "Shape of the Psalter," 61.

88. See also Ho, "Shape of Davidic Psalms."

structure. These three Sections further divide into four Groups each (twelve Groups in total), characterized by their respective Group Central Motif (GCM). Recall that the four GCMs in Section I are: (a) Yhwh's cosmic kingship and judgment from Zion, (b) Victorious Messianic king and Torah glorified, (c) Dedication of the Historical Zion-Temple and Yhwh's kingship, and (d) Supplication of the afflicted David.

In chapter 3, we stated that the three Sections parallel each other. The first GCMs in all three Sections are concerned with Yhwh's kingship and judgment. Likewise, the second and third GCMs are concerned with the Davidic king and Zion respectively. The fourth GCMs are consistently characterized as the Davidic supplication.

We have also seen a Metanarrative developing across the second and third GCMs of the three Sections. At the end of this Metanarrative, in Books IV–V, is the celebration of the victorious Yhwh-Messianic kingship and establishment of an ideal Zion. This comes *after* tracing the fall of the Davidic kingship and Zion-temple in Books II–III. Book I, or DC-I which is the longest of all the DCs, begins this trajectory.

The first Davidic Collection, in itself, is a concentric structure (see Figure 12). At the heart of DC-I is the establishment of these two institutions—the Davidic kingship and Zion-temple. This is understood by the GCMs in Pss 18–21 and 29–30, which are located at the center of Groups 2 and 3 (15–24 and 25–34). In Pss 18–21, human kingship is to be established through Torah-piety (18:1, 22–31; 19:8–15). The king is to take refuge in Yhwh's protection and deliverance from Zion/heaven (18:3, 7; 20:3, 7). His kingship at Zion is associated with the representative locale of Yhwh's presence and power. Hence, human kingship in DC-I is established through adherence to Yhwh's commandments and dependence on his power.

Psalm 18 begins with the superscription, "The LORD has delivered him from the hand of all his enemies and from the hand of Saul" (18:1). This historical information is unique[89] as it emphasizes David's ascendancy to Israel's throne after the fall of Saul's kingship. This superscription also alludes to the Davidic Covenant (cf. 2 Sam 7:1, 9, 11). Robertson argues that the focus and location of Pss 18–19 are "pivotal" as they usher in and highlight motifs associated with teaching, messiah, and sin in DC-I.[90] Psalm 18 depicts the steady kingship (18:37) that is victorious over foreign nations (18:38–46). This victorious rule is the result of Yhwh's delight (18:20), empowerment and deliverance (18:48–49; 20:7; 21:9–14). Psalm 19, with its focus on the Torah, stands not just at the center of the entire Group (15–24) but in the midst of four psalms that highlight the establishment of the Davidic kingship (18–21).[91] The motif

---

89. This is the only superscription out of 13 superscriptions with historical information that speaks positively of David (apart from Ps 60 which is rather "mixed").

90. Robertson has argued that beyond the Prologue (Pss 1–2), these three motifs remain silent until Pss 18–19: (a) The term Torah and its synonyms, which do not occur after Ps 1, but recur frequently after Pss 18–19; (b) the term "messiah" (משיח); (c) psalms associated with the guilt of sin. See Robertson, *Flow of the Psalms*, loc. 1721–1861.

91. Sumpter argues that Pss 20–21, "despite their lack of obvious eschatology and poetic vibrancy, function to clarify Psalm 18 by contextualizing it theologically within the divine economy" (Sumpter,

The Five Davidic Collections

of kingship is further expressed in Pss 15 and 24, in which the king takes his place at Zion.[92] In other words, Group 2 (15–24) does not only focus on the institution of the Davidic kingship but also on the manner which the king is to administer before God. As such, this Davidic king, by virtue of his godly rule, embodies the community of people living under God.[93] Scholars such as Miller, Brown, and Sumpter have reached a similar conclusion with regards to the primary place of the Davidic kingship in Pss 15–24.[94]

Psalm 29 in the third Group of DC-I (Pss 25–34) highlights the kingship of Yhwh over creation and nature.[95] At the end of the psalm, everything in his temple glorifies him as Yhwh sits enthroned as king forever. The predicate nominative, יהוה מלך "Yhwh is king," occurs only in Pss 10:16 and 29:10.[96]

The superscription of Ps 30, likely a later insertion, highlights the dedication of the "house," that is, the temple.[97] This superscription is also unique because it is the only superscription with reference to the house of God, or temple, despite little connection to the temple in the rest of the psalm.[98]

There are also good reasons to sustain the emphasis on the human king in Group 1 of DC-I (3–14). Reconsider the two central psalms (8–9) in Group 1 of DC-I, which highlight the concepts of Yhwh crowning a human king and his universal judgment. The distinctiveness of Pss 8–9 must not be overlooked. The enigmatic phrase, "According to *gittith*" (על-הגתית)[99] in Ps 8:1 is found three times in the Psalter and only once in

"Coherence of Psalms 15–24," 203).

92. Kraus argues that the setting of Ps 15 "can be reconstructed on the basis of its combination with Psalms 24. At the time of entrance into the sanctuary in Jerusalem, a liturgical act took place . . . The participants in the worship stand at the portals of the worship area and ask the question: 'O Yahweh, who may sojourn in your tent, who may dwell on your holy hill?' From the inside, a priestly speaker answers them with the declaration of the conditions of entrance (cf. Ps 24:3ff). Only then does the entry begin (Ps 24:7ff)" (Kraus, *Psalms 1–59*, 227).

93. Sumpter, "Coherence of Psalms 15–24," 200.

94. Sumpter, "Coherence of Psalms 15–24," 186–209; Miller, "Kingship, Torah Obedience, and Prayer," 127–42; Brown, "'Here Comes the Sun!'" 259–77.

95. It has been proposed that Ps 29 was adapted from "an older, Canaanite hymn to Baal," but scholarship remains divided over the origins of this psalm.

96. As opposed to יהוה מלך, "Yhwh reigns," in Pss 93:1; 96:10; 97:1; 99:1. For a discussion of this syntax, see Arnold and Choi, *Guide to Biblical Hebrew Syntax*, 6.

97. Clearly, David is not the one who dedicated the First Temple, Jacobson suggests that this insertion is possibly for the dedication of the Second Temple in 515 BCE (Ezra 6) or a rededication of the Second Temple in 165 BCE, after it had been profaned (1 Macc 4). It can also be a psalm used for the Festival of Hanukkah (*Sop.* 18.3), which is an annual festival of the 165 Event. See deClaissé-Walford et al., *Book of Psalms*, 289–90.

98. Cf. Pss 79, 122, 127, 134, 150. These psalms have reference to the Temple in the first verse of the psalm, but not in their superscriptions, if any.

99. The phrase might be (a): a musical instrument; (b) a tune or setting; (c) a festival of some kind. See Craigie, *Psalms 1–50*, 105; Mowinckel suggested that Pss 8, 81 and 84 "may have something to do with the 'Gittite' Obed-edom in 2 Sam. 6.10f, in whose house Yahweh's ark stayed till it was brought to the citadel of Jerusalem" (Mowinckel, *Psalms in Israel's Worship*, 2:215).

The Design of the Psalter

a Davidic psalm. The phrase, "on *muth-labban*" (עלמות לבן) in Ps 9:1 is the only occurrence in the entire Psalter.[100] As noted in chapter 2, these uncommon superscriptions could be used to mark their centralized location within a unit of psalms.[101]

Within Pss 3–14, only Pss 3 and 7 have historical information in the superscription, forming a frame around Pss 3–7.[102] While the superscription of Ps 3 identifies David's escape from Absalom, it is possible that "Cush, a Benjamite" mentioned in Ps 7:1 is identified with the Cushite who brought news to David about the death of Absalom in 2 Sam 18:31.[103] If we accept the superscription of Ps 7:1 as the Cushite's news of Absalom's death, Ps 7 would be a fitting prelude to the superscription in Ps 18:1 where all of David's enemies are subdued. This coheres well with the intertextual reading of 2 Sam 18–22.

This proposition for the identity of "Cush" is not without merit.[104] With this identification, the first three of four historical Davidic superscriptions in DC-I form a coherent group. First, they record David's escape from Absalom, and expulsion from Jerusalem (cf. 2 Sam 15; Ps 3:1). This is followed by the arrival of the news of Absalom's death (cf. 2 Sam 18; Ps 7:1). Finally, David is restored to his house in Jerusalem (2 Sam 20:3) and his reign over all Israel is complete with the death of Saul (cf. 2 Sam 22:1; Ps 18:1). It is helpful to link the historical superscription in Ps 18:1 with *both* 2 Sam 7:1 and 2 Sam 22:1, where David sang about Yhwh delivering him from Saul and all his enemies.

---

100. The phrase, "Muth-labben," literally means "death to his son," but it is possibly a designation for a tune (cf. על-עלמות in Ps 46:1). See Craigie, *Psalms 1–50*, 114; Mowinckel, *Psalms in Israel's Worship*, 2:216–17.

101. See Barbiero's arguments on the literary genre of Pss 3–14 and how they identify the centrality of Pss 8–9 in chapter 2.

102. The "Shiggaion" (שגיון) in Ps 7:1 is also unique (cf. Hab 3:1). Though its meaning remains unknown, it may be related to the Akkadian *šegu* which means "psalms of lamentation." See Craigie, *Psalms 1–50*, 97; Mowinckel, *Psalms in Israel's Worship*, 2:209.

103. "For the LORD has delivered you this day from the hand of all who rose up against you . . . May the enemies of my LORD the king and all who rise up against you for evil be like that young man." Several proposals attempt to identify "Cush, the Benjamite." (1) The Targum of Psalms identifies "Cush" as "Saul son of Kish"; (2) As the messenger in 2 Sam 18; (3) Sheba son of Bichri, possibly based on the roots in the LXX, Ιεμενι in 2 Sam 20:1; (4) "A Benjaminite from Saul's contingent who leveled allegations against David at this early stage of the conflict," recorded in 1 Chr 12; (5) Shimei be Gera (2 Sam 16; 1 Kgs 2:44). For the fourth proposal, see Berger, "David–Benjaminite Conflict," 283–84; Johnson, *David in Distress*, 133–39. For the second proposal, see Hutton, "Cush the Benjaminite," 123–37.

104. Hutton further notes, "It is suggested here, then, that the Cush of Ps 7: I, as problematic as it is, refers to the Cushi of 2 Samuel 18, who was sent by Joab as a runner to inform David of the death of his son Absalom. This tradition is at least as old as the LXX translation of Ps 7:1, and, though raising some minor problems of its own, avoids some of the major problems involved in associating the figure with Shimei or Saul." Hutton also points out that the superscriptions of "Psalms 7 and 18 [on the basis of their 'syntax and function'] do not appear to have arisen by the same hand or as a part of the same redactional or midrashic activity as did the other eleven [historical] superscriptions" (Hutton, "Cush the Benjaminite," 126, 130).

We have discussed how Pss 3–7 and 10–14 can be seen as separate units in chapter 2, especially with its alternating "day" and "night" features, in response to the phrase, "meditates day and night," in Ps 1:2. This alternation also makes Pss 8–9 central to the Group Pss 3–14.[105] The preceding arguments for the historical superscriptions of Pss 3, 7 and 18 show that the centrality of the kingship motif in DC-I has already developed from Ps 3.

In the following, I will show how the lexeme, "head" (ראש), which exemplifies the POS technique, helps to reveal this Davidic kingship motif in DC-I. The use of the lexeme, "head," contributes not only to the framing of Pss 3–7, but also reinforces our understanding of the CM of DC-I and the Metanarrative of the Psalter.

Psalms 3:4 and 7:17 are the only two instances in Pss 3–14 with ראש. These two instances also contain an interesting wordplay.[106] They reveal two different outcomes for the Davidic king and his enemies respectively. In Ps 3:4, Yhwh exalts David's head by "lifting" (רום) his head despite the derision of his enemies (3:3). Here, David is vindicated and victorious. In contrast, Ps 7:17 speaks of "mischief" (עמל) returning to the wicked's own "head" (ראש). The head of the wicked will be brought low in the end.

These two instances frame Pss 3–7.[107] The proposal becomes more plausible as we trace the occurrences of ראש across the Psalter. ראש occurs 34x in the Psalter, of which 28 (7x4)[108] of them refer to the human "head."

---

105. Auwers notes, "Psalm 8 is the only hymn, around which are organized two series of five individual lamentations (Ps 3–7; 9–14) [he considers Pss 9–10 as one psalm], where a 'just' person, threatened in its existence by its enemies, by disease, and by the socio-religious chaos, calls for Yhwh" (Auwers, *La Composition*, 43. My translation).

106. The word, "head," does not occur again until Ps 18 where Yhwh placed his anointed as the "head" of nations.

107. Smith argues for a framing of Pss 3–8 instead. He notes, "The selection of Psalm 8 is based on the fact that it is (a) the first praise psalm after a series of individual laments and (b) is closely tied to Psalm 7. In the context of Book I, which is dominated by laments, Psalm 8 is a unique psalm. It appears to have been inserted here to make the end of a first 'movement'" (Smith, "Redactional Criteria and Objectives," 6).

108. The ראש is translated as (a) "poison" (lxx χολή) in Ps 69:22; (b) "top" in Ps 72:16; (c) "chief men" in Ps 110:6; (d) "sum" in Ps 119:160; (e) "highest" in Ps 137:6; (f) "sum" in Ps 139:17.

The Design of the Psalter

	Book I		Book II		Book III		Book V	
3:4	King's head lifted up		44:15	Enemies mock		74:13–14	YHWH breaks heads		108:9	Ephraim as YHWH's head	
7:17	*Mischief returns to enemy's head*		60:9	Ephraim as YHWH's head		83:3	Enemies raised their heads		109:25	Enemies mock	DC-IV
18:44	**Kingship established**		66:12	Head overwhelmed by men					110:7	**Priestly-king lifts up head**	
21:4	**King crowned**		68:22	YHWH strikes head of enemies	DC-II				118:22	Rejected king become "head-stone"	
22:8	Enemies mock	DC-I	69:5	Overwhelmed by enemies					133:2	Unity of brothers like anointing Aaron's head	
23:5	**King anointed (crowning)**								140:8	David's head covered in battle	
24:7, 9	**YHWH's kingship exalted**								140:10	*Mischief returns to enemy's head*	DC-V
27:6	**David's head lifted in YHWH's house**								141:5 (2x)	Righteous' strike like the anointing of David	
38:5	Head overwhelmed by sin										
40:13	Head overwhelmed by evil										

Figure 55: ראש across the Psalter

Figure 55 lists all the occurrences of "head," revealing several interesting features. Consider these six observations: (1) The cells in bold show instances of "head" used in the contexts of enthronement (or exaltation) of either the human David, the Messianic king or YHWH (3:4; 18:44; 21:4; 23:5; 24:7, 9; 27:6; 110:7).[109] The word "head," when used in direct association with enthronement and exaltation of kings, is found only in Books I and V. The rest of the occurrences of ראש do not relate directly to kingship.

(2) It is significant that the phrase, "lifting of head" (רום with ראש), describing a human figure, is found only in three places (3:4; 27:6 and 110:7) and nowhere else.[110]

---

109. *BHS* notes that the reference to 18:44 is attested by Ms and 2 Sam 22:44 while Greek text of Lucian's recension has לאור.

110. In Ps 24:7, 9, נשא is used instead. While the combination of these two lexemes occurs in various places in the HB, interestingly, the "lifting of head" applied to a person is found in these three locations in the Psalter. For Ps 110:7, *BHS* notes that the Targum contains a final *yod* suffix; 2 Mss and Syriac has a 3ms suffix. These textual notes do not affect the POS of "head."

There is also a distinction between the two instances in Book I and the single instance in Book V. The phrase, "lifting of head," is possibly a metaphor for "honor" and reinstatement of "status and health."[111] While Pss 3:4; 27:6 refer to the human Davidic king, Ps 110:7 refers to a transcendent priestly-king.

The distinctiveness of 110:7 is also seen when we consider the geographical contexts associated with the lifting of "head." The "lifting of head" in Ps 3:4 is set within a literary context away from Jerusalem, in conjunction with David in the wilderness escaping from Absalom, (3:1, cf. 2 Sam 15–18). The immediate texts surrounding Ps 27:6 identify Yhwh's אהל (27:5, 6. Cf. 2 Sam 7:2), which suggest a non-permanent locale somewhere in the city of David (cf. 2 Sam 6:17).[112] However, in 110:7 the literary setting is the Zion-temple.[113] While Yhwh was the one lifting up the Davidic king's head in Pss 3:4 and 27:6,[114] it is the kingly figure himself who will "lift up" his own head in Ps 110. Psalm 110:7 is also the only instance after Book I to use "head" in a kingship setting.

(3) The rest of the cells in bold refer to the crowning of a king, forming more than two-thirds of all instances in DC-I and highlighting both the Davidic and Yhwh's kingship. This frequent association of "head" with kingship, especially in DC-I, supports our arguments that DC-I is centered on the establishment of the Torah-pious Davidic king and the earthly temple.

(4) The motifs, the king's honor and the fall of the wicked, are framed by two pairs of psalms (3:4; 7:17 and 110:7; 140:10). Psalms 7:17 and 140:10 (dotted-lined cells) are the only two instances in the Psalms where עמל ("mischief/evil") and ראש are used together.[115] These two instances occur strategically near the beginning of DC-I and at the end of DC-V, describing the fall of the wicked as mischief returns to his own "head." Furthermore, in these two pairs of references, the first describes the "lifting of head" of a Davidic king (3:4; 7:17) and the second describes עמל returning to the

---

111. In Ps 24:7, 9, the "lifting of heads," now addressed to the gates, is likely another metaphor that "connotes an acknowledgment of the Lord's kingship." The "Lord" in this case is the "Lord of Hosts," the "warrior-king," Yhwh, himself. See deClaissé-Walford et al., *Psalms*, 75, 252, 269. Kraus notes that "drinking by the brook" refers to "a 'sacramental' act that belongs to the ritual of the crowning" (Kraus, *Psalms 60–150*, 352). Jordaan and Nel note the while there are efforts to emend Ps 110:7a, entire phrase is supported by the Septuagint. See Jordaan and Nel, "From Priest-King to King-Priest," 236–37.

112. Although the "temple" in Jerusalem is already present in v. 4, it is interesting that the psalmist had chosen to use אהל instead of the temple surrounding the phrase "my head is raised up."

113. The נחל in Ps 110:7 could refer to the Gihon spring which "flows forth from the base of the old city hill" (Kraus, *Psalms 60–150*, 352).

114. While it is unclear who lifts up the head in Ps 27:6, the immediate preceding verse makes it clear that it is Yhwh who is doing the "lifting." Jacobson argues that the "LXX's *hypōsen* normally [here it is aorist active] renders the *hiphil* form (*yārîm*) with the implied subject being the Lord. The meaning is not dramatically altered since *my head* as the subject implies that the Lord was the one raising up the head" (deClaissé-Walford et al., *Psalms*, 266).

115. *BHS* notes that Ps 140:10 probably reads "their head" though this does not affect the POS of "head."

"head" of the wicked (110:7; 140:10) such that they not only parallel each other but also bookend *all* the occurrences of the word "head" associated with kingship. This contrasting motif of honor for the Davidic king and dishonor for the wicked recalls the Prologue where the righteous and the wicked are described by two contrasting outcomes in life.

(5) The anointing of the "head" in Pss 133:2; 141:5 of Book V is used figuratively to signify "brothers in unity" and "righteous admonishment" rather than kingship.[116] This stands in contrast to Ps 23:5 where the king is anointed before his enemies. The shift in the use of "head" in association with anointing between Books I and V show a further development in the motif of kingship across the Psalter. Psalm 133:2 and 141:5 in Book V depict the consecration of the priesthood and crowning of a king in the metaphorical sense. In Ps 133:2, the simile underscores the concept of living in unity and righteousness. Similarly, in Ps 141:5, this "crowning" is a mutual admonishment among the community of the righteous so that they may be delivered.

(6) The word "head" is associated with the building of the temple in Book V. We have seen that the figurative description of Aaron's anointing in Ps 133:2 "alludes to his solemn consecration in the sanctuary (cf. Exod 29:7; 30:30–32; Lev 8:12; 30)."[117] The occurrence of "head" in Ps 118:22 (the occurrence immediately before 133:2), is used in the construct form with "corner," forming the phrase, "head-stone/cornerstone" (לראש פנה).[118] This phrase is connected to house-building.[119] Like Pss 133:2 and 141:5, the use of "head" in Ps 118:22 is a metaphor. What the people reject as unworthy, Yhwh has chosen and placed it as the most important in the building of the house.

(6) Most of the occurrences in Books II and III depicting ראש are associated with (a) the rise of the enemies' head and their mocking ("shaking" of head);[120] (b) the psalmist overwhelmed by his enemies; and (c) Yhwh striking the "head" of the enemies. These characteristics of "head" in Books II and III correspond to our earlier findings that these two Books underscore the destruction of the Davidic dynasty and the Jerusalem temple.

---

116. Cf. Deut 25:5 which uses a similar phrasing. Zenger notes that it "unmistakably describes the dwelling of physical brothers in the same house" (Hossfeld and Zenger, *Psalms* 3, 475, 477). The first occurrence of "head" in Ps 141:5 is attested differently in Greek (and Syriac) as ἁμαρτωλοῦ, This affected the NRSV translation, which follows the Greek. It is possible that the Greek translators had interpreted this text. Since there is no Hebrew variant of this text, we should maintain the two occurrences of the word, ראש, in Ps 141:5.

117. Hossfeld and Zenger, *Psalms* 3, 480.

118. Zenger argues that since the stone can be seen by onlookers, it is unlikely to be a foundational cornerstone. It is more likely "a capstone that signals the completion of the building (cf. Zech 4:7)" (Hossfeld and Zenger, *Psalms* 3, 242).

119. Zenger explained, "the builders test each individual stone and sort out stones that are of no use, throwing them aside" (Hossfeld and Zenger, *Psalms* 3, 241).

120. BHS notes that many Mss and Greek has a *yod* before the first person plural suffix in the word, לראשנו, in Ps 66:12. This textual note does not affect the POS of "head."

In short, the word "head" displays the features of the POS technique and needs to be seen together with other lexemes that also display the POS characteristics. Our analysis of how it occurs across the Psalter shows that it is mostly associated with the Davidic kingship in DC-I. Furthermore, the occurrences of "head" in DC-II–IV and in Books II–III are often associated with mocking of enemies and Yhwh's judgment on them. As we move toward DC-V and Book V, there is a shift in the representation of "head." The motif of the Davidic (and Yhwh's) kingship, glorious and clear in Book I, is diminished as we move to Book V. Here, "head" is associated with the human David (without direct royal connotations), figurative descriptions of anointing, unity among brothers and the destruction of the wicked.

The study of the word, "head," supports our proposition that DC-I, as a whole, has a focus on the Davidic rule in Yhwh's house (3:4; 7:17; 18:44; 21:4; 22:8; 23:5; 24:7, 9; 27:6). These findings also correspond well with the Metanarrative of the Psalter. We will now proceed to analyze DC-II.

Second Davidic Collection (Pss 51–70)

The second Davidic Collection (DC-II) consists of 20 psalms.[121] We have discussed the CMs of Books II–III and how DC-II is structurally located in the second Group in the Section Books II–III. In chapters 2–3, we concluded that Books II–III highlight the fall of the human Davidic kingship and the Jerusalem temple. We have also discussed how the term, זנח ("to reject"), is almost exclusively found in Books II–III, highlighting Yhwh's "rejection" of his people and Zion. Furthermore, we have shown that the use of משיח ("Yhwh's anointed") is conspicuously absent in Book II (and DC-II) where most of the Davidic psalms with historical superscriptions are found. These historical descriptions of David record the gravest threats to David's life and kingship. It is in DC-II where the third dimension of intertextual reading is clearest. DC-II has a remarkable correspondence with the narratives of the life of David recorded in the Books of Samuel. In the following, we will discuss some features of DC-II, which I believe, unveil the central theological significance of DC-II.

(1) Descriptions of David's enemies are most *explicit* and *specific* in DC-II, and often in contexts of betrayal. From Ps 51, after the account of David's sin with Bathsheba, a host of names are mentioned. Psalm 52 begins with Doeg the Edomite who informed Saul that David had gone to Ahimelech the priest (cf. 1 Sam 22:9). Psalm

---

121. I have included Pss 66, 67 (without Davidic superscription) and excluded 71–72 in DC-II here. This is because Pss 66–67 are the two center psalms in the Subcollection Pss 65–68 united by the common terms, "for the choir direction" and "song" (למנצח, שיר) in the superscription, apart from the missing Davidic attribution. It is interesting that Pss 52 and 54 record "David" twice, perhaps as a "compensation" for the "missing" David in Pss 66 and 67. In contrast, Pss 71 and 72 have distinctively different superscriptions. It is entirely missing in Ps 71 and attributed to "Solomon" in Ps 72. If we include Ps 86 in DC-II, we will have a total of 19 (Davidic)+2 = 21 psalms in DC-II. See chapter 2 for our earlier discussion on the superscriptions in Books II–III of the Psalter.

The Design of the Psalter

54 records the Ziphites[122] who came to Saul to report David's whereabouts (1 Sam 23:19; cf. 26:1).[123] "Strangers" rose against David and "violent men" (עריצים) sought his life (54:4).[124] Psalm 55:14 speaks of a "man of equal" (אנוש כערכי), "my companion" (אלופי),[125] and "my friend" (מידעי), with whom the speaker (presumably David) had "sweet fellowship." Although they walked in Yhwh's house together, this "friend" turned against David. The repeated use of various synonyms of "friend" in the poem "[emphasize] the enormity of treason."[126]

Psalm 56 records David's captivity by the Philistines at Gath (cf. 1 Sam 21:10—22:1; 27:1—29:11),[127] and Ps 57 records David fleeing Saul and hiding in a cave (cf. 1 Sam 22:1, 24:3).[128] Psalm 59 highlights threats to David's life when Saul sent men to kill David at his house (cf. 1 Sam 19:11). The superscription of Ps 60 probably alludes to events in 2 Sam 8:1-15, 10:6-19.[129] Psalm 63:1 recalls 2 Sam 15-17 where David fled into the wilderness from his son Absalom and imagines David longing for Yhwh in his sanctuary at Zion (63:2). The reference of the Davidic flight from Absalom fits well with Ps 64.[130] It connects the "secret counsel of evildoers" (מסוד מרעים) in Ps 64:3 with the counsel of Ahithophel who betrayed David by defecting to Absalom and helping him with his "secret counsel" (סוד; 2 Sam 15:12—17:4).

This list of various individuals, identified as David's enemies, are often close to him, had served under him or lived with him, and in the end, betrayed David. Such specific and explicit accounts of David's encounters with his enemies in DC-II are not sustained with the same intensity elsewhere in the Psalter.

(2) The order and framing of historical superscriptions provide another important angle for reading DC-II. The historical superscriptions in DC-II depict David's

---

122. Ziphites "lived in a hill town southeast of Hebron" (Tate, *Psalms 51–100*, 47).

123. Johnson notes that "the titles attached to Pss 52 and 54 refer to people who speak words that have deadly consequences. In the case of Ps 52, Doeg speaks words against David which lead to the death of the priests and people of Nob, while in Ps 54, it is the Ziphites who speak words which nearly cost David his life" (Johnson, *David in Distress*, 67).

124. עריצים occurs only three times in the Psalter, of which the latter two are found in Books II and III (Pss 37:35; 54:5; 86:14).

125. The *pual* verb of ידע is found only in four places in the Psalter (31:12; 55:14; 88:9, 19) and means "close friend."

126. Schaefer, *Psalms*, 137.

127. Goldingay notes that neither of the two stories of David and Gath in the references "says that David was seized" (Goldingay, *Psalms*, 2:183).

128. Johnson argues that there is a stronger case for linking Ps 57 with 1 Sam 24 due to more lexical connections. See Johnson, *David in Distress*, 93.

129. Johnson notes several differences between Ps 60:1–2 and 2 Sam 8: (1) David, rather than Joab, was the one who killed the Edomites in 2 Sam 8; (2) 2 Sam 8:13 records 18,000 Arameans instead of 12,000 in Ps 60 (cf. 1 Chr 18:12); (3) the Aramean states involved are different. In 2 Sam 8, it is "Zobah and Damascus." See Johnson, *David in Distress*, 123. Goldingay thinks that the difference in the number of Edomites killed is probably due to "variant text forms" (Goldingay, *Psalms*, 2:226).

130. Cf. Ps 64: 4, 6 where the enemy of David plots "secret counsel" (סוד) and "hide snares" (לטמן מוקשים).

The Five Davidic Collections

distresses and downfall. If we identify the historical narrative behind Pss 63–64 as David's flight from Absalom, we would have come full circle from the first historical superscription in Ps 3:1 which notes David's escape from Absalom.[131] Thus, the common story of David's flight from Absalom, revealed by the superscriptions of Pss 3:1 and 63:1, frames the first twelve Davidic[132] superscriptions with historical references.

The following figure summarises the 13 Davidic superscriptions with historical references.

---

131. Besides the superscription, Johnson notes that the connection between 2 Sam 15–18 and Ps 3 is seen in the "allusion to sleep" in Ps 3:6. She notes that "the military counsel given to Absalom by his royal advisors at the time of his coup centered on when and where David would sleep." Both Ahithophel and Hushai's counsel are connected to where David will sleep. See Johnson, *David in Distress*, 16–18.

132. DC-I includes Pss 3, 7, 18, 34 (4x). DC-II includes 51, 52, 54, 56, 57, 59, 60, 63 (8x). The last historical reference in Ps 142 is found in DC-V.

The Design of the Psalter

	DC-I			
Psalm	Ps 3:1	7:1	18:1	34:1
Ref. (ESV)	2 Sam 15	2 Sam 18?	*2 Sam 7:1; 22:1*	1 Sam 21:13
	A Psalm of David, when he fled from Absalom his son.	A Shiggaion of David, which he sang to the LORD concerning Cush, a Benjamite.	*For the choir director. A Psalm of David the servant of the LORD, who spoke to the LORD the words of this song in the day that the LORD delivered him from the hand of all his enemies and from the hand of Saul.*	A Psalm of David when he feigned madness before Abimelech, who drove him away and he departed.
Thematic dev.	Davidic Kingship at stake	Absalom dies, Davidic kingship restored	Davidic kingship established (cf. Nathan's prophecy 2 Sam 7:1; 22:1)	David in distress. Supplication

	DC-II								DC-V
Psalm	51:1–2	52:1–2	54:1–2	56:1	57:1	59:1	60:1–2	63:1	142:1
Ref. (ESV)	2 Sam 12	1 Sam 21–22	1 Sam 23:19; 26:1	1 Sam 21, 27	1 Sam 22, 24	1 Sam 19:11	2 Sam 1/2 Sam 8–10	2 Sam 15–17	1 Sam 22, 24
	For the choir director. A Psalm of David, when Nathan the prophet came to him after he had gone in to Bathsheba.	To the choirmaster. A Maskil of David, when Doeg, the Edomite, came and told Saul, "David has come to the house of Ahimelech."	To the choirmaster: with stringed instruments. A Maskil of David, when the Ziphites went and told Saul, "Is not David hiding among us?"	To the choirmaster: according to The Dove on Far-off Terebinths. A Miktam of David, when the Philistines seized him in Gath.	To the choirmaster: according to Do Not Destroy. A Miktam of David, when he fled from Saul, in the cave.	To the choirmaster: according to Do Not Destroy. A Miktam of David, when Saul sent men to watch his house in order to kill him.	*To the choirmaster: according to Shushan Eduth. A Miktam of David; for instruction; when he strove with Aram-naharaim and with Aram-zobah, and when Joab on his return struck down twelve thousand of Edom in the Valley of Salt.*	**A Psalm of David, when he was in the wilderness of Judah.**	A Maskil of David, when he was in the cave. A Prayer.
Thematic dev.	Nathan's judgment: David's downfall begins	Recalls David's distress and threats to his life. Drawn from the Book of 1 Samuel.					Victorious state before David sins with Bathsheba	Bookends with Ps 3:1 for DC-I & II; Bookends DC-II with Ps 51:1–2	David in distress. Supplication

Figure 56: Parallel Thematic Development of Davidic Superscriptions with Historical Reference

The figure above captures thirteen historical Davidic superscriptions and their allusions to the Davidic narratives in 1–2 Sam. The first three superscriptions in DC-I (3:1; 7:1; 18:1) identify a sequential trajectory that traces David's escape from Absalom, news of Absalom's death to David being re-established as king in Jerusalem. They trace David's ascendancy to his kingship and are all drawn from the Book of 2 Samuel.

The prophet Nathan first enters the narrative of David in 2 Sam 7 and announces the well known Davidic Covenant.[133] This happens at a point in the narrative where "the LORD had given him rest from every side from all his enemies" (2 Sam 7:1; cf. 2 Sam 5:12; 22:1). The superscription of Ps 18:1, though more likely derived from 2 Sam 22:1, is also linked to 2 Sam 7.[134] Either way, the superscription of Ps 18:1 provides the imagery of the establishment of David's kingship, first upon the death of Saul (2 Sam 7:1), and a second time after the death of Absalom (2 Sam 22:1).[135] As such, Saul and Absalom are portrayed as two of David's most important nemeses in the Psalms.

The Davidic Covenant was given after the important initial remark that Yhwh had delivered David from all his enemies in 2 Sam 7:1. However, Nathan reenters the narrative to pronounce judgment on David a few chapters later in 2 Sam 12 after the Bathsheba incident. Nathan proclaims that the "sword shall never depart from [David's] house," and that the LORD would take David's wives before his eyes and give them to his "companion," who would sleep with them in broad daylight (2 Sam 12:10–11). Nathan then exits from the narrative.[136] Immediately after Nathan's pronouncement, David's child (with Bathsheba) fell sick and died. In the following chapters after 2 Sam 12, David's daughter was raped, his son Ammon killed by another (Absalom), and David's house was broken. By the end of 2 Sam 15, Absalom had usurped David's throne and David was driven away from his throne. His kingship was broken. Ahithophel's advice to Absalom to sleep with David's concubines in 2 Sam 16:21–22 fulfills Nathan's prophecies.

Nathan's words to David thus mark two important points in the Davidic narrative in the Books of Samuel. The first marks the establishment of the Davidic kingship through the Davidic Covenant when David was said to have subdued all his enemies in 2 Sam 7:1 (and 22:1). The second marks David's fall in 2 Sam 12:7–14 because of his sin.[137] The fall of David's house is situated in the narrative between the two references to his victorious kingship in 2 Sam 7:1 and 22:1.

---

133. Note that the word "covenant" is not used in 2 Sam 7.

134. The dependency direction between Psalms and the books of 1 and 2 Samuel cannot be fully ascertained. Weber argues that Ps 18 depended on 2 Sam 22. For a good discussion on how 2 Sam 22 and Ps 18 are connected, see Weber, "Das königlich-davidische Danklied," 189–90.

135. While Ps 18:1 follows 2 Sam 22:1 closely, they differ in at least three places. Psalm 18:1 contains a metheg between הציל and יהוה; has two *waw*s in the אותו; and uses ומיד instead of ומכף. 2 Samuel 7:1 has a common כל-איביו but uses מסביב instead of "Saul." The common phrase in 2 Sam 7:1; 22:1 and Ps 18:1 is כל-איביו. The common idea between them is that the LORD had established David's kingship (cf. 2 Sam 5–6), mentioned after Saul's death and after David's capture of Zion. This remark was given just before the Davidic Covenant (2 Sam 7). The second mention comes after Absalom's death when David was re-established as king (2 Sam 22).

136. Nathan no longer speaks after 2 Sam 12. He returns in 1 Kgs 1.

137. Nathan's role in 1 Kgs involves "manipulation" so that the Davidic kingship is passed on to Solomon. According to Sergi, "his main role is to provide divine legitimacy for the Davidic dynasty and to guarantee its existence" (Sergi, "Composition of Nathan's Oracle," 266).

Given the above, consider the 12 superscriptions in DC-II. The first historical superscription in DC-II (51:1–2) records Nathan coming to David *after* he had been in with Bathsheba. The preposition "after" is important because it locates Nathan pronouncing Yhwh's judgment on David due to his sin of murder and adultery, thereby marking the beginning of David's downfall with the superscription in 51:1–2.

The next five historical superscriptions that follow Ps 51 in DC-II[138] encapsulate the "sword" and life-threating experiences of David, but are all drawn from 1 Sam (52:1–2; 54:1–2; 56:1; 57:1; 59:1).[139] By Ps 63 (and 64),[140] the last of the historical superscriptions in DC-II, we arrive at a familiar place in the narrative in 2 Sam 15–17 where David had been dethroned by Absalom and was fleeing for his life.

The historical superscriptions of David in Pss 51 and 63 in DC-II frame the story of David's sin and his downfall. These frames of DC-II encapsulate the pronouncement of judgment on David's sin to the temporary defunct Davidic kingship after Absalom's successful coup. This corresponds exactly with the thematic focus we have proposed for Books II–III.

Those responsible for the historical superscriptions have skillfully placed stories that threatened David's life under the persecution of Saul in the Book of 1 Sam within the frames of Pss 51 and 63. In this way, the fall of David is historically associated with miseries under the hands of Saul and Absalom.[141]

The two other uses of 1 Sam references are found in the last historical superscriptions at the end of the parallel trajectories (34:1 and 142:1). These two references are distinct from the rest. The fourth superscription in DC-I (34:1), describing David's distress, may seem like an anomaly since it alludes to the Book of 1 Sam (instead of 2 Sam), disrupting the flow of David's ascendancy to kingship in the first three superscriptions (3:1; 7:1; 18:1). This is suggestive of an intentional structural phenomenon. It is consistent with the design of the five DCs and the macrostructure of the MT Psalter. Structurally, this final superscription in DC-I parallels the last superscription in DC-V (142:1). Both of them highlight David's distresses and his supplications to God (34:5; 142:1).

Recall in chapter 3 that there is always a structural phenomenon that depicts a final "frame" of Davidic distress and supplication. This "frame" is not necessarily the last psalm, rather, it is in a strategic location within a larger final textual unit (e.g., Group). Specifically, this frame of Davidic distress and supplication recurs in *all the*

---

138. Pss 52; 54; 56; 57; 59.

139. Except Ps 60:1–2, which we will return to subsequently.

140. Johnson notes five textual connections to the "wilderness" description in the superscription of Ps 63 in 2 Sam 15:23, 28; 16:2; 17:16, 29. She also highlights the connections between David crossing river Jordan in his flight from Absalom and not sleeping (cf. Ps 63:7; 2 Sam 17:15–16) and David longing to go back to Jerusalem (cf. Ps 63:3; 2 Sam 15:25–26). Johnson, *David in Distress*, 85–86.

141. Gillmayr-Bucher argues that the Davidic superscriptions function to link the readers' historical circumstances in the postexilic period with the Psalms texts. See Gillmayr-Bucher, "Psalm Headings," 247–54.

final GCMs of each Section of the entire Psalter (38; 86; 140–143). In other words, these 13 historical superscriptions suggest an intentional design that converges with the macrostructure and Metanarrative of the entire Psalter: They identify the establishment of the human Davidic kingship, his fall, and a recurring Davidic distress after his victory. They also situate the story of the "broken" house of David and the temporary defunct kingship between two records of his victories over his enemies in parallel to the Samuel narratives.[142]

Another "anomaly" is found in the historical superscription of Ps 60:1–2, the only superscription in DC-II that presents an awkward glimpse of David's victory in a psalm of Lament. The use of Pss 60 and 57 in the composition of Ps 108 is an important technique which we will return to for further analysis. At this point, it is helpful to note that the single reference in Pss 18:1 in DC-I and 60:1–2 in DC-II, respectively, are the only two victorious renditions of the Davidic kingship among all the historical superscriptions.

As an additional evidence for intentional shaping, Koorevaar sees that the number of these historical Davidic superscriptions occurring four times in Book I, eight times in Book II and once in Book V, giving rise to a 4+8+1 pattern. What is significant is that the number 13 is the numerical sum of אחד (1+8+4) occurring in the reverse. אחד "indicates Jhwh, who is אחד, *one*"[143] and according to Koorevaar, the final editor had deliberately infused the significance that "the one God is involved in the events in David's life"[144] in the historical superscriptions of the Psalms.

(3) A motif associated with acceptable sacrifice to Yhwh frames the fall of David's life in DC-II. It is clear that Pss 50 and 51, at the beginning of DC-II, highlight the sacrifice and atonement for sin. It is possible to see the motifs of sacrifice in Pss 66 and 69, as forming bookends with Pss 50–51 and framing the suffering Davidic king.

Three primary words associated with "sacrifice" in the Psalms are זבח ("sacrifice"), עלה ("whole burnt offering"), and פר ("bull"). The noun, זבח, occurs 11x in the Psalms.[145] In DC-I, this noun occurs three times (4:6; 27:6; 40:7). The first describes a kind of "righteous" sacrifice (4:6). The second is phrased as "sacrifices of shouts of joy" (27:6). However, the traditional understanding of animal sacrifices mentioned in the third is described as unnecessary to Yhwh (40:7).

Five further references to זבח in DC-II underscore the covenantal relationship between the psalmist and Yhwh. These references highlight the significance of "sacrifice" (50:5; 51:18). Important in these instances is the notion of the "sacrifice"

---

142. Based on our analyses here, we need not accept Anderson's conclusion that "there seems to be no real editorial purpose to either the existence or the present distribution of the historical superscripts" (Anderson, "Division and Order," 228).

143. Koorevaar, "Psalter as a Structured Theological Story," 587.

144. Koorevaar, "Psalter as a Structured Theological Story," 587.

145. Pss 4:6; 27:6; 40:7; 50:5, 8; 51:18–19, 21; 106:28; 107:22; 116:17. The Lemma in Ps 83:12 is translated as "Zebah," a Midianite king. The verb form occurs in Pss 4:6; 27:6; 50:14, 23; 54:8; 106:37–38; 107:22; 116:17. Note how they are similarly located with the noun form of זבח.

The Design of the Psalter

of a "broken spirit" (רוח נשברה) and a "contrite heart" (לב-נשבר, 51:19).[146] It is only when such sacrifices are offered, the "righteous" sacrifices mentioned in 51:21 (listed as "burnt offerings," "whole burnt offerings" and "bulls") are accepted. The phrase, "righteous sacrifice" (זבחי-צדק), appears in just two places (4:6; 51:21), framing all the occurrences between DC-I and II.[147] These 8 instances in DC-I and DC-II are the *only* instances found in the Davidic psalms.

The noun, "sacrifice," does not occur in Book III. In Book IV, it recurs, describing the sacrifices to a Moabite god (106:28). Two final instances found in Book V take on a different connotation and are identified with "sacrifices of thanksgiving" (זבחי תודה; cf. 107:22; 116:17).[148] Thus, two important concepts are associated with the noun, זבח, in the Psalms: one highlights the sacrifice of righteousness before traditional sacrifices are accepted in DC-I and II, and the other highlights a "sacrifice of thanksgiving" in Book V. The following figure captures an interesting scheme based on all the occurrences of זבח in the Psalter.

---

146. The textual note of Ps 51:19 in *BHS* suggests "read probably as זבחי."

147. Cf. Deut 33:19.

148. In Ps 50:14, the "sacrifice of thanksgiving" also occur, but it is used as a verb. In 50:23, the "sacrifice" in זבח תודה ("he who offers a sacrifice thanksgiving") is a participle. תודה also occur on its own as "offering of thanksgiving" without the noun "sacrifice" in 56:13.

Location	Struc-ture	Distinctive Motif	Text (NAU)	Ref.
DC-I	A	זבחי-צדק	Offer the sacrifices of righteousness, And trust in the LORD.	4:6
	B	Offer sacrifice with joy	And now my head will be lifted up above my enemies around me, And I will offer in His tent sacrifices with shouts of joy; I will sing, yes, I will sing praises to the LORD.	27:6
	C	Animal sacrifice not desired	Sacrifice and meal offering You have not desired; My ears You have opened; Burnt offering and sin offering You have not required.	40:7
DC-II	D	*chasidim* offer authorized sacrifice	Gather My godly ones to Me, Those who have made a covenant with Me by sacrifice.	50:5
	D′		I do not reprove you for your sacrifices, And your burnt offerings are continually before Me.	50:8
	C′	Animal sacrifice not desired	For You do not delight in sacrifice, otherwise I would give it; You are not pleased with burnt offering.	51:18
	B′	Offer sacrifice with a broken spirit	The sacrifices of God are a broken spirit; A broken and a contrite heart, O God, You will not despise.	51:19
	A′	זבחי-צדק	Then You will delight in righteous sacrifices, In burnt offering and whole burnt offering; Then young bulls will be offered on Your altar.	51:21
Book IV	D″	Rebellious offer unauthorized sacrifice	They joined themselves also to Baal-peor, And ate sacrifices offered to the dead.	106:28
Book V	Z	זבחי תודה	Let them also offer sacrifices of thanksgiving, And tell of His works with joyful singing.	107:22
	Z′	זבח תודה	To You I shall offer a sacrifice of thanksgiving, And call upon the name of the LORD.	116:17

Figure 57: Pan-Psalter Occurrence Scheme of זבח

In the column designated as "Structure," the eight instances in DC-I and II form a chiasmus. As noted above, the phrase, זבחי-צדק, defines the frames (A-A′). The next pair B-B′ has an interesting contrast of emotions associated with righteous sacrifice. One is associated with victorious joy and the other, broken contriteness. Both are accepted by God. The common motif in the C-C′ pair highlights the fact that YHWH does not delight in animal sacrifices *per se*, but at the center of the chiasmus, the D-D′ pair identifies the *chasidim* as those who are covenanted to offer authorized sacrifices to God. Hence, the 8 instances of sacrifice in DC-I and II are set within the context of righteous, acceptable and authorized sacrifice made by the godly in covenantal faithfulness. They express the right kind of covenantal relationship with God with the concept of sacrifice.

The 8 instances in DC-I and II and 3 instances in Books IV–V characterize the motif of sacrifice in the Psalter. Structurally, the pair of phrases, "sacrifice of righteousness" (A-A′) and "sacrifice of thanksgiving" (Z-Z′), bookend all the occurrences. An odd reference, Ps 106:28 (D″), stand at the center between them. This reference describes the rebellious people of God who offer unauthorized and unrighteous sacrifice to Baal-Peor and the dead. This reference is the antithesis to the center references (D, D′) within the A-A′ frame, which describe the righteous and acceptable sacrifices offered by the *chasidim* and represented by the Davidic figure.

The "sacrifices of thanksgiving" in Z and Z′ are made by God's people *after* they have been delivered from the jaws of death or captivity (107:16–21; 116:3, 8). It is now a sacrifice associated with thanksgiving rather than animal offerings. These two references are non-Davidic. They are found within a Subgroup of psalms with a movement toward Zion (104–107; 113–118). The last two characterizations in Z and Z′ correspond well to the structural and thematic shifts of our proposed Metanarrative of the Psalter.

The entire 11 instances of "sacrifice" can be seen as a three-part concentric structure: A-A′-D″-Z-Z′. They trace a straightforward trajectory that first describes the establishment of a right relationship with Yhwh through righteous sacrifice (A-A′). The absence of "sacrifice" in Book III corresponds to the Metanarrative of the Psalter in which Book III depicts the fall of the Zion-temple. Then people rebelled against Yhwh with their unauthorized sacrifices to idols (D″). Finally, they were delivered from their iniquities, and with the godly offering the sacrifice of thanksgiving (Z-Z′). The number "11" is also a symbolic number. The analysis of "sacrifice" is another exemplification of the POS technique.

The noun, עלה ("whole burnt offering"), occurs 7x in the Psalter and is *only* found in DC-I and II (20:4; 40:7; 50:8; 51:18, 21; 66:13, 15). Like זבח, the occurrences of עלה form an interesting shape. Consider Figure 58 which lists all their sequential occurrences in the Psalter.

Location	Structure	Distinctive Motif	Text (NAU)	Ref.
DC-I–II	A+Selah	*He* will remember; סלה	May He remember [יזכר] all your meal offerings And [he will] find your burnt offering acceptable! Selah.	20:4
	B	*You* have not desired; *You* have not required	Sacrifice and meal offering You have not desired; My ears You have opened; Burnt offering and sin offering You have not required.	40:7
	B'	*Your* sacrifices allowed; *Your* offerings; *Before Me*	I do not reprove you for your sacrifices, And your burnt offerings are continually before Me.	50:8
	C	*You* do not delight; *You* are not pleased	For You do not delight in sacrifice, otherwise I would give it; You are not pleased with burnt offering.	51:18
	C'	*You* will delight; *On Your altar*	Then You will delight in righteous sacrifices, In burnt offering and whole burnt offering; Then young bulls will be offered on Your altar.	51:21
	D	*I shall* come; *I shall* pay	I shall come [אבוא] into Your house with burnt offerings; I shall pay [אשלם] You my vows,	66:13
	D'+Selah	*I shall* offer; *I shall* make; סלה	I shall offer [אעלה] to You burnt offerings of fat beasts, With the smoke of rams; I shall make [אעשה] an offering of bulls with male goats. Selah.	66:15

Figure 58: Pan-Psalter Occurrence Scheme of עלה

All 7 instances are framed by Pss 20:4 and 66:15 (A-D'). Both of these verses contain the particle interjection, סלה ("*selah*"), which is not found in the rest of the occurrences. The distinctive motif that gives these 7 occurrences their shape is the selective use of first, second and third person speech. In Ps 20:4, the subject is Yhwh, expressed in the jussive form of the third person singular, who would "remember" and accept the offerings. This is in contrast with D and D' (66:13; 66:15), where the subject is the psalmist, expressed in the first person singular.

The B-B' and C-C' instances are two pairs of alternation. In the first reference of both pairs (B, C), there is a common motif of Yhwh not desiring (לא־חפצת; 40:7), requiring (לא שאלת; 40:7) or delighting (לא־תחפץ; 51:18) in the sacrifices. They are all expressed with the לא adverb to negate a verb in the second person singular form. The common idea of these two verses is reversed in B' and C' where Yhwh would *not* reprove the sacrifices (לא על־זבחיך אוכיחך; 50:8). Instead, he delights in sacrifices (אז תחפץ; 51:21).

These two references (50:8, 51:21) are also given locative references for the sacrifice. In 50:8, the sacrifices are made continually *before* Yhwh (לנגדי תמיד) and in 51:21, the sacrifices are offered *on* Yhwh's altar (על־מזבחך). Furthermore, the B-B' and C-C' references are expressed by a "Thou-I" language between Yhwh and the psalmist.

From the shape of these seven instances, we can detect a development. The opening frame (20:4) suggests a time when Yhwh will remember and accept sacrifices. However, in the next instance, Yhwh does not seem to delight in sacrifices. There appears to be a center core of four references (40:7; 50:8; 51:16; 51:21) that depict a deliberation on the kind of sacrifices that Yhwh would be pleased with. The last two instances of עלה in 66:13, 15 reflect the confidence of the psalmist. Expressed in the first person, the psalmist would now make sacrifices at Yhwh's house after having confidence in the kind of sacrifices that Yhwh will accept.

Crucially, these two instances fulfill the description of Ps 51:21, where such cultic sacrifices are accepted by Yhwh only when a "righteous sacrifice" of a broken spirit and a contrite heart are first offered.[149] Hence, they provide a denouement to the short trajectory traced by the noun, עלה. Again, a symbolic number, "7," is used.

While other terms relating to sacrifices are found in isolated parts of the Psalter,[150] the "acceptable atoning sacrifices to Yhwh" are sustained in three key locations in DC-II (Pss 50–51; 66:15–20;[151] and 69:31–32).[152] The motif of acceptable and pleasing offerings to Yhwh are found explicitly *only* in Pss 50:23; 51:19, 21; 66:19 and 69:32.

The POS analyses related to the concept of acceptable sacrifices provide an important interpretive framework for understanding David's brokenness in DC-II. In Pss 50–51, a sacrifice is deemed acceptable when it is offered as a sacrifice of "a broken spirit and a contrite heart." In a remarkable turn of events, the rejected animal sacrifices in Pss 50–51 are now accepted in Ps 66:15–20.

Following this train of thought, the word, "reproaches" (חרפות) of David, identified as the distresses, dishonor and shame associated with David's downfall,[153] is said to have *broken* David's heart in Ps 69:21 (חרפה שברה לבי). The contriteness of heart prospected in Ps 51 is procured with the contriteness of heart in Ps 69:21 by David's fall. As discussed, this fall, understood as the brokenness of the Davidic kingship, is depicted in Pss 51–64 which lie strategically between the two mentions of broken-heartedness. As a result, with the "broken-heartedness" in 69:21, sacrifices to Yhwh is now accepted.[154] Cultic sacrifices offered is once again pleasing to Yhwh (66:15–20).

---

149. The noun, פר, also referring to a sacrifice, occurs *only* in three places in the Psalter (Pss 50:9; 51:21; 69:32). עתוד, ("male goat") is found *only* in Pss 50 and 66.

150. E.g., consider also נדבה ("freewill offering") in Pss 54:8; 68:10; 110:3; 119:108; נסך ("drink offering") in 16:4; חטאה ("sin offering") in 40:7. Lone verses in DC-II that carry the idea of sacrifices include Pss 54:8 and 56:13.

151. The following forms of sacrifices are unique in the Psalter: עלות מחים ("fattened burnt offerings"); עם־קטרת אילים ("with the smoke of the sacrifice of rams"); בקר ("cattle"). Hossfeld notes, "The Psalms mention them [burnt offerings and slaughtered animal offerings] sparingly: the three passages in 40:7; 50:8; 51:18 speak of them in the context of critique of the cult. Of all the instances, only 20:4 (the king's sacrifice) and 66:13, 15 remain as examples of a positive attitude toward burnt offerings." On 66:25, Hossfeld added that "such offerings are mentioned in this detail otherwise only in Ps 50:9, 13" (Hossfeld and Zenger, *Psalms 2*, 146–47).

152. Note the following sacrifices: שור ("ox"); פר ("bull") and מקרן מפריס ("horns and hoofs").

153. Cf. Ps 69:8, 10, 11, 20, 21.

154. The connection between Pss 51 and 69 can also be marked by the expression, כרב רחמיך ("according to your abundant compassion"). This expression is found only in Pss 51:3 and 69:17 in the Psalter and is connected closely to עון ("iniquity"; 51:3; 69:28).

In other words, the motif of David's fall is at the heart of moving from unacceptable to acceptable sacrifices. This trajectory is bound by the motifs of rejected sacrifices on one end (50–51) and accepted sacrifices on the other (66–69). Between these two frames, there is a clear depiction of David's downfall, his brokenness and contriteness (51–64). The surfeit of historical superscriptions depicting David's distresses in these psalms reinforce the idea of David's fall. At the end of these negative depictions, the broken-hearted David becomes the pleasing sacrifice to Yhwh.

Apart from Ps 22, Ps 69 is the most referenced "psalm of Lament" in the NT.[155] Zenger points out that parts of Ps 69 were "quoted or alluded to in order to lend theological depth to the Christ-event."[156] For example, Ps 69:10 (John 2:17) is adopted in the temple cleansing event recorded in John 2:13–22. These words, applied to Jesus at the temple cleansing event, is to be seen in light of the whole of John's Gospel, that Jesus's action "will lead to his future death."[157] Zenger argues that the allusion of Ps 69:10 in John 2:17 requires an understanding of the whole context of Ps 69 in light of Jesus's death and resurrection. Zenger sees a similar trajectory in the Passion account where Jesus was given vinegar on the cross (cf. Ps 69:22; Matt 27:34, 48; John 19:29) and that "in light of Ps 69:35–37 the Christ-event achieves altogether cosmic dimensions."[158] Hence, the NT, as an early Christian interpretation of Ps 69, sees Jesus as the broken David, and as the acceptable atoning sacrifice for sin.

(4) The function of the postscript in Ps 72:20 marks the end of the Davidic story in DC-I and II. First, this postscript parallels 2 Sam 23:1,[159] marking a similar closing stage in David's story. Psalm 72:20 has eight features in common with 2 Sam 23:1:

a. Both instances use the plural construct form in the phrase(s), "prayers/words" of David (cf. תפלות דוד, 72:20; דברי דוד; 2 Sam 23:1).

b. Both instances identify David as בן־ישי ("son of Jesse").

---

155. See Ps 69:5* (cf. John 15:25); 69:10* (cf. John 2:17; Rom 15:3; [Heb 11:26]); 69:23–24 (cf. Rom 11:9–10); 69:25 (cf. Rev 16:1); 69:26 (Acts 1:20); 69:29 (cf. Phil 4:3; Rev 3:5; 13:8; 17:8; 20:12, 15; 21:27); 69:22*(cf. Matt 27:34, 48; Mark 15:23; Luke 23:36; John 19:29); 69:9* (cf. John 7:5; 1:11); 69:27 (cf. Isa 53:4); 69:14 (cf. Isa 49:8). Those with asterisks are applied or alluded to Jesus. Two OT allusions in Isaiah are applied to the "Suffering Servant." A similar list is found in Hossfeld and Zenger, *Psalms 2*, 184.

156. Hossfeld and Zenger, *Psalms 2*, 184–85.

157. Hossfeld and Zenger, *Psalms 2*, 185.

158. Hossfeld and Zenger, *Psalms 2*, 185.

159. Zenger likened the postscript in 72:20 to Job 31:40b ("the words of Job are ended"). He notes that "it does not simply indicate the end of a text, but marks a division *within* a larger textual complex." Following similar thoughts, Waltke notes that "the colophon in Ps 72:20 separates the earlier collections of books 1 and 2, which accent the triumphs of the kingdom, from book 3, which accents its defeat." Tanner also points out that "v. 20 serve to place these two books [Books II and III] with the story in 1 and 2 Samuel, where we meet and hear of David and Israel's beginning." See Hossfeld and Zenger, *Psalms 2*, 209, 219; Waltke, "Superscripts, Postscripts, or Both," 590; deClaissé-Walford et al., *Book of Psalms*, 579–80. None of them link Ps 72:20 with 2 Sam 23:1.

c. Both instances identify the terminative aspect of David's prayers/words (כלו, "they are finished"; 72:20; האחרנים נאם, "the last words"; 2 Sam 23:1).

d. These are the *only* two instances in the entire HB that connect the phrase, "David, the son of Jesse," with an expression that marks the end of David's speech/prayer.

e. In both instances, the "end" does not mean the absolute last occurrence of David's utterance/prayer. David's prayer clearly continues in Ps 86:1 (cf. 142:1; 143:1) following Ps 72:20. In a similar way, David continues to speak in the rest of 2 Sam 23 through 1 Kgs 2 before the record of his death in 1 Kgs 2:10.

f. Both instances appear in literary contexts where the Davidic king rules and judges Yhwh's people in righteousness (cf. 72:2; 2 Sam 23:3).

g. Both are given in contexts where Yhwh has delivered his anointed king from all his enemies and the king rules over his enemies (cf. 72:8; 2 Sam 22:1).

h. Both recall the Davidic Covenant in 2 Sam 7, where David's offspring will rule and the Davidic House will perpetuate (cf. 72:1–17; 2 Sam 23:5). These eight connections help us see that Ps 72:20 is meant to parallel 2 Sam 23:1.

Second, in view of the common features in the two texts, why did the editor(s) of the Psalter place this statement at the end of DC-II? Our consistent argument is that DC-I marks the establishment of David's kingship and by the end of DC-II, the fall of that *same* kingship is seen. The identification of "David the son of Jesse" at Ps 72:20 suggests a poignant marking of the end of the life and kingship of this historical David as with the Samuel narratives.[160] Designed without a Davidic superscription, Ps 71 is a backward reflection of David's life, from his birth and youth (71:6, 17) to his old age (71:9, 18). What happens in and beyond Ps 72 parallels what happens after 2 Sam 23, that is, David's kingship ends and the rule is given over to his offspring, a Solomonic figure. This Solomonic figure is, nonetheless, presented in an idealized manner.

The theological thrust, which Koorevaar rightly asserts, is that "[by] placing Solomon's psalm after a series of psalms of David, the canonical final editor wanted to signify with this last subscript in 72:20 that the psalms about David's conflict had reached their end objective."[161] Hence, we are to read DC-I and II intertextually. Both Ps 72:20 and 2 Sam 23:1 ("now these are the last words of David") mark the same point of the Davidic narrative.[162]

---

160. Auwers notes, "the last psalms of the series want to evoke the spiritual experience of David in the evening of his life (Pss 70–71) and his prayer for Solomon when he was going to succeed him on the throne (Ps 72)" (Auwers, *La Composition*, 47. My translation).

161. Koorevaar, "Psalter as a Structured Theological Story," 581.

162. Hence we need not adopt deClaissé-Walford's view that Book II, as a whole, underscores the reign of Solomon. Neither do we need to accept David Willgren's proposal that Ps 72:20 is a "frozen colophone." Rather, our analysis shows that it is a deliberate editorial move to highlight the fall of David.

When we compare Ps 3 at the beginning of DC-I and Ps 72 at the end of DC-II, we can see the victories of the two sons of David. In Ps 3, Absalom triumphs over David. In Ps 72, Solomon triumphs over Absalom (and all nations!). Thus, when seen together, the depiction of the Solomonic figure in Ps 72 and the postscript of 72:20 look prophetically to the promised Messianic king of the Davidic covenant and the final paradisical garden.

In sum, DC-II (and Book II) highlights the fall of the Davidic kingship. (1) Book II contains the most specific and explicit accounts of David's enemies and threats to his life; (2) The 13 historical Davidic superscriptions can be arranged in two parallel frames.

The second frame (Books II–IV) can be viewed as the beginning of David's fall with Nathan's judgment (51:1–2) through to his escape into the wilderness because of Absalom (63:1). Eight historical superscriptions in Book II depict David's distresses and the brokenness of his kingship. (3) The motif of an acceptable sacrifice to Yhwh at the beginning and end of DC-II frames the characterization of the fall of David. Through the brokenness of David's life, sacrifices to God are now accepted. (4) The postscript of Ps 72:20 at the end of Book II parallels with 2 Sam 23:1 and 1 Chr 23:27; 29:29, marking the end of David's life (cf. Figure 11). (5) The above points are derived from both tacit and formal elements such as structural shape and superscriptions.[163] Form and content correspond. With the nouns, "sacrifice" and "whole burnt offerings," the POS technique is also at work. Thus we can validate that DC-II, and Book II in general, speaks of the fall and brokenness of the Davidic kingship. Figure 59 illustrates the highlights of DC-I and DC-II:

---

163. Robertson may have presented a plausible argument that the second Davidic Psalter is a "communication" for "the nations regarding the establishment of the Davidic kingship and the ultimate defeat of every enemy that this kingship might face." Robertson based this on the use of "Elohim" in Books II and III in support of the theme of "communicating" the message to the nations. However, in note 99 of his book, Robertson admits that he remains unclear about the literary function of Davidic superscriptions with historical references. Robertson's "Elohim" argument must also be tested with the bulk of Book III, as it is part of the Elohistic Psalter. Robertson, *Flow of the Psalms*, loc. 2036, 2435–64.

The Design of the Psalter

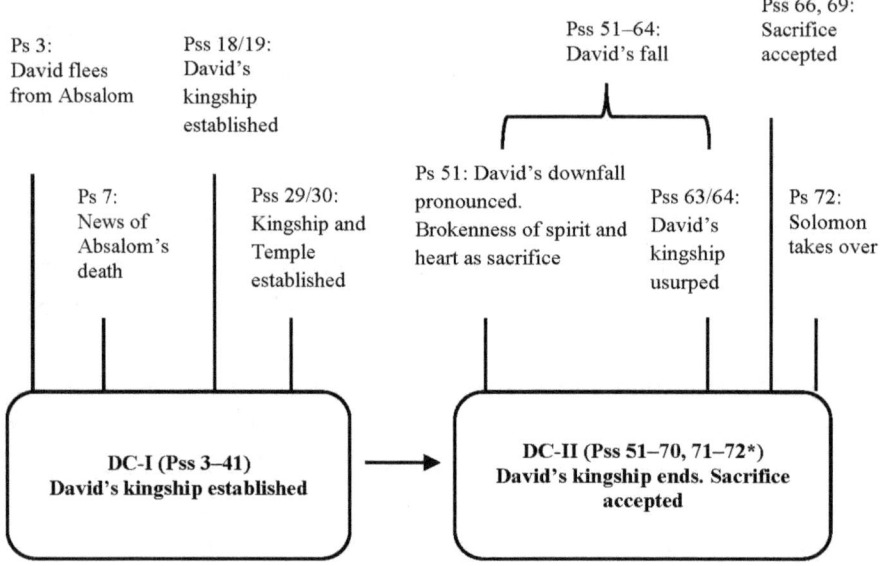

Figure 59: Highlights of Davidic Collections I and II

Third Davidic Collection (Pss 101–103)

To understand the role of DC-III in the five DCs, five phenomena of DC-III are first described:

(1) As explained in chapter 2, Pss 101–103 can be seen as a Davidic triptych even though Ps 102 does *not* have a Davidic superscription. Hossfeld notes,

> The framing of Ps 102:1 with two attributions to David in the neighboring psalms in itself suggests a link between the poor person in Ps 102:1 and David. Both the continuation of the Zion theme in Psalm 102 and the plausible sequence of Psalm 101 as a royal prayer, Psalm 102 as a reference to the king in distress, and Psalm 103 as praise and thanksgiving for rescue plead for an identification of the poor person with David make it possible to understand Psalms 101–103 as a David triad.[164]

Accepting Hossfeld's observation, the framing of the two Davidic psalms and common motifs that link these three psalms make up a unit are meant to be read together.

(2) The DC-III triptych parallels the triad Pss 90–92. As previously discussed, Pss 90–103 can be seen as Group 9.[165] These two triads (90–92, 101–103) frame the Y<small>HWH</small> *Malak* psalms (93–100) at the center. We have identified numerous arboreal lexemes (e.g., "grass") and concepts associated with the frailty of human life between

---

164. Hossfeld and Zenger, *Psalms 3*, 28.

165. The connections and disjunctions between Pss 101–103 and 104–106 at the end of Book IV are covered in chapter 2.

Pss 90–92 and 101–103. These concepts stand in contrast with the recurring motif of a righteous figure who flourishes in Yhwh's house in the same two triads of psalms.[166] Furthermore, four successive motifs: (a) the use of Moses's name; (b) Yhwh's everlasting nature; (c) the fleeting nature of mankind; (d) mankind being consumed by Yhwh's wrath because of sins in Ps 90:1–7, are spectacularly reversed in Ps 103:7–19 in a ABCD-A'D'C'B' fashion.

These structural evidence support our proposition that Group 9 is made up of three Collections (90–92; 93–100; 101–103). This arrangement suggests that Yhwh's preeminent kingship is framed by the twin motifs of Torah-pious life and Messianic kingship, which are also the leitmotifs in the Prologue (1–2), recurring in Pss 18–19; 118–19. Hence, it is important to read Pss 101–103 (DC-III) within the literary horizon of 90–103.

As we expand our perspective of the literary horizon, we see that Ps 90 comes immediately after the second Section (42–89) which highlights both the fall of the Davidic kingship and Zion-temple. At the end of Section 2, Psalm 89 had cast doubt on the Davidic Covenant. Subsequently, Pss 90–92 are sobering reflections, on one hand, recalling the transitoriness of life under God's judgment; on the other hand, reviewing the permanence of the righteous in the paradisical garden as depicted in the Prologue. In Pss 91–92, we see Yhwh's protection for those who take refuge in him and will eventually flourish in Yhwh's house. The following trajectory can be detected in Pss 90–92:

A Psalmist seeks to live right before Yhwh (90)
 B Psalmist expresses confidence in Yhwh's judgment and deliverance (91)
  C Psalmist praises Yhwh and flourishes before Yhwh (92).

This progression is mirrored in DC-III (101–103):

A' Davidic king administers right before Yhwh (101)
 B' Psalmist expresses confidence in Yhwh's judgment and deliverance (102)
  C' Psalmist praises Yhwh in a restored state (103).

Interestingly, the development of these motifs move across these two triads as well. Secret sins and iniquities of the psalmist in Ps 90:8 are now forgiven in Ps 103:3, 10.[167] These structural parallels and developments between DC-III and Pss 90–92 help us to locate the main thrust and message of DC-III.

(3) Coming immediately after the Yhwh *Malak* psalms, DC-III plays a crucial role of presenting a righteous Davidic kingship (101) and a restored Zion (102) *after* the destruction of these two elements in Books II–III.[168] Although the motif of a

---

166. See also Ribera-Mariné, "'El Llibre de les Lloances,'" 8.

167. Note that the term, "iniquity" (עון), occurs only in three psalms in Book IV: Pss 90:8; 103:3, 8; 106:43. Their locations bookend Pss 90–103 and Pss 90–106.

168. It is also interesting that in the book of Hebrews in the NT, both figures of David (Davidic

righteous person occurs from Ps 92,[169] a "blameless" (תמים)[170] and "wholesome" (תם)[171] Davidic king comes onto the scene only in Ps 101. Crucially, DC-III is the first presentation of a "blameless" Davidic king with an "intergrity of heart" *after* Yhwh's rejection (זנח) of his anointed in Books II–III.[172] This wholesome king in Ps 101 is contrasted with the "broken" David in Ps 69 at the end of DC-II. It is also the first Davidic psalm after Ps 86. Moreover, DC-III is the first concrete description of Yhwh's impending restoration of a ruined Zion-temple *after* Book III.[173] Thus DC-III prefigures a "change of fortunes" for both the Davidic kingship and Zion-temple.[174]

The prophetic presentation of an idealized Davidic king at the end of DC-II (the Solomonic figure in Ps 72) is now heightened in DC-III.[175] The characterization of the Davidic king as a human, earthly king has shifted to a *democratized* and *idealized* figure. By "democratization,"[176] the righteous requirements and blessings traditionally associated with the Davidic king is now appropriated and received by a certain community as a whole.[177] By "idealization," the David king is depicted as a once-for-all, universal and almighty king who will bring about a permanent utopic reality. This idealization is not simply a mimickry of the royal court-style presentation of the king

psalms) and Moses are connected in its argument for the supremacy of Jesus in Heb 3–4.

169. The word, "righteous" (צדיק), occurs only 6x in Book IV: Pss 92:12; 94:15, 21; 97:11–12; 103:6.

170. "Blameless" is used 12x in the Psalter. Almost all the instances are applied to a human being. (*) refers to the Davidic king or "anointed." Cf. Pss 15:2*; 18:24*, 26*, 31, 33*; 19:8; 37:18*; 84:12*; 101:2*, 6*; 119:1*, 80*. Hence, it is possible to view Ps 119 as the Torah-pious expression of the king in Ps 118.

171. "Wholesome/Completeness" occurs only 9x in the Psalter. All these instances are Davidic: Pss 7:9; 25:21; 26:1, 11; 37:37; 41:13; 64:5; 78:72; 101:2. Psalm 78:72, though a Asaphite psalm, identifies David as the one who shepherded Israel with תם.

172. Cf. Pss 43:2; 88:15; 89:39.

173. Especially after Ps 79:1 when Yhwh's holy temple is defiled and Jerusalem is "in ruins." This is reiterated in Ps 89:41. There are statements related to the Zion-temple between Pss 79–89, but they express praise or a longing for Zion rather than its restoration. Psalm 100 envisions entry into a restored Zion-temple, but it is only in Ps 102 where a concrete description of Zion's restoration is given.

174. In his study of Ps 102, Witt finds a similar conclusion. He notes, "As such, Psalm 102, alongside 101, represents an important *literary* turning point in the Hebrew Psalter." Emphasis his. Witt, "Hearing Psalm 102," 605.

175. The petitioner in Ps 101 is identified as a "postexilic righteous sage" rather than a Davidic king. Hossfeld and Zenger, *Psalms 3*, 13.

176. "Democratization" is defined as "the words written by a specific individual grounded in specific circumstances can be appropriated by all people in a wide variety of circumstances where the expression of the psalmist's thoughts and emotions reflect their own" (Grant, "Kingship Psalms," *DOTWPW*, 376). Separately, Tucker points out that one of the clearest representation of the democratization of the Davidic Covenant is found in Isa 55:3–5. Tucker, "Democratization," 164–66.

177. Auwers, "Le Psautier Comme Livre Biblique," 85. The concept of "democratization" of Books I–III has also been proposed by Rösel, Hossfeld, and Zenger. Tucker notes, "Hossfeld and Zenger aver that when Books I–III were arranged, the royal psalms (2; 72; 89) created a new hermeneutical horizon—one that suggested that the entire collection be read from a collective messianic perspective" (Tucker, "Democratization," 163, 169). See also Hossfeld and Zenger, *Die Psalmen I*, 15; Rösel, *Die Messianische Redaktion Des Psalters*, 95.

in ANE conventions.¹⁷⁸ For Starling, this imagery of a "king-ideal" is one that "pointed beyond the historical kings, who spoke the words of the royal psalms, or who were addressed or prayed for in them, and awaited a far greater fulfillment."¹⁷⁹ He adds,

> Just as the descriptions of the glory and power of the anointed king, and the scope and duration of his kingdom, outshone by far the experienced realities of life at the best of times under the monarchy, so the descriptions of the righteousness and justice of his reign soared above the actual attainment of any human king.¹⁸⁰

The Davidic Covenant, originally given to king David in 2 Sam 7, is already understood collectively with the *chasidim* by the end of Book III in Ps 89:20.¹⁸¹ The third Davidic Collection begins with a "blameless" (תמים) king walking in the "integrity of heart" (101:2) in his own house praying in the first person to Yʜᴡʜ.¹⁸² But a few verses later, the same attribute of "blameless" (תמים; 101:6) is now predicated on the community described as the "faithful of the land." They, too, will dwell with this "blameless" Davidic king and minister unto him in his house.

The absence of Davidic superscription in Ps 102 adds to the democratization. Identification of David as the distressed petitioner in Ps 102 can only be implied.¹⁸³ The petitioner in Ps 102 can possibly be someone other than a Davidic king¹⁸⁴ though its position in the Davidic triptych suggests that it is to be viewed with the royal Davidic figure in mind. In Ps 103:7, the Davidic figure addressed "the sons of Israel" in the third person but identified himself with the community using the first-person plural speech in verses 10, 12 and 14.

---

178. It has been suggested that the prayer in Ps 101 is akin to ancient Near Eastern royal court petition for a deity's visitation. The prayer is understood to also parallel "a model prayer for the instruction of students from the Nineteenth Egyptian dynasty." While such historical comparison is illuminating, they do not provide adequate explanation for the presence of Psalm 101. My contention is that individual psalms are to be understood through the macrostrategic placement of key content and motifs across the Psalter. We must be able to account for not just these "embellished" royal descriptions but also, the blatantly poor and afflicted expressions of the Davidic king in the Psalms. If Ps 101 is simply a royal court-style embellishment of David following ANE conventions, why then does Ps 102, immediately after it, depict David as an afflicted and suffering king (cf. Pss 108, 109, 110)? See Hossfeld and Zenger, *Psalms 3*, 14.

179. Starling, "Messianic Hope in the Psalms," 125.

180. Starling, "Messianic Hope in the Psalms," 125.

181. Tucker, "Democratization," 171.

182. Hossfeld notes that "only in the royal prayer of Ps 18:41 is the king the subject, as the petitioner is here [Ps 101]" (Hossfeld and Zenger, *Psalms 3*, 15).

183. It is the only superscription in the Psalter that is "intended for a particular instance in a person's life." deClaissé-Walford et al., *Book of Psalms*, 748.

184. Witt writes, "Scholars in the twentieth century have all but dismissed this idea, positing instead that the superscription points to the democratization of the psalm [102] for any common sufferer" (Witt, "Hearing Psalm 102," 590).

Psalm 103 is unique in the sense that it contains the highest instances of the *piel* imperative, "to bless,"[185] uttered by the psalmist David. The Davidic figure is made the exemplar of a praise leader, calling not only himself (103:1–2), but all of Yhwh's angels and heavenly hosts, all who do Yhwh's will, and all of Yhwh's works, to praise. Therefore, a democratization effect is at work. By the end of Ps 103, Yhwh's benefits is applied to many.

Hence, the presentation of a righteous, blameless, idealized "David" in DC-III is an important shift in the sweep of Davidic characterizations from DC-I to III. The David in DC-III is in stark contrast with the David of DC-II. Placed in Book IV of the Psalter, this shift in DC-III corresponds exactly with the shift in the larger Metanarrative of the entire Psalter. This shift anticipates clearer depictions of the idealized Davidic figure and the fate of the community represented by David in the rest of the Psalter.[186]

(4) Retrospectively from the vantage point of DC-III, we see a positive shift in the characterization of the Davidic figure from DC-I–II. But as we look forward from DC-III to DC-IV, a deepened characterization of this idealized Davidic figure is given. This forward perspective is accorded to us when we consider the structural parallels between DC-III and DC-IV (108–110). In fact, these two Collections provide the key to understanding all five DCs.

First, they are both triptychs of three psalms, placed between psalms without attributed authorship. *Prima facie*, the macrostructural shapes of DC-III and IV are very similar. The center psalms in each Collection (102, 109) are the longest, both identifying a broken petitioner. Second, the deliberate lexical parallels between the two center psalms (102 and 109) are noteworthy and detailed as follows:

(a) The clearest indication of their link lies in the use of the three lexemes, לצ + כ + נטה, in the phrase, "as the lengthening of a shadow," to describe the fleeting human life. Apart from Pss 102:12 and 109:23, this expression is not found anywhere in the HB.[187] Their co-locations as the center psalms of DC-III and IV require the reader to read these two Collections synchronically.

(b) The term, "prayer" (תפלה) occurs 10x in Books IV and V.[188] Its first instance is found in Ps 90:1 and subsequently, a total of five times in Pss 102 and 109 combined. It does not recur until Pss 141–43. The frequent occurrences in Pss 102 and 109, with

---

185. Pss 28:9; 66:8; 68:27; 96:2; 100:4; 103:1–2, 20–22*; 104:1, 35; 134:1–2; 135:19–20.

186. Recall our discussion on the "appointed time" (מועד) in chapter 3. Only three references of מועד are found in the entire Psalter, two of which are translated as "appointed time" (Pss 75:3; 102:14) and their contexts referring to the time of Yhwh's restoration of the fallen Zion-temple. This lexeme reinforces our contention that DC-III envisions a reversal of the misfortunes pertaining to the Davidic house and house of Yhwh.

187. These phrases are also the only two expressed in the first person by the psalmist. Cf. Ps 144:4, which uses עבר instead of נטה. There are ten occurrence of צל ("shadow") in the Psalter and only Pss 102:12; 109:23; 144:4 apply it as a simile to man's fleeting life.

188. Pss 90:1; 102:1–2, 18; 109:4, 7; 141:2, 5; 142:1; 143:1. In total, תפלה occurs 32x.

extended absence before, after, and between these two psalms, help to connect Pss 102 and 109.

The use of תפלה within a superscription occurs only 5x in the entire Psalter, forming a concentric shape around תפלה למשה (a prayer of Moses) at the center.

- A   A prayer of David (תפלה לדוד; 17:1)
- A'   A prayer of David (תפלה לדוד; 86:1)
  - B   A prayer of Moses, the man of God (תפלה למשה איש-האלהים; 90:1)
    - C   A prayer of the afflicted one (תפלה לעני; 102:1)
    - C'   A prayer (תפלה; 142:1)

The first two instances of תפלה are clearly attributed to David but the last two are not despite being in a Davidic triad (102:1) or a Davidic psalm (142:1). Johnson notes that the superscription of Ps 142 is the only one out of the thirteen historical superscriptions that does not "specify a personal or geographical name."[189] The thrust towards a more generic description in the last two superscriptions supports the "democratization" effect of the Davidic figure in DC-III and beyond.[190]

(c) The formulaic phrase, ואתה יהוה ("But you, O Lord"), also links Pss 102 and 109. The phrase, in this exact form, is found only 11x in the entire HB. In the Psalter, it appears seven times, all in DCs.[191] Psalms 102:13 and 109:21 are the only two references after Ps 59.[192]

(d) We have noted the specific motif of "broken/wounded heart" in Pss 51:19 and 69:21 earlier. This motif is uncommon in the Psalms and is possibly alluded to in only four other psalms (73:21; 102:5; 109:22; 143:4).[193] The presence of this motif in Pss 102 and 109 support their intentional pairing.

(e) The noun, בשר ("flesh"), used to describe the decrepit state of the physical body is found in six places in the Psalms.[194] It is unlikely to be a coincidence that they are found, again, only in Ps 102:6 and 109:24 in the entirety of Books III–IV.[195] These

---

189. Johnson argues that this vague superscription may be intended "to highlight the deity's involvement in David's escape from adversaries in general." She concludes that "the general nature of the heading lends itself to be used for any story that affirms David's need of his God to deliver him" (Johnson, *David in Distress*, 100–1, 108).

190. These five instances have also been noted by Witt, though he does not see that the last two references are similar and distanced from a Davidic attribution. See Witt, "Hearing Psalm 102," 593.

191. Pss 3:4; 22:20; 41:11; 59:6, 9; 102:13; 109:21.

192. Apart from the Psalter, they are found in the Davidic Covenant in 2 Sam 7:24 and 1 Chr 17:22, and in Jer 12:3; 18:23.

193. Note that different lexemes are used to describe "brokenness" of the heart. Cf. שבר ("to smash") in Pss 51:19 and 69:21; חמץ ("to embitter") in 73:21; יבש ("to be dry") in 102:5; חלל ("to pierce") in 109:22; and שמם ("to be appalled") in 143:4. The parallel between Pss 51:19 and 69:21 is the clearest as the same verb is used.

194. The noun is found in numerous places but only in the following psalms, it is used in connection with a "battered" or "broken-down" state of the human body: Pss 27:2; 38:4, 8; 63:2; 102:6; 109:24.

195. The one reference, בשר, in Ps 119:120 describe a fear of Yhwh rather than a decrepit

two references capture vivid descriptions of the afflicted petitioner in gauntness and in want of body fat.

(f) The noun, בגד ("garment"), is found only in four places in the Psalter (22:19; 45:9; 102:27; 109:19). Apart from Ps 45, the others are in DCs.[196] Among these four references, Pss 102 and 109 are the only two psalms found in the later two-thirds of the Psalter.

In Ps 22:19, "garment" is used together with another term, "clothing" (לבוש), in the same verse.[197] Psalm 102:27 is the only other reference in the Psalter that uses both בגד and לבוש in the same verse. Psalms 22 and 102 are also connected by their vivid descriptions of a decrepit, dry, broken and seemingly forsaken petitioner calling out to Yhwh (cf. 22:1–23; 102:1–12). Hence, we see lexical and thematic interconnections between Pss 22, 102 and 109.

At the same time, these three psalms are lexically interconnected with Ps 69, identifying a decrepit, despised and afflicted figure crying out to Yhwh. Psalms 22, 69 and 102 are linked by six lexemes (לבוש ["clothing"]; לב ["heart"]; בזה ["to despise"]; קרא ["to cry out"]; פנה ["to turn"]; עני ["afflicted"]). The use of these six lexemes that describe an afflicted figure is not found elsewhere in the Psalter.[198] Thus, Ps 102 is not only connected to 109, but connects Ps 109 with Pss 22 and 69.[199] Crucially, these connections identify a suffering Davidic king. However, in Pss 102 and 109, the suffering king is also an idealized, blameless and victorious Davidic king. This contrasts with the suffering human David presented in Pss 69–71.[200]

(g) Psalms 102 and 109 are also lexically connected with common motifs associated to "cursing" (cf. 102:9; 109:17–18, 28) and "fasting" (cf. 102:5, 10; 109:24). Therefore, the preceding seven lexical connections between Pss 102 and 109 prompt us to read the triptychs DC-III and IV together.[201]

(5) ברית is another lexeme that exemplifies the POS phenomenon and supports our argument for viewing DC-III and IV together.[202] The basic meaning of this word

---

description of the physical body.

196. Note that Ps 45 is a messianic psalm. While the Davidic psalms in *toto* identify a broken psalmist, Ps 45 identifies a victorious king.

197. Cf. לבוש (Pss 22:19; 35:13; 45:14; 69:12; 102:27; 104:6). Some of the common lexemes between Pss 22 and 102 include בזה ("to despise"); עני ("affliction"); עצם ("bone").

198. Common particles, prepositions and conjunctions are not considered in this count.

199. Mays connected Pss 3, 22, 31 and 69. Van der Lugt (and Allen) argues that Pss 102 and 69 correspond in their poetical structure. Robertson identifies a connection between the turning of an "intimate friend" to an enemy between Pss 41:9; 69:8–9; 109:4–5, 8. Mays, "'In a Vision,'" 7; Van der Lugt, *CAS III*, 123; Robertson, *Flow of the Psalms*, loc. 5374.

200. These psalms are mostly associated with Jesus in the NT.

201. This is not to say that Pss 102 or 109 do not have other lexical or thematic parallels with other psalms, adjacent or far. However, in our analysis, the interconnection between Pss 102 and 109 is clear. Witt, for instance, has found parallels between Ps 102 with Pss 86, 88 and 89 but curiously misses the connections with Ps 109. Witt, "Hearing Psalm 102," 595.

202. The following study on ברית is also published in my article, "Pan-Psalter Occurrence Scheme

is "imposition, liability or obligation."²⁰³ ברית is synonymous to law or commandment (Deut 4:13; 33:9; cf. ספר הברית, "Book of the Covenant" in Exod 24:7; 2 Kgs 23:2) and is understood as "the instruments by means of which a set of legal ordinances was imposed on the people."²⁰⁴ In the Pentateuch, this set of legal ordinances, the Mosaic covenant, is given by Yhwh to his people. Scholars have recognized that such a covenant, especially in written form and found in Deuteronomy, finds affinity with ANE Hittite treaties.²⁰⁵ However, a different kind of covenant (e.g., the Abrahamic and Davidic covenants), is characterized as unconditional and as a gift. "In contradistinction to the Mosaic covenants, which are of an obligatory type, the covenants with Abraham and David belong to the promissory type. God swears to Abraham to give the land to his descendants, and similarly promises to David to establish his dynasty without imposing any obligations on them."²⁰⁶

By the use of various royal psalms at key junctures (e.g., Pss 2, 72, 89), the Psalter in its final form "reflects exilic (or postexilic) evaluation of the hopes of the Davidic monarchy based on the covenant of David."²⁰⁷ While this is certainly the case, given the wide association with David in the Psalter, glimpses of the Sinaitic covenant within the Psalter is not entirely absent.

This can be seen in the five-book structure functioning to mimic the Pentateuch, the presence of a Mosiac Ps 90 immediately after Ps 89, and the presence of prominent Torah psalms (Pss 1 and 119).

---

of 'Jacob' and 'Covenant.'" I like to thank *JSOT* for giving me permission to reprint them here.

203. The etymology of the term is closely related to the Akkadian *biritu*, which means "clasp" or "fetter" (cf. Ezek 20:37). See Weinfeld, "ברית," *TDOT*, 2:255.

204. Weinfeld, "ברית," *TDOT*, 2:265.

205. The basic structure of such ANE covenantal documents consists of a title, a historical preamble, a list of stipulations and witnesses, blessings and curses and a ratification process. This has been proposed as early as 1954 by George Mendenhall, further studied and debated in the ensuing years, and upheld by a number of scholars recently. See Mendenhall, *Law and Covenant in Israel*, 2:26–44, 3:49–76. Cf. Taggar-Cohen, "Biblical Covenant," 461–88.

206. Like the Deuteronomic covenant, there are parallels of such the Abrahamic and Davidic covenants with the Assyrian and Hittite royal grants.The affinities between the phrasing of Yhwh's covenant with David and Ashurbanipal's grant to his servant below serve as an example. David served God in faithfulness and uprightness of heart; in truth and righteousness (cf. 1 Kgs 3:6; 9:4; 11:4, 6; 14:8). In comparison, Ashurbanipal gave to his servant, "[Balṭāya] . . . whose heart is whole to his master, stood before me with truthfulness, walked in perfection in mu palace . . . and kept the charge of my kingship (*iṣṣur maṣṣarti*) . . . I took thought of his kindness and decreed (therefore) his gi[f]t" (Weinfeld, "ברית," 270–271). Since Moshe Weinfeld's influential article, "The Covenant of Grant in the Old Testament and in the Ancient near East" published in the 1970, ANE royal grant are connected to the Davidic covenant in the OT and distinguished from the Suzerian-vassal treaty/Sinaitic covenant. While connections between the Davidic covenant and the royal grant continued to be maintained by some scholars (e.g., Jon Levenson), others have highlighted important differences (G. Knoppers). Cf. Weinfeld, "Covenant of Grant," 184–203. Levenson, "Davidic Covenant," 205–19; Knoppers, "Ancient Near Eastern Royal Grants," 670–97.

207. Wilson, "Use of Royal Psalms," 92.

There are 21 (7x3) instances of ברית across the five Books of the Psalter.[208] In the analysis of the POS of ברית below, associations to both the Mosiac and Davidic covenants can be seen. The techniques used for these 21 instances of ברית[209] across the five Books of the Psalter is remarkably similar to the POS of "Jacob" above.

Location	Structure	Ref	Distinctive Feature	Text (my translation)
Book I	A (DC-I)	**25:10**	Introduction: Blessings for covenant keepers	All the paths of Yahweh are lovingkindness and truth; **To those who keep** [לנצרי] his covenant and his testimonies.
		25:14		The secret of Yahweh is for those who fear him; And he makes known to them his covenant.
Books II–III	B (DC-II)	44.18	Godly vs wicked	"All this has come upon us, but we have not forgotten you, and we have not dealt falsely with your covenant."
		50:5		"Gather to me my godly ones, those who have made a covenant with me by sacrifice. [ברתי עלי־זבח]"
	B' (DC-II)	50:16		But to the wicked God says, "What right have you to recount my statutes and to take my covenant on your mouth? [ברתי עלי־פיך]"
		55:21		He has sent his hands against those who were at peace with him; he has violated his covenant.
	C	74:20	Wicked nations do not keep covenant nor walk in his law	Consider the covenant; for the dark places of the land are full of the dwellings of violence.
		78:10		**They did not keep** [לא שמרו] the covenant of God, and refused to walk in His law;
		78:37		For their heart was not steadfast toward him, they were not faithful in his covenant.
		83:6		For they have conspired together with one mind, against you they make a covenant.
	D	89:4	YHWH keeps Davidic covenant	"I have made a covenant with my chosen, I have sworn to David my servant."
		89:29		"My lovingkindness **I will keep** [אשמר] for him forever, and my covenant shall be confirmed to him."
		89:35		"My covenant I will not violate, and the utterance of my lips I will not change."
		89:40	YHWH fails Davidic covenant?	"You have spurned the covenant of your servant; you have violated his [David] crown in the dust."

---

208. Pss 25:10, 14; 44:18; 50:5, 16; 55:21; 74:20; 78:10, 37; 83:6; 89:4, 29, 35, 40; 103:18; 105:8, 10; 106:45; 111:5, 9; 132:12.

209. Pss 25:10, 14; 44:18; 50:5, 16; 55:21; 74:20; 78:10, 37; 83:6; 89:4, 29, 35, 40; 103:18; 105:8, 10; 106:45; 111:5, 9; 132:12.

Location	Structure	Ref	Distinctive Feature	Text (my translation)
Books IV–V	A' (DC-III)	103:18	Turning: To those who keep covenant and precept	**To those who keep** [לשמרי] his covenant, and to those who remember his precepts to do them.
	E	105:8	Everlasting covenant	He has remembered his **covenant forever** [לעולם בריתו], The word which He commanded to a thousand generations.
		105:10		Then He confirmed it to Jacob for a statute, to Israel as an **everlasting covenant** [ברית עולם].
	A"	106:45		And he remembered his covenant for their sake, and relented according to the greatness of His lovingkindness.
	E'	111:5		He has given food to those who fear him, he will remember His **covenant forever** [לעולם בריתו].
		111:9		He has sent a ransom to His people; he has ordained his **covenant forever** [לעולם בריתו]; Holy and awesome is his name.
	A'	132:12	Conclusion: blessings for covenant keepers	**If your sons will keep** [ישמרו] my covenant, and my testimony which I will teach them, their sons also shall sit upon your throne forever.

Figure 60: Pan-Psalter Occurrence Scheme of ברית

The occurrences of ברית can be organized along three sections of the Psalter (Books I, II–III, IV–V). The first two instances in Ps 25:10, 14 function as the introduction to the entire schema. They describe how Yhwh will treat his people who "keep" (לנצרי) his covenant. These two instances are designated as poetic unit A. The positive description of those who "keep" Yhwh's covenant is repeated only in 103:18; 132:12 with the lexeme שמר, they are designated as A'. Note that these references form the frames of Books IV–V in the POS of "covenant." These three units (A, A, A') are strategically located as the Introduction, Turning point and Conclusion in the POS structure of ברית by virtue of their common motif of Israel keeping the covenant.[210] This characteristic motif of the community keeping the covenant positively does not occur anywhere else in rest of the 21 instances. Note that 78:10 is phrased as a negative ("did not keep") and in 89:29, the subject of the covenant keeper is Yhwh.

Books II–III of the Psalter contain three sets of four references (B/B'-C-D) making a total of 12 references to the ברית. The B-B' units are two pairs of references (44.18; 50:5[211] and 50:16; 55:21) that distinguish those who have made a covenant with Yhwh (B) from those who do not (B'). The two references at the center (50:5, 16) consist of direct speeches of Yhwh regarding the godly and wicked. They are framed by 44.18; 55:21, respectively as parallel reflections regarding the godly and the wicked.

---

210. In the HB, the concept of "keeping" the covenant is expressed by three verbs, שמר, נצר and זכר. Cf. Gen 9:15; 17:9, 10; Exod 2:24; 19:5; Deut 33:9; Pss 25:10; 78:10; 103:18; 105:8; 132:12). See Weinfeld, *TDOT*, 2:260.

211. *BHS* notes that the Greek and Syriac has 3sg suffix. This critical note does not affect the POS of ברית.

The Design of the Psalter

The C unit consists of another four references that are entirely focused on the wicked as a collective who reject Yhwh's covenant. Unlikely to be a concidence, the two center references (78:10, 37), like the B-B' unit, are located within a single psalm.[212]

The D unit consists of four references entirely focused on Yhwh's covenant with David. They are all found within a single psalm (89:4, 29, 35, 40). The first and last references (89:4, 40) frame the entire D unit with their allusion to the Davidic king. The first three references are distinct from the fourth in that they are focused on Yhwh keeping the covenant to David (89:4, 29, 35). These three instances consistently identify Yhwh as the subject using the first person singular verbal forms and noun-suffixes. The last instance in 89:40 is an abnormaly, probably signaling the end of a compositional unit. The tone and the subject have changed, with the psalmist apparently accusing Yhwh for failing his covenant.

As a whole, the 12 references in Books II–II, with its three distinct units of four references each (B/B'-C-D), consist of different characterizations associated with parties of the covenant. The B-B' unit highlights the *godly* who would keep Yhwh's covenant. The C unit highlights the *wicked* who do not keep the covenant and the D unit highlights Yhwh as the covenant-keeper.

Section III contains the final seven references of ברית arranged concentrically. These seven instances are framed by two A' references, which are the Turning point and Conclusion. The Turning point (103:18; A') is the final occurrence of ברית in a Davidic psalm. Note that the phrase, "those who keep" (לשמרי; A') in 103:18, connects with the phrase "if your sons would keep" in 132:12 (אם-ישמרו בניך; A'). These two phrases identify positively those who keep Yhwh's covenant and together, they are linked to the phrase, "those who keep" in 25:10 (לנצרי; A). Once again, we observe how the poet uses repetitions of a certain motif as a technique to mark structural boundaries in a POS.

Situated at the center of Section III, Psalm 106:45 (A″) is the pivoting point of a striking symmetry. The location of 106:45 separates two pairs of references (105:8, 10 and 111:5, 9) designated by E and E'. What makes these two pairs (E, E') distinct in Section III is that they are located separately within a single psalm (Pss 105, 111) and they are the only four references that modify "covenant" with the adjective עולם.

The final reference in 132:12 identifies the sons of the Davidic king as those who would keep the covenant.[213] The motif of Yhwh teaching his covenant to "them" (the sons; אלמדם) as the final reference forms a fitting inclusio with 25:14 where Yhwh makes his covenant known to "them" (those who fear him; להודיעם).

---

212. *BHS* notes that the Greek and Syriac adds 2sg on ברית in 74:20. This critical note does not affect the POS of ברית.

213. This combination of Yhwh's teaching and covenant keeping recalls the New Covenant in Jer 31:31–34. See the following references that connect the motifs of Yhwh's teaching and covenant keeping: Deut 4:10–23; 31:19–20; 1 Kgs 8:25.

If we consider the four references in Ps 89 as two pairs of references, there are seven pairs of references that are found within a single psalm.²¹⁴ Apart from Ps 89, these pairs are interspaced across the 21 references in all the units A, B/B′, C, D, E/E′. The fourth and central pair (89:4, 29) marks an important first-person declaration by Yhwh of establishing a covenant with his chosen, the Davidic king.

From these 21 occurrences of ברית across the three sections (Books I, II–III and IV–V), we can detect a trajectory starting from Book I, with the establishment of relationship between Yhwh and those who keep his ברית. Then in Books II–III, distinctions are made between the godly and wicked. This section includes the emphatic description of the wicked who do not keep Yhwh's ברית, and a powerful declaration by Yhwh to keep his ברית with David. In the final Section, there is no longer any negative portrayal of the covenant keepers. Instead, there is an emphasis on the eternal covenant.

Fourth Davidic Collection (Pss 108–110)

Dubbed as a "trilogy," DC-IV comes immediately after the first psalm of Book V.²¹⁵ It is clearly unified by the Davidic superscription in each of the three psalms. The lexical motifs of "scepter,"²¹⁶ "dawn,"²¹⁷ and Yhwh's "right hand"²¹⁸ link Pss 108 and 110 which frame the Collection. Both Pss 108 and 110 highlight Yhwh's victorious battles against hostile nations and are set at the temple (cf. 108:8; 110:1).²¹⁹ While we have discussed the structural and lexical parallels between DC-III and DC-IV, we have not discussed how DC-IV deepened the characterization of the Davidic figure. We will proceed to explore how DC-IV deepens our understanding of David and analyze the function of DC-IV within the five DCs.

(1) Consider another structural connection between DC-III and IV. It is possible to see DC-III and DC-IV forming a chiasmus in an [A-B-C]-[C′-B′-A′] structure.

    A   Idealized Davidic king who rules from Zion (Ps 101)
        B   Broken petitioner (Ps 102)
            C   David praising Yhwh's steadfast love (Ps 103)
            C′   David praising Yhwh's steadfast love (Ps 108)
        B′   Broken petitioner (Ps 109)
    A′   Idealized Davidic king who rules from Zion (Ps 110)

---

214. Pss 25:10, 14; 50:5, 16; 78:10, 37; 89:4, 29; 89:35, 40; 105:8, 10; 111:5, 9.

215. Hossfeld and Zenger, *Psalms* 3, 3.

216. Cf. Pss 108:9 and 110:2. Cf. 45:7; 60:9*, 125:3. Note that Ps 60:9 is "reused" in Ps 108:9.

217. Cf. Pss 108:3 and 110:3.

218. Cf. Pss 108:7; 109:6, 31; 110:1, 5.

219. The word בקדשׁ in Ps 108:8 can be translated as "in his holiness" or "in his sanctuary." The latter is supported by Zenger and Botha. See Botha, "Psalm 108," 582; Hossfeld and Zenger, *Psalms* 3, 114.

This chiastic structure is visible through various parallels. In the A, A' units, Pss 101 and 110 sustain the motif of an idealized Davidic king.[220] They characterize a king who can annihilate all enemies. This motif of kingship, clearly forefronted in these two psalms, is softened in the rest of DC-III and IV.[221] Both psalms also identify a group of "blameless" people who minister before the king, an element not found in the rest (cf. 101:6; 110:3). The motif of the destruction of the king's enemies from Zion is also lacking in DC-III and IV, apart from these two psalms (cf. 101:1, 7–8; 110:2). The use of "morning/dawn" that characterizes the temporal settings in Pss 101 and 110 is not found in the rest.[222]

In the C, C' units, Ps 103 parallels 108 with the expression, "my soul/being" (cf. 103:1–2; 108:2). This phraseology is not found elsewhere in the chiasmus. While the word, חסד, is found in four psalms in DC-III and IV, only Pss 103:11 and 108:5 associate YHWH's חסד with the heights of the "heavens."[223] Psalms 103 and 108 are distinct because YHWH, rather than the king, is the object of emphasis and praise (cf. 103:19–22; 108:1–5).

Granted that the chiastic structure of DC-III and IV can be sustained, the bookends of these two Collections (A, A') feature an embellished Davidic king who is "blameless" and given victorious rule over all wickedness and hostile nations. At the center are two psalms (C, C') linked with the description of "heavens," focusing on YHWH's steadfast love. The centers of the two separate Collections (B, B'; 102 and 109) highlight the broken Davidic petitioner. As such, DC-III and IV are structurally united.

(2) DC-IV develops the characterization of the Davidic figure as the Messianic priest-king. In Ps 101, the Davidic figure is one who walks in the "blameless way" (בדרך תמים; 101:2). He is the champion of those who walk in the "blameless way" and the destroyer of wickedness in the city of the LORD (101:6–8). Botha even suggests that the Davidic characterization of a blameless king is "a good example of a pledge" to establish a righteous society.[224]

In contrast, the Davidic king in Ps 110 cannot function easily as an example. The speaker in the psalm is possibly "a court prophet" or a "temple functionary"[225] who

---

220. It has been proposed that the original setting of Ps 101 is a "royal proclamation issued at the enthronement festival of a prince of Judah in Jerusalem." The text, however, allows us to identify the speaker "as someone with great power and judicial authority over the whole land (vv. 5, 6, 7, and 8)." In the monarchic period, the speaker can be a royal figure, but in the postexilic period, he is likely to be a "religious functionary." See Botha, "Psalm 101," 725, 735.

221. The battle victories in Ps 108 are attributed to YHWH rather than the king.

222. Psalm 101:8 uses בקר ("morning") while Ps 110:3 uses the *hapax legomenon* משחר ("dawn").

223. In the Psalms, the description of "heavens" in relation to "steadfast love" is found only in Pss 36:6; 57:4, 11; 89:3; 103:11; 108:5.

224. Botha argues that this psalm is "a good example of a pledge to help with the establishment of an obedient and honorable society as envisaged in Psalm 1" (Botha, "Psalm 101," 735).

225. Longman III, *Psalms*, 381.

conveyed "the divine words to his 'LORD.'"²²⁶ With YHWH's help, this king would rule in the midst of his enemies from Zion. He is also identified as a "primeval" kingly-priest "in the order of Melchizedek" and given the prerogative to "judge" among the nations (110:6).²²⁷ The king's priesthood is also one that endures "forever" (cf. Isa 11:1–9; Ezek 34:23–24; Zech 6:9–15).²²⁸ Scholars have linked the kingly-priest descriptions to the El-Elyon cult,²²⁹ but this connection remains debatable. Others have adopted a messianic interpretation for this psalm. Routledge argues that the entire phrase "in the order of Melchizedek" in Ps 110:4 "might be suggesting just such a limitation: the Davidic king functions as a priest in the way we see Melchizedek functioning as a priest in Genesis 14:18–20, that is, as a means of blessing (the descendants of) Abraham."²³⁰ The integration of the offices of kingship and priesthood had never been definitively appropriated to a king in the history of Israel's nationhood. Hence, for Routledge, the dual king-priest office and the emphasis of the "order of Melchizedek" in Ps 110:4 "must point forward to the future Messiah"²³¹ (cf. Zech 6:12–14).²³²

Reading Ps 110 in the context of the postexilic period prompts us to see the Davidic priest-king as Messianic, through whom the promised blessings to Abraham and his descendants are perpetuated. Zenger, likewise, notes that the king described in Ps 110 is "impregnated" with Messianic concepts and the entirety of the psalm is "similar to Psalm 2."²³³ Following Routledge and Zenger, we see that Psalm 110 presents not just a blameless king (as in 101), but develops the Davidic figure as a Messianic priest-king.

(3) The afflicted David in Ps 109 is a *juridically* condemned figure, and not merely an afflicted figure. Both Pss 102 and 109 depict an afflicted Davidic king. Psalm 109 in DC-IV, however, develops this afflicted figure in two ways. First, the entirety of the psalm has a "judicial imprint." Zenger argued that "since the petition as a whole

---

226. Hossfeld and Zenger, *Psalms 3*, 147.

227. For a study of the relationship between David and Melchizedek, see Routledge, "Psalm 110," 1–16.

228. Zenger notes that the "priest" motif in Psalm 110 "is unique." Hossfeld and Zenger, *Psalms 3*, 146. There are three positions with regards to the origins of the psalm: (a) preexilic "enthronement" psalm in the "royal ritual of Jerusalem"; (b) Maccabean-Hasmonean dating with Simon as the "priest-king" (143–135 BCE); (c) postexilic expectation of a Davidic king. Hossfeld and Zenger, *Psalms 3*, 144.

229. Routledge argues against the connections between the use of "Melchizedek" in Ps 110 and the El-Elyon cult. See Routledge, "Psalm 110," 10.

230. Routledge, "Psalm 110," 14.

231. Routledge, "Psalm 110," 11.

232. On messianic passages in Zechariah, Petterson notes, "If these passages [e.g., Zech 12:10; 13:7] are treated in isolation from the wider context of Zechariah, then it is not clear that they refer to a future Davidic king or even that any identification is possible. However, if they are read as an integral part of the book of Zechariah, then the only identification of these figures that is coherent within the book is that they refer to the coming Davidic king, who is killed in the coming battle by Yahweh's intent. The result is a restored covenant relationship between Yahweh and his people (13:9; cf. 11:10). Zechariah 14 pictures the fruit of the coming king" (Petterson, "Shape of the Davidic Hope," 244).

233. Hossfeld and Zenger, *Psalms 3*, 144.

asks for the rescue of the person praying it in the face of or from a condemnation to death obtained through false testimony, we can call this a 'justice psalm.'"[234] If Zenger is right, it is possible to read Ps 109:1–3 as the psalmist's counteraction to his accusers before Yhwh, the judge, who stands at the "right hand of the needy one, to save him from those who condemn his soul to death" (109:31, ESV). Thus, while Ps 102 is presented as a supplication, Ps 109 is set like a scene in the court.

Second, it is plausible to view Ps 109:6–19 as a vivid account of the accusations made by hostile accusers against the petitioner. Four different views have been proposed for the identity of the speaker in verses 6–19.[235] The speaker can be: (a) the petitioner of the psalm, praying for punishment to befall his accusers;[236] (b) the petitioner *quoting* the words of his enemies; (c) the petitioner quoting the words of his enemies in vv. 6–15 *and* his own responses in vv. 16–19; or (d) Yhwh.

Zenger has taken the second position, and translated the decisive 109:20 as, "This is what they do, those who accuse me, calling on Yhwh and who speak evil against my life," taking פעלת as "work/deed" rather than "reward."[237] My argument for Ps 109:20 is fourfold. First, I agree with Zenger that פעלת can be translated as "work/deed" rather than "reward" since all other instances in the Psalms are understood as "work" (cf. 17:4; 28:5). Second, the phrase, מאת יהוה, occurs only in three other places in the Psalms (24:5; 27:4; 118:23) and in all three, the one who receives something מאת יהוה is associated with the Davidic king. This suggests that the recipient in Ps 109:20 is the psalmist (rather than the accusers). Third, syntactically the entire verse is a chiasmus:

---

234. Hossfeld and Zenger, *Psalms 3*, 128.

235. For details on the arguments for each position, see Hossfeld and Zenger, *Psalms 3*, 126–30.

236. Firth, holding onto the position that vv. 6–19 are the prayers of the psalmist, argues that in the psalmist's imprecatory prayer, he had applied the *lex talionis* principle on his accusers so that "the law required that a false witness suffer the fate that would have befallen the person accused had they been found guilty (Deut 19:16–21)" (Firth, *Surrendering Retribution*, 40–41).

237. Zenger's detailed argument is as follows: Much of the interpretation lies with how one understands the combination of words, פעלת and מאת יהוה in v. 20. The former, with the human being (or Yhwh) as subject, can refer to his actions or the result (reward) of his actions. As such, the nominal phrase, זאת פעלת שטני, can be interpreted in two ways: (1) descriptively, that is, "this is . . ." or (2) jussively, "let this be . . ." The phrase, מאת יהוה, can also be interpreted in two ways, either referring to the פעלה or wicked accusers. When they are seen together, the entire v. 20a can be read either as (a) "this(/let this be) is the act/reward of those who accuse me from Yhwh . . ." or (b) "this(/let this be) is the act/reward from Yhwh, for those who . . ." Moreover, Zenger argues that the "section in vv. 6–19 is so clearly distinct from it [vv. 1b–5], both syntactical and in content, that it cannot simply be regarded as a continuation of vv. 1–5. The following features of vv. 6–19 are particularly striking: in vv. 1–5 and 21–31, the petitioner always sees himself in contrast to a group of enemies (formulated in the plural); in contrast, the desire for destruction and accusation in vv. 6–19 are directed at an individual" (Hossfeld and Zenger, *Psalms 3*, 127–30). Van der Lugt's argument is also interesting. While he agrees that from v. 6 onwards, the psalmist quotes his accusers, he also argues for a caesura between verses 13 and 14. He notes that "from v. 14 onwards we are dealing with the wish of the supplicant himself that his opponents may decline." Then "in v. 20 the supplicant once again speaks of [his] accusers in the plural" (Van de Lugt, *CAS III*, 220–22).

זאת פעלת
שטני
מאת יהוה
והדברים
רע על-נפשי

The two words at the center, מאת יהוה, highlight the centrality of the causative factor of Yhwh. Three words before and after מאת יהוה mirror each other. The phrase, זאת פעלת שטני, translated as "this is the work of my adversary" parallels והדברים רע על-נפשי, "those who speak evil against my soul." The שטן and הדברים, refer to the psalmist's enemies. The first and last two words identifying "work/deed" of the שטן and הדברים respectively. From these three arguments, 109:20 reads as, "this is the work of my adversary, from Yhwh, those who speak evil against my soul." This translation may seem theologically difficult, assigning wicked accusations to God. However, this is the most unencumbered way to translate based on the syntax, which leads to my next point.

We have already connected Pss 109 and 102 with the heightened motif of the afflicted Davidic figure. We can further connect Ps 109:20 and Ps 118:23 with four common lexemes between these two verses.[238] The clause, מאת יהוה היתה זאת (118:23), refers to the antecedent where "the stone the builders rejected had become the chief cornerstone" (118:22). This enigmatic metaphor refers not just to the positive salvific motif in Ps 118, but also carries the element of affliction arising from Yhwh's judgmental work. This is shown in Ps 118:18, "Yhwh has disciplined me [Davidic figure] severely, but unto death he has not given me over." The connections of lexemes help us to understand Ps 109:20 in view of Ps 118:18–23. The theological dilemma of assigning the work of the adversary to Yhwh in 109:20 can be resolved through the larger rubric of Yhwh's chastisement in 118:18–23.

Though I do not agree with Zenger's translation,[239] I agree with Zenger's position that the "second [view] best corresponds to the overall dramaturgy of the psalm."[240] Taking Ps 109:6–19 as a quotation of the psalmist's accusers best fits the psalm's context as a judicial proceeding.

From this, we see an important development of the characterization of the afflicted king from DC-III to DC-IV—the afflicted Davidic figure in Ps 109 is unjustly accused by ingrate accusers with incredulous claims of crimes that demanded the death sentence of this Davidic figure.

---

238. (1) Attached preposition מן; (2) direct object marker את; (3) proper noun יהוה; (4) demonstrative pronoun זו.

239. It is grammatically difficult to translate מאת יהוה as "calling on Yhwh."

240. Hossfeld and Zenger, *Psalms 3*, 126.

(4) A third development of the Davidic characterization in DC-IV relates to the message of Ps 108 which underscores a time of triumph over specific nations.[241] Psalm 108 is a composite psalm made up of Pss 57:8–12 and 60:7–14.[242] Only the words, "David" and "song," in the superscriptions of Pss 57 of 60 are used in the superscription of Ps 108. Comparing these three psalms, we observe that negative laments are jettisoned from Pss 57 and 60, but "victorious" parts of the psalms are retained in Ps 108. Thus, Ps 108, as a recomposition of Pss 57 and 60, emphasizes a triumphalism of Israel's deliverance from her enemies. Botha's observation that "Psalm 108:8-10 no longer resides in a bed of complaint, but is given the character of a hopeful prophecy about the future triumph of Yhwh over the enemies of his people,"[243] affirms our contention.

In our analysis of the thirteen Davidic historical superscriptions earlier, Ps 60:1–2 is the only other "triumphant" superscription apart from Ps 18:1. However, the hope embedded in the superscription of Ps 60, where "twelve-thousands Edomites were struck down," is shrouded by the laments that follow in Ps 60:3–7. Why is this so? Our answer to this is that the *veiled* and *fettered* "triumphalism" of Ps 60 (and Ps 57) becomes a portrayal of hope under the brokenness of the Davidic kingship of DC-II within the Metanarrative of the Psalter.

However, the victories of Ps 60 and the reference to the defeat of Edom, both in Ps 60:2, 10–11, is given *unfettered* triumphal characterization in Ps 108 because DC-IV no longer presents a fallen Davidic king, but a victorious Davidic king. As Zenger has argued, the Messianic interpretations of Ps 110 and its "redactional" relationship with Ps 108 suggest an expression of "messianic" hope. Therefore the kingly figure in Pss 108 and 110 are to be seen together,[244] presenting an unfettered triumphalistic characterization of this Davidic king.

Moreover, by comparing Ps 108:12 with 60:12, the accusatory tone of Yhwh's "rejection" (זנח) has been softened by dropping the second-person pronoun, "you" (אתה).[245] The softening of this accusation fits well with the triumphant tone of the psalm. Psalm 108 is positive and confident, no longer a mere far-away glimpse of restorative hope.

(5) Psalm 108 comes immediately after a series of psalms that praise and trace Yhwh's deeds and lovingkindness, first with the formation and deliverance of the

---

241. Zenger argues that "[Ps 108] is an expression of the ('messianic') hopes of postexilic Israel, impregnated with royal theology" (Hossfeld and Zenger, *Psalms 3*, 123).

242. Zenger argues that a "reverse dependency can be excluded." A least ten differences are found by comparing Ps 108 with Pss 57 and 60. See Hossfeld and Zenger, *Psalms 3*, 114–16.

243. Botha, "Psalm 108," 585–86.

244. "Edom" in Pss 60:2, 10–11 and 108:10–11 has been linked to Amos 9:11–12 which reads, "'In that day I will raise up the fallen booth of David, And wall up its breaches; I will also raise up its ruins, And rebuild it as in the days of old; That they may possess the remnant of Edom, And all the nations who are called by My name,' Declares the LORD who does this" (ESV; See also Obad 1).

245. Refer to the discussion of the lexeme, זנח, in chapter 2.

nation Israel (104–5), followed by the rebellion and exile of Israel (106), and finally the call for Israel to be gathered from the nations to an "inhabited city" (107). The flow of canonical history captured in Pss 104–107 and the portrayal of the Davidic warrior-king leading victoriously against the various nations listed in Ps 108 recall the early chapters of the Book of Joshua where Joshua was about to lead Israel in the conquest of Canaan with the help of the captain of Yhwh's hosts (Josh 5:13–15).

This narrative horizon of the Joshua narrative compares well with Ps 108 as the preceding Pss 103–6 contain the most sustained reference to "Moses" and what he did in the wilderness after coming out of Egypt.[246] Seen under the literary horizon of Pss 104–8, the Davidic figure in Ps 108 is the "new" Joshua who is victoriously leading Yhwh's people into a new era—a better "Canaan."[247]

In sum, the five arguments above show how DC-IV develops several important aspects of the "new" Davidic figure and how it fits within the literary horizon from DC-III to DC-IV. These two DCs are parallel triptychs forming a chiasmus, inviting us to compare and contrast the development of the Davidic characterization. In Ps 108, he is connected with the Messianic hopes for the victories over the nations in and around Canaan. He is the "new" Joshua who assembles and leads the people of Israel from the nations to an "inhabited city." Although this Davidic figure is afflicted and condemned to death by hostile accusations in Ps 109, he is vindicated in Ps 110, crowned as the priest-king, ruling victoriously from Zion over the nations. The figure below summarizes the Davidic characterization from DC-I to IV:

---

246. Cf. Pss 77:21; 90:1; 99:6; 103:7; 105:26; 106:16, 23, 32. Note that "Moses" does not occur again after Ps 106.

247. Mitchell argues that the Messiah in the Psalms is both a Joshua (Ephraimite) and Davidic figure combined. See Mitchell, *Messiah ben Joseph*, 60.

The Design of the Psalter

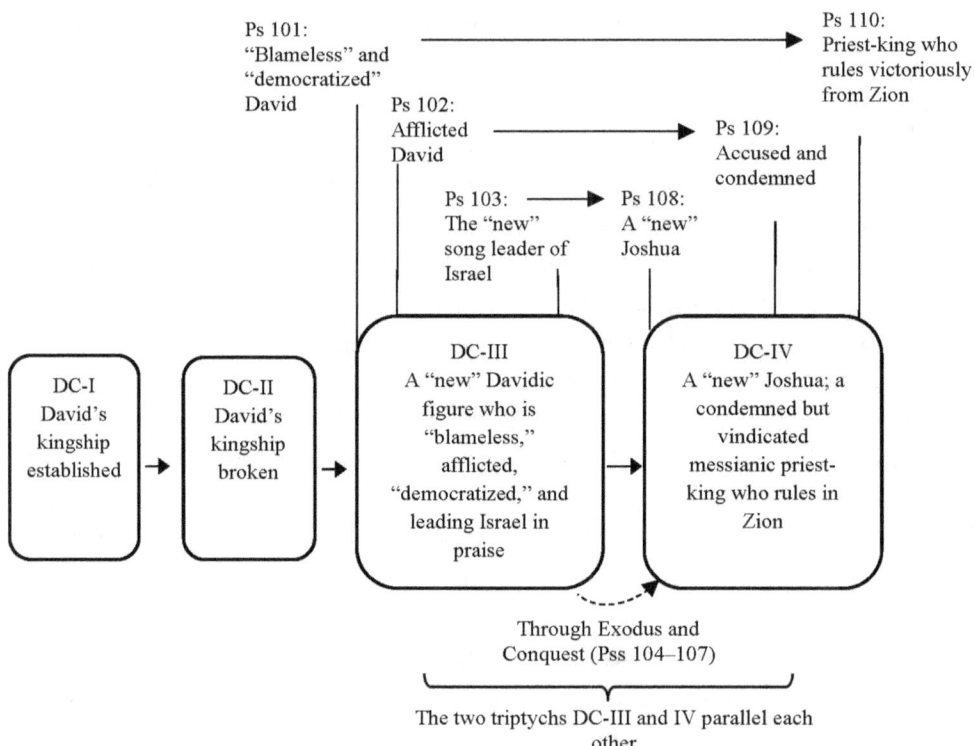

Figure 61: Summary of the Davidic Characterization from DC-I through IV

Fifth Davidic Collection (Pss 138–145)

One way of reading DC-V is to treat them as the collective responses to the horrors of exile in Ps 137.[248] Hossfeld sees a concentric structure in this collection that is also thematically progressive. The motif that frames this Collection is Yhwh's kingship in Pss 138 and 145.[249] Leuenberger argues that Yhwh's reign in DC-V is expressed clearly through the exercise of his sovereign providence and deliverance.[250] Ballhorn points out that DC-V, as the last DC in the Psalter, determines the final image of David. When this image of David is seen with the Final *Hallel* (146–150), they "administer an identity-forming program for Israel: the cast of the earthly Davidic king

---

248. This is argued from the contrasting use of שיר in Pss 137:3–4 and 138:5. The captors had requested for one of the Zion songs in Ps 137 but all the kings of nations will sing of "ways of the LORD" in Ps 138. Hossfeld and Zenger, *Psalms 3*, 531–32.

249. Hossfeld and Zenger, *Psalms 3*, 524–25.

250. Leuenberger, *Konzeptionen des Königtums Gottes*, 344.

is gently giving way to the kingdom of Yhwh."[251] This final Davidic king in Ps 145 "lays down his crown in view of the universal kingdom of Yhwh."[252] Ballhorn notes that this is the appropriate conclusion as one comes to the end of the Psalter, where the "messianic hope for the future is transformed theocentrically."[253] Buysch posits a different agenda for DC-V. He concludes that "the last Davidic Psalter… [is] a concise, practical teaching for approaching Yhwh in prayer with the forms of worship and confession."[254] The confessions and reflections therein express the essence of Yhwh, that is, his "righteousness," "creative power" and "historical power."[255] Psalm 145, at the end of DC-V, is essentially a focus on Yhwh's kingship.[256] Grol presents yet another view of DC-V. He argues that the exile in Ps 137 is used as a "*chiffre* [figure] for the crisis in the period of the redaction, the conflict with the Hellenists."[257] The aim of DC-V, following Ps 137, is "to strengthen the identity of the pious and orthodox, the *chasidim*, in their fight with the Hellenists."[258] And "David, whom the collection is attributed to, is role model for the *chasidim*."[259]

These conclusions on DC-V are helpful. The frames, Pss 138 and 145, are clearly focused on kingship and the latter has a theocratic emphasis. However, there remains a structural question as to why Pss 140–143, at the center of the Collection, sustain the motif of the Davidic distress and supplication. Why did the final editors of the Psalms revisit these laments and petitions if the intent was to move from messianic kingship to Yhwh kingship?

Before we study the features of DC-V, recall that in chapter 3, we argue that Pss 104–119, as a Group, parallels Pss 135–150 structurally. At the center of these two Groups are DC-IV and DC-V respectively, each bound by psalms that trace the canonical history of Israel up to the exile (104–107; 135–137) on the left, and psalms that praise Yhwh on the right, which interestingly, also trace the canonical story of creation to Israel's entry into Zion (111–118; 146–149). Also, an acrostic/alphabetical psalm at the right end (119 and 150) concludes both Groups. Hence, the first thing we note about DC-V is that it is carefully organized in the third Section of the Psalter with important macrostructural parallels. These structural features must provide the

---

251. Ballhorn, *Zum Telos des Psalters*, 297.

252. Ballhorn, *Zum Telos des Psalters*, 298.

253. Ballhorn, *Zum Telos des Psalters*, 298.

254. Buysch, *Der letzte Davidpsalter*, 326.

255. Buysch, *Der letzte Davidpsalter*, 327.

256. Van der Lugt argues that the verbal repetitions in the psalm form a concentric structure that emphasizes the kingship of Yhwh. He notes, "The concentric pattern of verbal recurrences on the level of the composition in its entirety highlights its quintessential train of thought [that is, Yhwh's kingship]" (Van der Lugt, *CAS III*, 540).

257. Van Grol, "David and His *Chasidim*," 336.

258. Van Grol, "David and His *Chasidim*," 336.

259. Van Grol, "David and His *Chasidim*," 336.

The Design of the Psalter

meaning and role of DC-V. In the following, we will explore three arguments for the role and function of DC-V.

(1) The key to understanding the role of DC-V lies in its central motif that follows a recurring emphasis of *Davidic supplication and distress* found at the centers of the last Group of every Section in the Psalter (i.e., Pss 38; 86; 140–143). We have seen this in Ps 86, where a lone Davidic psalm characterized by distress and supplication is precisely inserted at the center of the Psalms of Korah (84–88). Psalm 86 marks the motif of distress and supplication at the end of the entire Books II–III. Moreover, we have seen how the Davidic historical superscriptions in DC-I and DC-IV (cf. 34:1; 142:1), located as the final instances of two trajectories, share common motifs of *Davidic supplication and distress*. Motifs of distress and supplication not only fill the pages of the Psalter but also recur strategically toward the end of a unit, even after descriptions of victories. Hence, the motif of *Davidic supplication and distress* occurring as the last GCMs or last historical superscription along a trajectory is an intentional macrostructural phenomenon. This design provides the most important structural clue for the significance of DC-V. I present two (earlier) figures below illustrating the above argument.

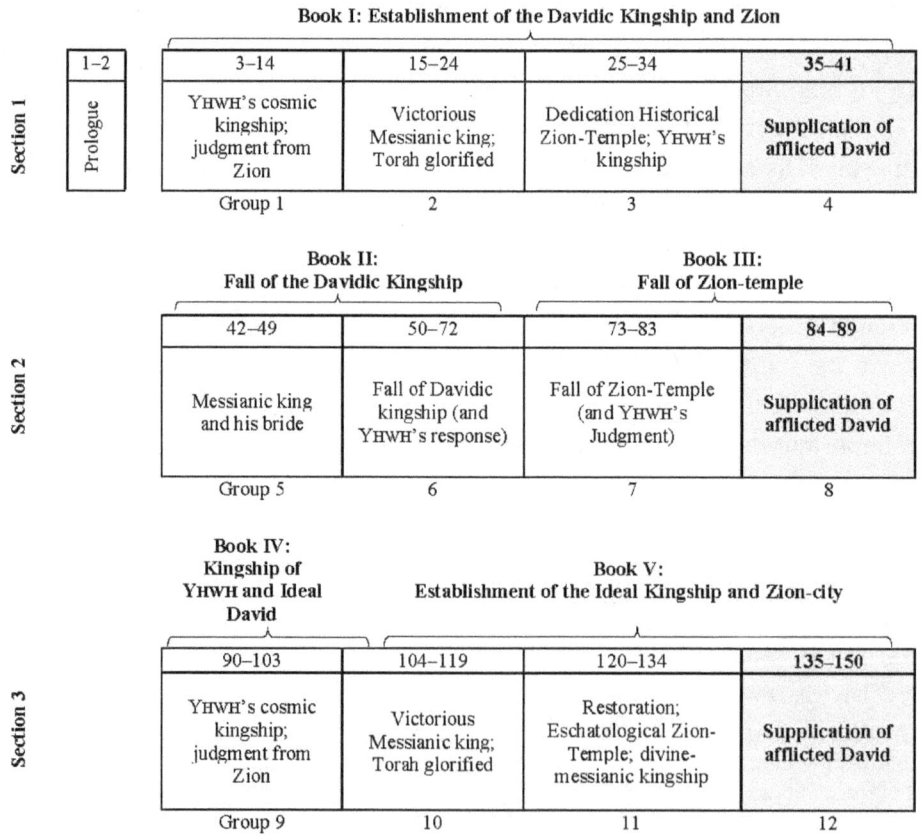

Figure 62: Common Final Group Central Motif of Davidic Supplication in Every Section

DC-I			
Ps 3:1	7:1	18:1	34:1
Davidic Kingship at stake	Absalom dies, Davidic kingship restored	Davidic kingship established (cf. Nathan's prophecy 2 Sam 7:1; 22:1)	David in distress. Supplication

DC-II								DC-V
51:1–2	52:1-2	54:1-2	56:1	57:1	59:1	60:1–2	63:1	142:1
Nathan's judgment – David's downfall begins	Recalls David's distress and threats to his life. Drawn from 1 Samuel.					Victorious state before David sins with Bathsheba	Book-ends with Pss 3:1 and 51:1–2	David in distress. Supplication

Figure 63: Common Motifs of the Distressed David in Supplication as Last Historical Superscriptions in Two Parallel Trajectories in DC-I and DC-II–V

We proceed to explore reasons for this structural feature. To do so, we first offer a brief sweep across the Metanarrative. In Figure 62, the motifs of distress and supplication at the end of Section 1 follow the establishment of David's kingship and temple. This suggests that even with the dual establishment of David's kingship and Zion-temple, affliction and supplication persist because of sin. The human king and earthly temple could not resolve the problems of sin and affliction. In Section 2, Ps 86, at the center of Group 8, sustains the motifs of Davidic affliction and supplication. With the emphasis on the fall of the kingship and Zion-temple in Section 2, affliction and supplication are understandably the preoccupations. A lone Davidic supplication psalm situated precisely at the structural center of a Korahite Collection provides an uncanny Davidic characterization. Note also how the Elohistic Psalter links Groups 5–7, leaving out Group 8.

With Section 3, there is a positive shift in the Metanarrative. Even with the dawn of an idealized Davidic figure in DC-III and IV, there are still issues of distress and affliction (102, 109). Then after DC-IV, Pss 111–119 further characterize the Torah-pious king.[260] Crutchfield argues that the righteous "man" referred to in Ps 112 is the messianic king.[261] He connects the "horn" in 112:9 with 132:17 and 148:14 (cf. 89:18,

---

260. For a study of the concept of Torah in Book V, esp. Ps 119, see the monograph by Mensah, "I Turned Back My Feet to Your Decrees."

261. Crutchfield argues, "First, the close relationship between these psalms [Pss 111–112] is explained: they are exegeting the unexplained relationship between God and messiah described in Psalm 110. Secondly, the hyperbolic language used to describe the God-fearer in Psalm 112 is fully explained, for this kind of language would find its fulfillment ultimately in the messiah in whom the pious would expect such virtues. Third, this seems to explain the messianic reference to the 'horn' of the righteous in Psalm 112:9" (Crutchfield, *Psalms in Their Context*, 35). See Ho, "Review of Crutchfield," 219–21.

25).²⁶² If parallels between Pss 112 and 1 can be sustained,²⁶³ then the Torah-pious and Messianic figures in Pss 1–2 are also demonstrated in Pss 110–112. Beyond Ps 119, we see an emphasis on the restoration of an idealized Zion city built by Yhwh (120–134), prefiguring an idealized society (cf. 132). Yet in spite of these positive depictions in Book V, DC-V ends with the motif of Davidic distress and supplication.

The motif of distress and supplication in DC-V is also increasingly associated with the *chasidim* of Israel (not just the Davidic figure). In fact, Grol argues that "Psalm 145 presents the *chasidim* as the ones David is referring to. The David of the collection [138–145] stands for them. He is their identification figure and symbol."²⁶⁴

The presence of affliction and supplication even after the advent of the Messianic king in DC-III and IV show that the ideal and victorious king has yet to *fully* establish the utopic social-reality of justice and bliss. This only happens as we approach Pss 144–145 at the end of DC-V. Here, the ideal Davidic king subdues all and hands over his kingship to Yhwh, *his* king (145:1). The final unambiguous transition from distress and lament to praise and peace occurs at 149:6–9, where the final judgment of the wicked is administered, leading to the praise of Yhwh at his sanctuary.

Hence, Pss 144–145 at the end of DC-V mark the beginning of a realized, ideal Davidic socio-community identified by ultimate justice, peace and praise.²⁶⁵ Regardless of how we perceive "Israel" in the Psalms, whether it refers primarily to the pre-exilic, exilic or postexilic community of faith or of the future generations (cf. 102:19; 145:4) of Yhwh's righteous pilgrims (e.g., Grol, identifying the setting to be at the Hellenistic period), the motif of affliction and supplication remain until a consummative shift in Pss 144–145.

Based on the structural phenomenon and development across the Metanarrative of the Psalter, the important theological message, both to the postexilic community at the final composition of the Psalter and to the reception of the MT Psalter tradition thereafter, is that distress and supplication would continue until a point when the victorious Davidic figure finally ushers in an ideal social-reality. The people, whose

---

262. Chester sees the "horn" in Ps 89 as messianic or "proto-messianic." Chester, *Messiah and Exaltation*, 247.

263. For connections between Pss 1 and 112, see Botha, "'Wealth and Riches,'" 118–19.

264. Grol argues that "names from divergent traditions" are integrated at the end "with the name of *chasidim*. The low and needy are found, the righteous (or justified) and the upright, the servant(s) of Yhwh (only singular!), those who revere God, and those who love him" (Grol, "David and His Chasidim," 325, 327).

265. Psalms 144–145 as a transition has been studied by Vignolo and Donatella Scaiola. Scaiola notes, "the last linking between doxology and macarism can be found in Ps 144, and suggests a signal of conclusion; secondly, the usual sequence is reversed, as the blessing in anticipated (144,1) with respect to the macarism which is being doubled (144,15). In his [Vignolo's] opinion, here is the beginning of the end of the fifth book, which develops throughout seven psalms. Psalm 145, which follows, can be considered an extended doxology, due to the inclusion within 145,1-2.21, which resumes 144,1. Pss 146–150 are doxological epilogue, well connected to Ps 145" (Scaiola, "End of the Psalter," 701–10, [702]). See also Vignolo, "Circolarita," 127–88.

God is Yhwh, must continue to persist in confident hope through petition until that defining shift.

The "blessed one" that begins the Psalter (אשרי-האיש; 1:1, 2:12) now finds fulfillment as "the blessed people" at the end of Ps 144:15 (אשרי העם). The people of God, as a collective, is to wait in supplication and hope until the time when they would be led into the paradisical city through the Davidic king.

Three other features of DC-V collaborate our arguments above.

(2) Accentuation of the Davidic idealization and democratization in DC-V. The Davidic characterization is increasingly predicated to the community.[266] We briefly rehearse this phenomenon from DC-III to V. In Ps 101:2, 6, "blamelessness" is both an attribute of the Davidic king and the people under him. The blessings sought for by the individual psalmist are given to the "children of Yhwh's servants" in 102:29.[267] Psalms that begin with an individual voice end with a collective voice (103:1, 20–22). Psalms 104–107 are community psalms. The king's personal questions are put before Yhwh *as* communal petitions in Psalm 108:11–14. Psalms 111–112 are contextualized within the "company" and "generation" of the "upright." Psalms 113 and 114 are identified with Yhwh's servants and the "house of Jacob." Psalm 114:2 even attributed "Judah" as "Yhwh's sanctuary" and "Israel" as Yhwh's dominion. That is, Yhwh's presence and victory are to be understood *as* his chosen people.

Psalms 115–118 conclude with communal praises to Yhwh. Although most of Ps 119 is expressed in the first person singular, the first four verses (119:1–4) introduce the psalm with generic characterization. As a whole, the SOA emphasizes the gathering (or return) of the multitude of Israel to the house of Yhwh in Zion even though some of them are expressed through an individual's voice (120–122).[268] Psalms 135–136 are communal psalms. In DC-V, four psalms (138–139, 142–143) are individual psalms. In Pss 140–141 and 144–145,[269] the individual is fused with the community.[270] Lama argues that Ps 145 is "the only psalm which explicitly presents

---

266. Robertson notes, "In the Psalter, the focus is on David as covenantal head of the nation. If he achieves victory, his people triumph. If he is overcome, the whole nation is defeated" (Robertson, *Flow of the Psalms*, loc. 5389).

267. Witt notes, "many recent commentators have also emphasized that the addition of the superscription strongly suggests that the psalm has now been democratized for an individual supplicant, who can relate to similar times of suffering" (Witt, "Hearing Psalm 102," 586).

268. Van der Lugt argues that "the word *m'lh* is never used for an ordinary pilgrimage, nor for one of the three annual feasts. The headings remind us of the return to Jerusalem from the exile in Babylon; see the expression *hm'lh mbbl* in Ezra 7, 9, used for a group of exiles returning to Palestine" (Van der Lugt, *CAS III*, 423).

269. This is not to say that distinction cannot be made between the individual Davidic king and the collective people. For example, Barbiero argues that Ps 144:1–11 identifies the individual king that is clearly set apart from the people in 144:12–15. See Barbiero, "Messianismus Und Theokratie," 44.

270. Cf. "poor" (אבינים; 140:13); "righteous" (צדיקים; 10:14); "upright" (ישרים; 140:14); "our bones" (עצמינו; 141:7); Pss 144:12–14; 145:4, 6–7, 10–21. Ballhorn notes that the movement in a psalm where an individual is mentioned, who confronts the wicked and the social structures they have created, followed by the voice of the righteous community is akin to how Psalm 1 is set up. This feature, to him,

Yhwh's kingdom[271] as universal and eternal."[272] Psalms 146–150 are all communal psalms as revealed by the *Hallelujah* superscriptions. Hence, apart from four psalms in DC-V and Pss 109–10 in DC-IV, most psalms (>85 percent) from DC-III onwards are communal and democratized to some extent.

Four other textual features in DC-V and the Final *Hallel* further explicate the democratizing phenomenon. First, there is a democratizing of the Davidic figure and associated Davidic blessings. In the POS analysis of the lexeme, "head," we have noted that this word, while clearly associated with the Davidic kingship in DC-I, is no longer clearly associated with it in the last three occurrences in DC-V (cf. 140:8, 10; 141:5). Specifically, Ps 141:5 notes that the wound by a righteous man is like the "anointing" of a Davidic king. In other words, the righteous community, in its fostering of mutual righteousness, *has become* a community of "priest-kings."

In Ps 144, Yhwh subdues the enemy of the Davidic king and by Ps 144:12–15, the paradisical community is ushered in.[273] Following this, the Davidic kingship begins to recede into the background and Yhwh's kingship comes to the foreground (145:1).[274] In Ps 145:11–12, the combination of three lexemes, "kingdom" (מלכות), "power" (גבורה), and "glory" (כבוד) used in close proximity with reference to Yhwh, is found elsewhere only in 1 Chr 29:28–30, referring to David's kingdom. The foregrounding of kingdom, rather than kingship, reinforces the concept of democratization in the Psalms.

Second, the community takes on the authoritative role of judge at the end of the Psalms. The congregation of the חסידים (149:1) in the Final *Hallel* is given the function to "execute vengeance" and judgment on the nations and kings based on "judgment written" (משפט כתוב; 149:9). This role of universal judgment and execution of "vengeance" (נקמה) is reserved solely as the prerogative of Yhwh elsewhere in the Psalter (18:48; 94:1).[275] Now, this prerogative is extended to the congregation of the godly.

---

reflects an "eschatological" connotation. See Ballhorn, *Zum Telos des Psalters*, 276.

271. At the center of Ps 145, the three consecutive use of "kingdom" (מלכות) in immediate succession is impressive (145:12–13) with an emphasis on Yhwh's eternal kingship. The noun, מלכות, occurs only six times in the entire Psalter, of which four instances are found in three successive verses in Ps 145:11–13. Cf. Pss 45:7; 103:19; 145:11–13.

272. Lama, *Placement of Psalm 145*, 5.

273. Todd highlights several important connections between Pss 137 and 144. In Ps 137, the captives could not sing a "song of Yhwh" in a foreign land but in Ps 144, the psalmist is to sing a "new song." The beatitude in Pss 137:8–9 and 144:15 further connect them. Todd argues that the enemies of Israel in Ps 137 ("Babylon" and "Edom") parallel the enemies of David in Ps 144. See Todd, *Remember, O Yahweh*, 119-22.

274. See also Howard, "Divine and Human Kingship," 206.

275. The noun, "vengeance" (נקמה), occurs only five times in the Psalter (18:48; 79:10; 94:1; 149:7). Apart from Ps 149:7; Yhwh is always the subject of executing "vengeance" on the nations (cf. 96:13; 98:9). This imagery is also found in Ps 2, where the messianic king executes judgment on the nations.

The Five Davidic Collections

This development is clear when we compare Ps 149 with Ps 101. In Ps 149, it is the community rather than the king who would execute judgment.[276]

Third, the idealized society takes centerstage as we move toward the end of the Psalter. Already in Ps 101, we see a "blameless" society ruled by a "blameless" Davidic king. This distinction between "blameless" king and "blameless" Israelites becomes increasingly vague. The Torah-pious lover of Yhwh's law[277] and the pilgrim at Yhwh's house[278] in Ps 119 can be interpreted as the Davidic king or otherwise. By the end of the Psalter, it is the חסידים (145:10; 148:14; 149:1, 5, 9), rather than the human king who is established in Zion.

The concept of justice and peace (שלום), envisioned of the communal life in Jerusalem in Pss 72 and 122, recur in Pss 127–28, where Yhwh, rather than man, is to be the builder of the house and city. The peaceful and just society seen in 132:13–18 and 144:12–15 are still associated with the Messianic king. However, in the Final *Hallel*, this blissful imagery of Zion is not associated with the human king (146:10; 147:2, 12–14; 149:1–2).[279] This idealized socio-community, free from distress and triumphant over nations, recalls the paradisical life envisioned in the Prologue. Bound by 1:1–2:12, the "blessed one" who walks in the Torah of Yhwh, is planted by streams of river, prospering and fruitful in all seasons. This blissful dwelling envisioned in the Prologue is now realized at the end of the Psalter.

Fourth, the Psalter concludes with the praise of Yhwh in the most extensive and all-embracing manner. All that has breath are called to praise Yhwh in Ps 150. Yhwh's sanctuary is now understood as "mighty heavens" (150:1). This praise of Yhwh, previously limited to the locale and congregation in Zion and Jerusalem (cf. 65:1; 102:22; 135:21; 146:10; 147:12), is now to be sounded universally in the "mighty heavens." Furthermore, the term, "prayer" (תפלה), with its last instance in 143:1, no longer recurs. Lament and prayers are transformed into praise.[280]

These features in DC-V and the Final *Hallel* show a development of the literary text as we move from DC-III to V.[281] The crescendo and convergence of idealization and democratization at the end of DC-V and the Final *Hallel* completes the Metanarrative of the Psalter. Here, the issues of injustice, ignominy, infirmity, and insecurity

276. See our discussion on Ps 108 in chapter 5.

277. Howard makes the case that, "Those kings who were the closest to the ideal—David, Hezekiah, and Josiah—were ones whom the texts especially emphasize as trusting in Yhwh and keeping the Law" (Howard, "Case for Kingship," 20). See also Pss 119:47, 48, 97, 113, 119, 127, 132, 159, 163, 165, 167.

278. Note that בבית מגורי in Ps 119:54 (cf. Gen 37:1; 47:9) is also translated "house of my pilgrimage."

279. The "king" in 149:2b refers to Yhwh rather than the human king because this "king" parallels the "maker" in 149:2a.

280. "Praise," on the other hand, is found in the last verse of the Psalter.

281. Ballhorn summarizes three theological shifts that can be detected as one move through the Psalter. First, there is a heightening of praise towards the end. Second, there is a shift from an emphasis on the Davidic kingdom to Yahweh's. Third, there is a tendency from individual speech to a collective mode, representing the entire congregation of Israel. See Ballhorn, *Zum Telos des Psalters*, 37.

suffered by the *chasidim* are finally resolved. Grol has rightly pointed out that when we arrive at 145:18–20—"the text sings of the global and universal kingship of God [over all creatures], but the attention is inescapably attracted by what this kingship means to the own group of chasidim."[282]

(3) All five DCs display a concentric structure. Each DC has a center. The first Davidic Collection *centers* around the establishment of the Davidic kingship and temple (18–21, 29–30), while DC-II centers around the fall of David (56–68). The superscriptions in Pss 38:1 and 70:1, near the end of DC-I and II, are the only two with the phrase, "for a memorial" (להזכיר).[283] These two instances are meant to be seen together as a commemoratory for the human David (cf. 1 Sam 4:18; 2 Sam 18:18; 1 Kgs 17:18). In contrast, the frames of DC-III–IV contrast a different royal Davidic figure that is both victorious and vindicated (101, 103, 108, 110). These two Collections also contain an afflicted Davidic figure at the center. The structures of DC-III–V are similar, having a Davidic or Yhwh kingship as bookends and the supplication/affliction of David at the center.[284] It is also striking that the last Davidic Psalm of DC-II, III, and V (86:15, 103:8, 145:8) repeats the formula "God is merciful and gracious, slow to anger and abounding in steadfast love and faithfulness" (Exod 34:6–7).[285]

In conclusion, the structural contours and profiles of all the DCs are similar. Like the Groups and Sections observed earlier, the DCs have a concentric structure around a central focus. At the same time, a linear development can be detected. The development begins with the establishment of David's kingship in DC-I followed by its fall in DC-II. At the end of DC-II, the Davidic kingship is turned over prophetically to a Solomonic-messianic figure. Then, the Davidic characterization shifts positively in DC-III, where a blameless and righteous Davidic king arises. Both DC-III and IV explicate and deepen the portrait of this Davidic king. At the end of DC-V, the Davidic kingship is now turned over to Yhwh. Between the kingships of the historical David (DC-I and II) and Yhwh (end DC-V), the kingship of an ideal messianic priest-king is pictured both as a condemned figure and vindicated ruler from Zion. Figure 64 summarizes and illustrates our entire study of the five DCs.

---

282. Grol, "David and His *Chasidim*," 323.

283. The *hiphil* infinite construct conjugation of זכר occurs only in these two locations in the Psalter.

284. Auwers, *La Composition*, 60.

285. If we consider Ps 86 as the last Davidic psalm of DC-II. The three psalms containing this formula has been highlighted by Groenewald in his study of the Yhwh's *hesed*, though he does not see that these three psalms are structurally significant. Groenewald, "God Abounding," 52–65.

Davidic Collection	Concentric Structure			Linear Progression
	Front	Center	End	
DC-I (3–41)	YHWH's kingship (8–9)	Establishment of David's kingship and Temple (18–21, 29–30)	Davidic distress and supplication (38)	Begins with YHWH's kingship. King David broken (sacrifice accepted). Kingship turned over to a Solomonic king ↓
DC-II (51–71, 86)	David's fall begins with Nathan's judgment (51)	David's life threatened (56–64)	David at the brink of death/Davidic distress and supplication (71/86)	
DC-III (101–103)	Blameless Davidite (101)	Afflicted figure (102)	David the Song leader (103)	Ideal, condemned-vindicated king-priest. ↓
DC-IV (108–110)	Victorious Davidic king entering Zion (108)	Afflicted and condemned Davidic figure (109)	Vindicated and victorious Davidic rule from Zion (110)	
DC-V (138–145)	YHWH's kingship (138)	Davidic distress and supplication (140–143)	Davidic figure handover kingship to YHWH (145)	Ideal king turned over kingship to YHWH in the end

Figure 64: Summary of the Five Davidic Collections

Messianic and Eschatological Program in The MT Psalter?

We began our study of the DCs by reviewing Gillingham's contentions that any Messianic or eschatological elements found in the Psalter are late and anachronistic. We questioned these contentions by pointing out that by the time of the LXX, Messianic (or proto-Messianic) and eschatological elements were already present (before the Maccabean times) and that the postexilic prophets had provided the fodder for Messianic and eschatological formulations. We are now in a good position to complete our argument for this chapter.

Our study of the five DCs has demonstrated that the Davidic characterization of the Psalter is not haphazard. There are clear structural and thematic developments. Specifically, its *telos* highlights an ideal and victorious Davidic king who would usher in an era of permanent social bliss. It is possible to argue that the Psalter, by its composition, arrangement, and trajectory, has a Messianic and eschatological program. The Psalter is, in other words, a reception of the Davidic Covenant.

By "Messianic," I mean an "expectation" or "hope" that refers to "a royal [Davidic] figure who will play a crucial role in the last days."[286] This is differentiated from

---

286. As understood in rabbinic and early Christian traditions. Juel, "Messiah," 889–90.

"the messiah" who is understood as a human monarch in the Davidic dynasty.[287] This "Messiah" is also deemed as "any figure expected to introduce an era of eternal bliss, regardless of the terminology used in the source."[288] Our understanding of "Messiah" in this book is similar to what Gillingham argues for as a "one-for-all figure coming either and the end of time or heralding it."[289]

Similarly, the term, "eschatological," can be best understood by Hoffman[290] and Ladd's definition. Hoffman posits three *prima facie* conditions for understanding "eschatological." It is future, universal, and miraculous, and as a whole, concerned with the elements of "doom" (judgment) and "salvation." Ladd, however, argues that it also has a present time aspect.[291]

For Ladd, the eschatological kingdom of God is "present" in history as long as the activity of the power of God is manifested within history.[292]

I have included the brief definitions of "Messianic" and "eschatological" only at this point as an independent verification so that our proposition of the Messianic

---

287. Murphy, "Notes on Old Testament," 7. See also Rose's definition and differentiation in Rose, "Messiah," *DOTP*, 566. Longman also differentiates "messianic expectations" from "Christological expectations." He notes that the messianic "expectation of a future royal or priestly deliverer" is not simply seen as Jesus Christ being the expected Messiah. Longman, "Messiah," *DOTWPW*, 467.

288. Messianic hope is also understood as "expectations of a definitive change in history which is not brought about by a particular deliverer." This concept appears "in studies by historians of religion and by social anthropologists, who use them in discussions of developments in Western history and in other cultures" (De Jong, "Messiah," *ABD*, 4:777–78).

289. Gillingham, "Messiah in the Psalms," 211. Elsewhere, she notes, "The broadest definition (upheld in different ways by Jews and Christians alike) is that the 'Messianism' is a general, idealized expression of hope for a new age of peace and justice-an age inaugurated by God himself, in order to restore his own ancient people, to be mediated through his chosen deliverer. The narrower definition (associated with a more particular Zionist expectation) is that it is about the national deliverance of Israel, involving the re-establishment of the Davidic monarchy, the reunification of the two kingdoms of Israel and Judah, the return of the Diaspora Jews, the reconstitution of Jerusalem Temple worship, and the destruction of hostile Gentile powers" (Gillingham, "Messianic Prophecy and the Psalms," 117).

290. Hoffman, "Eschatology in the Book of Jeremiah," 77.

291. This can be (a) "futuristic" in orientation; (b) present reality ("realized" or "existential") or (c) both futuristic and present. Dodd's "realized eschatology," according to Ladd, "has to do not with the last things, temporally conceived, but with those things which possess finality and ultimacy of meaning. The kingdom of God does not mean the eschatological order at the end of history, but the eternally present realm of God. The coming of the kingdom means the entrance of the eternal into time, the confrontation of the finite by the infinite." Those who argue from a non-eschatological perspective interpret them as an "event in which God becomes unmediated presence, and the result is 'the end of the world': before them stands either salvation or judgment. They sustain a new relationship with both their past and the future, in this sense, time has come to an end" (Ladd, *Presence of the Future*, 17, 36).

292. If the eschatological kingdom of God is the manifestation of God's power operative in that realm, then any manifestation of God's power can also be understood as the presence of the kingdom of God itself. Therefore, Ladd adds that "if however, the kingdom is the reign of God, not merely in the human heart but dynamically active in the person of Jesus and in human history, then it becomes possible to understand how the kingdom of God can be present and future, inward and outward, spiritual and apocalyptic. For the redemptive royal activity of God could act decisively more than once and manifest itself powerfully in more than one way in accomplishing the divine end" (Ladd, *Presence of the Future*, 42).

nature of the Psalter is not guided by these definitions to begin with. Consider the following points:

1. There is a trajectory moving from an initial establishment of Israel's kingship and temple (Books I), to its brokenness (Books II–III) and finally to salvation (Books IV–V) through the Psalter. The elements of "doom" and "salvation" are visible. The broken kingship and Zion-city-temple in Books II and III ("doom") are restored at the end of the Psalter ("salvation"; 144:12–15; 147:2). In the final *Hallel*, the doom of the wicked and salvation of the *chasidim* are also depicted.

2. The distinctions between an earthly and idealized Davidic king are observed as we move across the DCs. The idealized Davidic figure is a kingly figure (anointed) whose rule is universal, transcendent and victorious. This idealized figure is presented as the "blameless" king-priest in the order of Melchizedek who rules from Zion. The miraculous/transcendent nature can also be seen in how he is both afflicted and vindicated at the same time.

3. The definitive Messianic character is an ushering in of a paradisical, just and peaceful era in and after Pss 144–145 by a Davidic king. Supplications give way to exaltation and praise after Ps 143. Israel is depicted in gladness and honor, executing universal punishment on the nations (149). This new era of bliss identifies a time when the afflicted Israel is no longer in distress.

4. A trajectory of moving from the particular to the universal is increasingly seen (esp. Book V). At the end of the Psalter, all peoples are drawn towards the centrality of Yhwh kingship in the Final *Hallel*. All kings, peoples and nations, young or old, and all that have breath are to praise Yhwh at his sanctuary.

5. Miraculous events at the cosmic level are depicted in the Final *Hallel*. Angels and the created realm above fulfill Yhwh's word and praise him (147:15–18; 148:1–10). The sea monsters and the deep, likewise, praise him.

6. The dilemma between the present/future aspects of time is also especially evident from DC-III to V. On one hand, the Messianic figure is depicted as one who exerts his power over his enemies ushering in the blissful era (144–145). On the other hand, this same idealized figure is also presented in history as the suffering petitioner and victorious ruler from Zion in Pss 101–103, 108–110. This present/future, afflicted yet transcendental characterization of the messianic king represents Yhwh's operative power *both* in history and the *eschaton*.

In addition, our analysis corresponds well with Starling's identification of "five elements of messianic hope."[293] The Royal Psalms cannot be read in isolation from each

---

293. (1) The Messianic hope is a Davidic hope. It rests upon Yhwh's covenant with David; (2) The Messianic-Davidic hope represents the hope of Israel. The Davidic Covenant is also a "democratized" Covenant between Yhwh and Israel; (3) The Messianic hope is a hope for the nations. All the ends of the earth shall be blessed through this Messianic king; (4) The Messianic hope is a vindication of the

other and must be read in the context of the entire Psalter.[294] "It does appear that the editors of the Psalter sought to direct their readers to a particular understanding of the future Davidic king by placing some of the kingship psalms in a very specific interpretive context."[295]

Therefore, we have shown that Messianic and eschatological elements are present in the Psalter when we adopt a macrostructural perspective across the five DCs. There is no need to preclude Messianic or eschatological expectations at the time of the final composition of the Psalter as Gillingham and others have argued.

The reason why a number of Psalms scholars have deemed the Psalter to be devoid of any Messianic and eschatological references is twofold: Royal Davidic psalms are studied as individual psalms (without any macrostructural appreciation) and there is an over-dependence on historical royal court-style parallels found in the ANE. This is not to say that Royal Davidic psalms could not have origins associated with the ANE parallels but in the final composition, the editor(s) of the Psalter had "reprogrammed" the understanding of kingship within the concept of the Davidic covenant, which is Messianic in thrust.

The Five-Davidic Collections in The Horizon of the Psalter

Finally, to argue that the Psalter functioning with Messianic program which expounds, unfurls and realizes the entailments of the Davidic covenant, we need to further describe the role of the five Davidic Collections within the entire Psalter. The following figure captures this:

---

righteous suffering Messiah, who represents the suffering poor, who will become the "godly"; (5) The Messianic hope is the expression of the rule of Yhwh. The rule of the Messiah is inseparable from the rule of Yhwh. See Starling, "Messianic Hope in the Psalms," 127–30.

294. For instance, if we isolate the genre of Royal psalms, and view Pss 101, 110 without considering Pss 102–3 and 108–9, we would have missed the important structural parallel as argued in this chapter. This is the problem with Saur's work on the Royal Psalms. Saur argues that the Psalter is "*protomessianisch*." His thesis is similar although we arrive at the conclusions independently and differently. See especially, Saur, *Die Königspsalmen*; "Die Theologische Funktion," 693–96.

295. Grant, "Kingship Psalms," *DOTWPW*, 377.

The Five Davidic Collections

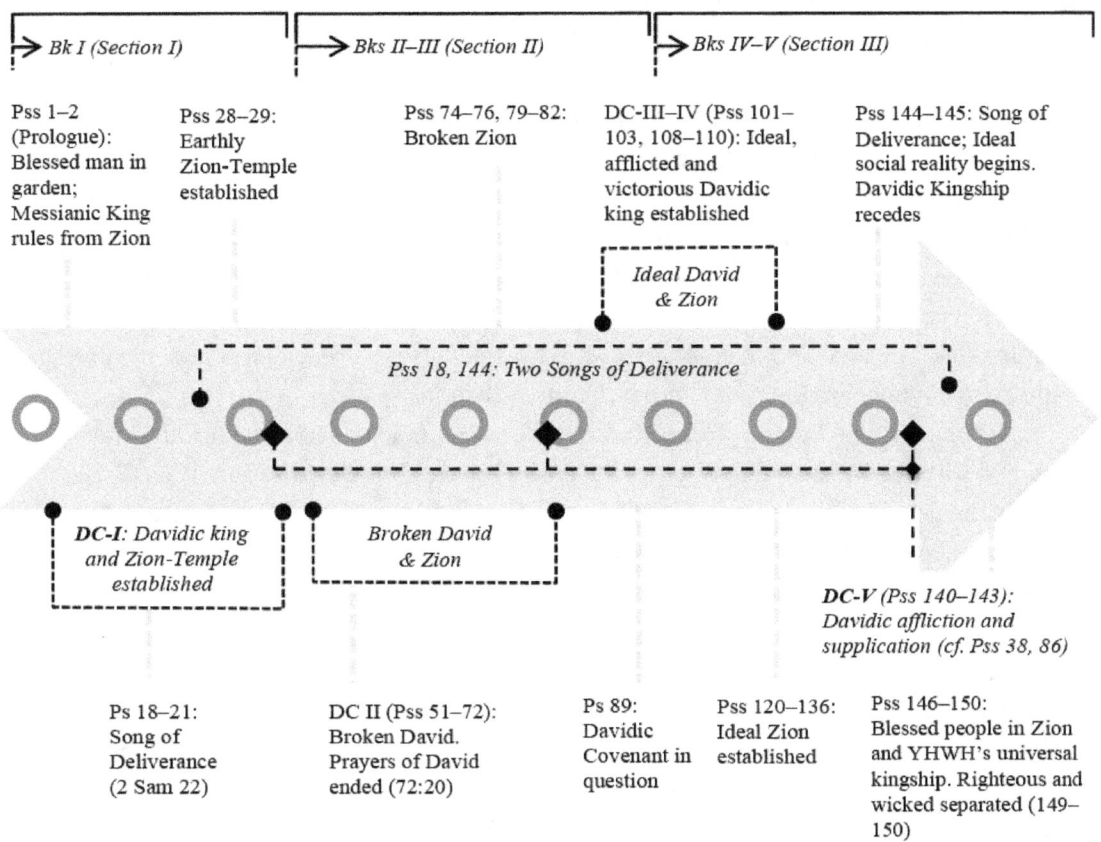

Figure 65: The Five Davidic Collections in the Horizon of the Psalter

In chapter one, the programmatic nature of the Prologue and the trajectory traced by the concentric and parallel triptychs of Pss 1 and 2 was established (Figure 9). The first and last panes of Pss 1–2 characterize the *way* and *outcome* of the righteous and wicked respectively. At the center of both psalms, the *attributes* of the righteous and Messianic king are highlighted respectively. The concept of the Davidic covenant (in particular 2 Sam 7), and how its motifs are placed at prominent locations in the Psalter have also been reviewed. Thematically, the Prologue which highlights the Torah-pious figure flourishing in the paradisical garden and the transcendental messianic king reigning over enemies is, in essence, a picture of the Davidic covenant. Through the rule of the Messianic king, the righteous will be blessed.

Structurally, the Prologue, as a triptych, parallels the entire Psalter, which is also a triptych in three Sections. Book I, the first pane of the Psalter (cf. first pane of Prologue), depicts the establishment of the Davidic kingship and Zion in the midst of opposition. This establishment is the central motif of DC-I. Books II–III, the center pane of the Psalter (cf. center pane of the Prologue), capture the broken Zion and Davidic king (DC-II), in vivid contrast with the Prologue which emphasizes a flourishing paradisical garden and transcendental king. Books IV–V, the third pane of the

261

Psalter (cf. third pane of Prologue), depict the blessed outcome of the righteous at Zion and judgment of wicked at the end, through the establishment of an ideal king (DC-III–IV) and Zion.

The Songs of Deliverance in Pss 18 and 144 are two strategic locations that mark the establishment of two Davidic kingships. The first the establishment of the human monarch and the second is that of the Messianic king, who will usher in a final period of bliss. These two locations also parallel two key references of David's victories over his enemies in 2 Sam 7 and 22. Between these two locations, the storyline of kingship and Zion go through a depressing brokenness in Books II–III before the turning point in Book IV. The final DC-V emphasizes David's (and also the *chasidim*'s) patient supplication, an unchanging motif across the three Sections.

Thus, the five Davidic Collections is a striking macro-design, skillfully intertwined with the Metanarrative across the entire Psalter. The Davidization of the Psalter by the design of these Davidic Collections allows the three (or four) identities and storylines to converge—the monarch David, the Messianic king and the *chasidim*. The reader of the Psalms is the fourth story, merging with the story of the *chasidim* and interfusing with the larger plotline of Yʜwʜ's purposes.

Before we conclude this chapter, let us reflect again on the plausibility of our interpretation from the perspective of the final editors or original readers. The structural design of the five Davidic Collections provides a clear parallel to the five-book structure of the Psalter and the Pentateuch. Such structural parallels are not difficult for readers to identify. If such macrostructural design was indeed intentional, why would the final editors choose to adopt such a shape? Scholars generally agree that the five-book structure was intended to lend canonical legitimacy to the Psalter.[296] This intention would be fulfilled with the five-book structure of the Psalter, but with the five Davidic Collections, there is a further invitation for the reader to connect and compare the dual Mosaic-Davidic figures. The figure of David is now set on par with Moses.

To be sure, the reader would be confronted with this comparison right at the beginning of the Psalter. Psalms 1 and 2 clearly contrast the motifs of Deuteronomic Torah piety with the messianic kingship. Our discussions on Book IV is another clear supporting point. The Mosaic Ps 90 and the entire Pss 90–92 form a series of three psalms associated with Moses.[297] These three psalms form an inclusio with the Davidic Pss 101–103 around the Yʜwʜ *Malak* psalms at the center. The idealized kingly (and "blameless") figure ruling with integrity in his house in Pss 101 invites comparison with Moses who is also faithful in God's house (Heb 3:2–5). Since Ps 92 clearly alludes to the Song of Moses (cf. Deut 32), a comparison between Moses and David as song leaders in Pss 92 and 103 is inevitable.

---

296. Studying the formation of the Psalter, this was one of the main conclusions reached by David Willgren. See Willgren, *Formation of the "Book."*

297. See esp. Gundersen, "Davidic Hope."

Grant's study on Pss 1–2, 18–19 and 118–19 in *The King as Exemplar* elaborates on the Mosaic-Davidic juxtaposition. From the perspective of the readers, these parallels are stark and consistent across the Psalter. Why did the final editors of the Psalms undertake such juxtaposition? I suggest that the timely theological message that proceeds from the structural design of the Psalter is twofold: an exhortation and encouragement. The horrors of the exile, the demise of Israel's kingship and the destruction of the temple *as* Yhwh's punishment of Israel's covenantal unfaithfulness must be grasped and internalized (Amos 2). Such reflections are not uncommon in exilic and postexilic texts (cf. Mic 3; Ezek 22:6; Neh 9:34; 2 Chr 28:19). In other words, there is a theological exhortation to return to covenantal faithfulness.

At the same time, one cannot reflect on Yhwh's covenant with his people without being encouraged by the covenantal promises. Readers would recall that God would raise up a better prophet (Deut 18:18), priest (1 Sam 2:35) and king (2 Sam 7:12–13). God would also rebuild Jerusalem that had been mired in ruins (Isa 44:26–28). Through a Righteous Branch, God will gather the scattered people of Israel and make them dwell securely (Jer 23:4–8; Jer 30:9–10). We have, at various junctures in the book, pointed out how messianic emphases in postexilic prophetic books (e.g., Micah and Zechariah) correspond to the messianic tendencies in the Psalter.[298] Likewise, we have also discussed the messianic emphases present in the LXX Psalter. Messianic themes were also present in various Second Temple literature.[299]

These texts cannot be separated from any serious reflections of Israel's future predicament in the postexilic period. Thus, the Psalter brings together two of the most important covenantal traditions of ancient Israel (Mosaic and Davidic) at a time when the experience of God's wrath for covenantal unfaithfulness (exile) was still raw and messianic hopes wanting.

In short, the message and theology arising from the juxtaposition of Moses and David, and integration of Torah piety and kingship in the Psalter is accomplished by skillful poetic structures and intertextual cognition. Our proposed overarching Metanarrative of the Psalter and democratization of the Davidic promises have a net effect consistent with the message we have proposed. Our reading of the Psalter shows that the final editors were sensitive to the theological and existential struggles of postexilic Israel readership and have crafted a coherent and significant message with poetical finesse to address these issues.

---

298. See esp. Mitchell, *Message of the Psalter*.

299. Wright identifies four different kinds of Second Temple literature with heightened messianic tones: Qumran texts [4Q174; 1QSa 2:11–21; 1QSb 5:23–29], Pseudepigrapha [*Psalms of Solomon* 17:21–32], historical texts [*Jewish War* 6.312–15], Apocryphal texts [*4 Ezra* 11–12]. Wright, *New Testament*, 307–20.

Summary

- In this chapter, we argue that the five Davidic Collections are carefully designed to identify, first, the establishment of a human monarch who later falls. This is then followed by the establishment of an ideal messianic Davidic king, who ushers in the paradisical shalom for the people of God.

- Precluding Messianic and eschatological concepts at the time of the final composition of the Hebrew Psalter need not be sustained.

- DC-I focuses on the Davidic rule in Yhwh's house. It is concerned with the establishment of human kingship and Yhwh's house. This is supported by the POS of "head."

- DC-II marks the fall of the Davidic king. This can be shown by the specific and explicit accounts of David's enemies, the design of the 13 historical Davidic superscriptions, motifs of an acceptable sacrifice to Yhwh in association with the brokenness of David, and the postscript in Ps 72:20 in parallel with 2 Sam 23:1.

- The 13 historical superscriptions can be organized into two trajectories comprising of 3+1 references in DC-I and 8+1 references in DC-II and V. The first trajectory in DC-I traces the establishment of David's victorious rule. The second trajectory in DC-II traces the brokenness of David. Both trajectories end with the motif of Davidic supplications.

- DC-III marks a turning point in the characterization of David and presents a blameless king. DC-III has structural and thematic parallels with the triptychs Pss 90–92 and Pss 108–110 (DC-IV).

- DC-IV deepens the characterization of the Davidic figure. He is simultaneously condemned by wrongful accusations and vindicated to rule victoriously over the nations from Zion. He is also presented as the "new" Joshua who leads Yhwh's people into the garden of bliss.

- DC-V has a central focus on supplication and distress and is framed by motifs of Yhwh's kingship. The important theological message, based on a recurring final literary frame, is that distress and supplication will continue to characterize the Davidic community until the ideal social-reality arrives (Pss 144–145).

- The five Davidic Collections correspond well with the Metanarrative of the Psalter. These five DCs display the three dimensions of reading. First, they contain a central focus because of their concentric structures. Second, a linear trajectory can be traced across the five Collections. Third, these five Collections can be read alongside the Samuel narratives. As a whole, the Psalter has a Messianic and eschatological *telos*.

- The five DCs expound, unfurl and realize the entailments of the Davidic covenant crystallized in the Prologue.

5

Numerical Devices, Alphabetic Acrostics or Compositions, and Superscriptions

When read on their own as self-contained units, this theological context escapes the reader's attention. When read with an eye for unifying thematic arrangement, however, we can begin to see how the editors of this collection perceived its fragmentary elements to cohere within a greater theological reality that encompassed their own day and age, namely the divine economy.[1]

—Philip Sumpter

The architecture that editors have given the Psalter is that of a book (ספר), adopting typically scribal techniques (such as the alphabetical process).[2]

—Jean-Marie Auwers

Once the function of the acrostic is understood, it can be seen as integral to the message of the psalm.[3]

—Reuven Kimelman

THE FOREGOING ANALYSES HAVE made it clear that a number of techniques have been used to structure the entire Psalter into its major sections or collections. These techniques include tacit, explicit, and thematic literary elements or devices. They also

---

1. Sumpter, "Coherence of Psalms 15–24," 209.
2. Auwers, "Le Psautier," 87. My translation.
3. Kimelman, "Psalm 145," 49.

operate at different levels. Parallelisms occur a the line level as well as across a number of psalms. A certain theme can develop and be traced across the Psalter.

Perhaps two of the most obvious formal devices in the macrostructure of the Psalter are book divisions and superscriptions. In the opening chapter, we have shown how numerological devices and alphabetical thinking contribute to the literary structure of the Psalms. Specifically, we have discussed individual psalms such as Pss 1, 2, 25, 37, 119, 106 and 150. A primary focus is the use of keyword(s) at the mathematical center of a psalm. This technique may work beyond (e.g., twin Pss 1–2) or within a psalm (e.g., *Aleph* and *Bet* stanzas of Ps 119). We have also seen how certain symbolic numbers (e.g., "7," "12") are associated with the POS technique.

We have previously noted the existence of extrabiblical Mesopotamian and Egyptian acrostics and poems that appropriate numerical sequences (e.g., the Babylonian theodicy; Prayer of *Nabu-ushebshi*; Hymn to the goddess Ishtar; Hymn to Amon), suggesting that Hebrew poets of the past were acquainted with such techniques. Moreover, epigraphic evidence of abecedary materials in ancient Israel (uncovered in Lachish, Arad, Kuntillat Ajrud) also suggests the possibility of ancient readers possessing such literary knowledge, though the extent of that knowledge cannot be ascertained.

Many of these acrostics embed cryptic messages within the poem, invoking deities or the identity of its composers. The use of mezostics in the poem indicates that the structural form and content are often integrated to the overall meaning. Within Palestine, inscriptions unearthed have revealed that abecedaries, literary features such as anaphoras, inclusions, introductions, and symbolism in written works were already widespread in the eighth century BCE. In particular, one of the earliest Hebrew poems (the Song of the Sea) uses techniques to centralize Yhwh's kingship and to develop a storyline integrated within a poem. Hence, we can assume that the final editors and readers of the Psalter would have been familiar with these techniques and rhetorical features.

In this chapter, I postulate that numerical devices, alphabetic acrostics, alphabetic compositions, and superscriptions work together as formal macrostructuring devices throughout the MT Psalter. I also argue that numerical techniques are used to structure individual psalms, denote alphabetical acrostics or compositions and codify headings in the Psalms. We will begin with numerical devices in the Psalms.

Numerical Devices and Mathematical Centers (Bazak, Labuschagne, and van der Lugt)

Jacob Bazak speaks of a certain poetic technique in biblical poetry, termed "numerical structure," a device that is "no longer in use today," which may "escape the eyes (or the ears) of a modern reader."[4] For Bazak, Labuschagne, van der Lugt, David Mitchell,

---

4. Bazak also quotes Alastair Fowler who wrote in the foreword of *Silent Poetry: Essays in Numerological Analysis*, that "numerological criticism analyses literary structures of various kinds, ordered by

and others,⁵ this technique emphasizes "a sentence which is of central importance by placing it in the numerical centre of the psalm, i.e., the beginning of that central sentence is a certain number of words from the opening of the psalm, while the end of the sentence is the same number of words from the end of the psalm."⁶

A common example cited is Psalm 23, where there are 26 words before the expression "for you are with me" (v. 4) and 26 words after. The number 26 is also the numerical sum⁷ of the Tetragrammaton, thus infusing the text with a symbolic meaning.⁸ This numerical phenomenon is also found in Ps 92, where 52 (26x2) words flank both sides of the center expression, ואתה מרום לעלם יהוה (92:9). Excluding the superscription, there are also 7 verses before and after this central expression. Furthermore, in Ps 92, the name of God is repeated 7x and there are 7 "different epithets" assigned to the wicked and righteous respectively. Bazak argues that "it is hardly possible that all these are mere coincidence; it would be more reasonable to conclude that numbers were of great significance to the poet."⁹

On many occasions, a *meaningful* or *rhetorical* center can also take the form of a central colon, verse, strophe or even canto. For instance, Labuschagne identifies the word עזרם as the center word in Ps 115, with 66 words on each side.¹⁰ However, the *entire* colon (v. 9b), עזרם ומגנם הוא ("he is their help and shield"), surrounded by 19

---

numerical symmetries or expressing number symbolism. In poetry, the numerological structure often forms a level of organization intermediate in scale and externality between metrical patterns on the one hand and structure as ordinarily understood on the other. As such, it constitutes a huge subject, perhaps even larger than most medieval and Renaissance scholars working today have begun to realize. It is probably no exaggeration to say that most good literary works—indeed, most craftsmanlike works—were organized at this stratum from antiquity until the eighteenth century at least. Moreover, numerological criticism is potentially a more fruitful subject than large-scale prosody, since it has more bearing on meaning, thematic content, structure and other adjacent strata" (Bazak, "Numerical Devices in Biblical Poetry," 333). Fowler's quote is also found in Labuschagne, "Significant Compositional Techniques," 585.

5. Labuschagne, "Significant Compositional Techniques"; *Numerical Secrets of the Bible*. See especially Labuschagne, "General Introduction," 1–19; van der Lugt, "Mathematical Centre," 643–51; Knohl, "Sacred Architecture," 189–97. In one of the latest studies, David Mitchell highlights the use of the numbers "8," "15," "25," "26," "34," and "51" in the organization of the Songs of Ascents. See Mitchell, *Songs of Ascents*, 15–26.

6. Bazak, "Numerical Devices in Biblical Poetry," 334.

7. Lubuschagne avoids the term, "*gematria*," as it is "generally associated with kabbalistic speculations and the pseudo-science of numerology" (Labuschagne, "Significant Compositional Techniques," 601).

8. Rand lists a number of examples supporting the use of the number 26 in the HB. He argues that "the urge to include the name if only in veiled, arithmetical form stems from the Israelites' need for constant reassurance of the presence of God. A central theme, repeated many times in the Pentateuch, is God's promise, 'and I will be with you,' and a 7 numerical code was a deliberate art form used by the biblical writer to suggest the divine presence" (Rand, "Numerological Structure in Biblical Literature," 53).

9. Bazak, "Numerical Devices in Biblical Poetry," 335. See also Auwer's comment on Bazak (Auwers, *La Composition*, 93–94).

10. Labuschagne "Psalm 115," 1–5; Van der Lugt, *CAS III*, 265–66.

cola on both sides, functions as the meaningful center at the level of the colon. The entire strophe (vv. 9–11), likewise, functions as a middle strophe, framed by three strophes on either side.[11] Hence, the "meaningful center" (by Labuschagne's definition) of a psalm can be the arithmetical center word or the poetical central colon, verse, strophe or canto.

Labuschagne names his technique "logotechnical quantitative structural analysis" (or "Logotechnique"[12]) and argues that such an analysis should be part of proper "literary analysis."[13] Besides the numbers 7 and 26, Labuschagne considers the numbers 10, 11 and 17 as significant text "structuring device[s]."[14] Other numbers such as 13, 14, 15, 43, 55 and 100 are also considered important.[15]

Pieter van der Lugt is another scholar who places an emphasis on the center of a text based on quantitative analysis.[16] His magnum opus, the three-volume *Cantos and Strophes in Biblical Hebrew Poetry*, is an extensive study of the higher poetical text structure where quantitative analysis figures prominently.[17] He argues that when "the focal idea of a composition is highlighted by one or more formal features—say,

---

11. For instance, van der Lugt argues that the two verses in Ps 140:7–8 are the rhetorical center of the psalm. These two verses stand as the four center cola surrounded by 12 cola on each side (also the two verselines are enveloped by 6 verselines on either side). Labuschagne argues that the meaningful center of Ps 148 can be considered at the canto level (vv. 7–10). See van der Lugt, "Mathematical Centre," 646; Labuschagne "Psalm 148," 1–5.

12. According to Labuschagne, this term was coined by Claus Schedl who saw it as "the art of numerical composition," "word-art," "language-art" or "compositional art." Labuschagne, *Numerical Secrets of the Bible*, 175. See also Schedl, *Baupläne des Wortes Einführung*, 22.

13. Labuschagne argues that this kind of analysis "is in fact *numerical criticism*; [it] is not a separate discipline but a supplementary branch of *literary criticism*, of which the first and foremost task is to explore and describe the literary architecture of a given text" (Labuschagne, "Significant Compositional Techniques," 587). See Labuschagne, *Numerical Secrets of the Bible*, 2.

14. The number "7" expresses "fullness, completeness, abundance and the maximum," and "imitates the shape of the Menorah"; "11," the sum of 7 and 4, and is a number of "fulfillment." "17" and "26" are related to the divine name. The "sum of positional values is "Y(10) + H(5) + W(6) + H(5) = 26"; and the sum of their digit values "Y(1+0) + H(5) + W(6) + H(5) = 17." The word, "glory" (כבד), also adds up to 17 (11+2+4) or 26 (20+2+4) as *kaph* can represent 11 or 20. The significance of this is that these two numbers "signify not only the name but the glory of God" (cf. Exod 33:17–23). Interestingly, Labuschagne considers the numbers "12" and "40," while occurring frequently in the Bible, not "text structuring numbers." "55" is the "triangular number of 10 or the sum of the numbers of 1 through 10." The word, "glory," can also be written as כבוד, and in this case, is represented by the numbers 23 (11+2+6+4) and 32 (20+2+6+4) which add up to 55. Labuschagne, "Significant Compositional Techniques," 586. For more information on the use of significant numbers in both the OT and NT, see Labuschagne, *Numerical Secrets of the Bible*, 22–40, 57–67, 69–73, 82–83, 89–91.

15. The number "13" is the sum of אחד (1+8+4=13) which indicates "Yhwh who is אחד one"; "14" is the sum of דוד "David" (4+6+4); "40" is used frequently in the Bible; "15" is the sum of יה "Yah" (10+5); "43" is 17+26 (the number of Yhwh's name); "100" is also the "number of completeness, perfection and full measure." See Koorevaar, "Psalter as a Structured Theological Story," 583, 587; Mitchell, *Songs of Ascents*, 17.

16. Van der Lugt, "Mathematical Centre," 643–45; *CAS II*, 505–551.

17. Ho, "Review of P. van der Lugt," 89–91.

by a quantitative phenomenon—[it is designated as] the *rhetorical center*."[18] However, he does not limit the search for a rhetorical center to quantitative means. He studies verbal repetitions, which include conjoined prepositions, conjunctions and suffixes, and undertakes an extensive review of how these repetitions occur at the strophe, canto and entire compositional levels. The manner which repetitions recur often is in line with his strophic structures and highlights the poem's rhetorical center. Van der Lugt provides a more detailed thematic discussion in the analysis of each psalm than Labuschagne.

The following points summarize the methodologies adopted by Labuschagne and van der Lugt in identifying a meaningful/rhetorical center in a text. (1) Their work is based on a synchronic analysis of the Codex L, while allowing for text-critical operations when strong evidence for emendation avails.[19] (2) Words, cola, verselines, strophes, cantos and divine names in each psalm are counted. Superscriptions and words such as *hallelujah* (as a header or coda), *selah* and doxologies (e.g., 106:48) are *not* counted.[20] (3) Words joined by *maqqef* are counted separately. (4) Meaningful/rhetorical centers are often "enveloped by an equal number of words on either side."[21] The smallest unit of such centers is usually a colon, though they can occur as verseline, strophe or even canto. (5) The identified center is deemed meaningful/rhetorical when it highlights a succinct theme or message, and word counts (either the number of words at the center or the enveloping words) are associated with divine name numbers (e.g., 7, 17, 26).[22] When these conditions are met, the centers are deemed as indicative of intentional design. (6) When the divine name (including אדני and אלהים) occurs with unusual frequency[23] or at pivotal locations (e.g., 39:8; 13:4), it

---

18. Pieter van der Lugt calls such a center identified quantitatively, a "rhetorical center" while Labuschagne calls it "meaningful center." Although the terms used by them are different, their method of counting is generally identical. For a comparison of "meaningful center" and "rhetorical center" of individual psalms between these two scholars, see Appendix A. While the centers identified by them are very similar, individual nuances, however, come from their delineations of poetical units (such as colon, verselines, strophes and cantos). They may differ in the pairing of certain psalms and addressing textual issues. Van der Lugt, *CAS II*, 506.

19. Labuschagne's approach is "strictly synchronic" while van der Lugt's is not. Van der Lugt is more open to text-critical operations. Cf. Labuschagne, "General Introduction," 9; van der Lugt, *CAS III*, 12.

20. For Labuschagne and van der Lugt, the smallest meaningful building block is the word. As such, syllables are not counted (contra Fokkelman and Freedman). Note that the header, *hodu* (e.g., 136:1) is counted. There is no apparently strict consensus on what constitutes headers. Van der Lugt notes that Fokkelmann counts *hallelujah* in Ps 146:1. Van der Lugt, *CAS III*, 544; Labuschagne, "Psalm 104," 1–9.

21. Van der Lugt, "Mathematical Centre," 643.

22. For Labuschagne, "In order to qualify as meaningful, an apparently suitable centre has to consist of a key-word or a phrase expressing a thought or idea that can be interpreted as crucial or essential from the perspective of the author." Labuschagne, "Significant Compositional Techniques," 596. For examples on how some of these numbers function in identifying the numerical center of a psalm, see *CAS II*, 526–36.

23. See the examples of Pss 8, 23, 39, 125 and 131 in van der Lugt, *CAS II*, 514–15.

may also indicate a rhetorical center.²⁴ (7) Rhetorical centers can also be detected by sudden shifts from the second person speech to the third or by the personal pronoun, אתה, used in addressing God. (8) The numerical compositional technique can be used as a "criterion to check the correctness of [the] delimitation of literary units"²⁵ or to uncover the latent key message of the psalm.

While I find their work intriguing and detailed, three concerns deserve attention. First, when a meaningful/rhetorical center of a poem is considered beyond the level of a single word or pair of words, the flexibility of identifying it as a center increases. For instance, in Psalm 139, the single center word is בבטן ("in the womb"; v. 13). This word, in itself, is not exactly meaningful but by expanding the number of words to the colon level, we arrive at the entire 139:13b ("You wove me in my mother's womb"). However, this colon is neither at the center by word-count nor by colon-count. It is possible, nonetheless, to add one colon *before* and two cola *after* to form a larger four-cola meaningful center (139:13a–14b). Yet stopping at Ps 139:14b is not completely satisfactory, so Labuschagne argues that the two verses Ps 139:13–14 (5 cola) is the meaningful center, at the strophe level!²⁶ Labuschagne explains,

> It stands to reason that every psalm has a pivot: 2 middle words in an even number and 1 in an odd number. Such a center is not necessarily deliberately designed or meaningful. Therefore, taking this center as starting point, one has to proceed to detect a larger center that is meaningful and presumably intended as such, either on word level or in terms of the rhetorical structure: the pivotal colon(s), verseline(s), or strophe.²⁷

In other words, there is flexibility to move from the word or colon level to higher level units such as the verse, strophe and beyond. At this point, the identified meaningful center is not necessarily centralized by equal word-counts on both sides but by poetical units, which is defined more fluidly.

---

24. At other times, the center may contain the only symmetric verseline in the poem. See van der Lugt's treatment of Pss 74, 58 and 79 in van der Lugt, "Mathematical Centre," 647–48.

25. Van der Lugt, *Rhetorical Criticism*, 536.

26. Van der Lugt, *CAS III*, 482–82; Labuschagne "Psalm 139," 1–6. Another example is Ps 110. At the word level, the meaningful center, ולא ("and not"), does not work. The entire colon in 110:4a, while meaningful, is not the central colon. As the search expands, the two verselines of six cola (110:3–4) form the meaningful center of the psalm. In this analysis, Labuschagne also identifies eight poetical verselines (van der Lugt counts seven) and 18 cola from seven Masoretic verses. Furthermore, Labuschagne and van der Lugt do not always agree on how poetical units (such as verses or strophes, e.g., Ps 110) are delimited in each psalm. The possibility of changing poetical units (e.g., verselines or strophes) to expand the search for a meaningful center somewhat dilutes the mathematical precision. See also Labuschagne, "Psalm 110," 1–5.

27. Labuschagne, "Significant Compositional Techniques," 595–96.

Second, textual emendations and various "exceptions" are often raised. In several instances, Labuschagne notes that the meaningful centers of a number of psalms[28] are designed to be read *with* the superscriptions. He admits,

> [i]f we include the 3-word heading [in Ps 20] and the word selah (v. 4b), the arithmetic center of the 70 words of the entire text (70 = 33 + 4 + 33) appears to coincide exactly with the meaningful center. This leads to the conclusion, in my opinion, that the editor has consciously chosen a 3-word heading and one selah precisely for this purpose.[29]

The phrase, בל-אמים, occurring in Pss 44:15, 57:10, 108:4 and 149:7 is also counted differently. In the first three instances, the *maqqef* plays a role and the entire phrase is counted as a single word whereas in the last instance (149:7), it is counted as two words.[30] And these inconsistencies must be considered.

A third issue relates to the integration of structural form and thematic content of a psalm. In both their works, Labuschagne and van der Lugt focus primarily on quantitative analyses and formal devices to account for poetical structures. Thematic development or semantic content in the psalm in question is often discussed secondarily. This is unavoidable as their methodologies require a focus on the form.[31]

Numerical Devices beyond a Single Psalm

Most quantitative analyses of the Psalms (including D. Freedman and Fokkelman's work on syllable counts[32]) are limited to the level of a single, or rarely, a pair of psalms.[33] To my knowledge, apart from Labuschagne, few have applied these numerical structuring techniques to the entire Psalter.[34] Cited by Auwers, Ramon Ribera-Mariné makes an interesting contribution.[35] He counts not just words, but the individual psalms, and finds that between Pss 2 and 89 (both kingship psalms), stands Ps 45 (also kingship psalm), and that Pss 18 and 72 (both kingship psalms as well) are located

---

28. E.g., Pss 15; 20; 21; 26; 35; 41; 66; 67.

29. Labuschagne "Psalm 20," 1–3.

30. Observation 1 in Labuschagne "Psalm 44," 1–5. The difficulty of this phrase has been treated by Barbiero and Pavan, "Pss 44,15," 598–605.

31. Both Labuschagne and van der Lugt note that the quantitative methodology has not found widespread acceptance among biblical scholars at this time. Van der Lugt, *CAS II*, 527.

32. Freedman, "Acrostics and Metrics," 367–92; "Pottery, Poetry, and Prophecy," 5–26; "Acrostic Poems," 408–31; Fokkelman, *MPHB*.

33. Van der Lugt applied the technique to the Songs of Ascents in van der Lugt, *CAS III*, 422–40. However, most of his structural arguments for this collection come from verbal rather than quantitative analyses.

34. Koorevaar is another scholar who has applied Logotechnique to understand the structuring of the Psalter. His analysis, in the form of a Book section, is too brief. Koorevaar, "Psalter as a Structured Theological Story," 579–92.

35. Ribera-Mariné, "'El Llibre de les Lloances,'" 1–19.

symmetrically around Ps 45.³⁶ This suggests that the Psalter is structured with careful numerical considerations associated with the kingship motif.

Labuschagne argues that "composers/editors used 7 and 11³⁷ as compositional tools to delimit the sub-groups within the five books … [and] they *finalized/canonized* the sub-groups and the books with minute care by means of a specific number of verselines, which are determined by the numbers 17 and 26, the numerical values of the name Yhwh."³⁸ Based on these numerical devices, Labuschagne structures the entire Psalter as follows:

Book I	1	2–8	9–18	19–29	30–31	32–41
# of psalms	1	7	9 (Pss 9–10 as one psalm)	11	2 (T)	11 (Ps 40 as two separate psalms)

Book II	42–49	50	51–57	58–64	65–71	72
# of psalms	7 (42-43 as one psalm)	1 (T)	7	7	7	1

Book III	73–83	84–89
# of psalms	11	6 ("mixed" psalms)

Book IV	90–100	101–106
# of psalms	11	6

Book V	107–117	118–119	120–126	127	128–134	135–145	146–150
# of psalms	11	1 (T)		15		11	5

Figure 66: Labuschagne's Structure of the Psalter based on Numbers "7" and "11"

The use of structuring numbers, 7 and 11, is clear.³⁹ On this basis, Labuschagne argues that Pss 9–10 must be seen as a "single composition"⁴⁰ and that Pss 30–31, 50, and 72 are "transition psalms" ("T") which do not belong to any subgroup. At the end of Book I, Pss 32–41 form a group of "ten or eleven" psalms so Ps 40 can either be seen as a single psalm or two separate psalms (i.e., 40:2–13, 14–18). In Book II, there are four groups of 7 psalms (42–49, 51–57, 58–64, 65–71) and two stand-alone psalms (50, 72).⁴¹ Divine name numbers ("17," "26") and their multiples play an important

---

36. Auwers, *La Composition*, 95.

37. He argues that "being *odd* numbers, 7 and 11 have the advantage of having a *pivot* and the ability to make the *middle* a strong focus of attention. This enabled the editors/composer to give pride of place to a key-psalm at the mathematical centre of the sub-group in question" (Labuschagne, "Significant Sub-Groups," 624).

38. Labuschagne, "Significant Compositional Techniques," 588–89; "Significant Sub-Groups," 624.

39. The table is drawn based on my reading of Labuschagne, "Significant Sub-Groups," 623–34. An expanded version, where he included a "one-time" Psalter structure and its formation, is found on Labuschagne's website. See Labuschagne, "Compositional Structure," 1–29.

40. Labuschagne, "Significant Sub-Groups," 625; "Psalm 9–10," 1–9.

41. Labuschagne considers Pss 42 and 43 as a single composition. Labuschagne's argument for

role as well.⁴² The 17 psalms in Book III are formed by 374 (22x17) verselines. Book IV, likewise, consists of 17 psalms with a total of 338 (13x26) verselines. Labuschagne concludes that these two Books are "sealed in terms of their verselines by a divine name number."⁴³ Book V is structured first with a group of 11 psalms (107–117), followed by two transition psalms (118–19), the SOA, and concluded by eleven Davidic psalms (135–45).

Labuschagne's work on the Psalter's structure based on the numbers 7, 11 and 26 is intriguing and deserves further attention. The strength of his argument lies in the precise recurrences of these numbers. Nonetheless, there are several issues that weaken his methodology. (a) The absence of absolute consistency in the numerical devices used creates a dilemma. The numbers 7 and 11 are not the only numbers used for the structuring of the Psalter.⁴⁴ Labuschagne also admits that not all "subgroups" are finalized/canonized with verselines that are factors of 17 or 26. The issue is that the attestation of partial data⁴⁵ works against a totalizing claim on the Psalter's structure with Logotechnique. In fact, Labuschagne also admits, "a conspicuous group of precisely 7 or 11 psalms is indeed a first (and important!) indication of a distinct grouping, but it needs to be underscored by thematic features and factors indicating coherence and unity."⁴⁶ However, it remains unclear how different compositional units relate to each other thematically, and how "transitional psalms," as he has conveniently designated, function to transit from a certain theme in one unit to another.⁴⁷ Labuschagne has not also shown in detail how thematic contents correlate with the Logotechnique in the structuring of the Psalter.

How can we reconcile the discrepancies between a structure based on numerical devices and an alternate structure based on thematic and literary evidence in the text?⁴⁸ While I agree with Labuschagne and van der Lugt that evidence of numeri-

---

considering Pss 42–43 as a single psalm is based on "several other manuscripts" which is not specified in the references below. His primary argument is that Pss 42–43 consist of "three refrains as a demarcating device (42:6, 12, and 43:5)" in the two psalms and a total of 187 (11x17) words. Labuschagne, "Significant Sub-Groups," 628; "Psalm 42–43," 1–4.

42. Considering only Davidic psalms in Book II, Labuschagne counts 289 (17x17) verselines in 18 Davidic psalms (51–65, 68–70). Including the non-Davidic psalms (Pss 66, 67, 71), Pss 51–71 consist of 340 (20x17) verselines. Together with Pss 42–49 (excluding Pss 50 and 72), the entire Book II consists of 459 (25x17) verselines. Labuschagne, "Significant Sub-Groups," 628–29.

43. Labuschagne, "Significant Sub-Groups," 631.

44. For instance, groups of five (146–150), six (84–89, 101–106), nine (9–18), ten (32–41) and fifteen (120–134) psalms are compositional units.

45. Besides exceptions that are not supported with clear qualifications.

46. Labuschagne, "Significant Sub-Groups," 625.

47. For more critique on Labuschagne's Logotechnical analysis, see Davies and Gunn, "Pentateuchal Patterns," 399–406.

48. For instance, Psalms 1 and 2, 111–117 can be seen as compositional units because of literary features such as the absence of superscriptions (Pss 1–2); lexical framing devices (e.g., אשרי in Ps 1:1; 2:12); the use of *hallelujah* lexemes (in Pss 111–117). It is important to consider content with its form. Cf. Zenger, "Composition and Theology," 91–92; Zakovitch, "Interpretative Significance," 215–27;

The Design of the Psalter

cal devices cannot be simply be dismissed, neither can thematic structure. Should not form and content cohere? Inherent in the numerical technique is an element of extreme precision. It is this precision that lends the argument its legitimacy. Yet, it is the same precision that renders non-conforming data problematic. Notwithstanding the possibilities of transmission and textual errors, why do the final editor(s) go to such lengths to render such precision in the composition of the psalms and yet leave various blatant non-conforming exceptions in the numerical organization of psalms?[49] These questions may never be answered with certainty, but they point out inconvenient gaps that remain in the quantitative analysis of texts. In short, how do we maintain a high view of the Codex L as the text that provides the numerical precision to certain textual unit-counts while at the same time, understand the inconsistencies?

(b) Regrettably, Labuschagne does not regard the superscriptions of the Psalms as playing a key structuring role in the Psalter.[50] He gives the numerical method priority over superscriptions in analyzing the Psalter's structure. For instance, he structures the Psalter across different superscript categories (e.g., Ps 2–8; 107–117) based on numerical considerations. However, Labuschagne also uses the superscriptions as a structuring device at other times (e.g., the Korahite psalms; Asaphite psalms; SOA; Davidic psalms). Psalms 135–137 are not Davidic psalms but are grouped as such. The dilemma of having the numerical method and superscriptions as competing structuring devices has not been adequately resolved by Labuschagne.

Nevertheless, Labuschagne and van der Lugt have brought the concept of the numerical method to the forefront and raised the concept of a meaningful/rhetorical center of a psalm. In view of the numerical analyses of Pss 1, 2, and 119 in the first chapter, we will further explore whether the numerical method plays a deeper role in the macrostructure of the Psalter.

An Alternative Method of Counting

To do so, I have explored a different method of word counting. First, I count words joined by *maqqef* as a single word. From the perspective of accentuation, "words joint

---

Cole, "Integrated Reading," 75–88.

49. For instance, the combination of Pss 9–10 as one psalm and separation of Ps 40 as two psalms may be plausible based on poetic, mathematical or thematic elements. They are also attested by extant manuscripts. However, these postulations are clearly not rendered by the editor(s) of L, on which Labuschagne based his calculations heavily on. It is also unclear if those manuscripts which Labuschagne alludes to consist of the same numerical structuring or verseline "finalizing" pattern.

50. Craigie notes, "the titles identify certain psalms in relation to particular persons or according to particular types and thus may be indicative of early collections of psalms, prior to the formation of the Psalter as a whole" (Craigie, *Psalms 1–50*, 28). In the Logotechnical analysis of individual psalms, Labuschagne includes word count of the texts with and without the headings of the Psalms. Unless stated otherwise, word counts or verseline-counts presented in his arguments do not include the headings.

by *maqqef* are considered as a single unit."⁵¹ In the study of the Masorah, Yeivin summarizes three main principles for the use of *maqqef*⁵² and determines that linguistic and musical reasons are two basic reasons for its usage. Yet he acknowledges that "in some cases, however, the linguistic and musical phenomena do not correspond."⁵³ Barbiero concurs with this difficulty. He notes that while "the *maqqef* customarily signals a link between two lexemes that are *distinct* in themselves but *united* with regard to the tonic accent,"⁵⁴ this is not always the case. He notes that the phrase בל-אמים ⁵⁵ in the MT is attested in the Aleppo Codex as בלאמים (without the *maqqef*). In his phonetic analysis of this phrase, he notes not just the difficulty of the scansion argument for *maqqef*, but questions if the *maqqef* has a different function:

> [T]he hypothesis that the *maqqep* was to be read as an »aid to the reading«, this would create some difficulties: indeed, the expression which results from this reading would have to be read as united although it was, in fact, »divided«. How else can the reader account for the different function of the *maqqep*?⁵⁶

In other words, while the function of *maqqef* can be explained by scansion principles in most cases, its full function in the MT Psalter remains a mystery.

Second, I have included all superscriptions, postscripts, doxologies (e.g., hallelujah) and the word, *selah*, in the word-count. Their presence has been attested from antiquity and from our study of superscriptions earlier, we conclude that they are careful compositions displaying numerical techniques and in line with the Metanarrative of the Psalter.

Third, I have restrained from making any emendation to the texts. By leaving the L intact, we obtain a single snapshot of the MT in the L Codex as it is.⁵⁷ This is

---

51. Yeivin, *Introduction to the Tiberian Masorah*, 232.

52. Yeivin notes that the use of the *maqqef* is: (1) to avoid "two main stress syllables one after the other"; (2) often used on short words which are treated as "enclitic"; (3) for "economy of accents." See Yeivin, *Introduction to the Tiberian Masorah*, 230–31.

53. For instance, Yeivin notes, "*ḥolem* is usually replaced by *qameṣ* before *maqqef*, as in Ex 21:11 ואם-שלש-אלה (where two stress syllables would come together but for the *maqqef*). In Jos 21:33 שלש-עיר עשרה (where two stress syllables would not come together) *ḥolem* is retained, despite the use of *maqqef*. Here it can be said that *maqqef* is used for musical reasons, but the linguistic situation does not require it." However, on accentuation (musical reasons), Yeivin conceded that "on the one hand, *maqqef* is often omitted from a word which has no accent [which it should be present], . . . but on the other, *maqqef* may be used on a word which has a conjunctive accent." The complexity of its function is further multiplied by its proliferation (more than 50,000 occurrences of *maqqef* in the HB) with different traditions in the use of *maqqef*. Yeivin, *Introduction to the Tiberian Masorah*, 23, 232–34. For his complete treatment on *maqqef*, see Yeivin, *Introduction to the Tiberian Masorah*, 229–36.

54. Barbiero and Pavan, "Pss 44,15," 601.

55. Pss 44:15; 57:10; 108:4; 149:7.

56. Barbiero and Pavan, "Pss 44,15," 601.

57. This is not to say that I am not open to text-critical issues where evidence is presented. As Maloney notes, "in many cases we have seen that a more plausible explanation for a difficult reading is found to be putatively poetic and artistic. That is, the poetic contribution of the difficult reading is motivation to keep the Masoretes' text and to reject suggested emendations—especially those

to prevent premature textual diagnosis when the design of the Psalter has not been understood.

Fourth, I list the result of my count in a terse form, which may consist of one or two words (the mathematical center for odd or even counts) and define it as "nexusword."[58] I may fill out the complete colon or beyond (in parenthesis) to get a fuller sense of the nexusword. I agree with Labuschagne that these words at the center could have been used to succinctly highlight an important theme or message for the entire psalm.

The method I have used to count words would theoretically alter the word count of the text in L significantly, in comparison to Labuschagne and van der Lugt's work.[59] However, by comparing my results with these two scholars, I have found that more than 67 percent of the nexuswords in Books I–III correspond to either or both of their identified meaningful/rhetorical centers. When Books IV and V are compared, it is surprising that more than 95 percent of the nexuswords that I have found are aligned with either or both of their counts. Appendix A records my findings compared with theirs. In the following, I will briefly demonstrate my word count using three psalms that we have already encountered.

In Ps 23, I count 50 words and the nexusword is the phrase, כי-אתה עמדי ("for you are with me"), which are the exact words Bazak, Labuschagne, and van der Lugt have identified. This nexusword is framed by 24 words on both sides. In Ps 92, the word count is 100 and the nexusword is מרום לעלם ("on high forever"). This nexusword is at the center of the entire verse of four words, ואתה מרום לעלם יהוה,[60] which Labuschagne and van der Lugt consider as the psalm's meaningful/rhetorical center. By extending one word on each side, I arrive at the same four words, surrounded by 48 words. They remain as the mathematical center of the psalm.

In Ps 115, the word-count is 118 and the nexusword (59th and 60th) is עזרם ומגנם ("[He is] their help and shield"). These two words also correspond to their count at the colon level. In these three psalms, we arrive at the same centers with two very different counting methods.

Moreover, it is possible that the alphabetical techniques at work in Pss 1–2 are featured in Ps 119. The first *two* lines (not just the first) of Ps 119 begin with the letter

---

emendations that have no textual support from other ancient witnesses" (Maloney, "Word Fitly Spoken," 183–86).

58. "Nexus" is a noun that can mean: (a) a connection; (b) a connected group; (b) center. "Nexusword," therefore, refers to word(s) at the center of a psalm text, which is connected in some way to other nexuswords across psalms.

59. I have written a macro in MS Excel to count the words of every psalm electronically. These word counts are then manually checked against the *BHS*.

60. Note the chiastic structure of these four words. The first and the last identify the subject (that is, Yhwh), and the two center words describe him.

א in the word אשרי. This recalls the two אשרי in Pss 1:1 and 2:12. It is interesting that the last word of Ps 119 also ends with the consonant ת.[61]

The last word of Ps 119 (שכח; "forget, ignore or wither") is a "terminative" word.[62] Interestingly, the לא שכחתי in Ps 119:176 is also found at the last colon of the ב stanza (119:16).[63] The last colon of the *aleph* stanza is yet another terminative word (עזב; "to forsake" 119:8). Terminative words occur at the end of Ps 1:6 and in the last verse of Ps 2:12 (אבד). Hence, the use of אשרי at the opening lines, as well as the terminative words at the end of Pss 1 and 2, and at the end of the first two stanzas of Ps 119,[64] help us to observe the parallels between these psalms.

The *aleph* stanza of Ps 119 has 39 words. At the center is מאד ("much") occurring as the last word of Ps 119:4.[65] When we count the words of the *beth* stanza (38 words), and the sum of words in both the *aleph* and *beth* stanzas (77 words), we have: (a) למדני ("teach me"; the 19th word) as the center in the *beth* stanza, beginning with ל, emphasizing its middle position; (b) and עד-מאד ("utterly," the 39th word) as the center of both the *aleph* and *beth* stanzas. מאד also occur as the last word of the *aleph* stanza. מאד also marks the division between the *aleph* and *beth* stanzas. The 39th word, when both *aleph* and *beth* stanzas are combined, is also the numerical figure of the total words in *aleph* (39 words). In other words, both *aleph* and *beth* are skillfully connected with the techniques of lexeme repetition, centering and word count.

The motifs, "teach me" (*beth*) and the double "much" (*aleph*), provide the overarching focus of Ps 119. Furthermore, our earlier discussions in chapter 1 on the verb אלף, "to teach," "to learn" or "to increase," depending on the stem, also correspond to our discussion of למד in Ps 119. Thus we have at least four convergences from the above analysis: (a) the use of the lexemes, למד,אלף, and מאד; (b) their use in acrostic/alphabetical compositions; (c) their precise location in the word-count; and (d) their use in the Prologue of the Psalter and the first introductory two stanzas of Ps 119.

Bearing in mind the recurring phenomenon that *introductions* to poetical structures often consist of two textual units, as seen in the POS of "Jacob," "whole burnt offering" and "covenant," the entire Psalter and the longest Ps 119 are similarly introduced by Pss 1–2 and 119:1–8, 9–16 respectively.

In relation to the word count analyses above, several implications of such precise matching can be raised. First, the high level of correspondence between my proposed nexusword and the meaningful/rhetorical centers of Labuschagne and van der Lugt, especially in Books IV–V, is uncanny. We can safely dismiss the notion of fortuitous

---

61. Without counting the final vowel in שכחתי.

62. Barré, "'Terminative' Terms," 207–15.

63. This is also found at the end of other colon junctures (cf. Ps 119:61, 83, 93, 109, 141, 153) with the exception of 119:93.

64. Soll notes, "the aleph and beth strophes function as a prologue; complaints and more general petitions for the psalmist's condition do not occur until the Gimel strophe" (Soll, *Psalm 119*, 90).

65. Note how this word disrupts rhyme at the end of Ps 119:2–3, 5–7.

coincidence. Perhaps my method was a complementary numerical technique, adopted by the final editor(s) of the Psalms who intended to include all the words in a psalm in the count. This would imply that the *maqqef* has an additional function of altering word count in a text.

The differences in the percentages of correspondence between Books I–III (>70 percent) and IV–V (>90 percent) support our contention that Books IV and V of the Psalter constitute a compositional unit although their redactional history remains elusive.[66] Labuschagne and van der Lugt's method of counting could have been an earlier technique.[67]

Second, Labuschagne and van der Lugt's views that the meaningful/rhetorical centers are somewhat detached from the texts themselves need not be maintained. Van der Lugt notes, "these rhetorical centres do not necessarily have relations with the structure of a psalm in terms of cantos and strophes. In most cases, they represent a rather individual aspect."[68] Neither of them considers these meaningful/rhetorical centers as functioning beyond the level of one or two psalms.[69] In other words, they neither assume any macrostructural links between these rhetorical centers nor do they present any evidence of such links.[70]

---

66. Citing Sanders, Frazer notes that the 4QPs[a] "arranges the Psalms and their titles as they still appear in the masora." It is likely there is no separation between the title and the text by the time of the Qumran Psalms scrolls. See Fraser, "Authenticity of the Psalms Titles," 17–18. For a further study, see Sanders, "Pre-Masoretic Psalter Texts," 114–23; *Psalms Scroll of Qumran Cave 11*; Skehan, "Psalm Manuscript from Qumran," 313–22.

67. When Books IV–V and other psalms are added or incorporated into existing collections, subsequently rearrangements, superscriptions and *maqqef* changes were also incorporated to maintain the meaningful centers and form the entire five-book structure at the final composition of the Psalter. This is not to say that *all* psalm superscriptions are of a later hand. Some of the superscriptions could have been composed with the poem; others could have been edited at the time of the Psalter's final composition. The addition of superscriptions, *selah* and *maqqef* changes do not affect the numerical counts in Bazak, Labuschagne and van der Lugt's works. Scholars such as Leuenberger and Ballhorn have also raised arguments on how Books IV and V can be seen as a unit. I deviate from Christensen's argument that Book II is the last Book to be incorporated in the Psalter. He notes, "A reasonable working hypothesis posits the insertion of Book 2 as the final addition to the Psalter, when the seventeen books of the deuteronomic canon were expanded to make the twenty-two books of the Pentateuchal canon in the time of Ezra. It appears that an original collection of psalms of David, preserved in Books 1 and 5 of the Psalms as we now have them, was edited into a Deuteronomic Psalter. The Pentateuchal Psalter of mainstream Jewish tradition appeared with the formation of the twenty-two-book canon of the Tanakh in the time of Ezra (ca. 400 BCE) when Book 2 (Pss 42–72) was inserted into existing collection" (Christensen, *Unity of the Bible*, 132).

68. Van der Lugt, *CAS III*, 8.

69. In "Significant Sub-Groups in the Book of Psalms," Labuschagne structures the entire Psalter based on numerical figures of word and verselines. However, the meaningful centers of individual psalms are not primarily used in the structuring. Neither did he provide a treatment on how the thematic content of the Psalter develops across the structure.

70. Van der Lugt analyzes Pss 120–134 as a Collection in van der Lugt, *CAS III*, 422–40. However, his treatment is based on verbal parallels rather than quantitative analyses or identified rhetorical centers.

Numerical Devices, Alphabetic Acrostics or Compositions, and Superscriptions

In contrast, I will explore if these nexuswords work at the macrostructural level, and, if they do, how. Are they also aligned with the macrostructural shape and Metanarrative of the Psalter?[71] I will identify the nexusword of all psalms and compare each with the macrostructural shape identified in chapters 2–3.[72] These nexuswords will also be analyzed for representations of the thematic genre, main motif or certain key insight of the psalm, in view of its location within a structural unit. I will demonstrate this process with Ps 108 and briefly discuss the other nexuswords in three Figures below.

Psalm 108

The composite Ps 108 consists of a number of textual edits from Pss 57 and 60 which are likely to be intentional.[73] Based on my count, there are 85 words in the psalm and the nexusword (43rd) is ועמק, "and the valley (of Succoth)"[74] in 108:8. *Prima facie*, this word is not significant in itself. What then is its role as a nexusword? It lies between two words, "Shechem"[75] and "Succoth," in the center of the five-word phrase, אחלקה שכם ועמק סכות אמדד, and at the numerical center of the psalm.[76] Psalm 108:8 is set within the context of vv. 8–10, commonly termed as the "divine oracles."[77] According

---

71. This possibility arose from our study of Pss 1; 2; and 150.

72. I have also reviewed the designations of psalm genre adopted by three recent commentaries in view of our discussions. See Goldingay, *Psalms*; Hossfeld and Zenger, *Psalms*; Longman, *Psalms*.

73. Textual issues that affect word count are listed here. Note that the phrase, נכון לבי in 57:8, is not found following נכון לבי אלהים in 108:2. Bardtke (*BHS*) suggests that the missing phase is to be inserted, in line with a few Mss, LXX and Syriac attestation. However, it must be noted that several intentional edits had been made in Ps 108 from Pss 57 and 60 (which may have been further redacted from an earlier Hebrew *Vorlage* on which the LXX was based on. This is the view of Anderson, "Politics of Psalmody," 313–32. The edits are likely to be intentional. For instance, Botha notes the replacement with "the particle אף [in 108:2] serves here as an expression of addition and emphasis and it more probably establishes a connection between לבי and כבודי than between אלהים and כבודי" (Botha, "Psalm 108," 575–78). *BHS* suggests אעל-זה, instead of אעלזה in v. 8a, which does not affect word count. The editors of Ps 108:10 added a *maqqef* for the phrase, עלי-פלשת and modified the word, רוע, as a first-person imperfect (rendering an easier reading). In 108:12, the word, אתה, in 60:12 is removed, and אלהים is attached to the negative. Zenger argues that the removal of "you" in 108:12 "softens the complaining accusation in Ps 60:12" (Hossfeld and Zenger, *Psalms 3*, 113–16).

74. Succoth lies in a valley. It is a "town on the eastern side of the Jordan near the wadi Jabbok, where Jacob put up shelters for his livestock (Gen 33:17)." Cf. Joshua 13:27. Longman, *Psalms*, 241.

75. Shechem is "an important northern city in Ephraim (Canaan) situated between Mount Ebal and Gerizim" (Longman, *Psalms*, 240–41).

76. Note the chiastic syntax of the phrase and the *athnak* just before our nexusword, ועמק "valley." Labuschagne and van der Lugt consider the entire Ps 108:8 as the meaningful/rhetorical center of the psalm. In Labuschagne's word count, he finds the word, "I will measure off" (אמדד), at the center of the psalm. While he considers v.8 as the meaningful center, he also notes that the 28-word oracle (vv. 8–10) can also be the meaningful center. Labuschagne, "Psalm 108," 1–6; van der Lugt, *CAS III*, 208.

77. Psalm 108:8–10, which Tate calls "divine oracle," is "interpreted as the response of a cult prophet or priest to the complaint and prayer of the preceding verses . . . In this sense, the oracle would be a message of assurance that Yahweh is the divine warrior who has conquered Israel's land and controls

to Botha, these three verses form the central strophe of the entire 5-strophe psalm, and is "an oracle telling of Yʜᴡʜ's future military triumph."[78] Thus, this divine oracle, at the poetical center of the psalm, provides the best contextual clue to understanding the significance of the nexusword in this psalm.

The oracle is a carefully composed unit. The words, אעלזה ("I will exult") at the beginning and אתרועע ("I will shout aloud") at the end, not only parallel each other phonetically and semantically, but they also bookend the entire oracle. They highlight the motif of joy associated with victory on the battlefield.[79] I have set Ps 108:8–10 in six lines below to illustrate parallel word-pairs. The first and last lines frame the oracles.[80] Between them, four pairs of words in four lines (lines 2–5) reveal Yʜᴡʜ's dealings/relationship with the named places (note the highlights). In every case, Yʜᴡʜ is the subject.

1 אלהים דבר בקדשו אעלזה
2 אחלקה שכם ועמק סכות אמדד
3 לי גלעד לי מנשה
4 ואפרים מעוז ראשי יהודה מחקקי
5 מואב סיר רחצי על־אדום אשליך נעלי
6 עלי־פלשת אתרועע

In the second line, the use of the word אמדד ("I will measure off"), carries the figurative meaning of "God's sovereignty, omnipotence, and omnipresence" in marking out geographical space.[81] Likewise, the use of אחלקה ("I will apportion")[82] signifies Yʜᴡʜ's ownership and authority over the land.

Yʜᴡʜ's ownership of Gilead and Manasseh is clear in the third line with the possessive first-person suffix on ל. In the fourth line, the words associated with Ephraim and Judah are מעוז ראשי (lit. "the fortress for my head") and מחקקי ("my scepter").[83]

---

the surrounding countries of Moab, Edom, and Philistia as well" (Tate, *Psalms 51–100*, 106).

78. Botha, "Psalm 108," 578.

79. The word, עלז, in Pss 60:8 and 108:8 shows God as the subject of rejoicing. Grisanti notes that these "passages in the Psalms offer hope to the afflicted people of God because Yahweh rejoices that he alone ultimately controls the status of peoples and lands" (Grisanti, "עלז," *NIDOTTE*, 3:420). The word, רוע, "is used to indicate the shout before or after a battle (Pss 60:8[10]; 108:9[10]). It is sometimes used more generally to simply indicate joyful exclamation in response to God" (Longman, "רוע," *NIDOTTE*, 3:1084).

80. Anderson recognizes the poetical unit of Ps 108:8–10 (=60:8–11) in the Divine oracle, but extends the oracle to v. 11. See Anderson, "Politics of Psalmody," 317, 319.

81. Cf. Isa 40:12. Fuller, "מדד," *NIDOTTE*, 2:850.

82. Van Dam, "חלק," *NIDOTTE*, 2:162.

83. Schoville notes that the phrase, מעוז ראשי, "may have one of two meanings: chief fortress (=NJPSV translation) or helmet (lit. 'fortress of the head'). While the latter would be a unique usage of the term, it is more likely the correct sense" (Schoville, "מעוז," *NIDOTTE*, 2:1015). The word מחקקי is a *polel* participle masculine singular construct with first person suffix from the root, חקק, and can mean

They carry the imagery of the battlefield and the trio-connotations of *refuge, kingship*, and *decree*, recalling the Central Motifs in chapters 2–3. In the next pair, the words, רחצי ("my washbowl") and נעלי ("my shoe"), are more than a derogatory remark against Moab and Edom representing their defeat and shame.[84] They can, according to Martens, be associated with the concept of the removal of uncleanness.[85] In short, we identify five motifs in the oracle: (1) the apportioning of land/plunder; (2) Yhwh's Lordship; (3) place of refuge, kingship, and decree; (4) removal of uncleanness; (5) victorious exultation in battle.

What is the significance of the named places in the oracle? They have been interpreted in several ways.[86] For Tate,

> Shechem and Succoth may recall the Jacob tradition of Gen 33:17–18 and 49:10; Edom and Moab allude to the Balaam oracle in Num 24:17–19 . . . Shechem, Succoth (in central Transjordan, perhaps, *Deir 'Alla* in the Jordan Valley), Gilead, Manasseh, and Ephraim represent the areas of the Northern Kingdom, while Judah, Moab, Edom, and Philistia represent the South.[87]

Tate links the "star" (Num 24:17), a kingly figure from the tribe of Judah who will rise from Jacob (Gen 49:10) to the one who will "crush" (Num 24:17–19) the forehead of Moab and possess Edom. These oracles, coming together in Ps 108:8–10, underscore how Yhwh, the divine warrior, will rule over the whole land[88] via a king from the tribe of Judah. Tate concludes that "the unidentified nature of the speaker is possibly an invitation to think of a new David, a king who would have the cooperation of

---

(a) "a decree; (b) leader (cf. Prov 8:15, Judg 5:14); (c) scepter (cf. Gen 49:10). Note that the LXX translates יהודה מחקקי as Ιουδας βασιλεύς μου ("Judah my king"). See Holladay, "חקק," *HOL*, BibleWorks. v. 10. For a textual study of יהודי מחקקי in Ps 60, see Anderson, "Politics of Psalmody," 329–30.

84. Goldingay notes, "Moab is the basin in which the warrior washes off the grime and blood after a battle. Edom is the place the warrior throws his shoes in doing so" (Goldingay, *Psalms*, 3:269).

85. Note that LXX has λέβης τῆς ἐλπίδος μου ("washbasin of my hope"). Anderson argues that the LXX follows a Hebrew *Vorlage* that fits well in the Hasmonean period when messianic hope was prevalent (Anderson, "Politics of Psalmody," 330); Martens notes that the verb רחץ is frequently used "in priestly legislation with instructions for the ceremonial washing of priests, and sometimes the washing of parts of the sacrifice (Num 19:7, 8; Lev 1:9, 13; 9:14) . . . Before stepping to the altar or into the tent of meeting, the priests were to wash hands and feet on penalty of death (Exod 30:19–21)" (Martens, "רחץ," *NIDOTTE*, 3:1098). Hence, the wash basin (used only twice as a noun in the Psalter) signifies a removal of uncleanness in the presence of God. The word, "sandal," also reflects uncleanness. Hamilton notes that both Moses and Joshua were told to remove their shoes in the presence of God (Exod 3:5; Josh 5:15). He also notes that "sandals, being made of animal skins, are impure in regard to the sacred and thus not to be worn into a sacred precinct" (Hamilton, "נעל," *NIDOTTE*, 3:120).

86. From the named places, Anderson dates the psalm to the period of John Hyrcanus I in the Hasmonean period. For a historical-critical interpretation and dating of Ps 60:8–11, see Anderson, "Politics of Psalmody," 321.

87. Tate, *Psalms 51–100*, 106–7; This is the view of Zenger as well. See Hossfeld and Zenger, *Psalms 3*, 119.

88. Goldingay notes, "To allocate Shechem and measure out Succot Valley to Israel is thus to allocate the land as a whole" (Goldingay, *Psalms*, 3:268).

Yahweh in new endeavors to fulfill old promises."[89] Zenger also notes that the oracle, "which traditionally would have been given to a king before the beginning of a battle, indicates the victorious end of the war in which the principal actor is Yhwh himself."[90]

I offer a further insight into our consideration. We have seen how the Samuel narratives, as intertextual reading (or re-reading), are important to the DCs in the last chapter. Likewise, it is important to consider the narratives' role in Ps 108:8–10.

In 1 Sam 20:15–16, Jonathan made a covenant with David not to "cut off" (כרת) his lovingkindness from his house when "the LORD cut off [כרת] every one of the enemies of David." This is likely the *first* prophetic oracle in the Samuel narratives to contain the motifs of David's enemies being destroyed and David reigning victoriously as king through Yhwh's help.[91] The motif of Yhwh cutting off *all* of David's enemies recurs in at least two key locations in the Samuel narratives.[92] First, it can be seen at the time when Yhwh made a covenant with David in 2 Sam 7:1, 9, 11, promising to establish his house and giving him rest from *all* his enemies. The motif recurs immediately in the following 2 Sam 8:1–15, where David subdued the Philistines, Moabites and the Edomites, and "reigned over *all* Israel."

The judgment of these nations described successively in Ps 108:10 cannot be seen apart from 2 Sam 8, where it describes the fall of David's numerous enemies in a single chapter. We come to a full circle in 2 Sam 9:1 with regards to David's oath to Jonathan. Three consecutive chapters, 2 Sam 7–9, provide a description of Yhwh's covenant with David, his victory over *all* enemies, and David fulfilling his covenantal promises to Jonathan.[93]

We can now consolidate an interesting intertextual reading. David was in trouble and sought Jonathan's help. Jonathan, who loved David as himself, saw (proleptically) that David would reign victoriously over his enemies. He urged David to show lovingkindness to his family in pronouncing an oath. Then David's enemies were cut off in 2 Sam 8 where the destruction of Moab, Edom, and Philistia are mentioned. By 2 Sam 9, David's promises to Jonathan were fulfilled. This mention of these three cities brings us to both Ps 108:10 and Num 24:17, where a Davidic "star" from the tribe of Judah will triumph over these cities and reign victoriously.

The places named in Ps 108:8–9 are also linked by a common motif of conspiracy described in narratives of Joshua and Judges. The mention of Succoth recalls both Josh 13:27–28 and Judg 8, where this town was apportioned to the tribe of Gad. But

---

89. Tate, *Psalms 51–100*, 107.

90. Hossfeld and Zenger, *Psalms 3*, 120.

91. Klein cites 1 Sam 25:26, 29, 39a; 2 Sam 3:18. See also 1 Sam 24:5. Klein, *1 Samuel*, 208.

92. See the dynamics of the word, "cut off," used to illustrate the relationships between David, Saul, Jonathan and their associates in 1 Sam 17:51; 18:3; 20:15–16; 22:8; 23:18; 24:5–6, 12, 22; 2 Sam 3:12–13, 21, 29; 5:3; 7:9; 20:22.

93. Anderson argues that the phrase, "to show consideration" (2 Sam 9:1), "belongs to covenant terminology and refers to loyal fulfillment of one's obligation previously undertaken" (Anderson, *2 Samuel*, 141).

through conspiration with Succoth's leaders, Israel was denied aid in her fight against the Midianites. However, when Gideon returned triumphantly from defeating Midian, he punished the leaders of Succoth (Judg 8:16).

In the same vein, Shechem was apportioned as a city of refuge in Josh 21:21. In Judges 9, we read about the conspiration of Abimelech with the elders of Shechem in the betrayal of Jerubaal, i.e., Gideon. By the end of the chapter, the curses of Jotham came true and both Abimelech and the men of Shechem were destroyed (Judg 9:56–57). Consider also the betrayal of the elders of Gilead, Ephraim and Manasseh against Jephthah (Judg 8:1; 11:1–3; 12:1–4). Like Succoth, Edom, and Moab refused to allow Israel passageway into Canaan (Judg 11:1–17). The betrayal and conspiracy of the Philistines against Samson are also clear in Judges 15:1–2; 16:5–21.

Elsewhere, the Psalter presents the same characterization of these nations. The Edomites' gloating over Israel's captivity is captured in Ps 137:7; while Edom, Moab and Philistia convening and conspiring against YHWH's people are seen in Ps 83:2–7.[94]

Apart from Judah, the eight places named in Ps 108:8–10 conspired to some extent against the people of God in their journey to Canaan, as portrayed in the book of Judges. In contrast, Judah is chosen as the first tribe designated to go up against the Canaanites (Judg 1:2) and the sons of Benjamin (Judg 20:18).

How does the common motif of a conspiracy of the eight nations against Israel in her conquest and entry into Canaan relate to our discussion? The leaders of these eight cities conspired against a "charismatic" deliverer (e.g., Jephthah, Samson, Jotham, and David).[95] They refused to help Israel. The common fate of these opposing nations is that they were eventually subdued by a victorious "ruler-deliverer."[96]

Reading the discussions of a deliverer in Judges alongside the Jonathan story, we see two kinds of responses and outcomes associated with the ruler-deliverer figures in the Judges/Samuel narratives. Those who conspired against the ruler-deliverer would be destroyed when he returns in victory (e.g., Succoth, Shechem, Edom, Moab, and Philistia). In contrast, those who loved and covenanted with the ruler-deliverer would receive his promised mercy upon his victorious return.

This intertextual understanding is embedded in the message in Ps 108. The Divine Oracle in 108:8–10 depicts YHWH's complete victory throughout land through the reign of a Judahite Ruler-deliverer. The places named, in view of the Samuel/Judges narratives, highlight the two kinds of outcomes for the victor's friends or enemies when the deliverer returns triumphantly.

---

94. "For behold, your enemies make an uproar; those who hate you have raised their heads. They lay crafty plans against your people; they consult together against your treasured ones. They say, 'Come, let us wipe them out as a nation; let the name of Israel be remembered no more!' For they conspire with one accord; against you, they make a covenant—the tents of Edom and the Ishmaelites, Moab and the Hagrites, Gebal and Ammon and Amalek, Philistia with the inhabitants of Tyre" (ESV).

95. Weisman, "Charismatic Leaders," 399–411.

96. Judg 2:16, 18; 3:9; 8:22–23; 9:2, 16.

Based on this interpretation of Ps 108:8–10, the nexusword of Ps 108 (ועמק, "and the valley [of Succoth]"), which does not seem significant *prima facie*, is unveiled. This nexusword identifies the divine oracle, highlighting not just Yhwh's victory, but also how he will deal with those who conspired against him upon overcoming the Ruler-deliverer's adversaries in Ps 108.

It is also pertinent to see that this interpretation accords with the trajectory of DC-IV (108–110).[97] The prophetic imagery of the victorious king ("new Joshua") in Ps 108 who received a temporary setback because of the conspiracy of his accusers (109), will subsequently reign victoriously from Zion with his mighty sceptre in Ps 110, executing judgment against his enemies. This development fits well with Ps 2 in the Prologue.

Consider also the nexuswords of Pss 109 and 110. The nexusword, כאה ("to dishearten"; 109:16), corresponds not just to the content genre of Ps 109 but aligns itself with the nexus-trajectory of Pss 108–110. This word occurs only three times in the HB (109:16; Ezek 13:22; Dan 11:30). In all three instances, this word is used in a context where the righteous are "disheartened" by their wicked oppressors. The nexusword of Ps 109 thus indicates the temporary setback of the king identified in Ps 108. The nexusword of Ps 110 is the enigmatic phrase, "the dew of your youth" (110:3), which may refer to "young warriors who comprise the army."[98] According to Zenger, the imagery presented in Ps 110 is "not about a 'real' enthronement in the royal palace but rather a 'throne community' with God."[99] The king is surrounded by his holy array, including his youth. The nexusword of Ps 110 thus characterizes the king's mighty army. It also underlies the fact that his people will come forth in the day of his power, as the dew at dawn.

The trajectory seen in Pss 108–110 is not unique. This development is also seen in Pss 144–145 and 149, where the victorious Davidic king, who suffered under the wicked (144:7–11), will eventually reign over his enemies. With their king, the *chasidim* of Yhwh is given the task of executing their enemies (149:7). Hence, our analysis of the nexusword in Ps 108 (and briefly, 109–110) suggests that the nexusword, is a technique (brachygraphy/steganography?), which possibly functions as a kind of short-hand to highlight certain motifs or ideas associated with the larger macrostructural unit.[100] Such short-hand techniques are not unheard of in the Masoretic texts. Yeivin, a Masorah scholar, notes that "some Tiberian MSS found in the Cairo Geniza were written in a form known as '*serugin*' ('shorthand,' 'brachygraphy'). In the oldest

---

97. See also our discussion in chapter 4.
98. Goldingay, *Psalms*, 3:295.
99. Hossfeld and Zenger, *Psalms 3*, 145.
100. Yeivin, *Introduction to the Tiberian Masorah*, 10–11. See also Fischer and Würthwein, *Text of the Old Testament*, 244–45, for an illustration of Oxford Ms. Heb e. 30, fol. 48b (which is a text on Isa 7:11–9:8) that shows the Hebrew text in an abbreviated form, where only the first word of a verse is written in full but subsequent words are written only with a single letter.

examples, the first word of a verse is written in full, followed by a single letter from each of the other important words in the verse."

In our study here, a nexusword is usually in alignment with the psalm's content genre (or genre motif[101]). The nexusword of a psalm points to a word (or a pair of words), which in turn, designates a larger motif in the immediate rhetorical context (in this case, the divine oracle in 108:8–10). This context may be a colon, a verse or more. The meaning of this nexus-context, abbreviated by the nexusword, gives the psalm its content-thrust and provides the link to a larger unit of psalms, forming a nexus-trajectory. This nexus-phenomenon is in line with our proposed macrostructure and Metanarrative of the Psalter.[102]

With Ps 108 in view, consider the nexuswords of Book I, based on my word count method, presented in Figure 67.

---

101. In this case, Ps 108 can be seen as both a Song and Petition, capturing the entire essence of the psalm. Although the classification of the genre of a psalm cannot be precise at times, associated motifs can be grouped within a certain genre. For instance, Grol sees the motifs of supplication and complaint under the genre of "prayer," or the motifs of blessing and praise under "hymn." See Van Grol, "David and His Chasidim," 316.

102. Although the nexusword (or nexus-context) in my study correspond well to the meaningful/rhetorical centers identified by Labuschagne and van der Lugt (about 70 percent in Books I–III and more than 90 percent in Books IV–V), I have arrived at it using a very different method of count and a different understanding of its implication. Labuschagne and van der Lugt do not consider these centers to have any macrostructuring roles.

The Design of the Psalter

Book I

Ps	Nexusword	Word count	MT verse	Alphabetic Acrostic (AA)/ Alphabetic Poem (AC)	Macro-structure and Super-script	Content or Genre Motifs
1	which (yield its fruit in its season)	57	3	AC	ashre	Torah
2	(You are) my Son	77	7		Un-titled	Kingship
1–2	against the LORD, and against his anointed	134	2:2	AC		
3	from his (holy) hill	63	5		hist	Lament Day; External hostilities
4	be angry and do not sin	68	5	PAC		Lament Night; Personal distress
5	(I will enter) your house	89	8			Lament Day; External hostilities
6	(no) remembrance of you; in Sheol	74	6			Lament Night; Personal distress
7	judge me, O LORD (according to my righteousness)	124	9	PAC (7:9–18)	hist	Lament Day; External hostilities
8	for you are mindful of, and the son of man	66	5	PAC		Lament night; *Central focus: kingship
9	(the LORD) who dwells in Zion	150	12			Lament Day; *Central focus: judgment
10	(he seizes the) poor when he draws	146	9		Untitled	Com Lament, Day
9–10	they are but man	296	9:21			
11	(the LORD's) throne is in heaven	62	4			Ind Lament, Night; CF
12	(who is) master over us?	72	5			Com Lament, Day
13	"answer me O LORD"	48	4			Ind Lament, Night
14	(do) all the workers of wickedness (not know?)	64	4	AC		Com Lament, Day
15	not take up (reproach) against his neighbour	44	3			Entrance liturgy
16	to me. I will bless	78	6, 7	PAC		CF
17	you will hide me; from the face (of the wicked)	116	8, 9			Lament
18	the LORD rewarded (me)	345	25		hist Sup	Kingship
19	to make wise (the simple)	113	8			*Central focus: Cosmic and Torah Praise
20	all your petitions. Now I know that the LORD saves his anointed	62	6, 7	AC	Davidic	*Central focus: Kingship
21	your presence, for the king (trust)	92	7, 8			Kingship
22	evildoers encircle me	224	17			Lament
23	for you are with me	50	4	PAC		CF
24	Jacob	81	6			Entrance liturgy
25	his testimonies	133	10			Ind Lament; Justice for the poor
26	and I go about (your altar)	73	6			Ind Lament; Avoiding wickedness

Ps	Nexusword	Word count	MT verse	Alphabetic Acrostic (AA)/ Alphabetic Poem (AC)	Macro-structure and Super-script	Content or Genre Motifs
27	(I will offer) in his tent, sacrifices (with shouts of joy)	126	6	AC		Ind Lament; Avoiding wickedness
28	render them their due reward	80	4			Ind Lament; Avoiding wickedness
29	(he makes) Lebanon (skip like a calf)	81	6	AC		Kingship; YHWH enthroned
30	O LORD, (by your favor)	87	8	AC		TK; Dedication of Temple
29–30	*the house of David (superscription)*	*168*	*30:1*			
31	(become) a broken vessel	200	13			TK; Avoiding wickedness
32	(therefore let all godly pray) to you (at a time you may be found)	99	6	PAC		TK; Avoiding wickedness
33	(his heart) to generation (after generations)	137	11	AC	Untitled	TK; Avoiding wickedness
34	the fear of (the LORD)	139	12		hist	Justice for the poor
35	I bowed down (in mourning)	203	14			Sup
36	(your judgments are like the great) deep	81	7			Hymn
37	(they vanish) like smoke (they vanish)	259	20			Sapiential hymn
38	they stand, my nearest kin (stand far off)	144	12	AC	For a memorial	Sup
39	(does not know) who will gather?	108	7	PAC		Sapiential hymn
40	*I will not restrain (my lips O LORD)*	*168*	*10*	PAC		TK
41	(united) against me they whisper	104	8			Sup

Figure 67: Nexusword, Content/Genre Motifs, and Macrostructure Juxtaposition in Book I[103]

Without a detailed exegesis of every psalm, it is difficult to show how every nexusword captures a core theme in the psalm and its macrostructural implications. Nonetheless, we will review the nexusword in relation to the psalm's content/genre motif,[104] and

---

103. In the "nexusword" column, words in parenthesis are added to give sense to the otherwise terse expression. In many cases, I have filled out the entire colon. Words that are not in parenthesis are the identified single-word nexusword (in odd word count) or a pair of words (in even word count). There are several instances where two psalms are considered as one (e.g., Pss 9–10), or a single psalm is divided into two (e.g., Ps 40). I have italicized the rows where such analyses occurred. Legend: AA: Alphabetical Acrostic; AC: Alphabetical Composition; PAC: Probable Alphabetical Composition; hist: historical superscription; Sup: Supplication psalm; TK: Thanksgiving; CF: Confidence psalm.

104. This is to capture the literary character of the psalm. For Book I, I have adopted the genre classifications out forth by G. Barbiero (see chapter 2). For Books II–III, I have adopted the classifications by Gillingham. For Books IV and V, I have adopted the classifications by Hossfeld, Zenger, and Howard. In addition, I have referenced further genre classifications of the psalms in this chapter from the works of Longman, Craigie, Tate, Terrien, and Goldingay. Terrien makes an important point, stating that the general classification of an individual psalm into its type or genre, cannot be separated from its "contents, style, emotive accent, and existential situation" (Terrien, *Psalms*, 42); My use of the

explore possibilities of a nexus-trajectory across a unit of psalms. Consider the following observations for Book I:

(1) I have found at least 30 psalms (73 percent) where the nexusword I have identified corresponds to Labuschagne and van der Lugt's results of meaningful/rhetorical center.[105]

(2) The nexuswords of Pss 1 and 2, and the entire colon where they appear,[106] coincide with the meaningful centers identified by the two scholars. Recall in chapter 1 when we consider Pss 1–2 as a single composition, the nexusword is found at the last colon of Ps 2:2: "against the LORD and against his holy one." Even when I apply Labsuschagne and van der Lugt's method, the meaningful center is *also* the term, "against" (2:2), in the same colon.[107] Despite two different methods of counting, we have arrived at the same colon defining the meaningful centers of the Prologue, whether it is viewed as separate psalms or a single composition.

(3) Considering the Group Pss 3–14,[108] the alternation of "Day" and "Night" psalms in this Group provides an interesting comparison with their nexuswords. Notice that the Day psalms in Pss 3, 5, 7[109] are associated with *external hostility* and the Night psalms in Pss 4, 6 are associated with *personal distress*.[110] By comparing this alternation with their nexuswords, the Day/external-hostility psalms are also associated with the motifs of Zion, temple, and YHWH's judgment.[111] The connection between external hostility and seeking YHWH as judge is an important motif in the Psalms. In contrast, the nexuswords associated with the Night/personal-distress psalms are more

---

term, "content/thematic genre," seeks less to postulate the *functional* use of the psalm in its original *Sitz im Leben* but more as a generalized literary description of an individual psalm as a whole. While I concede that genre classification is not always accurate or possible (e.g., the presence of mixed genre), the general literary character of a psalm can still be qualified with proper analysis of its content. Differences in genre classifications between different authors are a matter of nuance or emphasis. Regardless, genre classification provides a succinct way to capture the essence or character of a psalm's content.

105. In Book I, only Pss 3; 4; 9–10; 12; 16; 18; 19; 25; 39; 41 are incongruous. However, in several of these psalms, there are issues in Labuschagne and van der Lugt's word count as well. For instance, neither scholar finds meaningful centers in Pss 12, 19, 25, 39, 41. Headers are included in the count in order to find a rhetorical center (e.g., Ps 12) and textual emendations are adopted (Pss 18 and 25). See Appendix A.

106. Ps 1:3a, "which yield its fruit in its season" and 2:7a, "You are my son."

107. There is no superscription nor *selah* in Pss 1–2. Hence, the word count change of the two psalms arises only from considering the words joined by *maqqef* as a single word.

108. For details on how these structural units are delineated, see chapters 2–3.

109. We have discussed "morning" and "evening" psalms earlier (chapter 2, cf. Pss 3:6, 8; 4:5, 9; 5:4, 6:7; 7:7; 8:4; 9:20; 10:12; 11:2; 12:6; 13:4; 14:2, 5). Longman classifies them as "lament" and associate them with "morning" or calling God "to arise." Longman, *Psalms*, 64, 69, 75; Craigie calls this "morning" or "evening prayers" (Craigie, *Psalms 1–50*, 30).

110. Psalms 4, 6 are "laments" and "evening prayer" (Longman, *Psalms*, 67, 72).

111. The respective nexuswords are: "from his [holy] hill" (3:5); "your house" (5:8); "judge me, O LORD," (7:9).

self-reflective and contemplative in nature (Ps 4, "do not sin"; Ps 6, "no remembrance of you in Sheol"). They address the psalmist's inner struggles.

The Day Pss 10, 12, 14 are classified as Communal Laments[112] whereas the Night Pss 11, 13 are classified as Individual Laments/Confidence.[113] The nexuswords associated with Day/Communal-Lament psalms (10:9, "the poor"; 12:5, "master over us"; 14:4, "workers of wickedness") are associated with the motifs of public denunciation of wicked doers, whereas the nexuswords associated with Night/Individual-Lament psalms focus on the psalmist's reflection of Yhwh's relationship with him, recalling Yhwh's dealings with the righteous and Yhwh's covenantal faithfulness (11:4, "the Lord's throne is in heaven"; 13:4, "answer me O Lord"). The two center psalms in this Group correspond with this theme as well. Psalm 8 (Night) highlights Yhwh's dealing with his chosen man whereas Ps 9 (Day) highlights Yhwh's kingship and judgment from Zion.[114]

(4) The nexuswords of the Group, Pss 15–24, correspond not only to the content/genre motifs of these psalms but also to its chiastic structure. Psalms 15 and 24, at the frames of this Group, are Entrance Liturgies.[115] These two psalms raise the question of who would enter through the gates into the temple. Strikingly, the nexuswords in Pss 15:3, 24:6 answer this question with those "who does not take up a reproach with his friend," and "Jacob."[116]

Moving inwards from the frames, Pss 16 and 23 are Confidence psalms[117] and their nexuswords (16:6, 7 "to me, I will bless"; 23:4, "for you are with me") reflect the psalmist's confidence in Yhwh. Similarly, the nexuswords in Pss 17:8, 9 and 22:17 ("you will hide me, from the face of the wicked"; "evildoers encircle me") encapsulate the nature of Lament.[118] Two Kingship psalms[119] (18, 21) surround two central psalms (19, 20) having the motifs of Torah and kingship respectively.[120] The nexuswords lo-

---

112. Longman, *Psalms*, 84, 92, 97.

113. Although Longman considers this a Confidence psalm, he notes that "Psalm 11 is a prayer of a righteous person in the midst of persecution." See Longman, *Psalms*, 90, 92, 95.

114. Barbiero argues that the Day-night alternation is a compositional principle. Barbiero, "Le Premier Livret Du Psautier," 468.

115. Longman, *Psalms*, 100, 138; Craigie, *Psalms 1–50*, 150, 211.

116. Auwers argues that the common theme unifying Pss 15–19 is the concept of "human conduct and standards that defined behaviors of integrity" (Auwers, "Les Voices de L'exégèse," 7).

117. Longman, *Psalms*, 103, 133; or "*Prayer*" by Craigie, *Psalms 1–50*, 155, 197, 204. The genre of Lament and Prayer, though distinguishable, remains slight.

118. Longman, *Psalms*, 107, 128; or "*Prayer*" Craigie notes that Ps 22:2–22 is a "*lament*," within which vv. 12, 20–22 are "*prayer*." Psalm 22:23–32 are "*praise* and *thanksgiving*." Craigie, *Psalms 1–50*, 161, 197.

119. Longman, *Psalms*, 110, 124; Craigie notes that Ps 22 is a "*royal liturgy*" but "should be interpreted in the setting of thanksgiving for a military victory." Psalm 20, according to Craigie is a *royal liturgy*. See Craigie, *Psalms 1–50*, 180, 185.

120. Longman, *Psalms*, 118, 121. Craigie argues that Ps 19 is "a unity (in its present form, at least), and should probably be classified as a *wisdom psalm* (though it also has some features of a prayer, vv.

cated in Pss 18:25; 19:8; 20:6, 7 and 21:7, 8 correspond directly to the content/genre motifs of these four psalms respectively.[121] This is graphically illustrated in Figure 68.

Ps	Nexusword	Distinctive Motif/Genre	Structure
15	[those who does] not take up (reproach) against his neighbor	Who?	A
16	to me. I will bless	Confidence	B
17	you will hide me; from the face (of the wicked)	Lament	C
18	the LORD rewarded (me)	Kingship	D
19	to make wise (the simple)	Torah	E
20	all your petitions. Now I know that the LORD saves his anointed	Kingship	E'
21	your presence, for the king (trusts)	Kingship	D'
22	evildoers encircle me	Lament	C'
23	for you are with me	Confidence	B'
24	Jacob	Who?	A'

Figure 68: Nexusword Structure of Pss 15–24

(5) The Group, Pss 25–34, is also a chiasmus structured according to content/genre motifs of individual psalms and arrangements of AAs or ACs.[122]

The frames, Pss 25 and 34, both AAs, are Laments expressing strong trust in YHWH, and characterized with a concern for justice to the poor.[123] Psalms 26–28 are Individual Laments[124] with a focus on avoiding wickedness. Psalms 31–33 are Thanksgiving psalms,[125] also with a focus on avoiding wickedness. The nexuswords of Pss 26, 27, 31 and 32 ("I go about your altar," "I will offer in his tent sacrifices," "I have become

---

13–14)" (Craigie, *Psalms 1–50*, 180).

121. Note that Labuschagne has to emend Pss 18 and include the headings of Pss 20, 21 to find a meaningful center. Van der Lugt does not consider Pss 19 and 24 as having any rhetorical centers. This is because they have retained their perspective at the level of a single psalm and not Pss 15–24 as a Group.

122. We will discuss AA and AC in the following section.

123. Their nexuswords are "YHWH's testimonies" (25:10) and the "fear of the LORD" (34:12). Longman, *Psalms*, 145, 171; Craigie argues that Ps 25 is likely a *"prayer of confidence,"* or *"individual lament."* On Ps 34, Craigie notes that "the latter portion of the psalm (vv. 10–23) has the general characteristics of wisdom or *didactic* poetry" (Craigie, *Psalms 1–50*, 217, 278). Terrien classifies Ps 34 as a "Sung Meditation by a sage who wishes to teach musically the fear of the LORD" (Terrien, *Psalms*, 303).

124. Longman, *Psalms*, 146, 149, 152. Craigie notes that Ps 26 had been classified as an *"individual lament"* by Gunkel, but he argues that the psalm should be an *"entrance liturgy"* instead. Psalm 27 consists of statements of confidence, a prayer addressed to God and an oracle. He notes that Ps 28 is "commonly classified as an *individual lament.*" See Craigie, *Psalms 1–50*, 224, 231, 236.

125. Longman considers Ps 31 as a Lament but "ending with an expression of thanksgiving." He calls Ps 33 a "victory hymn." Longman, *Psalms*, 160, 163, 166; Similarly, Craigie argues that Ps 31 is a "prayer (vv. 2–19), followed by thanksgiving and praise (vv. 20–25)." On Ps 32, it is "a basic thanksgiving psalm [which] has been given literary adaptation according to the wisdom tradition." Psalm 33, according to Craigie, is a *"hymn of praise"* which contains the call to praise. See Craigie, *Psalms 1–50*, 258, 265, 270.

a broken vessel," "let all godly pray to you") highlight the psalmist's brokenness. This is expressed outwardly in seeking God at the sanctuary in Pss 26 and 27, and internally in Pss 31 and 32. The nexuswords of Pss 28 and 33 are concerned with Yhwh's "reward" to the wicked and his "counsel standing to all generations."

In short, we can detect the nexuswords of Pss 25–34 aligning in genre and content in an A-B-C-B'-A' structure, as seen in Figure 69:

Ps	Nexusword-Motif	Distinctive Motif/Genre	Structure
25	Justice for the poor; Yhwh's testimonies	AA; Justice/Testimonies	A
26–28	Avoiding wickedness; seeking Yhwh at the sanctuary	Individual Lament	B
29–30	Yhwh's kingship and the Zion-temple	Kingship-Temple	C
31–33	Yhwh's purposes for the wicked	Thanksgiving	B'
34	Justice for the poor; fearers of Yhwh	AA; Justice/God-fearers	A'

Figure 69: Nexusword-Motif Structure of Pss 25–34

(6) The nexuswords of Pss 35–41 are aligned with respect to its content and form in this final Group in Book I. Like the previous Group, the content/genre motifs reveal a chiastic structure. The bookends (35, 41) and the center psalm (38) are Supplication psalms.[126] The nexuswords of Pss 35, 38 and 41 ("I bowed down in mourning," "nearest kin stand far off," "against me they whisper") are in alignment to their content. They highlight the brokenness of the psalmist and his cries to Yhwh because of the deeds of his enemies (and even of the closest kin). In a similar way, the nexuswords of Pss 36 and 40 ("your judgments are like the great deep," "I will not restrain my lips") align with their hymnic Praise and Thanksgiving genre respectively.[127]

Two Sapiential Pss 37 and 39 enclose the center Ps 38. The nexusword of Ps 37 ("they vanish like smoke") is a metaphorical comparison between the wicked and perishing nature of pastures and smoke (37:20; cf. 1:4). In Ps 39:7 ("who will gather"), the psalmist asks a rhetorical question: what must he do in light of man's passing nature. Clearly, these two nexuswords are connected in their thought-content. The following Figure 70 summarizes the nexusword structure of Pss 35–41:

---

126. Psalms 35, 38 can also be a Lament where the psalmist calls on God. A clear classification for Lament/Supplication psalm may be difficult. See Longman, *Psalms*, 172, 182, 190. Craigie describes Ps 25 as an *"individual lament* or a *prayer"* and Ps 38 as a *"prayer"* (Craigie, *Psalms 1–50*, 285, 302).

127. Scholars differ in the categorizing of Ps 36 because it contains elements of lament, confidence and thanksgiving. Longman also sees a wisdom element in this psalm. See Longman, *Psalms*, 175, 187. Craigie notes that Ps 36 has been classified as *"individual lament, national lament,* and *wisdom poetry."* However, it is "hymnic" in vv. 6–10, and a "prayer" in vv. 11–13. In Ps 40, Craigie also notes that Ps 40 begins with *"thanksgiving,"* but moves on to *"lament* and *prayer"* (Craigie, *Psalms 1–50*, 290, 314).

The Design of the Psalter

Ps	Nexusword	Distinctive Motif/Genre	Structure
35	I bowed down (in mourning)	Supplication against deeds of enemy or friend	A
36	(your judgments are like the great) deep	Praise	B
37	(they vanish) like smoke (they vanish)	Outcomes of the Wicked	C
38	they stand, my nearest kin (stand far off)	Supplication	D
39	(does not know) who will gather?	Outcomes of the Wicked	C'
40	I will not restrain (my lips O LORD)	Praise	B'
41	(united) against me they whisper	Supplication against deeds of enemy or friend	A'

Figure 70: Nexusword Structure of Pss 35–41

These six observations for Book I affirm that nexuswords correspond well both to the content/genre and poetical structures of various Groups. This is a crucial observation as it suggests that formal numerical devices are designed to correspond with the tacit thematic character of individual psalms. Furthermore, they also correspond to the structural divisions of Book I and the shapes of Groups.

Numerical Devices, Alphabetic Acrostics or Compositions, and Superscriptions

Books II–III

Ps	Nexusword	Word count	MT verse	Alphabetic Acrostic (AA)/ Alphabetic Poem (AC)	Macro-structure and Superscript	Content/ Genre Motifs
42	my God my (soul)	114	7		Korah (*maskil*)	Ind Lament
43	(let them bring me) to thy holy hill	46	3		Untitled	Ind Lament (longing for Zion)
42–43	and in the night, his song (is with me)	*160*	*9*			
44	(you have made us) a scorn (to our neighbors)	173	14		Korah (*maskil*)	Com Lament
45	cassia (are your robes)	139	9			Kingship Song
46	the kingdoms (totter)	87	7	AC		Divine Response (YHWH's kingship)
47	the Lord with the sound (of a trumpet)	64	6		Korah	Divine Response
48	in the city of the LORD of host	100	9			Divine Response
49	generations (the foolish) called (their lands)	144	12			Ind Lament, Wisdom
50	(world's) fullness are mine	149	12	AC	Asaph	
51	(create in me a clean heart) O God!	137	12		hist	Petition
52	forever, he will snatch you (up)	82	7	AC	2x	Lament
53	(have the workers of wickedness no) knowledge	67	5			Lament
54	my life, not!	58	5		2x	Lament
55	but it is you, a man	174	14			Lament
56	Against their crime	107	8		hist; *mikhtam*	Petition, Trust
57	sharp. Be exalted	94	5, 6		hist; *al-tashheth*	Petition, Trust
58	(O God, break the teeth) in their mouths	85	7	PAC	*al-tashheth*	Petition, Trust
59	his strength for you!	134	10	AC	hist; *altashheth*	Petition, Trust
60	answer us, O God	102	7, 8		hist; *shushan*	Petition, Trust
61	*selah*. For you	60	5, 6			CF
62	(I will not) be shaken. On God (rest my salvation)	96	7, 8		*Jeduthun*	CF
63	and my lips	81	6		hist	CF
64	snares, they say.	74	6			CF
65	the roaring (of waves)	101	8			TK
66	you have tried us	131	10		A Psalm	TK
67	(let the) peoples (sing for joy)	49	5		A Song	TK
68	your captives	295	19			TK
69	(O Lord) turn (to me)	251	17			Lament
70	"Aha! (Aha!)"	43	4	AC	for a memorial	Lament
71	dishonor, who seek to injure me.	174	13		Untitled	Petition, Trust
72	(he delivers) the needy's cry for help	140	12		Solomon	Kingship
71–72	*I will sing praise to you with the lyre, O holy one of Israel*		71:22 c–d			
73	every morning	171	14		Asaph	Didactic

The Design of the Psalter

Ps	Nexusword	Word count	MT verse	Alphabetic Acrostic (AA)/ Alphabetic Poem (AC)	Macro-structure and Superscript	Content/ Genre Motifs
74	salvation in the midst (of the land)	174	12	AC		Com Lament
75	for (not from the east or west)	77	7	AC		Divine Response
76	deep sleep, rider (and horse)	78	7			Divine Response
77	it (is my grief)	141	11			Ind Lament
78	they repented (and sought God)	473	34			Didactic
79	do not remember against us (our former sins)	115	8	PAC		Com Lament
80	(and it took) deep root and fill the land	124	10			Com Lament
81	(I will admonish) in you	111	9			Divine Response
82	no understanding	51	5			Divine Response
83	as Jabin	109	10			Ind Lament
84	early rain	101	7		Korah	Ind Lament (towards Zion)
85	grant to us (your salvation)	83	8			Communal Lament (Petition)
86	for you are great	128	10		Dav	Kingship Psalm (Lament)
87	(behold) Philistia (and Tyre)	47	4		Korah	Divine Response
88	(not) go out	131	9			Individual Lament
89	I will strike down (those who hate him), my faithfulness, (and lovingkindness will be with him)	334	24, 25	AC	Ethan	Ind Lament, Royal

Figure 71: Nexusword, Content/Genre Motifs and Macrostructure Juxtaposition in Books II–III[128]

Consider the following observations on Books II–III: (1) Beginning with the first Group of Korahite psalms (42–49), we note that it is bound by Laments (42–43, 44, 49)[129] with a single Kingship and three Divine Response psalms at the center (45, 46–48).[130] The nexuswords of these psalms are Laments, a longing for Zion-temple from a distant land, which correspond to their content/genre motifs. The nexusword in 44:14 ("you have made us a scorn") expresses a Communal Lament. In Ps 45, the

---

128. Legend: AA: Alphabetical Acrostic; AC: Alphabetical Composition; PAC: Probable Alphabetical Composition; hist: historical superscription; Sup: Supplication psalm; TK: Thanksgiving; CF: Confidence psalm.

129. Psalms 42–43 are Individual Laments and Ps 44 is a Communal Lament. Scholars view Ps 49 as having genre elements of both Wisdom and Lament. See Longman, *Psalms*, 193, 198, 213. Craigie considers Pss 42–43 as "*individual lament*" and Ps 44 as a "*national* (or communal) *lament.*" Psalm 49, according to him, is a "*wisdom psalm*" (Craigie, *Psalms 1–50*, 325, 331, 358).

130. Longman considers Pss 46 and 48 as a "Zion Hymn" where "God makes his presence known to his people." Psalm 47 is also a psalm that celebrates "God as King" (Longman, *Psalms*, 201, 204, 209). Craigie categorized Pss 46 and 48 as "*Songs of Zion*," a subcategory of hymns. See Craigie, *Psalms 1–50*, 342, 352.

nexusword ("cassia are your robes") is part of a description of the anointed king (45:8-9). The nexuswords for Pss 46-48 highlight the "tottering of the kingdoms" (46:7) upon the voice of Yhwh, with Yhwh mounting as king "with the sound of a trumpet" (47:6) and him establishing in "the city of the Lord of host" (48:9).[131] These three nexuswords identify Yhwh's kingship over Israel and the foreign nations. In short, the nexuswords of the first Group of Korahite psalms correspond well with its characteristic content/genre.

(2) The second Group of Korahite psalms (84-89) is structured like the first. They are bound by Laments (84-85; 88-89).[132] Similarly, two psalms at the center of the Group are identified as Kingship (Davidic) and Divine Response psalms respectively.[133] Psalm 84:5-7 describes the worshippers enroute to Zion, passing through the valley of "Baka" ("dryness").[134] Longman notes the worshippers "bring life-giving water to the area in the form of springs and rains."[135] Thus the nexusword, "early rain" (84:7), is a metaphor for "blessing," found at the valley of weeping (Lament).

The nexusword in Ps 85:8 ("grant to us your salvation") is a cry to Yhwh for salvation, while that of Ps 86 ("for you are great") highlights Yhwh's kingship.[136] All nations will come to worship him. This universality of Yhwh, likewise, characterizes the nexusword of Ps 88 ("I am shut up and cannot to go out"). In Ps 89, the nexusword ("lovingkindness will be with him") identifies Yhwh's steadfast love for his son whose kingship will be established. Yhwh would also strike down all those who hate him.[137] Like the first Korahite Group, the nexuswords of the second Korahite Group correspond to its genre content to some extent.

---

131. Longman views Yhwh as the Divine Warrior in Ps 46:8-10 with his ascendancy to kingship in 47:5-7. See Longman, *Psalms*, 205, 208. Craigie views Ps 47 as "*enthronement psalm*" or "*victory hymn*" (Craigie, *Psalms 1-50*, 348).

132. Longman identifies Ps 84 as a Zion Hymn; Ps 85 as a Communal Lament; Ps 88 as an Individual Lament; and Ps 89 as both a Royal hymn and Community Lament. See Longman, *Psalms*, 310, 312, 319, 322. Tate notes Ps 84 as a psalm containing "mixed elements although it is usually described as a hymn which expresses devotion to the temple in Jerusalem." He argues that Ps 85 is a "prayer for the favor and saving work of Yahweh." For him, Ps 88 is an individual lament and Ps 89 is a mixed genre, consisting of lament and "Hymnic praise" (vv. 2-3, 6-19), "Recall of divine oracle about David" (vv. 4-5, 20-38) and Lament (vv. 39-52). See Tate, *Psalms 51-100*, 355, 367, 413.

133. Longman argues that Ps 87 is "about Zion" and "God makes his presence known in the world" (Longman, *Psalms*, 317). Tate classifies Ps 87 as "a poem which praises Zion as the city of God and the center of life" (Tate, *Psalms 51-100*, 387).

134. Longman, *Psalms*, 311. This also recalls the place of "weeping" (הבכים) in Judges 2:1, 5. Perhaps we can see a parallel between this place of "weeping" in Judges 2 and the "valley of weeping" in Ps 84. Both contexts locate Israel's disobedience and falling into the hands of foreigners, accompanied by a longing to be established at Zion or Canaan, the land of the promised inheritance.

135. Longman, *Psalms*, 311.

136. Psalm 86 may be classified as a Lament. However, its center core relates to Yhwh's kingship and supremacy. Zenger also notes that the Davidic superscription describes the king "not as the battling and victorious king, but rather as the suffering servant of Yhwh" (Hossfeld and *Zenger, Psalms 2*, 370-71).

137. The nexusword of Ps 89 highlights Yhwh's kingship in a psalm that consists of both lament

(3) When we compare the first and second Korahite Groups, they parallel each other, not just in genre structure, but also in nexusword content. The Individual Laments at the beginning of each Korahite Group (42–43, 84) are expressed vis-à-vis the Zion-temple. The Communal Laments that follow (44, 85) use nexuswords that are speeches directed to God. The Kingship songs (45, 86) and Divine Responses (46–48, 87) are descriptions of the king and how he is to act. The final psalm in each Group (49, 89) is mixed in genre. Psalm 49 is both a Lament and a Wisdom[138] psalm, whereas Ps 89 is both a Lament and a Kingship psalm.

Korahite Group I	Genre	Nexusword Motif	Korahite Group II
42–43	Individual Lament	Zion-centered	84
44	Communal Lament	People's cry to God	85
45	Kingship Song	Descriptions of the king	86
46–48	Divine Response (YHWH's kingship)	YHWH's response	87
49	Mixed genre. Lament, Wisdom	Psalmist's despondence and YHWH's kingship	88, 89

Figure 72: Genre-nexusword Parallels in the Korahite Groups

Together, the first and last psalms in these two Korahite Groups (42–43 and 84; 49 and 88–89) contain the leitmotifs of Wisdom (or Torah)-Kingship-Zion, seen throughout the Psalter (e.g., 1–2, 18–19). These two Korahite Groups bind the Davidic and Asaphite[139] Groups at the center, which will be discussed below.

(4) Consider the nexuswords in Pss 51–71. The nexusword in Ps 51 is a petition cry, "O God," and the nexuswords in Pss 52–55 ("forever he will snatch you and tear you up from your tent," "workers of wickedness have not knowledge," "trying to seek my life," "but it is you, a man") identify the psalmist's complaint to YHWH against his enemies.[140] In Ps 56, the nexusword ("against their crime") reflects a trust in YHWH that he will punish the wicked. The nexusword of Ps 57 ("sharp swords," "YHWH's

---

and praise.

138. Craigie calls Ps 49 a "wisdom psalm" with similar didactic themes as the Book of Job. See Craigie, *Psalms 1–50*, 358

139. Psalm 50 will be treated together with Pss 73–83.

140. The difficulty of assigning genre category for Ps 52 is acknowledged as it can be seen as a "prophetic judgment discourse," "wisdom psalm," or a "lament," depending on which part of the psalm is in focus. Similarly, Ps 53 is hard to categorize. It can be considered as a "prophetic lament." Hossfeld categorizes Ps 54 as a "petitionary prayer with integrated lament." He has not assigned a genre for Ps 55, but repeatedly characterized it as "a plea to God" (Hossfeld and Zenger, *Psalms 2*, 28, 40, 46, 52). This difficulty of classifying Ps 52 is noted by Tate. For him, Ps 53 contains a "lament by the speaker regarding personal and social conditions." Psalm 54 is an "individual lament" with elements of "thanksgiving." Likewise, Ps 55 is an "individual lament, though it has strong statements of assurance and exhortation" (Tate, *Psalms 51–100*, 35, 41, 45, 55).

"highness") straddles across two Masoretic verses. The first expresses of accusations by his enemies whereas the second word exalts Yhwh. Together, they express the psalmist's trust in Yhwh. The nexuswords of Pss 58–60 ("O God, break the teeth in their mouth," "his strength for you," "answer us, O God!") express the psalmist's trust in Yhwh's victory over his enemies.[141] In similar ways, the nexuswords of Pss 61–63 are all found to express trust in God ("For you," "I will not be shaken, on God," "and my lips offer praises"),[142] corresponding to their characteristic content/genre motifs. While the nexusword in Ps 64:6 ("laying snares secretly") speaks of the psalmist's enemies, its complete expression underscores the confidence that they will not escape Yhwh's judgment.

The nexuswords in Pss 65–67 describe Yhwh stilling the "roaring of waves" (65:8),[143] "the purifying" of his people (66:10) and that his "people would sing joyfully" (67:5). The nexusword of Ps 68 highlights Yhwh's ascendancy to the throne, victoriously leading a train of "captives." The nexusword in Pss 69 ("O Lord, turn to me") shows a turn from exaltation to lamentation,[144] and highlights the desperate condition of the psalmist and the oppression of his enemies. The nexusword in Ps 70 ("Aha!") captures the enemies' mocking voice and that of Ps 71 ("who seek to injure me") expresses the psalmist's trust in Yhwh and petitions against his enemies.[145] The nexusword of Ps 72 ("he delivers the needy's cry for help") does not correspond directly to Kingship. However, when read with the preceding verse, it describes the actions of the king of kings.[146]

Note that DC-II is framed by a Didactic/Prophetic (50) and a Kingship psalm (72).[147] Both psalms also contain the Zion motif but in this case, the perfect beauty of Yhwh shines forth and his rule "produces" from Zion (ינון; 72:17; cf. 50:2; 72:8).

141. Hossfeld notes that "Psalm 58 can most properly be assigned to the mixed genre "Wisdom song." Psalm 59 consists of a movement "from petition via lament to expression of trust" (Hossfeld and Zenger, *Psalms 2*, 79, 86–87). Tate argues that Ps 58 begins with an "Arraignment of unjust leaders" and ends with an "Assurance of the righteous." In similar ways, Ps 59 begins with a "Call for help, lament and prayer" and ends with a "Refrain about confidence in God" (Tate, *Psalms 51–100*, 85, 96).

142. Hossfeld and Zenger, *Psalms 2*, 106, 113, 121. Tate describes Ps 61 as "more affirmation than it is petition." Psalm 62 is "clearly one of trust and affirmation" and Ps 63, based on vv. 4–9, "indicate clearly that this is a psalm of confidence" (Tate, *Psalms 51–100*, 112, 119, 125).

143. Goldingay notes that the stilling of waves underscore Yhwh's power over the "tumultuous dynamic forces" of nature (Goldingay, *Psalms*, 2:279). On genre classification of these psalms, see Longman, *Psalms*, 250–55.

144. Longman, *Psalms*, 262; Tate, *Psalms 51–100*, 192.

145. Pss 50, 66, 67, 71 and 72 in Book II are not Davidic. Book II is not bound by Davidic psalms.

146. If we include three words (words joined by *maqqef* are taken as a single word) from either side of אביון משוע ("needy's cry for help" in 72:12), the nexusword will be כל-גוים יעבדוהו כי-יציל אביון משוע ועני ואין-עזר לו ("For all nations will serve him, for he delivers the needy's cry for help, the poor and those who have no helper"). This entire phrase is still the arithmetic center based on my method of count.

147. While many scholars consider it as a Prophetic psalm, didactic or wisdom element may be seen in Ps 50:7–14, recalling Yhwh's responses to Job at the end of the book.

(5) Like the Korahite Groups, the Asaphite psalms are structurally divided into two Groups that parallel each other (50, 73–77 and 78–83). The nexusword of Ps 50 ("world's fullness is mine") recalls Yhwh's responses to Job, explicating a didactic knowledge of God's ownership of the natural world. Being stricken "every day," Psalm 73:14–15 show us the psalmist struggling to know Yhwh's purposes with regards to the prosperity of the wicked.

The nexusword of Psalm 74 ("salvation in the midst of the land") relates to Yhwh's kingship more than a Communal Lament. Longman identifies this as a Lament[148] and Goldingay calls this psalm a "community prayer."[149] This may be an anomaly in our analysis, though the context of the nexusword is an appeal to Yhwh's character and deeds in the midst of a Lament.[150] The nexuswords of Pss 75 and 76 ("for not from the east of the west," "rider and horse were cast into deep sleep") are both expressions of divine judgment and deliverance. The final psalm in the first group of Asaphite psalms has the pronoun "it" as its nexusword (77:11), appealing to Yhwh's outstretched hand in the midst of his grief.

Psalm 78, the first in the second group of Asaphite psalms (akin to its parallel, Ps 50), is a Didactic/Historical psalm.[151] The nexusword ("they repented and sought God") captures Israel's returning to Yhwh (78:34). Psalms 79 and 80 are Communal Laments.[152] The nexusword in 79:8 ("do not remember against our former sins") highlights the community under the wrath of God. Like Ps 74, the nexusword of Ps 80 ("it [the people] took deep root and fill the land") is an appeal to Yhwh's character and deeds in the midst of a Lament. The figurative imagery of the clearing of the ground and of the flourishing vine (nexusword in Ps 80) refers to the conquest of Canaan and Israel's establishment,[153] though subsequent descriptions show that the vine will be cut down and burnt (80:17). Like Ps 74, Ps 80 is the first of three psalms (cf. 74–76, 80–82) that emphasizes divine power and deliverance.

The nexusword of Ps 81 ("I will admonish in you") recalls Yhwh's testing of the people in Exod 15:26, and a call for Yhwh to rescue the poor and needy from the wicked respectively.[154] The nexusword in Ps 82:5 ("without understanding") may refer to the "wicked" in the previous verse. It expresses the ignorance and tottering of the wicked before Yhwh who is the judge of the earth. It is unclear whether Ps 83 is an

---

148. Longman, *Psalms*, 278.

149. Goldingay, *Psalms*, 2:423. Tate notes that the "language of vv. 1–11 and vv. 18–23 is clearly that of communal lament" (Tate, *Psalms 51–100*, 246).

150. Psalm 81 is also an Alphabetic Composition (AC). The AC usually marks strategic psalms with key motifs of Torah/wisdom and kingship.

151. Longman argues that the opening stanza "presents itself well within the tradition of wisdom literature" (Longman, *Psalms*, 289).

152. Longman, *Psalms*, 294, 297.

153. Longman, *Psalms*, 299–300.

154. Goldingay, *Psalms*, 2:552, 2:565–66.

Individual or Communal Lament,[155] but it is a complaint against the nations plotting against Yʜᴡʜ. The nexusword in Ps 83 ("Jabin") recalls the Canaanite king (cf. Judg 4:2–3) who had, at one time, oppressed Israel for twenty years. Discussions related to the Asaphite Groups are summarized in Figure 73.

Asaphite Group I	Genre	Nexusword Motif	Asaphite Group II
50, 73	Didactic, Sapiential	Repentance and seeking God	78
74	Communal Lament	Appeal to character and deeds of Yʜᴡʜ in the midst of lamenting for Zion	79–80
75–76	Divine Response	Divine judgment and deliverance	81–82
77	Lament	Calling out to Yʜᴡʜ	83

Figure 73: Genre-nexusword Parallels in Asaphite Groups

In brief, we observe that the nexuswords of the psalms in Books II–III generally correspond well to their characteristic content/genre motifs and various macrostructural trajectories there they occur. While the link between some nexuswords and the psalm content may not be obvious *prima facie*, it is possible to show that they still elicit a certain characteristic motif that is important and coherent in the larger context. To complete our analysis, we will now focus on Books IV–V.

---

155. Tate notes that this psalm "contains mixed elements, although it is usually described as a hymn which expresses devotion to the temple in Jerusalem" (Tate, *Psalms 51–100*, 355).

The Design of the Psalter

Books IV–V

Ps	Nexusword	Word count	MT verse	Alphabetic Acrostic (AA)/ Alphabetic Poem (AC)	Macro-structure and Superscript	Content/ Genre Motifs
90	we bring to an end, our years like a sigh	125	9		Moses	Sapiential, Supplication
91	you will look (with your eyes)	99	8		Untitled	Trust
92	(you, O LORD) are on high forever!	100	9		A Psalm, Song	TK, Didactic
93	floods	41	3		YHWH *Malak*	YHWH *Malak*; Praise/Trust
94	to give him rest (both words start with lamed)	146	13	AC	Untitled	YHWH *Malak*; CF
95	for (he is our God)	77	7	AC	Untitled	YHWH *Malak*; Praise
94, 95	*your steadfast love, O LORD, held me up. (3-word center)*	*223*	*94:18*			
96	ascribe (to the LORD)	95	8	PAC	Un-titled	YHWH *Malak*; Praise
97	all who serve idols	84	7		YHWH *Malak*	YHWH *Malak*; Praise
98	sing praises	67	4		A Psalm, Song	YHWH *Malak*; Praise
99	holy (is he)	77	5		YHWH *Malak*	YHWH *Malak*; Praise
100	we are his people	36	3	PAC	TK	TK, Praise
101	secretly his neighbor	70	5		David	Royal
102	for (your servants) find pleasure (in her stones)	183	15		Afflict	Ind Lament
103	(he removed) our transgression (from us)	141	12	AC	David	TK Prayer
104	(the cliffs are) a refuge (for rock badgers)	233	18		*bless*	Song on Creator and Sustainer
105	Jacob sojourned (in the land of ham)	256	23	PAC	*hodu*	Remembrance; Canonical history
106	they did not believe (his word)	287	24	AC	Hallelujah	Remembrance; Canonical history
107	let them recount (his works with joy)	253	22		*hodu*	TK, Canonical history/wisdom
108	(I will measure out) the valley (of Succoth)	85	8			Petition, a song
109	despondent (in the heart)	201	16		David	Ind Lament, Psalm of Justice
110	your youth	55	3			Kingship; Divine Response
111	to his people, to give [note *lamed*]	68	6		Hallelujah	Confessional Hymn;
112	remembered forever	72	6		Hallelujah	Torah/wisdom
111 – 112	*praise God, blessed is the man!*	*140*	*112.1*			
113	who (is like the LORD)?	51	5		Hallelujah	Praise; Theocentric
114	what was it?	47	5			Praise; Theocentric
115	(he is) their help and their shield	118	9		Untitled	Praise; Theocentric
116	I believe	109	10			Ind TK or Confession; Universal

Numerical Devices, Alphabetic Acrostics or Compositions, and Superscriptions

Ps	Nexusword	Word count	MT verse	Alphabetic Acrostic (AA)/ Alphabetic Poem (AC)	Macro-structure and Superscript	Content/ Genre Motifs
117	for he is great [12-word psalm]	12	2		Hallelujah	Praise; Universal
113 – 117	trust!	337	115:11			
118	the (right hand of) the LORD has done (valiantly)	178	15		hodu	TK; Kingship
119	(forever) your word will stand (in the heavens [first line of the *lamed* canto])	934	89		ashre	Torah/Wisdom Song
120	warriors' sharpened (arrows)	42	4		Songs of Ascents	Lament
121	(no) sleep, watcher (of Israel)	46	4			Com Trust
122	for (there the thrones are set for judgment)	57	5			Zion hymn
123	our eyes (look to the LORD God)	35	2			Lament/ Petition
124	(the stream would have) swept over our soul	54	4			TK
125	the wickedness (not rest over the righteous)	43	3			CF, Trust; Rule of the wicked
126	the LORD	45	3			Mixed; TK/Prayer/ Lament
127	he gives (to his beloved)	49	2			Wisdom/Zion
128	(shoots of) olive (around your table)	43	3			Wisdom
129	turned backwards (those who hate Zion)	50	5			Mixed; TK/Petition/ Lament; Rule of the wicked
130	(I wait) for the LORD	47	5			Lament
131	(surely) I have composed (calmed myself)	27	2			CF
132	the LORD has sworn (to David)	109	11			Royal, CF; Zion
133	the beard of Aaron	29	2			Wisdom
134	in the night; lift up your hands	20	1, 2			Praise
133 – 134	*(for there the LORD has) commanded (the blessing, life forevermore)*	*49*	*133.3c*			
120 – 134	*(he gives) to his beloved, sleep.*	*696*	*127.2*			
135	(king) of Amorite, and Og (king of Bashan)	144	11		Hallelujah	Great Hallel
136	(to him who divided the Red Sea in two, for his steadfast love) endures forever	159	13		hodu	Great Hallel
137	let my tongue cling	68	6		Untitled	Janus psalm
138	Lord. For (great is the glory of the LORD)	62	5	AC	David	YHWH's kingship
139	in the womb of my mother	160	13			Prayer, Meditation
140	(give ear to the) voice of my pleas for mercy, O LORD!	104	7			Ind Lament

301

The Design of the Psalter

Ps	Nexusword	Word count	MT verse	Alphabetic Acrostic (AA)/ Alphabetic Poem (AC)	Macro-structure and Superscript	Content/ Genre Motifs
141	for continually (my prayer is against their evil deeds)	81	5			Ind Lament
142	no refuge remains (for me)	68	5		David (hist)	Ind Lament
143	answer me O LORD	102	7			Ind Lament
144	O God, a (new) song!	120	9	PAC	David	Praise
145	they tell of your power!	126	11			YHWH's kingship
138 – 145	*a prayer (superscription of Ps 142:1)*	823	142:1			
146	the one who keeps faith (forever)	74	6			Individual
147	his delights is not in the leg (of man)	126	10			Israel
148	hail	87	8		*hallelujah*	Cosmic and Israel
149	(let the) godly (exult in glory)	57	5			Faithful Israel
150	harp and lyre	34	3	AC		Universal
146 – 150	*his words to Jacob*	378	147:19			

Figure 74: Nexusword, Content/Genre Motifs and Macrostructure Juxtaposition in Books IV–V[156]

Psalm 90 is a prayer with wisdom elements.[157] Its nexusword ("we bring to an end, our years like a sigh") captures the motif of the transitoriness of human life, a common feature of sapiential works. The nexusword in Psalm 91:8 as a whole ("you will look with your eyes") encapsulates the psalmist's trust[158] in YHWH. Psalm 92 is a Praise and Thanksgiving hymn[159] and its nexusword proclaims "YHWH is forever on high!" The nexuswords of these three opening psalms of Book IV thus evoke man's transitoriness (90), express an unwavering trust that YHWH will judge the wicked (91), and exults YHWH (92). They are connected with the contrasting concept of human transitoriness and permanent establishment (90:1; 91:1, 9, 10; 92:12–13). Between the two

156. Legend: AA: Alphabetical Acrostic; AC: Alphabetical Composition; PAC: Probable Alphabetical Composition; hist: historical superscription; Sup: Supplication psalm; TK: Thanksgiving; CF: Confidence psalm; Ind: Individual; Com: Communal. See chapters 1–3 and the subsequent section for details on how superscriptions play a role in the macrostructure of the Psalter based on numerical techniques.

157. Goldingay, *Psalms*, 3:22; Tate notes that the psalm is "a communal prayer composed of grateful reflection, complaint, and petitions for a gracious divine action" (Tate, *Psalms 51–100*, 437).

158. Goldingay notes that this is an individual declaration of YHWH's protection addressed to the king (cf. Ps 20). See Goldingay, *Psalms*, 3:39. Tate saw this as "a prayer with didactic/sermonic intention" (Tate, *Psalms 51–100*, 451).

159. Goldingay notes that it is a Thanksgiving hymn with didactic elements. See Goldingay, *Psalms*, 3:52–53; Tate, *Psalms 51–100*, 464.

metaphoric and arboreal descriptions of transitoriness and permanence (90:5–6; 92:7, 12–13), the psalmist envisages the way to escape the transitoriness in Ps 92. He will see the deliverance (92:3–7, 10–13) and "recompense of the wicked" (92:8) when he makes Yhwh his place of refuge and trust (92:1–2, 14–16). This trajectory culminates with Ps 93 in praise of Yhwh as the one who destroys the wicked and establishes the righteous. The three nexuswords identified in Pss 90–92 correspond exactly with this trajectory.

Psalms 90–92 prepare us for the nexusword characterization of the Yhwh *Malak* psalms (93–100). In the latter, the nexuswords "exult" (98:4) Yhwh's kingship and holiness (96:8, "ascribe"; 99:5, "holy is he"), Yhwh's relationship with his people (94:13,[160] "to give him rest"; 95:7, "for he is our God"; 100:3, "we are his people"), as well as Yhwh's power over the forces of nature (93:3, "floods"),[161] and other gods (97:7, "all who serve idols"). The Yhwh *Malak* psalms are primarily psalms of Trust, Confidence or Praise[162] and nexuswords in these psalms correspond well to their genre content.

If Psalms 94 and 95 can be seen as a single AC,[163] the nexusword based on my method of counting is "Yhwh" in 94:18, which corresponds to the main idea in Pss 93–100. This nexusword is at the center of the three-word colon that reads, "your steadfast love, Yhwh, held me up." This colon also summarizes the focus of the entire Yhwh *Malak* group that Yhwh rules and acts faithfully.

The nexuswords of the three Davidic psalms (101–103; DC-III) express the quintessential thoughts of each psalm and its content/genre motifs respectively. The nexusword of Ps 101 ("I will destroy he who slanders his neighbor secretly") highlights the righteous administration of the king eliminating wickedness from his house.[164] Psalm 102:15 ("for your servants find pleasure in her stones") expresses the lament of Yhwh's servants regarding the ruins of Zion. In Psalm 103:12 ("he removed our transgression from us"), the psalmist gives thanks to Yhwh for removing his transgressions.[165]

The nexuswords of Pss 104–106 also accord with their content/genre motifs. Psalm 104 "celebrates God as the Creator and Sustainer of all life on earth."[166] Its

---

160. Both words in the nexusword in 94:13 begin with *lamed* (להשקיט לו).

161. On Ps 93:3, Goldingay referenced Isa 17:12–13, where the "roar of waters is a figure for the roar of the nations. The river might thus be political powers such as the great empires" (Goldingay, *Psalms*, 3:69). Tate notes that Ps 93 is a "hymn or praise psalm" (Tate, *Psalms 51–100*, 474).

162. Goldingay, *Psalms*, 3:64, 3:75, 3:88, 3:101; 3:110; 3:119; 3:126; 3:134.

163. Alphabetic Compositions (AC) will be discussed in the following section.

164. Longman sees Ps 101 as a Royal song, Ps 102 as an Individual Lament and Ps 103 as a Thanksgiving Prayer. See Longman, *Psalms*, 350, 352, 355.

165. A parallel thought progress between the triad Pss 90–92 and 101–103 can be seen: they underscore the righteous administration of the king (cf. 90:12, 17; 101:5–8); two different outcomes befalling the wicked and Yhwh's servants (cf. 91:8; 102:14, 28), and finally the psalmist's restored state before Yhwh (cf. 92:12–13; 103:12–13).

166. Longman, *Psalms*, 358,

nexusword ("the cliffs are a refuge") captures this content/genre motif. Psalms 105 and 106 are both "remembrance psalms"[167] that trace the canonical history of ancient Israel. The nexusword of Ps 105 ("Jacob sojourned") identifies Jacob's journey and that of Ps 106 ("they did not believe his word") identifies the crux of the issue, that is, Israel's inability to enter the land due to disbelief. This nexusword locates the final psalm at the juncture between Books IV and V, as Israel yearns to be gathered up from wherever she has been dispersed to become once again an inhabited city.

Book V begins with Ps 107, a wisdom psalm that is closely related to Pss 104–106.[168] The nexusword of Ps 107 ("recount his works with joy") encapsulates the entirety of the psalm and corresponds to the genre of Thanksgiving, recalling with joy the works of Yhwh in Israel's canonical history. The three Davidic psalms that follow are a Petition,[169] an Individual Lament,[170] and a Kingship hymn.[171]

Psalms 111–112 are a pair of Confessional AAs with clear Torah and sapiential elements. Like Ps 1, they address Yhwh's blessings to the righteous man who delights in his law. The nexusword of Ps 111 ("to give to his people") is a confession that Yhwh will לעמו לתת the inheritance of the nations. The nexusword of Ps 112 ("remembered forever") confesses that the righteous will be לזכר עולם. Both nexuswords begin with a *lamed*. When these two AAs are counted as a single composition, their combined nexusword is found in the first verse of Ps 112, "Praise God, blessed is the man," which corresponds to both ideas found in the separate nexuswords.

Framed by *hallelujah* in the superscriptions, Pss 113–15, 117 are deemed as psalms of Praise or Confidence.[172] Psalm 116 has been classified as an Individual Thanksgiving or Confession psalm.[173] The nexuswords of Pss 113 ("who is like the Lord"), 115 ("he is their help and shield") and 117 ("for he is great"), and the rhetorical question in Ps 114:5 are all theocentric in nature, clearly capturing the content/genre motif of Praise. Likewise, the nexusword of Ps 116 ("I believe") expresses a confession of trust in Yhwh for the present and future because of his grace (חנון; 116:5) and mighty deeds in the past. The nexusword of Ps 116, "I believe," clearly expresses confidence and trust in Yhwh. When I count the words in Pss 113–117 as a single composition, the nexusword is "trust" at the center colon of Ps 115:11, corresponding exactly with the nexusword of Ps 116!

---

167. Longman, *Psalms*, 364, 268.

168. Zenger argues that "Psalm 107, *as a whole*, is so strongly linked, both semantically and conceptually, with the preceding Psalm 106 that it must be regarded as a deliberate continuation, though with an altered perspective" (Hossfeld and Zenger, *Psalms 3*, 101).

169. Hossfeld and Zenger, *Psalms 3*, 117.

170. Hossfeld and Zenger, *Psalms 3*, 128; Goldingay, *Psalms*, 3:276.

171. Hossfeld and Zenger, *Psalms 3*, 144–45.

172. Goldingay, *Psalms*, 3:316, 3:321, 3:327, 3:349. Longman sees Pss 113; 114 as celebratory songs. Longman, *Psalms*, 389, 391.

173. Goldingay, *Psalms*, 3:338.

Longman considers Ps 118 as a "corporate thanksgiving that celebrates a military victory" brought about by God, and Ps 119 is an acrostic "wisdom song" exulting the qualities of Yhwh's law.[174] The nexusword of Ps 118, based on my count, falls exactly on the two words at the center of the phrase, ימין יהוה עשה חיל ("Yhwh does"; 118:15). These two words, with its entire colon of four words (still the arithmetic center), coincide exactly with the meaningful/rhetorical centers identified by Labuschagne and van der Lugt.[175] Such a correlation is uncanny. The nexusword, "your [Yhwh] word will stand" in Ps 119:89, falls exactly on the first line of the *lamed* canto and captures the quintessential thought of Ps 119.

Psalm 120 is a Lament.[176] Its nexusword ("warriors' sharpened arrow") is a complaint against the enemies' vicious attacks. Psalm 121 is a Communal psalm of Confidence/Trust.[177] Its nexusword ("watcher of Israel does not slumber") is a profession of trust in the unceasing keeping of Israel by Yhwh. Psalm 122 is a Hymn of celebration and Prayer for Zion.[178] The verse which the nexusword ("for there the thrones are set") resides in identifies two crucial features in Zion—judgment thrones and the house of David. In chapter 2, we have seen how Pss 122, 127–28 and 132 develop the motif of the Zion city.[179] The nexuswords in Pss 122, 127 ("he gives to his beloved") and 132 ("Yhwh has sworn to David") capture this trajectory, highlighting the locale of Zion where justice is sought; blessings through Yhwh's provision alone, and Yhwh's promises to David.[180]

The nexusword of Ps 123 ("our eyes look to Yhwh") is a lament/petition to Yhwh while the nexusword of Ps 124 ("the stream swept over our soul") is a collective thanksgiving in recognition of what Yhwh has done.[181] The nexuxword's proclamation that the "wicked will not rest over the allotment of the righteous" in Ps 125:3 expresses the confidence of the psalm.[182] Psalm 126 is a Mixed psalm. Zenger deems this as a "petition for daily demonstration of Yhwh's power to bless."[183] The colon that

---

174. Longman, *Psalms*, 399, 402–403, 408.

175. Labuschagne, "Psalm 118," 1–6; van der Lugt; *CAS III*, 288.

176. Longman, *Psalms*, 410; Goldingay, *Psalms*, 3:448.

177. Longman, *Psalms*, 413; Goldingay, *Psalms*, 3:455; Hossfeld and Zenger, *Psalms 3*, 320.

178. Longman, *Psalms*, 416; Goldingay, *Psalms*, 3:462; Hossfeld and Zenger, *Psalms 3*, 343.

179. First, in Ps 122:5, the pilgrims desire a city of justice that is administered through a Davidic king. Second, this seems to be envisioned in Pss 127–28, enabled by Yhwh's providence for his beloved people. Third, this motif of a righteous rule through the Davidic house envisioned as an ideal, well-provisioned and just society, becomes clearer in Ps 132:15–18.

180. Psalms 127 and 132 are deemed as wisdom poem and royal/confidence hymn. Longman, *Psalms*, 425, 440; Goldingay, *Psalms*, 3:498, 3:542; Hossfeld and Zenger, *Psalms 3*, 381, 384, 457.

181. Longman, *Psalms*, 418, 420; Goldingay, *Psalms*, 3:470, 3:477; Hossfeld and Zenger, *Psalms 3*, 346, 353.

182. Zenger considers this psalm a petition and psalm of Zion. See Hossfeld and Zenger, *Psalms 3*, 362, 363; Longman, *Psalms*, 421; Goldingay, *Psalms*, 3:484, 3:542.

183. Hossfeld and Zenger, *Psalms 3*, 375. Cf. Longman, *Psalms*, 423; Goldingay, *Psalms*, 3:490.

carries the nexusword in Ps 126:3 ("Yhwh has done great things for us") expresses the core thought of the psalm.

The nexusword, "olives" (זית) in 128:3, is a simile for many children around the table, identifying a flourishing scene in the house of those who fear the LORD. This recalls Ps 52:10 (cf. 92:12), the only other occurrence of זית in the Psalms. Furthermore, both instances of this word are used in connection with the "house," and describe the protection and providence of a child under the father's household. In other words, the lexeme "olive" in the Psalter has a very clear and distinct usage. Together with Ps 1:3, where the righteous are planted in "Zion," the nexusword encapsulates the growth of the righteous under the care and house of God.[184] This nexusword is an example of the technique of *Fernverbindung*.[185] Yhwh's providence from Zion (his house) in 127:1 and 128:5 frame the entire imagery of blessings in the house of those who fear the LORD. Hence, the nexuswords of Pss 127 ("beloved") and 128 ("olive shoots") capture the quintessential focus of these two psalms.

Psalm 129 is a Mixed psalm.[186] It focuses on the rule of the wicked, referring to those who hate Zion. The nexusword ("those who hate Zion turned backward") in Ps 129:5 captures this thematic focus, that the enemies will eventually be יסגו אחור. Psalm 130 is a Lament/Petition.[187] The colon where the nexusword ("I wait for Yhwh") resides expresses the psalmist's lament. In contrast, the nexusword of Ps 131 ("I have calmed myself") expresses the psalmist's trust.[188]

The count revealing the nexusword of Ps 133 falls on an interesting expression, "the beard of Aaron," that has been well discussed.[189] The focus on the anointing is emphasized by the repetitions of "beard" (זקן). If the entire colon, "Aaron's beard," is missing,[190] the anointing in Ps 133:2 can be associated only with the anointed king in 132:10 in the immediate context. Following Dobbs-Allsopp, Armstrong notes that "the only other biblical instance of ירד being used in connection with a beard is when spit ran down David's beard in 1 Sam 21:14," further reinforcing the association between anointing and the king in Ps 132:10.[191] The mention of "Aaron's beard,"

---

184. See our earlier discussion on Pss 1–2 where we argue that the locale of the streams of water in Ps 1 parallels Zion in Ps 2. On the genre of Ps 128, see Longman, *Psalms*, 427; Goldingay, *Psalms*, 3:507.

185. Lexical or certain phonological, semantic, syntactical, and grammatical parallels that bind distant psalms.

186. Zenger notes that it "oscillates between thanksgiving song, psalm of confidence, popular psalm of Lament and of vengeance" (Hossfeld and Zenger, *Psalms 3*, 409).

187. Longman, *Psalms*, 430; Goldingay, *Psalms*, 3:522; Hossfeld and Zenger, *Psalms 3*, 426.

188. Longman, *Psalms*, 432; Goldingay, *Psalms*, 3:534; Hossfeld and Zenger, *Psalms 3*, 448.

189. Hossfeld and Zenger, *Psalms 3*, 470–71, 474–77; Armstrong compares Pss 133 and 134 in the MT with various extant Qumran manuscripts. He links the priestly anointing of Aaron in Pss 133 with 132. Armstrong, "Psalms Dwelling Together in Unity," 499.

190. Note Bardtke's suggestion (in *BHS*) that the entire phrase, "the beard of Aaron, running down on the collar of his robes" may be deleted.

191. Armstrong, "Psalms Dwelling Together in Unity," 499.

however, limits this association. As stated earlier, the mention of Aaron highlights the "completion" of YHWH's house which he will build (127:1). The role of Psalms 133–36 describes what follows after the completion of the Zion temple—the anointing of Aaron, the installation of the Levitical priests to minister day and night, and the call to bless YHWH.[192] The nexuswords in Pss 133 ("the beard of Aaron") and 134 ("in the night, lift up your hands") capture the motifs of the anointing of Aaron and the installation of the Levitical priests.

We have already pointed out how Pss 135–36 function as Janus psalms, in relation to Pss 133–34[193] and 137. The framing of the ministers in the house of the LORD, and of the house of Aaron and Levi in Ps 135:1–2, 19–21, relate to the completion of the YHWH's house. The 26 lines of כי לעולם חסדו in Ps 136 recall 2 Chr 7, where the Levites and the priests gave praise to YHWH using this formula at the consecration of YHWH's house. At the same time, the trace of the canonical history in Ps 135:4–18 and the first half of every verse in Ps 136:4–24[194] is a trajectory toward Ps 137. The nexuswords of Pss 135 ("king of Amorite, and Og"), 136 ("to him who divided the Red Sea into two, his steadfast love endures forever") identify with this latter trajectory. Once again, we observe that the nexuswords of Pss 133–36 correspond well to its macrostructural thematic-trajectory.

Van der Lugt considers Pss 133 and 134 as a single composition.[195] By his method, he arrives at Ps 133:3c-d as the rhetorical center of the composition. I have also arrived at Ps 133:3c by my method. The meaningful phrase, "for there [Zion], YHWH has commanded blessings," is a fitting expression of the entire SOA. When I count the entire SOA as a single composition, the colon carrying the nexusword for the entire Pss 120–134 is at Ps 127:2c—"he gives to his beloved sleep." This colon is the exact colon for the nexusword of Ps 127. It is striking that the entire SOA and the individual Ps 127 (at the center) share the same colon as their arithmetic centers!

Psalm 137 is a Community Lament. Its nexusword ("let my tongue cling") expresses a sense of dryness when one is far from Zion, corresponding well to the content/genre motif of the psalm. The following eight Davidic psalms are framed by two YHWH's kingship psalms (138; 145) with four Laments at the center (140–143). Psalms 139 and 144 are psalms of Meditation and Praise respectively.[196] All their nexuswords correspond to their respective genre content accurately. When I counted all the words in Pss 138–145 as a single composition, the count falls on the last word of Ps 142:1, תפלה ("a prayer"). Its location, the mathematical center of the entire final DC, is also

---

192. Zenger notes that Ps 134 is like "a 'farewell' to the pilgrims as they return to their daily world, especially if Ps 134:3a is understood as an introductory quotation of the whole of the Aaronic blessing in Num 6:24–26." See Hossfeld and Zenger, *Psalms 3*, 487.

193. Note that Ps 133 has been classified as a poem with wisdom elements and Ps 134 a praise psalm. Longman, *Psalms*, 438, 440; Goldingay, *Psalms*, 3:564, 3:571.

194. Bazak, "Geometric-Figurative Structure," 130.

195. Van der Lugt, *CAS III*, 416.

196. Hossfeld and Zenger, *Psalms 3*, 524–25.

the only historical superscription after Book II. This nexusword of the entire Collection—"a prayer"—reinforces our argument that there is always a recurring motif of Davidic supplication in the final Group of each Section of the Psalter. Here, we have another example of our quantitative technique corresponding to our macrostructural and metanarratival arguments.

The final five psalms in the Psalter are *hallelujah* psalms, expressing a totality of praise to Yhwh. The nexuswords of these five psalms identify Yhwh as the "one who keeps faith" (146:6) and who "does not delight in the legs [strength]" of men (147:10). For nature obeys him (148:8) and so the "godly" can exult in glory (149:5) and praise Yhwh with the "harp and lyre" (150:3).[197]

The life of praise in Ps 150 is also the "blessed" life in Psalm 1.[198] The glory of the godly in Ps 149 and their execution of the wicked (149:6–9) reflect the Son's vengeance over the nations in Ps 2:8–12.[199] In a striking reversal, the rage of the rulers of the earth in Ps 2:3, will eventually be bound by the *chasidim* in Ps 149:8. The motifs associated with the nexuswords of Pss 149 and 150 are the theological climax expressed vis-à-vis the combined nexusword of Pss 1–2 ("against the LORD, and against his anointed one").

Fittingly, the nexusword of Pss 146–150 as a single composition is the phrase, "his word to Jacob" (147:19), recalling the call to Torah-piety in Ps 1. This expression is also the last reference in our study of the POS of "Jacob." In sum, we see the twin motifs of Yhwh's kingship and the Torah in the nexusword of the final Hallel.

Hence, we conclude our discussion on the numerical techniques:

(1) The numerical technique of meaningful/rhetorical centers highlighted by Bazak, Labuschagne, van der Lugt and others provide the platform on which we built our analysis. Their analyses are limited primarily to a single or a pair of psalms and do not view the meaningful centers as linked to the macrostructure of the Psalter. Taking a departure from their work, I included *all* words in a psalm for word count (including superscriptions, postscripts and *selah*). Words joined by the *maqqef* are counted as a single word.

(2) My results show that most, if not all, of the nexuswords correspond to the thematic and genre focus of the individual psalms.[200] They do not appear to be a sepa-

---

197. Apart from Pss 57, 108, and 150, the combination of "harp" and "lyre" is not found in a single verse elsewhere in the HB.

198. Cha notes, "Psalms 1 and 2 as the twofold introduction to the Hebrew Psalter invite us to make a decision to live a life of blessedness, which takes full account of the realities of life with valleys and peaks. Psalms 146–150 as the fivefold grand doxology to the entire Hebrew Psalter, one for each book, call us to lead a life of praise in spite of the valleys in our lives. Such a life is what the Hebrew Psalter calls 'blessed'" (Cha, "Psalms 146–150," 208–9).

199. Note that Pss 2:3, 9; 105:18; 107:14–16; 149:8 are the only few psalms that use the terms, "iron" and "fetters" in close proximity and in the same context.

200. I recognize that genre categories are not always easy to assign, with scholars differing in their opinions. This is usually the case when a psalm consists of various elements of lament, confidence, or praise. A detailed treatment of each psalm is not possible here. What I have tried to do was to

rate aspect of the psalm as van der Lugt supposes. Furthermore, the nexusword of a particular psalm is not detached from the contextual shape of that Collection/Group (e.g., the alternating Day-Night compositions of Pss 3–14).

(3) The quantitative technique is employed beyond the level of a single psalm. For instance, pairs of psalms such as Pss 1–2, 9–10, 29–30, 42–43, 94–95, 111–112, 133–134, and entire Collections such as 113–117, 138–145 and 146–150 show the nexusword method at work.

(4) The correspondence and alignment of the nexusword to the macrostructure and Metanarrative of the Psalter suggest that the quantitative technique is a formal technique in the design of the Psalter. The nexuswords function to capture or condense, in terse form, an important motif in a psalm, explicating the macrostructure.

(5) By comparing the nexusword via my technique with the meaningful/rhetorical centers of Labuschagne and van der Lugt's work, we observe a striking correspondence (see Appendix A). In Books I–III, our findings converge with those of these scholars in at least 70 percent of the psalms. In Books IV–V, this correspondence is more than 90 percent.[201]

In the next section, we will explore how AAs and ACs function as macrostructuring devices.

Alphabetical Acrostic (AA) and Alphabetic Composition (AC) as Macrostructuring Devices

It was mentioned in the first chapter that acrostic poems in ancient Mesopotamia and Egypt likely predate biblical acrostics. These ancient acrostics display interesting structuring techniques, as well as embed cryptic messages. We have also noted that epigraphic evidence of abecedaries has been found in Palestine in the preexilic period. Recall also that in Israel's earliest poetry, the Song of the Sea, important poetic techniques such as the locating YHWH's kingship at the center of a psalm were already in use. These points allow us to appreciate how postexilic final editors and readers would have the skills and competency to compose and understand carefully crafted acrostic poems.

We begin our analysis of biblical acrostics poems with some definitions. The Alphabetical Acrostic (AA) is defined as an abecedarian (or *alefbetic*) poem in which each poetic line (or the MT verseline[s]) begins with a successive letter of the Hebrew alphabet. There are eight commonly accepted AAs in the Psalms (9–10, 25, 34, 37, 111, 112, 119, 145). The Alphabetic Composition (AC) is a poem that does not have

---

determine if the nexusword corresponds with the content/genre motif of the psalm and macrostructural thematic trajectory. I have shown that most, if not all, nexuswords are illuminating of the macrostructural and metanarratival perspectives of the Psalter.

201. Perhaps the final editor(s) had adopted multiple modes of word count in the Psalter. This, clearly, is speculative. A possible future work would be to study and compare the presence of *maqqef* in various Hebrew manuscripts of the Psalter.

a full set of the alphabetic sequence but nonetheless displays features of alphabetical thinking similar to the AA (e.g., 22 verselines).

Besides the eight (or nine) clear AAs in the Psalter, there are a number of established ACs as well. As discussed earlier, both Pss 1 and 150[202] begin with a word starting with א and end with a word starting with ת. Thus, Pss 1 and 150, with their display of alphabetizing features, are considered ACs, framing the entire Psalter. Furthermore, it is interesting that Books I and V are the only two Books that contain AAs,[203] symmetrically mirroring each other in the first and last Books of the Psalter.

When the eight AAs are lined up, they exhibit a linear trajectory beginning with three Lament/Petition AAs (9/10, 25, 34), followed by four Wisdom AAs (37, 111, 112, 119) and are concluded by a Kingship-Praise AA (145). In other words, there is a movement from Lament/Petition to Torah-centeredness and finally to Praise in these eight AAs.

Choi has also noted that the four Wisdom AAs (37, 111, 112, 119) are more or less "perfect" acrostics with 22 clear lines. In contrast, the rest of the AAs are "transformed or imperfect."[204] *Prima facie*, the presence of these structuring phenomena associated with AAs or ACs suggest that these compositions play an important role in the macrostructure of the Psalter.

Identification Features of AA and AC[205]

Recent theses on AAs have focused on lexical connections, textual problems, poetic structure, and comparative origins.[206] Although AAs and ACs are compositionally related, research on AAs and ACs is disproportionate. Noted earlier, there is currently no agreed consolidation of all recognized ACs in the Psalter. Based on various scholarly discussions of AAs and ACs and the analyses, ten identifiable alphabetic signatures that can be used to designate ACs are listed as follows:

1. *Alphabetic in full or part.* Most, if not all, of the letters of the Hebrew alphabet are attested in an AA. In contrast, ACs, however, contain only several representative alphabets, such as *aleph*, *lamed* or *tav*, and they are usually featured at the beginning, middle, and end of the poem. Sometimes, the halfway mark of the poem is indicated by successive consonants such as *kaf*, *lamed*, and *mem*.[207]

202. For Ps 150, this is seen by ignoring the anacrusis הללו יה in the first and last word, and noting the suffix אל in the second word of Ps 150:1. The choice of אל here is significant because it is unique in the Psalms.

203. Considering Pss 9–10 as a single AA.

204. Choi, "Understanding the Literary Structures," 20–21.

205. With permission, the following section is also published as Ho, "Macrostructural Logic." The article consolidates materials here and in chapter 1 and argues that alphabetical poems, by their locations in the Psalter, carry structuring functions.

206. Choi, "Understanding the Literary Structures," 12.

207. For instance, In Ps 1, van der Lugt notes that the pivotal cola is v. 3c–d which consists of 26

2. *In AAs (e.g., Pss 25, 34), there may be an* aleph, lamed *and* peh *combination to indicate the first, middle and last line.* These three alphabets are the consonants of the name of the first alphabet, אלף. There is also a tendency for AAs or ACs to start the poem with a word of blessing beginning with the alphabet *aleph* (אשרי; cf. 1:1; 112:1) and ending with a word of destruction beginning with *tav* (תאבד; cf. 1:6; 2:12; 9:19; 73:27; 83:18; 119:176; 143:12).[208]

3. *Numerical devices are important in AAs and ACs.* Recurring numbers such as 11, 22 and 23, or multiples of 11 usually function as alphabetizing devices.[209] For instance, the AAs Pss 25 and 34 have 22 and 23 verses respectively. The AC Ps 103 consists of 22 verses and exactly 11 occurrences of the Tetragrammaton.[210]

4. *The structural beginning and end of AAs and ACs are usually emphasized in different ways.* Giffone shows that in Ps 9:2–3 (beginning of the AA), there is "a striking number of first-person imperfect verb" (words beginning with *aleph*). At the end of Ps 10:17, there is a series of words beginning with *tav*, "contributing to the overall feel of the verse as oriented to Y<small>HWH</small>."[211] We have also seen how the AC Ps 150 is emphasized on both ends.

5. *Words at the center of AAs or ACs are often marked by the letter* lamed. We have noted how a ל occurs at the two center words in Ps 150 and at the beginning of the second halves of the ACs Pss 1–2 and 9–10. In the AA Ps 145, the three lines at the center (כ, ל, מ) carry the highlight of Y<small>HWH</small>'s kingship in the poem.[212]

6. *The alphabetical poem can traverse beyond a single psalm.* This is clearly displayed by the AA Pss 9–10 and has been discussed in chapter 1.

7. *The alphabetic poem has an average syllable count of 8 in a colon.* Freedman and Miano argue that "the basic pattern is an [alphabetic] poem of 22 lines or bicolons with an average syllable count of 8 in each colon . . . and 3-4 stresses per colon."[213] This technique of syllable count is beyond the scope of this paper but included here for completeness.

---

letters. At the center of these letters (12+2+12) is the alphabets *kaph* and *lamed* (from וכל), which are the eleventh and twelve letters (middle-two) of the Hebrew alphabet. See Van der Lugt, *Cantos*, 1:584.

208. Botha, "'Wealth and Riches Are in His House,'" 119–20.

209. The use of these numbers is seen in the counts of consonants, words, cola, verselines, and strophes. Soll, *Psalm 119*, 10–11. See also Freedman and Miano, "Non-Acrostic," 88–89; Ceresko, "ABCs of Wisdom," 101; "Endings and Beginnings," 34.

210. Van der Lugt, *Cantos*, 3:130–31.

211. Giffone, "'Perfect' Poem," 57.

212. Note that the three letters of the alphabets in reverse read מלך, "king."

213. Freedman and Miano, "Non-Acrostic," 87–88; Freedman, "Acrostics and Metrics," 392.

The Design of the Psalter

8. *Mezostics*. As noted above, Hurowitz and Ceresko have shown how אלף patterns bracket all four sides of the AA Ps 34.[214] Nonetheless, their observations have not found widespread acceptance. As such, this criterion is held tentatively.

9. *Limited repertoire of words*. Watson argues that a limited repertoire of words and phrases is a characteristic of acrostics.[215] He also sees alliteration and *hendiadys* as features of acrostics. This feature, admittedly, is more subjective.

10. *No single AA or AC displays all the above features*. However, the three most distinguishing and common identification features of ACs are the alphabetical order, the use of the numbers "11" or "22," and structural/literary emphases at the beginning, center, and end of a poem.

A list of Alphabetic Compositions in the Psalter

Based on the above characterizations of AAs and ACs, I have complied a list of psalms that qualify as ACs. Further research, though, is required to confirm this list. There are a number of psalms designated as *Probable Alphabetic Compositions* (or PAC), that is, they show only faint features of AC, which could be incidental. Subsequently, all AAs, ACs, and PACs are arranged in relation to the 150 psalms to explore the logic to their arrangement.

---

214. Hurowitz, "Additional Elements," 326–33; Ceresko, "Endings and Beginnings," 34–37; Barré has also discovered a similar framing device in the Prayer of Habakkuk. Barré, "Newly Discovered Literary Devices," 446–62.

215. Watson, *Classical Hebrew Poetry*, 196.

Numerical Devices, Alphabetic Acrostics or Compositions, and Superscriptions

- Book I (9 ACs and 8 PACs): Pss 1–2;[216] 4?;[217] 7:9b–18?;[218] 8?;[219] 14;[220] 16?;[221] 20;[222]

---

216. For the references to various psalms in the five books of the Psalter (nn. 40–75), I have interacted primarily with van der Lugt, Labuschagne, and Fokkelman as their works have addressed the counting of words, cola, verselines, and strophes extensively. Note that Psalms 1–2 are two separate psalms in the MT-150. They are counted as one AC.

217. This is considered a PAC. Using his method, van der Lugt counts 77 (7x11) words, including the header and *selah*. This word count is confirmed by Labuschagne. Van der Lugt, *Cantos*, 1:114; Labuschagne, "Psalms 4."

218. This is considered a PAC. Psalms 7 and 40 have been considered as composite psalms. For instance, van der Lugt divides Ps 7 into two compositions and detects 11 verselines and 22 cola in Ps 7:9b–18 (van der Lugt, *Cantos*, 1:139). Nonetheless, our purpose here is to detect whether there are alphabetical thinking underlying the final form of the psalm and this is based on a synchronic analysis of the psalm. Diachronic concerns (how the composite components of the psalm came together) do not form the basis of our argument here. Based on our synchronic observations, we have indicated that alphabetic compositions (AC/PAC) usually display only a partial form of the alphabetic acrostics (AA). We have also observed how two independent Pss 9 and 10 can combine to form a single AA. If we are able to accept such alphabetic features traversing across boundaries of separate psalms, there is no reason why, synchronically speaking, alphabetical thinking cannot occur within a limited part of a psalm (as in the case of Pss 7 and 40) regardless of its diachronic history.

219. Both van der Lugt and Labuschagne count 77 (11x7) words (including the header and *selah*) in this psalm. Van der Lugt, *Cantos*, 1:144; Labuschagne, "Psalms 8."

220. Van der Lugt points out that the number "11" plays an important structuring role in this psalm, indicating an AC. Labuschagne finds a number of numerical features that are associated with the number "11." For instance, he sees that the five words at the center is framed by 33 words on each side and that the center colon is the 22nd colon. Van der Lugt, *Cantos*, 1:180; Labuschagne, "Psalms 14."

221. Giffone calls this psalm a "pseudo-acrostic." Giffone, "'Perfect' Poem," 72.

222. The alphabetic features are recognized by Freedman and Miano. Van der Lugt counts a total of 66 (6x11) words in the poem with 33 (3x11) words in each half. He considers the number "11" playing an important structuring role in this psalm. Likewise, this is confirmed by Labuschagne also sees the number "11" and its factors occurring throughout. The psalm consists of 66 words (without superscription) and its arithmetic center of 4 words is framed by 33 words on each side. Moreover, in vv. 2–6 and 7–10, there are 33 words "addressed to the king" and 33 words "spoken about the king." Cf. Freedman and Miano, "Non Acrostic," 88–89; Van der Lugt, *Cantos*, 1:228–29; Labuschagne, "Psalms 20."

The Design of the Psalter

23?;[223] 27;[224] 29;[225] 30;[226] 32?;[227] 33;[228] 38;[229] 39?;[230] 40:2–13?[231]

223. Van der Lugt counts 55 words (5x11) in this psalm. The use of the numerals "11" and "23" plausibly indicate the psalm as an AC. Labuschagne counts 33 words in the first canto of this psalm and 22 words in the second, making a total of 55 words (5x11). Cf. van der Lugt, *Cantos*, 1:252; Labuschagne, "Psalms 23."

224. Van der Lugt sees 10 strophes and 22 verselines in this psalm and considers this an "alphabetizing" poem. While Labuschagne also sees 22 verselines, he sees one more strophe than van der Lugt. Cf. van der Lugt, *Cantos*, 1:283–84; Labuschagne, "Psalms 27."

225. Labuschagne and van der Lugt concur that there are 10 verselines and 23 cola by taking vv. 7–9 as two tricolic verses. Fokkelman identifies 12 verselines. Admitedly these differences are difficult to resolve. The use of these numbers plausibly indicates the psalm as an AC. Cf. van der Lugt, *Cantos*, 1:297; Labuschagne, "Psalms 27."

226. Van der Lugt and Labuschagne note that four words at the rhetorical center are framed by 44 (4x11) words on each side. The use of the number "11" plausibly indicate the psalm as an AC. Van der Lugt, *Cantos*, 1:304; Labuschagne, "Psalms 30."

227. Neither Labuschagne nor van der Lugt has indicated this psalm as alphabetic. However, by my count (counting words joined by *maqqef* as one word), there are 99 (9x11) words, including the heading, and 11 verses. The first word after the superscription begins with *aleph* and the last word ends with *bet*. The center consonant of the center word, אליך (32:6), is a *lamed*. We will consider this as a PAC.

228. This psalm is recognized as alphabetic by a number of scholars. Botha also cites Pss 33, 38, 94 and 103 as ACs, and Van der Lugt, Fokkelman and Labuschagne count 22 verselines and 44 cola. While van der Lugt calls this an "alphabetizing poem," Labuschagne calls this an "alphabetic acrostic psalm." Van der Lugt, *Cantos*, 1:330–31; Botha, "Wealth and Riches," 107; Labuschagne, "Psalms 33"; Fokkelman, *MPHB*, 2:497.

229. Van der Lugt counts 11 strophes and 23 verselines. The center verse (v. 12) is framed by 11 verselines. Van der Lugt considers this psalm an "alphabetizing poem." Labuschagne notes that the central colon (framed by 23 cola on each side) is located within the center verseline (framed by 11 verselines on each side) and that the center verseline is located at the center of 11 strophes in the psalm. Cf. van der Lugt, *Cantos*, 1:385–86; Labuschagne, "Psalms 38."

230. Van der Lugt notes that the pivotal verse (v.8) "has exactly 7 words and 26 (15+11) letters. Further, it is the only line of the poem where God is designated *'dny*.' Moreover, the invocation *'dny'* is the exact pivot of this line: 3+1+3 words and 11+4+11 consonants!" For Labuschagne, he sees that the vv. 13–14 are clearly a unit (a final prayer and coda) and that they are made up of exactly 22 words. Van der Lugt, *Cantos*, 1:393; Labuschagne, "Psalms 40."

231. The unity of Psalm 40 has been debated. Van der Lugt argues that vv. 2–13 and 14–18 are two separate compositions. In vv. 2–13, there are 20 verselines and 44 (4x11) cola. The central cola, v. 7b–c, has 26 (11+15) letters. He notes that "the noun *'wlh'* ('burnt offering') is the exact pivot of the cola in question (>3+1+3 words and 11+4+11 consonants!)." Fokkelman and Labuschagne see Psalm 40 as a unity, though the boundary between two independent compositions remains visible. Van der Lugt, *Cantos*, 1:403;

314

- Book II (5 ACs and 1 PAC): Pss 46;[232] 50;[233] 52;[234] 58?;[235] 59;[236] 70.[237]
- Book III (3 ACs and 1 PAC): Pss 74;[238] 75;[239] 79?;[240] 89.[241]
- Book IV (4 ACs and 3 PACs): Pss 94,[242] 95,[243] 96?[244] 100?[245] 103,[246] 105?[247] 106.[248]

232. Both van der Lugt and Labuschagne count 11 verselines and 23 cola, Labuschagne argues that vv. 7–8a constitute an 11-word meaningful center of the psalm and that the first canto (vv. 2–8) form a 55word (5x11) unit. Cf. van der Lugt, *Cantos*, 2:47; Labuschagne, "Psalms 46."

233. Van der Lugt counts 23 verselines and considers this an "alphabetizing poem." He argues that v. 12 is the middle verseline framed by 11 verselines on both sides. Van der Lugt, *Cantos*, 2:87.

234. Fokkelman, Labuschagne, and van der Lugt count 11 verselines and 24 cola in this psalm. The two cola, in verse 8, are the central cola of the poem, framed by 11 cola on each side. He argues that vv. 7b–8 are the meaningful center consisting of 11 words. Van der Lugt, *Cantos*, 2:108; Fokkelman, *Major Poems*, 2:501; Labuschagne, "Psalms 52."

235. Freedman and Miano, "Non Acrostic," 88–89; Van der Lugt counts 11 verselines and 22 cola. Van der Lugt, *Cantos*, 2:152.

236. According to van der Lugt, there are 44 cola in the poem and a total of 143 (13x11) words. He calls this a "quasi-alphabetic" poem. Van der Lugt, *Cantos*, 2:161.

237. Both Labuschagne and van der Lugt counts 44 (4x11) words in this psalm and considers the number "11" to "have a structuring function." Cf. van der Lugt, *Cantos*, 2:269; Labuschagne, "Psalms 70."

238. Ceresko, "Endings and Beginnings," 33. Van der Lugt notes that the 23 verselines in this poem can be considered an "alphabetizing feature of the poem." Van der Lugt, *Cantos*, 2:313.

239. Fokkelman, van der Lugt and Labuschagne count 11 verselines though they differ in the counting of cola in this poem. Van der Lugt notes that the pivotal colon, v. 7a, is framed by 11 cola on each side. Van der Lugt, *Cantos*, 2:322; Fokkelman, *MPHB*, 2:506; Labuschagne, "Psalms 75."

240. This is considered a PAC. There are only very faint connections with alphabetic thinking in this psalm. The count of verselines, words or cola does not arrive at 11 or its multiples. Van der Lugt, however, notes that the two middle cola in v. 7 are made up of "11+11 letters." Van der Lugt, *Cantos*, 2:373.

241. Van der Lugt notes that vv. 25–26 are the central strophe of the psalm. He argues that this strophe is "made up of 11 words, symbolically representing the idea of fulfillment" (Van der Lugt, *Cantos*, 2:471).

242. Van der Lugt notes, "The 23 poetic verselines (which coincide with the Masoretic verses) probably indicate that we are dealing with an alphabetizing composition" (Van der Lugt, *Cantos*, 3:57). Freedman, "Acrostic Poems," 416, 423; Botha, "Wealth and Riches," 107.

243. Van der Lugt counts 11 verselines in this poem. The number "11" in this psalm may plausibly indicate that it as an AC. Van der Lugt, *Cantos*, 3:65.

244. Eijzeren notes that the first consonants in the first four words of Ps 96:11, ישמחו השמים ותגל הארץ, form the Tetragrammaton. Eijzeren, "'Halbnachts Steh' Ich Auf,'" 26; Van der Lugt counts 11 occurrences of the divine name. Van der Lugt, *Cantos*, 3:74.

245. Freedman and Miano, "Non Acrostic," 88–89.

246. Van der Lugt, *Cantos*, 3:132; Freedman and Miano, "Non Acrostic," 88–89; Botha, "Wealth and Riches," 107.

247. Freedman and Miano, "Non Acrostic," 88–89.

248. Ceresko, "Endings and Beginnings," 37–41.

The Design of the Psalter

- Book V (2 ACs, 1 PAC): Pss 138,[249] 144?[250] 150.[251]

In summary, I have identified a total of 46 AAs, ACs, and PACs. Book I consists of 22 such compositions (5 AAs + 9 ACs + 8 PACs). Books II–III consist of 8 ACs + 2 PACs and Books IV–V consist of 4 AAs + 6 ACs + 4 PACs.

The Arrangement of AAs and ACs as a Macrostructuring Device

It is interesting that Books I and V of the Psalter are the only two books that contain AAs,[252] symmetrically mirroring each other as the first and last books of the Psalms. When the eight AAs are lined up, they exhibit an interesting linear genre trajectory. These AAs begin with three Lament/Petition psalms (9/10, 25, 34),[253] followed by four Wisdom psalms (37, 111, 112, 119) and are concluded by a Kingship-Praise psalm (145). Based on genre categories, there is a movement from Lament/Petition to

---

249. Skehan and Hurowitz have argued for alphabetic thinking based on the sequence of consecutive alphabets found in a string of words. These letters can be located anywhere in a word in the string and need not always be located at the beginning of a word. For instance, Skehan argues that the first two pairs of words in Deut 32:30 (איכה ירדף אחד אלף) begin and ends with א and פ. He proceeds to suggest that the poet had in mind the words, אלף (Skehan, *Studies in Israelite Poetry*, 75–76). Hurowitz has adopted this concept in his "Additional Elements of Alphabetical Thinking in Psalms XXXIV" (an acrostic psalm), he argues that the א line (34:2) consists of an אלף sequence based on the first, fourth and eighth words. Moreover, he has argued that the use of "acrosticizing letters more deeply in the verse than the initial position" occurs in the Nah 1:1–10. He adds, "The use of alphabetizing letters in post-primary position is known in later acrostics," citing Sephardic medieval prayer rite (see esp. Hurowitz, "Additional Elements," 328). Skehan's and Hurowitz's research on alphabetical thinking may have shown us that the use of alphabetical features in poetry is more complex than we have understood. Based on their work, I wonder if the first four words of Psalm 138 after the superscription, אוֹדְךָ בְכָל־לִבִּי נֶגֶד אֱלֹהִים, contain the alphabets, ה, ד, ג, ב, א, in successive sequence. Note that the last two words joined by the *maqqef* begin with an א and ת. Elsewhere, Van der Lugt also notes, "the poem as a whole displays all kinds of quasi-alphabetic acrostic devices. It opens with a verb beginning with an 'aleph ('wdk) and closes with a verb beginning with a taw (trp)" (Van der Lugt, *Cantos*, 3:475). See Ceresko, "Endings and Beginnings," 33, 35.

250. The entire v. 12, אֲשֶׁר בָּנֵינוּ כִּנְטִעִים מְגֻדָּלִים בִּנְעוּרֵיהֶם בְּנוֹתֵינוּ כְזָוִיֹּת מְחֻטָּבוֹת תַּבְנִית הֵיכָל, consists of an impressive sequence of the alphabet from *aleph* to *lamed*. Verse 12 also marks a shift in the psalm. This sequence breaks after the first word in v. 13.

251. See also Ceresko, "Endings and Beginnings," 32–44.

252. Considering Pss 9–10 as a single AA.

253. Admittedly, characterizing the genres of these psalms is difficult because elements of laments and praise are found. Jacobson's struggle with this is on Psalm 9 well captured: "Perhaps the purpose of the psalm is instruction in prayer and praise. More likely the purpose is a prayer for help." He notes that Ps 9:1–12 consists of praise whereas 9:13–20 focuses on petition. On the other hand, Psalm 10:1–11 begins with a series of complaints and then closes (10:12–18) with a note of trust. Psalm 34 begins with a historical superscription that pictures David acting mad so that he is driven away from Abimelech. David is pictured in dire straits, yet praise, thanksgiving elements are not absent in this psalm. Lament, trust, and petition elements are found in vv. 4, 6, 15, 17. Yet, elements of call to praise, thanksgiving and exhortation are also found (vv. 1–3, 9–11). See deClaissé-Walford et al., *Book of Psalms*, 130, 321.

Numerical Devices, Alphabetic Acrostics or Compositions, and Superscriptions

Torah-centeredness[254] and finally, to Praise. Choi notes that the four Wisdom AAs (37, 111, 112, 119) are more or less "perfect" acrostics with 22 clear lines. In contrast, the rest of the AAs are "transformed or imperfect."[255] These organizational features of the AAs are interesting but how do they contribute to the overall shape of the MT-150? Is there a strategic intent to their locations and if so, how do they inform us of the design of the Psalter? A striking picture emerges when all the 46 AAs, ACs, and PACs are set against the entire macrostructure of the Psalter.

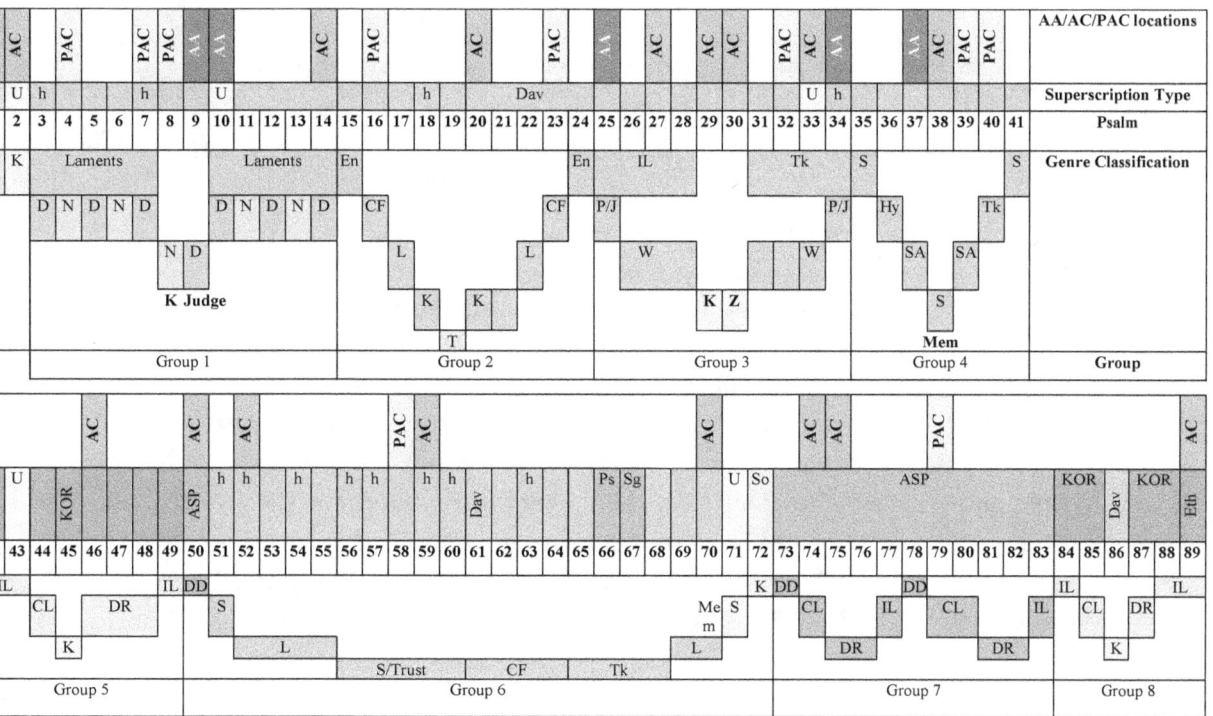

---

254. While the Torah-centeredness of Pss 111, 112 and 119 is clear, Ps 37's torah-centeredness is seen by its emphases on justice (vv. 30, 33), Torah-piousness (v. 31), and binary views of the ways and outcomes righteous and the wicked. The righteous is to watch his "steps" (v. 23), to be "blameless" (v. 18) and to "do good" (v. 27). The entire psalm is akin to Psalm 1, 112 and 119. For instance, contrasts of the righteous and the wicked are clear in Ps 37 (vv. 1, 6, 9); the wicked will pass away like grass, will not stand in judgment and will perish (vv. 2, 9–10, 20, 38), whereas the righteous are called the "blessed" (v. 22). They will be established, be in delight and be known by God (vv. 10–11, 18).

255. Choi, "Understanding the Literary Structures," 20–21.

The Design of the Psalter

				AC	AC	PAC			PAC		AC		PAC	AC			AA	AA					AA
M	U	Ps	mlk		U		mlk	Ps	mlk	Tk	Dav	Aff	Dav	brk	hd	hll	hd		Dav		hll	hll	hll	U		hll	hd	a
90	91	92	93	94	95	96	97	98	99	100	101	102	103	104	105	106	107	108	109	110	111	112	113	114	115	116	117	118	119
S	Trust	Tk								PR	S	Bless	BRK	HD	HLL	HD	Plea		DR		T		HLL						T
				YHWH *Malak*															L					Theo		Uni			
				Group 9														Group 10											

															AC							PAC	AA						AC
				Songs of Ascents											hll	hd	U			h				hll	hll	hll	hll	hll	
120	121	122	123	124	125	126	127	128	129	130	131	132	133	134	135	136	137	138	139	140	141	142	143	144	145	146	147	148	149	150
L		Z		PR				L		Z		PR		G-Hallel	Jns	YK	Dir	Dir				Dav	Dav	YK	I	Isr	Cos+Isr	Faithful	Uni
			W		Z		W										Med		IL			PR							
				Group 11															Group 12										

Figure 75: Distribution of Alphabetic Acrostics and Alphabetic Compositions across the Three Main Sections of the Psalter

In the figure above, the Psalter has been structured into three major Sections with each having four Groups (Book I: Pss 1–41, Books II–III: Pss 42–89 and Books IV–V: Pss 90–150).[256] Each Section is characterized by five categories (see top right column).[257] While much can be said about how the Psalter is structured, the details need not distract us for our purposes here. The Prologue and four-Group structure in Book I are well documented.[258] Similarly, the four major Groupings of Books II–III are commonly acknowledged by virtue of their superscriptions.[259] The structuring of Books IV–V is more involved but even without granting this, our arguments in the following will not be affected.

---

256. Legend: a: *ashre*; U: Untitled psalm; h: Historical superscription; Dav: Davidic Psalm; KOR: Korahite psalm; ASP: Asaphite psalm; Ps: A psalm; Sg: A song; So: Solomonic psalm; Eth: Ethan; M: Moses; *mlk*: YHWH *Malak* psalm; Tk: Thanksgiving; Aff: Psalm of affliction; brk: Bless; hd: *Hodu* psalm; hll: *Hallelujah* psalm; T: Torah motif; K: Kingship psalm; D: Day psalm; N: Night psalm; En: Entrance Liturgy; CF: Confidence psalm; L: Lament; P/J: Motifs of justice and the poor; W: Motif of the wicked; Z: Motif of Zion; S: Supplication psalm; SA: Sapiential psalm; Hy: Hymn; Mem: A Memorial; IL: Individual Lament; CL: Communal Lament; DR: Divine Response psalm; DD: Didatic psalm; Theo: Theocentric in focus; Uni: Universal in focus; PR: Praise psalm; G-Hallel: Great Hallel; Jns: Janus psalm; YK: YHWH kingship psalm; Med: Meditation psalm; Dir: For the Director of Music; Isr: Israel; Cos + Isr: Cosmic and Israel; Pro: Prologue.

257. For "Genre Classifications," I have relied on Psalms commentaries of Hossfeld, Zenger, Longman, Craigie, Tate, Terrien and Goldingay.

258. Barbiero, *Das erste Psalmenbuch*; Zenger, "Das Buch der Psalmen," 356; Auwers, *La Composition*, 43–46.

259. Gillingham, "Zion Tradition," 322–26; Koorevaar, "Psalter as a Structured Theological Story," 589–90.

Book I

Consider the Prologue and Group 1 (3–14) of Section 1. As noted earlier, the pair of ACs (Pss 1–2) marks the beginning of the Psalter and Book I. These two psalms contain the twin motifs of Torah-piety and Yhwh's kingship at Zion. They mark the seam between the Prologue and Group 1. Psalm 14 is another AC, marking the right frame of Group 1. The four Psalms (7–10) at the center of Group 1 are marked by two pairs of PACs (7–8) and AAs (9–10). They are located with the two central Pss 8–9 containing the motifs of Yhwh's kingship (and judgment). We will refer to these motifs at the center of a Group as *Group Central Motifs* (GCM).

Group 2 (15–24) is framed by Entrance Liturgies (15, 24). The second psalm and penultimate psalm (16, 23), both Confidence psalms, are PACs. These two PACs form a second frame just inside the Entrance Liturgies. A single AC (20) marks a Kingship psalm at the center.

Group 3 (25–34) is framed by two AAs (25, 34) and consists of four ACs. Two of them mark precisely the motifs of kingship and Zion-temple (29–30). Psalms 27 (AC), 32 (PAC) and 33 (AC) act like a secondary frame around the center. Again, the GCM is marked by either an AA and/or AC.

The alphabetizing features of Pss 29–30 may not be clear *prima facie*. Labuschagne and van der Lugt argue that Ps 29 contains 10 verselines and 23 cola. This allows the center colon, v.6a, to be framed by exactly 11 cola on each side. The use of the number "11" recalls the alphabetizing technique. Psalm 30 contains 12 verselines and by their count, the four words at the center are framed by 44 (4x11) words on both sides,[260] making a well-balanced structure. From their analyses, these two psalms together contain 22 verselines.

I agree that each of these two psalms is structured in balanced halves. I offer the following additional evidence. In Ps 29, the letters that begin the verselines are symmetric about the center verse (29:6) in a striking ה-ה-ק-ק-ו-ק-ק-ק-ק-י-י sequence. The nexusword, "Lebanon," begins with *lamed*.[261] Likewise, Ps 30 can be seen in two halves. There are 9x references to "Yhwh." By my count, the fifth and middle instance (30:8) coincides with the nexusword, separating the two halves of the composition. In the first half of Ps 30, immediately after the superscription, the poem begins with an *aleph* (ארוממך; "I will extol you"; 30:2)[262] and ends with a word that begins with a *lamed* (לעולם; 30:7; just before the nexusword, "Yhwh"). Then the composition

---

260. They argue that Ps 29:7–8 is one tricolic poetic verseline and the header in Ps 30:1 is not included in the verseline-count. Van der Lugt, *CAS III*, 304; Labuschagne "Psalm 29," 1–4; "Psalm 30," 1–3.

261. Labuschagne and van der Lugt argue for 5 strophes (with the center at vv. 5–6). The first (vv. 1–2; excluding the header in their count) and the last strophe (vv. 10–11) contain 16 words each. Together, the 32 words correspond to the numerical value of *kbwd* (20 + 2 + 6 + 4 = 32; "glory"). In other words, the composition is enveloped by the two strophes that underscore the "glory of God."

262. In the Psalter, the exact form of ארוממך ("I will extol you") is found only in three places (30:2; 118:28; 145:1) which are significant as they locate the concept of kingship.

continues immediately in the second half with a word that begins, again, with an *aleph* (אליך; 30:9) and ends with two words לעולם אודך (30:13) which also start with a *lamed* and *aleph*. The two לעולם in 30:7, 13 thus locate the ends of the two halves. The entire poem is bound by two words of praise that begin with *aleph*. These features are characteristic of ACs.

When these two compositions (29–30) are considered together, I counted 168 words and the two-word nexusword הבית לדוד ("the temple, of David"; 30:1), identifying both the Davidic king and Yhwh's temple. These words capture the CM of Group 3 (25–34).²⁶³ The expression, "a song of dedication" (שיר-חנכת) in the superscription of Ps 30 is a *hapax legomenon*. The noun, "dedication" (חנכה) occurs only 7x in the HB, all associated with either the sanctuary altar or temple.²⁶⁴ Hence, these two ACs (29–30) mark the CMs of kingship and Zion-temple.

Group 4 (35–41) is not framed on both ends but its three center psalms (37–39) are marked by an AA, AC, and PAC respectively. The CGM of Group 4, which is the supplication of an afflicted David (38), is marked by an AC.

Book I shows the highest number of AAs, ACs, and PACs. These alphabetic poems are observed to locate transitions between Groups, act as frames (e.g., Groups 2, 3) and mark GCMs.

Books II–III

There is an absence of AAs in Books II–IV. Nonetheless, the ACs and PACs distributed in Books II–III continue to reveal a similar phenomenon as seen in Book I.

Psalm 46, as an AC in the first Korahite Group, marks the start of a series of three Divine Response psalms. The nations tremble before Yhwh and the stream in the city of God in Ps 46, evidently recall Pss 1–2. The transition between the first Korahite psalm-group and the second Davidic Psalter is marked by an AC (Ps 50). Psalms 52 and 70, as the second and penultimate psalm of the second Davidic Collection (Group 6) are ACs. At the center, a PAC (58) and AC (59) mark David's trust when his life was threatened. The motifs of Yhwh judging (58:10–12), his "laughing" (שחק) and "scoffing" (לעג) at the nations (59:9) in these two psalms, also unmistakably recall Ps 2. The combination of these two words is found only in Pss 2:4 and 59:9 in the entire Psalter.²⁶⁵

In the Asaphite psalms (Group 7), two ACs mark the Communal Lament and Divine Response in Pss 74–75 respectively. Psalm 74 highlights the fallen Zion-temple and Ps 75, Yhwh as the judge who will cut off the prideful horn²⁶⁶ of the wicked.

---

263. This superscription is also often considered as a late redaction or used because of the association with David and the temple. Craigie, *Psalms 1–50*, 252.

264. Num 7:10–11, 84, 88; 2 Chr 7:9; Neh 12:27; Ps 30:1.

265. Apart from the Psalms, they are found only in Prov 1:26, occurring in close proximity.

266. Psalm 75 contains four instances of the noun, קרן (Ps 75:5–6, 11), the highest frequency

Motifs of the wicked's arrogance and Yhwh's impending judgment bring us back to the leitmotifs in the Prologue. Like Ps 74, the PAC Ps 79 marks the fallen Zion-temple. These two ACs and a single PAC mark descriptions of Yhwh's kingship and the broken Zion.

At the end of the second Korahite psalm-group (Group 8), we find a single AC, Ps 89, which highlights the Davidic Covenant and Yhwh's establishment of his anointed king (89:4–38). The motifs of the anointed king (89:21), his sonship to Yhwh (89:27) and his triumph over his enemies (89:23–24), recall the motifs of Ps 2. In this Group, the GCM is marked not by alphabetic poems but the lone Davidic supplication Ps 86.

In sum, the locations of ACs and PACs in Books II–III correspond remarkably to the observations and GCMs found in Book I. As with Book I, the alphabetical poems in Books II–III continue to mark GCMs, frame a literary unit or identify a transition seam.

Books IV–V

There are two ACs (94, 95) and two PACs (96, 100), marking the Yhwh *Malak* Collection (93–100). Apart from Ps 98, all the psalms in this Collection that do not begin with יהוה מלך are either an AC or PAC. We note that AC/PAC typically mark Yhwh's kingship. Thus it is appropriate that Pss 94–96 and 100, which do not begin with יהוה מלך, also mark Yhwh's kingship as well. Together with the psalms that begin with יהוה מלך, the entirety of Collection (93–100) carries the mark of Yhwh's kingship. The ACs in Pss 103 and 106 mark the end of the third Davidic Collection (101–103) and Book IV.

Alphabetic acrostics return in Book V of the Psalter. The twin Pss 111–112 is situated at he beginning of a unit of non-attributed authorship Pss 111–118. Psalm 111 focuses on the righteous deeds of Yhwh and Ps 112 presents his representative righteous figure. Psalm 119, which carries the same motif of a Torah-pious figure who "delights" in Yhwh's commandments (חפץ; cf. 112:1; 119:35), is located at the end of the literary unit. Like Pss 103 and 106, the AA Ps 119 is precisely located at the transition to Song of Ascents.

Psalm 145 marks the end of the last Davidic Collection and the transition into the Final Hallel. The entire Davidic Group (138–145) is framed by an AC (138) and an AA (145). Psalms 138 and 145, together with the PAC Ps 144, all highlight Yhwh's kingship.

From the above, there is a striking consistency in the use of AAs, ACs, and PACs to mark leitmotifs of the prologue of the Psalms (Pss 1–2), frame literary units and identify transitions.

---

within a single psalm of the Psalter.

Alphabetic Acrostics and Davidizations in Books I and V of the Psalter

Located symmetrically at both ends of the Psalter, each of the four AAs in Books I and V respectively forms two distinct compositional units to present two contrasting Davidizations of the Psalter. The last four AAs function as an "acrostic foil" to the first four AAs. The first four AAs (9/10; 25; 34; 37) frame the image of an earthly Davidic kingship and Zion and the last four AAs (111; 112; 119; 145) characterize a representative ideal Davidic community. The framing is achieved by creating common motifs between the first and last AAs of each set (i.e., between Pss 9/10 and 37; and Pss 111 and 145).

There is a striking parallel between the AAs Pss 111 and 145. Both of these AAs mark the end (or beginning) of a compositional unit. Both of these psalms come at the end of a Davidic group (Pss 108–110 and 138–145). Consider two texts of three verses each in Pss 111:2–4 and 145:3–5 below:

111:2–4
גדלים מעשי יהוה דרושים לכל-חפציהם:
הוד-והדר פעלו וצדקתו עמדת לעד:
זכר עשה לנפלאתיו חנון ורחום יהוה:

145:3–5
גדול יהוה ומהלל מאד ולגדלתו אין חקר:
דור לדור ישבח מעשיך וגבורתיך יגידו:
הדר כבוד הודך ודברי נפלאותיך אשיחה:

The two isolated pairs of three consecutive verses in Pss 111 and 145 contain six shared lexemes (גדול, יהוה, מעשה, הדר, הוד, פלא).²⁶⁷ Apart from these two places, these lexemes appearing in such close proximity do not occur elsewhere in the entire HB. Common to both literary contexts is the motif of Yhwh's creation, power, and providence over nature.²⁶⁸ The common thematic and poetic features of Pss 111 and 145 suggest that these two AAs may be functioning as an inclusio around the four AAs in Book V.

Likewise, it is possible to see that Pss 9–10 and 37 form a frame around the first four AAs as well. We have already discussed parallels between Pss 1–2 and 9–10 above. While Ps 37 (last AA in Book I) shares a number of lexemes with Pss 9–10 (first AA in Book I), it is remarkable that Ps 37 and Pss 1–2 (first AC in Book I) also share

---

267. Two sets of associated lexemes that relate to Yhwh's "works/acts" are used in Ps 111 (עשה, "work," v. 4; פעל, "deed," v. 3) and Ps 145 (דבר, "work," v. 5; גבורה, "mighty acts," v. 4).

268. The concept of Yhwh providing food for his creation so that they may be satisfied and flourish in life is also shared by Pss 111:5 and 145:15–16. Cf. Pss 8:1–9; 104:1, 24, 30–31; Job 37.

at least 15 nouns, verbs or adjectives.²⁶⁹ Besides these common lexemes, there is an overlap between Ps 1 and the first few verses of Ps 37.²⁷⁰ In short, Pss 1–2 (or 9–10) and 37 form a frame in Book I by virtue of their unique poetic and thematic parallels.

When the structural framework of the first and last four AAs are perceived, the next logical question is why are they acting as frames. Based on the macrostructure proposed above, the first four AAs (9/10, 25, 34, 37) frame the important Group Central Motifs of earthly Davidic kingship and Zion in Book I. The last four AAs (111, 112, 119, 145) characterize a representative ideal Davidic community based on the Group Central Motifs in Book V. These four AAs are associated with a blameless, righteous, Torah-pious Davidic community who would dwell in that paradisiacal city by Ps 145.²⁷¹

Seen from this perspective, the last four AAs represent a development in the understanding of Davidic kingship. In the first four AAs capture an individual human Davidic king. The last four AAs capture a democratized people represented by the Davidic kingship. Between these two sets of AAs, the Psalter depicts the "fall" of the Davidic kingship (entire Book II)²⁷² and the appearing of an ideal Davidic king (in Pss 101–103; 108–110).

---

269. Cf. ידע, שחק, עשה, משפט, מעט, יום, תורה, הגה, דרך, איש אדון, צדיק, ארץ, רשע, יהוה.

270. The opening verse in both psalms calls for non-association with the wicked. The image of wicked doers fading away like grass in Ps 37:2 (cf. 37:20) mirrors a similar picture in Ps 1:4. The motif of "delight" (ענג) in Ps 37:4, 11, likewise, parallels the psalmist's "delight" (חפץ) in the Torah in Ps 1:2. It is striking that the combined depictions of the wicked plotting against the righteous and Yhwh laughing at the wicked are found nowhere else in the Psalter, except in Pss 37:12–13; 2:1–2. The semblance of the phrase כל־חוסי בו ("all who take refuge in him") at the end of Ps 2 and כי־חסו בו ("for they take refuge in him") at the end of Ps 37 is striking!

271. They come onto the scene *only* after Ps 110, in which the Davidic priest-king triumph emphatically over the nations. Hence, Ps 110 marks an important milestone in the overall structure of the Psalter. It defines a new reality brought about by the triumphant Davidic king of Ps 110. Subsequent to Ps 110, there is an intensified characterization of the righteous *community* (112:4, 6; 118:15, 20; 125:3; 140:14; 142:8) and Yhwh's building of a Zion-city (Ps 127). Moreover, all the traditional Hallels are found only after Ps 110 (Egyptian [113–118], Great [135–136] and Final [146–150] Hallels).

272. Following Wilson's analysis, many scholars have adopted his understanding that Book II of the Psalter is a "celebration of the faithfulness of YHWH to his covenant with David." This is correct only if the final Ps 72 in Book II is allowed to represent the weight of Book II. However, the weight of Book II actually highlights a broken David and the apparent "demise" of the earthly Davidic kingship. This is shown by the high number of historical superscriptions (e.g., 51, 52, 54, 56, 57, 58, 59, 63) that depict David as a fugitive whose life is constantly under threat. Stefan Attard argues that the exilic imageries in the Korahite Pss 42–44 set the tone for the persecution of David in the second Davidic Psalter (Pss 51/52–71/72). I suggest that the sins and spiritual brokenness of David and issues of acceptable sacrifices depicted in Ps 51 seem to find resolution only later in Pss 66:13–19. This resolution is made possible because the reproaches that David experienced throughout second Davidic Psalter had "broke his heart" (69:20–21), recalling Ps 51:17. Psalms 70–71 then address David's waning years (esp. 71:18–20). It is under this horizon that Ps 72 finds its theological significance, that is, God is looking beyond the earthly Davidic king to keep his covenant. Wilson, *EHP* 208; Attard, *Implications of Davidic Repentance*, 443.

The Function of Alphabetic Acrostics and Alphabetic Compositions

Based on our observations above, the functions of AAs and ACs can be summarized in four ways. First, they mark the theological highpoints of Yhwh's kingship, the messianic king, the fall and restoration of both the Davidic kingship and Zion-temple. Second, they clarify the shape of the Psalter. There is a tendency for alphabetic poems marking the leitmotifs found in the Pss 1–2 as Group Central Motifs.[273] The AAs and ACs/PACs also provide structural clarity to literary units at the levels of composition. Third, the eight AAs in Books I and V capture a remarkable message. The last four AAs function as an "acrostic foil" to the first four. These two sets of AAs present two contrasting Davidizations of the Psalter—the earthly Davidic king and the ideal/democratized Davidic figure. Within the horizon of the entire Psalter, they frame the fall of the human king and the rise of an ideal Davidic king.[274]

Finally, it is plausible that the alphabetic poems carry numerical symbolism. By counting the number of individual psalms[275] identified as AAs, ACs, and PACs in the three Sections, we observe that they add up to symbolic numbers.[276] Scholars have also found that the numbers "4," "10," "14," "17" and "22" are associated with the divine name and as a symbol of completeness.

Section	Books	ACs+PACs	AAs	Total
1	I	17	5	22 (2x11)
2	II–III	10	0	10
3	IV–V	10	4	14 (2x7)

Figure 76: Count of Alphabetic Acrostics, and (Probable) Alphabetic Compositions

273. The AAs and/or ACs tend to also work in pairs when they mark the leitmotifs of Yhwh's kingship, the anointed king and Zion-temple. Cf. Pss 1–2; 7–8; 9–10; 29–30; 58–59; 74–75; 94–95; 105–106; 111–112; 144–145.

274. We need to reconsider the plausibility of the 14 PACs (4, 7, 8, 16, 23, 32, 39, 40, 58, 79, 96, 100, 105, 144) functioning as intentional ACs. Even if we remove all the PACs in our list, our conclusions based on just AAs and ACs remain intact. Further research is needed to validate PACs.

275. Hence, we count Pss 1, 2 or 9, 10 as four individual separate psalms (but they are a single AC [Pss 1–2] and AA [Pss 9–10]).

276. The number "7" [and "10"] expresses "fullness, completeness, abundance and the maximum," and "imitates the shape of the Menorah"; "11," the sum of 7 and 4, is a number of "fulfillment." "17" and "26" are related to the divine name. The "sum of positional values is "Y(10) + H(5) + W(6) + H(5) = 26"; and the sum of their digit values "Y(1+0) + H(5) + W(6) + H(5) = 17." The significance of this is that these numbers "signify not only the name but the glory of God" (cf. Exod 33:17–23). Labuschagne, "Significant Compositional Techniques"; *Numerical Secrets of the Bible*, 22–40, 57–67, 69–73, 82–83, 89–91. Cf. van der Lugt, "Mathematical Centre," 643–51; Knohl, "Sacred Architecture," 189–97; Mitchell, *Songs of Ascents*, 15–26.

I have demonstrated how alphabetical poems, when their structural locations and content are properly understood in the Psalter, can provide additional macrostructural meanings. Beginning with alphabetic acrostics, quintessential features of these acrostics are characterized and used as criteria to identify other less obvious alphabetic compositions. In total, forty-six alphabetical poems are proposed. When all these poems are viewed under the entire Psalter, they are observed to provide several important macrostructuring functions. They are used to recall and repeat leitmotifs of the prologue of the Psalter, mark the seams of literary units, frame the respective fall and rise of the earthly and ideal Davidic king, and develop two Davidizations of the Psalms. Under this scrutiny, the alphabetic poems in the Psalms have a macrostructural logic that is subservient to the overarching theological thrust of the Psalter. If the above proposal can be sustained, our understanding of acrostic poems and the Psalter is significantly altered. At the same time, our respect for the poetic finesse of ancient Hebrew poets will be greatly enhanced!

However, it is also clear that in our analyses, several locations are certainly not as well explained by our proposals (e.g., absence of any acrostics in the SOA; not every Group has an acrostic at the center or as frames; or the use of PAC). This lack of consistency may be attributed to several reasons. The final editors could have applied a combination of techniques and the prominence of one technique over another may be at work. For instance, the final editors may sacrifice marking a psalm as the arithmetic center of a literary unit. In its place is the intentional marking of an off-centered psalm with significant connections to the leitmotifs of the Prologue. In this case, the connection with the Prologue as a rhetorical feature is the overriding technique at work. Separately, the possibility that texts had undergone multiple editorial layers cannot be dismissed. It is also possible that the final editors tried to leave earlier layers unaltered or that they had redacted a poetic design that was lost on them. Or simply, certain technique or logic intended by the poets are still not understood.[277]

The nature of numerical devices lies in their precision in correspondence. Hence, when numerical devices do not correspond consistently, they lose their credibility as a technique. To be sure, we must also recognize that the suggestion of any technique at work is not argued on the basis of impeccable consistency. No interpretative method is absolutely foolproof and without exceptions. Rather, many poetical techniques are expressed along a spectrum of variations. For instance, scholars have long recognized that acrostic structures may be full or quasi (e.g., Pss 119 or 9–10). The presence of quasi- or semi-acrostics does imply that the acrostic technique is not monolithic. As such, we need to leave room for different expressions of the techniques. Even in Labuschagne's Logotechnical analyses where precision is important, he recognizes different counting methods in certain psalms (whether to include words in the superscription or not).

---

277. Wilson, *EHP*, 207–8.

Controls of validity of interpretation, especially from the perspective of the final editors and readership have been discussed and noted throughout this book. Externally, we have also shown that such techniques were not uncommon in the ancient Near East. What we have found compelling is not merely the accumulation of various observations identified in this study but how they independently converge and present themselves with a consistent message across the Psalter. Our study of AAs and ACs in this chapter correspond surprisingly well with our entire argument. The AAs and ACs, as formal devices, work together with its thematic content to capture and unveil the central theological thrust and trajectory of the MT Psalter.

This study of AAs and ACs may have broken new ground in Psalms scholarship. In 2012, Eijzeren compiled at least thirteen possible functions of alphabetic or acrostic compositions identified by various scholars. They can function as[278] (a) symbolism of completeness,[279] (b) mnemonic or memory aid devices,[280] (c) aesthetic or artistic compositions,[281] (d) displays of poetical skills,[282] (e) symbolism of order, (f) enhancement to the message of the poem, (g) magic or cultic purposes, (h) didactical aids, (i) signposts to an embedded message, (j) clues to reading the texts, (k) responsive (or liturgical) structures, (l) dedications or references to people or gods, or (m) identifications of authorship.

Schuliger adds to this list by arguing that the alphabetic acrostic "serves as a covenant reminder, a metaphor for hope, a message-sign of the covenant reality of God."[283] According to Seybold, acrostics are crucial to "the systematic doctrine"[284] of the Psalter as the alphabetical structure is symbolic of completeness.[285]

Nonetheless, there is no clear consensus on the function of alphabetic compositions at the current state of Psalms scholarship. In our discussions, we have demonstrated how the statements of Schuliger and Seybold can stand. We propose that AAs and ACs serve the crucial macrostructural function of *marking transitions* and leitmotifs of the Prologue of the Psalter. They also illustrate the Metanarrative with two sets of contrasting AAs in Books I and V, *depicting two Davidizations* of the texts and framing the fall of the Davidic kingship in DC-II and rise of an ideal Davidic king in DC-III and IV. We surmise that the trio—form, content and intent—are carefully

---

278. For arguments and references to these functions, see Eijzeren, "'Halbnachts Steh' Ich Auf,'" 30–37.

279. Labuschagne, *Numerical Secrets of the Bible*, 13; Van der Lugt, CAS III, 584.

280. See also Vesco, *Le psautier de David*, 1:29; Robertson, *Flow of the Psalms*, loc. 1873; loc. 5294.

281. Lindars, "Is Psalm 2 an Acrostic Poem," 63

282. Watson, *Classical Hebrew Poetry*, 198.

283. Schuliger, "Theological Significance," iii, 126, 137.

284. Seybold, *Introducing the Psalms*, 152; Maloney, "Word Fitly Spoken," 31.

285. Soll calls the alphabet "a metaphor for totality." He adds that "the acrostic is a kind of 'concealed art' that is not apparent when the poem is read out loud . . . it is hidden in order to be revealed, so there has to be some way of indicating to the reader that an acrostic pattern is at work." Soll, *Psalm 119*, 27, 31.

integrated into the message of the entire Psalter and collaborated by the design of AAs and ACs.

In light of our analysis, these AAs or ACs (which may or may not have arisen from "wisdom-inspired editors")[286] should not be merely associated with sapiential or Deuteronomic concerns but more so with the Davidic program.[287] Scholars consider that the acrostic style reflects the concerns of "Israel's wisdom movement" because "writing" and "composition" were closely linked to the "wisdom circles."[288] While these suggestions cannot be proved or disproved,[289] we can now be more certain from our study that AAs and ACs have been embedded with macrostructural and thematic roles in the overall program of the MT-150.

Superscriptions

We have considered the macrostructuring roles of superscriptions and the historical superscriptions of the Davidic psalms in earlier chapters. In light of our study on the numerical technique, we now consolidate them to show that formal poetic devices such as numerical techniques, acrostics or alphabetical compositions, and superscriptions all work together coherently to shape the macrostructure of the MT Psalter. The following figure highlights how numerical symbolism function when all the superscriptions of the Psalter are categorized accordingly.

---

286. Botha argues that "the alphabetic acrostic psalms were composed and inserted by the wisdom-inspired editors of the Psalter to influence the way we have to understand the Psalms." He further argues that the message they wanted to convey is "to draw a clear distinction between the righteous and the wicked so that the reader or hearer would experience these psalms as exhortations to a certain style of living." Botha, "'Wealth and Riches,'" 108–9, 126.

287. The Midrash states that Torah would have started with the Hebrew alphabet א "had a ב not been preferred for theological reasons." Raymond Apple points out that the "Decalogue (Exod 20:2; Deut 5:6) does open with the aleph of *anokhi*, 'I.' Retelling the history of mankind from the beginning, Chronicles starts with a large *aleph*. Even if it was considered significant that the Psalter begins with the letter *aleph*, it does not yet explain why the specific word chosen was *ashrei*. According to *Yalkut Shimoni* on the first verse of this psalm, David, the traditional author of Psalms, wanted to begin his book where Moses had left off in the Torah. Moses said, *ashrekha Yisra'el* (*Fortunate are you, O Israel*; Deut 33:29); here David begins with the words *ashrei ha-ish*" (Apple, "Happy Man of Psalm 1," 179–80).

288. Ceresko, "ABCs of Wisdom," 99.

289. Ho, "Review of John Kartje," 100–1.

The Design of the Psalter

As Superscriptions	Psalm	Number of Pss	Superscription	Number of Pss	Numerical Symbolism
Davidic	3–9; 11–32; 34–41; 51–65; 68–70, 86, 101, 103, 108–110, 138–145 ("David" in Songs of Ascents is not included)	69	With names	98	98 (14x7)
Solomon	72 ("Solomon" in the Songs of Ascents is not included)	1			
Moses	90	1			
Korah	42, 44–49, 84–85, 87–89	12			
Asaph	50, 73–83	12			
Yhwh *Malak*	93, 97, 99	3			
Clear superscription but without names	66–67; 92; 98; 100; 102; 104 (*piel* impv fs)*	7	Without names	7	52 (2x26)
Hodu (Impv mp)	105, 107, 118, 136	4	Praise Impv. Masc. Plural	15	
Hallelujah (impv mp)	106, 111–113, 117, 135, 146–150	11			
Songs of Ascents	120–134	15	SOA	15	
No Clear Superscription	2; 10; 33; 43; 71; 91; 94–96; 114–116; 137	13	Psalms without clear superscription	15	
No Clear Superscription (*ashre*)	1, 119	2			
			Total Psalms	150	

Figure 77: **Numerical Techniques in the Superscriptions of the MT Psalter**

We have discussed how certain psalms (e.g., *hodu*, *hallelujah* and Yhwh *Malak* psalms) traditionally understood as "untitled" psalms, can be considered as a form of *intended* superscription. I have noted fifteen psalms that do not have clear superscriptions (last two rows in the table) as a category by itself. These psalms are often found in twin-psalms (e.g., 1–2, 9–10, 33–34, 94–95).

I have also divided all superscriptions into two main categories. The first category consists of superscriptions with names. Since the שיר המעלות is clearly a standalone structural unit, psalms within this category that has a name in the superscription are not counted. As such, I have excluded the additional "David" or "Solomon" in Pss 122:1; 124:1; 127:1; 131:1; 133:1 in the count (to avoid double counting). These five psalms are listed in the category of SOA.

I have also excluded *additional* mentions of "David" in the superscriptions of Pss 52:2, 54:2 as they belong to the historical part of the superscriptions (again, to avoid double counting). I have, on the other hand, included the three Yhwh *Malak* psalms in the category of superscription with names as these psalms (93; 97; 99) begin with the divine name. If these identifications are valid, the total number of psalms with names add up to 98 (14x7). The number, "7," and its multiples symbolize completeness.

The second major category is psalms that do not carry names in the superscription. This major category is subdivided into psalms with clear superscription and psalms that do not have clearly identifiable superscription. There are 7 psalms with clear superscription but do not include names. The *Hodu* and *Hallelujah* psalms are another group of psalms with identifiable superscription but do not include. These psalms begin with formulaic words of praise/thanks in the *imperative masculine plural* conjugation. While Psalm 104 also begins with a similar formula of praise (ברכי), this word has the *piel* imperative feminine singular form which occurs only once. Since this form is different from the *Hodu-Hallelujah* category, I have placed this psalm under the category "Clear superscriptions but without names."

The three categories, *Hodu-Hallelujah* praise psalms, SOA, and psalms with "No clear superscription" consist 15 psalms each. Together with the 7 psalms having "Clear superscriptions but without names," there is a total of 52 psalms in the larger category of superscriptions without names. The number, "52" (2x26), is a multiple of the divine name.[290]

Superscriptions are clearly from antiquity (e.g., 82:1 in MasPs[a]).[291] Our study reinforces the importance and integrity of Psalms superscription. They should not simply be relegated to secondary relevance. Rather, they are carefully designed and cannot be separated from the psalm texts.

Summary

- In this chapter, we argue that numerical elements, alphabetic acrostics, alphabetic compositions, and superscriptions can function as macrostructuring devices.

- Labuschagne, van der Lugt, and others have shown that the Psalter is designed with numerical devices. Numbers such as "17" and "26" express divine presence, and numbers such as "7" and "11" function to structure texts. They also argue that there is usually a meaningful or rhetorical message at the center of a psalm.

- Adopting a different method, I counted all words in a psalm, including headers and words such as *selah*. Based on word counts, I term word(s) at the center as "nexusword." More than 70 percent of the nexuswords in Books I–III and more than 90 percent in Books IV–V correspond to Labuschagne and/or van der Lugt's meaningful/rhetorical centers.

- The nexusword of a psalm points to a word (or a pair of words), which in turn, designates a larger motif in the immediate context. The meaning of this nexus-context, abbreviated by the nexusword, gives the psalm its content-thrust and provides the link to a larger unit of psalms, forming a nexus-trajectory.

---

290. Koorevaar makes an interesting case for a "recount" total of 147 psalms in the Psalter. He considers the pairs of Pss 9–10, 42–43, and 114–15 as three single compositions. His discussion on superscriptions as possible structuring principle reinforces our contention of the structuring function of superscriptions. However, his conclusion remains tentative in view of our analysis. Koorevaar, "Psalter as a Structured Theological Story," 586–92.

291. Anderson notes, "Not only are they evidenced in MT, Qumran, LXX, and Targums, but it ought also to be noted that even by the time of the LXX translation (second or third century BC?) the technical terms contained there were so antiquated and obscure that the translators had a fair degree of trouble interpreting them. This is true also for the Targums. Furthermore, we find similar super/postscripts in other parts of Scripture (cf. Hab 3:1, 19b; Isa 38:9). There thus seems to be no reason not to take the super/postscripts seriously." Anderson, "Division and Order," 226.

The Design of the Psalter

- Book I consists of 22 AAs and ACs/PACs. Books II–III consist of 10 AAs and ACs/PACs and Books IV–V have a total of 14 AAs and ACs/PACs.

- The AA contrast two Davidizations of the Psalms and frame the fall of the Davidic king and rise of an ideal Davidic king. Psalm 110 marks an important milestone in the Metanarrative of the Psalter.

- AA, ACs, and PACs function to mark leitmotifs found in the Prologue and are strategically located as CM of Collections and Groups. They also mark seams/transition points between Collections, Groups, and Books.

- Numerical symbolism is embedded in the superscriptions of the Psalter. They can be grouped into two main categories (those that include names and those that do not) and add up to symbolic numbers. They are part of the composition and should not be viewed as secondary glosses.

- Numerical devices correspond well with other structuring techniques and the design of the Psalter.

6

Conclusion

I believe the messianic thrust of the OT was the whole reason the books of the Hebrew Bible were written.[1]

—John Sailhamer

Context, however, changes the way in which we read everything.[2]

—Jamie Grant

For me, a primary indicator for larger groupings within the Hebrew Bible is symmetry–symmetry defined by structures and numbers, usually of a simple binary or bilateral kind. When symmetry is established or confirmed by examination, it must be the result of conscious planning of deliberate decisions. Therefore I contend that the selection, arrangement, and organization of the books of the Hebrew Bible follow from the deliberate and purposeful decisions and actions of an individual or a small group of people at a particular time and in a particular place, thus producing a unified whole.[3]

—David Freedman

We began with the aim of understanding the logic and *design* of the MT-150 Psalter to ascertain if an overarching architectural logic can be assigned to it. In this

---

1. Sailhamer, "Messiah and the Hebrew Bible," 23.
2. Grant, "Psalms and the King," 107.
3. Freedman, *Unity of the Hebrew Bible*, vi.

conclusion, we will review the highlights of our analyses, briefly posit the implications of this work, and identify areas for future work.

Overall Summary and Key Propositions

The main points of each chapter have been summarized in bullet points at the end of each chapter. Here, I will revisit the three research questions that guided this study: (1) What are the main organizing principles of the Psalter? (2) How is the Psalter organized macrostructurally? (3) Is there a coherent overarching theme and logical design to the Psalter?

Key Macro-organizing Principles of the MT-150

Despite various discoveries of structuring techniques of Hebrew poetry and the rise of canonical approaches to the Psalms in the last few decades, there remains little consensus to the techniques of shaping or the Psalter's macrostructure. Therefore, consolidating the various techniques and approaches to understand the organization of the Psalter is timely and pertinent. The following six points summarize the macrostructuring principles of the MT-150.

First, the Psalter employs a variety of organizing techniques at different levels of composition. In chapter 1, I have consolidated at least 32 formal and tacit techniques. Formal techniques are likely known conventions existing at the time of the composition. The distinction between *formal* and *tacit* is not always clear and may overlap at different levels of composition.

Second, despite the multiplicity of these techniques, they collaborate with each other coherently in the structuring of the entire Psalter. They do not operate in conflicting ways when viewed under the overall scheme—a necessary feature for the Psalter to have an overarching unified design and logic. The coherence of these organizing principles suggests intentionality and unity of the MT-150. This does not necessitate that every observation presented in this book must fit into a perfect structural model. The effect of multiple editorial layers is such that the final editing did not always eliminate every non-conforming data.[4] Certain structural logic could remain elusive (e.g., the arrangements of AAs, ACs, and PACs, or the POS). Nonetheless, cumulative observations presented in this work have displayed exceptional consistency and coherence. Significantly, the correspondence and convergence of various independent techniques or observations support a unified and intentional logic to the design of the Psalter.

Third, the principles of the organization of the MT-150 should be viewed from a macro-perspective. Certain principles of organization cannot be easily detected

---

4. Wilson, *EHP*, 207–8, 214–15.

without a macrostructural perspective (e.g., the thematic parallel between Pss 104–119 and 135–150). Semi-macrostructural studies (limited to a Collection or several psalms), while helpful, cannot speak for the entire Psalter.

Fourth, the MT-150 is organized to afford at least three dimensions of reading. It should be read linearly, concentrically (palindromically) and intertextually. The linear dimension detects shifts, develops concepts and traces a thematic trajectory. The concentric dimension highlights recurring leitmotifs located centrally at various compositional units. Intertextually, the Psalter re-reads the Davidic covenant and its various expressions in the Historical books such as 1–2 Sam. The Psalter frames two high points of Davidic triumphs (cf. 2 Sam 7, 22; Pss 18, 144) around his brokenness, especially from Pss 51, where David's sin with Bathsheba is recorded. I propose that the MT-150 has a fourth dimension that is numerical. Numerical symbolism is also built into various techniques. Certain numbers associated with the Tetragrammaton (e.g., "17," "26") and acrostic/alphabetical compositions (e.g., "11," "22") recur strategically, uniting content and form. The convergence of the numerical technique with other techniques gives strong credence to our our structural proposals.

Fifth, the Prologue (Pss 1–2) is programmatic of the structural *shape* and *thematic* development of the Psalter. The Prologue is a triptych that has both concentric and linear dimensions. Linearly, it develops the *ways* and *outcomes* of the righteous and wicked. Their concentric focal points characterize the blessed state of the righteous man in the paradisical garden (Ps 1) which is enabled by the triumphant messianic king at Zion (Ps 2). In a similar way, the MT-150 is structured as a larger triptych (Books I, II–III, IV–V), capturing the righteous' journey to an ideal Zion via an ideal Messianic king.

Sixth, the macrostructural shape of the MT-150 is unveiled at the compositional levels of *Groups, Collections, and Subcollections*. Many studies are positioned at the semi-macrostructural level analyzing a Collection or several adjacent psalms in detail. But it is the "in-between" category, between Collections, Books and the entire Psalter, that lacks treatment. Eight of the most important macrostructuring techniques pertaining to this "in-between" category are as follows:

i. Concentric structure highlighting a Central Motif at the compositional levels of the Collections and beyond

ii. Placement and logic of Davidic psalms/Collections

iii. Placement and logic of alphabetical acrostics/compositions

iv. Formulation of superscription, their numerical design, the 13 historical superscripts and the coda at Ps 72:20

v. Recurring thematic trajectory towards Zion. This is also an expression of the techniques of *Steigerung* ("development") and *Fernverbindung* ("distant-binding")

vi. The use of individual psalm *genre* in structuring a compositional unit

vii. Pan-Psalter lexeme Occurrences Scheme—an exhaustive sequence of certain word/phrases at strategic locations across the entire Psalter to make or reinforce a rhetorical point in collaboration with the macrostructural shape of the Psalter

viii. Numerical devices and symbolism associated with the Tetragrammaton or motif of completeness.

Macrostructure of the MT-150

The second research question on the macrostructure of the MT-150 is fundamental to understanding the design of the entire Psalter. In its entirety, the Psalter is structured concentrically into three Sections (Books I, II–III, IV–V) and each Section consists of four Groups (1–4, 5–8, 9–12). The 12 Groups are delineated as follows: Pss 3–14; 15–24; 25–34; 35–41 (Book I); Pss 42–49; 50–72; 73–83; 84–89 (Books II–III); Pss 90–103; 104–119; 120–134; 135–150 (Books IV–V). My structural proposals are laid out graphically in four important Figures (12, 17, 27, 28).

The structural divisions of Books I–III are easier to detect because of their well-delimited superscriptions. An important key to understanding the structure of Books IV–V is to see Pss 104–107 and 135–137 as compositional units, and functioning as Janus Collections. The macrostructural distant-parallel between Pss 104–119 and 135–150 reinforces our overall structural proposition. Remarkably, the four respective Group Central Motifs (GCMs) in every Section parallel each other, giving the Psalter concentric and linear reading dimensions. The following figures summarize the 12 GCMs and macrostructural design of the MT-150.

Conclusion

		Book I: Establishment of the Davidic Kingship and Zion			
		3–14	15–24	25–34	35–41
	1–2				
Section 1	Prologue	YHWH's cosmic kingship; judgment from Zion	Victorious Messianic king; Torah glorified	Dedication Historical Zion-Temple; YHWH's kingship	Supplication of afflicted David
		Group 1	2	3	4

	Book II: Fall of the Davidic Kingship		Book III: Fall of Zion-temple	
	42–49	50–72	73–83	84–89
Section 2	Messianic king and his bride	Fall of Davidic kingship (and YHWH's response)	Fall of Zion-Temple (and YHWH's Judgment)	Supplication of afflicted David
	Group 5	6	7	8

	Book IV: Kingship of YHWH and Ideal David		Book V: Establishment of the Ideal Kingship and Zion-city	
	90–103	104–119	120–134	135–150
Section 3	YHWH's cosmic kingship; judgment from Zion	Victorious Messianic king; Torah glorified	Restoration; Eschatological Zion-Temple; divine-messianic kingship	Supplication of afflicted David
	Group 9	10	11	12

Figure 78: Central Motifs of all 12 Groups in the 3 Sections of the MT Psalter

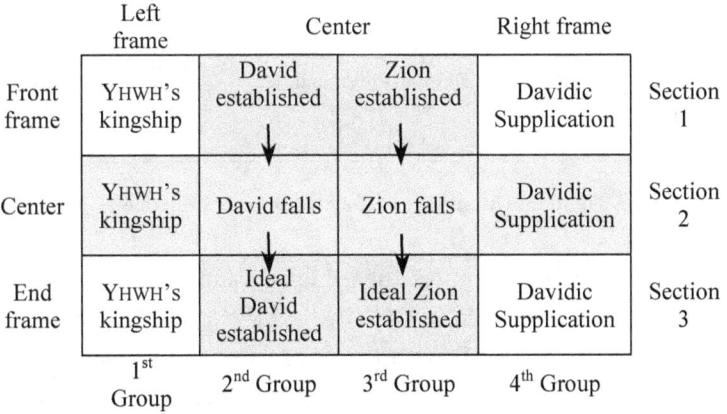

Figure 79: Concentric and Linear Structures of Group Central Motifs

Figure 78 shows how the 12 Groups across 3 Sections are characterized by a distinctive Central Motif.

The Design of the Psalter

Figure 79 shows how they are remarkably interlinked, and providing both linear and concentric dimensions to reading the MT-150. The two middle GCMs vertically down the three Sections provide the linear Metanarrative. The second GCMs (Groups 2, 6 and 10) develop the establishment, fall and the (re)establishment of an ideal Davidic king whereas the third GCMs (Groups 3, 7 and 11) develop a similar trajectory for Zion. As a whole, the concentric-linear structure envisions the establishment of the ideal kingship and ideal Zion, framed by two persistent motifs of Yhwh's universal kingship (1, 5, 9) and Davidic supplication (4, 8, 12).

In Figure 80, we see that five Davidic Collections (DC-I–V) are skillfully interwoven into the five-Book structure of the Psalter. Each DC can be viewed as a triptych. Together, they trace a linear development and characterize, more clearly, the ideal Davidic king.

Davidic Collection	Concentric Structure			Linear Progression
	Front	Center	End	
DC-I (3–41)	Yhwh's kingship (8–9)	Establishment of David's kingship and Temple (18–21, 29–30)	Davidic distress and supplication (38)	Begins with Yhwh's kingship. King David broken (sacrifice accepted). Kingship turned over to a Solomonic king ↓
DC-II (51–71, 86)	David's fall begins with Nathan's judgment (51)	David's life threatened (56–64)	David at the brink of death/Davidic distress and supplication (71/86)	
DC-III (101–103)	Blameless Davidite (101)	Afflicted figure (102)	David the Song leader (103)	Ideal, condemned-vindicated king-priest. ↓
DC-IV (108–110)	Victorious Davidic king entering Zion (108)	Afflicted and condemned Davidic figure (109)	Vindicated and victorious Davidic rule from Zion (110)	
DC-V (138–145)	Yhwh's kingship (138)	Davidic distress and supplication (140–143)	Davidic figure handover kingship to Yhwh (145)	Ideal king turned over kingship to Yhwh in the end

Figure 80: Summary of the Five Davidic Collections

The first Davidic Collection captures the establishment of the Davidic kingship but the storyline takes a negative turn in DC-II where the kingship is depicted as broken. A positive shift occurs in DC-III with the appearing of an ideal, victorious but afflicted king. This characterization of the ideal king deepens in the parallel DC-IV. The final DC-V democratizes a supplicational Davidic figure and concludes with the Davidic king submitting to Yhwh's kingship.

The 150 poems may appear to be a series of independent units chronologically linked to each other. But they are a nexus of overlapping motifs skillfully structured

Conclusion

into a single composition through a range of formal and tacit devices for emphasis, artistry, and rhetoric.

Overarching Logic and the Design of the MT-150

The logic of the MT-150 is a reception of the Davidic covenant wrapped in the clothing of Hebrew poetry. The primary leitmotifs of the Psalter, found in the Prologue (Pss 1–2), is an interweaved ternion of Kingship, Zion and Torah-piousness. These motifs are usually sustained at the seams of the five Books of the Psalter and at the palindromical center of compositional units. The GCMs of Book I trace the establishment of the Davidic kingship and Zion-temple. This is followed by a sustained focus on the historic fall of David's kingship and Zion in Books II–III respectively. A turning point in the Metanarrative occurs in Book IV with the foregrounding of Yhwh's kingship (93–100) and the appearance of a blameless, suffering Davidic ruler (DC-III–IV; 101–103; 108–110). Book V of the Psalter begins with a call for Yhwh to lead his people to an inhabited city. It highlights the establishment of an ideal Zion city that Yhwh builds (120–136), to which the psalmist and the *chasidim*, through persistence in supplication and the triumphs of the Davidic king (138–44), will eventually arrive (145–150). The Davidic promises prevail because of Yhwh's covenantal faithfulness.

The macrostructural logic of the Psalter is thus an unfurling and relecture of the Davidic covenant (in 2 Sam 7 and other texts). It is a search for blessedness, made possible under a larger trans-temporal reality that traces the establishment, fall and "re-establishment" of the Davidic promises via an ideal anointed king. The posture hitherto of the *chasidim* is that of trusting prayer and patience because of Yhwh's unfailing חסד.

From extrabiblical and internal literary evidence, many of the stylistic and rhetorical techniques (e.g., symmetry and the use of kingship motif at the center of a compositional unit) in the Psalter were already in use by the time of the final editing in the postexilic period. Moreover, important developing motifs across the Psalter, such as the sojourn to God's dwelling at Zion, are central in the Song of the Sea, one of Israel's earliest poetry. Sharing a common socio-political and theological setting, the final editors of the Psalter and implied readers alike would have been more familiar with these poetic, theological and structural devices than modern readers today.

The marvel of the Psalter's design lies in the synergizing of at least four narratives—first, a larger Metanarrative of God's purposes expressed through a prophetic re-reading of the Davidic covenant. Then it develops two smaller narratives representing the life-journeys of the individual Davidic king and the community of *chasidim* respectively. Finally, the story of the reader of the Psalter is fused into these three narratives. The Davidization of the psalms and the democratization of the Davidic blessings integrate all four narratives. Our reading of the Psalter shows that the final editors were sensitive to the theological and existential struggles of postexilic Israel readership and had crafted a coherent and significant message with poetical finesse to address these issues.

Implications and Further Work

Significant implications and opportunities for further research are briefly captured in the following:

Sitz im Psalter

The design of the Psalter reflects a synchronic-theological reading rather than historical-critical one. While the Psalter may have been composed under different layers historically, the generic nature of the final MT-150 form is designed for trans-temporal reception. By its own theological horizon, the Psalter remains a book that looks to the future. This feature is not unlike other canonical books in the HB. Reading individual psalms via their *Sitz im Leben*, though useful, speculates on one historical slice of the Psalms and fails to grasp its role in the larger programmatic message as we have shown. The interpretation of an individual psalm is best elucidated via its *Sitz im Psalter*. Perhaps we can use the analogies of a photo mosaic,[5] a television serial, or a horological masterpiece to describe it. The parts, assembled in sequential, parallel, and overlapping installments, bring about an overall architectonic movement and purpose.

The meaning of individual psalms is radically enriched when read within the immediate literary unit and under the whole, through which the theological thrust of the Psalms, especially its connection with the Davidic covenant, can be understood. This book may articulate the plausibility of a macrostructural design but a detailed exegetical study of individual psalms within the *Sitz im Psalter* based on our proposal is still necessary. In other words, the message of each psalm read historically or form-critically, may radically change when it is read with its *Sitz im Psalter*.

The logic and design the MT-150 not only *describes* a certain reality for humankind and the world before Yhwh, it *prescribes* the way through which humans find bliss at a paradisical city, and *ascribes* the role and significance of each psalm under its *Sitz im Psalter*.

Sitz in der Literatur

It is important to situate the poetical principles and the Psalter's theological re-reading of the Davidic covenant within the larger Hebrew canon and literature of the Second Temple period. Where biblical texts are concerned, there is a need to further clarify the

---

5. A photo mosaic is a coherent picture made with many small pixelated images carefully arranged.

relationship between the MT-150 and the Torah, Historical books, post-exilic Prophets, and the New Testament (e.g., Epistle to the Hebrews). It must be acknowledged that the Psalter's re-reading of the Davidic covenant, especially in the brokenness of the Davidic king becoming an acceptable sacrifice, and the appearing of a blameless, afflicted and victorious messianic king, coheres strikingly with the Christological interpretation of the Psalms.[6]

If the sequential order is important and intentional, we need to understand why the Psalter is ordered differently in different traditions of the HB.[7] Partly due to the fragmentary nature, it is also unclear if the various poetical techniques identified in this book were already developed in extant pre-Masoretic non-Qumran psalms manuscripts (e.g., MasPs^a). Another area for study is the Qumran Psalms Scrolls (e.g., 11QPs^a), which deviate from the MT-150 in the repertoire, sequence, and orthography of psalms.

Strawn, after tracing the textual history of the Psalms in the pioneering project, *The Textual History of the Bible*, concludes that "future studies of shape and shaping should be conducted in comparative modes, such that a study of, say, MT-150 would not be conducted without some awareness of at least one (ideally more) alternative 'shape' known from the manuscript tradition."[8] This volume provides a good platform for such comparative work.

---

6. The Christological interpretation is a formidable and reasonable re-reading of the MT-150. Consider Jesus's statement about the Psalms in Luke 24:44 and the following Christological re-readings of Psalms by the NT: (1) The characterization of the ideal Davidic figure as ideal, blameless (John 8:46; cf. Pss 101–103), shepherd (Matt 2:6; 26:30; John 10:11–14; cf. Pss 78:70–72; 80:1), victorious (1 Tim 6:15; Rev 19:16; cf. Ps 108), messianic priest-king (Matt 16:16; Heb 3:1; 7:14–24; cf. Ps 110), Torah-pious (Matt 4; Mark 10:17–18; cf. Pss 112; 119), and Son of God (Matt 16:16; Luke 1:32; cf. Pss 2:7, 12; 8:5; 72:1); (2) The king is both afflicted and victorious (Acts 4:27; Rom 15:16; cf. Pss 101–102; 109–10); (3) Two triumphant depictions of victory over death and one depiction of his death (1 Cor 15:23–28; Rev 20:5–6; cf. Pss 18; 144–145); (4) The raging of the nations against Jesus and false accusations that led to his condemnation (Matt 26:59–62; Acts 4:25–26; cf. Ps 2:2; 109:6–20); (5) Jesus ushers in the sure blessings of the Davidic promises and submits his kingship to God the father at the end (Acts 13:33–41; 1 Cor 15:28; cf. Pss 144–145); (6) Through the brokenness of Jesus, sacrifice is accepted to God (Rom 3:24; Heb 10:19; cf. Pss 51–69); (7) Jesus as the better Moses and David (Heb 3:2–6; Acts 2:29–36; cf. Pss 90–92, 101–103); (8) The rejection of Jesus and building of God's house (Matt 16:16; 1 Pet 4:4–8; Ps 109:20; 118:22); (9) The concept of "new song" in the Book of Revelation as the dawn of a new era (Rev 5:9; 14:3; cf. Pss 33:4; 40:4; 96:1; 98:1; 144:9; 149:1); (10) Persistent supplication of the people of God until the coming of a new era (Eph 6:18; 1 Thess 5:17; Jas 5:13–20; cf. Pss 38; 86; 140–143). (11) The appearing of a paradisical Zion city with the river of life and fruit-bearing trees, where the people of God dwells in security and bliss (Rev 21:1–3; 22:1–3; cf. Pss 1:3; 46:4); (12) The people of God will reign with Jesus at Zion (Rev 20:4; cf. Pss 149:1–9); (13) A concluding call for the people of God to heed the word of God (Rev 22:7; cf. Ps 147:19; Nexusword of Pss 146–150); (14) The expression, Hallelujah and eschatological consummative praise (Rev 19:1–6; cf. Pss 145–150). For discussions on the use of Psalms in the NT, see Moyise and Menken, *Psalms in the New Testament*. On reception of the Psalms in the Epistle of Hebrews in the New Testament, see Human and Steyn, *Psalms and Hebrews*.

7. Even within the MT tradition, differences in book order are attested. For instance, in the Aleppo Codex, the Psalms comes after Chronicles.

8. Strawn, "10.2.2 Masoretic Texts."

Sitz im Leben

There is a prescriptive call to hope and supplication in the MT-150 but how does this prescriptive thrust inform, cohere or respond to the historical setting of its original readership? Who are the people most capable and equipped to compose the MT-150 and under what circumstance was the Psalter finally composed? Were the composers Levites associated with the Second Temple, or were they scribes associated with the Wisdom circle?[9] While these issues are unlikely to be addressed with certainty, our study can contribute to the understanding of these circumstantial settings. Since the LXX follows the MT-150 well, it is plausible that a proto-Masoretic 150 *Vorlage* was already extant before the mid-second century BCE. Proto-Masoretic Psalms manuscripts such as MasPs^a (30–1 BCE), MasPs^b (50–25 BCE) and 5/6HevPs (50–68 CE) support the existence of a proto MT-150 by the time of the first century BCE.[10]

From the logic and design of the MT-150, I suggest that a single editor or a small group of editors may be responsible for the Psalter's final shape. These editors were highly skilled and familiar with a range of formal and tacit poetical techniques. The use of techniques such as the POS and numerical devices presumed a literary whole and required focused reading rather than a partial recitation, though the latter need not be rejected. While a reading audience with access to a copy of the entire Psalter and having the sophistication to work through the text in detail is suggested by the Psalter's design, it is not a necessary condition for reception. This is to say that the Psalter is not merely used as an occasional liturgical work (e.g., as a hymnal) but also a book to be read from the beginning to the end, and to be meditated on continually (Ps 1:2).

Many compositional techniques were already seen in various Mesopotamian and Egyptian acrostics poems, as well as, the Song of the Sea, one of Israel's earliest poems. Extended chiastic or acrostic structures across large portions of texts also find parallels elsewhere across the Hebrew Bible (e.g., Lamentations, Judg 3:7—16:31). It is plausible that the Psalms editors and the implied readers would have been familiar with these literary rhetorics.

The final editors of the Psalter were clearly concerned with the fulfillment of YHWH's promises through the Davidic covenant and were well-versed in the historical narratives (e.g., 1–2 Samuel).[11] While it is unclear if the editors of the Psalms were also those behind 1–2 Chronicles, the Chronicler seemed to understand the design

---

9. For authorship associated with the Levitical priests in the post-exilic period, see Jonker, "Revisiting the Psalms Headings," 102–22; Gillingham, "Levites and The Editorial Composition," 201–13.

10. These three texts are very close to the MT-150 and are deemed as "proto-MT" Psalms texts. Tov, *Textual Criticism of the Hebrew Bible*, 3:328.

11. Dated to 50–25 BCE, 4QSam^a (4Q51) is found to be closer to the LXX translation rather than the MT. This suggests that a pre-Masoretic *Vorlage* of the book of Samuel, on which the LXX was dependent was already extant at around the time the LXX was translated. Fischer and Würthwein, *Text of the Old Testament*, 66.

of the Psalter by his selective use of the Zion-Temple motifs and the formulaic *hodu* from Books IV–V of the Psalter. The MT-150 is likely composed through a period of social strain.[12] Even though the Second temple was still standing, worshippers were looking forward to a better Zion-city-temple. The combination of motifs of messianic hope and ideal Zion, vis-à-vis a less than ideal depiction of social life in Book V of the Psalter, suggests a state of challenging circumstances that required a re-reading of Davidic promises and exhortations to persist in prayer and Torah-piousness. This is so that the original readers would continue in hope until that transition (Pss 144–145) into the blissful eschatological social-reality. At the same time, the Psalter has a trans-temporal character such that readers today can also hold on to that same Davidic hope regardless of their circumstances, and persist in prayer until that final *hallelujah*!

---

12. On Persian influence, see Tucker, *Constructing and Deconstructing Power*.

Appendix

Ho-Labuschagne-van der Lugt Comparison of the Rhetorical Center in An Individual Psalm

Note:

1. *Asterisk denotes that either textual emendations, expansions beyond the word level, or the meaningful center can be found with a different methodology (e.g., adding the header counts), is required for that psalm.

2. In the "nexusword" column, I have filled out the entire colon in parenthesis to provide a clearer sense of the immediate context. Word(s) not in parenthesis are the identified nexusword.

3. When the nexusword identified corresponds with either the *meaningful center* of Labuschagne's study or the *rhetorical center* of van der Lugt's analysis, I indicate it as "Y" in the last column. I have totaled up the number of psalms with "Y" for each Section and expressed it as a percentage of correspondence at the bottom of the column.

4. In certain cases, I have italicized and highlighted the rows where two psalms are considered as one (e.g., Pss 9–10); a single psalm is divided into two (e.g., Ps 40); or the nexusword is for a compositional unit larger than a single psalm (e.g., Pss 1–2).

5. For further references on Labuschagne and van der Lugt's work, see http://www.labuschagne.nl/psalms.htm; *CAS* I–III.

Appendix

Ps	Ho Nexusword	Word count	MT verse	Labuschagne Meaningful center	MT verse; level of poetic unit	van der Lugt Rhetorical center	MT verse; level of poetic unit	Correspondence?
1	which (yield its fruit in its season)	57	3	Which yields its fruit in its season, And its leaf does not wither	3a; word	which brings forth its fruit in due season and whose foliage does not fade	3c–d; word, colon, verse	Y
2	(you are) my Son	77	7	I will tell of the decree: The LORD said to me, "You are my Son"	7a–b; colon	I will tell of the decree: The LORD said to me, "You are my Son"	7a–b; colon	Y
1–2	against the LORD, and against his anointed	134	2:2	Disregarding considering maqqef, centerword = "against" (2:2), entire colon = against the LORD, against his anointed				Y
3	from his (holy) hill	63	5	I lay down and slept; I woke again, for the LORD sustained me	6; word	I lay down and slept; I woke again, for the LORD sustained me	6; word	N
4	be angry and do not sin	68	5	meditate in your hearts, on your beds, and be silent	5b; word	ponder in your own hearts on your beds, and be silent	5b; word	N
5	(I will enter) your house	89	8	I will worship at your holy temple in awe of you	8b; word, colon	because of your steadfast love I will appear in your presence	8; colon, verse	Y
6	(no) remembrance of you; in Sheol	74	6	I am wearied with my moaning	7a; colon	For in death there is no remembrance of you . . . I am weary with my moaning	*6 –7a; word (with words in headings)	Y
7	judge me, O LORD (according to my righteousness)	124	9	new	9b–10a–b; words (entire poem)	my enemy without cause	7:1–9a = 5b; word	Y
						he has bent and readied his bow	*7:9b–18 = No meaningful center	
8	For you are mindful of, and the son of man	66	5	What is a human being that you think of him, . . . glory and honour crowned him	5–6; word, colon	a human being seems insignificant, . . . mastery in your creation	5–6; word, colon, verse	Y
9	(the LORD) who dwells in Zion	150	12	Treated as a single psalm.				
10	(he seize the) poor when he draws	146	9					
9–10	they are but man	296	9:21	Why, YHWH, do you stand far off? Why hide away in times of trouble?	10:1; word	Why, O Lord, do you stand far off	10:1; word, colon	N
11	(the LORD's) throne is in heaven	62	4	YHWH, in heaven is his throne	4b; word	the Lord's throne is in heaven	4b; word, colon	Y
12	(who is) master over us?	72	5	because of the plundering of the poor . . . in the safety for which he longs"	6; verse	God will rescue the afflicted	*6a–b; colon (with headings, 5-word center)	N
13	answer me O LORD	48	4	Look now and answer me, YHWH my God	4a; word	look answer me, O Lord my God	4a; word	Y
14	(do) all the workers of wickedness (not know?)	64	4	Have they no knowledge, all those evildoers?	4a; word	Have they no knowledge, all the evildoers	4a; word, verse, strophe	Y
15	not take up (reproach) against his neighbour	44	3	And (he) tells no tales against his neighbour	3c; word	nor takes up a reproach against his friend	3c; word, colon, verse	Y
16	to me. I will bless	78	6, 7	Yes, I am well content with my inheritance	6b; colon.	indeed, I have a beautiful inheritance	6b; word, colon	N
17	you will hide me; from the face (of the wicked)	116	8, 9	Guard me like the apple of your eye in the shadow of your wings hide me	8; word	Keep me as the apple of your eye	8; colon, verse	Y
18	the LORD rewarded (me)	345	25	with the blameless you show yourself blameless	*26b; word	with the blameless man you show yourself blameless	26b; word, colon	N

Appendix

Ps	Ho			Labuschagne		van der Lugt		Correspondence?
	Nexusword	Word count	MT verse	Meaningful center	MT verse; level of poetic unit	Rhetorical center	MT verse; level of poetic unit	
19	to make wise (the simple)	113	8	The precepts of the LORD are right, rejoicing the heart . . . enlightening the eyes	*9; verse	The precepts of the LORD are right	*9a; word (no meaningful center)	N
20	all your petitions. Now I know that the LORD saves his anointed	62	6, 7	May YHWH fulfil your every request	*6c; colon (with header and *selah*)	May God fulfil all the request of the king	*6c; colon (with header and *selah*)	Y
21	your presence, for the king	92	7, 8	For the king trusts in YHWH	*8a; word	For the king trusts in the LORD	8a; word	Y
22	evildoers encircle me	224	17	A band of evildoers encircle me piercing my hands and my feet	17b–c; colon level	a company of evildoers encircles me . . . they stare and gloat over me	17b–18; word	Y
23	for you are with me	50	4	For you are with me	4d; word	For you are with me	4d; word	Y
24	Jacob	81	6	Those who seek your presence are the people of Jacob!	6b; colon	Such is the generation of those who seek him	*6a; word (not rhetorical center)	Y
25	his testimonies	133	10	For your name's sake, YHWH	*11; word	For your name's sake, O LORD	*11a; word (no rhetorical center)	N
26	and I go about (your altar)	73	6	I wash my hands in innocence . . . and recounting all your wondrous deeds	*6, 7; verseline	and I will go about	6b; word	Y
27	(I will offer) in his tent, sacrifices (with shouts of joy)	126	6	Yes, I shall acclaim him in his tent with sacrifice. I shall sing and make music for YHWH	*6c, colon; 6d; word	and I will offer in his tent sacrifices with shouts of joy	6c; colon	Y
28	render them their due reward	80	4	Render them their due reward	4d; word	Render them their due reward.	4d; word	Y
29	(he makes) Lebanon (skip like a calf)	81	6	He makes them skip like a calf	6a; word level	He makes Lebanon to skip like a calf	6a; colon	Y
30	O LORD, (by your favor)	87	8	O LORD, by your favour you have established me as a strong mountain	8a; colon (or vv. 7–8)	By your favor, (O LORD), you made my mountain stand strong	8a; word	Y
29–30	house of David (superscription)	168	30:1					
31	(I have become) a broken vessel	200	13	I have become like a broken vessel for I hear the whispering of many	*13b–14a; no meaningful center	I have become like a broken vessel. For I hear the whispering of many	*13b–14a; word (no rhetorical center)	Y
32	(therefore let all godly pray) to you (at a time you may be found)	99	6	Therefore, let every faithful one pray . . . great waters will not reach him	6; colon	Therefore let everyone who is godly . . . great waters, they shall not reach him	6; verse	Y
33	(his heart) to generation (after generations)	137	11	The counsel of YHWH stands forever . . . the people he has chosen as his heritage	11–12; word (center = *ashre*)	The counsel of the LORD stands forever . . . the people whom he has chosen as his heritage	11–12; colon, verselines	Y
34	the fear of (the LORD)	139	12	I will teach you the fear of YHWH	12b; word	I will teach you the fear of the LORD	12b; word	Y
35	I bowed down (in mourning)	203	14	I walked, bowed in grief . . . unknown assailants crowded against me	*14–15b; colon	I went about as though I grieved . . . I bowed down in mourning	*14; verseline (no rhetorical center)	Y

345

Appendix

Ps	Ho			Labuschagne		van der Lugt		Correspondence?
	Nexusword	Word count	MT verse	Meaningful center	MT verse; level of poetic unit	Rhetorical center	MT verse; level of poetic unit	
36	(your judgments are great) deep	81	7	YHWH, your righteousness extends to heaven . . . and beast you save, YHWH	6, 7; verselines (no meaningful center)	Your steadfast love, O LORD, extends to the heavens, . . . man and beast you save, O LORD	7b–c; colon, 6, 7; strophe	Y
37	(they vanish) like smoke (they vanish)	259	20	Like the glory of the pastures, they vanish—like smoke they vanish	20; word	the godless borrow and do not pay	21a; colon (no rhetorical center)	Y
38	they stand, my nearest kin (stand far off)	144	12	and my kinsfolk keep far off	12b; word	and my nearest kin stand far off	12b; word, colon	Y
39	(does not know) who will gather?	108	7	And now, YHWH, what do I wait for? My hope is in you	8; verse (no meaningful center)	And now, O Lord, for what do I wait? My hope is in you	8; verse (no rhetorical center)	N
40	I will not restraint (my lips O LORD)	168	10	I do not restrain my lips, . . . saving power I announced	10b–11b; colon	but you have given me an open ear . . . offering you have not required	*40:2–13 = 7b–c; colon	Y
						Aha, Aha!	*40:14–18 = 16b; word	
41	(united) against me they whisper	104	8	he goes out and tells it abroad	*7c; word	when he goes out, he tells it abroad	*7c; word (not rhetorical center)	N
				Correspondence (Book I) = 30/41 (73%)				
42	my God my (soul)	114	7					N
43	(let them bring me) to thy holy hill	46	3					N
42–43	and in the night, his song (is with me)	160	9	By day YHWH grants his love, . . . a prayer to the God of my life	42:9; verse (no meaningful word)	By day the LORD commands . . . prayer to the God of my life	42:9; verse	Y
44	(you have made us) a scorn (to our neighbours)	173	14	You have sold your people . . . the derision and scorn of those about us	*13, 14; verseline	You have sold your people . . . the derision and scorn of those around us	13–14; colon	Y
45	cassia (are your robes)	139	9	Your robes are all fragrant . . . At your right hand stands the queen in gold of Ophir	*9, 10; strophe	daughters of kings . . . queen in gold of Ophir	10; verse	Y
46	the kingdoms (totter)	87	7	Nations rage, kingdoms totter, . . . YHWH of Hosts is with us	7–8a; word, verse	The nations rage, . . . the earth melts	7b; colon or 7, verse	Y
47	the Lord with the sound (of the trumpet)	64	6	God has gone up to the shout of triumph . . . praise our king, sing praises	6, 7; colon	God has gone up to the shout of triumph . . . praise our king, sing praises	6–7; colon, verse	Y
48	in the city of the LORD of host	100	9	As we have heard, so we have . . . God establishes it forever	9; colon, verse	As we have heard, so have we seen . . . which God will establish forever. *Selah*	*9; word (not rhetorical center)	Y
49	generations (the foolish) called (their lands)	144	12	Their graves are their homes forever, their dwelling places for all generations they call their names over their lands	12; verse (no meaningful center)	Their graves are their homes forever, their dwelling places to all generations	12a–b; colon	Y
50	(world's) fullness are mine	149	12	If I were hungry, I would not tell you for the world and all that is in it are mine	12; verse or entire vv. 7–13 (no meaningful center)	If I were hungry, I would not tell you, . . . drink the blood of goats?	12–13; strophe	Y

346

Appendix

Ps	Ho Nexusword	Word count	MT verse	Labuschagne Meaningful center	MT verse; level of poetic unit	van der Lugt Rhetorical center	MT verse; level of poetic unit	Correspondence?
51	(create in me a clean heart) O God!	137	12	Create in me a pure heart, O God, and renew within me a steadfast spirit	12; colon	a clean heart create for me, O God, and a steadfast spirit renew within me	12; colon	Y
52	forever, he will snatch you (up)	82	7	The righteous will look on, will be awestruck and will laugh at him	8; verse	The righteous will look on, will be awestruck and will laugh at him	8; colon, verse	N
53	(have the workers of wickedness no) knowledge	67	5	All are unfaithful, altogether corrupt, . . . if eating bread, and never call upon God?	4–5; verse	They have all fallen away; . . . as they eat bread, and do not call upon God?	4–5; verse	Y
54	my life, not!	58	5	Behold, God is my helper, the Lord the sustainer of my life	6; verse	Behold, God is my helper; the Lord is the upholder of my life	6; verse	N
55	but it is you, a man	174	14	a man of my own sort, my comrade, my familiar friend	14; word (selah in the wrong place)	within God's house we walked in the throng	15b; colon (not rhetorical center)	Y
56	for what crime?	107	8	You yourself record my wailing (v.9a); Meaningful Center 1—In God whose word I praise, in God I trust, I fear not; what can flesh do to me? (v.5); Meaningful Center 2—In God whose word I praise, . . . what can man do to me?	(1) 9a; colon; (2) 5, 11, 12. Multiple meaningful centers	you keep a record of misery	9a; colon	N
57	sharp. Be exalted	94	5, 6	Let your glory be all over the earth	6b; word	Let your glory be over all the earth	6b; word	N
58	(O God, break the teeth) in their mouths	85	7	God, smash their teeth . . . Let them vanish like water that runs away	7–8a; word	O God, break the teeth in their mouths; . . . the young lions, O LORD	7; colon, verse	Y
59	his strength for you	134	10	Yes, God is my bulwark, a God of steadfast love for me	10b–11a; word			N
60	answer us, O God	102	7, 8	Gilead is mine and Manasseh is mine.	9a; colon	mine is Gilead, and mine is Manasseh.	9a; colon	N
61	selah. For you	60	5, 6	for you, God, have heard my vows	6a; word	For you, O God, have heard my vows	6a; word	Y
62	(I will not) be shaken. On God	96	7, 8	my safety and my honour, my rock of refuge, my shelter is in God	8b; word	the rock of my strength, my refuge, is in God	8b; colon	N
63	and my lips	81	6	When I think of you on my bed	7a; word	when I remember you upon my bed	7a; word	N
64	snares, they say	74	6	They confirm their wicked resolves; they talk of hiding snares	7a–b; colon (no meaningful center)	They confirm their wicked resolves; they talk of hiding snares	7a–b, colon (no rhetorical center)	N
65	the roaring (of waves)	101	8	You calm the roaring of the seas, . . . the tumult of the nations	8; off-center words	who stills the roaring of the seas, . . . the tumult of the peoples	8; colon	Y
66	you have tried us	131	10	For you tested us, God you refined us as silver is refined	10; word (include headers and selah)	you put a trammel on our loins	11b; colon	Y
67	(let the) peoples (sing for joy)	49	5	you judge the peoples with equity	5b; word	surely, you rule the peoples in equity	5b; colon noun "peoples"	Y
68	your captives	295	19	You went up the high mount, . . . you received gifts from men	19a–b; word	You went up the high mount, . . . you received gifts from men	19a–b; word	Y
69	(O Lord) turn (to me)	251	17	In your great compassion . . . Make haste, answer me	17b–18; word	For I am in distress; answer me quickly	18b; colon	Y

347

Appendix

Ps	Ho Nexusword	Word count	MT verse	Labuschagne Meaningful center	MT verse; level of poetic unit	van der Lugt Rhetorical center	MT verse; level of poetic unit	Correspondence?
70	Aha (Aha!)	43	4	Let them withdraw in their shame, . . . all who seek you	4–5b; word	Let them withdraw in their shame, . . . all who seek you	4–5b; colon, verse	Y
71	dishonour, who seek to injure me	174	13	God, be not far from me . . . they be covered who seek my hurt	12, 13; word, strophe	May my accusers . . . they be covered who seek my hurt	*13; verse (no rhetorical center)	Y
72	needy when they call	140	12	kings of Tarshish . . . kings of Sheba and Seba bring gifts	10; strophe	kings of Tarshish . . . kings of Sheba and Seba bring gifts	10; colon, verse and strophe	N
71–72	I will sing praise to you with the lyre, O holy one of Israel		71:22 c–d					
				Correspondence (Book II) = 21/ 31 (68%)				
73	every morning	171	14	For all day long I suffer . . . I would have betrayed your people	14, 15; verse	If I had said, "I will speak thus"	*15a; colon (not rhetorical center)	Y
74	(yet God is my king . . .) salvation in the midst (of the land)	174	12	Yes, God is my king from of old working salvation in the midst of the earth	12; verse	Yet God my King . . . salvation in the midst of the earth	12; verse	Y
75	for (not from the east or west)	77	7	Not from the east or from the west and not from the wilderness comes lifting up	*7; verse (no meaningful center word)	For not from the east or from the west and not from the wilderness comes lifting up	7; verse	Y
76	deep sleep, rider (and horse cast into deep sleep)	78	7	you, awesome are you	8a; word	you, awesome are you	8a; word	N
77	it (is my grief)	141	11	I will call to mind the deeds of YH, I will remember your wonders of old	*12; colon (no meaningful center word)	Then I said, "I will appeal to this, . . . meditate on your mighty deeds	11–13; strophe	Y
78	they repented (and sought God)	473	34	They remembered that God . . . their redeemer	v. 35; verse	They remembered that God . . . their redeemer	35; verse	N
79	do not remember against us (our former sins)	115	8	For they have devoured Jacob and laid waste his homeland	*7; colon (no meaningful center word)	For they have devoured Jacob and laid waste his habitation	7; colon	N
80	(and it took) deep root and fill the land	124	10	A vine from Egypt you dug out you drove out nations and planted it . . . and to the River its shoots	*9–12; canticle (no meaningful center word)	A vine from Egypt you dug out . . . and to the River its shoots	9–12; canticle	Y
81	(I will admonish) in you	111	9	O that you would listen to me, Israel	9b; word, colon	O Israel, if you would but listen to me	9b; word, colon	Y
82	no understanding	51	5	They know nothing and understand nothing; in darkness they walk about.	5a–b; word	They have neither knowledge . . . walk about in darkness	5a; word, colon	Y
83	as Jabin	109	10	Deal with them as with Midian, . . . became dung for the ground	10–11; verse (no meaningful center word)	Deal with them as with Midian . . . dung for the ground	10–11; verse	Y
84	early rain	101	7	Blessed are those whose strength is in you, . . . hear my prayer; give ear, O God of Jacob! *Selah*	6–9; canto	Blessed are those whose strength . . . heart are the highways to Zion	6; verse	Y

Appendix

Ps	Ho Nexusword	Word count	MT verse	Labuschagne Meaningful center	MT verse; level of poetic unit	van der Lugt Rhetorical center	MT verse; level of poetic unit	Correspondence?
85	grant to us (your salvation)	83	8	Let me hear what God YHWH will speak . . . let them not turn back to folly	9; strophe	Restore us again . . . your indignation toward us! (v. 5); Steadfast love and faithfulness meet (11a)	*Two centers, 5, 11a.	N
86	for you are great	128	10	There is none like you among the gods, . . . do wondrous things you alone are God	8–10; strophe	all nations will honor God	9; verse	Y
87	(behold) Philistia (and Tyre)	47	4	I shall mention Rahab and Babylon . . . This one and that one were born in her	*4–5a; colon (no meaning center word)	I shall mention Rahab and Babylon . . . This one and that one were born in her	*4–5a; colon (no meaning center word)	Y
88	(not) go out	131	9	My eyes grow dim through anguish I invoke you, YHWH, every day	10a–b; colon	my eye grows dim through sorrow	10a; word	N
89	I will strike down (those who hate him), my faithfulness, (and steadfast love will be with him)	334	24, 25	My faithfulness and my steadfast love shall be with him. . . Rock of my salvation"	25–27; strophe (excluding coda)	My faithfulness and my steadfast love . . . his right hand on the rivers	25–26; strophe	Y
				Correspondence (Book III) = 12/17 (71%)				
90	we bring to an end, our years like a sigh	125	9	we bring our years to an end like a sigh	9b; word	we spend our years like a sigh	9b; word	Y
91	you will look (with your eyes)	99	8	you will see the retribution on evildoers	8b; colon (no meaningful center word)	and you will see the downfall of the godless	8b; word, colon	Y
92	(you, O LORD) are on high forever	100	9	but you are on high forever, O LORD	9; word	but you, O LORD, are on high forever	9; word	Y
93	floods	41	3	floods have lifted up . . . the floods lift up their roaring	3; word	floods have lifted, . . . the floods lift up their roaring	3; word	Y
94	to give him rest (both words start with *lamed*)	146	13	happy the one whom you instruct, YH and whom you teach from your law	12; verse	blessed is the man . . . you teach out of your law	12; verse, strophe	N
95	for (he is our God)	77	7	For he is our God	7a; word	yes, he is our God	7a; word, colon	Y
94–95	*your steadfast love, O LORD, held me up.*	223	9:18					N
96	ascribe (to the LORD)	95	8	ascribe to the Lord the glory of his name	8a; word	ascribe to the Lord the glory of his name	8a	Y
97	all who serve idols	84	7	all worshipers of images . . . bow down before him	7; word	all worshipers of images . . . worship him, all you gods	7; colon	Y
98	sing praises	67	4	break forth and exult and sing praises	4b; colon	break forth and shout joyfully and sing praise	4b; colon	Y
99	holy (is he)	77	5	holy is he	5c; colon	holy is he	5c; word	Y
100	we are his people	36	3	and we are his, his people and the flock of his pasture	3b; word or 4a, colon	none	none	Y
101	secretly his neighbour	70	5	whoever secretly slanders . . . I will not tolerate	5; strophe	none	none	Y
102	for they are pleased	183	15	for your servants hold her stones dear and have pity on her dust	15; verse (no meaningful center word)	for your servants hold her stones dear and have pity on her dust	15; verse	Y

349

Appendix

Ps	Ho Nexusword	Word count	MT verse	Labuschagne Meaningful center	MT verse; level of poetic unit	van der Lugt Rhetorical center	MT verse; level of poetic unit	Correspondence?
103	our transgression (from us)	141	12	For as the heavens are high . . . he remove our transgressions from us	12b; word	so far does he remove our transgressions from us	12b; colon	Y
104	a refuge	233	18	In them the birds build their nests; . . . a refuge for the rock badgers	*17–18; word. ("hallelujah" left out)	In them the birds build their nests; . . . the rocks are a refuge for the rock badgers	*17–18; word. ("hallelujah" left out of count)	Y
105	Jacob sojourned (in the land of ham)	256	23	Then Israel came to Egypt; Jacob sojourned in the land of Ham	23; verse	Then Israel came to Egypt; Jacob sojourned in the land of Ham	23; colon, verse	Y
106	they did not believe (his word)	287	24	he purposed to destroy . . . having no faith in his promise	23, 24; verse	Therefore he said he would destroy . . . his wrath from destroying them	*23 center words	Y
	Correspondence (Book IV) = 16/17 (94%)							
107	let them recount (his works with joy)	253	22	and let them offer sacrifices . . . his deeds in songs of joy	22; verse	and let them offer sacrifices . . . his deeds in songs of joy	22; colon, verse	Y
108	valley (of Succoth)	85	8	God has spoken in his sanctuary . . . I will measure off!"	8 verseline	God has promised in his holiness . . . Valley of Succoth"	8; verse	Y
109	despondent (in the heart)	201	16	afflicted and poor	16b; word	he loved to curse; let curses come upon him	17a center words of canto II.1	Y
110	your youth	55	3	your people will participate when you take up arms . . . you are a priest for ever after the order of Melchizedek	3, 4; verse (no meaningful center word)	holiness, priests	3, 4; word, colon	Y
111	to his people, to give	68	6	his powerful works he demonstrated to his people giving them the land of the nations	6; colon (no meaningful center word)	he has shown his people the power of his works, in giving them the inheritance of the nations	6; colon	Y
112	remembered forever	72	6	for never shall he be moved in eternal memory shall be the just person	6; word, verse ("for memory")	to remember	6; colon	Y
111–112	*Praise God, blessed is the man!*	*140*	*112.1*			blessed is the man who fears the LORD	*112.1*	Y
113	who (is like the LORD)?	51	5	who is like YHWH our God who is seated on high?	5; verse	who is like the LORD our God, who is seated on high	5; colon, verse	Y
114	what was it?	47	5	the sea looked and fled; . . . O hills, like lambs?	3–6; 26 words (off-center)	None	None	Y
115	(he is) their help and their shield	118	9	O Israel, trust in YHWH! . . . Their help and their shield is he! (strophe level)	9b; word	he is their help and their shield.	9b; colon; 9–11, strophe	Y
116	I believe	109	10	I shall walk before the LORD in the land of the living. I believed when I said, "I am greatly afflicted." I said in my alarm, "All men are liars"	9–11; verse (no meaningful center word)	I believed, even when I spoke: "I am greatly afflicted"	10; word	Y
117	for he is great (12-word psalm)	12	2	peoples	1b; word	None	None	N
113–117	*trust!*	*337*	*115:11*					

350

Appendix

Ps	Ho			Labuschagne		van der Lugt		Correspondence?
	Nexusword	Word count	MT verse	Meaningful center	MT verse; level of poetic unit	Rhetorical center	MT verse; level of poetic unit	
118	the (right hand of) the LORD has done (valiantly)	178	15	the right hand of YHWH acts with power	15c; word, or 15–16, strophe	the right hand of the LORD does valiantly	15c	Y
119	(forever) your word will stand (in the heavens)	934	89	that I may follow the instruction of your mouth	88b; word (1063 words, but 1064 words in MT)	that I may keep the testimonies of your mouth	88b; word	N
118–119	I will learn your commandments		119:73					
120	warrior's sharpened (arrows)	42	4	sharpened arrows of a warrior! Moreover, red-hot coals of broom	4; verse	a warrior's sharp arrows, with glowing coals of the broom tree	4; verse (not a rhetorical center)	Y
121	(no) sleep, watcher (of Israel)	46	4	behold, he never slumbers, never sleeps . . . is your shade on your right hand	4, 5; verse	None	no rhetorical center (divides into two equal halves)	Y
122	for (there the thrones are set for judgment)	57	5	it is a decree for Israel to give thanks . . . thrones of the house of David	4c–5; strophe (no meaningful center)	there thrones for judgment were set	5a; word	Y
123	our eyes (look to the LORD God)	35	2	So our eyes are turned to YHWH our God	2c; word	so our eyes look to the LORD our God, (till he has mercy upon us)	2c–d; word, verse	Y
124	(the stream would have) swept over our soul	54	4	Then over us would have swept the raging waters	5; verse	then the waters would have engulfed us, . . . torn by their teeth	4–6; strophe	Y
125	the wickedness (not rest over the righteous)	43	3	Surely, the sceptre . . . not extend their hands to wrongdoing	3; strophe	For the sceptre . . . stretch out their hands to do wrong	3; strophe	Y
126	the LORD	45	3	great things indeed YHWH did for us we were glad	3; word	the LORD has done great things for us; we are glad	3; word	Y
127	he gives (to his beloved)	49	2	he provides his beloved with sleep	2d; word (including header)	None	None	Y
128	(shoots of) olive (around your table)	43	3	around your table	3c–d+4a–b; word	Your children like olive plants . . . man be blessed who fears the LORD	v.3c–4; word	Y
129	turned backwards (those who hate Zion)	50	5	may they be put to shame and turned back	5a; colon	may they be put to shame and fall back	5a; colon	Y
130	(I wait) for the LORD	47	5	I wait for YHWH, my soul waits and in his word I put my hope	5; word, colon	I wait for the Lord, my soul waits, and I hope for his word	5; word	Y
131	(surely) I have composed (calmed myself)	27	2	on the contrary, I have remained calm and quieted my soul	2ab; verse	I have composed and quieted . . . child rests against his mother	2a–b; colon, verse	Y
132	the LORD has sworn (to David)	109	11	YHWH has sworn an oath to David	11a; word	the LORD has sworn to David	11a; word	Y
133	the beard of Aaron	29	2	It is like the fragrant oil on the head, . . . flowing down on the mountains of Zion	2–3b, strophe	None	None	Y
134	In the night; lift up your hands	20	1, 2,	lift up your hands towards the sanctuary and bless YHWH	2; verse			Y

351

Appendix

Ps	Ho Nexusword	Word count	MT verse	Labuschagne Meaningful center	MT verse; level of poetic unit	van der Lugt Rhetorical center	MT verse; level of poetic unit	Correspondence?
133-134	(For there the LORD has) commanded (the blessing, life forevermore)		133:3c			For there the LORD commanded—the life forever	133:3c–d; colon (Pss 133/34 combined as one)	
120-134	(he gives) to his beloved, sleep	696	127:2					
135	(king) of Amorite, and Og (king of Bashan)	144	11	the defeat of Sihon and Og demonstrating YHWH's power (21 words)	10–12; strophe	who struck down many nations . . . a heritage to his people Israel	10–12; verse, strophe	Y
136	(to him who divided the Red Sea in two, for his steadfast love) endures forever	159	13	to him who struck down the firstborn . . . his steadfast love endures forever	10–15; 40-word center	to him who struck down the firstborn . . . for his steadfast love endures forever	10–15; 40-word center	Y
137	Let my tongue cling	68	6	if I forget you, Jerusalem, . . . if I do not remember you	5–6a; colon	woe is me, O Jerusalem, if I should forget your ruins (v. 5) and your (former) beauty (v. 6a–b)	5–6b; colon, verse	Y
138	Lord. For (great is the glory of the LORD)	62	5	all the kings of the earth will praise you, YHWH, when they hear the words of your mouth	4; verse	all kings of the earth praising the words spoken by God	4; colon	N
139	in the womb of my mother	160	13	for you yourself fashioned my inward parts . . . you know me through and through	13–14b MC a colon level.	you knit me in the womb of my mother	13–14a–b; word, colon (center word = "womb")	Y
140	(give ear to the) voice of my pleas for mercy, O LORD	104	7	I say to YHWH: "You are my God! . . . you shield my head on the day of battle"	7–8; colon	I said to the LORD, "You . . . You have covered my head in the day of battle"	7–8; colon, verse	Y
141	for continually (my prayer is against their evil deeds)	81	5	may a just person strike me . . . but my prayer is against their evil deeds	5; strophe	a righteous man strikes me . . . continually against their evil deeds	5; colon, verse, strophe	Y
142	no refuge remains (for me)	68	5	flight has fled from me; no one cares for me	5c–d; word	no refuge remains to me; no one cares for my soul	5c–d; word, colon, verse	Y
143	answer me O LORD	102	7	hasten to answer me, YHWH my spirit fails	7a–b; verse	I am longing . . . hasten to answer me	6–7b; colon, verse, strophe	Y
144	O God, a (new) song	120	9	O God, I shall sing a new song to you	9a; word, colon	O God, I will sing a new song to you	9a; word, colon	Y
145	they tell of your power	126	11	a kingship for all times	13a; word	to make known to the children of man your mighty deeds	12a; colon	Y
138-145	a prayer (superscription of Ps 142:1)	823	142:1					
146	the one who keeps faith (forever)	74	6	happy is he whose helper is the God of Jacob . . . who gives food to the hungry	5–7b; strophe	who keeps faith forever	6c; colon, verse	Y
147	his delights is not in the leg (of man)	126	10	he does not delight in the strength of a horse nor does he take pleasure in men's legs	*10; word, verse	He does not take pleasure in the legs of a man	10b; word	Y
148	hail	87	8	praise YHWH from the earth you sea monsters . . . you creeping creatures and winged birds	7–10; canto (off-center)	praise the LORD from the earth, sea monsters . . . stormy wind, fulfilling His word	7–8; word (off-center) verse, strophe	Y
149	(let the) godly (exult in glory)	57	5	let the faithful exult in glory	*5a; word, verse	let the godly exult in glory	5a; word	Y
150	harp and lyre	34	3	None	None	praise Him with harp and lyre.	3b; colon	Y
146-150	his words to Jacob	378	147:19					

Appendix

Ps	Ho			Labuschagne		van der Lugt		Correspondence?
	Nexusword	Word count	MT verse	Meaningful center	MT verse; level of poetic unit	Rhetorical center	MT verse; level of poetic unit	
	Correspondence (Book V) = 41/44 (93%)							

353

Bibliography

Abernethy, Andrew T. "God as Teacher in Psalm 25." *VT* 65 (2015) 339–51.
Albright, William Foxwell. *The Proto-Sinaitic Inscriptions and Their Decipherment.* HTS 22. Cambridge: Harvard University Press, 1966.
Alden, Robert L. "Chiastic Psalms (I): A Study in the Mechanics of Semitic Poetry in Psalms 1–50." *JETS* 17 (1974) 11–28.
———. "Chiastic Psalms (II): A Study in the Mechanics of Semitic Poetry in Psalms 51–100." *JETS* 19 (1976) 191–200.
———. "Chiastic Psalms (III): Study in the Mechanics of Semitic Poetry in Psalms 101–150." *JETS* 21 (1978) 199–210.
Alexander, T. Desmond, and David W. Baker, eds. *Dictionary of the Old Testament: Pentateuch.* IVP Bible Dictionary. Downers Grove, IL: InterVarsity, 2003.
Alonso Schökel, Luis. *A Manual of Hebrew Poetics.* SubBi 11. Rome: Editrice Pontificio Istituto Biblico, 1988.
Alter, Robert. *The Art of Biblical Poetry.* New York: Basic, 1985.
Anderson, A. A. *2 Samuel.* WBC 11. Waco: Nelson, 1989.
Anderson, Craig. "The Politics of Psalmody: Psalm 60 and the Rise and Fall of Judean Independence." *JBL* 134 (2015) 313–32.
Anderson, R. Dean, Jr. "The Division and Order of the Psalms." *WTJ* 56 (1994) 219–41.
Angel, Hayyim. "The Eternal Davidic Covenant in II Samuel Chapter 7 and Its Later Manifestations in the Bible." *JBQ* 44 (2016) 83–90.
Apple, Raymond. "The Happy Man of Psalm 1." *JBQ* 40 (2012) 179–82.
Armstrong, Ryan M. "Psalms Dwelling Together in Unity: The Placement of Psalms 133 and 134 in Two Different Psalms Collections." *JBL* 131 (2012) 487–506.
Arnold, Bill T., and John H. Choi. *A Guide to Biblical Hebrew Syntax.* New York: Cambridge University Press, 2003.
Attard, Stefan. "Establishing Connections between Pss 49 and 50 within the Context of Pss 49–52: A Synchronic Analysis." In *Composition of the Book of Psalms*, edited by Erich Zenger, 413–42. BETL 238. Leuven: Peeters, 2010.
Auffret, Pierre. "Essai Sur La Structure Littéraire des Psaumes 111 et 112." *VT* 30 (1980) 257–79.
Augustine. *Sancti Aurelii Augustini Opera.* Paris: Apud Parent-Desbarres, 1837.
Auwers, Jean-Marie. *Composition Littéraire du Psautier: Un état de la Question.* CahRB. Paris: Gabalda, 2000.
———. "Le David des Psaumes et les Psaumes de David." In *Figures de David à Travers la Bible: XVIIe Congrès de l'ACFEB, Lille, 1er–5 Septembre 1997*, edited by L. Desrousseaux and J. Vermeylen, 187–224. LD 177. Paris: Cerf, 1999.

———. "Le Psautier Comme Livre Biblique: Édition, Rédaction, Fonction." In *Composition of the Book of Psalms*, edited by Erich Zenger, 67–90. BETL 238. Leuven: Peeters, 2010.

———. "Les Psaumes 70–72: Essai de Lecture Canonique." *RB* 101 (1994) 244–57.

———. "Les Voices de L'exégèse Canonique Du Psautier." In *Biblical Canons*, edited by Jean-Marie Auwers and H. J. de Jonge, 5–26. BETL 163. Leuven: Peeters, 2003.

———. "L'organisation Du Psautier Chez Les Pères Grecs." In *Psautier Chez Les Pères*, edited by J. Irigoin, 37–54. Strasbourg: Centre d'Analyse et de Documentation Patristiques, 1994.

Balentine, Samuel E. "The Royal Psalms and the New Testament : From 'messiah' to 'Messiah.'" *TTE* 29 (1984) 56–62.

Ballard, Harold Wayne, Jr. *Divine Warrior Motif in the Psalms*. North Richland Hills, TX: D&F Scott, 1998.

Ballhorn, Egbert. "Das Historische und das Kanonische Paradigma in der Exegese." In *Der Bibelkanon in der Bibelauslegung: Methodenreflexionen und Beispielexegesen*, edited by Egbert Ballhorn and Georg Steins, 9–30. Stuttgart: Kohlhammer, 2007.

———. *Zum Telos des Psalters: Der Textzusammenhang des Vierten und Fünften Psalmenbuches (Ps 90–150)*. BBB 138. Berlin: Philo, 2004.

Bar-Efrat, Shimeon. "Some Observations on the Analysis of Structure in Biblical Narrative." *VT* 30 (1980) 154–73.

Barbiero, Gianni. *Das erste Psalmenbuch als Einheit: eine synchrone Analyse von Psalm 1–41*. ÖBS 16. Frankfurt: Lang, 1999.

———. "Le Premier Livret Du Psautier (Ps 1–41): Une étude Synchronique." *RevScRel* 77 (2003) 439–80.

———. "Messianismus und Theokratie: Die Verbindung der Psalmen 144 und 145 und Ihre Bedeutung für die Komposition des Psalters." *OTE* 27 (2014) 41–52.

———. "Psalm 132: A Prayer of 'Solomon.'" *CBQ* 75 (2013) 239–58.

———. "The Risks of a Fragmented Reading of the Psalms: Psalm 72 as a Case in Point." *ZAW* 120 (2008) 67–91.

Barbiero, Gianni, and Marco Pavan. "Ps 44,15; 57,10; 108,4; 149,7: Bl'mym or Bl-'mym?" *ZAW* 124 (2012) 598–605.

Barkay, Gabriel, et al. "The Amulets from Ketef Hinnom: A New Edition and Evaluation." *BASOR* 334 (2004) 41–71.

———, et al. "The Challenges of Ketef Hinnom: Using Advanced Technologies to Reclaim the Earliest Biblical Texts and Their Context." *NEA* 66 (2003) 162–71.

Barré, Michael L. "'Terminative' Terms in Hebrew Acrostics." In *Wisdom, You Are My Sister: Studies in Honor of Roland E. Murphy, O.Carm on the Occasion of His Eightieth Birthday*, edited by Michael Barré, 207–15. CBQMS 29. Washington, DC: Catholic Biblical Association of America, 1997.

Barr, James. *The Concept of Biblical Theology: An Old Testament Perspective*. Minneapolis: Fortress, 1999.

———. *Holy Scripture: Canon, Authority, Criticism*. Oxford: Oxford University Press, 1983.

Barton, John. "Classifying Biblical Criticism." *JSOT* 29 (1984) 19–35.

———. *The Old Testament Canon, Literature and Theology: Collected Essays of John Barton*. Aldershot, UK: Ashgate, 2007.

———. *Reading the Old Testament: Method in Biblical Study*. Philadelphia: Westminster, 1984.

Bazak, Jacob. "The Geometric-Figurative Structure of Psalm 136." *VT* 35 (1985) 129–38.

———. "Numerical Devices in Biblical Poetry." *VT* 38 (1988) 333–37.

Beaucamp, Évode. "L'unité du recueil des montées: Psaumes 120–134." *LTP* 36 (1980) 3–15.

Becker, Joachim, and David E. Green. *Messianic Expectation in the Old Testament*. Edinburgh: T. & T. Clark, 1980.

Bee, Ronald E. "The Use of Syllable Counts in Textual Analysis." *JSOT* 4 (1978) 68–70.

Bellinger, William H. "The Psalter as Theodicy Writ Large." In *Jewish and Christian Approaches to the Psalms: Conflict and Convergence*, edited by S. E. Gillingham, 148–60. Oxford: Oxford University Press, 2013.

———. "Reading from the Beginning (Again): The Shape of Book I of the Psalter." In *Diachronic and Synchronic: Reading the Psalms in Real Time: Proceedings of the Baylor Symposium on the Book of Psalms*, edited by Joel S. Burnett, et al., 114–26. LHBOTS 488. New York: T. & T Clark, 2007.

Berger, Yitzhak. "The David–Benjaminite Conflict and the Intertextual Field of Psalm 7." *JSOT* 38 (2014) 279–96.

Bergler, Siegfried. "Der Längste Psalm—Anthologie oder Liturgie." *VT* 29 (1979) 257–88.

———. "Threni v—Nur ein Alphabetisierendes Lied: Versuch einer Deutung." *VT* 27 (1977) 304–20.

Berlin, Adele. *Dynamics of Biblical Parallelism*. Bloomington: Indiana University Press, 1985.

———. *Poetics and Interpretation of Biblical Narrative*. BLS 9. Sheffield: Almond, 1983.

Berry, Donald K. *Psalms and Their Readers: Interpretive Strategies for Psalm 18*. JSOTSup 153. Sheffield: Sheffield Academic, 1993.

Bertman, Stephen. "Symmetrical Design in the Book of Ruth." *JBL* 84 (1965) 165–68.

Booij, Thijs. "Psalm 144: Hope of Davidic Welfare." *VT* 59 (2009) 173–80.

———. "Psalms 120–136: Songs for a Great Festival." *Bib* 91 (2010) 241–55.

Bosma, Carl J. "Discerning the Voices in the Psalms. [1]: A Discussion of Two Problems in Psalmic Interpretation." *CTJ* 43 (2008) 183–212.

Botha, Phil J. "Psalm 101: Inaugural Address or Social Code of Conduct?" *HTS Theological Studies* 60 (2004) 725–41.

———. "Psalm 108 and the Quest for Closure to the Exile." *OTE* 23 (2010) 574–96.

———. "'Wealth and Riches Are in His House' (Ps 112:3): Acrostic Wisdom Psalms and the Development of Antimaterialism." In *Shape and Shaping of the Book of Psalms: The Current State of Scholarship*, edited by Nancy deClaissé-Walford, 105–27. AIL 20. Atlanta: SBL Press, 2014.

Braude, William G. *Midrash on Psalms*. 2 vols. New Haven: Yale University Press, 1959.

Braulik, Georg P. "Psalter and Messiah. Towards a Christological Understanding of The Psalms in the Old Testament and the Church Fathers." In *Psalms and Liturgy*. Edited by Dirk J. Human and C. J. A. Vos. JSOTSup 410, 15–40. London: T. & T. Clark, 2004.

Breck, John. "Biblical Chiasmus: Exploring Structure for Meaning." *BTB* 17 (1987) 70–74.

———. *The Shape of Biblical Language: Chiasmus in the Scriptures and Beyond*. Crestwood, NY: St. Vladimirs Seminary. 2008.

Brennan, Joseph P. "Psalms 1–8: Some Hidden Harmonies." *BTB* 10 (1980) 25–29.

———. "Some Hidden Harmonies of the Fifth Book of Psalms." In *Essays in Honor of Joseph P. Brennan by Members of the Faculty, Saint Bernard's Seminary, Rochester, NY*, edited by Robert F. McNamara, 126–58. Rochester, NY: St. Bernard's Seminary, 1976.

Briggs, Charles A., and Emilie Grace Briggs. *A Critical and Exegetical Commentary on the Book of Psalms*. 2 vols. ICC. Edinburgh: T. & T. Clark, 1907.

Brooke, George J. "The Psalms in Early Jewish Literature in the Light of the Dead Sea Scrolls." In *The Psalms in the New Testament*, edited by Steve Moyise and Maarten J. J. Menken, 5–24. NTSI. London: T. & T. Clark, 2004.

Brown, William P. "'Here Comes the Sun!' The Metaphorical Theology of Psalms 15–24." In *The Composition of the Book of Psalms*, edited by Erich Zenger, 259–77. BETL 238. Leuven: Peeters, 2010.

Brownlee, William H. "Psalms 1–2 as a Coronation Liturgy." *Bib* 52 (1971) 321–36.

Broyles, Craig C. "The Psalms and Cult Symbolism: The Case of the Cherubim-Ark." In *Interpreting the Psalms: Issues and Approaches*, edited by Philip Johnston and David Firth, 139–56. Downers Grove, IL: InterVarsity, 2005.

Brueggemann, Dale A. "Brevard Childs' Canon Criticism: An Example of Post-Critical Naiveté." *JETS* 32 (1989) 311–26.

———. "The Evangelists and the Psalms." In *Interpreting the Psalms: Issues and Approaches*, edited by Philip Johnston and David Firth, 243–78. Downers Grove, IL: InterVarsity, 2005.

Brueggemann, Walter. "Bound by Obedience and Praise: The Psalms as Canon." *JSOT* 50 (1991) 63–92.

———. *The Message of the Psalms: A Theological Commentary*. Minneapolis: Augsburg, 1984.

———. "Psalms and the Life of Faith: A Suggested Typology of Function." *JSOT* 17 (1980) 3–32.

———. "The Psalms and the Life of Faith: A Suggested Typology of Function." In *Soundings in the Theology of Psalms*, edited by Rolf Jacobson, 1–25. Minneapolis: Fortress, 2011.

Brueggemann, Walter, and Patrick D. Miller. "Psalm 73 as a Canonical Marker." *JSOT* 72 (1996) 45–56.

Brug, John F. "Biblical Acrostics and Their Relationship to Other Ancient Near Eastern Acrostics." In *The Bible in the Light of Cuneiform Literature*, edited by William W. Hallo, et al., 283–304. Ancient Near Eastern Texts and Studies 8. New York: Mellen, 1990.

———. "Near Eastern Acrostics and Biblical Acrostics: Biblical Acrostics and Their Relationship to Other Ancient Near Eastern Acrostics." Paper presented at The Bible and Near Eastern Literature, NEH Seminar. Yale, New Haven, 1987.

Burnett, Joel S. "Forty-Two Songs for Elohim: An Ancient Near Eastern Organizing Principle in the Shaping of the Elohistic Psalter." *JSOT* 31 (2006) 81–101.

———. "A Plea for David and Zion: The Elohistic Psalter as Psalm Collection for the Temple's Restoration." In *Diachronic and Synchronic*, edited by Joel S. Burnett, et al., 95–113. LHBOTS 488. London: T. & T. Clark, 2007.

Butler, Trent C. "Forgotten Passage from a Forgotten Era (1 Chr 16:8–36)." *VT* 28 (1978) 142–50.

Butterworth, Mike. "נחם." In *NIDOTTE* 3:81–83.

Buysch, Christoph. *Der Letzte Davidpsalter: Interpretation, Komposition und Funktion der Psalmengruppe Ps 138–145*. SBB 63. Stuttgart: Katholisches Bibelwerk, 2010.

Callaham, Scott N. "An Evaluation of Psalm 119 as Constrained Writing." *HS* 50 (2009) 121–35.

Cassuto, Umberto, and Joshua A. Berman. *Documentary Hypothesis*. Jerusalem: Shalem, 2006.

Ceresko, Anthony R. "The ABCs of Wisdom in Psalm 34." *VT* 35 (1985) 99–104.

———. "Endings and Beginnings: Alphabetic Thinking and the Shaping of Psalms 106 and 150." *CBQ* 68 (2006) 32–46.

———. "Function of Chiasmus in Hebrew Poetry." *CBQ* 40 (1978) 1–10.

Cha, Kilnam. "Psalms 146–150: The Final Hallelujah Psalms as a Fivefold Doxology to the Hebrew Psalter." PhD diss., Baylor University, 2006.

Chester, Andrew. *Messiah and Exaltation: Jewish Messianic and Visionary Traditions and New Testament Christology.* WUNT 207. Tübingen: Mohr/Siebeck, 2007.

Childs, Brevard S. "Analysis of a Canonical Formula: It shall be recorded for a future generation." In *Die Hebräische Bibel und ihre zweifache Nachgeschichte: Festschrift für Rolf Rendtorff zum 65. Geburtstag*, edited by Erhard Blum, et al., 357–64. Neukirchen-Vluyn: Neukirchener, 1990.

———. *Biblical Theology of the Old and New Testaments: Theological Reflection of the Christian Bible.* Minneapolis: Fortress, 1993.

———. "Canonical Shape of the Prophetic Literature." *Int* 32 (1978) 46–55.

———. *Introduction to the Old Testament as Scripture.* Philadelphia: Fortress, 1979.

———. "Psalm Titles and Midrashic Exegesis." *JSS* 16 (1971) 137–50.

Choi, Junho. "Understanding the Literary Structures of Acrostics Psalm: An Analysis of Selected Poems." PhD diss., Stellenbosch University, 2013.

Christensen, Duane L. "The Book of Psalms Within the Canonical Process in Ancient Israel." *JETS* 39 (1996) 421–32.

———. *The Unity of the Bible: Exploring the Beauty and Structure of the Bible.* New York: Paulist, 2003.

Clayton, J. Nathan. "An Examination of Holy Space in Psalm 73: Is Wisdom's Path Infused with an Eschatologically Oriented Hope?" *TJ* 27 (2006) 117–42.

Clements, Ronald E. "Beyond Tradition-History: Deutero-Isaianic Development of First Isaiah's Themes." *JSOT* 31 (1985) 95–113.

———. "The Messianic Hope in the Old Testament." *JSOT* 43 (1989) 3–19.

———. "Psalm 72 and Isaiah 40–66: A Study in Tradition." *PRSt* 28 (2001) 333–41.

Clifford, Richard J. *Psalms 73–150.* AOTC. Nashville: Abingdon, 2003.

———. "The Temple in the Ugaritic Myth of Baal." In *Symposia Celebrating the Seventy-Fifth Anniversary of the Founding of the American Schools of Oriental Research (1900–1975)*, 137–45. Cambridge, MA: ASOR, 1979.

———. "Tent of El and the Israelite Tent of Meeting." *CBQ* 33 (1971) 221–27.

Clines, David J. A. "Contemporary Methods in Hebrew Bible Criticism." In *From Modernism to Post-Modernism: The Nineteenth and Twentieth Centuries*, edited by Magne Saebø, 148–69. Vol. 3.2 of *Hebrew Bible/Old Testament: The History of Its Interpretation.* Göttingen: Vandenhoeck & Ruprecht, 2015.

Cole, R. Dennis. *Numbers.* NAC 3B. Nashville: Broadman & Holman, 2000.

Cole, Robert Alan. "An Integrated Reading of Psalms 1 and 2." *JSOT* 98 (2002) 75–88.

Cole, Robert L. *Shape and Message of Book III.* JSOTSup 307. Sheffield: Sheffield Academic, 2000.

———. *Psalms 1–2: Gateway to the Psalter.* HBM 37. Sheffield: Sheffield Phoenix, 2013.

Collins, John J. "Mowinckel's *He That Cometh* Revisited." *ST* 61.1 (2007) 3–20.

Craigie, Peter C. *Psalms 1–50.* WBC 19. Waco: Word, 1983.

Creach, Jerome. "The Destiny of the Righteous and the Theology of the Psalms." In *Soundings in the Theology of Psalms*, edited by Rolf Jacobson, 49–61. Minneapolis: Fortress, 2011.

———. "Like a Tree Planted by the Temple Stream: The Portrait of the Righteous in Psalm 1:3." *CBQ* 61 (1999) 34–46.

———. "The Shape of Book Four of the Psalter and the Shape of Second Isaiah." *JSOT* 80 (1998) 63–76.

Bibliography

———. *Yahweh as Refuge and the Editing of the Hebrew Psalter*. JSOTSup 217. Sheffield: Sheffield Academic, 1996.

Crenshaw, James L. "Education in Ancient Israel." *JBL* 104 (1985) 601–15.

———. *Education in Ancient Israel: Across the Deadening Silence*. New York: Doubleday, 1998.

Crow, Loren D. *Songs of Ascents (Psalms 120–134): Their Place in Israelite History and Religion*. SBLDS 148. Atlanta: Scholars, 1996.

Crutchfield, John C. *Psalms in Their Context: An Interpretation of Psalms 107–118*. Milton Keynes, UK: Paternoster, 2011.

Culley, Robert C. *Oral Formulaic Language in the Biblical Psalms*. Toronto: University of Toronto Press, 1967.

Davies, Philip R., and David M. Gunn. "Pentateuchal Patterns: An Examination of C. J. Labuschagne's Theory." *VT* 34 (1984) 399–406.

Davis, Barry C. "A Contextual Analysis of Psalms 107–118." PhD diss., Trinity Evangelical Divinity School, 1996.

———. "Is Psalm 110 a Messianic Psalm?" *BSac* 157 (2000) 160–73.

Day, John. *Psalms*. Old Testament Guides 14. Sheffield: JSOT Press, 1990.

De Hoog, John. "A Canonical Reading of Psalm 119." MTh. Thesis, Australian College of Theology, 2011.

De Jong, Marinus. "Messiah." In *ABD* 4:777–88.

deClaissé-Walford, Nancy. "Anzu Revisited: The Scribal Shaping of the Hebrew Psalter." *WW* 15 (1995) 358–66.

———. "The Canonical Approach to Scripture and the Editing of the Hebrew Psalter." In *The Shape and Shaping of the Book of Psalms: The Current State of Scholarship*, edited by Nancy deClaissé-Walford, 1–11. AIL 20. Atlanta: SBL Press, 2014.

———. "The Canonical Shape of the Psalms." In *Introduction to Wisdom Literature and the Psalms: Festschrift Marvin E. Tate*, edited by Harold Wayne Ballard and W. Dennis Tucker, 93–110. Macon, GA: Mercer University Press, 2000.

———. "An Intertextual Reading of Psalms 22, 23, 24." In *The Book of Psalms: Composition and Reception*, edited by Peter W. Flint and Patrick D. Miller, 139–52. VTSup 99. Leiden: Brill, 2004.

———. "The Meta-Narrative of the Psalter." In *Oxford Handbook of the Psalms*, edited by William P. Brown, 363–75. Oxford: Oxford University Press, 2014.

———. "Psalm 145: All Flesh Will Bless God's Holy Name." *CBQ* 74 (2012) 55–66.

———. "Reading Backwards from the Beginning: My Life with the Psalter." *LTQ* 41 (2006) 119–30.

———. *Reading from the Beginning: The Shaping of the Hebrew Psalter*. Macon, GA: Mercer University Press, 1997.

———. "The Structure of Psalms 93–100." *RevExp* 95 (1998) 290–91.

———, et al. *Book of Psalms*. NICOT. Grand Rapids: Eerdmans, 2014.

DeSilva, David Arthur. "X Marks the Spot?: A Critique of the Use of Chiasmus in Macro-Structural Analyses of Revelation." *JSNT* 30 (2008) 343–71.

Dickie, George, and W. Kent Wilson. "The Intentional Fallacy: Defending Beardsley." *JAAC* 3 (1995) 233–50.

Dietterich, Inagrace T. "Sing to the Lord a New Song: Theology as Doxology." *CurTM* (2014) 23–28.

Doan, William, and Terry Giles. "The Song of Asaph: A Performance-Critical Analysis of 1 Chronicles 16:8–36." *CBQ* 70 (2008) 29–43.

Dobbs-Allsopp, F. W. "The Syntagma of *Bat* Followed by a Geographical Name in the Hebrew Bible: A Reconsideration of Its Meaning and Grammar." *CBQ* 57 (1995) 451–70.

Dorsey, David A. *Literary Structure of the Old Testament: A Commentary on Genesis–Malachi.* Grand Rapids: Baker Academic, 2005.

Driver, Daniel R. "Brevard Childs : The Logic of Scripture's Textual Authority." PhD diss., University of St. Andrews, 2009.

Eijzeren, M. J. van. "'Halbnachts Steh' Ich Auf.' An Exploration into the Translation of Biblical Acrostics." MA Thesis, Utrecht University, 2012.

Firth, David G. "More than Just Torah: God's Instruction in the Psalms." *STR* 6 (2015) 63–82.

———. *Surrendering Retribution in the Psalms: Responses to Violence in the Individual Complaints.* PBM. Milton Keynes: Paternoster, 2005.

———. "The Teaching of the Psalms." In *Interpreting the Psalms: Issues and Approaches*, edited by Philip Johnston and David Firth, 159–74. Downers Grove, IL: InterVarsity, 2005.

Fischer, Alexander Achilles, and Ernst Würthwein. *Text of the Old Testament: Revised Edition of Ernst Würthwein's Introduction to Biblia Hebraica.* Translated by Errol F. Rhodes. 3rd ed. Grand Rapids: Eerdmans, 2014.

Fish, Stanley. *Is There a Text in This Class?: The Authority of Interpretive Communities.* Cambridge, MA: Harvard University Press, 1980.

Fishbane, Michael. *Biblical Interpretation in Ancient Israel.* Oxford: Clarendon, 1985.

———. "Inner-Biblical Exegesis." In *Antiquity: From the Beginnings to the Middle Ages (Until 1300)*, edited by Magne Sæbø, 33–48. Vol. 1.1 of *Hebrew Bible/Old Testament: History of Its Interpretation.* Göttingen: Vandenhoeck & Ruprecht, 1996.

Flint, Peter W. "The Book of Psalms in the Light of the Dead Sea Scrolls." *VT* 48 (1998) 453–72.

———. *Dead Sea Psalms Scrolls and the Book of Psalms.* STDJ 17. Leiden: Brill, 1997.

Floyd, Michael H. "Welcome Back, Daughter of Zion!" *CBQ* 70 (2008) 484–504.

Fokkelman, Jan P. *85 Psalms and Job 4–14.* Vol. 2 of *Major Poems of the Hebrew Bible: At the Interface of Hermeneutics and Structural Analysis.* SSN 41. Assen: Van Gorcum, 2000.

———. *Ex. 15, Deut. 32, and Job 3.* Vol. 1 of *Major Poems of the Hebrew Bible: At the Interface of Hermeneutics and Structural Analysis.* SSN 37. Assen: Van Gorcum, 1998.

———. *Psalms in Form: The Hebrew Psalter in Its Poetic Shape.* Leiden: Deo, 2002.

———. *Reading Biblical Poetry: An Introductory Guide.* Louisville: Westminster John Knox, 2001.

———. *The Remaining 65 Psalms.* Vol. 3 of *Major Poems of the Hebrew Bible: At the Interface of Hermeneutics and Structural Analysis.* SSN 43. Assen: Van Gorcum, 2003.

Forbes, John. *Studies on the Book of Psalms: The Structural Connection of the Book of Psalms, Both in Single Psalms and in the Psalter as an Organic Whole.* Edited by James Forrest. Edinburgh: T. & T. Clark, 1888.

Foulkes, Francis. "Jacob." In *NIDOTTE* 4:738–43.

Fraser, James H. "The Authenticity of the Psalms Titles." ThM Thesis, Grace Theological Seminary, 1984.

Freedman, David Noel. "Acrostic Poems in the Hebrew Bible: Alphabetic and Otherwise." *CBQ* 48 (1986) 408–31.

———. "Acrostics and Metrics in Hebrew Poetry." *HTR* 65 (1972) 367–92.

———, ed. *Anchor Bible Dictionary*. 6 vols. New Haven: Yale University Press, 1992.

———. "Patterns in Psalms 25 and 34." In *Priests, Prophets, and Scribes*, edited by Eugene Ulrich, et al., 125–38. Sheffield: JSOT, 1992.

———. "Pottery, Poetry, and Prophecy: An Essay on Biblical Poetry." *JBL* 96 (1977) 5–26.

———. *Pottery, Poetry, and Prophecy: Studies in Early Hebrew Poetry*. Winona Lake, IN: Eisenbrauns, 1980.

———. *The Unity of the Bible*. Distinguished Senior Faculty Lecture Series. Ann Arbor: University of Michigan Press, 1991.

Freedman, David Noel, and David Miano. "Non-Acrostic Alphabetic Psalms." In *Book of Psalms, Composition and Reception*, edited by Peter W. Flint and Patrick D. Miller, 87–96. VTSup 99. Leiden: Brill, 2004.

———, et al., eds. *EDB*. Grand Rapids: Eerdmans, 2000.

———, et al. *Psalm 119: The Exaltation of Torah*. Winona Lake, IN: Eisenbrauns, 1999.

Fuller, Russell. "מדד." In *NIDOTTE* 2:850–51.

George, Mark K. "Fluid Stability in Second Samuel 7." *CBQ* 64 (2002) 17–36.

German, Brian T. "Contexts for Hearing: Reevaluating the Superscription of Psalm 127." *JSOT* 37 (2012) 185–99.

Gerstenberger, Erhard S. "Der Psalter als Buch und als Sammlung." In *Neue Wege der Psalmenforschung*, edited by Klaus Seybold and Erich Zenger, 3–13. HBS 1. Freiburg: Herder, 1994.

———. "Die ‚Kleine Biblia': Theologien Im Psalter." In *The Composition of the Book of Psalms*, edited by Erich Zenger, 391–400. BETL 238. Leuven: Peeters, 2010.

———. *Psalms, Part 1, with an Introduction to Cultic Poetry*. FOTL 14. Grand Rapids: Eerdmans, 1991.

———. *Psalms, Part 2, and Lamentations*. FOTL 15. Grand Rapids: Eerdmans, 2001.

Giffone, Benjamin D. "A 'Perfect' Poem: The Use of the Qatal Verbal Form in the Biblical Acrostics." *HS* 51 (2010) 49–72.

Gillingham, Susan. "Entering and Leaving the Psalter: Psalms 1 and 150 and the Two Polarities of Faith." In *Let Us Go up to Zion*, edited by Iain Provan and Mark Boda, 383–93. VTSup 153. Leiden: Brill, 2012.

———. "From Liturgy to Prophecy: The Use of Psalmody in Second Temple Judaism." *CBQ* 64 (2002) 470–89.

———. "The Levites and the Editorial Composition of the Psalms." In *The Oxford Handbook of the Psalms*, edited by William P. Brown, 201–13. Oxford: Oxford University Press, 2014.

———. "The Levitical Singers and the Editing of the Hebrew Psalter." In *The Composition of the Book of Psalms*, edited by Erich Zenger, 91–124. BETL 238. Leuven: Peeters, 2010.

———. "The Messiah in the Psalms: A Question of Reception History and the Psalter." In *King and Messiah in Israel and the Ancient Near East*, 209–37. Sheffield: Sheffield University Press, 1998.

———. "Messianic Prophecy and the Psalms." *Theol* 99 (1996) 114–24.

———. "The Reception of Psalm 137 in Jewish and Christian Traditions." In *Jewish and Christian Approaches to the Psalms: Conflict and Convergence*, edited by Susan Gillingham, 64–82. Oxford: Oxford University Press, 2013.

———. "Studies of the Psalms: Retrospect and Prospect." *ExpT* 119 (2008) 209–16.

———. "The Zion Tradition and the Editing of the Hebrew Psalter." In *Temple and Worship in Biblical Israel*, edited by John Day, 308–41. Oxford Old Testament Seminar. London: T. & T. Clark, 2005.

Gillmayr-Bucher, Susanne. "The Psalm Headings: A Canonical Relecture of the Psalms." In *The Biblical Canons*, edited by Jean-Marie Auwers and H. J. de Jonge, 247–54. BETL 163. Leuven: Peeters, 2001.

———. "Relecture of Biblical Psalms: A Computer Aided Analysis of Textual Relations Based on Semantic Domains." In *Bible and Computer: The Stellenbosch AIBI-6 Conference: Proceedings of the Association Internationale Bible et Informatique, "From Alpha to Byte,"* edited by Johann Cook, 259–82. Leiden: Brill, 2002.

Goldingay, John. "The Compound Name in Isaiah 9:5(6)." *CBQ* 61 (1999) 239–44.

———. *Psalms*. 3 vols. Edited by Tremper Longman III. BCOTWP. Grand Rapids: Baker Academic, 2006–2008.

Goswell, Greg. "The Shape of Messianism in Isaiah 9." *WTJ* 77 (2015) 101–10.

Goulder, M. D. "Asaph's History of Israel (Elohist Press, Bethel, 725 BCE)." *JSOT* 65 (1995) 71–81.

———. *Prayers of David (Psalms 51–72): Studies in the Psalter, II*. JSOTSup 102. Sheffield: JSOT, 1990.

———. *Psalms of Asaph and the Pentateuch: Studies in the Psalter, III*. JSOTSup 233. Sheffield: Sheffield Academic, 1996.

———. *Psalms of the Return (Book V, Psalms 107–150): Studies in the Psalter, IV*. JSOTSup 258. Sheffield: Sheffield Academic, 1998.

———. *Psalms of the Sons of Korah*. JSOT 20. Sheffield: JSOT Press, 1982.

———. "The Social Setting of Book II of the Psalter." In *The Book of Psalms: Composition and Reception*, edited by Peter W. Flint and Patrick D. Miller, 349–67. VTSup 99. Leiden: Brill, 2004.

———. "The Songs of Ascents and Nehemiah." *JSOT* (1997) 43–58.

Grant, Jamie A. "The King as Exemplar: The Function of Deuteronomy's Kingship Law in the Shaping of the Book of Psalms." PhD diss., University of Gloucestershire, 2002.

———. *King as Exemplar: The Function of Deuteronomy's Kingship Law in the Shaping of the Book of Psalms*. ABib 17. Atlanta: Society of Biblical Literature, 2004.

———. "The Psalms and the King." In *Interpreting the Psalms: Issues and Approaches*, edited by Philip Johnston and David Firth, 101–18. Downers Grove, IL: InterVarsity, 2005.

Grisanti, Michael. "עלז." In *NIDOTTE* 3:419–21.

Groenewald, Alphonso. "A God Abounding in Steadfast Love: Psalms and Hebrews." In *Psalms and Hebrews*, edited by Dirk Human and Gert Steyn, 52–65. LHBOTS 527. London: T. & T. Clark, 2010.

Grol, Harm van. "1 Chronicles 16: The Chronicler's Psalm and Its View of History." In *Rewriting Biblical History: Essays on Chronicles and Ben Sira in Honor of Pancratius C. Beentjes*, edited by Jeremy Corley and Harm van Grol, 97–121. DCLS 7. New York: de Gruyter, 2011.

———. "David and His Chasidim: Place and Function of Psalms 138–145." In *Composition of the Book of Psalms*, edited by Erich Zenger, 309–38. BETL 238. Leuven: Peeters, 2010.

———. "Emotions in the Psalms." *Deuterocanonical & Cognate Literature Yearbook 2011*, (2012) 69.

Grossberg, Daniel. *Centripetal and Centrifugal Structures in Biblical Poetry*. SBLMS 39. Atlanta: Scholars, 1989.

Gundersen, David. "Davidic Hope in Book IV of the Psalter (Psalms 90–106)." PhD diss., Southeastern Baptist Theological Seminary, 2015.

Gunkel, Hermann. *Die Psalmen*. HKAT. Göttingen: Van-denhoeck & Ruprecht, 1926.

Gunkel, Hermann, and Joachim Begrich. *Einleitung in die Psalmen: Die Gattungen der religiosen Lyrik Israels*. Gottingen: Vandenhoeck & Ruprecht, 1933.

———. *Introduction to Psalms: The Genres of the Religious Lyric of Israel*. Translated by James D. Nogalski. Mercer Library of Biblical Studies. Macon, GA: Mercer University Press, 1998.

Haakma, Garmt J. "Die Zahlenmässige Strukturanalyse: Ein Kürze Einführung in die Methode und die Problematik der Logotechnik oder Zahlenmässige Strukturanalyse." *CV* 32 (1989) 273–83.

Halle, Morris, and John McCarthy. "The Metrical Structure of Psalm 137." *JBL* 100 (1981) 161–67.

Hamilton, Victor. "נַעַל." In *NIDOTTE* 3:120–21.

Hanson, K. C. "Alphabetic Acrostics: A Form Critical Study." PhD diss., Claremont Graduate School, 1984.

———. "How Honorable! How Shameful! A Cultural Analysis of Matthew's Makarisms and Reproaches." *Semeia* 68 (1996) 81–112.

Hengstenberg, Ernst Wilhelm. *Commentary on the Psalms*. Translated by P. Fairbairn and J. Thomson. 3 vols. Edinburgh: T. & T. Clark, 1845.

Hirsch, E. D. *Validity in Interpretation*. New Haven: Yale University Press, 1977.

Ho, Peter C. W. "The Design of the MT Psalter: A Macrostructural Analysis." PhD diss., University of Gloucestershire, 2017.

———. "Pan-Psalter Occurrence Scheme of "Jacob" and "Covenant."" *JSOT* (forthcoming)

———. "The Macrostructural Logic of the Alphabetic Poems in the Psalter." *VT* (forthcoming).

———. "Review of Ernst R. Wendland. *Studies in the Psalms: Literary-Structural Analysis with Application to Translation*." *Them* (forthcoming).

———. "Review of John Crutchfield, *Psalms in Their Context: An Interpretation of Psalms 107–118*." *JESOT* 4 (2015) 219–21.

———. "Review of John Kartje, *Wisdom Epistemology in the Psalter: A Study of Psalms 1, 73, 90, and 107*." *Them* 41 (2016) 100–101.

———. "Review of Nancy deClaissé-Walford, et al., *The Book of Psalms*." *Them* 41.3 (2016) 496–497.

———. "Review of Pieter van der Lugt, *Cantos and Strophes in Biblical Hebrew Poetry III Psalms 90–150 and Psalm 1*." *JESOT* 5.1 (2016) 89–91.

———. "Review of W. Dennis Tucker, *Constructing and Deconstructing Power in Psalms 107–150*." *JESOT* 4.1 (2015) 121–23.

Hoffman, Yair. "Eschatology in the Book of Jeremiah." In *Eschatology in the Bible and in Jewish and Christian Tradition*, edited by Henning Reventlow, 75–97. JSOTSup 243. Sheffield: Sheffield Academic, 1997.

Hoftijzer, Jacob. "Holistic or Compositional Approach? Linguistic Remarks to the Problem." In *Synchronic or Diachronic?: A Debate on Method in Old Testament Exegesis*, edited by Johannes C. de Moor, 98–114. OtSt 34. Leiden: Brill, 1995.

Hong, Koog P. "Synchrony and Diachrony in Contemporary Biblical Interpretation." *CBQ* 75 (2013) 521–39.

Hossfeld, Frank-Lothar, and Erich Zenger. *Die Psalmen I: Psalm 1–50*. HThKAT. Würzburg: Echter, 1993.

———. *Die Psalmen II: Psalm 51–100*. HThKAT. Würzburg: Echter, 2002.

———. *Die Psalmen III: Psalm 101–150*. HThKAT. Würzburg: Echter, 2012.

———. "Neue und Alte Wege der Psalmenexegese: Antworten auf die Fragen von M. Millard und R. Rendtorff." *BibInt* 4 (1996) 332–43.

———. *Psalms 2: A Commentary on Psalms 51–100*. Hermeneia. Minneapolis: Fortress, 2005.

———. *Psalms 3: A Commentary on Psalms 101–150*. Hermeneia. Minneapolis: Fortress, 2011.

Houk, Cornelius B. "Syllables and Psalms: A Statistical Linguistic Analysis." *JSOT* (1979) 55–62.

Howard, David. "The Case for Kingship in the Old Testament Narrative Books and the Psalms." *TJ* 9 (1988) 19–35.

———. "A Contextual Reading of Psalms 90–94." In *The Shape and Shaping of the Psalter*, edited by J. Clinton McCann, 108–23. JSOTSup 159. Sheffield: JSOT Press, 1993.

———. "Divine and Human Kingship as Organizing Motifs in the Psalter." In *The Psalms: Language for All Seasons of the Soul*, edited by Andrew Schmutzer and David Howard, 197–207. Chicago: Moody, 2014.

———. "Editorial Activity in the Psalter: A State-of-the-Field Survey." *WW* 9 (1989) 274–85.

———. "The Proto-MT Psalter, the King, and Psalms 1 and 2: A Reponse to Klaus Seybold." In *Jewish and Christian Approaches to the Psalms: Conflict and Convergence*, edited by Susan Gillingham, 182–89. Oxford: Oxford University Press, 2013.

———. "Psalm 94 among the Kingship-of-Yhwh Psalms." *CBQ* 61 (1999) 667–85.

———. *The Structure of Psalms 93–100*. Winona Lake, IN: Eisenbrauns, 1997.

Human, Dirk J., and Gert Jacobus Steyn, eds. *Psalms and Hebrews*. LHBOTS 527. New York: T. & T. Clark, 2010.

Hurowitz, Victor Avigdor. "Additional Elements of Alphabetical Thinking in Psalm XXXIV." *VT* 52 (2002) 326–33.

Hutchinson, James H. "The Psalms and Praise." In *Interpreting the Psalms: Issues and Approaches*, edited by Philip Johnston and David Firth, 85–100. Downers Grove, IL: InterVarsity, 2005.

Iser, Wolfgang. *Act of Reading: A Theory of Aesthetic Response*. Baltimore: Johns Hopkins University Press, 1980.

———. *Implied Reader: Patterns of Communication in Prose Fiction from Bunyan to Beckett*. Baltimore: Johns Hopkins University Press, 1974.

Japhet, Sara. *I & II Chronicles: A Commentary*. OTL. London: SCM, 1993.

Jebb, John. *Sacred Literature*. London: T. Cadell, 1828.

Joffe, Laura. "The Answer to the Meaning of Life, the Universe and the Elohistic Psalter." *JSOT* 27 (2002) 223–35.

Johnson, Vivian L. *David in Distress His Portrait through the Historical Psalms*. LHBOTS 505. New York: T. & T. Clark, 2009.

Johnston, Philip. "The Psalms and Distress." In *Interpreting the Psalms: Issues and Approaches*, edited by Philip Johnston and David Firth, 63–84. Downers Grove, IL: InterVarsity, 2005.

Jones, Christine Brown. "The Message of the Asaphite Collection and Its Role in the Psalter." In *Shape and Shaping of the Book of Psalms: The Current State of Scholarship*, edited by Nancy deClaissé-Walford, 71–85. AIL 20. Atlanta: SBL Press, 2014.

———. "The Psalms of Asaph : A Study of the Function of a Psalm Collection," PhD diss., Baylor University, 2009.

Jonker, Louis. "Revisiting the Psalms Headings: Second Temple Levitical Propaganda." In *Psalms and Liturgy*, edited by Dirk J. Human and C. J. A. Vos, 102–22. JSOTSup 410. London: T. & T. Clark, 2004.

Jordaan, Gert, and Pieter Nel. "From Priest-King to King-Priest." In *Psalms and Hebrews*, edited by Dirk Human and Gert Steyn, 229–40. LHBOTS 527. London: T. & T. Clark, 2010.

Kapelrud, Arvid S. "Eschatology in the Book of Micah." *VT* 11 (1961) 392–405.

Kartje, John. *Wisdom Epistemology in the Psalter: A Study of Psalms 1, 73, 90, and 107*. BZAW 472. Berlin: de Gruyter, 2014.

Keck, Leander E., et al. *1 & 2 Maccabees, Job, Psalms*. NIB. Nashville: Abingdon, 1996.

Keet, Cuthbert Cubitt. *Study of the Psalms of Ascents: A Critical and Exegetical Commentary upon Psalms CXX to CXXXIV*. London: Mitre, 1969.

Kim, Hyung Jun. "The Structure and Coherence of Psalms 89–106." PhD diss., University of Pretoria, 2009.

Kim, Jinkyu. "The Strategic Arrangement of Royal Psalms in Books IV–V." *WTJ* 70 (2008) 143–57.

Kimelman, Reuven. "Psalm 145: Theme, Structure, and Impact." *JBL* 113 (1994) 37–58.

Kimmitt, Francis Xavier. "Psalms 44, 45, 46: We Need A King!" Paper presented at the ETS 55th Annual Meeting, Atlanta, November 20, 2003.

———. "The Shape of Psalms 42–49." PhD diss., New Orleans Baptist Theological Seminary, 2000.

Klein, Ralph W. *1 Chronicles*. Hermeneia. Minneapolis: Fortress, 2006.

———. *1 Samuel*. WBC. Waco: Word, 1983.

———. "Psalms in Chronicles." *CurTM* 32 (2005) 264–75.

Klingbeil, Martin. "Off the Beaten Track: An Evangelical Reading of the Psalms without Gunkel." *BBR* 16 (2006) 25–39.

Knierim, Rolf. "Old Testament Form Criticism Reconsidered." *Int* 27 (1973) 435–68.

Knohl, Israel. "Sacred Architecture: The Numerical Dimensions of Biblical Poems." *VT* 62 (2012) 189–97.

Koorevaar, Hendrik J. "The Psalter as a Structured Theological Story with the Aid of Subscripts and Superscripts." In *Composition of the Book of Psalms*, edited by Erich Zenger, 579–92. BETL 238. Leuven: Peeters, 2010.

Körting, Corinna. "The Psalms—Their Cultic Setting, Forms, and Traditions." In *From Modernism to Post-Modernism: The Nineteenth and Twentieth Centuries*, edited by Magne Saebø, 531–58. Vol. 3.2 of *Hebrew Bible/Old Testament: The History of Its Interpretation*. Göttingen: Vandenhoeck & Ruprecht, 2015.

Köster, Johann F. B. *Die Psalmen nach Ihrer Strophischen Anordnung übersetzt*. Königsberg: Gebrüder Bornträger, 1837.

Kraus, Hans-Joachim. *Psalms 1–59: A Commentary*. Translated by Hilton C. Oswald. Continental Commentaries. Minneapolis: Augsburg, 1988.

———. *Psalms 60–150: A Commentary*. Translated by Hilton C. Oswald. Continental Commentaries. Minneapolis: Augsburg, 1989.

———. *Worship in Israel: A Cultic History of the Old Testament*. Translated by Geoffrey Buswell. Richmond: John Knox, 1966.

Kratz, Reinhard Gregor. "Die Tora Davids: Psalm 1 und die Doxologische Fünfteilung des Psalters." *ZTK* 93 (1996) 1–34.

Kristeva, Julia. *Desire in Language: A Semiotic Approach to Literature and Art*. New York: Columbia University Press, 1982.
Kugel, James L. *The Idea of Biblical Poetry: Parallelism and Its History*. New Haven: Yale University Press, 1981.
Kugel, James L., and Rowan A. Greer. *Early Biblical Interpretations*. LEC 3. Philadelphia: Westminster, 1986.
Labuschagne, Casper. "The Compositional Structure of the Psalter." Groningen: Labuschagne, 2012. http://www.labuschagne.nl/psalterstructure.pdf.
———. "General Introduction to Logotechnical Analysis." Rev. ed. Groningen: Labuschagne, 2016. http://www.labuschagne.nl/aspects.pdf.
———. "Psalm 9–10: Logotechnical Analysis." Groningen: Labuschagne, 2011. http://www.labuschagne.nl/ps009-10.pdf.
———. "Psalm 20: Logotechnical Analysis." Groningen: Labuschagne, 2008. http://www.labuschagne.nl/ps020.pdf.
———. "Psalm 25: Logotechnical Analysis." Groningen: Labuschagne, 2008. http://www.labuschagne.nl/ps025.pdf.
———. "Psalm 30: Logotechnical Analysis." Groningen: Labuschagne, 2008. http://www.labuschagne.nl/ps030.pdf.
———. "Psalm 42–43: Logotechnical Analysis." Groningen: Labuschagne, 2008. http://www.labuschagne.nl/ps042-43.pdf.
———. "Psalm 44: Logotechnical Analysis." Groningen: Labuschagne, 2008. http://www.labuschagne.nl/ps044.pdf.
———. "Psalm 104: Logotechnical Analysis." Groningen: Labuschagne, 2011. http://www.labuschagne.nl/ps104.pdf.
———. "Psalm 108: Logotechnical Analysis." Groningen: Labuschagne, 2008. http://www.labuschagne.nl/ps108.pdf.
———. "Psalm 110: Logotechnical Analysis." Groningen: Labuschagne, 2011. http://www.labuschagne.nl/ps110.pdf.
———. "Psalm 115: Logotechnical Analysis." Groningen: Labuschagne, 2011. http://www.labuschagne.nl/ps115.pdf.
———. "Psalm 118: Logotechnical Analysis." Groningen: Labuschagne, 2012. http://www.labuschagne.nl/ps118.pdf.
———. "Psalm 139: Logotechnical Analysis." Groningen: Labuschagne, 2012. http://www.labuschagne.nl/ps139.pdf.
———. "Psalm 148: Logotechnical Analysis." Groningen: Labuschagne, 2008. http://www.labuschagne.nl/ps148.pdf.
———. "Neue Wege und Perspektiven in der Pentateuchforschung." *VT* 36 (1986) 146–62.
———. *Numerical Secrets of the Bible: Rediscovering the Bible Codes*. North Richland Hills, TX: Bibal, 2000.
———. "Significant Compositional Techniques in the Psalms: Evidence for the Use of Number as an Organizing Principle." *VT* 59 (2009) 583–605.
———. "Significant Sub-Groups in the Book of Psalms." In *Composition of the Book of Psalms*, edited by Erich Zenger, 623–34. BETL 238. Leuven: Peeters, 2010.
Ladd, George Eldon. *Presence of the Future: The Eschatology of Biblical Realism*. Grand Rapids: Eerdmans, 2000.
Lama, Ajoy K. "Placement of Psalm 145 in Book V: A Compositional Analysis." PhD diss., Trinity Evangelical Divinity School, 2007.
Lambdin, Thomas O. *Introduction to Biblical Hebrew*. New York: Scribner, 1971.

Lange, Armin, and Matthias Weigold, eds. *Biblical Quotations and Allusions in Second Temple Jewish Literature*. JAJSup 5. Göttingen: Vandenhoeck & Ruprecht, 2011.

LeFebvre, Michael. "Torah-Meditation and the Psalms: The Invitation of Psalm 1." In *Interpreting the Psalms: Issues and Approaches*, edited by Philip Johnston and David Firth, 213–25. Downers Grove, IL: InterVarsity, 2005.

Leiman, Sid Z. "The Inverted Nuns at Numbers 10:35–36 and the Book of Eldad and Medad." *JBL* 93 (1974) 348.

Leonard, Jeffery M. "Identifying Inner-Biblical Allusions: Psalm 78 as a Test Case." *JBL* 127 (2008) 241–65.

Leuchter, Mark. "Eisodus as Exodus: The Song of the Sea (Exod 15) Reconsidered." *Bib* 92.3 (2011) 321–46.

Leuenberger, Martin. *Konzeptionen des Königtums Gottes im Psalter: Untersuchungen zu Komposition und Redaktion der theokratischen Bücher IV–V im Psalter*. ATANT 83. Zürich: TVZ, 2004.

Levenson, Jon D. "The Davidic Covenant and Its Modern Interpreters." *CBQ* 41 (1979) 205–19.

———. *Sinai and Zion: An Entry into the Jewish Bible*. Minneapolis: Winston, 1985.

Lim, Johnson T. K. *A Strategy for Reading Biblical Texts*. StBibLit 29. New York: Lang, 2002.

Lindars, Barnabas. "Is Psalm 2 an Acrostic Poem." *VT* 17 (1967) 60–67.

Longman, Tremper, III. "רוע." In *NIDOTTE* 3:1081–1084.

———. *Literary Approaches to Biblical Interpretation*. FOCI 3. Grand Rapids: Zondervan, 1987.

———. "The Messiah: Explorations in the Law and Writings." In *Messiah in the Old and New Testaments*, edited by Stanley E. Porter, 13–34. MNTS 9. Grand Rapids: Eerdmans, 2007.

———. *Psalms: An Introduction and Commentary*. TOTC 15–16. Downers Grove, IL: InterVarsity, 2014.

Longman, Tremper, III, and Peter Enns, eds. *Dictionary of the Old Testament: Wisdom, Poetry & Writings*. Downers Grove, IL: InterVarsity, 2008.

Lowth, Robert. *Lectures on the Sacred Poetry of the Hebrews*. Translated by G. Gregory. London: Tegg, 1825.

Lugt, Pieter van der. *Cantos and Strophes in Biblical Hebrew Poetry: With Special Reference to the First Book of the Psalter*. OtSt 53. Leiden: Brill, 2006.

———. *Cantos and Strophes in Biblical Hebrew Poetry II: Psalms 42–89*. OtSt 57. Leiden: Brill, 2010.

———. *Cantos and Strophes in Biblical Hebrew Poetry III: Psalms 90–150 and Psalm 1*. OtSt 63. Leiden: Brill, 2013.

———. "The Mathematical Centre and Its Meaning in the Psalms." In *Composition of the Book of Psalms*, edited by Erich Zenger, 643–52. BETL 238. Leuven: Peeters, 2010.

———. *Rhetorical Criticism and the Poetry of the Book of Job*. OtSt 32. Leiden: Brill, 1995.

Lynch, Matthew J. "Zion's Warrior and the Nations: Isaiah 59:15b–63:6 in Isaiah's Zion Traditions." *CBQ* 70 (2008) 244–63.

Maloney, Les. "Intertextual Links: Part of the Poetic Artistry within the Book I Acrostic Psalms." *ResQ* 49 (2007) 11–21.

———. "A Word Fitly Spoken Poetic Artistry in the First Four Acrostics of the Hebrew Psalter." PhD diss., Baylor Uuniversity, 2005.

Man, Ronald E. "The Value of Chiasm for New Testament Interpretation." *BSac* 141 (1984) 146–57.

March, W. Eugene. "Psalm 86: When Love Is Not Enough." *ASB* 105 (1990) 17–25.

Marrs, Rick R. "'Back to the Future': Zion in the Book of Micah." In *David and Zion: Biblical Studies in Honor of J. J. M. Roberts*, edited by Bernard F. Batto and Kathryn L. Roberts, 77–96. Winona Lake, IN: Eisenbrauns, 2004.

Martens, Elmer. "רחץ." In *NIDOTTE* 3:1098–99.

Mays, James Luther. "The David of the Psalms." *Int* 40 (1986) 143–55.

———. "'In a Vision': The Portrayal of the Messiah in the Psalms." *ExAud* 7 (1991) 1–8.

———. *The Lord Reigns: A Theological Handbook to the Psalms*. Louisville: Westminster John Knox, 1994.

———. "The Place of the Torah-Psalms in the Psalter." *JBL* 106 (1987) 3–12.

———. *Psalms*. Interpretation. Louisville: Westminster John Knox, 1994.

———. "The Question of Context in Psalm Interpretation." In *Shape and Shaping of the Psalter*, edited by J. Clinton McCann, 14–20. JSOTSup 159. Sheffield: JSOT Press, 1993.

McCann, J. Clinton. "Books I–III and the Editorial Purpose of the Hebrew Psalter." In *The Shape and Shaping of the Psalter*, edited by J. Clinton McCann, 93–107. JSOTSup 159. Sheffield: JSOT Press, 1993.

———. "The Psalms as Instruction." *Int* 46 (1992) 117–28.

———. "Reading from the Beginning (again): The Shape of Book I of the Psalter." In *Diachronic and Synchronic*, edited by Joel Burnett, et al., 129–42. LHBOTS 488. New York: T. & T. Clark, 2007.

———. "The Shape and Shaping of the Psalter: Psalms in Their Literary Context." In *Oxford Handbook of the Psalms*, edited by William P. Brown, 350–62. Oxford: Oxford University Press, 2014.

———. "The Shape of Book I of the Psalter and the Shape of Human Happiness." In *Book of Psalms: Composition and Reception*, edited by Peter W. Flint and Patrick D. Miller, 340–48. VTSup 99. Leiden: Brill, 2004.

———. "The Single Most Important Text in the Entire Bible: Toward a Theology of the Psalms." In *Soundings in the Theology of Psalms*, edited by Rolf Jacobson, 63–75. Minneapolis: Fortress, 2011.

———. *Theological Introduction to the Book of Psalms: The Psalms as Torah*. Nashville: Abingdon, 1993.

———. "Wisdom's Dilemma: The Book of Job, the Final Form of the Book of Psalms, and the Entire Bible." In *Wisdom, You Are My Sister: Studies in Honor of Roland E. Murphy, O. Carm., on the Occasion of His Eightieth Birthday*, edited by Michael L Barré, 18–30. CBQMS 29. Washington, DC: Catholic Biblical Association of America, 1997.

McCarthy, Dennis J. "2 Samuel 7 and the Structure of the Deuteronomic History." *JBL* 84 (1965) 131–38.

McConville, Gordon. "Messianic Interpretation of the Old Testament in Modern Context." In *The Lord's Anointed: Interpretation of Old Testament Messianic Texts*, edited by P. E. Satterthwaite, et al., 1–18. Grand Rapids: Paternoster, 1995.

McEvenue, Sean E. "The Old Testament, Scripture or Theology." *Int* 35 (1981) 229–42.

Meek, Russell. "Intertextuality, Inner-Biblical Exegesis, and Inner-Biblical Allusion: The Ethics of a Methodology." *Bib* 95 (2014) 280–91.

Mensah, Michael Kodzo. *"I Turned Back My Feet to Your Decrees."* ÖBS 45. New York: Lang, 2016.

Milgrom, Jacob. *Numbers: [Ba-Midbar]*. JPS Torah Commentary. Philadelphia: Jewish Publication Society, 1990.

Millard, Matthias. *Die Komposition des Psalters: Ein Formgeschichtlicher Ansatz*. FAT 27. Tübingen: Mohr/Siebeck, 1994.

Miller, Patrick D. "The Beginning of the Psalter." In *The Shape and Shaping of the Psalter*, edited by J. Clinton McCann, 83–92. JSOTSup 159. Sheffield: JSOT Press, 1993.

———. "The End of the Psalter: A Response to Erich Zenger." *JSOT* (1998) 103–10.

———. "Kingship, Torah Obedience, and Prayer: The Theology of Psalms 15–24." In *Neue Wege der Psalmenforschung: Für Walter Beyerlin*, edited by Klaus Seybold and Erich Zenger, 127–42. HBS 1. Freiburg: Herder, 1994.

———. "Psalm 127: The House That Yahweh Builds." *JSOT* 22 (1982) 119–32.

———. "Synonymous-Sequential Parallelism in the Psalms." *Bib* 61 (1980) 256–60.

Mitchell, David C. "Lord, Remember David: G. H. Wilson and the Message of the Psalter." *VT* 56 (2006) 526–48.

———. *Message of the Psalter: An Eschatological Programme in the Books of Psalms*. JSOTSup 252. Sheffield: Sheffield Academic, 1997.

———. *Messiah Ben Joseph*. Newton Mearns: Campbell, 2016.

———. *Songs of Ascents: Psalms 120–134 in the Worship of Jerusalem's Temples*. Newton Mearns: Campbell, 2015.

Moon, EunMee. "The Sapiential Reading of Psalms 107–18 in the Framework of Books IV and V of the Psalter." PhD diss., Trinity International University, 2008.

Mournet, Krista. "Moses and the Psalms: The Significance of Psalms 90 and 106 within Book IV of the Masoretic Psalter." *CBW* 31 (2011) 66–79.

Mowinckel, Sigmund. *He That Cometh*. Translated by G. W. Anderson. New York: Abingdon, 1956.

———. *The Psalms in Israel's Worship*. Translated by D. R. Ap-Thomas. 2 vols. Oxford: Basil Blackwell, 1962.

———, et al. *Psalmenstudien 6*. Kristiania, Norway: Dybwad, 1924.

Moyise, Steve, and Maarten J. J. Menken, eds. *The Psalms in the New Testament*. London: T. & T. Clark, 2004.

Muilenburg, James. "Form Criticism and beyond." *JBL* 88 (1969) 1.

Mullen, E. Theodore. "The Divine Witness and the Davidic Royal Grant: Ps 89:37–38." *JBL* 102 (1983) 207–18.

Müller, D. H. *Die Propheten in ihrer ursprünglichen Form*. Vienna: Hölder. 1896.

Murphy, John M. "John W. Welch Chiasmus Papers Collection, 1818–2004 (bulk: 1953–2004)." 2007. Revised, Provo, UT: Brigham Young University, 2011. https://chiasmusresources.org/sites/default/files/hbll_chiasmus_archive_finding_aid_9-final_2013.pdf.

Murphy, Roland E. "Notes on Old Testament Messianism and Apologetics." *CBQ* 19 (1957) 5–15.

Murray, D. F. "Mqwm and the Future of Israel in 2 Samuel 7:10." *VT* 40 (1990) 298–320.

Nasuti, Harry P. *Defining the Sacred Songs: Genre, Tradition, and the Post-Critical Interpretation of the Psalms*. JSOTSup 218. Sheffield: Sheffield Academic, 1999.

———. "The Interpretive Significance of Sequence and Selection in the Book of Psalms." In *Book of Psalms*, edited by Patrick D. Miller and Peter W. Flint, 311–39. VTSup 99. Leiden: Brill, 2005.

Ndoga, Samuel S. "Revisiting the Theocratic Agena of Book 4 of the Psalter for Interpretive Premise." In *The Shape and Shaping of the Book of Psalms: The Current State of Scholarship*, edited by Nancy deClaissé-Walford, 147–60. Ancient Israel and Its Literature 20. Atlanta: SBL Press, 2014.

Nogalski, James D. "From Psalm to Psalms to Psalter." In *Introduction to Wisdom Literature and the Psalms*, edited by Harold Wayne Ballard and W. Dennis Tucker, 21–36. Macon, GA: Mercer University Press, 2000.

Ollenburger, Ben C. *Zion, the City of the Great King a Theological Symbol of the Jerusalem Cult*. Sheffield: JSOT Press, 1987.

Olson, Dennis T. "Zigzagging through Deep Waters: A Guide to Brevard Childs's Canonical Exegesis of Scripture." *WW* 29 (2009) 348–56.

Oswalt, John. "משח." In *NIDOTTE* 2:1123–27.

Pardee, Dennis. "Acrostics and Parallelism: The Parallelistic Structure of Psalm 111." *Maarav* 8 (1992) 117–38.

Parrish, V. Steven. *A Story of the Psalms: Conversation, Canon, and Congregation*. Collegeville: Liturgical, 2003.

Patterson, Richard D. "Singing the New Song: An Examination of Psalms 33, 96, 98, and 149." *BSac* 164 (2007) 416–34.

Pavan, Marco. *"He Remembered That They Were but Flesh, a Breath That Passes and Does Not Return."* Translated by Michael Tait. ÖBS 44. New York: Lang, 2014.

Petersen, David L. "Hebrew Bible Form Criticism." *RelSRev* 18 (1992) 29–33.

Petterson, Anthony R. *Behold Your King: The Hope For the House of David in the Book of Zechariah*. London: T. & T. Clark, 2009.

———. "The Shape of the Davidic Hope across the Book of the Twelve." *JSOT* 35 (2010) 225–46.

Pietersma, Albert. "Messianism and the Greek Psalter: In Search of the Messiah." In *The Septuagint and Messianism: Colloquium Biblicum Lovaniense LIII*, edited by M. A. Knibb, 49–75. BETL 195. Leuven: Peeters, 2006.

Piotrowski, Nicholas G. "'I Will Save My People from Their Sins': The Influence of Ezekiel 36:28b–29a; 37:23b on Matthew 1:21." *TynBul* 64 (2013) 33–54.

Prinsloo, G. T. M. "The Role of Space in the Shire Hama'lot (Psalms 120–134)." *Bib* 86 (2005) 457–77.

———. "Sheol > Jerusalem < Samayim: Spatial Orientation in the Egyptian Hallel (Psalms 113–118)." *OTE* 19 (2006) 739–60.

Pritchard, James, ed. *The Ancient Near East: An Anthology of Texts and Pictures*. Reprint. Princeton: Princeton University Press, 2011.

Rad, Gerhard von. *Old Testament Theology*. Vol. 1. Translated by D. M. G. Stalker. Edinburg: Oliver and Boyd, 1962.

Rand, Herbert. "Numerological Stucture in Biblical Literature." *JBQ* 20 (1991) 50–56.

Reindl, Joseph. "Weisheitliche Bearbeitung von Psalmen: Ein Beitrag zum Verstaendnis der Sammlung des Psalters." In *Congress Volume, Vienna, 1980*, edited by John Emerton, 333–56. VTSup 32. Leiden: Brill, 1981.

Rendtorff, Rolf. *Canon and Theology*. Translated by Margaret Kohl. Overtures to an Old Testament Theology. Minneapolis: Fortress, 1993.

Reynolds, Kent Aaron. *Torah as Teacher the Exemplary Torah Student in Psalm 119*. VTSup 137. Leiden: Brill, 2010.

Rezetko, Robert. *Source and Revision in the Narratives of David's Transfer of the Ark: Text, Language, and Story in 2 Samuel 6 and 1 Chronicles 13, 15–16*. The LHBOTS 470. New York: Bloomsbury, 2007.

Ribera-Mariné, Ramon. "'El Llibre de les Lloances.' Estudi redaccional del salteri." *RCT* 16 (1991) 1–19.

Ridderbos, N. H. *Die Psalmen: Stilistische Verfahren und Aufbau mit besonderer Berücksichtigung von Ps 1–41*. BZAW 117. Berlin: de Gruyter, 1972.

Roberts, J. J. M. "The Old Testament's Contribution to Messianic Expectations." In *Messiah: Developments in Earliest Judaism and Christianity*, edited by James H. Charlesworth, 39–51. Minneapolis: Fortress, 1992.

Robertson, O. Palmer. *Flow of the Psalms: Discovering Their Structure and Theology*. Kindle ed. Philipsburg: P&R, 2015.

Robinson, Geoffrey D. "The Motif of Deafness and Blindness in Isaiah 6:9–10: A Contextual, Literary, and Theological Analysis." *BBR* 8 (1998) 167–86.

Rohde, Michael. "Observations on the Songs of Ascents: A Discussion about the So-Called Zion-Theology of Psalms 120–134." *BT* 1 (2009) 24–42.

Rose, Wolter H. "Messianic Expectations in the Early Post-Exilic Period." *TynBul* 49.2 (1998) 373–76.

———. *Zemah and Zerubbabel: Messianic Expectations in the Early Postexilic Period*. LHBOTS 304. London: T. & T. Clark, 2000.

Rösel, Christoph. *Die Messianische Redaktion des Psalters: Studien zu Entstehung und Theologie der Sammlung Psalm 2–89*. CTM 19. Stuttgart: Calwer, 1999.

Routledge, Robin L. "Psalm 110, Melchizedek and David: Blessing (the Descendants of) Abraham." *BT* 1 (2009) 1–16.

Sailhamer, John. "The Messiah and the Hebrew Bible." *JETS* 44 (2001) 5–23.

Sanders, James A. "Pre-Masoretic Psalter Texts." *CBQ* 27 (1965) 114–23.

Satterthwaite, P. E. "Zion in the Songs of Ascents." In *Zion City of Our God*. Edited by Richard S. Hess and Gordon J. Wenham, 105–28. Grand Rapids: Eerdmans, 1999.

Saur, Markus. *Die Königspsalmen: Studien zur Entstehung und Theologie*. BZAW 340. Berlin: de Gruyter, 2004.

———. "Die Theologische Funktion der Königspsalmen innerhalb der Komposition des Psalters." In *Composition of the Book of Psalms*, edited by Erich Zenger, 689–700. BETL 238. Leuven: Peeters, 2010.

Sawyer, John F. A. "The Psalms in Judaism and Christianity: A Reception History Perspective." In *Jewish and Christian Approaches to the Psalms: Conflict and Convergence*, edited by Susan Gillingham, 134–43. Oxford: Oxford University Press, 2013.

Scaiola, Donatella. "The End of the Psalter." In *Composition of the Book of Psalms*, edited by Erich Zenger, 701–10. BETL 238. Leuven: Peeters, 2010.

Schaefer, Konrad. *Psalms*. Berit Olam. Collegeville, MN: Liturgical, 2001.

Schaper, Joachim. *Eschatology in the Greek Psalter*. WUNT 2/76. Tübingen: Mohr/Siebeck, 1995.

Schedl, Claus. *Baupläne des Wortes Einführung in die biblische Logotechnik*. Vienna: Herder, 1974.

———. "Die Alphabetisch-Arithmetische Struktur von Psalm 136." *VT* 36 (1986) 489–94.

Schniedewind, William. "Understanding Scribal Education in Ancient Israel: A View from Kuntillet ʿAjrud." *Maarav* 21 (2014) 271–93.

Schoville, Keith N. "מעוז." In *NIDOTTE* 2:1013–15.

Schroeder, Christoph. "'A Love Song': Psalm 45 in the Light of Ancient Near Eastern Marriage Texts." *CBQ* 58 (1996) 417–32.

Schuliger, Jeffrey Wayne. "The Theological Significance of Alphabetic Acrostics in the Psalter." ThM Thesis, Regent College, 2009.

Schultz, Richard L. "The Ties That Bind: Intertextuality, the Identification of Verbal Parallels, and Reading Strategies in the Book of the Twelve." In *Thematic Threads in the Book of the*

Twelve, edited by Paul Redditt and Aaron Schart, 27–45. BZAW 325. Berlin: de Gruyter, 2003.

Schunck, Klaus D. "Der Fünfte Thronname des Messias, Jes 9:5-6." *VT* 23 (1973) 108–10.

Seitz, Christopher R. *The Bible as Christian Scripture: The Work of Brevard S. Childs*. Atlanta: SBL, 2013.

Seow, C. L. "An Exquisitely Poetic Introduction to the Psalter." *JBL* 132 (2013) 275–93.

Sergi, Omer. "The Composition of Nathan's Oracle to David (2 Samuel 7:1–17) as a Reflection of Royal Judahite Ideology." *JBL* 129 (2010) 261–79.

Seybold, Klaus. *Die Psalmen*. HAT 15. Tübingen: Mohr/Siebeck, 1996.

———. *Die Wallfahrtspsalmen: Studien zur Entstehungsgeschichte von Psalm 120–134*. BthSt 3. Neukirchen-Vluyn: Neukirchener, 1978.

———. *Introducing the Psalms*. Translated by R. Grame Dunphy. Edinburgh: T. & T. Clark, 1990.

———. "The Psalter as a Book." In *Jewish and Christian Approaches to the Psalms: Conflict and Convergence*, edited by Susan Gillingham, 168–81. Oxford: Oxford University Press, 2013.

———. "Zur Geschichte des Vierten Davidpsalters (Pss 138–145)." In *The Book of Psalms: Composition and Reception*, edited by Peter W. Flint and Patrick D. Miller, 368–90. VTSup 99. Leiden: Brill, 2004.

Shea, William H. "Chiasm in Samuel." *LB* 9/10 (1971): 21–31.

———. "Chiasmus and the Structure of David's Lament." *JBL* 105 (1986) 13–25.

———. "The Chiastic Structure of the Song of Songs." *ZAW* 92 (1980) 378–96.

———. "The Earliest Alphabetic Inscription and Its Implications for the Writing of the Pentateuch." In *Inicios, Paradigmas y Fundamentos*, edited by Gerald Klingbeil, 45–60. River Plate Adventist University Monograph Series in Biblical and Theological Studies 1. Editorial Universidad Adventista del Plata: Argentina, 2004.

———. "Further Literary Structures in Daniel 2–7: An Analysis of Daniel 5, and the Broader Relationships Within Chapters 2–7." *AUSS* 23 (1985): 277–95.

———. "The Literary Structure of Zechariah 1–6." In *Creation, Life and Hope*, edited by Jiří Moskala, 83–100. Berrien Springs, MI: Seventh-day Adventist Theological Seminary, Andrews University, 2000.

Sheppard, Gerald T. "Theology and the Book of Psalms." *Int* 46 (1992) 143–55.

Shipp, R. Mark. "'Remember His Covenant Forever': A Study of the Chronicler's Use of the Psalms." *ResQ* 35 (1993) 29–39.

Singer, Dwight Charles. "The Literary Context of the Fourth Davidic Grouping in the Psalter (Psalms 138–145)." *WTJ* 75 (2013) 373.

Skehan, Patrick William. "Broken Acrostic and Psalm 9." *CBQ* 27 (1965) 1–5.

———. "Psalm Manuscript from Qumran (4QPs^b)." *CBQ* 26 (1964) 313–22.

———. "Structure of the Song of Moses in Deuteronomy (Deut 32:1–43)." *CBQ* 13 (1951) 153–63.

Smith, Kevin G. "The Redactional Criteria and Objectives Underlying the Arrangement of Psalms 3–8." ThD Diss., South African Theological Seminary, 2007.

Smith, Kevin G., and William R. Domeris. "The Arrangement of Psalms 3–8." *OTE* 23 (2010) 367–77.

Smith, Robert. "Chiasm in Sumero-Akkadian." In *Chiasmus in Antiquity: Structures, Analyses, Exegesis*, edited by John W. Welch, 17–35. Hildesheim: Gerstenberg Verlag, 1981.

Snearly, Michael K. "The Return of the King: Book V as a Witness to Messianic Hope in the Psalter." In *Psalms: Language for All Seasons of the Soul*, edited by Andrew Schmutzer and David Howard, 209–17. Chicago: Moody, 2014.

———. "The Return of the King: An Editorial-Critical Analysis of Psalms 107–150." PhD diss., Golden Gate Baptist Seminary, 2012.

———. *The Return of the King: Messianic Expectation in Book V of the Psalter*. LHBOTS 624. New York: T. & T. Clark, 2015.

Soll, William Michael. "Babylonian and Biblical Acrostics." *Bib* 69 (1988) 305–23.

———. *Psalm 119: Matrix, Form, and Setting*. Washington, DC: Catholic Biblical Association of America, 1991.

———. "The Question of Psalm 119:9." *JBL* 106 (1987) 687–88.

Starling, David. "The Messianic Hope in the Psalms." *RTR* 58 (1999) 121–34.

Stensvaag, John M. "Recent Approaches to the Psalms." *LQ* 9 (1957) 195–212.

Stinespring, William Franklin. "No Daughter of Zion: A Study of the Appositional Genitive in Hebrew Grammar." *Enc* 26 (1965) 133–41.

Strawn, Brent A. "10.2.2 Masoretic Texts and Ancient Texts Close to MT." In *Textual History of the Bible Online*, edited by Armin Lange, et al. Leiden: Brill, 2016. http://www.brill.com/products/online-resources/textual-history-bible-online.

Strugnell, John, and Ḥanan Eshel. "It's Elementary: Psalms 9 and 10 and the Order of the Alphabet." *BRev* 17 (2001) 41–44.

Sumpter, Philip. "The Coherence of Psalms 15–24." *Bib* 94 (2013) 186–209.

———. "Substance of Psalm 24: An Attempt to Read Scripture after Brevard S. Childs." PhD diss., University of Gloucestershire, 2011.

Swanson, Dwight D. "Qumran and the Psalms." In *Interpreting the Psalms: Issues and Approaches*, edited by Philip Johnston and David Firth, 247–61. Downers Grove, IL: InterVarsity, 2005.

Sweeney, Marvin A., and Ehud Ben Zvi. *The Changing Face of Form Criticism for the Twenty-First Century*. Grand Rapids: Eerdmans, 2003.

Tanner, Beth LaNeel. *The Book of Psalms through the Lens of Intertextuality*. StBibLit 26. New York: Lang, 2001.

Tate, Marvin E. "King and Messiah in Isaiah of Jerusalem." *RevExp* 65 (1968) 409–21.

———. *Psalms. 51–100*. WBC 20. Dallas: Word, 1990.

Tate, W. Randolph. *Biblical Interpretation: An Integrated Approach*. Peabody, MA: Hendrickson, 1991.

———. *Interpreting the Bible: A Handbook of Terms and Methods*. Grand Rapids: Baker Academic, 2006.

Taylor, John B. *Ezekiel*. TOTC 22. London: Tyndale, 1971.

Terrien, Samuel L. *Psalms: Strophic Structure and Theological Commentary*. Grand Rapids: Eerdmans, 2003.

Todd, James M. "A Poetic and Contextual Analysis of Psalms 135–137." PhD diss., Southeastern Baptist Theological Seminary, 2010.

———. *Remember, O Yahweh: The Poetry and Context of Psalms 135–137*. Eugene, OR: Wipf & Stock, 2015.

Tov, Emanuel. *Textual Criticism of the Hebrew Bible, Qumran, Septuagint: Collected Essays*. Vol. 3. VTSup 167. Leiden: Brill, 2015.

Toy, Crawford Howell. "On the Asaph-Psalms." *Journal of the Society of Biblical Literature and Exegesis* 6 (1886) 73–85.

Tucker, Dennis, Jr. *Constructing and Deconstructing Power in Psalms 107–150*. Atlanta: SBL, 2014.

———. "Democratization and the Language of the Poor in Psalms 2–89." *HBT* 25 (2003) 161–78.

———. "Empires and Enemies in Book V of the Psalter." In *The Composition of the Book of Psalms*, edited by Erich Zenger, 723–32. BETL 238. Leuven: Peeters, 2010.

———. "A Polysemiotic Approach to the Poor in the Psalms." *PRSt* 31 (2004) 425–39.

———. "The Role of the Foe in Book 5: Reflections on the Final Composition of the Psalter." In *Shape and Shaping of the Book of Psalms: The Current State of Scholarship*, edited by Nancy deClaissé-Walford, 147–60. AIL 20. Atlanta: SBL Press, 2014.

Van Dam, Cornelis. "חלק." In *NIDOTTE* 2:161–163.

Van Gogh, Vincent. *Terrace of the café on the Place du Forum in Arles in the evening*, 1888. Oil on canvas, 81 cm by 65.5 cm. Otterlo, Netherlands, Kröller-Müller Museum. Wikimedia Commons. https://commons.wikimedia.org/wiki/File:Van_Gogh_-_Terrasse_des_Caf%C3%A9s_an_der_Place_du_Forum_in_Arles_am_Abend1.jpeg.

Van Leeuwen, Raymond C. "Why Do the Trees of the Forest Sing a New Song? (Psalms 96 and 98)." *CQ* 62 (2004) 22–34.

Vesco, Jean-Luc. *Le psautier de David traduit et commenté*. 2 vols. Paris: Cerf, 2006.

Vincent, Marvin A. "The Shape of the Psalter: An Eschatological Dimension?" In *New Heaven and New Earth—Prophecy and the Millennium*, edited by P. J. Harland and C. T. R. Hayward, 61–82. VTSup 77. Leiden: Brill, 1999.

Viviers, Hendrik. "The Coherence of the Maʿalôt Psalms (Pss 120–134)." *ZAW* 106 (1994) 275–89.

Waaler, Erik. "A Revised Date for Pentateuchal Texts?: Evidence from Ketef Hinnom." *TynBul* 53 (2002) 29–55.

Waltke, Bruce K. "Superscripts, Postscripts, or Both." *JBL* 110 (1991) 583–96.

Weber, Beat. "Das Königlich-Davidische Danklied 2 Samuel 22/Psalm 18 Im Kontext von Psalm 1–18. Eine (proto)kanonische Lesung vom Ende der Samuelbücher her zum Anfangsbereich des Psalters Hin." In *Canterò in Eterno Le Misericordie Del Signore" (Sal 89,2)*, edited by Stefan Attard and Marco Pavan, 187–204. AnBib 3. Roma: Gregorian & Biblical, 2015.

———. "Die Doppelte Verknotung des Psalters: Kanonhermeneutische Erwägungen zu den 'Schnittstellen' Psalm 18 // 2 Samuel 22 und Psalm 96; 105; 106 // 1 Chronik 16." *BZ* 60 (2016) 14–27.

———. "'Gelobt Sei der HERR, Mein Fels . . . !' (Ps 144,1): Wirkung und Bedeutung von Psalm 18 (// 2 Samuel 22) im Nachfeld des Psalters." *OTE* 29 (2016) 195–220.

———. "Toward a Theory of the Poetry of the Hebrew Bible: The Poetry of the Psalms as a Test Case." *BBR* 22 (2012) 157–88.

Wegner, Paul D. "A Re-Examination of Isaiah IX 1–6." *VT* 42 (1992) 103–12.

Weinfeld, M. "בְּרִית." In *TDOT* 2:253–79.

———. "The Covenant of Grant in the Old Testament and in the Ancient near East." *JAOS* 90 (1970) 184.

Weiser, Artur. *Psalms. A Commentary*. Translated by Herbert Hartwell. 5th ed. OTL. London: SCM, 1962.

Weisman, Zeev. "Charismatic Leaders in the Era of the Judges." *ZAW* 89 (1977) 399–411.

Welch, John W., ed. *Chiasmus in Antiquity: Structures, Analyses, Exegesis*. Provo, UT: Neal A. Maxwell Institute for Religious Scholarship, 1998.

Wendland, Ernst R. *Analyzing the Psalms: With Exercises for Bible Students and Translators.* 2nd ed. Winona Lake, IN: SIL International, 2002.

———. *Studies in the Psalms: Literary-Structural Analysis with Application to Translation.* Dallas: Summer Institute of Linguistics, Academic, 2017.

Wenham, Gordon J. *Psalms as Torah: Reading Biblical Song Ethically.* Grand Rapids: Baker Academic, 2012.

———. "Towards a Canonical Reading of the Psalms." In *Canon and Biblical Interpretation*, edited by Craig Bartholomew and Anthony Thiselton, 333–51. Vol. 7. SHS. Milton Keynes: Paternoster, 2006.

Westermann, Claus. *Praise and Lament in the Psalms.* Translated by Keith Crim and Richard Soulen. Atlanta: John Knox, 1981.

———. *Psalms: Structure, Content & Message.* Translated by Ralph Gehrke. Minneapolis: Augsburg, 1980.

Whybray, Norman. *Reading the Psalms as a Book.* JSOTSup 222. Sheffield: Sheffield Academic, 1996.

Willgren, David. *Formation of the "Book" of Psalms: Reconsidering the Transmission and Canonization of Psalmody in Light of Material Culture and the Poetics of Anthologies.* FAT 2/88. Tübingen: Mohr/Siebeck, 2016.

Williams, Tyler. "Towards a Date for the Old Greek Psalter." In *Old Greek Psalter: Studies in Honour of Albert Pietersma*, edited by Robert Hiebert, et al., 248–76. JSOTSup 332. Sheffield: Sheffield Academic, 2009.

Willis, Timothy M. "'So Great Is His Steadfast Love': A Rhetorical Analysis of Psalm 103." *Bib* 72 (1991) 525–37.

Wilson, Gerald H. *The Editing of the Hebrew Psalter.* SBLDS 76. Atlanta: Scholars, 1985.

———. "Evidence of Editorial Divisions in the Hebrew Psalter." *VT* 34 (1984) 337–52.

———. "A First Century CE Date for the Closing of the Book of Psalms." *JBQ* 28 (2000) 102–10.

———. "King, Messiah, and the Reign of God: Revisiting the Royal Psalms and the Shape of the Psalter." In *Book of Psalms: Composition and Reception*, edited by Peter W. Flint and Patrick D. Miller, 391–406. VTSup 99. Leiden: Brill, 2005.

———. "The Qumran Psalms Scroll (11QPs^a) and the Canonical Psalter." *CBQ* 59 (1997) 448–64.

———. "The Qumran Psalms Scroll [11QPs^a] Reconsidered : Analysis of the Debate." *CBQ* 47 (1985) 624–42.

———. "The Shape of the Book of Psalms." *Int* 46 (1992) 129–42.

———. "Shaping the Psalter: A Consideration of Editorial Linkage in the Book of Psalms." In *Shape and Shaping of the Psalter*, edited by J. Clinton McCann, 72–82. JSOTSup 159. Sheffield: JSOT Press, 1993.

———. "The Structure of the Psalter." In *Interpreting the Psalms: Issues and Approaches*, edited by Philip Johnston and David Firth, 229–46. Downers Grove, IL: InterVarsity, 2005.

———. "Understanding the Purposeful Arrangement of Psalms in the Psalter: Pitfalls and Promise." In *Shape and Shaping of the Psalter*, edited by J. Clinton McCann, 42–51. JSOTSup 159. Sheffield: JSOT, 1993.

———. "The Use of Royal Psalms at the 'Seams' of the Hebrew Psalter." *JSOT* 35 (1986) 85–94.

———. "The Use of 'Untitled' Psalms in the Hebrew Psalter." *ZAW* 97 (1985) 404–13.

Wilson, Lindsay. "On Psalms 103–106 as a Closure to Book IV of the Psalter." In *Composition of the Book of Psalms*, edited by Erich Zenger, 755–66. BETL 238. Leuven: Peeters, 2010.

Wimsatt, W. K., and M. C. Beardsley. "The Intentional Fallacy." *SR* 54 (1946) 468–88.

Witt, Andrew. "Hearing Psalm 102 within the Context of the Hebrew Psalter." *VT* 62 (2012) 582–606.

Wolfe, Kenneth R. "The Chiastic Structure of Luke–Acts and Some Implications for Worship." *SJT* 22.2 (1980) 60–71.

Xun, Chen. *Theological Exegesis in the Canonical Context: Brevard Springs Childs' Methodology of Biblical Theology*. StBibLit 137. New York: Lang, 2010.

Yarchin, William. "Were the Psalms Collections at Qumran True Psalters?" *JBL* 134 (2015) 775–89.

Yeivin, Israel. *Introduction to the Tiberian Masorah*. Translated by E. J. Revell. MasS 5. Missoula, MT: Scholars, 1980.

Zakovitch, Yair. "The Interpretative Significance of the Sequence of Psalms 111–112. 113–118. 119." In *Composition of the Book of Psalms*, edited by Erich Zenger, 215–27. BETL 238. Leuven: Peeters, 2010.

———. "On the Ordering of Psalms as Demonstrated by Psalms 136–150." In *Oxford Handbook of the Psalms*, edited by William P. Brown, 214–28. Oxford Handbooks. Oxford: Oxford University Press, 2014.

Zandee, Jan. "Le Roi-Dieu et le Dieu-Roi dans l'Égypte Ancienne." *Numen* 3 (1956) 230–34.

Zenger, Erich. "The Composition and Theology of the Fifth Book of Psalms, Psalms 107–145." *JSOT* (1998) 77–102.

———. "Das Buch der Psalmen." *Einleitung in das Alte Testament*. Edited by Erich Zenger. KSTS 1. Stuttgart: Kohlhammer, 1995.

———. "Das Weltenkönigtum des Gottes Israels." In *Der Gott Israels und die Völker: Untersuchungen zum Jesajabuch und zu den Psalmen*, edited by Erich Zenger and Norbert Lohfink, 151–78. SBS 154. Stuttgart: Katholisches Bibelwerk, 1994.

———. "Der Jüdischer Psalter: Ein Anti-Imperiales Buch?" In *Religion und Gesellschaft: Studien zu Ihrer Wechselbeziehung in den Kulturen des Antiken Vorderen Orients*, edited by Rainer Albertz, 95–105. AOAT 248. Münster: Ugarit-Verlag, 1997.

———. "Der Psalter als Buch." In *Der Psalter in Judentum und Christentum*, edited by Erich Zenger and Norbert Lohfink, 1–58. HBS 18. Freiburg: Herder, 1998.

———. "Der Zion als Ort der Gottesnähe: Beobachtungen zum Weltbild des Wallfahrtspsalters Ps 120–134." In *Gottes Nähe im Alten Testament*, edited by Gönke Eberhardt and Kathrin Liess, 84–114. SBS 202. Stuttgart: Katholisches Bibelwerk, 2004.

———. "Komposition und Theologie des 5. Psalmenbuchs 107–145." *BN* 82 (1996) 97–116.

———. "Psalmenexegesis und Psalterexegese: Eine Forschungsskizze." In *Composition of the Book of Psalms*, edited by Erich Zenger, 17–65. BETL 238. Leuven: Peeters, 2010.

———. "Psalmenforschung nach Hermann Gunkel und Sigmund Mowinckel." In *Congress Volume Oslo 1998*, edited by André Lemaire and Magne Sæbø, 399–435. VTSup 80. Leiden: Brill, 2000.

———. "Torafrömmigkeit. Beobachtungen zum Poetischen und Theologischen Profil von Psalm 119." In *Freiheit und Recht: Festschrift für Frank Crüsemann zum 65*, edited by Christof Hardmeier and Frank Crüsemann, 380–96. Gütersloh: Kaiser, 2003.

———. "Was Wird Anders bei Kanonischer Psalmenauslegung." In *Ein Gott, Eine Offenbarung: Beiträge zur biblischen Exegese, Theologie und Spiritualität: Festschrift für Notker Füglister*, edited by Friedrich V. Reiterer, 397–413. OSB 60. Würzburg: Echter, 1991.

Bibliography

Zimmerli, Walther. "Zwillingspsalmen." In *Wort, Lied und Gottesspruch: Festschrift für Joseph Ziegler*, edited by Joseph Ziegler and Josef Schreiner, 105–16. Würzburg: Echter, 1972.

Zobel, "יעקב." In *TDOT* 6:185–208.

Zogbo, Lynell, and Ernst R. Wendland. *Hebrew Poetry in the Bible: A Guide for Understanding and Translating*. New York: United Bible Society, 2000.

Scripture Index

OLD TESTAMENT

Genesis
12:7	187
33:17	281
49:10	281

Exodus
3:15	130
15	48, 129, 137
15:1–11	137
15:1	49
15:9–11	49
15:11–13	137
15:11	50
15:12–18	137
15:17–18	49
15:18	50
15:26	298
24:7	237
29:7	214
30:7	159
30:30–32	214
34:6–7	256
40	159
40:1–15	159

Leviticus
8:12	214
8:30	214
8:35	159

Numbers
3–4	159
9:2–3	183
10	187
10:12–13	187
10:33–36	186, 188–89
24:17–19	281
24:17	282

Deuteronomy
4:13	237
6:4	33
9:27	171
17	90
17:14–20	50, 194
18:18	263
31–32	12
31:22–24	12
32–33	103, 145
32	262
33:9	237
33:29	50

Joshua
1:7–8	23
5:13–15	237
13:27–28	282
21:21	283

Judges
1:2	283
5	48
8	282
8:1	283
8:16	283
9:56–57	283
11:1–3	283
12:1–4	283
15:1–2	283
16:5–21	283
20:8	283

Ruth
4:11	152n

Scripture Index

1 Samuel

2:35	263
4:18	256
15:11	185
19:11	216, 218
20:15–16	282
21–22	218
21:10—22:1	216
21	218
21:13	218
21:14	306
22	218
22:1	216
22:9	215
23:19	216, 218
24	218
24:3	216
26:1	218
27:1—29:11	216
27	218

2 Samuel

1	218
2:2	168
2:6	168
4–9	75–77
5–6	71
5:1	76
5:12	219
6	70
6:6–7	77
6:12–19	170
6:13	77
6:17–18	77
6:17	213
7	41, 70–71, 73, 77, 194, 219, 233, 262, 337
7:1	71, 75, 78, 208, 210, 218–19, 282
7:2	213
7:4	73
7:5	73
7:7	72
7:8–16	25
7:9	71, 75, 78, 208, 282
7:10	71, 73
7:11	71, 78, 208, 282
7:12–16	153
7:12–13	263
7:12	73, 77
7:13	71–73, 160
7:14–17	200
7:14	72
7:15	71, 75
7:16	72–73
7:17	73
7:18–29	73
7:19	72
7:23–26	73
7:24–26	72
7:26	72
7:29	72
8	77
8:1–15	216, 282
8:1–14	99
8:15	154
9	77
9:1	282
10:6–19	216
11	94
12—1 Kgs 1	97
12	218–19
15–18	213
15–17	216, 218
15	210, 218–19
16:21–22	219
18–22	210
18	210, 218
18:18	256
18:31	210
19–24	75–77
19:12–13	76
20:3	76, 210
21–24	76
21	75, 77
22	74, 75, 77–78, 262
22:1–51	74
22:1	75, 77–78, 210, 218–19, 228
22:2–7	75
22:8–46	75
22:51	74, 77
23	77, 228
23:1	227, 228–29, 264
23:1–3	75, 171
24	75
24:17	75
24:25	77

1 Kings

1	94
2	228
5	152
8	187
11:39	163
17:18	256

2 Kings
23:2	237

1 Chronicles
16	22, 34, 70, 78
16:8	74
16:7–36	74, 77, 187
16:34	74, 160
17:11–14	153
18:1–13	99
23:13	159
23:27	229
23:28–29	159
29:28–30	254
29:29	229

2 Chronicles
3:1	77
6	78, 79
6:41–7:3	160, 186–89
6:41–42	74, 77, 154
7:3	160
7:6	160
7:12–22	78
28:19	263
36	80
36:23	80

Ezra
3:11	160n
6	168n

Nehemiah
9:34	263

Esther
2:15	67n

Job
15:5	63n
31:35–37	48
31:40	227n
33:33	63n
35:11	63n
37	322n
38:4	122n

Psalms
1–119	59
1–41	35, 157, 318
1–2	18, 20, 23–24, 26, 33, 36, 39–41, 59, 62, 65–66, 68–70, 82, 84, 88, 96, 126, 161, 194, 207, 231, 250, 252, 255, 261, 263, 276–77, 288, 296, 308, 313, 319, 322–24, 337
1	15, 20, 22–23, 31, 64, 66–67, 71, 84, 237, 252, 262, 266, 288, 308–10
1:1–2	69
1:1	7, 67, 253, 277
1:2	12, 37, 211
1:3–4	71
1:3	3, 50, 67, 69, 89
1:4–6	69
1:4	68
1:6	277
2–41	26
2	15, 20, 23, 29, 65, 67, 72, 84, 96, 166, 197, 206–07, 237, 243, 262, 266, 271, 288, 320
2:1–3	68, 69
2:1–2	65
2:1	67
2:2	67, 288
2:3	308
2:4–9	68–69, 89
2:6–12	71
2:6	71
2:7	6
2:8–12	308
2:10–12	20, 68–69
2:10	68
2:12	25, 59, 67, 253, 277
3–41	26, 35, 96, 194, 207, 257, 336
3–14	18, 20, 37, 39, 83, 85, 88–89, 94, 132, 138, 160, 194, 209–11, 250, 288, 319, 334
3–7	17, 18, 85, 211
3	210, 229–30, 288
3:1	210, 213, 217–18, 251
3:4	213
3:9b	17
4	288, 313
5	288
6	288
7–8	319
7	210–11, 230, 288
7:1	210, 218, 251
7:9b–18	313
7:17	213
8–9	86, 138, 209, 211, 257
8	17, 20, 138–39, 289, 313
8:1	209

Psalms (continued)

Reference	Pages
8:3–6	88
8:7–9	138
9–14	17
9–10	62, 65, 272, 309, 310, 319, 322
9	45, 65, 85, 138–39, 289
9:1	210
10–14	85–87, 211
10	45, 65, 86, 96, 289
10:16	50, 209
11	86, 289
12	86, 289
12:2	17
12:6	17
13	86, 289
13:3b	17
13:6	49
14	86, 289, 313, 319
14:7	17, 174
15–24	18, 20, 39, 83, 86, 88–89, 132, 139, 161, 208, 209, 250, 289, 319, 334
15–17	86
15	86, 209, 289–90, 319
15:1	168
16	86, 289, 290, 313
16:10	6, 143
17	290
17:1	235
18–22	86
18–21	88, 139, 208, 256, 257, 261
18–19	194, 231, 263, 296
18	37, 71, 74, 78–79, 139, 211, 230, 262, 271, 290
18:1	208, 218–19, 251
18:3	208
18:7	208
18:22–31	208
18:37	208
18:38–47	208
18:51	139
19	27, 33, 138–39, 208, 230, 289, 290
19:1–11	140
19:15	139
20	139, 289–90, 313
20:2	174
20:3	208
20:4	225
20:7	139, 208
20:10	139
21	29, 139, 290
21:2	139
21:8	139
22	227, 236, 290
22:24	174
23–24	86
23	267, 276, 290, 314
23:5	214
24	139, 209, 289–90, 319
24:6–9	170, 174
25–34	18, 39, 83, 88–89, 132, 139, 161, 168, 208–09, 250, 290, 319, 334
25–28	87, 139
25	31, 62–64, 86, 87, 266, 291, 309, 310, 322
25:13	17
25:15	17
25:16	17
25:22	17
26–28	17, 290–91
26	290
27	290, 314
27:6	213
28–29	261
29–31	87
29–30	72, 87, 138–39, 179, 208, 256–57, 291, 309, 319–20
29	87, 139, 314, 319
29:1	140
29:9–11	87–88, 140, 168
29:10–30:1	72
29:10	50, 209
30–32	17
30–31	272
30	71, 87, 139, 168, 209, 314, 319
30:1	168
31–34	87, 139
31–33	291
31	290
31:21–22	87
32	17, 290, 314
33	96, 178, 180, 314
33:4	178
33:13–15	87
34	62, 63, 87, 291, 309–10, 322
34:1	218, 220, 251
34:2	63
34:12	17, 63
34:16	17, 87
34:17	17
34:23	17
35–41	18, 39, 83, 85, 87–89, 132, 144, 161, 179, 250, 291, 320, 334
35	291
35:10	50
35:27	88

36	291	50	18, 20, 30, 33, 39, 90, 92, 94, 96, 298–99, 315, 320
36:1	88	50:8	225
37–39	140, 320	50:9–13	22
37	62, 64, 87, 266, 291, 309–10, 322	51–72	18, 26, 39, 40, 90, 93–94, 132, 250, 261
38	88, 138, 140, 144, 157, 179, 220, 250, 257, 291, 314, 320	51–71	20, 257, 296, 336
38:1	141, 256	51–70	35, 94, 96, 142, 194, 215
38:4	89	51–66	37
38:19	89	51–64	22, 93, 227, 230
38:23	140	51–55	142
39–41	87	51	37, 93, 94, 96, 98–99, 198, 215, 220–21, 226, 230, 257, 296
39	87, 291, 314	51:1–2	218, 220, 229, 251
39:2	89	51:18–21	17
40–41	22, 84	51:18	222, 225
40	180, 291	51:19	222, 235
40:2–13	314	51:21	222, 225
40:4–7	22, 178, 180	52–55	93–94, 296
40:7	225	52	198, 215, 315, 320
40:14–18	141	52:1–2	218, 251
41	87, 291	52:10	50
41:5	89	53:6–7	174–75
41:7	122	54	198
41:14	36, 59, 177	54:1–2	218, 220, 251
42–89	157, 231, 318	54:5	97
42–83	24, 35, 101	55:5–6	97
42–72	35	55:14	216
42–49	18, 20, 22, 39, 90, 132, 141, 161, 250, 338	56–68	142, 256
42–44	142	56–64	142, 257
42–43	22, 91, 294, 296, 309	56–60	93–94, 142
42	24	56–59	94
43	91, 96–97	56	95, 198, 216, 296
43:2	97	56:1	218, 220, 251
44–46	92	56:3	97
44	91–92, 97, 294, 296	57	198, 216, 220, 246, 279, 296
44:5	172, 175	57:1	218, 220, 251
44:10	97	57:5	97
44:15	271	57:8–12	246
44:24	97	57:10	271
45–48	22	58–60	297
45	30, 72, 91–92, 99, 141–42, 236, 271–72, 294, 296	58	315, 320
46–49	142	59	97, 198, 216, 235, 315, 320
46–48	91, 294–96	59:1	218, 220, 251
46	91–92, 315, 320	59:4	97
46:8–12	175	60–64	94
47–48	74	60	94, 97, 99, 220, 246, 279
47	92	60:1–2	97, 100, 199, 218, 220, 251
47:5	175	60:1	99
48	91–92	60:3	97, 199
49	22, 91, 294, 296	60:7–14	246
50–72	141–42, 161, 334	60:12	97, 246
50–51	17, 221, 226	61–64	93–94, 97, 142
		61–63	297

383

Scripture Index

Psalms (*continued*)

Reference	Pages
61	94
61:7	97
63–64	217, 230
63	198, 220
63:1	216–18, 229, 251
64	216, 220
64:3	216
65–68	93–94, 142
65–67	22, 93, 297
65	94
65:9–13	94
66–69	227
66–67	96
66	96, 230
66:13	225
66:15	225
67	50, 96
68–72	93
68	142
69–72	22
69–71	93–94, 142, 236
69–70	94
69	37, 94, 227, 230, 231, 236, 297
69:10–13	170–71
70	96, 141, 195, 297, 315, 320
70:1	140–41, 256
71–72	94, 96
71	96, 257, 297
71:19	50
72–83	141
72	13, 15, 20, 30, 59, 93–94, 96, 153–154, 166, 228–30, 232, 237, 255, 271, 297
72:1	152
72:2	228
72:17–19	36, 59, 73, 177, 200
72:20	59, 97–98, 144, 194, 227–29, 264
73–89	35
73–83	18, 20, 22, 30, 39, 90, 132, 161, 250, 334
73–77	92, 96, 143, 298
73–76	144
73	20, 22, 24, 31, 98, 143–44, 299
73:1	7
73:17	98
73:28	26
74–76	143, 144, 261
74	22, 92, 97, 142–44, 168, 183, 298–99, 315, 320–21
74:1	97
74:3	142
75–76	22, 92, 96, 99, 299
75	183, 298, 320
75:3	183, 185
75:10	175
76	298
76:6–7	175
77	22, 92, 97, 186, 299
77:8	97
77:16	92, 175
78–83	92, 96, 143, 298
78	22, 73, 92, 298–99
78:5	175
78:21	175
78:71	175
79–82	143, 144, 261
79–80	22, 92, 142, 144, 299
79	98, 142–43, 168, 298, 315, 320
79:7	56, 175–76
80	98, 298
80:2	92
80:3	92
81–82	22, 92, 96, 99, 299
81	298
81:2–6	92, 175
83	22, 90, 92, 143, 298–99
83:2–7	283
84–89	18, 20, 22, 39, 90, 132, 141, 144, 161, 250, 295, 334
84–88	250
84–85	22, 295
84	17, 91, 296
84:5–7	295
84:9	176
85	17, 91, 296
85:2	176
86	33, 91, 99, 144, 157, 195, 220, 232, 250, 257, 295–96, 320, 336
86:1	144, 228, 235
86:15	256
87–88	22
87	22, 91, 170, 296
87:2–5	170
88–89	295, 298
88	22, 91, 97, 295
88:1	10
88:15	97, 150
89	15, 20, 24, 89, 72, 97, 100, 150, 237, 241, 261, 271, 295–96, 315, 320
89:5	73
89:9	50
89:20–38	72
89:20	233
89:22	73
89:38–39	15

Scripture Index

89:39	97	101	103–04, 121, 147, 194, 230–32, 241, 243, 248, 255–57, 262, 303
89:44	44	101:2	253
89:48	24	101:6	253
89:50–51	24, 194	102–106	104
89:53	36, 59, 73, 177	102	104, 145, 147, 230, 231, 233–36, 241–43, 245, 248, 257
90–150	157–58, 318		
90–119	116, 149	102:1–12	13, 150, 183
90–106	30, 35	102:1	235
90–103	133, 145–47, 149, 161, 230–31, 250, 334	102:14	170
		102:19	12, 41, 183
90–100	39, 104, 167	102:23	122
90–94	103	102:24–25a	13
90–92	18, 20, 22, 27, 39, 103, 123, 145–46, 149, 230–31, 262, 264, 303	102:29	73
		103–107	120
		103–106	247
90–91	26	103–104	118–19
90	15, 20, 31, 103, 146–47, 149, 158, 231, 237, 262, 302	103	31, 104, 117–19, 145–47, 230–31, 234, 241–42, 248, 256–57, 262, 315, 321
90:1–7	231		
90:1	7, 145, 234, 235, 302	103:1–2	119, 234
91–92	231	103:7–19	231
91	103, 145, 149, 231, 302	103:8	256
91:1	302	103:22	119
91:9	25, 145, 302	104–119	124–26, 133, 148–49, 157, 161, 249–50, 334
92–100	39		
92	26, 103, 146, 147, 231, 262, 267, 276, 302–03	104–108	247
		104–107	117, 120–26, 133, 147–49, 151, 157, 160, 183–84, 224, 249
92:9	267		
92:12–13	302	104–106	104, 108, 117–21, 133, 157, 159, 303–04
92:13–15	50, 145		
93–100	18, 22, 34, 39, 103–04, 123, 127, 145, 147, 149, 160, 170, 180, 230–31, 303, 321, 337	104	103, 118–19, 121, 122, 124, 150, 183
		104:1	119
93	303, 328	104:19	183
93:1	50, 117	104:33	49, 122
94–95	309	104:34	122
94	26–27, 103–04, 303, 315, 321	104:35	119, 123
95–100	103–04	105–107	79, 120, 124
95	167, 303, 315, 321	105–106	15, 184
96	79, 118, 178, 180, 182, 315, 321	105	118, 122, 148, 240, 303, 315
96:1–13	74, 77, 178, 180, 182	105:1–15	74, 77
96:10	50	105:1	14, 117, 120, 123
97	33, 328	105:3	122
97:1	50	105:38	122
98	178, 180, 182	105:40–44	124
98:1	178, 180, 182	105:45	122
99	328	106–107	123
99:1	50	106	20, 24, 120, 122–23, 148, 247, 266, 304, 315, 321
100	104, 118, 167, 315		
101–110	120	106:1	14, 45, 74, 77, 117, 120
101–106	20, 22, 39, 103	106:5	122
101–103	35, 37, 104, 117–21, 123, 145–47, 183, 195, 230–31, 257, 259, 261–62, 303, 321, 336–37	106:23–27	124
		106:41	123

385

Psalms (continued)

Reference	Pages
106:46	123
106:47	122–23
106:48	36, 59, 73, 177, 269
107–150	35
107–136	114
107–119	110, 115
107–117	22
107	15, 18, 20, 31, 71, 108, 120–24, 147–48, 157, 184, 186, 247, 304
107:1	14, 120
107:2	7, 123
107:3	122, 123, 157
107:7	157
107:14	157
107:23–26	124
107:30	122
107:40	124
107:42–43	108
108–110	18, 24, 35, 37, 108, 110, 120–21, 126–27, 147–49, 157, 160, 194–95, 234, 241, 257, 259, 261, 264, 284, 334, 337
108	147, 241, 246–48, 256–57, 279, 284–85
108:4	271
108:8–10	246, 280–85
108:8	279
108:12	246
109	121, 147, 234–36, 241–45, 247–48, 257, 284
109:1–3	244
109:6–19	244–45
109:20	244–45
110–112	252
110	30, 72, 147, 186, 194, 214, 241–43, 246–48, 256–57, 284
110:1–2	71
110:3–4	186, 200
110:6	243
110:7	213
111–137	18
111–119	110, 126–27, 147–49, 151, 158–59, 251
111–118	30, 249, 321
111–117	20, 108, 159
111–113	159
111–112	18, 21, 36, 109–110, 126, 253, 304, 309, 321
111	62, 240, 304, 309–10, 321–22
111:7–8	7
111:10	9
112	62, 64, 252, 304, 309–310, 321–22
112:9	251
112:10	9
113–118	24, 109, 110, 224
113–117	148, 309
113–115	110, 184, 304
113	109, 184, 253, 304
114	158, 184, 253
114:2	253
114:5	304
114:7	177
115–118	253
115–116	159
115	184, 267, 276, 304
115:11	304
116–118	110
116	304
117–119	40
117–118	39, 124
117	21, 109, 159, 304
118–137	115
118–135	22
118–119	20, 194, 231, 263
118	21, 79, 108–109, 148, 245, 305
118:18–19	171
118:18	245
118:22	214
118:23	245
118:27	148
119–134	60
119	21, 22, 24, 33, 45, 47, 62, 64, 108, 110, 114, 126–27, 149, 150, 157, 159, 237, 249, 252–53, 255–66, 276–77, 305, 309–310, 321–22
119:1–8	277
119:4	277
119:9–16	277
119:16	277
119:96	127
119:176	277
120–150	116
120–136	110, 113, 261, 337
120–134	21, 25, 30, 36, 80, 108, 115, 118, 133, 151, 155, 161, 167, 250, 252, 307, 334
120–124	111, 151, 154, 156
120–122	155–56, 168, 253
120	111, 153–55, 305
121	153–54, 305
122	111–12, 127, 151–56, 160, 168, 255, 305
122:1	328
122:2–3	171
122:4	112

386

Scripture Index

Reference	Pages
122:5	200
122:8	167
123–125	155
123	155, 305
123:1	155
124	111–12, 155, 305
124:1	328
125–129	111, 117, 151, 155–56
125	111, 117, 155
125:1	167
126–128	155
126	155, 305
126:1	71, 151, 167–68
127	33, 72, 79, 111–12, 117, 127, 151–56, 160, 168, 169, 305–07
127:1	71, 152, 155, 168, 306–07, 328
128	155, 306
128:5	167, 306
129–131	155
129	111, 117, 306
130–134	111, 151, 156
130	111, 306
130:3	112
131	112, 306
131:1	328
132–136	159, 169, 189
132–135	160
132–134	155, 156
132	29, 71, 77, 79, 111, 127, 151, 153–56, 159, 160, 168
132:7	155
132:8–10	74, 154, 189
132:8	79, 155
132:10–12	155, 200
132:10	306
132:13	167
132:15–18	146, 168, 200
132:17	251
133–136	307
133–134	309
133	112, 155, 306–307
133:1	328
133:2	159, 214, 306
134–135	118, 119
134	111, 113, 118–19, 155, 307
135–150	114–15, 125–26, 133, 156, 157, 159, 161, 249–250, 334
135–137	39, 40, 108, 124, 125, 157, 249
135–136	113, 156–57, 159–160, 253, 307
135	21, 108, 119, 157, 307
135:4	125
135:6–7	125
135:8–12	125
136–150	21, 22
136–137	21
136	72, 73, 79–80, 113, 125, 157, 160, 307
137	108, 113, 125, 157, 160, 249, 307
137:1	125, 157
137:7	283
138–145	18, 21, 35, 108, 113–14, 117, 126–27, 156–57, 163, 194–95, 248, 252, 257, 307, 309, 321, 336–37
138	113, 156, 248, 257, 307, 316, 321
139	270, 307
139:13–14	270
140–143	21, 113, 156–57, 160, 220, 249–50, 257, 261, 307
140:7	156
140:10	213
141–143	234
141:2	156
141:5	214
142	235
142:1	156, 218, 220, 235, 250–51, 307
143	259
143:1	156, 255
143:12	71
144–150	169
144–145	21, 207, 252, 259, 261, 264, 284
144	15, 37, 71, 74, 78–79, 180–81, 254, 262, 307, 316, 321
144:9–15	79, 178, 180
144:12–15	73, 177, 180, 254, 257
144:15	253
145	15, 18, 62, 80, 113, 126, 156, 181, 207, 248–49, 252–53, 257, 307, 309–310, 321–22
145:1	252
145:8	256
145:18–20	256
145:19–20	108
145:21	15, 73
146–150	17, 59, 108, 113, 121, 126–27, 156, 158–59, 163, 167, 248, 254, 261, 309, 337
146–149	126, 249
146–147	124
146	114, 124, 165
146:5–10	123, 177
147	114, 165
147:1	123
147:2	259
147:13	171

Psalms (continued)

147:15–18	259
148–150	21
148	114, 165
148:11	20
148:14	251
149–150	33
149	17, 114, 165, 178, 180, 181, 255, 259, 284, 308
149:1	178, 181–83, 254
149:2	167
149:5–9	181
149:6–9	252, 308
149:7	271
149:9	254
149:19	73
150	30, 64, 69, 114, 117, 126–27, 157, 165, 181, 249, 255, 266, 308, 311–12, 316
150:1	127, 255
150:3	64

Proverbs

22:17–21	48

Isaiah

2:5–6	172
6:9–13	182
9:5–6	185
11:1–9	243
28:9–13	48
40	182
40:11	72
42	182
42:7–10	178, 182–83
43:8–13	182
44:26–28	263
48:6	182
49:8	227
50:4–9	48
53:4	227
55:3	6
59:15–21	185
62:2	182
63:1–6	185
65:17	182
66:22	182

Jeremiah

17:8	3
23:4–8	263
23:5	202
30:9–10	263
31:7	172
33:14	177

Lamentations

1	64
2	64
4	64

Ezekiel

12:28	177
13:22	284
14:22	185
22:6	263
34:23–24	243
37:23–24	72

Daniel

9:25	202
11:30	284

Amos

2	263
9:8	172

Obadiah

1:17	172

Micah

2:12	172
3	263
4:1–2	185
4:7–8	185
5:4	72

Nahum

1:2–9	64

Zephaniah

3:14	170n

Haggai

2:20–23	202

Zechariah

3:8	202
6:9–15	202, 243
6:12–14	243

Scripture Index

9–14	29, 30
9:11–10:12	29
12:1	177
12:3	29
12:10–14	29
13:7–9	29
14:1	29
14:2–15	29
14:16–21	29

Malachi

1:2	172
3:18	20

NEW TESTAMENT

Matthew

2:6	339n
4	339n
16:16	339n
26:30	339n
26:59–62	339n
27:34	227n
27:48	227

Mark

10:17–18	339n
15:23	227n

Luke

1:32	339n
23:36	227n
24:44	6, 339n

John

1:11	227n
2:17	227n
2:13–22	227
2:17	227
7:5	227n
10:11–14	339n
15:25	227
19:29	227n

Acts

1:20	227
2:29–36	339n
4:26–26	339n
4:27	339n
13:22–23	6
13:33–35	6

Romans

3:24	339n
11:9–10	227
15:3	227
15:16	339n

1 Corinthians

15:23–28	339n

Ephesians

6:18	339n

Philippians

4:3	227n

1 Thessalonians

5:17	339n

1 Timothy

6:15	339n

Hebrews

3:1	339n
3:2–5	262
7:14–24	339n
10:19	339n

James

5:13–20	339n

1 Peter

4:4–8	339n

Revelation

3:5	227n
5:9	178, 339n
14:3	339n
19:1–6	339n
19:16	339n
20:4	339n
20:5–6	339n
21:1–3	339n
22:1–3	339n
22:7	339n

www.ingramcontent.com/pod-product-compliance
Lightning Source LLC
Chambersburg PA
CBHW081147290426
44108CB00018B/2469